Daily Devotions of

Ordinary People -

Extraordinary God

I0224521

by Jody Neufeld

Energion Publications
P. O. Box 841
Gonzalez, FL 32560
850-968-1001
http://energion.com
pubs@energion.com

Ordinary People - Extraordinary God, Daily Devotions of,
by Jody Neufeld
Published by **Energion Publications**.
P.O. Box 841
Gonzalez, FL 32560
Website: energion.com

Cover Design by PhotoMD (www.photomd.net)
Cover Photograph © Carol Everhart Roper

Copyright © 2004 by Jody Neufeld
All rights reserved.
Neufeld, Jody 1954 –
Includes bibliographical references.
ISBN# 1-893729-15-X

Dedication

This book and all the ones to come is humbly dedicated
to my Heavenly Father.

Jesus prayed, *"Father, the time has come for you*
to bring glory to your Son,
in order that he may bring glory to you...
I have brought glory to you here on earth
by doing everything you gave me to do.   John 17:1, 4 (CEV)

Acknowledgements

I thank God for the pastors (shepherds) that God has brought into my life: Rev. Perry Dalton, Dr. Robert McKibben, Rev. Bruce Sheffield, Rev. Riley Richardson, and Rev. Ted Wood, who like Jesus, open their cloaks and show me their heart for Christ each Sunday morning.

All the "ordinary" people that my Extraordinary God has used to touch my life, molding me like clay on the potter's wheel. I am thankful that God is willing to break me and start again.

My children who have taught me so much about being a child of God: Janet, who truly has the *gift* of faith, John, a gentle warrior for the weak, and James, who showed more Godly courage and peace in his life than most of us know is available to us.

My husband, Henry, who encourages me, teaches me, and loves me because God said so.

Introduction

August 2000 was an extraordinary time in my life because it was 'so God'. I had been through a divorce four years previously, just finished a year with my youngest son in cancer treatment that had a 1 in 4 chance of survival, my daughter got married, and my oldest son had been drafted by Major League Baseball. The best was yet to come as I said 'yes' to God when He called me to full-time ministry with the husband He gave me, Henry Neufeld.

This meant that my 'season' of 32 years in nursing was finished. I began as a candy striper in high school and continued as a nursing assistant while in college. I had worked as a registered nurse in critical care units and physician's offices and spent the last 12 years in hospice care as a home nurse, patient care manager, and education director. For over 30 years, God taught me so much about His healing power and the various ways He works to heal body, mind, and spirit. And now a new season would begin.

While in the workplace I watched and experienced the daily 'fight' that a Christian must wage to walk in God's path and His will. The enemy is crafty and sly as he throws obstacles of frustration and ill will in our paths. It is a daily choice that I must make to speak God's words and act in God's way. I knew that spending time with the Lord every morning gave me HIS start, a point of 'right relationship' as Paul describes in Romans.

Now that I was 'free' of a frantic morning schedule, I could spend time with the Lord that was limited only by my own schedule. I felt the Lord telling me to share some of our times together with others. The sharing began with 12 people from my workplace. It has grown to more than I know as people pass the 'daily devotions' on to others.

The vision that God has given me is for us to begin each day with Him. Whether it is this devotion book or another, I believe that the Lord is sending His Spirit to inspire writers to provide 'tools' so that His children may deepen their study with Him and about Him. In this way, we gain strength and maturity for the battles ahead. As we follow Jesus' example and take time 'away' with the Father in prayer and study, our lives become the bright lamps that Jesus said were to be put on stands to give light to the whole world.

The people that I have included are just 'ordinary' people that God has used in my life. Each of you who pick up this book know 'ordinary' people who put themselves into the hands of an 'extraordinary' God and say, "Here I am! Use me!"

January 1

A new year with possibilities and opportunities has now begun. It seems like just a week ago that I was looking at the year through the same day!

Each and every day, I have a choice: Choose God or choose the world's way of living my life. I sat on the fence for a long time, most of my life actually. I thought I could love God and do pretty much what I wanted the other six days of the week.

Then came that night in July when I knew that Jesus did it all for me, for my sins! All of a sudden the whole 'salvation' concept wasn't just a theory. It was personal. It was about a relationship. If I was to have a relationship with Jesus, then it was going to be more than a once a week conversation! A marriage wouldn't work if the husband and wife only spoke one day a week! Neither, would my relationship with Jesus grow and become the relationship that would finally fill that emptiness that I had always had.

"I am the vine; you are the branches. If a man remains in me and I in him, he will bear much fruit; apart from me you can do nothing. If anyone does not remain in me, he is like a branch that is thrown away and withers; such branches are picked up, thrown into the fire and burned. If you remain in me and my words remain in you, ask whatever you wish, and it will be given you. This is to my Father's glory, that you bear much fruit, showing yourselves to be my disciples. As the Father has loved me, so have I loved you. Now remain in my love."   *John 15:5-9*

Rejoice in the Lord always. I will say it again: Rejoice! Let your gentleness be evident to all. The Lord is near. Do not be anxious about anything, but in everything, by prayer and petition, with thanksgiving, present your requests to God. And the peace of God, which transcends all understanding, will guard your hearts and your minds in Christ Jesus.   *Philippians 4:4-7*

I will start today with God and put my feet in HIS footsteps. There will be no worldly New Year's resolutions. I am just going to open my heart to Jesus and watch what happens!

Additional text: Philippians 2, Psalm 1

January 2

v.2 O LORD my God, I called to you for help and you healed me.
v. 3 O LORD, you brought me up from the grave; you spared me from going down into the pit.
v.4 Sing to the LORD, you saints of his; praise his holy name.
v.5 For his anger lasts only a moment but his favor lasts a lifetime;
weeping may remain for a night, but rejoicing comes in the morning.

Psalm 30:2-5

Verse 2 of this Psalm is such a statement of fact: "I called and you answered." Period. God <u>did</u> respond. He met my expectation that He would answer.

Verse 3 seems to say that God did even more than I expected. That His grace and mercy kept me from death (physical, emotional, spiritual) and from the "pit" that I was walking toward. I have been in situations that I KNEW was bad news and I seemed to spin in a circle or wander around and not be able to find my footing. The worse case scenario was rushing toward me and I couldn't seem to change course. God saved me.

Verse 4 is a moment of relief and praise. HALLELUJAH!!! God is WORTHY of my praise!

Verse 5 is like a "philosophical review" of the event. I am a sinner. I chose an un-Godly path but I KNOW I am a Child of God, saved by grace. I know that He is a righteous parent – angry when I am disobedient but continues to show me love – may I always know that I am loved. I cry during the discipline. It isn't fun. It isn't fun when I have to go through the consequences of an "unwise" (I'm being kind to myself!) decision. And so I weep.

Joy DOES come. It may not be literally "in the morning" – like 8 or 12 hours from now. When I turn control over to God, joy does come. The "weeping" may last for a 'season' – and that 'season' may be hours, days, weeks, and yes, even years, but JOY, <u>real</u> JOY that has NOTHING to do with my circumstances <u>WILL</u> come. Yes, I argue with God's timing when I am going through the un-joyful time. But I stand and testify today that God's timing <u>IS</u> perfect and the joy, the relief, the "aahhh" of the cool water after being on God's anvil, does come!

Sing a new song to the Lord! Sing it everywhere around the world! Sing out his praises! Bless his name. Each day tell someone that he saves.
Publish his glorious acts throughout the earth. Tell everyone about the amazing things he does. For the Lord is great beyond description, and greatly to be praised. Worship only him among the gods! For the gods of other nations are merely idols, but our God made the heavens! Honor and majesty surround him; strength and beauty are in his Temple.

Psalm 96:1-6 (TLB)

I will praise You today, Lord, for: _____

_____

Additional Text: Psalm 5, John 14

Laziness leads to poverty; hard work makes you rich.   *Proverbs 10:4 (CEV)*

With a new year comes great temptation to make resolutions. Resolutions aren't bad things but for me they rarely produce much fruit. They are usually rash and not well thought out to make them attainable – because I usually do not ask GOD what HE wants me to do differently! I just plow ahead trying to lose weight, exercise every day, read my Bible 4 hours every day, and agree to sit on three more committees or charitable organizations without checking whether all those resolve and good works is from God or not!

Proverbs tells me to work just as Paul told the Thessalonians that if they didn't work they would not eat! But MY work must be balanced with listening to the Lord's guidance.

My friends, we are talking this way. But we are sure that you are doing those really good things that people do when they are being saved. God is always fair. He will remember how you helped his people in the past and how you are still helping them. You belong to God, and he won't forget the love you have shown his people. We wish that each of you would always be eager to show how strong and lasting your hope really is. Then you would never be lazy. You would be following the example of those who had faith and were patient until God kept his promise to them.   *Hebrews 6:9-12 (CEV)*

The writer of Hebrews also does not want me to be lazy but encourages me to imitate the FAITH and PATIENCE of those before me. God does tell me to "GO" and make disciples but He also says, "BE STILL" and know that He is God. Ask, listen, then do.

If I make THIS my resolution, it will soon become my life – not just a choice. *I am the true vine, and my Father is the vinedresser. Every branch of mine that does not bear fruit he takes away, and every branch that does bear fruit he prunes, that it may bear more fruit. Already you are clean because of the word that I have spoken to you. Abide in me, and I in you. As the branch cannot bear fruit by itself, unless it abides in the vine, neither can you, unless you abide in me...If you abide in me, and my words abide in you, ask whatever you wish, and it will be done for you. By this my Father is glorified, that you bear much fruit and so prove to be my disciples.*   *John 15:1-4, 7-8 (ESV)*

My best resolution is to do everything that will encourage that branch that connects me to the vine and produces fruit to glorify the Father. It's all about You, Lord!

Additional text: John 15, Titus 3

"What man of you, having a hundred sheep, if he has lost one of them, does not leave the ninety-nine in the open country, and go after the one that is lost, until he finds it? And when he has found it, he lays it on his shoulders, rejoicing. And when he comes home, he calls together his friends and his neighbors, saying to them, 'Rejoice with me, for I have found my sheep that was lost.' Just so, I tell you, there will be more joy in heaven over one sinner who repents than over ninety-nine righteous persons who need no repentance." Luke 15:4-7(ESV)

Have you ever lost your child at the mall or the fair? Just for 30 seconds is enough to give a parent a heart attack!!! My twins were about 3 when their dad and I were in Atlanta's mall looking in shop windows. In just a moment, they were GONE! They were right beside me looking in the window with me – and then they were GONE!!! I think my heart stopped! Two small children! Who would take two of them? Janet would have howled if someone she didn't know grabbed her. She wasn't much on strangers, thank the Lord! John, being a 'social' kind of guy, might have initially went but even at an early age, he was protective of Janet and if she yelled in fear or pain he would have decided this wasn't a good thing and kicked and screamed too. Then, in less than 3 minutes of looking – there they were -- standing in front of a recessed shop window, looking at all the "pretties". I think their dad and I grabbed them and began hugging and kissing them and babbling about "don't ever doing THAT again"! (I'm not sure they knew what THAT was since they didn't know they were lost!)

My experience gives me a 'glimpse' into the JOY the shepherd feels as he finds the lost sheep and puts it on his shoulders. Jesus wants me to realize that the grief and fear that I felt when Janet and John were lost is 'the same but different' that He feels when one of His sheep is lost – eternally! He will pursue and pursue, calling in that voice full of love no matter how much the sheep might run and hide behind whatever bushes. He doesn't give up even when the sheep turns and says, "NO! I don't want you!" In His loving heart He still desires that 'all men come to Him' [1 Timothy 2:4].

Do I welcome 'sinners' into my church? Do I welcome them with Jesus' heart? This parable doesn't say that the Shepherd "WASHED" the sheep before He put it on His shoulders! The Shepherd didn't care if it had mud all over it – it says He JOYFULLY lifted the sheep to His shoulders and carried it. Do I 'carry' sinners close to me? Do I disciple them with love and acceptance at where they are – desiring with the love of Jesus that they grow to where HE wants them to be?

Do I rejoice when someone stands up in church (or wherever!) and testifies that they have turned from their "old life" and accepted Jesus as their Savior? Do I applaud? Hug them? Lift a prayer of thanksgiving? According to Jesus – it's worth a brass band at least!!!

Taking that step of faith into the assurance of eternal salvation through Jesus is a difficult step to most of us. It is SO simple and yet is like taking that final step in a bungee jump! It is SO worth celebrating!

January 5

Taste and see that the LORD is good; blessed is the man who takes refuge in him. Fear the LORD, you his saints, for those who fear him lack nothing. The lions may grow weak and hungry, but those who seek the LORD lack no good thing.
Psalm 34:8-10

When I taste something new, I'm a little slow to move it from the fork/spoon to my mouth – especially in public! After all – if I don't like it, well, it's 'tacky' to spit it out!!!

The psalmist testifies that the Lord 'tastes GOOD'! If someone tells me that something tastes <u>really</u> good, I am more likely to give it a try!

Every day I have opportunities to tell people that the Lord 'tastes' good. It doesn't have to be an OVERT testimony. Every day God does wonderful ordinary (or EXTRAORDINARY!) things. Do I give Him credit? Or do I just shrug it off as "coincidence" or "circumstance"? It is an opportunity for me to give God credit for what He is doing in my life and just <u>maybe</u> someone might "taste and see that the Lord is good"!!!

If I ignore the opportunities because someone might question or criticize my 'story' and enthusiasm for God, I think the verse that suggests I should fear God more than I fear some <u>person's</u> opinion of me might be something to consider! I want the promise that I will "lack nothing" and "lack no good thing" if – IF I am obedient.

[Jesus said,] *"But blessed are your eyes, for they see, and your ears, for they hear. Truly, I say to you, many prophets and righteous people longed to see what you see, and did not see it, and to hear what you hear, and did not hear it."*
Matthew 13:16-17 (ESV)

Jesus goes on to explain the parable of the sower to His disciples. God desires that we GROW in our relationship with Him, that we learn new things, and come to new levels of intimacy with Him. A friendship or marriage cannot be healthy if it doesn't grow. What 'new thing' has the Lord told me this week? Have I taken time to just be quiet and listen?

Additional text: Matthew 13, Psalm 117, James 1

January 6

Where could I go to escape from your Spirit or from your sight?
Psalm 139:7 (CEV)

Henry and I enjoy Chattanooga, TN. My husband had spent some of his growing up years there and suggested that we visit one of their local attractions called *Ruby Falls*. An underground waterfall discovered around 1930 by a local young man, it is not nearly as popular as the attractions of Gatlinburg. But going there was worth a 7-hour drive and a 1-mile walk to me.

First, I descended almost 300 feet down in an elevator. The shaft had been dug through solid rock. Then I walked a half-mile – up, down, ducking low, and squeezing through rock crevices that barely accommodated my size – one spot was called "Weight Watchers' Pass". (I resemble that remark!) Remember – this was all 285+ feet below the surface. Light was dim and I noticed that our guide carried a flashlight and there were what appeared to be foot lockers along the way with emergency torches, etc.

Finally, I am told that I have reached my destination. I am sweaty, slightly out of breath, and my feet hurt – and I know that I still have to walk back! This is not Disney World – there are no people-movers!

It is dark. Pitch black except for the guide's flashlight. I hear the sound of – rushing water. I think to myself that this waterfall is not a trickle from a crack in the rock. It must be big!

And suddenly – a light comes on – the waterfall is not big – it is beyond my imagination HUGE! It is illuminated by white lights, then blue, then red – the water – the color of the water – it cannot be described! I begin to weep. They allow us to walk behind the falls – all around it – still I silently weep – my heart is pounding.

Or suppose I said, "I'll hide in the dark until night comes to cover me over."
But you see in the dark because daylight and dark are all the same to you.
You are the one who put me together inside my mother's body,
And I praise you because of the wonderful way you created me.
Everything you do is marvelous! Of this I have no doubt.
Nothing about me is hidden from you!   *Psalm 139:11-15 (CEV)*

My walk back to the elevator is made in almost silence. I pass several groups going to the falls. They have to wait for us to pass them in the narrow places. In the darkness, 300 feet below the earth, a river runs and then falls into a pool and disappears again beneath the earth.

My Heavenly Father made it.

My Heavenly Father made me.

How far am I willing to travel? How much effort will I put into moving closer to my Creator? My Heavenly Father? My Lord? What price will I pay to spend time in His Presence? Seems like a good time to pray and ponder those questions.

Additional text: Psalm 139, Psalm 34

Then, at the evening sacrifice, I rose from my self-abasement, with my tunic and cloak torn, and fell on my knees with my hands spread out to the LORD my God and prayed: "O my God, I am too ashamed and disgraced to lift up my face to you, my God, because our sins are higher than our heads and our guilt has reached to the heavens. From the days of our forefathers until now, our guilt has been great. Because of our sins, we and our kings and our priests have been subjected to the sword and captivity, to pillage and humiliation at the hand of foreign kings, as it is today."   *Ezra 9:5-9*

Then he called the crowd to him along with his disciples and said: "If anyone would come after me, he must deny himself and take up his cross and follow me. For whoever wants to save his life will lose it, but whoever loses his life for me and for the gospel will save it. What good is it for a man to gain the whole world, yet forfeit his soul? Or what can a man give in exchange for his soul? If anyone is ashamed of me and my words in this adulterous and sinful generation, the Son of Man will be ashamed of him when he comes in his Father's glory with the holy angels."   *Mark 8:34-38*

'Shame' and 'guilt' are powerful words and feelings. They bring me to repentance for my sins. That's a good thing. That is what Ezra was talking about. The shame brought him to his knees. Because he KNEW the love and graciousness of God, he didn't stay there! He accepted the grace and gave thanks. I suspect his tears flowed from one to the other without a pause in between! HALLELUJAH! If I become 'stuck' in shame, that is not God holding me back. God desires feelings of shame and guilt in me ONLY to convict me – not to emotionally beat me into a pulp! He NEVER withholds His grace and mercy from me when I come with a sincere and repentant heart.

Jesus speaks to me about being ashamed of HIM! Now that's a WHOLE 'nother ballgame!!! Sometimes I get a little 'puffed' and think that He isn't speaking to <u>me</u> because I think of the story of Peter and self-righteously stand up and declare that "I've NEVER denied You, Lord!" But actually I have. It may have been passively or by omission – but I've done it! Usually it is in a situation when I KNOW I shouldn't be watching a movie or smiling at a joke that the Lord is clearly convicting <u>me</u> that it is not pleasing to Him. He may be telling me to verbally say something but I think more often He is telling me to gently and with love turn and walk away and by my example let the Holy Spirit do the rest in others' hearts. Jesus was gentle and loving with everyone but the Pharisees. That seems like a good example to me. When I become 'in-your-face' to most people about sin, I think I sell the Holy Spirit short on what <u>HE</u> can do. I believe what God is asking me to do is stand up for what HE is saying to <u>me</u> about <u>my</u> sin.

On the Day of Judgment, it is going to be <u>VERY</u> personal between Jesus and me. I think it will cut my heart the most to have Jesus turn to me with regret in His eyes and I will see the times when I denied Him, when I rejected Him. Right here, in this discussion about 'shame' – have I rejected His grace and mercy? Am I living my life in victory?

January 8

On the last day, the climax of the holidays, Jesus shouted to the crowds, "If anyone is thirsty, let him come to me and drink. For the Scriptures declare that rivers of living water shall flow from the inmost being of anyone who believes in me." (He was speaking of the Holy Spirit, who would be given to everyone believing in him; but the Spirit had not yet been give, because Jesus had not yet returned to his glory in heaven.)   John 7:37-39 (TLB)

"For my people have done two evil things: They have forsaken me, the Fountain of Life-giving Water; and they have built for themselves broken cisterns that can't hold water!"   Jeremiah 2:13 (TLB)

I have "water savers" on my toilets and kitchen sink. These are little devices that are 'environmentally appropriate' as they save the amount of water that would normally rush out of these pipes and give you only what is absolutely needed. I am sure some scientist who doesn't know anything about washing vegetables in a kitchen sink made that determination.

Jesus knows how much I need to drink from Him. When I connect to Him (and it is my choice!) and allow Him to determine the type and rate of water I need, I will be perfectly satisfied. I will grow well in His garden – not over-watered or dry and parched.

"Over-watered" could mean that my flesh has made me less Holy Spirit-filled and more emotional in the Lord. I begin to walk only from experience to experience and not in the true power of God.

"Dry and parched" could mean that I have chosen to walk in the safe and comfortable and not in the true power of God that comes through the Holy Spirit and can certainly push the parameters that I thought I had found and settled down.

God's words to Jeremiah are arrows that rightly pierce my heart and illuminate the truth. I MUST choose to connect to the Lord's "living water" – drinking only from His stream that is sweet and perfect and flowing, not stagnant. I must not step off into a stream that seems right just because I've been there before or it's not too swift. It looks 'FUN'! So it must be GOD! And I must not "dig in" and design my own pool that's mine, ALL MINE! Never to be shared! That is not God's water!

Jesus spoke of living water flowing from us if we believed in Him (John 7:38). It is water we are to FREELY give to others. I must keep this 'water' (or Holy Spirit) flowing through me so that the path stays clean and without any discoloration that I might put in it. This means I must seek time with the Lord in worship, Bible study, and prayer so that I stay 'filled up' and overflowing. As a stream that has its source in the Lord, it will bring healing to broken hearts and lives, cleansing from sin and the chains of oppression that come with sin. This River of Living Water that is Jesus Christ has no beginning and no ending.

Additional text: Psalm 1, Zechariah 14, Revelation 22

On another day the angels came to present themselves before the LORD, and Satan also came with them to present himself before him. And the LORD said to Satan, "Where have you come from?"

Satan answered the LORD, "From roaming through the earth and going back and forth in it."

Then the LORD said to Satan, "Have you considered my servant Job? There is no one on earth like him; he is blameless and upright, a man who fears God and shuns evil. And he still maintains his integrity, though you incited me against him to ruin him without any reason."

"Skin for skin!" Satan replied. "A man will give all he has for his own life. But stretch out your hand and strike his flesh and bones, and he will surely curse you to your face."

The LORD said to Satan, "Very well, then, he is in your hands; but you must spare his life."   *Job 2:1-6*

But you, O God, do see trouble and grief; you consider it to take it in hand. The victim commits himself to you;   you are the helper of the fatherless.

Psalm 10:14

"My sheep listen to my voice; I know them, and they follow me. I give them eternal life, and they shall never perish; no one can snatch them out of my hand. My Father, who has given them to me, is greater than all; no one can snatch them out of my Father's hand. I and the Father are one."   *John 10:27-30*

It is wonderful – no, beyond 'wonderful' – to know that I am in God's hand. I know that He loves me without conditions. I know that He sees the Big Picture and desires to give me good gifts (Luke 11:13). He rejoices with me during the blessings and the miracles. He comforts me in ways no person is able.

HOWEVER, because God IS all-powerful, because He IS GOD, He also has control over what satan does. Some people would say that Job is only a story and did not truly happen. I believe we need to be "vawry, vawry careful" at what we 'discount' (I'm not going to say "throw out") in Scripture. It is logical that if I believe that God is GOD then I also believe that EVERYTHING is under His control. Even the 'bad' things? Yup. Even the 'troubles' as well.

I am THANKFUL that the Lord has control of my troubles. I wouldn't want anybody else to have that control! With the knowledge that God has power over my trials or test, I can take that step of faith, into trust, and begin to learn from them. That's not an easy step. Discipline is not easy and it isn't something that I request! It is necessary for me to grow. I do not want to live on a plateau. I do not want to stagnate in my Christian life. If an organism doesn't grow – it is DEAD. I want to LIVE for God. I want to truly LIVE.

Therefore, I urge you, brothers, in view of God's mercy, to offer your bodies as living sacrifices, holy and pleasing to God--this is your spiritual act of worship. Do not conform any longer to the pattern of this world, but be transformed by the renewing of your mind. Then you will be able to test and approve what God's will is--his good, pleasing and perfect will.   *Romans 12:1-2*

January 10

And while they were there, the time came for her to give birth. And she gave birth to her firstborn son and wrapped him in swaddling cloths and laid him in a manger, because there was no place for them in the inn. Luke 2:6-7(ESV)

That very day two of them were going to a village named Emmaus, about seven miles from Jerusalem and they were talking with each other about all these things that had happened. While they were talking and discussing together, Jesus himself drew near and went with them. But their eyes were kept from recognizing him. And he said to them, "What is this conversation that you are holding with each other as you walk?" And they stood still, looking sad. Then one of them, named Cleopas, answered him, "Are you the only visitor to Jerusalem who does not know the things that have happened there in these days?" And he said to them, "What things?" And they said to him, "Concerning Jesus of Nazareth, a man who was a prophet mighty in deed and word before God and all the people...And he said to them, "O foolish ones, and slow of heart to believe all that the prophets have spoken! Was it not necessary that the Christ should suffer these things and enter into his glory?" And beginning with Moses and all the Prophets, he interpreted to them in all the Scriptures the things concerning himself.

So they drew near to the village to which they were going. He acted as if he were going farther, but they urged him strongly, saying, "Stay with us, for it is toward evening and the day is now far spent." So he went in to stay with them. When he was at table with them, he took the bread and blessed and broke it and gave it to them. And their eyes were opened, and they recognized him. And he vanished from their sight. They said to each other, "Did not our hearts burn within us while he talked to us on the road, while he opened to us the Scriptures?" Luke 24:13-19, 25-32 (ESV)

The disciples asked the right question: "Did our <u>hearts</u> not burn?" They knew that they should have recognized Jesus through their hearts if not their eyes. In tough times when life seems pretty dark and uncertain and we wonder where Jesus is – He's right there!

Psalm 30 says*, " weeping may remain for a night, but rejoicing comes in the morning".*

During a recent worship song, I heard the leader say that "morning is not just a number on a clock – it's when you WAKE UP!" Waking up to the presence of Jesus is when I rejoice. I leave behind the darkness of my own way of thinking and doing things and SEE JESUS! I begin again to follow the way and life that is Jesus.

At the Bethlehem inn and on the way to Emmaus, there was no room for Jesus in preconceived lives. Jesus is asking me to OPEN my life and let HIM create in me what He will.

Additional text: Psalm 30, Job 42

"And why worry about a speck in the eye of a brother when you have a board in your own? Should you say, 'Friend, let me help you get that speck out of your eye,' when you can't even see because of the board in your own? Hypocrite! First get rid of the board. Then you can see to help your brother."

Matthew 7:3-5 (TLB)

The great evangelist, D.L. Moody, was once asked, "Who has caused you the most trouble in your ministry?" Thinking that Rev. Moody would respond with the name of another preacher or congregation member or elder – the man was quite surprised when he answered, "Who has given me the most trouble?!! Why, D. L. Moody!!!"

Rev. Moody spoke truly. Scripture doesn't tell me to take the plank out of someone else's eye. I am to remove MY plank!

Check up on yourselves. Are you really Christians? Do you pass the test? Do you feel Christ's presence and power more and more within you? Or are you just pretending to be Christians when actually you aren't at all?

2 Corinthians 13:5 (TLB)

Do I blame everyone else <u>except</u> myself for problems in my life? Wisdom is seeking the Lord so that He can discern for me what IS mine to accept as poor choices and what was beyond my scope and can I learn something from it? Then I will walk forward in His truth and victory, knowing that I am on the right path – His path!

The year King Uzziah died I saw the Lord! He was sitting on a lofty throne, and the Temple was filled with his glory...Such singing it was! It shook the Temple to its foundations, and suddenly the entire sanctuary was filled with smoke.

Then I said, "My doom is sealed, for I am a foul-mouthed sinner, a member of a sinful, foul-mouthed race; and I have looked upon the King, the Lord of heaven's armies."

Then one of the seraphs flew over to the altar and with a pair of tongs picked out a burning coal. He touched my lips with it and said, "Now you are pronounced 'Not guilty' because this coal has touched your lips. Your sins are all forgiven.

Then I heard the Lord asking, "Whom shall I send as a messenger to my people? Who will go?"

And I said, "Lord, I'll go! Send ME."   *Isaiah 6:1, 4-8 (TLB)*

It is truly awesome that it is God's will to use ME to spread the Good News of salvation through Jesus Christ. Even with that first thought, it is SO EASY to get in the way of God's plan for every situation and person that He puts me in contact with. It's all about Him, not me! It is HIS HOLY SPIRIT that wins souls, not my evangelism plan! God asks me to be just His vessel to carry the treasure.

Additional text: Psalm 51, 2 Corinthians 4

While Jesus was having dinner at Matthew's house, many tax collectors and "sinners" came and ate with him and his disciples. When the Pharisees saw this, they asked his disciples, "Why does your teacher eat with tax collectors and `sinners'?"

On hearing this, Jesus said, "It is not the healthy who need a doctor, but the sick. But go and learn what this means: `I desire mercy, not sacrifice.' For I have not come to call the righteous, but sinners."   *Matthew 9:10-13*

For I desire mercy, not sacrifice, and acknowledgment of God rather than burnt offerings.   *Hosea 6:6*

Why have we fasted,' they say, `and you have not seen it?
 Why have we humbled ourselves, and you have not noticed?'
 "Yet on the day of your fasting, you do as you please
 and exploit all your workers.
Your fasting ends in quarreling and strife, and in striking each other with wicked fists. You cannot fast as you do today and expect your voice to be heard on high.   *Isaiah 58:3-4*

What did I do yesterday for the Lord? Jesus says that it is "mercy" not "fasting" that is desirable. This causes me to examine my motives for going to church or Bible study or even doing my morning devotion! What are my motives? Am I doing it because it is "expected", to check it off my spiritual list for the day/week? Does it give me something to hold up when I lead my Sunday school class or fill out my annual report to the district church every year?

"So when you give to the needy, do not announce it with trumpets, as the hypocrites do in the synagogues and on the streets, to be honored by men. I tell you the truth; they have received their reward in full. But when you give to the needy, do not let your left hand know what your right hand is doing, so that your giving may be in secret. Then your Father, who sees what is done in secret, will reward you.

And when you pray, do not be like the hypocrites, for they love to pray standing in the synagogues and on the street corners to be seen by men. I tell you the truth; they have received their reward in full. But when you pray, go into your room, close the door and pray to your Father, who is unseen. Then your Father, who sees what is done in secret, will reward you."   *Matthew 6:2-8*

It's a 'heart thing'. Isaiah 58 speaks to me about mercy, compassion, love, and kindness. The Lord promises that these "true fastings" (from judgment, quarreling, strife) will bring blessings of His righteousness. He will hear my prayers, guide me, and satisfy my needs when I am in tough times. I will be filled with His joy that is not dependent on circumstances and I will grow in Him and "feast" on my inheritance. That sounds GOOD! I want to GROW UP and GLORIFY my Father!

God's love is SO <u>EXTRAVAGANT</u>! I don't think I really knew what that word meant until I began to know and <u>accept</u> the love of my Heavenly Father. He wants <u>so much</u> for me to be well and whole. He actually wants that more than <u>I</u> do! Yes, He does! Let's look at some scenes from Jesus' ministry. He speaks the Father's heart-messages.

Later, Jesus went to Jerusalem for another Jewish festival. In the city near the sheep gate was a pool with five porches, and its name in Hebrew was Bethzatha. Many sick, blind, lame, and crippled people were lying close to the pool.

Beside the pool was a man who had been sick for thirty-eight years. When Jesus saw the man and realized that he had been crippled for a long time, he asked him, "Do you want to be healed?"   *John 5:1-6 (CEV)*

DO I want to be healed? Seems like the answer would be obvious. When I have a physical illness, the 'cure' in the natural will involve an examination by a doctor, possibly medication and/or surgery. The same principles apply in the spiritual. I must be willing to be examined by the Great Physician. Be real. Be open. And that may involve some personal pain. The medicine He prescribes may not taste good and it may be inconvenient to my routine. The Lord may tell me I need to spend more time with Him or I may need to be submissive and obedient to someone <u>He</u> has put in authority over me – a pastor, my spouse, a mentor! Surgery can provide a relatively quick cure if I am willing to 'give up' something. Am I willing to have the 'boil' lanced open or the 'tumor' of un-forgiveness removed or give up <u>my</u> right – to be <u>right</u>??!! <u>DO</u> I want to be healed?

"When an evil spirit leaves a person, it travels through the desert, looking for a place to rest. But when it doesn't find a place, it says, 'I will go back to the home I left.' When it gets there and finds the place clean and fixed up, it goes off and finds seven other evil spirits even worse than itself. They all come and make their home there, and that person ends up in worse shape than before."

While Jesus was still talking, a woman in the crowd spoke up, "The woman who gave birth to you and nursed you is blessed!"

Jesus replied, "That's true, but the people who are really blessed are the ones who hear and obey God's message!"   *Luke 11:24-28 (CEV)*

OK. I've decided that I <u>do</u> want to be healed and I've been obedient to the treatment from the Lord that absolutely does bring on a cure – then what? In the physical, if I do not want to be re-infected I may have to change some habits. There is always <u>more</u> in my relationship to God. There's always another level of intimacy with God. I find those new levels through prayer, worship, study, and *<u>listening</u>* to God. That means I must practice silence on MY part so I can hear HIS wisdom and truth.

I am no one special. I'm just an average child of God that is loved – extravagantly – by an extra-ordinary God.

Their work won't be wasted, and their children won't die of dreadful diseases.
I will bless their children and their grandchildren.
I will answer their prayers before they finish praying. Isaiah 65:23-24 (CEV)

"Sometimes I wonder if God hears me." "Sometimes I wonder if He cares." These are not unusual thoughts when going through troubled times. How do I really know God is concerned about me and my problems? How does my concern for my son who is far away from home stack up against a major war and famine to my Heavenly Father?

God told us through Isaiah that even before I 'call' to Him – He answers. While I am still 'splaining things to Him – He hears. God is not constrained by multiple cries for help nor does He have 'off' hours when He takes vacation or sleeps. Isaiah testified himself that:

Don't you know? Haven't you heard?
The LORD is the eternal God, Creator of the earth.
He never gets weary or tired; his wisdom cannot be measured.
The LORD gives strength to those who are weary.
Even young people get tired, then stumble and fall. Isaiah 40:28-30 (CEV)

The night He died, Jesus prayed for us. The Son of God, in the moments when He was about to begin the final walk of His life here on earth, when He was about to complete the mission that He had been given to do – prayed for me.

"I am not praying just for these followers. I am also praying for everyone else, who will have faith because of what my followers will say about me. I want all of them to be one with each other, just as I am one with you and you are one with me. I also want them to be one with us. Then the people of this world will believe that you sent me...I told them what you are like, and I will tell them even more. Then the love that you have for me will become part of them, and I will be one with them." John 17:20-21, 26 (CEV)

Jesus prays for me that I will not only be united with ALL who call themselves believers in Him but that I will be completely united with HIM.

Stormie Omartian shared in her recent book, *Praying Through Life's Problems*, that she had walked with the Lord for 32 years and more time she spent with Him the less discouragement and fear she experienced when troubles occurred. She found she hung on to God's hope, knowing that He was in control. Continuous prayer keeps her in close touch with her Lord, remembering that she cannot live without Him and so He needs to be in charge of her life.

I give my burdens to Jesus because He DOES care for me.

Additional Text: Matthew 6, John 17

January 15

Always be joyful and never stop praying. Whatever happens, keep thanking God because of Jesus Christ. This is what God wants you to do.

1 Thessalonians 5:16-18 (CEV)

Praying is a good thing. It is communicating with God. Like any communication it is a whole lot easier when life is going well and I know the light at the end of the tunnel isn't a train! How do I pray when the times are difficult?

My friends, be glad, even if you have a lot of trouble. You know that you learn to endure by having your faith tested. But you must learn to endure everything, so that you will be completely mature and not lacking in anything.

If any of you need wisdom, you should ask God, and it will be given to you. God is generous and won't correct you for asking.   *James 1:2-5 (CEV)*

Praying for wisdom is a good place to start. Making good choices sure keeps me from increasing my stress and suffering during painful situations. Asking for wisdom on a daily basis 'covers' me with God's ability to see the larger picture. Sometimes decisions allow me to seek the Lord and wait upon His answer. Sometimes I don't have time to even form a prayer in my mind before I must act. It is good to have sought Him daily and KNOW His will.

"Then I will ask the Father to send you the Holy Spirit who will help you and always be with you. The Spirit will show you what is true. The people of this world cannot accept the Spirit, because they don't see or know him. But you know the Spirit, who is with you and will keep on living in you.

John 14:16-17 (CEV)

Asking the Holy Spirit for His comfort and healing is another good step. In the midst of tragedy and loss, when the world seem to have tipped on its axis, asking the Holy Spirit to just "Come" and minister to me, in WHATEVER WAY He knows I need, is a positive and constructive prayer. I do not need to be any more specific than that. He will come in power AND revelation to meet every need.

But it is just as the Scriptures say, "What God has planned for people who love him is more than eyes have seen or ears have heard. It has never even entered our minds!"   *1 Corinthians 2:9 (CEV)*

When Jesus was in Gethsemane, in His humanness He sweated blood thinking of what was to come. In His humanness, He asked the Father three times if what was to happen could pass by Him. He found the strength to continue while on His knees and by the power of the Holy Spirit to focus His mind on the atonement that the ultimate sacrifice would bring instead of the misery and suffering of the moment.

Additional Text: Luke 3, Acts 7

I was sharing yesterday about how to pray when times are difficult.

- Praying for wisdom.
- Asking for the Holy Spirit to come and minister to me
- And by the power of the Holy Spirit, pray to focus on the good that may come and not on the misery of the moment

I love the LORD, for he heard my voice; he heard my cry for mercy.
Because he turned his ear to me, I will call on him as long as I live.
The cords of death entangled me, the anguish of the grave came upon me;
I was overcome by trouble and sorrow.
Then I called on the name of the LORD:
"O LORD, save me!"
The LORD is gracious and righteous; our God is full of compassion.
The LORD protects the simple-hearted; when I was in great need, he saved me.
Be at rest once more, O my soul, for the LORD has been good to you.
For you, O LORD, have delivered my soul from death, my eyes from tears,
my feet from stumbling, that I may walk before the LORD
in the land of the living.   *Psalm 116:1-9*

Praying for <u>more</u> of God's presence in my life increases my faith and causes doubt to flee. His presence helps me to STAND strong and not be swayed by my emotions and the lies of satan.

Paul said he had "learned to be content whatever the circumstances" (Philippians 4:11). Do I think that Paul never felt the grief of the death of a loved one or never felt completely alone? Of course he did. But Paul also sought and asked for the presence of God to be so tangible in his life that his fears were removed and hope was always there.

Praying to stay in God's Word and being obedient is also good. When the hurricane is blowing in my life, I must have something solid that I can sink my anchor into. God's word is a solid rock. It lifts me and strengthens me. God's promises are free and worth more to me than any quick fix I can try to buy.

Disappointment is a common occurrence in this life. People will inevitably disappoint me. Placing my expectations on God and counting on HIM to meet my needs surely takes the pressure off of others to meet my needs! Expecting too much of others AND myself takes a spotlight that was only meant for God and mis-focuses it. Misplaced expectations lead to bitterness and un-forgiveness.

He tends his flock like a shepherd: He gathers the lambs in his arms
and carries them close to his heart...   *Isaiah 40:11*

Let us RUN to the Father and allow HIS arms to hold us!

Additional Text: Proverbs 19, Philippians 4

In the morning, O LORD, you hear my voice;
   in the morning I lay my requests before you
   and wait in expectation.   *Psalm 5:3*

This life, or anyone in it, can NEVER meet all my expectations. When I put my expectations in the Lord and know that my help comes from Him, that surely takes the pressure off those around me! It is God's desire that I rely fully on Him. Others will bring only bitterness and un-forgiveness. Relying on God brings hope and peace with the assurance that the Lord will hold and sustain me.

"If you forgive others for the wrongs they do to you, your Father in heaven will forgive you. But if you don't forgive others, your Father will not forgive your sins."   *Matthew 6:14-15 (CEV)*

Forgiveness. Yes, I will definitely say that I need to pray for forgiveness. Oh – Lord! You want me to pray that I will forgive OTHERS?!

During some of the most difficult times of my life, forgiving others was the second hardest thing to do. I think it goes along with the 'expectation thing' that we just talked about. People hurt me. They're human! But when it is people who are closest to me – husband, parents, children – even a pastor or fellow Believer – it seems to add a layer that makes forgiveness just a bit more difficult. I 'expect' more, don't I? Even though He doesn't need it – I admit that sometimes I even need to forgive GOD! Forgiveness removes the root of bitterness that can grow branches of offense and depression, etc. etc. and blocks God's joy from my life.

And then there's the hardest thing I need to pray to receive – God's grace to forgive MYSELF!!! It's the pits when I think that I have failed or I'm responsible for a bad thing that has happened. Maybe I really haven't failed but I let regret and condemnation pound away at me. Someone recently said that as a child of God "I may fail but I am NOT a failure!". This is a weight I was NEVER meant to carry. "Could've and should've and would've" are SOOOO counterproductive!

Prayer IS communication with God. It is my time to lay it all out for God. Yes, He DOES already know what's going on in my life and going through my mind but laying it out – verbalizing it or journaling it – is the beginning of my releasing it. It is also my time to LISTEN to God. Hear Him speak to me. Yes, even audibly but also in His written word, the Scriptures, and in His Holy Spirit to my spirit.

The result is peace, encouragement, forgiveness, thanksgiving, joy comfort, and love. Praying is a good thing!

Additional Text: 1 Chronicles 5, Mark 11

January 18

When the man heard this, he was sad, because he was very rich.
Jesus saw how sad the man was. So he said, "It's terribly hard for rich people to get into God's kingdom! In fact, it's easier for a camel to go through the eye of a needle than for a rich person to get into God's kingdom."
When the crowd heard this, they asked, "How can anyone ever be saved?"
Jesus replied, "There are some things that people cannot do, but God can do anything."   *Luke 18:23-27(CEV)*

There was a very popular worship song a few years ago "All Things Are Possible" (Darlene Zschech. 1997). It was based on this 27th verse from Luke. I sang this song sometimes with tears of hope born of desperation in the circumstances I was in. God heard my voice and I could feel His very presence as He would pick me up off the floor and assure me that He was already walking before me and had all those 'pesky little problems', that seem so HUGE to me, well under control!

And then, as I saw God work in my life and in the lives of those I loved, I would sing the song with joyful abandon! I would put it in my CD player and just dance around the house! I confess to you that someone also gave me a 'bootlegged' copy of the videotape and I so loved watching adults and children alike sing this song. I could see by the expressions on their face that they KNEW that ALL things were possible with God!!

I know what it is to be poor or to have plenty, and I have lived under all kinds of conditions. I know what it means to be full or to be hungry, to have too much or too little. Christ gives me the strength to face anything.
                                                Philippians 4:12-13 (CEV)

Another translation says: *I know how to live on almost nothing or with everything. I have learned the secret of contentment in every situation, whether it be a full stomach or hunger, plenty or want; for I can do everything God asks me to with the help of Christ who gives me the strength and power.*   *(TLB)*

Paul wasn't speaking of just physical hunger. Sometimes I hunger for … unconditional love … wisdom and clear sight in a particular circumstance … 'gifting' to accomplish a task I have been given. God is already there. He already knows the need. He can fulfill the need.

You are kind, LORD, so good and merciful.
You protect ordinary people, and when I was helpless,
you saved me and treated me so kindly that I don't need to worry anymore.
                                                Psalm 116:5-7 (CEV)

Additional text: Psalm 116, Matthew 6

We know that everything in the Law was written for those who are under its power. The Law says these things to stop anyone from making excuses and to let God show that the whole world is guilty. God doesn't accept people simply because they obey the law. No, indeed! All the Law does is to point out our sin. Now we see how God does make us acceptable to him. The Law and the Prophets tell how we become acceptable, and it isn't by obeying the Law of Moses. God treats everyone alike. He accepts people only because they have faith in Jesus Christ. All of us have sinned and fallen short of God's glory. But God treats us much better than we deserve, and because of Christ Jesus, he freely accepts us and sets us free from our sin. Romans 3:19-24 (CEV)

I am basically a 'T' cross-er and an 'I' dot-ter. I like things to be in their place and tasks to be completed. God will not allow me to do that with my spiritual life. Of course, all I have to do is go back and start reading all those laws in Exodus, Leviticus, and other Old Testament books, to find out rather quickly that I cannot possibly adhere to all those edicts! I can't even get the "Top Ten" right!!!

Paul, the Big Pharisee, assures me that HE couldn't get it all right either. He says *ALL of us have sinned and fallen short* of where God wants us to be. Praise God for GRACE and MERCY! Undeserved love and undeserved forgiveness!

Charles Wesley wrote a song in the 1700's, *And Can It Be That I Should Gain?*. The story goes that while involved in prison ministry in London that he had the opportunity to visit with a man who was to be executed the next day. He led that man to Christ (thank You, Lord!). Wesley was so overwhelmed by God's grace and mercy that he returned to his apartment and sat down and wrote the song in one sitting.

And can it be that I should gain an interest in the Savior's blood!
Died he for me? who caused his pain! For me? who him to death pursued?
Amazing love! How can it be that thou, my God, shouldst die for me?
Amazing love! How can it be that thou, my God, shouldst die for me?

Long my imprisoned spirit lay, fast bound in sin and nature's night;
thine eye diffused a quickening ray; I woke, the dungeon flamed with light;
my chains fell off, my heart was free, I rose, went forth, and followed thee.
My chains fell off, my heart was free, I rose, went forth, and followed thee.
Amazing love! How can it be that thou, my God, shouldst die for me?
Amazing love! How can it be that thou, my God, shouldst die for me?

Jesus died for me. Jesus died for you. There's nothing hidden or mystical about it. He did it out of love. I can't earn it even with my obedience. My obedience should come because of love. Love for my Lord who first loved me.

Additional Text: Mark 14, Romans 5

Some time later God tested Abraham. He said to him, "Abraham!"
"Here I am," he replied.
Then God said, "Take your son , your only son, Isaac, whom you love, and go to the region of Moriah. Sacrifice him there as a burnt offering on one of the mountains I will tell you about."
Early the next morning Abraham got up and saddled his donkey. He took with him two of his servants and his son Isaac. When he had cut enough wood for the burnt offering, he set out for the place God had told him about. On the third day Abraham looked up and saw the place in the distance. He said to his servants, "Stay here with the donkey while I and the boy go over there. We will worship and then we will come back to you."
Abraham took the wood for the burnt offering and placed it on his son Isaac, and he himself carried the fire and the knife. As the two of them went on together, Isaac spoke up and said to his father Abraham, "Father?"
"Yes, my son?" Abraham replied.
"The fire and wood are here," Isaac said, "but where is the lamb for the burnt offering?"
Abraham answered, "God himself will provide the lamb for the burnt offering, my son." And the two of them went on together.
When they reached the place God had told him about, Abraham built an altar there and arranged the wood on it. He bound his son Isaac and laid him on the altar, on top of the wood.   *Genesis 22:1-9*

I wonder what Isaac thought at that moment! Did he look at his father like, "Are you NUTS?!!!" Or given the time and social mores and maybe even the relationship of trust that Abraham and Isaac might have had, did Isaac quietly relinquish his control in absolute trust to his father?

Since I made that 180 degree turn in 1995, acknowledging that I was a sinner and accepting Jesus as my Lord and Savior, it seems that God has asked me many times to relinquish my control and let Him have His way. Prior to 1995, I was so hell-bent (an accurate term!) on my own way of doing things that I never heard God's question of 'Will you obey me?' much less answered it! Or I guess I answered it with my actions, didn't I? My answer to the control question has usually been more toward the "Are you NUTS?!!!" side than the peaceful release. I KNOW that God knows best but it's taking that step away from ME to HIM that trips me up! And besides, how do I know it's REALLY God?

Rejoice in the Lord always. I will say it again: Rejoice! Let your gentleness be evident to all. The Lord is near. Do not be anxious about anything, but in everything, by prayer and petition, with thanksgiving, present your requests to God. And the peace of God, which transcends all understanding, will guard your hearts and your minds in Christ Jesus. Finally, brothers, whatever is true, whatever is noble, whatever is right, whatever is pure, whatever is lovely, whatever is admirable--if anything is excellent or praiseworthy--think about such things. Whatever you have learned or received or heard from me, or seen in me--put it into practice. And the God of peace will be with you.

Philippians 4:4-9

This is just one of the Scriptures that comes to my mind when I wonder if what I am hearing is God. Yes, I also consider what I feel in my spirit and what God has done in my experience. But in any given situation, I could hold up this Scripture and get a 'reading' on which path/answer is truly God. Look:

Which path would glorify God with my gentleness and show that the Lord is near?

Which path brings on 'anxiety' and which brings 'peace' in my spirit?

When I lift the situation in prayer, which path does thanksgiving overflow and which path do I want to present before God if I am staring Him right in the face?

Which path is true, noble, right, pure, lovely, admirable, excellent, or praiseworthy?

Trust in the LORD with all your heart and lean not on your own understanding; in all your ways acknowledge him, and he will make your paths straight.
Do not be wise in your own eyes; fear the LORD and shun evil.

Proverbs 3:5-7

~

January 21

How sweet are your words to my taste, sweeter than honey to my mouth!
Through your precepts I get understanding; therefore I hate every false way.
Your word is a lamp to my feet and a light to my path.
Psalm 119:103-105 (ESV)

Again Jesus spoke to them saying, "I am the light of the world. Whoever follows
me will not walk in darkness, but will have the light of life." John 8:12 (ESV)

Light and darkness. I'm getting up in the middle of the night and I am <u>positive</u>
I know the way in my own house to the bathroom so I don't turn on the light.
Besides, I'm being a loving wife by not turning on the light and disturbing
Henry! (Like the light is going to wake him from a dead sleep!) **WHAM!** I
bang my toe into the edge of the doorway because I misjudged the space! Now
Henry is awake because I just made noise! Why didn't I use the light? As I
'stumble' around in my everyday life trying to stay on the path in a world of
darkness, why don't I use the Light?

It's become very apparent to me recently that some questions or decision
require more than logic and reasoning. Although God did make my mind and
provide opportunities for education and experiences, events in my life seem to
defy or go beyond the scope of this God-given power. God is not limited. He is
<u>limit-less</u> in His provision. He spoke to me this morning in these words, His
words, that they are a "*lamp*" to me. That if I search <u>Him</u> and know <u>Him</u> that I
will gain <u>His</u> wisdom and <u>His</u> knowledge and walk in <u>His</u> perfect way, not
stumbling and misjudging the distance.

In the darkness that 'hovers' over events in my life, God's Spirit is still there.
My life may seem 'formless and empty', BUT God's Spirit hovers over me and
when I reach toward the Light, very often that means picking up His Word. I
become plugged in to the Light and the darkness flees. His light may only
extend one step ahead of me. He KNOWS me so well that He gives me only
one step ahead so I won't get arrogant and start improvising my own steps!!!
But the Light is there and it's true and it's faithful. Praise God!

"No one after lighting a lamp puts it in a cellar or under a basket, but on a
stand, so that those who enter may see the light." *Luke 11:33 (ESV)*

Additional text: Psalm 139, Luke 11

For my name's sake I defer my anger, for the sake of my praise I restrain it for you, that I may not cut you off.

Behold, I have refined you, but not as silver; I have tried you in the furnace of affliction.

For my own sake, for my own sake, I do it, for how should my name be profaned? My glory I will not give to another. Isaiah 48:9-11 (ESV)

God loves me right now – just as I am. But I want to grow, not remain stagnate and He wants the same thing for me. That refining and pruning is not always fun and the enemy sees it as an opportunity to begin <u>his</u> mischief.

We are afflicted in every way, but not crushed; perplexed, but not driven to despair; persecuted, but not forsaken; struck down, but not destroyed;

2 Corinthians 4:8-9 (ESV)

We have to be willing to turn everything over to Jesus, holding nothing back:

I said, "Everything?" He said, "Yes, everything."

I said, "Everything?" He said, "Yes."

I said, "Some of it is perverse, sad, embarrassing."

He said, "Nevertheless..."

I said, "What will You do with it?"

He said, "If I can make an ax head float, turn water into wine, and cover this universe with one drop of My blood, I can take your mistakes and make them My victories!"

I said, "What about <u>my</u> victories?" He said, "Those would only be more mistakes..." [ouch!] from *Friendly Fire* by Mike Warnke

I <u>like</u> walking in victory! That's a wonderful 'church' phrase! But 'victory' implies that there was a <u>battle</u> to win or lose, doesn't it? Historically, I've not read about 'bloodless' battles. Henry is a history buff and specifically likes to read or watch historical biographies so I have learned more about battles and wars than I ever thought I would! I do read and teach a lot about 'spiritual warfare'. There is a lot to be learned from what I can 'see' in the natural and draw the parallels about what God is doing in the spiritual realm:

-- Know your enemy (the Accuser! The scumbag!)

-- Know the strengths and weaknesses of your allies (including the smart thing – aligning myself with God, in which case, HE doesn't have weaknesses!)

-- Learn from history so I do not repeat it! (Study Scripture and learn from my past)

-- Fight smart! Using weapons available and in the proper time and place and way

-- Don't forget: the War is <u>already</u> won! So follow orders from the Commander-in-chief, entering only the battles I am assigned and always remembering His priority to set free any prisoners I meet along the way! Give God <u>all</u> the praise and <u>all</u> the glory!

Additional Text: 2 Chronicles 32, Psalm 18

My dear friends, you always obeyed when I was with you. Now that I am away, you should obey even more. So work with fear and trembling to discover what it really means to be saved. God is working in you to make you willing and able to obey him.

Do everything without grumbling or arguing. Then you will be the pure and innocent children of God. You live among people who are crooked and evil, but you must not do anything that they can say is wrong. Try to shine as lights among the people of this world, as you hold firmly to the message that gives life... *Philippians 2:12-16 (CEV)*

I saw a new heaven and a new earth. The first heaven and the first earth had disappeared, and so had the sea. Then I saw New Jerusalem, that holy city, coming down from God in heaven. It was like a bride dressed in her wedding gown and ready to meet her husband.

I heard a loud voice shout from the throne: God's home is now with his people. He will live with them, and they will be his own. Yes, God will make his home among his people. He will wipe all tears from their eyes, and there will be no more death, suffering, crying, or pain. These things of the past are gone forever. *Revelation 21:1-4 (CEV)*

Salvation. Eternity. Sometimes I wonder if I can really grasp the concept of "eternity". I live in a microwave, instant potatoes, and disposable world. What is "eternal" and "forever and ever" to me?

If I draw a line on a piece of paper and put a zero at the left end, that marks the year I was born. Then I go down the line and mark "16", "21", "30" etc. until I get to ...well, how ever many years I think I am going to live. I would probably mark "85" unless the Lord comes before that! Now, think about that timeline in the concept of "eternity". There isn't enough paper, is there? For me, there are also children, grandchildren, a spouse, siblings, and others who would be a mark on my timeline. Will they also join me in "eternity"?

Paul tells us to work out our salvation with *"fear and trembling"*. I believe he is speaking of 'holy fear'. That AWE-SOME-NESS of what God has done through His Son, Jesus Christ. That unconditional, knows-no-end love that has given ME – "ETERNITY"! Paul goes on to tell us to be a light – a lighthouse – in a dark world.

The apostle, John, attempts to describe to us the Judgment Day as he saw it in a vision. I have had a few visions. Mere English words become totally inadequate to describe the colors, much less the actual event. The larger picture that we can grasp is – God wins, satan loses – I know WHOSE side I want to be on!!

Additional text: Revelation 20 and 21

There is a time for everything, and a season for every activity under heaven:
a time to be born and a time to die, a time to plant and a time to uproot,
a time to kill and a time to heal, a time to tear down and a time to build,
a time to weep and a time to laugh, a time to mourn and a time to dance,
a time to scatter stones and a time to gather them,
a time to embrace and a time to refrain, a time to search and a time to give up,
a time to keep and a time to throw away, a time to tear and a time to mend,
a time to be silent and a time to speak, a time to love and a time to hate,
a time for war and a time for peace.   *Ecclesiastes 3:1-8*

On the third day a wedding took place at Cana in Galilee. Jesus' mother was there, and Jesus and his disciples had also been invited to the wedding. When the wine was gone, Jesus' mother said to him, "They have no more wine."

"Dear woman, why do you involve me?" Jesus replied. "My time has not yet come."

His mother said to the servants, "Do whatever he tells you."   *John 2:1-5*

It is recorded that Jesus' <u>public</u> life began at this wedding. I've often wondered at how many lepers he passed or how many funerals He attended prior to that time. I believe it goes back to obedience; perfect obedience to the will and timing of the <u>Father</u>.

They did not understand that he was telling them about his Father. So Jesus said, "When you have lifted up the Son of Man, then you will know that I am the one I claim to be and that I do nothing on my own but speak just what the Father has taught me. The one who sent me is with me; he has not left me alone, for I always do what pleases him." Even as he spoke, many put their faith in him.   *John 8:27-30*

I <u>want</u> to be closer to God, to understand His heart and mind. To see what He sees and in the way He sees things. Obedience draws me closer to God. Many times that means obedience without knowing the 'why'. That's tough for me. I was one of those little kids that when their daddy told them to do something I responded with "Why?" instead of "Yes, sir."

God's timing is <u>perfect</u>. Now – How is my obedience to His timing??

Additional text: Proverbs 3, John 1

Have you ever heard someone say, "I am waiting on the Lord?" Since accepting Jesus as my Savior and making the decision to live for Him, God has cleaned up much of my life (as I allow Him!) – not the least of which is my mouth! I used to be able to curse with the best of sailors! (My apologies to all you naval personnel!) I think 'wait' is now my least favorite '4-letter word' and the one I hear from the Lord too often, in MY opinion! I am an organizer and I recognize that the shortest route between two points is a straight line! I am willing to show anyone who hesitates MY way of doing things so we can 'get on with it'! More often than not, that straight line is inside a tunnel. I am on a 'mission' and I do not see all the other important 'points' along the way. God does.

For thus said the Lord GOD, the Holy One of Israel, "In returning and rest you shall be saved; in quietness and in trust shall be your strength."

But you were unwilling, and you said, "No! We will flee upon horses"; therefore you shall flee away; and, "We will ride upon swift steeds"; therefore your pursuers shall be swift.

A thousand shall flee at the threat of one; at the threat of five you shall flee, till you are left like a flagstaff on the top of a mountain, like a signal on a hill.

Therefore the LORD waits to be gracious to you, and therefore he exalts himself to show mercy to you. For the LORD is a God of justice; blessed are all those who wait for him.   *Isaiah 30:15-18 (ESV)*

And while staying with them, he ordered them not to depart from Jerusalem, but to wait for the promise of the Father, which, said, "...you heard from me; for John baptized with water, but you will be baptized with the Holy Spirit, not many days from now."

So when they had come together, they asked him, "Lord, will you at this time restore the kingdom to Israel?" He said to the, "It is not for you to know times or seasons that the Father has fixed by his own authority...And when he had said these things, as they were looking on, he was lifted up, and a cloud took him out of their sight   *Acts 1:4-7, 9 (ESV)*

And so I wait when I am told to wait. I am but a part of God's plan. God desires that I be an integral part of HIS plan, using me with the talents and gifts that He has given. If I will say, "Here am I. Send me." (Isaiah 6:8) and be obedient in the details of when and how. God blesses me in ways I can only imagine when I am obedient.

For in this hope we were saved. Now hope that is seen is not hope. For who hopes for what he sees? But if we hope for what we do not see, we wait for it with patience.   *Romans 8:24-25 (ESV)*

Additional text: Romans 8, Acts 1

"You have heard that it was said, 'You shall love your neighbor and hate your enemy.' But I say to you, Love your enemies and pray for those who persecute you, so that you may be sons of your Father who is in heaven. For he makes his sun rise on the evil and on the good, and sends rain on the just and on the unjust. For if you love those who love you, what reward do you have? Do not even the tax collectors do the same? And if you greet only your brothers, what more are you doing than others? Do not even the Gentiles, do the same? You therefore must be perfect, as your heavenly Father is perfect."

Matthew 5:43-48 (ESV)

I've read the passage from Matthew often wondered about the sun and the rain coming to the righteous and the <u>un</u>righteous. The usual discussion involves the "fairness" of God. I'm not sure that my lil' ol' finite mind could possibly be equipped to "judge" God's fairness to His children.

My soul yearns for you in the night; my spirit within me earnestly seeks you.

For when your judgments are in the earth, the inhabitants of the world learn righteousness. If favor is show to the wicked, he does not learn righteousness; in the land of uprightness he deals corruptly and does not see the majesty of the LORD.

Isaiah 26:9-10 (ESV)

This passage in Isaiah tells me that God <u>does</u> extend grace to <u>ALL</u> of His children. <u>I</u> make the choice to accept it, asking and receiving forgiveness and learning righteousness, learning about a 'right relationship' with God. That is <u>MY</u> choice.

And finally, I found it interesting today that Jesus put the passage that trials (or rain) will come to the unrighteous AND the righteous in the same paragraph with His clear word that I am to love those who are unlovable AND who persecute me. He tells me to lift my goals higher than the unbelievers and compare myself or set my standard to God, not another man.

Against you, you only, have I sinned and done what is evil in your sight, so that you may be justified in your words and blameless in your judgment...

Create in me a clean heart, O God, and renew a right spirit within me.

Cast me not away from your presence, and take not your Holy Spirit from me.

Restore to me the joy of your salvation, and uphold me with a willing spirit.

Psalm 51:4, 10-12

Additional text: Psalm 51, 1 Corinthians 13

Jesus left and went into one of the Jewish meeting places, where there was a man whose hand was crippled. Some Pharisees wanted to accuse Jesus of doing something wrong, and they asked him, "Is it right to heal someone on the Sabbath?"

Jesus answered, "If you had a sheep that fell into a ditch on the Sabbath, wouldn't you lift it out? People are worth more than sheep, and so it is right to do good on the Sabbath." Then Jesus told the man, "Hold out your hand." The man did, and it became as healthy as the other one. The Pharisees left and started making plans to kill Jesus.   *Matthew 12:9-14 (CEV)*

Now let's look at what the LORD said originally to Moses:

Keep the Sabbath holy. You have six days to do your work, but the Sabbath is mine, and it must remain a day of rest. If you work on the Sabbath, you will no longer be part of my people, and you will be put to death.

Every generation of Israelites must respect the Sabbath. This day will always serve as a reminder, both to me and to the Israelites, that I made the heavens and the earth in six days, then on the seventh day I rested and relaxed.   *Exodus 31:14-17 (CEV)*

Every day belongs to the Lord. I am to use every day to God's glory and honor. I am not to 'desecrate' any day! As a nurse, I usually had to work two Sundays a month. I never felt that I was committing a sin. God had given me talents and had made it possible for me to become a nurse. When the opportunity opened up, I was most grateful that I no longer had to work on weekends. And this was before I was a believer!

Now I want to draw even closer to God. I want to walk so that my footprints are hidden in His. So what is God speaking into my heart about the Sabbath? I want Him to receive my love in this area by being obedient.

-- I want to spend time with Him in a place of worship with other Believers. I want to worship Him through music, prayer, His Word, and testimonies of what He is doing. I want to be on <u>His</u> schedule with this.

-- I don't want to 'work' on that day. I want the day to be totally 'OPEN' to listening to Him and sharing with others, keeping the focus on God the whole day. This means I need to make arrangements for meals and any other task that seems like 'work' for me.

-- I want to praise the Lord all day. No negatives. Just thanksgiving and praise for what God has done and is doing and will do.

I don't want to become a 'Pharisee' about the Sabbath. I want to be an obedient child! I want my Heavenly Father to smile with pleasure to see me! It is a good thing when <u>my</u> wants come into alignment with <u>GOD'S</u> wants!!!

Additional text: Romans 12, Deuteronomy 6

When the foundations are being destroyed, what can the righteous do?"
The LORD is in his holy temple; the LORD is on his heavenly throne.
He observes the sons of men; his eyes examine them.   *Psalm 11:3-4*

What is there to say in the midst of war? What do I say to my friends who have been notified that their son or daughter has been killed in combat? Where will my eyes be when the next terrorist attack comes? Glued to the television or focused on the One who has the power to do something about EVERY situation?

We have seen pictures and reel after reel of what war looks like. We have to hunt for the pictures of soldiers praying, soldiers being baptized in the desert, and reporting miraculous events of protection and care. God isn't sleeping through this war. He isn't *distracted* by some other single incident and missing our concerns.

During the days, months, and years ahead, we as Christians have an opportunity to hold up God's banners of truth, hope, compassion, power, and unconditional love. Whether it is family, friends, fellow members of our local church, co-workers, or even unknown people on the street, we are Christ's ambassadors with opportunities to share God's peace that DOES pass understanding through prayer, fellowship, and witnessing to the character of God.

God's temple, His dwelling on earth is ME. It's YOU. We are His temple. We carry His light into the WHOLE world. Jesus said to *"GO into ALL the world"*. Do I think that Jesus spoke carelessly and didn't really mean "ALL"? I must lift my head out of my own little universe and see the opportunities that the Lord has placed in my path. I can do NOTHING without Him. Sharing that testimony in these uncertain days is being a conduit of God's light – His lighthouse – in a world that would want me to believe that all is lost! Just before He died, Jesus said to His disciples and to me,

"I have much more to say to you, more than you can now bear. But when he, the Spirit of truth, comes, he will guide you into all truth. He will not speak on his own; he will speak only what he hears, and he will tell you what is yet to come. He will bring glory to me by taking from what is mine and making it known to you. All that belongs to the Father is mine. That is why I said the Spirit will take from what is mine and make it known to you... "I have told you these things, so that in me you may have peace. In this world you will have trouble. But take heart! I have overcome the world."   *John 16:12-15, 32*

As we pray each day, let us remember to always pray through to the victory that has already been won!

Additional text: 2 Chronicles 2, Psalm 19

January 29

The LORD is a mighty tower where his people can run for safety.

Psalm 18:10 (CEV)

What an AWESOME promise and testimony! That's what I want – an anchor that holds in ANY storm! No matter WHAT happens, I can count on the power of the Lord that is there for me to run toward and be safe.

Someone sent me this story in an email. Even though it is VERY funny – it is also VERY true!

A burglar broke into a house one night. He shone his flashlight around, looking for valuables, and when he picked up a CD player to place in his sack, a strange, disembodied voice echoed from the dark saying, "*Jesus is watching you.*" He nearly jumped out of his skin, clicked his flashlight out and froze.

When he heard nothing more after a bit, he shook his head, clicked the light back on and began searching for more valuables. Just as he pulled the stereo out so he could disconnect the wires, clear as a bell he heard, "*Jesus is watching you.*"

Freaked out, he shone his light around frantically, looking for the source of the voice. Finally, in the corner of the room, his flashlight beam came to rest on a parrot.

"Did you say that?" he hissed at the parrot.

"Yep," the parrot confessed, "I'm just trying to warn you."

The burglar relaxed. "Warn me, huh? Who are you?"

"Moses," replied the bird.

"Moses!" the burglar laughed. "What kind of stupid people would name a parrot Moses?"

"Probably the same kind of people that would name a Rotweiller 'Jesus'," the bird answered.

The name of Jesus is not just a name – it is the POWER behind the name that is our anchor of hope in ANY circumstance. The writer of Hebrews said:

This hope is like a firm and steady anchor for our souls. In fact, hope reaches behind the curtain and into the most holy place. Jesus has gone there ahead of us, and he is our high priest forever, just like Melchizedek.

Hebrews 6:19-20 (CEV)

Jesus is always there in the Holy of Holies with the Father and I can come in there ANY TIME because of JESUS! In the darkest days and nights of my life when things are happening that I totally do not understand and see absolutely NO reason behind it, I can go to the Holy of Holies and Jesus will sit down with me and we will talk it out! As long as it takes! There are still things that happen in my life that I don't understand and for the most part I have made the choice to accept God's greater wisdom and sight. But when I do have further questions, God is there. Because of the power of His name and what He did on the cross, Jesus is the strong tower I run toward!

Additional Text: Daniels 2, Hebrews 6

"Yes, the way to identify a tree or a person is by the kind of fruit produced.
Not all who sound religious are really godly people. They may refer to me as
'Lord', but still won't get to heaven. For the decisive question is whether they
obey my Father in heaven."   Matthew 7:20-21 (TLB)

I am a Christian; not just by what I profess but by the fruit of my profession.
The apostle Paul preached a lot about faith. He was a Pharisee and rejoiced at
the new covenant that comes to us through Jesus' perfect and eternal atonement.
We were set FREE from the chains of the law.

The disciple, James, preached that, "faith without deeds is dead" (2:26). He
certainly was not erasing faith from the equation but in fact was adding faith and
works makes a BALANCED equation.

At the Judgment many will tell me, 'Lord, Lord, we told others about you and
used your name to cast out demons and to do many other great miracles.' But I
will reply, 'You have never been mine. Go away, for your deeds are evil.'"

                                                               Matthew 7:22-23 (TLB)

Ah – so it seems that Jesus is telling me that OBEDIENCE is the key to Jesus'
reprimand. It's not just that I CALL Jesus 'Lord' but do I act like He is 'Lord'.
Do my actions and my heart set Him as Lord and Savior in my life? Do I submit
everything to Him INCLUDING His ministry that I do at HIS command? Or do
I cast out demons and perform miracles in Jesus' name but for MY glory and
honor? Ouch.

Remember the story of Simon the Sorcerer in Acts 8? Simon was known for
his 'powers', which the people thought were 'amazing'. Phillip came to the area
to preach the Good News and Simon believed! He followed Phillip around and
was fascinated by the signs and wonders he saw. Peter and John come to the
town. Simon again sees miracles that even he, the 'magician', cannot explain!
So he offers Peter some money if he will lay hands on him so he can 'get it'!
Peter replies very strongly that the power of the Holy Sprit is NOT for sale and
pokes at the root of Simon's heart, his bitter, sinful heart.

I am known to be a true disciple when my heart is obedient and humble. The
Holy Spirit flows through a heart like a knife through soft butter. I become only
a conduit between God and His children. I am only an instrument of an extraordinary God!

Additional text: Isaiah 6, Acts 8

January 31

And behold, a man came up to him, saying, "Teacher, what good deed must I do to have eternal life?" And he said to him, "Why do you ask me about what is good? There is only one who is good. If you would enter life, keep the commandments."
"...All these I have kept. What do I still lack?"
Jesus said to him, "If you would be perfect, go, sell what you possess and give to the poor, and you will have treasure in heaven; and come follow me." When the young man heard this he went away sorrowful, for he had great possessions.

Matthew 19:16-17, 20-22 (ESV)

"I want to be good." I've said that since I took tap dancing as a 4-year-old. Every time my parents punished me, I said that in my heart. Every time I confessed my sins as a child to a priest and had to stand in long lines on a Saturday afternoon to do it, I promised to be good so I wouldn't have to do THAT again!!!

What is 'good'?

Jesus tells me that 'good', is being obedient to the Father's commandments. I knew, as a child that being 'good' was being obedient, didn't I? 40 years later, I'm still trying to find a way to wiggle around the obvious!

'Good' comes from obedience and obedience comes from two factors: love and fear.

Scripture speaks of the 'fear of the Lord' and rightly so. It's a 'holy fear'; an 'awed' fear. Scripture tells me that God can hold the oceans in the palm of His hand. He's so BIG. I am small. He could destroy me with a thought, a breath. He blesses me with more than I could ask or imagine!

I believe that like me with my own children, the Father desires that I be obedient every time because of my LOVE for Him. He's willing to use the 'fear factor' because He wants me to grow and mature in a 'good' way but He'd like me to learn about Him so clearly and grab on to our relationship drawing so close to Him that I am motivated out of love. I feel His love all the time and return that love with obedience and joy. That's intimacy!

When I want to know about 'good', I can turn to Jesus and look at His example. He is my example and guide.

Additional text: Hebrews 4, Matthew 19

Marybelle Schulte Grossheider
1919-2003

This is about my mom. I don't remember discussing 'faith' with my mother until the last five years or so of her life. But I remember even as a young child watching her kneel in church and a 'look' would come over her face of such peace…I knew she was talking with her Lord. I didn't understand but I knew I wanted whatever she had.

Marybelle Grossheider was third generation American, growing up during the post-war depression in the 'heartland' of the United States. She thought of herself as a farm girl and was proud of the work ethic that she had learned from her parents who, though very poor, always had 'some to share'. As the oldest of five children, she was given adult responsibilities early in life and was able to only complete the eighth grade.

She grew up with a strong faith that was walked out in the everyday life of her family. Though they never considered themselves 'poor like other people', food came from what they raised on the farm and clothing was self-made and handed down. God was a central figure in the home and recognized as the One who had provided all that they needed.

She married a man who was raised in a different denomination in a time when this was not often done. She was not even allowed to marry inside the church but instead they were married in the pastor's house. My brother and I were raised in Mother's faith but we went to both churches for Christmas and Easter. We were taught that we all believed in Jesus Christ as Savior and Lord but that we were traveling slightly different roads in the same direction to live eternally with Jesus.

One of my earliest memories of my mother was seeing her sitting on the side of her bed, praying. Later, she would sit in a chair beside the bed, morning and night, quietly and fervently praying. Whenever some 'bad news' would come, I would find Mother sitting in her chair or out in the garden or down in the basement washing clothes, her mouth whispering prayers.

Late in her life, her mind weakened by multiple strokes and frequent confusion, making it impossible for her to live alone, she still found peace when she was taken to prayer services. All my life, Mom showed me the peace that could be found when I sought the presence of God in prayer. She was just an ordinary farm girl used by an extra-ordinary God.

February 1

Have you ever thought about the breath of God? Just His breath?

By the word of the LORD were the heavens made, their starry host by the breath of his mouth. He gathers the waters of the sea into jars; he puts the deep into storehouses. Let all the earth fear the LORD; let all the people of the world revere him. For he spoke, and it came to be; he commanded, and it stood firm.

Psalm 33:6-9 (CEV)

And then the lawless one will be revealed, whom the Lord Jesus will overthrow with the breath of his mouth and destroy by the splendor of his coming.

2 Thessalonians 2:8 (CEV)

Today I feel God's presence, the essence of His very being, in looking at the concept of His breath. All of these writers, Moses, David, and Paul, give us a look into the magnitude of God. His BREATH!

Breathing in a human is part of the "autonomic nervous system" of the body. It is a function that we do not have to consciously think about. Somewhere in the neighborhood of 20 times a minute, I take a breath and keep blood cells supplied with oxygen, which in turn keeps my body functioning, from my brain to my skin. How wondrous! As AWESOME as that is, I cannot **create** with that breath. I cannot **destroy** with that breath. God can. God does.

Just a breath. In a moment...my grandson, my granddaughter...is created. In a moment...the evil that torments or that destroys...is gone.

I did not see a temple there. The Lord God All-Powerful and the Lamb were its temple. And the city did not need the sun or the moon. The glory of God was shining on it, and the Lamb was its light.

Nations will walk by the light of that city, and kings will bring their riches there. Its gates are always open during the day, and night never comes. The glorious treasures of nations will be brought into the city. But nothing unworthy will be allowed to enter. No one who is dirty-minded or who tells lies will be there. Only those whose names are written in the Lamb's book of life will be in the city...

God's curse will no longer be on the people of that city. He and the Lamb will be seated there on their thrones, and its people will worship God and will see him face to face. God's name will be written on the foreheads of the people. Never again will night appear, and no one who lives there will ever need a lamp or the sun. The Lord God will be their light, and they will rule forever.

Revelation 21:22-27, 22:3-5 (CEV)

Whenever I am troubled by circumstances in my life or in the lives of those I love – I remember that my Father is MIGHTY GOD! I know how the story ends. I receive God's eternal promises.

Additional Texts: Habakkuk 2, Acts 17

If I must boast, I will boast of the things that show my weakness.
2 Corinthians 11:30 (ESV)

A song of ascents.
I lift up my eyes to the hills. From where does my help come from?
My help comes from the LORD who made heaven and earth..
He will not let your foot be moved; he who keeps you will not slumber.
Behold, he who keeps Israel will neither slumber nor sleep.
The LORD is your keeper; the LORD is your shade on your right hand.
The sun shall not strike you by day, nor the moon by night.
The LORD will keep you from all evil; he will keep your life;
the LORD will keep your going out and coming in from this time forth
  and forevermore. *Psalm 121 (ESV)*

"If I must 'boast', I'll boast of things that show how weak I am." Not a frequent statement of mine! In fact, I would say without hesitation – and certainly not bragging! – I am a person who is determined not to show weakness. I'm not going to varnish it – it is a CONTROL issue!!!

"I lift up my eyes – where is the help going to come from?" That usually happens as a last resort and God has frequently pulled me out of the fire! But He has also left me there! You'd think I'd learn!

"The LORD watches over" me. Cool! Then why do 'bad' things happen? Is God watching the trials and tribulations? When I get laid off my job, is God watching? When my child becomes seriously ill, is God watching? Yes. God doesn't take vacations or 'doze off'. I would not attempt to explain the mind of God but if I look at Jesus' words, it would encourage me to look beyond this world:

"I have said these things to you, that in me you may have peace. In the world you will have tribulation. But take heart; I have overcome the world."
John 16:33 (ESV)

I have begun to spend some 'different' kind of quiet with the Lord the last few months. As I awake in the morning and as I drift off to sleep at night, I begin to thank the Lord for the events of the day and just lay them out for Him to direct and clarify; a sort of 'before and after' view. It seems to help me come along side of GOD'S perspective. I am finding I really like that even though I continue to be puzzled by His response sometimes! Guess I haven't quite got His view yet! I want to be "*CONTENT*" in every situation and this seems to be helping me. HALLELUJAH!

I rejoiced in the Lord greatly that now at length you have revived your concern for me. You were indeed concerned for me, but you had no opportunity. Not that I am speaking of being in need, for I have learned to be content. I know how to be brought low, and I know how to abound. In any and every circumstance, I have learned the secret of facing plenty and hunger, abundance and need. I can do all things through him who strengthens me.
Philippians 4:10-13 (ESV)

February 3

Praise God, the Father of our Lord Jesus Christ. God is so good, and by raising Jesus from death, he has given us new life and a hope that lives on. God has something stored up for you in heaven, where it will never decay or be ruined or disappear.
You have faith in God, whose power will protect you until the last day. Then he will save you, just as he has always planned to do. On that day you will be glad, even if you have to go through many hard trials for a while. Your faith will be like gold that has been tested in a fire. And these trials will prove that your faith is worth much more than gold that can be destroyed. They will show that you will be given praise and honor and glory when Jesus Christ returns.
You have never seen Jesus, and you don't see him now. But still you love him and have faith in him, and no words can tell how glad and happy you are to be saved. That's why you have faith.   *1 Peter 1:3-9 (CEV)*

One Sunday my pastor's message was entitled "Why Christians Are Tested!" He said, "God allows us to be tested in order to <u>increase</u> our SURRENDER to Him."
Once you corrected me for not obeying you, but now I obey.
Psalm 119:67 (CEV)

His second point was "And God allows us to be tested in order to <u>inspire</u> others who struggle."
Now most of the Lord's followers have become brave and are fearlessly telling the message.   *Philippians 1:14 (CEV)*

It's all about faith and how God works with me to build <u>my</u> faith, which allows me to share with others and then they, too, are building a faith relationship with God. As I look within and then look out into the world, I <u>do</u> desire that my faith be refined like gold. When I lay the crown that I will receive (2 Timothy 4:8, James 1:12, 1 Peter 5:4) at God's feet, because HE is the only one that deserves it (!), I want it to be 24K gold – no gold-plated piece of wanna-be! And the world is not going to be impressed with 10K gold – anybody can get that. People are looking for "the REAL thing" – something that will last!
You know that many runners enter a race, and only one of them wins the prize. So run to win! Athletes work hard to win a crown that cannot last, but we do it for a crown that will last forever.   *1 Corinthians 9:24-25 (CEV)*
I have fought well. I have finished the race, and I have been faithful. So a crown will be given to me for pleasing the Lord. He judges fairly, and on the day of judgment he will give a crown to me and to everyone else who wants him to appear with power.   *2 Timothy 4:7-8 (CEV)*

I receive the encouragement of my Heavenly Father. I press on toward the goal that He has given me in Jesus. It is an 'eternal' goal that I do not see clearly now but will one day. It is more than I could ever ask or imagine.

Additional Text: 1 Corinthians 9, 2 Timothy 4

Lord, you have been our dwelling place in all generations. Before the mountains were brought forth, or ever you had formed the earth and the world, from everlasting to everlasting you are God.

You return man to dust and say, "Return, O children of man!" For a thousand years in your sight are but as yesterday when it is past, or as a watch in the night.   *Psalm 90:1-4 (ESV)*

I drew a line on a piece of paper this morning … oh, probably about 12" long. I put a zero on the left end and wrote "eternity on the right end. Then I decided that I would probably live to be 85. "Now where do I put THAT mark if 12" is 'eternity'?" This not only gave me some perspective about how fleeting my life is but also how TRULY fleeting my "momentary troubles" are.

So we do not lose heart. Though our outer nature is wasting away, our inner nature is being renewed day by day. For this slight momentary affliction is preparing for us an eternal weight of glory beyond all comparison, as we look not to the things that are seen but to the things that are unseen. For the things that are seen are transient, but the things that are unseen are eternal.

2 Corinthians 4:16-18 (ESV)

This has also given me another glimpse into the power and vastness of my God. That His promises are true because He can make good on them!!! My trust level went up another notch!!!

He who dwells in the shelter of the Most High will abide in the shadow of the Almighty. I will say to the LORD, "My refuge and my fortress, my God, in whom I trust."

For he will deliver you from the snare of the fowler and from the deadly pestilence. He will cover you with his pinions and under his wings you will find refuge; his faithfulness is a shield and buckler.

You will not fear the terror of the night, nor the arrow that flies by day, nor the pestilence that stalks in darkness, nor the destruction that wastes at noonday.

A thousand may fall at your side, ten thousand at your right hand, but it will not come near you. You will only look with your eyes and see the recompense of the wicked.

Because you made the LORD your dwelling place – the Most High, who is my refuge – no evil shall be allowed to befall you, no plague come near your tent.

For he will command his angels concerning you and to guard you in all your ways. On their hands they will bear you up, lest you strike your foot against a stone. You will tread on the lion and the adder, the young lion and the serpent you will trample underfoot.

"Because he holds fast to me in love, I will deliver him; I will protect him, because he knows my name. When he calls to me, I will answer him; I will be with him in trouble; I will rescue him and honor him. With long life I will satisfy him and show him my salvation."   *Psalm 91 (ESV)*

Additional Text: Judges 7, Esther 2-4

Our God, you bless everyone whose sins you forgive and wipe away. You bless them by saying, "You told me your sins, without trying to hide them, and now I forgive you." Before I confessed my sins, my bones felt limp, and I groaned all day long. Night and day your hand weighed heavily on me, and my strength was gone as in the summer heat. So I confessed my sins and told them all to you. I said, "I'll tell the LORD each one of my sins." Then you forgave me and took away my guilt. Psalm 32:1-5 (CEV)

I was recently reading some words from Susannah Wesley. Mrs. Wesley was the mother of John and Charles Wesley, along with 17 other children. As a woman of the 1700's, she was not a high official in the church. What she was was a wife and mother, exerting great influence in her children's lives and so even into our lives now with her God-given wisdom and desire to serve and be more intimate with God. Mrs. Wesley said this, *When judging the lawfulness or unlawfulness of pleasure, take this rule: whatever weakens your reason, impairs the tenderness of your conscience, obscures your sense of God, or takes off the relish of spiritual things; in short, whatever increases the strength and authority of your body over your mind, that is sin to you, however innocent it may be in itself.*

Many things that seem very innocent by the world's standard or perspective distract and weaken my walk with the Lord. Listening to gossip and "trash talk" around the water cooler of my office OR of the church I attend are insidious or subtle little jabs into my Godly armor. Spending more time with the readings and seminars of others than I do with reading God's word and attending to my prayer time – listening time to Him – obscures the truth of who GOD is. I become an expert in everyone and everything BUT God! I can't tell you how many emails I have received from people who feel they are being tormented by satan and tell me all the books they have read about satan and his demons and principalities and still do not have answers about what is happening to them. But when I ask how much they have increased their time in GOD'S word and increased their time in worship of HIM – there is a pause and silence.

We worship you, Lord, and we should always pray whenever we find out that we have sinned. Then we won't be swept away by a raging flood. You are my hiding place! You protect me from trouble, and you put songs in my heart because you have saved me.

You said to me, "I will point out the road that you should follow. I will be your teacher and watch over you. Don't be stupid like horses and mules that must be led with ropes to make them obey."

All kinds of troubles will strike the wicked, but your kindness shields those who trust you, LORD. And so your good people should celebrate and shout.

Psalm 32:6-11 (CEV)

Let us be vigilant in our everyday lives. Jesus told us that the greatest commandment was *Love the Lord your God with all your heart and with all your soul and with all your mind.* OK – "ALL" my heart, emotions, and mind means there is no room for anything else.

"Ask and it will be given to you; seek and you will find; knock and the door will be opened to you. For everyone who asks receives; he who seeks finds; and to him who knocks, the door will be opened.

"Which of you, if his son asks for bread, will give him a stone? Or if he asks for a fish, will give him a snake? If you, then, though you are evil, know how to give good gifts to your children, how much more will your Father in heaven give good gifts to those who ask him!"   *Matthew 7:7-11*

What causes fights and quarrels among you? Don't they come from your desires that battle within you? You want something but don't get it. You kill and covet, but you cannot have what you want. You quarrel and fight. You do not have, because you do not ask God. When you ask, you do not receive because you ask with wrong motives, that you may spend what you get on your pleasures.

James 4:1-3

Well, if Jesus says to ask and it will be given and James says I should ask God – why don't I get everything that I ask for? Uh-oh. I think it's those words that come after both of these that are hanging me up!

The Father gives <u>good</u> gifts. James says I ask with wrong motives. OOOHH! I should ask for good gifts and with the right motives! How do I tell what good gifts to ask for <u>are</u> and how do I 'test' my motives?

Jesus is my example. Jesus tells me that everything that He did was to glorify the Father. So – what do I NEED to glorify the Father?

The gifts of the Spirit are a good place to start: love, joy, peace, patience, kindness, goodness, faithfulness, gentleness, and self-control. These also keep my motives on the right track. I think the question to ask myself is: Do my motives glorify God and build the Body of Christ? Because those things show my obedience to the two most important commandments according to Jesus: loving God and loving my neighbor as myself.

Then the mother of Zebedee's sons came to Jesus with her sons and, kneeling down, asked a favor of him. "What is it you want?" he asked.

She said, "Grant that one of these two sons of mine may sit at your right and the other at your left in your kingdom."

"You don't know what you are asking," Jesus said to them. "Can you drink the cup I am going to drink?"   "We can," they answered.

Jesus said to them, "You will indeed drink from my cup, but to sit at my right or left is not for me to grant. These places belong to those for whom they have been prepared by my Father."

When the ten heard about this, they were indignant with the two brothers. Jesus called them together and said, "You know that the rulers of the Gentiles lord it over them, and their high officials exercise authority over them. Not so with you. Instead, whoever wants to become great among you must be your servant, and whoever wants to be first must be your slave-- just as the Son of Man did not come to be served, but to serve, and to give his life as a ransom for many."

Matthew 20:20-28

Ask for the Lord's GOOD gifts and ask with HIS motives. It's all about HIM – not about ME!

When Jesus saw the crowd, he went across Lake Galilee. A teacher of the Law of Moses came up to him and said, "Teacher, I'll go anywhere with you!" Jesus replied, "Foxes have dens, and birds have nests. But the Son of Man doesn't have a place to call his own." ...

After Jesus left in the boat with his disciples, a terrible storm suddenly struck the lake, and waves started splashing into their boat. Jesus was sound asleep, so the disciples went over to him and woke him up. They said, "Lord, save us! We're going to drown!"

But Jesus replied, "Why are you so afraid? You surely don't have much faith." Then he got up and ordered the wind and the wave to calm down. And everything was calm...

Two men with demons in them came to him from the tombs. They were so fierce that no one could travel that way...Jesus told them to go, and they went out of the men and into the pigs...Everyone in the town came out to meet Jesus. When they saw him, they begged him to leave their part of the country.

Matthew 8:18-20, 23-26, 28, 32, 34 (CEV)

God is so good! In these 16 verses the blessings and the cost of being a disciple of Jesus is shown to me. I love a balanced truth!

The teacher who comes to Jesus and, with initial abandonment, says he will follow Jesus <u>wherever</u> He goes! In my mind's eyes, I see Jesus' eyes soften with love as He lays a hand on the man's shoulder and reminds him that they won't be going to the Ritz hotel of the day or eat filet mignon.

This segues into the boat in the storm giving me the reassurance that even though following Jesus means difficult choices in keeping Him the top priority in my life – He is there, always there, in the midst of any storm and HE IS LORD OF LORDS AND KING OF KINGS! No storm will get the best of me when I allow Jesus to be in charge!

Then there are the demons. It would be foolish of me to think that evil/satan does not exist. I only have to read the paper or catch CNN to hear of terrorist attacks and serial killers and know that evil exists and is REAL. It is important for me to note the question that the demons ask: *"Have you come here to torture us before the appointed time?"* Even the demons know who will eventually win the war. Evil will touch my life. But like Elisha and King Hezekiah I must remember and walk in the victory that greater is He who is <u>with</u> me than he who is <u>against</u> me.

The war for souls is real. It is Jesus and His disciples against satan and his followers. The people of the town, while 'WOW'd' by the power and the authority – didn't deny it – they *really* didn't want "that kind of stuff" happening in their town. I guess they'd rather have the demoniacs running around acting crazy! Would I rather that those who are tormented by 'demons' like depression, alcohol, drugs, rage, etc. just run around outside <u>my</u> church instead of dealing with their freedom inside Jesus' house? It won't be neat and clean. It will be powerful and victorious and glorifying to <u>GOD</u>!!! Being a follower of Jesus has a tangible cost. So does the alternative.

Additional Text: Matthew 8, 2 Kings 6, 2 Chronicles 32

February 8

"Come to me, all who labor and are heavy laden, and I will give you rest."
Matthew 11:29 (ESV)

Jesus' words are recorded as He walks the many miles encouraging the people to repent and turn their hearts to God. He has just given His "woe" rebuke, telling the people that miracles have been performed in their midst and yet they continue to harden their hearts and not repent. It seems like the righteous anger leaves Jesus and He tries once again to meet the people with compassion, affirming that He sees their hardship and invites them to come to Him where they will find true rest.

The Spirit and the Bride say, "Come." And let the one who hears say, "Come." And let the one who is thirsty come; let the one who desires take the water of life without price.
Revelation 22:17 (ESV)

From Old Testament to New we are invited to refresh ourselves in the "living water" that comes from God. Psalms and Proverbs tell us of streams of refreshing that only God can give. Jesus told the Samaritan woman that if she drank from the "living water" that she would never be thirsty again. Jesus exhorted the people in John chapter 7 that if we would believe in Him, "streams of living water will flow from within" us, meaning the Holy Spirit.

Our days here on this earth seem to be increasingly filled with suffering from disease and war and atrocities that humans commit against one another. Self-help books and hours of talk shows on relationships are not going to alleviate the pain. Only through mighty God, Jehovah, the Alpha and Omega, the One who has always been and will always be – can I find 'rest' and a quenching of the thirst that has not end. Looking in any other place will only bring more disappointment and frustration in my life as I attempt to find 'rest' in distractions that produce no solutions and a 'quenching' in substances that only demand that I drink more!

Is God too abstract, too nebulous like a cloud that blows across my life? No. God is real and tangible when I reach out and turn towards Him. It's just a step. It's just an admission: "Lord, I've looked everywhere and found nothing that I can count on. I'm sorry that I turned to You last. I need You. Come into my life and be my Lord and Savior."

God told Joshua, *"No man shall be able to stand before you all the days of your life. Just as I was with Moses, so I will be with you. I will not leave you or forsake you."*
Joshua 1:5 (ESV)

David said in Psalm 27, *"For my father and my mother have forsaken me, but the LORD will take me in."*
Psalm 27:10 (ESV)

The writer of Hebrews repeats God's words to Moses from Deuteronomy 31, *"I will never leave you nor forsake you."* and goes on to say, *"So we can confidently say, 'The Lord is my helper; I will not fear; what can man do to me?"*
Hebrews 13:5-6 (ESV)

Though you have not seen him, you love him. Though you do not now see him, you believe in him and rejoice with joy that is inexpressible and filled with glory, obtaining the outcome of your faith, the salvation of your souls.
1 Peter 1:8-9 (ESV)

And the Philistine moved forward and came near to David, with his shield-bearer in front of him. And when the Philistine looked and saw David, he disdained him, for he was but a youth, ruddy and handsome to appearance. And the Philistine said to David, "Am I a dog that you come to me with sticks?" And the Philistine cursed David by his gods...

Then David said to the Philistine, "You come to me with a sword and with a spear and with a javelin, but I come to you in the name of the LORD of hosts, the God of the armies of Israel, whom you have defied. This day the LORD will deliver you into my hand, and I will strike you down and cut off your head...and...all this assembly may know that the LORD saves not with sword and spear. For the battle is the LORD's, and he will give you into our hand."

When the Philistine arose and came and drew near to meet David, David ran quickly toward the battle line to meet the Philistine. And David put his hand in his bag and took out a stone and slung it and struck the Philistine on his forehead. The stone sank into his forehead, and he fell on his face to the ground.

So David prevailed over the Philistine with a sling and with a stone, and struck the Philistine and killed him. There was no sword in the hand of David...When the Philistines saw that their champion was dead, they fled.

1 Samuel 17:41-43, 45-51 (ESV)

How did David KNOW that God was going to not only give him the wisdom to pick the right rocks but also the keen sight to line the slingshot up with Goliath's forehead? How did he have the *courage* to go out in the middle of a battlefield and face the biggest guy he had ever seen? Alone!

David KNEW God. God was not a casual acquaintance of David's. David spent a lot of time with God every day. David even sang to the Lord, making up little songs that expressed his joy and yes, even his doubts and questions. They had built a relationship and it was built on trust. This relationship had not come quick and had not come easy. If I was totally willing – it could have been quick and easy. I am the one who has to give up past experiences and see God for who He is.

David also KNEW based on his experiences. God had given him the strength to kill a lion that was attacking his sheep. David could count on God in life threatening situations.

David also KNEW based on the traditions of His forefathers. He had heard the stories of generations before he was even born!

Give ear, O my people, to my teaching; incline your ears to the words of my mouth! I will open my mouth in a parable; I will utter dark sayings from of old, things that we have heard and known, that our fathers have told us. We will not hide them from their children, but tell to the coming generation the glorious deeds of the LORD, and his might and the wonders that he has done.

Psalm 78:1-4 (ESV)

Let us walk with confidence into this day, knowing that our Lord is faithful and has already gone before us!

What is a friend? A friendship is truly an 'open' relationship. Unlike marriage, there is no legal binding or separating of the relationship. But like marriage, it will last a long time and produce wondrous fruit if I allow God to make the choices, set the standards, and be the binding that causes it to grow for many years. Let's see what God says about friends. Proverbs is a good place to start.

Gossip is no good! It causes hard feelings and comes between friends.

Proverbs 16:28 (CEV)

Sounds like I need to be careful whom I listen to! Does the one that I call 'friend' speak constructively of other people or does he/she constantly find fault with everyone? If she is a faultfinder – it will sure makes me wonder what she may say about me when I'm not around! Also, is there a spirit of loyalty to the friends that God has given me? I need to remember that what God says about me or about my friends is the truest thing – not the 'gossip' that is spoken by others!

A friend is always a friend, and relatives are born to share our troubles.

Proverbs 17:17 (CEV)

In good times and tough times, the friend that God has brought into my life loves me in spite of myself. That person sees me as a 'work in progress' and rejoices when I repent and grow in faith. They take their cue from God and forgive and forget!

Some friends don't help, but a true friend is closer than your own family.

Proverbs 18:24 (CEV)

This is a 'hard Word' from the Lord. It tells me that God is sending me friends that will walk as Jesus did. I remember when I came to realize that while I would always care about my friends, those that I had known for many years, even from childhood, but that there were some that I was going to have to 'cut loose'. Jesus was not a #1 priority in their life and they led a life that was MY 'old life' and I couldn't sit on the fence anymore. I could care about them and pray for them but I couldn't hang with them anymore. Many of them couldn't accept the 'new Jody'. It was a very painful time. Some have remained in touch and we can 'agree…to disagree' about many things. Others decided that the change was too much and so they have left.

You can trust a friend who corrects you, but kisses from an enemy are nothing but lies. *Proverbs 27:6 (CEV)*

This might be translated that the truth from a friend is always better than flattery from an enemy. An arrow from God, 'shot', so to speak, through a friend can bring about a painful truth but the Holy Spirit will confirm God's truth to me and I will be glad and rejoice in that friend who was obedient to speak what the Lord gave them…speaking always in love.

I'm going to stop right now and pray for my God-given friends. I am going to pray that God will bless them with all that they need to come closer to Him and know Him more intimately.

Additional Text: Proverbs 22, James 2

Let's continue learning more from God about friends.

Jesus also spoke of friends. He gave us the command for unconditional love. *"Now I tell you to love each other, as I have loved you. The greatest way to show love for friends is to die for them. And you are my friends, if you obey me."* *John 15:12-14 (CEV)*

Paul said, *Christ encourages you, and his love comforts you. God's Spirit unites you, and you are concerned for others. Now make me completely happy! Live in harmony by showing love for each other. Be united in what you think, as if you were only one person. Don't be jealous or proud, but be humble and consider others more important than yourselves. Care about them as much as you care about yourselves.* *Philippians 2:1-4 (CEV)*

This passage could be used to describe the Body of Christ, the Church, but it certainly shows us true friendship. There is a trust that must be there with a friend that assures me that I do not have to 'watch my own back' because my friend is already there! She is sensitive to my interests and more often than not, has already prayed for me before I even request it! The Holy Spirit KNEW who to wake up and say, "PRAY FOR JODY!"

You people aren't faithful to God! Don't you know that if you love the world, you are God's enemies? And if you decide to be a friend of the world, you make yourself an enemy of God. *James 4:4 (CEV)*

Here again is that hard 'Word' that my friends must be God-chosen. Even as I write this …I remember friends that continue to be of the world and reject God. Tears come to my eyes as I pray for them, asking God to continue to extend to them the mercy that He has shown me. I want eternity for these friends and family that are lost now. I want Jesus for them! God is gracious and good. He desires … even more than I do … that ALL come to the saving knowledge of Him (1 Timothy 2). It is because of this truth that I can allow God to chose my friends and be obedient to His choices. His way is perfect and He has proven that to me over and over. It is a Rock I stand on.

Do I have friends who do not know or do not accept Jesus as Savior and Lord? Sure. But they aren't my close friends. They aren't the ones that I turn to first. That was a difficult lesson for me to wrestle. Jesus had twelve disciples. Did He take all of them everywhere? No. Only Peter, James, and John were present when He raised the little girl from the dead. They were the only ones to actually see their transfigured Lord. And they were the ones next to Him in the Garden.

Who are the God-chosen friends in my life? They are certainly a 'pearl of great price' and I stop now to lift them in prayer.

Additional Text: Proverbs 16 and 17, 1 Corinthians 13

February 12

In case someone out there has forgotten, Valentine's Day is just two short days away. Sometimes I think that there is more media pressure to get a gift for this occasion 'RIGHT' than there is at Christmas! Whether you are a guy or a girl, God has a suggestion for the PERFECT GIFT! It is not a dozen roses. It is not a diamond ring, necklace, or bracelet. It is more precious than that. It is FIVE MINUTES of your time in prayer <u>EVERY DAY</u> for your wife or husband or friend. Let's see what Jesus says:

"Have faith in God! If you have faith in God and don't doubt, you can tell this mountain to get up and jump into the sea, and it will. Everything you ask for in prayer will be yours, if you only have faith. Whenever you stand up to pray, you must forgive what others have done to you. Then your Father I heaven will forgive your sins." Mark 11:22-25 (CEV)

Jesus tells us clearly about the <u>power</u> of prayer AND He tells us that the prayer must be coupled with forgiveness. Whether you are married or seeking God's will in a relationship, it is hard work. It <u>requires</u> GOD'S grace and mercy and LOVE each and every day. Prayer is the secret ingredient.

A wonderful Christian author, Stormie Omartian, has written a series of books "The Power of the Praying Wife", "The Power of the Praying Husband", and "The Power of the Praying Parent". I am not working on commission here! But Mrs. Omartian has done a wonderful job in writing down some guidelines for us to help us pray for our spouse and children – regardless if we are <u>going</u> to be married, if we have <u>been</u> married for 1 year or 50, whether our children are infants or 40 years old.

Let us give our loved ones the BEST Valentine ever – lifting them in prayer EVERY DAY. They will know it! They will see and feel the blessings of the Lord in their life as you lift them in prayer. 1 Corinthians 13 from the CEV:

What if I could speak all languages of humans and of angels? If I did not love others, I would be nothing more than a noisy gong or a clanging cymbal. What if I could prophesy and understand all secrets and all knowledge? What if I had faith that moved mountains? I would be nothing, unless I loved others. What if I gave away all that I owned and let myself be burned alive? I would gain nothing, unless I loved others.

Love is kind and patient, never jealous, boastful, proud, or rude. Love isn't selfish or quick tempered. It doesn't keep a record of wrongs that others do. Love rejoices in the truth, but not in evil. Love is always supportive, loyal, hopeful, and trusting. Love never fails.

Everyone who prophesies will stop, and unknown languages will no longer be spoken. All that we know will be forgotten. We don't know everything, and our prophecies are not complete. But what is perfect will someday appear, and what isn't perfect will then disappear.

When we were children, we thought and reasoned as children do. But when we grew up, we quit our childish ways. Now all we can see of God is like a cloudy picture in a mirror. Later we will see him face to face. We don't know everything, but then we will, just as God completely understands us. For now there are faith, hope, and love. But of these three, the greatest is love.

February 13

I will always praise the LORD. With all my heart, I will praise the LORD. Let all who are helpless, listen and be glad. Honor the LORD with me! Celebrate his great name. I asked the LORD for help, and he saved me from all my fears...

When his people pray for help, he listens and rescues them from their troubles. The LORD is there to rescue all who are discouraged and have given up hope. The LORD's people may suffer a lot, but he will always bring them safely through.   *Psalm 34:1-4, 17-19 (CEV)*

Late one Sunday night, a man (Kenny) came into the church I was attending. It was during our prayer ministry time. He sat down with his head in his hands. He had been hitchhiking and the smell of alcohol and marijuana was strong on him.

After talking quietly with him for a time, we asked if we could anoint him and pray for him and he agreed. In fact, it seemed like he had experienced this before. As we continued to talk later, he said he had "been a born-again Christian for over 20 years". "I'm not perfect," he said.

Give me your tired, your poor, your huddled masses yearning to be free...
                                                               The Statue of Liberty

My own great-great grandparents came to America on a boat tired and poor, yearning to be free from what was then Prussia. Thousands came into the harbors of the United States and found a new life. They came very long distances, making a step of faith that the unknown they were coming towards must be better than the hardships they were leaving.

What about the 'Kenny's' that are coming toward the beacon of Jesus here on earth...His Church? Kenny was tired, poor, and yearning to be free. Do I welcome him into the light of God's presence? That same light that drew me in? Maybe I smelled a little better than Kenny. Maybe my 'sin' wasn't as apparent but I was certainly dirty and smelly in God's eyes.

Kenny had heard about the Way to Jesus. He could quote the Bible verses but was too hurt and afraid or felt too unworthy to accept the free gift into his heart...yearning...but not free...yet.

I believe we are ALL called to be evangelists. When I accepted Jesus as my Savior, I also accepted His command to *"Go...and make <u>disciples</u>"*. WHERE I evangelize is for God to direct. Evangelism could be here in the U.S. or anywhere in the world. <u>OR</u> it could be in my own home church. There are many sitting in the pews of the church that do NOT know Jesus as Savior, their <u>personal</u> Savior. They do not live in freedom that comes with the assurance of their salvation. Some of them are well-dressed and clean and been members for 30 years. Some are a 'Kenny' and come in out of the darkness one night. They have a divine appointment. God have mercy on us if we put out the 'Do not disturb' sign!!!

The LORD then stood beside Samuel and called out as he had done before, "Samuel! Samuel!" "I'm listening," Samuel answered. "What do you want me to do?"   *1 Samuel 3:10 (CEV)*

I am listening to You, Lord. What do <u>You</u> want me to do?

February 14

Praise be to God, who has not rejected my prayer or withheld his love from me!
Psalm 66:20

AMEN! I agree with the author of the psalm. Here it is – another Valentine's Day. What is the history of this love-soaked day? The Encyclopedia Britannica says that: Under the rule of Emperor Claudius II, Rome was involved in many bloody and unpopular campaigns. Claudius the Cruel was having a difficult time getting soldiers to join his military leagues. He believed that the reason was that the Roman men did not want to leave their loved ones or families. As a result, Claudius <u>cancelled</u> all marriages and engagements in Rome. (And we accuse Congress and the President of being interfering and heavy-handed!!!) The good Saint Valentine was a priest at Rome in the days of Claudius II. It is reported that he and Saint Marius, also a priest, aided the Christian martyrs and secretly married couples, and for this kind deed Saint Valentine was apprehended and dragged before the Prefect of Rome. He was condemned and beaten to death with clubs and then beheaded. He suffered martyrdom on the 14th day of February, about the year 270 A.D.

Here we are 1800 years and a lot of media effort later!

I have had many disappointing Valentine's days. I came away feeling no one cared. Others received bouquets of flowers, were taken out to dinner, and received 'truckloads' of jewelry! But for me, it was a day like any other. I could start my own pity-party and stay in it <u>ALL</u> day! BUT I also had "Kodak days" with crayon-drawn cards from my children. Lop-sided hearts and a simple "I love you, Mom!" that were more precious than I can express and reduced me to a puddle!

I woke up early one Valentine's Day. The house was quiet except for the gentle snore of our dog at my feet. Valentine's Day. I had sent my husband of two years some 'e-cards' – that's electronic cards – expressing my humorous and heartfelt feelings. He was also going to take me to lunch that day! All of a sudden I remembered One that I had not sent greetings! Before I could form the words in my mind, I heard "I love you, Jody". Tears came to my eyes as I realized that <u>every</u> morning, when I allow the quiet moments to be known before I LEAP into the day – EVERY MORNING, I hear the Lord's quiet, rumbling voice say, "I love you, Jody." He loves us, people! There are NO conditions to His love! Listen to what our Lord says to us:

The LORD your God is with you, He is mighty to save. He will take great delight in you, He will quiet you with his love, He will rejoice over you with singing.
Zephaniah 3:17

I have loved you with an everlasting love; I have drawn you with loving-kindness.
Jeremiah 31:3

This is how God showed us His love among us: He sent his one and only Son into the world that we might live through him.
1 John 4:9

Rejoice and <u>LIVE</u> – in God's love today and every day. SHARE with those you meet that not only do <u>you</u> love them on this Valentine's Day but also that <u>God</u> loves them <u>every day</u>!!!

February 15

Know therefore that the LORD your God is God; he is the faithful God, keeping his covenant of love to a thousand generations of those who love him and keep his commands.   *Deuteronomy 7:9*

Have mercy on me, O God, according to your unfailing love;
according to your great compassion blot out my transgressions.   *Psalm 51:1*

It was just before the Passover Feast. Jesus knew that the time had come for him to leave this world and go to the Father. Having loved his own who were in the world, he now showed them the full extent of his love.   *John 13:1*

Do I even begin to grasp *"the full extent of his love"*? NO! It is impossible. But let me meditate on some of the manifestations of that love.

I have been given a life and free choice in that life. As I traveled in Eastern Europe, the endless blessings that God has given me by placing me in the USA, the 'land of the free', took form and substance. My friends there also rejoice at the freedom they have. After decades of Communism where individuals were <u>forced</u> to conform to the government's decrees in EVERYTHING, many of these countries now have the freedom to vote and argue and think! More importantly, they can WORSHIP when and however they want. No one can take that away – even the government!

I have been given ETERNAL life through JESUS CHRIST. ETERNAL!!! It never ends! Death and disease does not have a hold on me! My life has no end!

His love is unfailing! *"..we can never do anything to make God stop loving us because we never did anything to make Him start."* Mike Warnke in his new book, *Friendly Fire.* This is difficult for me to grasp because the human love that I have experienced and give — well, it has conditions on it. God's example to me is <u>un</u>conditional, <u>un</u>failing. WOW!

For this reason I kneel before the Father, from whom his whole family in heaven and on earth derives its name. I pray that out of his glorious riches he may strengthen you with power through his Spirit in your inner being, so that Christ may dwell in your hearts through faith. And I pray that you, being rooted and established in love, may have power, together with all the saints, to grasp how wide and long and high and deep is the love of Christ, and to know this love that surpasses knowledge--that you may be filled to the measure of all the fullness of God.

Now to him who is able to do immeasurably more than all we ask or imagine, according to his power that is at work within us, to him be glory in the church and in Christ Jesus throughout all generations, for ever and ever! Amen.   *Ephesians 3:14-21*

Additional Text: Romans 5, Ephesians 3

February 16

From east to west, the powerful LORD God has been calling together everyone on earth.   *Psalm 50:1 (CEV)*

Blow the trumpet in Zion, declare a holy fast, call a sacred assembly.

Joel 2:15

"Then the sign will appear in the sky. And there will be the Son of Man. All nations on earth will weep when they see the Son of Man coming on the clouds of heaven with power and great glory. At the sound of a loud trumpet, he will send his angels to bring his chosen ones together from all over the earth."

Matthew 24:30-31 (CEV)

Then I looked and saw a lone eagle flying across the sky. It was shouting, "Trouble, trouble, trouble to everyone who lives on the earth! The other three angels are now going to blow their trumpets."   *Revelation 8:13 (CEV)*

I have "Caller ID". I admit that I do look first to see the identification. Usually my curiosity is greater than my uncertainty at the "unknown" number!!! My husband on the other hand, doesn't need to think twice if it says "unknown" – he puts the phone down and goes back to what he was doing!

God speaks to us daily. Yes, every day. He speaks intimately and personally. He speaks to us as His people. A 'call' – a Holy Spirit call – is something that we don't want to miss. I wish I had 'caller ID' so I could check each voice that runs through my head and KNOW when it's God calling! But you know what? If I spend more and more time with God – studying His word, praying (which involves listening to <u>His</u> voice, right?), and in worship – I will become SOOOOO familiar with His voice – <u>THAT'S</u> my 'caller ID'!!!

Sometimes the Lord uses <u>me</u> to make one of His calls, like the examples in Joel and Jesus. The example in Revelation could be an evangelist, pastor, teacher, prophet, or apostle who warns of things to come and that NOW is the time to repent. This 'call' from the prophet Joel continues to ring in my ears today.

"Blow the trumpet in Zion; sound the alarm on my holy hill.
Let all who live in the land tremble, for the day of the LORD is coming.
It is close at hand—...

Be glad, O people of Zion,
    rejoice in the LORD your God, for he has given you
    the autumn rains in righteousness.
He sends you abundant showers, both autumn and spring rains, as before.
The threshing floors will be filled with grain;
    the vats will overflow with new wine and oil.
I will repay you for the years the locusts have eaten--
    the great locust and the young locust, the other locusts and the locust swarm--
my great army that I sent among you.
You will have plenty to eat, until you are full,
    and you will praise the name of the LORD your God,
    who has worked wonders for you;
    never again will my people be shamed."   *Joel 2:1, 23-26*

February 17

Then they returned to Jerusalem from the mount called Olivet, which is near Jerusalem, a Sabbath day's journey away. And when they had entered, they went up to the upper room, where they were staying, Peter and John and James and Andrew, Philip and Thomas, Bartholomew and Matthew, James the son of Alphaeus and Simon the Zealot and Judas son of James. All these with one accord were devoting themselves to prayer, together with the women and Mary the mother of Jesus and his brothers. Acts 1:12-14 (ESV)

Rejoice in the Lord always; again I will say, Rejoice. Let your reasonableness be known to everyone. The Lord is at hand; do not be anxious about anything, but in everything by prayer and supplication with thanksgiving let your requests be made known to God. And the peace of God, which surpasses all understanding, will guard your hearts and your minds in Christ Jesus.

Finally, brothers, whatever is true, whatever is honorable, whatever is just, whatever is pure, whatever is lovely, whatever is commendable, if there is any excellence, if there is anything worthy of praise, think about these things. What you have learned and received and heard and seen in me – practice these things, and the God of peace will be with you. Philippians 4:4-9 (ESV)

Why is it that even after all this time with the Lord and all that He has done in my life I still find myself going down that thought road of "well, when I can't do anything else I can still pray for you."? Prayer = POWER

It's not just the power that God answers me in the way I want Him to do so. It is coming to the Lord with situations or burdens or questions and laying them out before Him. God sifts through dividing truth and lies, Spirit and flesh, me and Him. It's going from indecision and uncertainty to His peace, even when the imperative answer may not be apparent.

Prayer is corporate whether with my spouse or child or the whole church Body, local or worldwide. Prayer is personal and every day. It is moment-to-moment conversation with my Lord. It comes in thanksgiving and joy with answered prayer and watching Him work! It is moments of frustration in my office. Instead of getting mad, I turn to God and say, "What now?" and then be open to the answer! It is the answer to despair and depression when the world seems too much. God is more! Nothing is bigger than Him! Nothing overwhelms my Lord! Prayer is peace. It is a refuge. It is a place to plug into God's power.

Is anyone among you suffering? Let him pray. Is anyone cheerful? Let him sing praise. Is anyone among you sick? Let him call for the elders of the church, and let them pray over him, anointing him with oil in the name of the Lord. And the prayer of faith will save the one who is sick, and the Lord will raise him up. And if he has committed sins, he will be forgiven. Therefore, confess your sins to one another and pray for one another, that you may be healed. The prayer of a righteous person has great power as it is working. James 5:13-16 (ESV)

Additional Text: Philippians 4, 1 Thessalonians 4 and 5

The people of Israel are treated as God's enemies, so that the good news can come to you Gentiles. But they are still the chosen ones, and God loves them because of their famous ancestors. God doesn't take back the gifts he has given or forget about the people he has chosen.

At one time you Gentiles rejected God. But now Israel has rejected God, and you have been shown mercy. And because of the mercy shown to you, they will also be shown mercy. All people have disobeyed God, and that's why he treats them as prisoners. But he does this, so that he can have mercy on all of them.

Who can measure the wealth and wisdom and knowledge of God? Who can understand his decisions or explain what he does?

"Has anyone known the thoughts of the Lord or given him advice?

Has anyone loaned something to the Lord that must be repaid?"

Everything comes from the Lord. All things were made because of him and will return to him. Praise the Lord forever! Amen.

Dear friends, God is good. So I beg you to offer your bodies to him as living sacrifice, pure and pleasing. That's the most sensible way to serve God. Don't be like the people of this world, but let God change the way you think. Then you will know how to do everything that is good and pleasing to him.

Romans 11:28-12:2 (CEV)

Does God still want me? I mean in ministry. I know He loves me. I know I was made to worship and serve Him. But — is the 'call' that I've thought was so clear — still clear, still valid.

Verse 29 of Romans 11 in the NIV says *"for God's gifts and his call are irrevocable"*. Sometimes when opportunities seem to 'dry up' or as in my life, my son's illness seems to fly straight into the face of the call to prayer ministry for those seeking the Lord for healing of body or spirit, and questions and despair seem to overwhelm me. Confusion sets in.

I am reminded of Peter. Three times he denied Jesus. Scripture tells us he went out and "wept bitterly". Isn't it interesting that in John 21:15-17 Jesus asks Peter three times "Simon, do you love me?"? Coincidence? Maybe. I think Jesus was restoring. When Peter might think that his relationship was so damaged and that surely God couldn't and wouldn't use him in a position of leadership. Jesus went back to the basics with Peter — "Do you love me?"

Do I love Jesus? "Yes, Lord, YOU know I love you!" "Yes, Lord, You KNOW I love you!" "Yes, Lord, You know I love YOU!"

When I go back to the basics, when I go with an open heart, when I go willing to repent and be obedient to whatever God's plan may be — then His call becomes clear and I see His faithfulness to that 'call'.

Have Thine own way, Lord! Have Thine own way!

Thou art the potter, I am the clay.

Mold me and make me after Thy will, while I am waiting, yielded and still.

Have Thine own way, Lord! Have Thine own way!

Wounded and weary, help me, I pray.

Power, all power surely is Thine!

Touch me and heal me, Savior divine.   by Adelaide A. Pollard (public domain)

February 19

You were doing so well until someone made you turn from the truth. And that person was certainly not sent by the one who chose you. A little yeast can change a whole batch of dough...
Galatians 5:7-9 (CEV)

Jesus also said: "The kingdom of heaven is like what happens when a woman mixes a little yeast into three big batches of flour. Finally, all the dough rises."
Matthew 13:33 (CEV)

The disciples had forgotten to bring any bread when they crossed the lake. Jesus then warned the, "Watch out! Guard against the yeast of the Pharisees and Sadducees."

The disciples talked this over and said to each other, "He must be saying this because we didn't bring along any bread."

Jesus knew what they were thinking and said: "You surely don't have much faith! Why are you talking about not having any bread? Don't you understand? Have you forgotten about the five thousand people and all those baskets of leftovers from just five loaves of bread? And what about the four thousand people and all those baskets of leftovers from just seven loaves of bread? Don't you know by now that I am not talking to you about bread? Watch out for the yeast of the Pharisees and Sadducees!"

Finally the disciples understood that Jesus wasn't talking about the yeast used to make brad but about the teaching of the Pharisees and Sadducees.
Matthew 16:5-12 (CEV)

Yeast is a fungus that when mixed with sugar – it agitates and causes growth in a substance.

When I accepted Jesus as my Lord and Savior, I signed up for the "race" that Paul mentions in Galatians. It is the best race. I began to run. I trained. What happened?

Maybe I picked up some yeast along the way. I went to Bible study and sang in the choir. Went to Sunday School. I even had "social" time with other Believers. I began to grow.

BAM!

The world gave me a punch and that nice full feeling *wooshed* out of me! Did I stay there and let it keep pounding me? No. I moved on.

I need the Lord's wisdom to stay "mixed up" with live yeast. If I get "mixed up" in dead yeast – I won't grow. Life in Christ is contagious. So is dead religion. It takes God's wisdom to give me eyes to see and a heart to seek the "live" yeast that is only found in Jesus.

Additional Text: John 1, Matthew 7, 2 Peter 1

As Jesus was walking down a road, a man ran up to him. He knelt down, and asked, "Good teacher, what can I do to have eternal life?"

Jesus replied, "Why do you call me good? Only God is good. You know the commandments. 'Do not murder. Be faithful in marriage. Do not steal. Do not tell lies about others. Do not cheat. Respect your father and mother.'"

The answered, "Teacher, I have obeyed all these commandments since I was a young man."

Jesus looked closely at the man. He liked him and said, "There's one thing you still need to do. Go sell everything you own. Give the money to the poor, and you will have riches in heaven. Then come with me."

When the man heard Jesus say this, he went away gloomy and sad because he was very rich.   *Mark 10:17-22 (CEV)*

The man wanted eternal life. Jesus said he didn't lack. He didn't need to get anything. He needed to give up in order to make room for God as his top priority.

What do I need to give up so that God is the top priority in my life? Yes, that means BEFORE my family! If my husband or children are more important than my relationship to God then I believe God does back me into a corner so that I have to choose. Does that sound extreme?

"This is what you must write to the angel of the church in Laodicea:

I am the one called Amen! I am the faithful and true witness and the source of God's creation. Listen to what I say.

I know everything you have done, and you are not cold or hot. I wish you were either one or the other. But since you are lukewarm and neither cold nor hot, I will spit you out of my mouth. You claim to be rich and successful and to have everything you need. But you don't know how bad off you are. You are pitiful, poor, blind, and naked."   *Revelation 3:14-17 (CEV)*

Jesus rebukes me for trying to be hot AND cold about my relationship with Him. He even says it would be better for me to be one or the other!

Have you ever been to a family reunion or a church picnic? What a feast of food! But did you ever notice that all the food is the same temperature? YUK! The flavor even becomes bland.

God does NOT want me lukewarm and bland about Him.

That is a heart thing. It's not whether I raise my hands and shout and sing LOUD! It's whether my heart burns with love for my Lord. It's a hunger for His Word and time with Him that only HE can fill.

It's time to stop right now and take my temperature!

Additional Text: Psalm 42, Isaiah 59

February 21

So you see that God is kind and also very strict. He punishes those who stop following him. But God is kind to you, if you continue following in his kindness. If you do not, you will be cut off from the tree.   *Romans 11:22 (NCV)*

"Kindness". I'm not sure how to define it but I know what it is when I see it. Webster's says it's "sympathetic, friendly, gentle, tender-hearted, generous, etc." That works for me. It is an aspect of God that I want to just sit and soak in, ya' know? But my Heavenly Father is also fair, just, and righteous.

You can be sure of this: No one will have a place in the kingdom of Christ and of God who sins sexually, or does evil things, or is greedy. Anyone who is greedy is serving a false god. Do not let anyone fool you by telling you things that are not true, because these things will bring God's anger on those who do not obey him.   *Ephesians 5:5-6 (NCV)*

As a new parent (that was a few years ago!), I mistakenly thought that my children (I had two the first time!) would always be sweet, happy cherubs and that I would never have to raise my voice. Discipline would be something that 'other parents' would have to do and that's why James Dobson wrote Dare to Discipline! My children would be obedient because I poured out enough love and attention on them that they would want to do whatever Mommy asked them because they would just know that Mommy knew best!

Sometime before the end of the first year, I received the revelation that unless I wanted to known as the mother of spoiled, rotten children that no one wanted to be around, I would have to use discipline to teach my children that there were consequences for their actions. I wanted them to be kind. So sometimes I would have to be stern. Discipline did not just mean corporal punishment. Spanking can be a part of discipline. Before someone gets upset by my 'allowance' of spanking, let me tell you that from my personal experience I KNOW the difference between spanking and beating a child. I have been on the receiving end of that but I have also felt the anger or frustration as a parent that puts me in the wrong place to *discipline* my child. I do not believe a parent should ever give any kind of discipline when they are so angry that they cannot speak to a child with respect and control. I have learned from my Heavenly Father that when my child's behavior has pushed me to the edge – it is time for my 'time out' with God first and then deliver discipline to my child. Discipline is correction to Godly behavior. I must be in Godly behavior before I can set the example and discipline my child toward Godly behavior.

So let us be thankful, because we have a kingdom that cannot be shaken. We should worship God in a way that pleases him with respect and fear, because our God is like a fire that burns things up.   *Hebrews 12:28-29 (NCV)*

Our Heavenly Father is the perfect parent combining unconditional love with fair and loving discipline. I think loving discipline keeps the focus on the child and his/her growth and does not seek to produce temporary relief for the parent.

My son described his baseball career the other day as a "a marathon not a sprint". God thinks in "eternal" terms and His thinking and discipline for me is not limited by the circumstances of THIS life. He is "consuming" through all matters of time and space. What an awesome Father He is!!!

"To the angel of the church in Ephesus write:
These are the words of him who holds the seven stars in his right hand and walks among the seven golden lampstands: I know your deeds, your hard work and your perseverance. I know that you cannot tolerate wicked men, that you have tested those who claim to be apostles but are not, and have found them false. You have persevered and have endured hardships for my name, and have not grown weary.
Yet I hold this against you: You have forsaken your first love.   Revelation 2:1-4

The Church of Ephesus was a busy church. They were doing all kinds of 'stuff'. The Lord acknowledged their hard work and perseverance in hard times. They did not grow weary in doing good.   But they had forgotten the most important thing – loving God – pleasing <u>Him</u>.

First love. Paul had some things to say about marriage. Mostly, he was advocating that we all stay single! BUT – let's see what he says about the important things:

I want all of you to be free from worry. An unmarried man worries about how to please the Lord. But a married man has more worries. He must worry about the things of this world, because he wants to please his wife. So he is pulled in two directions. Unmarried women and women who have never been married worry only about pleasing the Lord, and they keep their bodies and minds pure. But a married woman worries about the things of this world, because she wants to please her husband.   1 Corinthians 7:32-34 (CEV)

A marriage that has selfishness in it will not survive. My eyes must be on pleasing my partner. Isn't that what the Lord desires for His 'marriage' with me? A bride whose goal is to please the heart of her groom?

Jesus went on to say, "When you have lifted up the Son of Man, you will know who I am. You will also know that I don't do anything on my own. I say only what the Father taught me. The one who sent me is with me. I always do what pleases him, and he will never leave me."   John 8:28-29 (CEV)
Then you will live a life that honors the Lord, and you will always please him by doing good deeds. You will come to know God ever better. His glorious power will make you patient and strong enough to endure anything, and you will be truly happy.   Colossians 1:10-11 (CEV)
We always thank God for all of you, mentioning you in our prayers. We continually remember before our God and Father your work produced by faith, your labor prompted by love, and your endurance inspired by hope in our Lord Jesus Christ.   1 Thessalonians 1:2-3

Ah-ha! There we go. Works that come <u>from</u> faith and labor that comes <u>from</u> love, and endurance that is inspired <u>by</u> hope in JESUS! There's the difference. There's the point!

Additional Text: 1 Corinthians 7, Colossians 1, 1 Thessalonians 1

Then Amalek came and fought with Israel at Rephidim. So Moses said to Joshua, "Choose for us men, and go out and fight with Amalek. Tomorrow I will stand on the top of the hill with the staff of God in my hand." So Joshua did as Moses told him, and fought with Amalek, while Moses, Aaron, and Hur went up to the top of the hill. Whenever Moses held up his hand, Israel prevail, and whenever he lowered his hand, Amalek prevailed. But Moses' hands grew weary, so they took a stone and put it under him, and he sat on it, while Aaron and Hur held up his hands, one on one side, and the other on the other side. So his hands were steady until the going down of the sun. And Joshua overwhelmed Amalek and his people with the sword. Exodus 17:8-13 (ESV)

Well, Joshua won the battle but it wasn't the number of men or swords that he had that did the trick! It was WHO that was with him! God wanted to show Joshua that he needed more than just himself. And Joshua didn't win just because the great MOSES was backing him up. Moses needed help. God could have sent him supernatural strength to be able to hold his arms up all day. Maybe God wanted to show <u>Moses</u> that even HE needed more than just himself. God used Joshua and Moses AND Aaron AND Hur – as a team – to lead His army into battle and win.

"Again I say to you, if two of you agree on earth about anything they ask, it will be done for them by my Father in heaven. For where two or three are gathered in my name, there am I among them." Matthew 18:19-20 (ESV)

God established a BODY of Believers from the beginning. He gave each of us talents and strengths. But He also gave us weaknesses. I believe He made me weak so that He could be strong for me. Sometimes He is strong just directly – from Him to me. But sometimes He uses others – people I know, some even that I don't know – to hold me up in times of need. Do you have Aaron's and Hur's in your life? I bet you do – but maybe you just don't see them.

Sometimes it's just a friendly smile or wink at the local fast food place. Sometimes it's a person who sends you a card or email – just because! Maybe it's your spouse that brings you a single flower that they got when they stopped for milk on the way home from work or they put a note in your lunch bag that said "I love you" or had a smiley face! Maybe it's someone in your church that is SO GOOD at giving hugs when you see them! They might have even said they were praying for you. Now how did they know you needed prayer? Hmmmm....

Isolating myself in times of hardship is the devil's best weapon to get me depressed and oppressed! Yes, it's hard to get up and get dressed and brush my hair – and putting on make-up seems like a Mt. Everest climb.

"Come to me, all who labor and are heavy laden, and I will give you rest. Take my yoke upon you, and learn from me, for I am gentle and lowly in heart, and you will find rest for your souls. For my yoke is easy, and my burden is light."
Matthew 11:28-30 (ESV)

Reach out and touch the Aaron and Hur folks in your life. They're standing by – because God already told them your need!

The word of the LORD came to Jeremiah a second time, while he was still shut up in the court of the guard. "Thus says the LORD who made the earth, the LORD who formed it to establish it – the LORD is his name: Call to me and I will answer you, and will tell you great and hidden things that you have not known. For thus says the LORD, the God of Israel, concerning the houses of this city and the houses of the kings of Judah that were torn down to make a defense against the siege mounds and against the sword: They are coming in to fight against the Chaldeans and to fill them with the dead bodies of men whom I shall strike down in my anger and my wrath, for I have hidden my face from this city because of all their evil. Behold I will bring to it health and healing, and I will heal them and reveal to them abundance of prosperity and security. I will restore the fortunes of Judah and the fortunes of Israel, and rebuild them as they were at first. I will cleanse them from all the guilt of their sin against me, and I will forgive all the guilt of their sin and rebellion against me. And this city shall be to me a name of joy, a praise and a glory before all the nations of the earth who shall hear of all the good that I do for them. They shall fear and tremble because of all the good and all the prosperity I provide for it.

Jeremiah 33:1-9 (ESV)

I, along with several million other Americans, have a cell phone. Most of the time I find it a blessing. Like my math skills since I started using a calculator, my memory for the telephone numbers of friends and family have become rusty because I can just access my 'phone book' in my cell phone and push a button to 'reach out and touch' – never seeing the person's actual number.

My pastor has titled this passage of Jeremiah as "Knowing God's phone number". The really cool thing is – it requires no real brainpower on my part – just a simple choice – call God first! As His child, I have a direct line into Him. No line, no waiting.

As Jesus passed on from there, he saw a man called Matthew sitting at the tax booth, and he said to him, "Follow me." And he rose and followed him.

And as Jesus reclined at table in the house, behold, many tax collectors and sinners came and were reclining with Jesus and his disciples. And when the Pharisees saw this, they said to his disciples, "Why does your teacher eat with tax collectors and sinners?" But when he heard it, he said, "Those who are well have no need of a physician, but those who are sick. Go and learn what this means, 'I desire mercy, and not sacrifice.' (Hosea 6:6) *For I came not to call the righteous, but sinners."*

Matthew 9:9-13 (ESV)

There is NOTHING that blocks my call to God – except me. If I'm hearing lies in my head that I'm not good enough or holy enough or – WHATEVER – enough – well, duh! That's right, I'm not but Jesus is my communication link. He came to heal and to save ME, a sinner. He walks right into the throne room of HIS heavenly Father and says, "Father, I need You to hear what Jody is saying. She needs you to listen to her." No problem. I walk in JESUS' righteousness, not my own. I am special – because of Jesus.

Additional Text: Hebrews 4 and 5

Psalm 22 v. 3 tells me that God inhabits – lives – in the praise of His people. The power of God is present when I praise Him.

Early the next morning, as everyone got ready to leave for the desert near Tekoa, Jehoshaphat stood up and said, "Listen my friends, if we trust the LORD God and believe what these prophets have told us, the LORD will help us, and we will be successful."

Then he explained his plan and appointed men to march in front of the army and praise the LORD for his holy power by singing: "Praise the LORD! His love never ends." 2 Chronicles 20:20-21 (CEV)

As soon as they began singing, the LORD confused the enemy camp, so that the Ammonite and Moabite troops attacked and completely destroyed those from Edom. Then they turned against each other and fought until the entire camp was wiped out!...

Jehoshaphat led the crowd back to Jerusalem. And as they marched, they played harps and blew trumpets. They were very happy because the LORD had given them victory over their enemies, so when they reached the city, they went straight to the temple.

When the other nations heard how the LORD had fought against Judah's enemies, they were too afraid to invade Judah. The LORD let Jehoshaphat's kingdom be at peace. 2 Chronicles 20:20-23, 27-30 (CEV)

King Jehoshaphat was obedient to a pretty risky order that he got from God. Send singers and musicians and dancers out in front of the army. Praise God before the battle even begins.

How does that work in my life? Well, how do I usually react when tough times come in my life? Do I think about calling my close brothers and sisters to come pray with me or do I think they'd be too busy? Do I check to see when – even how many times – I can go to church and attend worship and enter in to a time with the Lord and body of Believers or do I crawl into my hole at home and pull the covers over my head? Do I turn on my CD player for praise and worship music, seeking to get my 'eternal eyes' back on track, allowing God to guide me out of the pit, or do I turn on the TV to lose myself in whatever sitcom – never to be seen again that day in God's presence. Jesus is waiting to sit down and hear my woes and help me sift through the truth with the power of His Holy Spirit – if I will just choose that option!

Even more importantly, if I will make praising God the first priority of each day, then I AM praising Him before any battle begins. I have a friend of mine named Janet, who gets up each morning and spends an hour or so outside in her backyard just walking and talking with the Lord. But her children and husband tell me that she also has been known to dance and leap across the yard as she praises her heavenly Father who made this glorious day. What a testimony!

Additional Text: Psalm 8, Psalm 136

Instruct them to do as many good deeds as they can and to help everyone. Remind the rich to be generous and share what they have. This will lay a solid foundation for the future, so that they will know what true life is like.

1 Timothy 6:18-19 (CEV)

I'll tell you what it really means to worship the LORD. Remove the chains of prisoners who are chained unjustly. Free those who are abused! Share your food with everyone who is hungry; share your home with the poor and homeless. Give clothes to those in need; don't turn away your relatives.

Then your light will shine like the dawning sun, and you will be quickly healed. Your honesty will protect you as you advance, and the glory of the LORD will defend you from behind. When you beg the LORD for help, he will answer, "Here I am!"

Isaiah 58:6-9 (CEV)

Someone once said, "I've been poor and I've been rich…and rich is better!"

It would be hard for me to stand today and say that the period of my life when I had my telephone and electricity turned off because of unpaid bills was a "better" time! Realizing that there was going to be <u>nothing</u> for Christmas did not uplift me to a new spiritual 'high'! HOWEVER, I did <u>learn</u> a lot of things during that time. There are certainly fewer distractions in the valleys and pits of life!!!

I don't think I will ever watch with the same judgmental attitude as a person pleads with the lady behind the counter to help them find a way to turn the electricity back on in the middle of July so that children and elderly relatives will have fans, much less air conditioning!

I won't go through a Christmas season without looking around at my friends, relatives, and acquaintances and ask the Lord to reveal anyone to me that needs a 'blessing'. When the Lord speaks to my heart to <u>give</u> to someone, I am NOT in the judging business demands that I know what '<u>legitimate</u>' place my gift will be used! God will deal with <u>them</u> as He has dealt with <u>me</u>!!! I obey by giving and leave the rest to Him.

Jesus treated everyone with unconditional love and compassion <u>except</u> the Pharisees. By allowing His love to just flow through me like I am a 'pipe' will produce fruit that will glorify him and bring me closer to Him. That is where I want to be! I want the abundant life that comes through Jesus!

Jesus said: "I tell you for certain that I am the gate for the sheep. Everyone who came before me was a thief or a robber, and the sheep did not listen to any of them. I am the gate. All who come in through me will be saved. Through me they will come and go and find pasture.

A thief comes only to rob, kill, and destroy. I came so that everyone would have life, and have it in its fullest. I am the good shepherd, and the good shepherd gives up his life for his sheep."

John 10:7-11 (CEV)

Additional Text: 2 Corinthians 4, Galatians 5

I have a pair of beautiful earrings. They appear to be a square cut ½ carat diamond. But they're not! They're cubic zirconium. Imitations. They are beautiful and serve the function that I need without the expense of the originals. Let's look at what Scripture says about "imitations":

Therefore be imitators of God, as beloved children. And walk in love, as Christ loved us and gave himself up for us, a fragrant offering and sacrifice to God.
Ephesians 5:1-2 (ESV)

And we desire each one of you to show the same earnestness to have the full assurance of hope until the end, so that you may not be sluggish, but imitators of those who through faith and patience inherit the promises.
Hebrews 6:11-12 (ESV)

Remember your leaders, those who spoke to you the word of God. Consider the outcome of their way of life, and imitate their faith. *Hebrews 13:7 (ESV)*

Beloved, do not imitate evil but imitate good. Whoever does good is from God; whoever does evil has not see God. *3 John 11*

Did you know that I am a 'copy cat'? I want to be such an imitation of Jesus that when people meet me or spend time with me – all they remember is Jesus! How do I imitate Jesus?!!!

Rich Little is probably one of the greatest impersonators of all times. He used to be on Bob Hope's shows and he would pretend to be Johnny Carson, John Wayne, George Burns, and many, many others. (Am I showing my age or what?!) I heard him tell an interviewer once that he would study hours and hours of videotape to get the perfect voice tone and physical mannerisms of the person he was imitating. He studied the person thoroughly. Hmmm…Do I study Jesus that thoroughly? Do I know His character, His very nature? Do I know Jesus so well that I could tell you exactly what He would do in a given situation?

It is not great talents God blesses so much as great likeness to Jesus. A holy minister is an awful weapon in the hand of God. *Robert M. McCheyne*

Listen to this story:

Some Jewish men started going around trying to force out evil spirits by using the name of the Lord Jesus Christ. They said to the spirits, "Come out in the name of that same Jesus that Paul preaches about!"

Seven sons of a high priest named Sceva were doing this, when an evil spirit said to them, "I know Jesus! I have heard about Paul. But who are you?" Then the man with the evil spirit jumped on them and beat them up. They ran out of the house, naked and bruised.

When the Jews and Gentiles in Ephesus heard about this, they were so frightened that they praised the name of the Lord Jesus. Many who were followers now started telling everyone about the evil things they had been doing.
Acts 19:13-18 (CEV)

Am I such an imitator of Jesus that the demons – the enemy – know about me? Do they tremble because of WHO stands with me?

Additional Text: Acts 19, Ephesians 6

February 28

Do two walk together unless they have agreed to do so?   *Amos 3:3*

When I was a kid we had "Field Day" at school. I guess it's like the school fairs they have now only we didn't have mechanical rides, unless you want to count those old ponies that the local farmer brought in! We had games. Did you ever run in a 3-legged race? It's fun if you have a partner who will work with you! When I was in the 5th grade this one <u>really</u> tall girl and I finally got wisdom and figured out that 'hooking up' together would be a lot smarter than binding our LOONNGG leg to our individual best friends who happened to barely come up to our shoulder! So we tied our legs together and with our long strides perfectly matched – we left the rest of them literally in the dust!!! We were in unity! We were a team!

We are careful not to judge people by what they seem to be, though we once judged Christ in that way. Anyone who belongs to Christ is a new person. The past is forgotten, and everything is new. God has done it all! He sent Christ to make peace between himself and us, and he has given us the work of making peace between himself and others.

What we mean is that God was in Christ, offering peace and forgiveness to the people of this world. And he has given us the work of sharing his message about peace. We were sent to speak for Christ and sincerely ask you to make peace with God. Christ never sinned! But God treated him as a sinner, so that Christ could make us acceptable to God.   *2 Corinthians 5:16-21 (CEV)*

When Jesus said that He was coming back, He talks about <u>a</u> Bride – ONE Bride – and He says His Church – one Church. If I am reconciled to God, then I am in unity with Him. So I am to be in unity with the Bride – with the Church. Reconciliation is BOTH parties desiring to come together and be in unity. Not just one side <u>giving in</u> to the other. Both desire reconciliation or it just will not work!!!

Oh, that God's spirit of reconciliation would permeate the entire Body of Christ! Can we not major on the major – that is Jesus Christ and Him crucified – and let the 'minor details' be clarified by the Holy Spirit and maybe even that 'great heavenly doctrinal committee' that will determine what is God's right and God's wrong?!!!

Let us walk together in unity by the power of the Holy Spirit. Let us keep our focus on Jesus, who took fishermen, tax collectors, and other assorted sinners and made them into Fishers of Men. Let us work together to win souls and bring glory to God who is the only one worthy of all the PRAISE and GLORY!

Additional Text: 2 Corinthians 5, 1 Corinthians 12-14

February 29

When Israel was a child I loved him as a son and brought him out of Egypt. But the more I called to him, the more he rebelled, sacrificing to Baal and burning incense to idols. I trained him from infancy, I taught him to walk, I held him in my arms. But he doesn't know or even care that it was I who raised him.

As a man would lead his favorite ox, so I led Israel with my ropes of love. I loosened his muzzle so he could eat. I myself have stooped and fed him. But my people shall return to Egypt and Assyria because they won't return to me..

Oh, how can I give you up, my Ephraim? How can I let you go? How can I forsake you like Admah and Zeboiim? My heart cries out within me; how I long to help you!   *Hosea 11:1-5, 8 (TLB)*

There is so much to learn from the Old Testament passages about God's love for me and for the Church. In these few verses of Hosea, I hear God's 'extravagant love' and yet He is not oblivious to disobedience and sin. He is aware that His children reject Him and He allows the consequences of those actions to occur. He is merciful but that does not mean God condones. I used to think that prophecy was just for encouragement and exhortation. It isn't. It is also for correction and discipline. God is SO MERCIFUL that He allows the pain of correction to bring me to the joy of victorious, obedient living!

If you haven't read Hosea recently I encourage you to do so and put yourself into the writing in place of Israel. This is one of those books that have taught me a lot about the Father's love.

I am a sinner. My Father doesn't want me to sin. He wants me to be obedient -- not for HIS benefit -- but for my 'life', my eternal life.

If we say we have no sin, we are only fooling ourselves, and refusing to accept the truth. But if we confess our sins to him, he can be depended on to forgive us and to cleanse us from every wrong. [And it is perfectly proper for God to do this for us because Christ died to wash away our sins.] If we claim we have not sinned, we are lying and calling God a liar, for he says we have sinned.

My children, I am telling you this so that you will stay away from sin. But if you sin, there is someone to plead for you before the Father. His name is Jesus Christ, the one who is all that is good and who pleases God completely. He is the one who took God's wrath against our sins upon himself, and brought us into fellowship with God; and he is the forgiveness for our sins, and not only ours but all the world's.   *1 John 1:8-2:2 (TLB)*

February 29th is observed only every four years for scientific reasons. God's love is not restrained by this world or it's passage of time. God's love was mine before I was born. It was waiting like the best gift I could imagine. Once I said, "Yes, I am a sinner and need Jesus Christ as Savior", the gift <u>completely</u> covered me and just kept on giving!

If you have never read the book of Hosea or have not read it this week, do so today. It gives me a <u>glimpse</u> of the magnitude of the Father's love for <u>me</u>!

Additional Text: Hosea 1-14 (the chapters are short!)

'Nana Webb'
Lillie Corrine Brewton Webb (1897 – 1980)

Lillie Brewton was born in Robertsdale, AL. Her father was a truck farmer growing his own vegetables and selling them from the back of his truck with the help of his wife and seven children. He was known as a polite man with conservative Christian views. Lillie grew up in a 'circuit church'. Just as John Wesley created in the 1700's, a pastor would travel a 'circuit' serving families covering hundreds of square miles. Services were held in one-room churches, buildings, barns, and even in just a tent. In her day-to-day world, when someone became sick, the pastor could not always get to the home to visit and offer prayers. Many diseases that are curable or manageable today brought devastating illness and even death prior to World War II. Lillie was a part of the group of people who visited the sick and prayed for them. God answered those prayers with miraculous results.

She met her husband, John Webb, when she was 19-years-old and he was 24. Of course, they met at church. They had four children. They were married over 60 years when he died in 1980.

Lillie continued throughout her life to do whatever she could to serve the Lord, whether it was visiting and praying for people, selling (and giving away!) Bibles, bringing food to those in need, and feeding the indigents who were just passing through. She loved to attend tent revivals led by such preachers as Luther Horne, Billy Graham, and Oral Roberts.

Nana Webb was a great influence on my life as she was with her four children, 16 grandchildren, and twenty-something great-grandchildren. Having come from a much smaller Midwest family, I found moving to the south and integrating into a large 'clan' rather overwhelming at first. Nana and Daddy John always had time to talk, telling me family stories until I began to feel like I belonged. This was a trait that has been carried on to this day.

I suspect Nana prayed for me quite a bit. It would not have taken her long to sense that her grandson had married a woman who knew 'about' God but very little on how He was in her daily life. Nana showed me by example how to pray through decisions and concerns. Shortly after I told her that I was pregnant with our first child, she told me that she knew it was twins. She may have had one of her visions. Three ultrasounds during my pregnancy showed only one child but on delivery day – there was a beautiful baby girl – and a handsome baby boy! It was then that I shared with her that I had had an abortion several years before and had been afraid throughout the pregnancy that I would be *punished* for my sin. Nana just smiled and told me God didn't work that way. "Have you asked forgiveness for you sins?" "Oh, yes, ma'am," I said. She smiled again and suggested we pray about that right then so "the ol' devil can't EVER bring it up again because I'm a witness!" Nana was a good teacher of the Good News.

She would be proud of her children and grandchildren because they have continued to spread Jesus' love to others around the world.

Grandchildren are the crowning glory of the aged; parents are the pride of their children   *Proverbs 17:6 (NLT)*

March 1

How lovely is your dwelling place, O LORD of hosts!   *Psalm 84:1 (ESV)*

When I accepted Jesus as my Lord and Savior, the Redeemer of my life, He came to dwell in me. His Holy Spirit became a part of me. I suspect the writer of Psalm 84 was not talking about me or even himself when he exclaimed that God's home was "*LOVELY*". However, Scripture tells us that God lives within us. Hmm…I wonder what the '*dwelling*' looks like?

What is in the 'Living Room' of my life? Do I live like God is a part of my day-to-day life? The TV I watch, the movies I see, the jokes I laugh at, and do I walk that life with my children and spouse?

How about the 'Kitchen'? Do I "cook up" good stuff in my spirit, my soul? Do I mix pleasing portions of personal Bible study, private and corporate worship and private and corporate prayer?

Finally, brothers, whatever is true, whatever is honorable, whatever is just, whatever pure, whatever is lovely, whatever is commendable, if there is any excellence, if there is anything worthy of praise, think about these things. What you have learned and received and heard and seen in me – practice these things, and the God of peace will be with you.   *Philippians 4:8-9 (ESV)*

What happens in my bedroom, including the closet? What is my relationship with God? I can be totally honest here because this is the place where NOBODY sees – except Him.

Then Job answered the LORD and said: "I know that you can do all things, and that no purpose of yours can be thwarted. 'Who is this that hides counsel without knowledge?' Therefore I have uttered what I did not understand, things too wonderful for me, which I did not know.

'Hear, and I will speak; I will question you, and you make it known to me.' I had heard of you by the hearing of the ear, but now my eye sees you; therefore I despise myself, and repent in dust and ashes."   *Job 42:1-6 (ESV)*

Not to be indelicate, but what about the bathroom? Have my past sins that I have repented and are covered by Jesus' Blood from the cross truly been flushed away? Or do I continue to revisit them and the stench affects every part of my 'dwelling'?

Thus says the LORD, who makes a way in the sea, a path in the mighty waters, who brings forth chariot and horse, army and warrior; they lie down, they cannot rise, they are extinguished, quenched like a wick.

"Remember not the former things, nor consider the things of old. Behold, I am doing a new thing; now it springs forth, do you not perceive it? I will make a way in the wilderness and rivers in the desert."   *Isaiah 43:16-19 (ESV)*

And finally, there is my front porch and yard. Is it beautiful and fragrant with good fruit and flowers? Or does it look deserted like no one lives there any more? Whether prophet or not, I will be known by my fruit.

"You will recognize them by their fruits…"   *Matthew 7:16 (ESV)*

I look around my physical dwelling and place and I consider how much time and effort I spend in keeping that 'up' and cleaned and repaired. How does that balance with the time and effort I put into my spiritual dwelling that <u>GOD</u> lives in?!!?

Then Jesus said, "I am the bread that gives life. Whoever comes to me will never be hungry, and whoever believes in me will never be thirsty. But as I told you before, you have seen me and still don't believe. The Father gives me my people. Every one of them will come to me, and I will always accept them. I came down from heaven to do what God wants me to do, not what I want to do. Here is what the One who sent me wants me to do: I must not lose even one whom God gave me, but I must raise all on the last day. Those who see the Son and believe in him have eternal life, and I will raise them on the last day. This is what my Father wants."

The Jews began to complain about Jesus because he said, "I am the bread that comes down from heaven." They said, "This is Jesus, the son of Joseph. We know his father and mother. How can he say, 'I came down from heaven?'

John 6:35-42 (NCV)

What wonderful Good News Jesus gives <u>us</u> in those first two sentences. <u>HE</u> is the answer to the question that we ask from the moment we are born — "I want. I want. What is it that I want?" We are all born with this "lack" in us. I remember hearing a song when I was a teenager "Is that all there is?" – I think Peggy Lee sang it. (OK. I feel old!) No matter what I have accomplished in my career, or my children and their accomplishments and success; none of that is an <u>eternal</u> answer to the need inside me.

In the next few sentences, Jesus says He will not drive me away — for <u>I</u> am the reason He came. <u>ME</u>! Later in this chapter of John's gospel, Jesus speaks of "eat my flesh, drink my blood" and it is recorded that many of His disciples stopped following Him. Jesus will not drive me away but I may have times in my life with Him that His teaching is difficult. I may have to spend more time with Him to gain more clear understanding.

And how did he accomplish the last part of what He says — to raise us up, give us eternal life, to not lose us? <u>HE DIED</u>! He didn't come on a white horse and destroy the disgusting hordes of satan. He died. He became the perfect sacrifice. The atonement.

Now before we get too puffed up about how <u>we</u> don't react to those words like the Jews did, let's consider our actions. Jesus is all we need. Jesus did everything that was needed to <u>give</u> me eternal life. I didn't EARN it — He <u>gave</u> it to me. Where is He on my priority list today? Do I walk like the child of a King? Do I represent Him in truth like a disciple should? Do I <u>serve</u> others like He did? When the lesson Jesus is teaching me seems difficult and my day-to-day life is a battle, do I come closer to Him or dig my toe in the ground and begin to back away until I get to the place where it's more comfortable? Those are questions I need to ask myself and look in the mirror when I do it!

The religious leaders of Jesus' day did not 'see' Him as 'Messiah' because He was too *ordinary*. They thought they 'knew' Jesus and there was nothing extraordinary in His family or education so how could God use HIM! Today, there may be some (or many!) who wonder how God could use ME! He does!

Additional Text: John 6, Hebrews 11

Then they came to the town of Jericho. As Jesus was leaving there with his followers and a great many people, a blind beggar named Bartimaeus son of Timaeus was sitting by the road. When he heard that Jesus from Nazareth was walking by, he began to shout, "Jesus, Son of David, have mercy on me!"
Many people warned the blind man to be quiet, but he shouted even more, "Son of David, have mercy on me!"
Jesus stopped and said, "Tell the man to come here."
So they called the blind man, saying, "Cheer up! Get to your feet. Jesus is calling you." The blind man jumped up, left his coat there, and went to Jesus.
Jesus asked him, "What do you want me to do for you?"
The blind man answered, "Teacher, I want to see."
Jesus said, "Go, you are healed because you believed." At once the man could see, and he followed Jesus on the road.   *Mark 10:46-52 (NCV)*

Faith. Does God answer prayer according to my faith? Is the will of the Almighty contingent upon what I believe?

Faith means being sure of the things we hope for and knowing that something is real even if we do not see it.   *Hebrews 11:1 (NCV)*

That is one of the most well known verses in the Bible about faith. The next 36 verses tell us about these wonderful "ancients" and their faith, implying that they were extra-ordinary, void of doubt. Looking on into chapter 11 of Hebrews…Hmmm…Abel — well, he ends up murdered.

Abraham — let's see: he lied to a king about his wife, he doubted God and manipulated His promise, causing a whole mess of problems with the begetting of Ishmael and Isaac.

Jacob — manipulated his brother, his father, living most of his adult years in exile.

Joseph – is sold as a slave, is wrongfully accused of adultery, and ends up in prison. Then becomes #2 man in Egypt — and then manipulates his brothers out of revenge before forgiving them.

Moses — whined his way through his call from God until God's anger "burned" against him.

Israelites — whined and complained for 40 years on a trip that should have been done in a couple of weeks.

We have around us many people whose lives tell us what faith means. So let us run the race that is before us and never give up. We should remove from our lives anything that would get in the way and the sin that so easily holds us back.
Hebrews 12:1 (NCV)

And, for me, here is the answer to my original question. It is not my faith that is counted when I petition God. It is my complete weakness in Jesus. It is Jesus' sacrifice that covers my sin that gives me favor with God. My life is FULL of doubts and whining and complaining and disobedience. I come to God to ask for healing, for mercy, for help in a given situation, help for my family and loved ones, — and I'm stinky with sin. I turn and Jesus steps in front of me — a cleansing rain — steps in front of me so that all the Father sees is a beautiful daughter with a request.

This made me hate life. Everything we do is painful; it's just as senseless as chasing the wind.

Suddenly I realized that others would someday get everything I had worked for so hard, then I started hating it all. Who knows if those people will be sensible or stupid? Either way, they will own everything I have earned by hard work and wisdom. It doesn't make sense.

I thought about all my hard work, and I felt depressed. When we use our wisdom, knowledge, and skill to get what we own, why do we have to leave it to someone who didn't work for it? This is senseless and wrong. What do we really gain from all of our hard work? Our bodies ache during the day, and work is torture. Then at night our thoughts are troubled. It just doesn't make sense. Ecclesiastes 2:17-23 (CEV)

We are like clay jars in which this treasure is stored. The real power comes from God and not from us. We often suffer, but we are never crushed. Even when we don't know what to do, we never give up. In times of trouble, God is with us, and when we are knocked down, we get up again. We face death every day because of Jesus. Our bodies show what his death was like, so that his life can also be seen in us. This means that death is working in us, but life is working in you. 2 Corinthians 4:7-12 (CEV)

My husband, Henry, the Bible scholar, calls *Ecclesiastes*, <u>Solomon's Whine Book</u>. While I agree that it is not a book I particularly enjoy because I do hear a whiney voice when I read it for content, it is easy for "despair" to get a hold of me, too! There's a lot being 'dished out' at me each day. When I look at it, weigh it, and try to reason it out – it's pretty overwhelming! It's not like I'm paranoid or delusional – it <u>is</u> reality!

But I have a choice. I <u>ALWAYS</u> have a choice. Yes, I do! I can stand there and take it – and eventually break <u>OR</u> I can sink to my knees and ask for help. Going to my knees many times feels weak and even scary. But I've found out that this is the <u>ONLY</u> place I can find peace. It is called the 'peace that passes understanding'. That is CERTAINLY the truth!!! It takes some time. It may require some 'wrestling' and a searching that is ABSOLUTELY without blinders. I call it my "Come to Jesus Moments". Truth and openness to GOD's wisdom is tough but I testify that EVERY TIME – EVERY TIME – God's way, His answer, His direction in my life, is ALWAYS correct…ALWAYS!

Additional Text: Isaiah 61, Ephesians 5

Elisha's servant got up early, and when he went out, he saw an army with horses and chariots all around the city. The servant said to Elisha, "Who, my master, what can we do?"
Elisha said, "Don't be afraid. The army that fights for us is larger than the one against us."
Then Elisha prayed, "LORD, open my servant's eyes and let him see."
The LORD opened the eyes of the young man, and he saw that the mountain was full of horses and chariots of fire all around Elisha.
2 Kings 6:15-17 (NCV, emphasis mine)

"Oh my Lord, what shall I do?" I've been there – wore that t-shirt down to a rag – and I am here today to testify to the fear that tried to isolate and destroy me.

Fear and deception are the great weapons of the enemy. If he can convince me that I am overwhelmed and outnumbered, then I will give up. I will pull in and try to find some cave to hide away.

"Open His eyes so he may see." That's the answer. Give me eyes to see YOUR truth, Lord. There is not a situation that God does not have control. God is Creator, Ruler, Savior, King of King, Alpha and Omega, beginning and end.

I testify to you today that He has brought me through abuse, shame, poor choices, divorce, raising three children (through their teen years!), ministry, financial catastrophes, cancer, and the list goes on – GOD brought me through. WHO WAS WITH ME WAS GREATER THAN THOSE WHO WERE WITH 'THE OTHER GUY'!!!

The angel of the LORD camps around those who fear God, and he saves them.
Examine and see how good the LORD is. Happy is the person who trusts him. You who belong to the LORD, fear him! Those who fear him will have everything they need.
Psalm 34:7-9

When situations seem overwhelming – God hasn't deserted me! In fact, He's gone before me!

Those who go to God Most High for safety will be protected by the Almighty.
I will say to the LORD, "You are my place of safety and protection. You are my God and I trust you.
God will save you from hidden traps and from deadly diseases.
He will cover you with his feathers, and under his wings you can hide. His trust will be your shield and protection.
Psalm 91:1-4 (NCV)

God is faithful. Even the darkness of my troubles is like light to Him (Psalm 139). He is ready to meet with me any time of the day or night. When turmoil comes, stopping right then and laying it all out to God will bring peace and clarity to my overloaded mind and spirit. Allowing God to separate truth from lies and shift the priorities to His will produces the strength that I need for the day.

Additional Text: 2 Kings 6, Romans 8, Deuteronomy 7:7-26

The Lord took me again to Jesus' parable of the prodigal son. This time, He wanted me to look at the father. What did he do?

And he said, "There was a man who had two sons. And the younger of them said to his father, 'Father, give me the share of property that is coming to me.' And he divided his property between them.   Luke 15:11-12 (ESV)

Sometimes God will allow me to have what I ask – even if it is not a good choice!

"But when he came to himself, he said, 'How many of my father's hired servants have more than enough bread, but I perish here with hunger. I will arise and go to my father, and I will say to him, "Father, I have sinned against heaven and before you. I am no longer worthy to be called your son. Treat me as one of your hired servants." ' And he arose and came to his father. But while he was still a long way off, his father saw him and felt compassion, and ran and embraced him and kissed him.   v.17-20

My Heavenly Father is always looking for me to come back under His wing. He wants to guide and protect me, giving me wisdom and knowledge to make good choices. He wants me in His house, worshipping Him. When I leave and go my way, He continues to look for me and sends His Holy Spirit to tell me, "It's OK to come back. Come back!"

Notice the prodigal's father did not have him bathe first! He threw his arms around the boy – pig smell, maybe even (excuse me!) 'doo-doo' on the clothes and all – and hugged him!

"And the son said to him, 'Father, I have sinned against heaven and before you. I am no longer worthy to be called your son.'   v. 21

God lets me repent. It lifts the burden of my sin.

"But the father said to his servants, 'Bring quickly the best robe, and put it on him, and put a ring on his hand, and shoes on his feet. And bring the fattened calf and kill it, and let us eat and celebrate. For this my son was dead, and is alive again; he was lost, and is found.' And they began to celebrate.   v.22-24

God's mercy and forgiveness is freely and quickly given. He doesn't ask me to beg or humiliate myself – He just forgives me when I ask out of His extravagant love.

The rest of this chapter tells us about the older son, the 'faithful' son, and how he feels slighted because his 'sinful' brother received a party and he didn't. The father listens to the son, listens to everything he has to say and then replies:

"And he said to him, 'Son, you are always with me, and all that is mine is yours. It was fitting to celebrate and be glad, for this your brother was dead, and is alive, he was lost, and is found.' "   v. 31-32

My Heavenly Father wants me to always remember – it's all about saving souls. God blesses me for being His obedient child and everything He has is mine as His child. BUT – God REJOICES over a saved soul!

Additional Text: Matthew 18, Colossians 3

You are my God and protector. Please answer my prayer. I was in terrible distress, but you set me free. Now have pity and listen as I pray...
I can lie down and sleep soundly because you, LORD, will keep me safe.

Psalm 4:1,8 (CEV)

Have you ever had trouble sleeping at night? Worry can give me insomnia! Sometimes I do not even recognize it as 'worry'. After all, as a Christian, a believer in a sovereign Lord and compassionate Savior, I should <u>never</u> worry...right? That's the theory! Or should I say, 'theology'? Well, even Paul could get overwhelmed –

During my many travels, I have been in danger from rivers, robbers, my own people, and foreigners. My life has been in danger in cities, in deserts, at sea, and with people who only pretended to be the Lord's followers I worked and struggled and spent many sleepless nights.   *2 Corinthians 11:26-27 (CEV)*

Paul and worry! Sometimes I set a standard for myself that is a good ideal to set as my aim but the 'reality' of my life and the weakness in me should come as no surprise. God isn't surprised! He has given me instructions and directions to walk towards when those times of worry come upon me. Even though I <u>know</u> that God is in control and is faithful there are still times when the worries of this world seem to cover me like a large dark blanket. How do I know which way to go and how to move to get out from under it? Paul tells me from his own experience –

Do not be anxious about <u>anything</u>, BUT in <u>everything</u>, by PRAYER and petition, with <u>thanksgiving</u>, present your requests to GOD. <u>And</u> the peace of God, which transcends <u>all</u> understanding, <u>will guard</u> your hearts and your minds in CHRIST JESUS.
<u>Finally</u>, brothers, whatever is <u>true</u>, whatever is <u>noble</u>, whatever is <u>right</u>, whatever is <u>pure</u>, whatever is <u>lovely</u>, whatever is <u>admirable</u>—if anything is <u>excellent</u> or <u>praiseworthy</u>—think about such things.

Philippians 4:6-7 (emphasis mine)

When I am weak and overwhelmed with thoughts about bills or someone I love, job promotions or security, even the unknown strikes of terrorists, God says, *"Come to me, all you who are weary and burdened, and I will give you rest. Take my yoke upon you,*[come walk with me] *and learn from me, for I am gentle and humble in heart, and you will find rest for your souls."*[Matthew 11:28-29]. This may seem simplistic and too easy … but I think that's actually the point! If I believe God is sovereign and creator-God of all, then who better to take all my worry, frustration, and fear? I believe that where I fall short is in thinking that a quick 5 minute prayer will always 'do the trick'. Maybe I am so desperate and ready that in 5 minutes I can lay it all down. But it may take a little more focused time –

Be joyful always; pray <u>continually</u>; give thanks in <u>all</u> circumstances, for <u>THIS</u> is God's will for you in Christ Jesus.   *1 Thessalonians 5:16-18 (emphasis mine)*

More time in prayer = less time in worry.

Additional Text: 2 Corinthians 12

So I bow in prayer before the Father from whom every family in heaven and on earth gets its true name. I ask the Father in his great glory to give you the power to be strong inwardly through his Spirit. I pray that Christ will live in your hearts by faith and that your life will be strong in love and be built on love. And I pray that you and all God's holy people will have the power to understand the greatness of Christ's love – how wide and how long and how high and how deep that love is. Christ's love is greater than anyone can ever know, but I pray that you will be able to know that love. Then you can be filled with the fullness of God.

With God's power working in us, God can do much, much more than anything we can ask or imagine. To him be glory in the church and in Christ Jesus for all time, forever and ever. Amen.

I am in prison because I belong to the Lord. God chose you to be his people, so I urge you now to live the life to which God called you. Always be humble, gentle, and patient, accepting each other in love. Ephesians 3:14-4:2 (CEV)

What a wonderful prayer from Paul for the people of Ephesus! He prays for their spiritual strength to continue to move <u>toward</u> Jesus, that their relationship with Him would GROW, not become stagnant, no matter how great and Spirit-filled they might think they were!

I would be wise to heed and accept that prayer for myself. There is always MORE to my relationship with Jesus. I heard someone say once that the reason the angels continue to say, "Holy, Holy, Holy" in God's presence is because He is continuously showing them another facet of His character and every time He does, they can not help but drop to their knees and cry "Holy, Holy, Holy".

Paul then says that Christ's love is wider and longer and higher and deeper than anything they have experienced or could attempt to imagine. His love, just like His power, or creative word, or grace, or mercy – has no end.

Most of the experiences with love in my life have had definite conditions or limits. Jesus' love is so bound-less that He left heaven – left the <u>glory</u> – and died a horrible, disgusting death – for ME. Even knowing that, I fail. I sin. And with a timid word of repentance, He restores me to full relationship with Him. The past is *erased* without a trace! That's love. That's Jesus.

Then Paul reminds me that God does more than I ask. Not only did He heal my son, but also He is turning him into a warrior, a worshipper, that will lead the army of God into battle. When days were uncertain and we were reeling from the initial word that James' cancer had reoccurred, God revealed Himself in truth to James and James said, "What's the worse that could happen, Mom? I die and go to heaven and see Jesus and Dad?" Fear tucked its tail between its legs and ran with disease yelping behind it! More than I could ask or imagine!

Paul continues on because he knows that the love of Christ is only the beginning for the Church. Jesus' love cannot <u>just</u> be personal for me – I've been given it freely – freely I must give it away. To be worthy involves humility. It's all about Jesus anyway. It's not about me. Never has been. By the power of the Holy Spirit, we are bound together. We are one with the Father, just as Jesus is one. Let us focus on THAT!

March 9

"But when the Father sends the Comforter instead of me – and by the Comforter I mean the Holy Spirit – he will teach you much, as well as remind you of everything I myself have told you.
I am leaving you with a gift – peace of mind and heart! And the peace I give isn't fragile like the peace the world gives. So don't be troubled or afraid."
John 14:26-27 (TLB)

Thomas Watson, a 16th century poet, once said, "Gladly the man, when he dies, enters into peace; but while he lives, peace must enter into him."

As I grow older I think *peace* is the manifestation of God that I desire and the confirmation that I receive when I am <u>in</u> the will of God and stepping in the path that HE desires for me. It's not being comfortable or complacent. It is truly that *peace that passes ALL understanding* that Paul wrote about. It is *peace* that is not affected by the circumstances of my life or people in my life.

Henry Drummond, an evangelist who may have been the original 'campus crusader' with his work in the student movement in the late 1800's, gave this illustration about true peace:

Two painters each painted a picture to illustrate his conception of rest. The first chose for his scene a still, lone lake among the far-off mountains. The second drew on his canvas a thundering waterfall with a fragile birch tree bending over the foam; at the fork of the branch, almost wet with the white water's spray, a robin sat on its nest. The first [painting] *was only stagnation; the last was rest.*

Jesus' life was certainly one of troubled times. His early life of poverty and heavy responsibility as He cared for his mother and siblings segued into even more pressure and attacks from every angle as He fought with the ruling powers of His society, the Pharisees and Sadducees. Even during Jesus' final hours when He was put under excruciating torture and ending with a crucifixion, His spirit was at rest. His statement of peace in John 14 is recorded as spoken during the Last Supper as Jesus was giving the best of His wisdom, sharing His heart with those who would be the conduits to me and to you. It is His legacy to me…peace.

So now, since we have been made right in God's sight by faith in his promises, we can have real peace with him because of what Jesus Christ our Lord has done for us. For because of our faith, he has brought us into this place of highest privilege where we now stand, and we confidently and joyfully look forward to actually becoming all that God has had in mind for us to be.
We can rejoice, too, when we run into problems and trials for we know that they are good for us – they help us learn to be patient. And patience develops strength of character in us and helps us trust God more each time we use it until finally our hope and faith are strong and steady. Then, when that happens, we are able to hold our heads high no matter what happens and know that all is well, for we know how dearly God loves us, and we feel this warm love everywhere within us because God has given us the Holy Spirit to fill our hearts with his love.
Romans 5:1-5 (TLB)

A large crowd followed and pressed around him [Jesus]. And a woman was there who had been subject to bleeding for twelve years. She had suffered a great deal under the care of many doctors and had spent all she had yet instead of getting better she grew worse. When she heard about Jesus, she came up behind him in the crowd and touched his cloak, because she thought, "If I just touch his clothes, I will be healed." Immediately her bleeding stopped and she felt in her body that she was freed from her suffering.

At once Jesus realized that power had gone out from him. He turned around in the crowd and asked, "Who touched my clothes?"

"You see the people crowding against you," his disciples answered, "and yet you can ask, `Who touched me?' "

But Jesus kept looking around to see who had done it. Then the woman, knowing what had happened to her, came and fell at his feet and, trembling with fear, told him the whole truth. He said to her, "Daughter, your faith has healed you. Go in peace and be freed from your suffering."   Mark 5:24-34

As someone who has been in the medical profession for over 25 years, this story is a wonderful miracle that blesses me in my own life.

Let's look at this:

First, the woman had been bleeding for 12 years. That brings the question to me – is there something in MY life that I have been 'battling' for more than 12 years?

The woman had suffered! She had not only physical pain and weakness but financial ruin, isolation, rejection, and the stigma of being 'unclean'. This is a place in Scriptures where I believe that Jesus says to me, "Yes, Jody, there is going to be suffering and I am going to be there while it is going on."

The woman decides just to touch Jesus' clothes. She's not going to throw herself on Him. She's not going to get radical and call attention to herself. Just being in the same room with Jesus is enough to 'rock' my world, isn't it? Just His presence is enough to change my life!

In an *instant*, the woman was healed! Just like that! No formulas or incantations... just a simple 'word' from Jesus. I noticed in this instance, however, that Jesus asked for TRUTH that the woman was relying only on Him. God gets all the glory and praise for the miracle! Do I admit to what God has done in my life TODAY in front of others? Do I brush them off as unimportant or coincidences or that I did it in my own power? Can I really do ANYTHING in my own power?

I waited patiently for the LORD; he turned to me and heard my cry.
He lifted me out of the slimy pit, out of the mud and mire;
He set my feet on a rock and gave me a firm place to stand.
He put a new song in my mouth, a hymn of praise to our God.
Many will see and fear and put their trust in the LORD.   Psalm 40:1-3

Additional Text: Psalm 40, Luke 7

March 11

And he said, "Listen, all Judah and inhabitants of Jerusalem and King Jehoshaphat: Thus says the LORD to you, 'Do not be afraid and do not be dismayed at this great horde, for the battle is not yours but God's...
And they rose early in the morning and went out into the wilderness of Tekoa. And when they went out, Jehoshaphat stood and said, "Hear me, Judah and inhabitants of Jerusalem! Believe in the LORD your God, and you will be established; believe his prophets, and you will succeed." And when he had taken counsel with the people, he appointed those who were to sing to the LORD and praise him in holy attire, as they went before the army, and say, "Give thanks to the LORD, for his steadfast love endures forever." And when they began to sing and praise, the LORD sent an ambush against the men of Ammon, Moab, and Mount Seir, who had come against Judah, so that they were routed... And the fear of God came on all the kingdoms of the countries when they heard that the LORD had fought against the enemies of Israel. So the realm of Jehoshaphat was quiet, for his God gave him rest all around.
2 Chronicles 20:15, 20-22, 29-30 (ESV)

I was made by God to love Him. I was made to worship Him.

King Jehoshaphat's story tells me that praise and worship goes <u>before</u> any battle. I do not battle against flesh and blood so God's battle plans reflect His understanding of the enemy. My true enemies cannot stand in the presence of praise and worship of God so they will do ANYTHING they can to discourage me from worship whether that is whispering in my ear that I <u>really</u> don't need to go to church or whether it's a distraction from my quiet time. When I praise and worship God, the enemies flee!!! Discouragement, depression, fears – they all GO! In the presence of praising God!!!

I also need to remember that there is always an 'avenue of praise' for me. I can praise as I drive down the rode in my car. I can praise as I fly across the country – even using headphones and CDs! If I no longer have an opportunity to play piano and praise like I use to – maybe some praise team or choir can use my voice. Even if my voice is not the greatest by some world standards – God just said, "Let everything that has breath..." notice that there is no mention of pitch or tone or how great I look standing in front of people!!! Sometimes when I am praising God, I close my eyes and in my spirit, I am dancing all around the room!!! I have no constraints by my physical abilities or gravity --- I'm flying!!!

What do I have to praise Him about? Some things are obvious – others are more 'veiled'. Sometimes I even 'count my blessings'. There are lots of ways to do that but I am a simple person so I just start with the letter 'A' and think of everything that I am grateful to God that begins with the letter 'A': Alex (my grandson), crisp juicy apples – and so on.

I even feel better right now than I did when I first got up this morning. PRAISE THE LORD!!!

Additional Text: Luke 19, John 4

"God alone sees the heart; the heart alone sees God."

John Donne (1573-1631)

The LORD saw that the wickedness of man was great in the earth, and that every intention of the thoughts of his heart was only evil continually. And the LORD was sorry that he had made man on the earth, and it grieved him to his heart. So the LORD said, "I will blot out man whom I have created from the face of the land, man and animals and creeping things and birds of the heavens, for I am sorry that I have made them." But Noah found favor in the eyes of the LORD.

Genesis 6:5-8 (ESV)

If God is love, then God is about emotion. It is not an emotion that can be manipulated but it is about emotion that stirs the heart and makes a change. This passage in Genesis tells me that God had seen such great evil that His heart was touched by it as He saw the atrocities done to His children BY His children. He would not stand for it any longer! There would be consequences.

God sees my heart. He sees in truth and in'fairness' that I am not capable of comprehending. His eyes see every corner of my intentions and sift through the "could-uv's" and "should-uv's" and weighs the "did's" and judges in Spirit and in truth.

In the recounting of Noah despite the evil that was so grieving to God, the Lord saw a man named Noah and judged in fairness. He gave Noah a task, however, that would bring trials of ridicules and disbelief. I don't want to think that Noah got an easy pass to an escape from the terminal water ride that God was planning! Moses had to pass the test of obedience to enter the ark of salvation. God gives us tests so we have test-imonies!

Having purified your souls by your obedience to the truth for a sincere brotherly love, love one another earnestly from a pure heart, since you have been born again, not of perishable seed but of imperishable, through the living and abiding word of God.

1 Peter 1:22-23 (ESV)

When I allow God to 'purify' my uncertain and wayward heart so that I love in His truth and see others with HIS eyes, then I have an imperishable life. My love for others is not contingent upon their actions or their love but it flows through me with God's UNCONDITIONAL power. Thanks be to God!

Additional Text: Jeremiah 1, Romans 7

Pride only leads to arguments, but those who take advice are wise.
Proverbs 13:10 (NCV)

"You have heard that it was said to our people long ago, 'You must not murder anyone. Anyone who murders another will be judged.' But I tell you, if you are angry with a brother or sister, you will be judged. If you say bad things to a brother or sister, you will be judged by the council. And if you call someone a fool, you will be in danger of the fire of hell.

So when you offer your gift to God at the altar, and you remember that your brother or sister has something against you, leave your gift there at the altar. Go and make peace with that person, and then come and offer your gift.

If your enemy is taking you to court, become friends quickly, before you go to court. Otherwise, your enemy might turn you over to the judge, and the judge might give you to a guard to put you in jail. I tell you the truth, you will not leave there until you have paid everything you owe."   *Matthew 5:21-26 (NCV)*

Disagreements. Quarrels. Conflicts in relationships. Whatever I want to call them – Jesus clearly tells me to settle these matters. I can think of many reasons not to do this. "He doesn't want to make up." "<u>I</u> was right!" "She's too far away and I don't want to do this over the phone!" It all comes down to MY feelings, MY wants, MY pride.

So what if the other person doesn't want my forgiveness or hear my forgiveness? God does. So what if I was right? Jesus was the "most right" one of all and He forgave me <u>and</u> His executioners as we nailed Him to a cross. So what if the person I quarreled with is now on the other side of the country? I don't want to be on the other side of the room on Judgment Day. I want to be sitting together at the Feast with Jesus. I want Him to look at us with joy, not regret.

It is good and pleasant when God's people live together in peace!
It is like perfumed oil poured on the priest's head and running down his beard.
It ran down Aaron's beard and on to the collar of his robes.
It is like the dew of Mount Hermon falling on the hills of Jerusalem.
There the LORD gives his blessing of life forever.   *Psalm 133 (NCV)*

Jesus tells me not to murder. OK. I can do that! But He brings it even further and tells me not to be *angry* with my brother or sister. Remember whom He defined as my brother and sister? (Mark 3:31) I need the help of the Holy Spirit to show the kindness and compassion that Jesus did. Spending time with the Lord <u>every</u> <u>day</u>, learning from His Word, reasoning with my mind, and allowing the Holy Spirit to reveal God's truth and guide me is the way to grow in the Lord.

"You have heard that it was said, 'Love your neighbor and hate your enemies.' But I say to you, love your enemies. Pray for those who hurt you. If you do this, you will be true children of your Father in heaven."   *Matthew 5:43-45 (NCV)*

Additional Text: Matthew 6, 1 Timothy 5

You were an anointed guardian cherub. I placed you; you were on the holy mountain of God; in the midst of the stones of fire you walked.

You were blameless in your ways from the day you were created, till unrighteousness was found in you. In the abundance of your trade you were filled with violence in your midst, and you sinned; so I cast you as a profane thing from the mountain of God, and I destroyed you, O guardian cherub, from the midst of the stones of fire.

Your heart was proud because of your beauty; you corrupted your wisdom for the sake of your splendor. I cast you to the ground; I exposed you before kings, to feast their eyes on you.   *Ezekiel 28:14-17 (ESV)*

Many theologians believe this passage is about Lucifer or satan and his fall. Some believe it is more literal, speaking of Baal, the 'head' god of that time. To me – either way – it's about PRIDE!

About six years ago, I spent three days flat on my back with pain in my low back that was --- excruciating! Turning, reaching for a glass of water, getting up for the 'necessities' was indescribable torture. I decided all I could do was rest and read.

Well, trust our Lord not to waste an opportunity! He took me through Scriptures on a word study about PRIDE! It was an experience – a wondrous blessing. I awoke on the 4th day without ANY pain and a real insight into the root – the very root of my sins – PRIDE.

But whatever gain I had, I counted as loss for the sake of Christ. Indeed, I count everything as loss because of the surpassing worth of knowing Christ Jesus my Lord. For his sake I have suffered the loss of all things and count them as rubbish, in order that I may gain Christ, and be found in him, not having a righteousness of my own that comes from the law, but that which comes through faith in Christ, the righteousness from God that depends on faith – that I may know him and the power of his resurrection, and may share his sufferings, becoming like him in his death, that by any means possible I may attain the resurrection from the dead.   *Philippians 3:7-11 (ESV)*

There is nothing about me that is worthy to receive the love, the gifts that God has for me and what He has already done for me. I cannot serve Him enough to even make a dent in the sacrifice of Jesus. My pride is a stench to God. Humility is beautiful in His eyes.

"With what shall I come before the LORD, and bow myself before God on high? Shall I come before him with burnt offerings, with calves a year old?

Will the LORD be pleased with thousands of rams, and ten thousands of rivers of oil?

Shall I give my firstborn for my transgression, the fruit of my body for the sin of my soul?"

He has told you, O man, what is good; and what does the LORD require of you but to do justice, and to love kindness, and to walk humbly with your God?
                                       Micah 6:6-8 (ESV)

Additional Text: 2 Chronicles 32, Isaiah 2

March 15

"If the people of this world hate you, just remember that they hated me first. If you belonged to the world, its people would love you. But you don't belong to the world. I have chosen you to leave the world behind, and that is why its people hate you. Remember how I told you that servants are not greater than their master. So if people mistreat me, they will mistreat you. If they do what I say, they will do what you say.

People will do to you exactly what they did to me. They will do it because you belong to me, and they don't know the one who sent me. If I had not come and spoken to them, they would not be guilty of sin. But now they have no excuse for their sin.

Everyone who hates me also hates my Father. I have done things that no one else has ever done. If they had not seen me do these things, they would not be guilty. But they did see me do these things, and they still hate me and my Father too. That is why the Scriptures are true when they say, 'People hated me for no reason.'

I will send you the Spirit who comes from Father and shows what is true. The Spirit will help you and will tell you about me. Then you will also tell others about me, because you have been with me from the beginning.

I am telling you this to keep you from being afraid. You will be chased out of the Jewish meeting places. And the time will come when people will kill you and think they are doing God a favor. They will do these things because they don't know either the Father or me. I am saying this to you now, so that when the time comes, you will remember what I have said."   John 15:18-16:4 (CEV)

Have you ever felt like the world hated you? Or at least people you care about hated you? I have. Jesus knows how I feel. His own brothers and sisters did not believe in him. (John 7:5) They rarely came around and certainly didn't support His ministry! After all – they might get put out of the synagogue! Jesus was intimately acquainted with rejection and humiliation and grief. He knows what it's like to be ridiculed for being 'different'.

"The time will come and is already here when all of you will be scattered. Each of you will go back home and leave me by myself. But the Father will be with me, and I won't be alone. I have told you this, so that you might have peace in your hearts because of me. While you are in the world, you will have to suffer. But cheer up! I have defeated the world."   John 16:32-33 (CEV)

Jesus <u>has</u> overcome. It's done! Let us throw off the oppression of this world and walk in the victory with Jesus! It <u>is</u> a choice! I can stare at the closed door <u>OR</u> I can look up for the new open doors. I can replay the words of rejection and criticism or I can open God's word and read His words of truth about me, <u>HIS</u> child. It seems I have spent most of my life looking to my parents, my husband, my boss, my friends, even my children to give me the recognition and validation that would make my life seem worthwhile. God was there all the time telling me how much He loved me. I am HIS child and He does NOT make JUNK!

May I begin today to seek to know the width, length, height, and depth of God's love for me! (Ephesians 3:14) Let me choose God's way – RIGHT NOW!

March 16

"I will bless you with a future filled with hope – a future of success, not of suffering. You will turn back to me and ask for help, and I will answer your prayers. You will worship me with all your heart, and I will be with you and accept your worship. Then I will gather you from all the nations where I scattered you, and you will return to Jerusalem."   *Jeremiah 29:11-14 (CEV)*

"I am the gate. All who come in through me will be saved. Through me they will come and go and find pasture.

A thief comes only to rob, kill, and destroy. I came so that everyone would have life, and have it in its fullest.   *John 10:9-10 (CEV)*

People of Jerusalem, you don't need to cry anymore. The Lord is kind, and as soon as he hears your cries for help, he will come. The Lord has given you trouble and sorrow as your food and drink. But now you will again see the Lord, your teacher, and he will guide you. Whether you turn to the right or to the left, you will hear a voice saying, "This is the road! Now follow it."

Isaiah 30:19-21 (CEV)

Adversity. Tribulation. These are all part of this life and we all can tell of our own experiences. I believe they come from three sources.

1) Satan, the Enemy. This is the 'easy' source for me. Satan is 'easy' for me to blame. Frankly, I think I give him more credit than he deserves. He does "steal, kill, and destroy". He <u>is</u> the enemy. Solution: <u>Submit</u> to God. <u>Resist</u> the devil <u>AND</u> he <u>WILL</u> flee! [James 4:7]

2) My flesh. My own mistakes and poor choices. They are the consequences of my actions. Solution: *The fear of the Lord is wisdom, and knowledge of the Holy One is understanding.* [Proverbs 9:10] Learn from these mistakes and move on in the Lord. Walk in the victory of precepts learned!!!

3) God. Whew! This is a tough one. Scripture speaks clearly about the Lord's discipline [Proverbs 1, Hebrews 12, Revelation 3] and how He treats us as sons/daughters not slaves. The words seem to admonish me to <u>embrace</u> the Lord's discipline and learn <u>His</u> lessons. God <u>ALLOWS</u> the adversity, the tribulation to refine me because He desires that I be His favored child —

"Nowhere in the land will more than a third of them be left alive. Then I will purify them and put them to the test, just as gold and silver are purified and tested. They will pray in my name, and I will answer them. I will say, 'You are my people,' and they will reply, 'You, LORD, are our God!' "

Zechariah 13:8-9 (CEV)

Yes, adversity and tribulation are experiences and events I would rather avoid like construction in rush hour traffic! BUT I know how the story ends. I <u>KNOW</u> that I overcome adversity and tribulation by the Blood of Jesus Christ, the word of my testimony, and my willingness to give up my life, my plan, my control for His.

But thank God for letting our Lord Jesus Christ give us the victory!

1 Corinthians 15:57

Additional Text: John 10, 1 Corinthians 15

March 17

Now when the Philistines heard that the people of Israel had gathered at Mizpah, the lords of the Philistines went up against Israel. And when the people of Israel heard of it, they were afraid of the Philistines. And the people of Israel said to Samuel, "Do not cease to cry out to the LORD our God for us that he may save us from the hand of the Philistines." So Samuel took a nursing lamb and offered it as a whole burnt offering to the LORD. And Samuel cried out to the LORD for Israel, and the LORD answered him. As Samuel was offering up the burnt offering, the Philistines drew near to attack Israel. But the LORD thundered with a mighty sound that day against the Philistines and threw them into confusion, and they were routed before Israel. And the men of Israel went out from Mizpah and pursued the Philistines and struck them, as far as below Beth-car.

Then Samuel took a stone and set it up between Mizpah and Shen and called its name Ebenezer, for he said, "Til now the LORD has helped us." So the Philistines were subdued and did not again enter the territory of Israel. And the hand of the LORD was against the Philistines all the days of Samuel.

1 Samuel 7:7-13 (ESV)

The Philistines may have been Israel's enemy but they weren't stupid! Attacking when your enemy is most vulnerable is good military strategy. Israel had gathered to pray. When they realized that the Philistines were upon them — they cried out to Samuel, "Don't stop praying!!!" It is unfortunate that too often we turn to the "God Option" only when we think there is no other one!

When the going gets tough — the tough PRAY!

Likewise the Spirit helps us in our weakness. For we do not know what to pray for as we ought, but the Spirit himself intercedes for us with groanings too deep for words. And he who searches hearts knows what is the mind of the Spirit, because the Spirit intercedes for the saints according to the will of God.

Romans 8:26-27 (ESV)

When the word "overwhelming" comes to my mind in describing my life, I want a red flag to raise and furiously begin waving!!! If I feel this emotion, then I am off God's track, timing, and priorities and have taken too many burdens as mine. Like Israel, like Jesus, and as Paul passed on to the Romans, I need to hit my knees and lay it all out for God to sort and meet Him in that place of peace — again. I know that I KNOW — that no matter WHAT is going on in my life, no matter what is thrown my way — God's peace is ALWAYS there. I haven't faced what Jesus did but I have His example when *"My soul is overwhelmed"*. My soul is my emotions. Prayer is where my soul finds God's peace, God's truth, God's love.

My prayer time MUST have #1 priority in my day. Prayer is not just me talking. It's LISTENING!!! It's being quiet enough to hear His quiet voice. "Speak, Father. Your servant is listening."

Additional Text: Matthew 27, Romans 8

So do not fear, for I am with you; do not be dismayed, for I am your God.
I will strengthen you and help you; I will uphold you with my righteous right hand.   *Isaiah 41:10*

I have shared with you before a testimony about the Lord's battle against cancer through my son. I want to revisit that today. "Cancer" was a secondary enemy. Fear was where the front line was drawn in this war.

For our struggle is not against flesh and blood, but against the rulers, against the authorities, against the powers of this dark world and against the spiritual forces of evil in the heavenly realms.   *Ephesians 6:12*

For those who have had cancer, or any other life-threatening illness, or a loved one has been in this situation, the minute the word comes out of the physician's mouth, your life – <u>all</u> aspects of your life, physical and spiritual, are never the same. In fact, many of us feel we are frozen in time. Our mind seems to narrow and completely focus on the one word – cancer. That's fear. Total, all-consuming fear and it is <u>NOT</u> God.

I've been in the medical profession in one capacity or another, since I was 14. I started as a candy striper! I have worked in critical care units, surgery, physician's office, and I retired from nursing after 12 years with hospice. When I think back on those 30+ years, it's fear that has been expressed to me by those I have been honored to care for. Fear came out in anger, humor, silence, tears, and every emotion in between.

"I am the good shepherd; I know my sheep and my sheep know me— just as the Father knows me and I know the Father—and I lay down my life for the sheep."
                                                                                    John 10:14-15

Questions are raised: Why? What is this going to do to my family? What does this mean financially? Have I made a difference in this life? I can tell you that 'why' questions rarely have good answers. I guess that is why I believe only <u>GOD</u> can answer that one. I wonder if that is what Jacob wrestled with God about? Why has my life gone this way? Why is this happening to me? How this life-threatening illness affected a family's life, including financially, -- well, count yourself blessed that it <u>will</u> increase your prayer time. I look back and I don't <u>know</u> how we managed with ½ my salary in a one-salary family, but we did.

Taking these questions – the manifestations of our fear – to the Lord and laying them at <u>HIS</u> feet so that He can answer and deal with them – takes the weapon of fear and knocks it down to size – even <u>squashes</u> it!!!

Humble yourselves, therefore, under God's mighty hand, that he may lift you up in due time. Cast all your anxiety on him because he cares for you.
                                                                                    1 Peter 5:6-7

He <u>IS</u> mighty God – El Gibbor – who says to each of us: *"I will not leave you – I will not forsake you"*.

Additional Text: Matthew 6, 1 Peter 4 and 5

The LORD is my light and the one who saves me. I fear no one. The LORD protects my life; I am afraid of no one.   *Psalm 27:1 (NCV)*
Being afraid of people can get you into trouble, but if you trust the LORD, you will be safe.   *Proverbs 29:25 (NCV)*
"I tell you, my friends, don't be afraid of people who can kill the body but after that can do nothing more to hurt you. I will show you the one to fear. Fear the one who has the power to kill you and also to throw you into hell. Yes, this is the one you should fear."   *Luke 12:4-5 (NCV)*

And so as each day passes, I hear that more and more troops are being deployed. Men and women are standing on ships or walking across tarmacs to waiting planes sometimes with a backward glance and a wave – but more often then not, a set face and caps that are pulled low over eyes that are moist with unshed tears. Commentaries on TV multiply with 'rumors of war and more rumors'. Speculation run amuck!

I am given clear counsel from my heavenly Father that HE is the 'light' that will guide me. HE has all the 'eternal' answers. Any fear for my loved ones who may be deployed, for homeland safety, even the decision-making of our leaders belongs at the foot of the Cross. My worries are cancelled when I kneel in prayer.

A prayer journal is an awesome tool to build my faith. A simple spiral notebook or legal pad sitting next to my Bible allows me to make a quick note of prayer requests or needs. Leaving 3-4 blank lines after the need allows me to then make a note on how God answered the prayer. THAT's a faith-builder!!!

Then Judas (not Judas Iscariot) said, "But, Lord, why do you plan to show yourself to us and not to the rest of the world?"
Jesus answered, "If people love me, they will obey my teaching. My Father will love them, and we will come to them and make our home with them. Those who do not love me do not obey my teaching. This teaching that you hear is not really mine; it is from my Father, who sent me.
I have told you all these things while I am with you. But the Helper will teach you everything and will cause you to remember all that I told you. This Helper is the Holy Spirit whom the Father will send in my name."
John 14:22-27 (NCV)

The strength and the power of these words and the VERY PRESENCE of my Father through His Holy Spirit will be that solid rock on which I will stand in the days to come. Let's take time today to pray for our leaders and those who advise them. Let us pray for our troops and their families who wait for them at home.

Additional Text: Psalm 27, Luke 12

I look upon all the world as my parish; that in whatever part of it I am, I judge it meet, right and my bounden duty to declare unto all that are willing to hear, the glad tidings of salvation. — *John Wesley, 1703-1791*

Do you remember who shared the Good News of Jesus Christ with you? Maybe it was your mom or dad when you were so young that it seems like you've always known Jesus as a personal Savior who died just for you. Maybe it was a Sunday School teacher that brought those wonderful gospels alive until one day it just "clicked" and you KNEW that it was all about your sin – it was all about your Savior, Jesus Christ. Or maybe you were like me – sat in church all your life but didn't know or accept that it was about me and Jesus. That He did it for ME! He loved ME so much! I am so unworthy of You, Lord! "Yes, but I LOVE YOU, Jody! I love YOU!"

But how are they to call on him in whom they have not believed? And how are they to believe in him of whom they have never heard? And how are they to hear without someone preaching? And how are they to preach unless they are sent? As it is written, "How beautiful are the feet of those who preach the good news!" But they have not all obeyed the gospel. For Isaiah says, "Lord, who has believed what he has heard from us?" So faith comes from hearing, and hearing through the word of Christ. Romans 10:14-17 (ESV)

I heard a question the other day that really peaked my interest: "Would you want even your worse enemy in hell for all eternity?" I admit that I thought of someone – not really an enemy but someone I struggle to like – and, no, I thought, I don't wish them that! Eternal life with Jesus is not an exclusive club – just a blessed one! God desires that all would come to a saving knowledge of Him and Jesus told me to "GO!" and tell the world.

And I heard a loud voice in heaven, saying, "Now the salvation and the power and the kingdom of our God and the authority of his Christ have come, for the accuser of our brothers has been thrown down, who accuses them day and night before our God. And they have conquered him by the blood of the Lamb and by the word of their testimony, for they loved not their lives even unto death. Therefore, rejoice, O heavens and you who dwell in them! But woe to you, O earth and sea, for the devil has come down to you in great wrath, because he know that his time is short!" Revelation 12:10-12 (ESV)

Satan's time is short but then so is mine to share this Good News that saved my soul. I overcome day-to-day 'attacks' of depression and despair and frustration by the word of my testimony AND receiving the testimony of others. It occurs to me that going to lunch or dinner with a fellow Christian is satisfying food for the spirit AND the body when testimonies of what God has done is shared.

Additional Text: Hebrews 10, Revelation 21

Now the LORD said to Abrahm, "Go from your country and your kindred and your father's house to the land that I will show you. And I will make of you a great nation, and I will bless you and make your name great, so that you will be a blessing. I will bless those who bless you, and him who dishonors you I will curse, and in you all the families of the earth shall be blessed." So Abram went, as the LORD had told him, and Lot went with him. Abram was seventy-five years old when he departed from Haran. Genesis 12:1-4 (ESV)

Abram was 75 years old. His new name of "Abraham" and the conception of his son, Isaac, AND the promise from God that he would be a "father of nations" was still in his FUTURE! I do not believe the word "retirement" was in the picture!

I suspect many of us use age as an excuse to avoid God's call to His ministry. We may begin our life with Jesus by saying we are "too young" to serve. Paul clearly told Timothy that he was not to believe that lie. We have MANY examples in David, Daniel, Samuel, and even Jesus empowering His "baby" disciples to GO and teach and serve that tell us clearly not to sit back and wait for some arbitrary age when Wisdom will just fall down on us.

Next, we become very involved with raising children and determine that we don't have 'time' for anything outside our family. Excuses became easier to justify at this point in my life! I had three children, a husband, and a career to juggle. I didn't need anything else!

Then we move along and decide, "Well, I've done my time. It's time for someone else to work. I'm going to retire and just relax!"

And Peter said, "See, we have left our homes and followed you." And he [Jesus] said to them, "Truly, I say to you, there is no one who has left house or wife or brothers or parents or children, for the sake of the kingdom of God, who will not receive many times more in this time, and in the age to come eternal life." Luke 18:28-30 (ESV)

To serve God is all about Him. It's about having a willing heart that will receive God's 'call' to serve and let HIM set the priorities in my life, let HIM run the schedule in my life. When I let go of that tight-fisted grip on the reins of my moment-to-moment, day-to-day, even year-to-year schedule, AWESOME things occur in all aspects of my life that I certainly could not have achieved in my own power and puny wisdom.

Therefore, since we are surrounded by so great a cloud of witnesses, let us also lay aside every weight, and sin, which clings so closely, and let us run with endurance the race that is set before us,... Hebrews 12:1 (ESV)

Who is the cloud of witnesses in my life? There's Bill who brings men to Jesus through the gifts of discipleship and encouragement. There's Trudell who sees young sailors sitting on a bench in front of the mall and in that sweet 'grandma' way, goes over to inquire where they are from and where they are going to go and with joy all over her face asks, "Do you know Jesus?"

Am I willing to leave all of me behind for the sake of God's kingdom? Am I willing to count on God's <u>non</u>-retirement plan and believe that His "eternal life benefits" will be more than I could ever ask or imagine? Am I willing?

I replied, "I'm not a good speaker, LORD, and I'm too young."

"Don't say you're too young," the LORD answered. "If I tell you to go and speak to someone, then go! And when I tell you what to say, don't leave out a word! I promise to be with you and keep you safe, so don't be afraid."

The LORD reached out his hand, then he touched my mouth and said, "I am giving you the words to say, and I am sending you with authority to speak to the nations for me. You will tell them of doom and destruction, and of rising and rebuilding again."   *Jeremiah 1:6-10 (CEV)*

God EMPOWERS me to DO the mission He has given me to do. Pastor Greg Burns of *New Dimensions Christian Center* shared this thought with us one Sunday. I sat there and gave a good, hearty "Amen!" ...and then I remember something that I had felt the Lord tell me to "Go!" and DO and that I was reluctant to begin. The Scripture seems clear and good in theory but putting it into practice in my daily life is like applying brakes on a bobsled run!!! "What's around the curve?" "What if I hit an icy patch?" Do I think God will bail out on me during the scary part? And who gets scared? Not GOD!!!

I look to the hills! Where will I find help? It will come from the LORD, who created the heavens and the earth.   *Psalm 121:1-2 (CEV)*

When I am obedient and seek the Lord in ALL things and at ALL times, He will go before me and be my rear guard! He's 'got my back'!

We don't have the right to claim that we have done anything on our own. God gives us what it takes to do all that we do. He makes us worthy to be the servants of his new agreement that comes from the Holy Spirit and not from a written Law. After all, the Law brings death, but the Spirit brings life.   *2 Corinthians 3:5-6 (CEV)*

God has equipped me for every mission that He has called me to participate in. He is the Commander-in-Chief and has the perfect plan. He knows where each of His children are to serve because He knows the gifts that He has given each of us and how we fit together for the good of the entire Body.

Each of you has been blessed with one of God's many wonderful gifts to be used in the service of others. So use your gift well. If you have the gift of speaking, preach God's message. If you have the gift of helping others, do it with the strength that God supplies. Everything should be done in a way that will bring honor to God because of Jesus Christ, who is glorious and powerful forever. Amen.   *1 Peter 4:10-11 (CEV)*

It's all about glorifying God. It's all about Him. It's not about me or my ideas except as He has released them in me.

Additional Text: Titus (yes, the book! It isn't long!)

You tricked me, LORD, and I was really fooled. You are stronger than I am, and you have defeated me. People never stop sneering and insulting me. You have let me announce only destruction and death. Your message has brought me nothing but insults and trouble.

Sometimes I tell myself not to think about you, LORD, or even mention your name. But your message burns in my heart and bones, and I cannot keep silent.

I heard the crowds whisper, "Everyone is afraid. Now's our chance to accuse Jeremiah!" All of my so-called friends are just waiting for me to make a mistake. They say, "Maybe Jeremiah can be tricked. Then we can overpower him and get even at last."

But you, LORD, are a mighty soldier, standing at my side. Those troublemakers will fall down and fail—terribly embarrassed, forever ashamed.

LORD, All-Powerful, you test those who do right, and you know every heart and mind. I have told you my complaints, so let me watch you take revenge on my enemies. I sing praises to you, LORD. You rescue the oppressed from the wicked.   *Jeremiah 20:7-13 (CEV)*

Jeremiah began this passage with just telling the Lord what he thinks of the way He is doing things! It reminds me of the story of Jonah where Jonah goes and sulks because the city of Nineveh repented and so the Lord showed them mercy and didn't destroy them. Jonah wanted to see some VENGEANCE!!! Jeremiah is complaining because he is taking some flack from the locals for what he is saying. So he decides he won't say the Lord's words, His convicting words, any more. Jeremiah finds that idea not so good when the words become like a fire in his bones. He comes to the revelation that the <u>Lord</u> is his own mighty warrior and that it is the <u>Lord</u> who is actually being ridiculed. It's only personal to the Lord, not Jeremiah.

God's Holy Spirit is given to me to equip me to do His will and complete His plan. The Spirit glorifies the Father, not me. The baptism of the Holy Spirit is all about the empowerment that comes enabling me to glorify the Father so much that no one remembers me…only the Father and His Son, Jesus. It is not about speaking in tongues, although that is a wonderful, powerful gift to me from the Father. It doesn't come to me to call attention to <u>me</u>. It's all about helping me to glorify God. I become more <u>in</u>visible so that God becomes more <u>visible</u> to others.

All of you angels in heaven, honor the glory and power of the LORD!

Honor the wonderful name of the LORD, and worship the LORD most holy and glorious.   *Psalm 29:1-2 (CEV)*

Additional Text: Psalm 29, 1 Corinthians 2 and 3

The Lord said to me, "I knew you before you were formed within your mother's womb; before you were born I sanctified you and appointed you as my spokesman to the world." Jeremiah 1:4-5 (TLB)

I have a mission. God has given <u>every</u> <u>one</u> of us a mission and a purpose. Jeremiah was a prophet. Some are pastors. Some are preachers or evangelists. Some of us are to be encouragers. Sounds like I am talking about the 'offices' or 'gifts' that are given to us by God's Holy Spirit. That's part of it but each of us has a <u>mission</u>.

God made me because He loves me. I show my love for Him by my worship and my service and obedience to Him. When God 'calls' me and makes His mission known to me, there is no excuse not to respond. He has already gone before me. He has already supplied all that I need. His grace (which covers <u>everything</u>!) is sufficient!

If you will stir up this inner power, you will never be afraid to tell others about our Lord, or to let them know that I am your friend even though I am here in jail for Christ's sake. You will be ready to suffer with me for the Lord, for he will give you strength in suffering.

It is he who saved us and chose us for his holy work, not because we deserved it but because that was his plan long before the world began – to show his love and kindness to us through Christ. 2 Timothy 1:8-9 (TLB)

My mission is to testify about my Lord. In some form or fashion, each and every day, maybe even several times a day, I am to testify! In a growing relationship, there is ALWAYS something NEW to testify about! That doesn't mean that I stand up on a tree stump in a park and preach (although it could!) but maybe it means seeing an old friend in Wal-Mart who needs a hand of encouragement and a testimony that I know that God is still on the throne and sees me and knows my needs. His grace is sufficient.

My mission is also about allowing God to heal ME from my past, which allows me to complete my present and future missions. His grace is sufficient for that, too! God's power – His grace – is sufficient to heal me from EVERY wound; there is not a wound too big for HIM! Just like it is my choice to go to a physician or let a wound fester and become more infected and more painful, I have the choice on allowing God to heal me. He's waiting and willing to do it RIGHT NOW!!!! He wants me to be 100% fit and ready to GO on the mission He has given me. His grace IS sufficient. HALLELUJAH!!!

Additional Text: Psalm 85, Ezra 8

May grace and peace be multiplied to you in the knowledge of God and of Jesus our Lord. His divine power has granted to us all things that pertain to life and godliness, through the knowledge of him who called us to his own glory and excellence, by which he has granted to us his precious and very great promises, so that through them you may become partakers of the divine nature, having escaped from the corruption that is in the world because of sinful desire.

2 Peter 1:2-4 (ESV)

No temptation has overtaken you that is not common to man. God is faithful, and he will not let you be tempted beyond your ability, but with the temptation he will also provide the way of escape, that you may be able to endure it.

1 Corinthians 10:13 (ESV)

God desires that I be holy because <u>HE</u> is holy. He wants to be so close in my life that I cannot tell where I end and He begins. In order for that to happen, I must be holy. Me? How can <u>I</u> possibly be 'holy'? I am <u>so</u> fallible and <u>so</u> very human. Jesus came to be my example.

Since therefore the children share in flesh and blood, he himself likewise partook of the same things, that through death he might destroy the one who has the power of death, that is, the devil, and deliver all those who through fear of death were subject to lifelong slavery. For surely it is not angels that he helps, but he helps the offspring of Abraham. Therefore he had to be made like his brothers in every respect, so that he might becomes a merciful and faithful high priest in the service of God, to make propitiation for the sins of the people. For because he himself has suffered when tempted, he is able to help those who are being tempted. *Hebrews 2:14-18 (ESV)*

and –

For we do not have a high priest who is unable to sympathize with our weaknesses, but one who in every respect has been tempted as we are, yet without sin. Let us then with confidence draw near to the throne of grace, that we may receive mercy and find grace to help in time of need.

Hebrews 4:15-19 (ESV)

"No, Jesus was God. He's not like me!" Scripture tells us He was tempted in <u>every</u> way and was made like us in <u>every</u> way. It seems like my excuses are a little flimsy!

I heard a wise preacher say, "How do you avoid temptation? — You RUN in the opposite direction!!"

If lust is my temptation, turn my head! Click off that TV show! If lying or cursing is my temptation, don't hang around people who influence me to do so! OR <u>pray</u> and ask God to "prick" my consciousness <u>EVERY</u> <u>TIME</u> an untruth or foul word pops into my head, before it leaves my mouth, and causes me to be <u>FILLED</u> with remorse! Repentance! A powerful tool in coming back around into right relationship with God!!!

Remember, God <u>desires</u> that I be in right relationship with Him. He is NOT sitting there on His golden throne waiting to WHACK me when I mess up! He <u>wants</u> me to succeed and has given me the PERFECT ADVOCATE — JESUS CHRIST HIS ONLY SON!

And this is my prayer: that your love may abound more and more in knowledge and depth of insight, so that you may be able to discern what is best and may be pure and blameless until the day of Christ, filled with the fruit of righteousness that comes through Jesus Christ--to the glory and praise of God.   *Philippians 1:9-11*

Therefore, as God's chosen people, holy and dearly loved, clothe yourselves with compassion, kindness, humility, gentleness and patience. Bear with each other and forgive whatever grievances you may have against one another. Forgive as the Lord forgave you. And over all these virtues put on love, which binds them all together in perfect unity.

Let the peace of Christ rule in your hearts, since as members of one body you were called to peace. And be thankful. Let the word of Christ dwell in you richly as you teach and admonish one another with all wisdom, and as you sing psalms, hymns and spiritual songs with gratitude in your hearts to God. And whatever you do, whether in word or deed, do it all in the name of the Lord Jesus, giving thanks to God the Father through him.   *Colossians 3:12-17*

Paul spent a lot of time praying, guiding, rebuking, and leading the churches (people) into maturity. By what he taught (sometimes <u>over</u> and <u>over</u>!) there is a sense that he could have 'pounded the pulpit' and said, "For <u>God's</u> sake, GROW UP!" The persecution of the Believers by the civil authorities that was supported by the — dare I say it — mainline church of that day — was fierce as well as insidious. Instead of recognizing the enemy for who he really was, Paul was grieved that the backbiting and fighting <u>within</u> the Body was causing division and wounding. Where was the love that Jesus taught? The compassion? The kindness? Gentleness with each other? Forgiveness?

Now you are the body of Christ, and each one of you is a part of it. And in the church God has appointed first of all apostles, second prophets, third teachers, then workers of miracles, also those having gifts of healing, those able to help others, those with gifts of administration, and those speaking in different kinds of tongues...

And now I will show you the most excellent way. If I speak in the tongues of men and of angels, but have not love, I am only a resounding gong or a clanging cymbal. If I have the gift of prophecy and can fathom all mysteries and all knowledge, and if I have a faith that can move mountains, but have not love, I am nothing. If I give all I possess to the poor and surrender my body to the flames, but have not love, I gain nothing.   *1 Corinthians 12:27-28,13:1-3*

In the first part of this Scripture, every one of us is mentioned. What?!!! If you walk up to someone and say, "Hi! It is so good to see you!" You are an encourager. You are exhibiting one of the "gifts of healing". We are all part of the Body. We all have gifts. But the "most excellent way" is LOVE. In <u>EVERYthing</u> I do, there MUST be love or I am not with God.

Additional Text: Philippians 2 and 4

The ways of the God are without fault. The LORD's words are pure. He is a shield to those who trust him. Who is God? Only the LORD. Who is the Rock? Only our God. God is my protection. He makes my way free from fault. He makes me like a deer that does not stumble; he helps me stand on the steep mountains. He trains my hands for battle so my arms can bend a bronze bow. You protect me with your saving shield. You support me with your right hand. You have stooped to make me great.   *Psalm 18:30-35 (NCV)*

I have taken your words to heart so I would not sin against you.

Psalm 119:11 (NCV)

[This is an excerpt from Rick Joyner's book *The Final Quest*. The man is going up the mountain (his spiritual life) and the sword — is the Word of God.]

Our swords grew after we reached each level, but I almost left mine behind because I did not seem to need it at the higher levels. I almost casually decided to keep it, thinking that it must have been given to me for a reason. Then, because the ledge I was standing on was so narrow, and becoming so slippery, I drove the sword into the ground and tied myself to it while I shot at the enemy. The voice of the Lord then came to me, saying: "You have used the wisdom that will enable you to keep climbing. Many have fallen because they did not use their sword properly to anchor themselves." No one else seemed to hear this voice, but many saw what I had done and did the same.

God's Word IS my anchor on the narrow slippery slope of my life. Besides the conditions of where I stand, I am also in a battle at the same time.

I was watching an old Jimmy Stewart movie the other night, *Shenandoah*. I always liked that movie but I was struck at the new lesson that I saw. It's the story about a man and his family during the Civil War, much like the more recent movie, *Patriot*, about a man and his family during the Revolutionary War. Both men argued and declared that their family was NOT going to get involved in a fight that had nothing to do with them! Both stories told of how innocent children were shot and killed and so the family did become involved.

I am involved in a war. We all are whether we like it or not, whether we recognize it or not. There is a real enemy who is violent and destructive. The Good News is — we know how it ends! God wins and we are His children so we win, too!!! However, there are still battles to be waged and we can either fight smart — God's way — or get shot as innocent bystanders or stupid ostriches with our head in the sand!

God's Word is our Sword and Anchor. Each day, He teaches me something new as I read His Word. Each day that I listen to Him, my sword gets bigger and He gives me lessons on how to handle it better to encourage His children, keep me on the path and in the battle He has 'called' me to, and destroy the accuser of the Brethren!!!

Your word is like a lamp for my feet and a light for my path.

Psalm 119:10 (NCV)

Additional Text: Matthew 13, Psalm 99

How beautiful upon the mountains are the feet of him who brings good news, who publishes peace, who brings good news of happiness, who publishes salvation, who say to Zion, "Your God reigns."
The voice of your watchmen – they lift up their voice; together they sing for joy; for eye to eye they see the return of the LORD to Zion.   Isaiah 52:7-8 (ESV)

I guess when I think of a messenger in Isaiah's time I think of a man who walks barefoot, or at best in sandals, over dusty or muddy roads. He/she has calluses and hasn't seen a pedicure in their life!!! "Beautiful feet"?

There are 'watch<u>persons</u>' in my life who truly do have "beautiful feet". Some have young smooth feet. Some have feet with arthritic joints. Some have feet of color. They are all beautiful because they bring me God's Good News just when I need it. Some are pastors or teachers but more importantly they are brothers and sisters in the Body of Christ. They are the ones who come when I am at the end of my rope. Many times they don't know my need but they are obedient to the message they have been given and obedient to deliver it!!!

I was thinking of a particular incident this morning when God's Good News came to me at just the moment I needed to hear it. I ran the scenario of what might have happened or the road I might have walked if that Good News had not come to me because the messenger was 'afraid' to deliver it or was too 'tired' or the hundred other excuses that I have heard in MY head from my flesh or the enemy when <u>I</u> have been given a message to give.

I lift up these messengers of God who have been faithful and I ask the Lord to return to them a thousand-fold for what they have brought to me. I also lift up those who have struggled in the message and the delivery and ask our merciful Father to strengthen their feeble limbs as He has strengthened mine.

Like the cold of snow in the time of harvest is a faithful messenger to those who send him; he refreshes the soul of his masters.   Proverbs 25:13 (ESV)
When he had washed their feet and put on his outer garments and resumed his place, he [Jesus] said to them, "Do you understand what I have done to you? You call me Teacher and Lord, and you are right, for so I am. If I then, your Lord and Teacher, have washed your feet, you also ought to wash one another's feet. For I have given you an example that you also should do just as I have done to you. Truly, truly, I say to you, a servant is not greater than his master, nor is a messenger greater than the one who sent him. If you know these things, blessed are you if you do them."   John 13:12-17 (ESV)

Additional Text: Psalm 78, Isaiah 40

March 29

When Jesus had finished praying, he shouted, "Lazarus, come out!" The man who had been dead came out...

Many of the people who had come to visit Mary saw the things that Jesus did, and they put their faith in him. Others went to the Pharisees and told what Jesus had done. Then the chief priests and the Pharisees called the council together and said, "What should we do? This man is working a lot of miracles. If we don't stop him now, everyone will put their faith in him. Then the Romans will come and destroy our temple and our nation."...

A lot of people came when they heard that Jesus was there. They also wanted to see Lazarus, because Jesus had raised him from death. So the chief priests made plans to kill Lazarus. He was the reason that many of the people were turning from them and putting their faith in Jesus.

John 11:43, 45-47, 12:9-11 (CEV)

Raising Lazarus from the dead moved Jesus from the frying pan right on into the fire! This miracle could not be explained away! Lazarus had been in the tomb three days. It would be impossible to say that he had just been asleep. Too many witnesses had prepared his body, wrapped him in grave clothes, and carried him to the tomb. Only GOD could raise the dead.

Prophets for hundreds and hundreds of years had encouraged the people with the hope of the Messiah. The 70-member Sanhedrin had preached to the people about Messiah, about His power, about how He would set them free. But when the miracles began and the prophecies were fulfilled, pride, ambition, greed, and self-absorption blinded them to God's truth. *"If we don't stop him now, everyone will put their faith in him. Then the Romans will come and destroy our temple and our nation."*

Well, they were right! When I put my faith in Jesus, everything and everyone else in my life dropped down to a definite lower place. As the Lord grew me in the faith and worked miracles in me, like Lazarus, I too became a target. It is certainly my desire that Jesus INCREASE in me and 'self' DECREASE so that all that people remember is Jesus. That will get on the enemy's 'last nerve'!

Jesus said: The time has come for the Son of Man to be given his glory. I tell you for certain that a grain of wheat that falls on the ground will never be more than one grain unless it dies. But if it dies, it will produce lots of wheat. If you love your life, you will lose it. If you give it up in this world, you will be given eternal life. If you serve me, you must go with me. My servants will be with me wherever I am. If you serve me, my Father will honor you."

John 12:23-26 (CEV)

I am a disciple of Jesus not because of me or who or what I am but because of Jesus and who and what HE is. It is His grace and mercy that has brought me this far. What a gift! I worship You, O LORD! But being a disciple is not just about waving palm branches and dancing. It is also about dying. It is about all that I am in my flesh, dying so that I become all that JESUS is in Spirit.

Additional Text: Galatians 5, Isaiah 41

"For I will pass through the land of Egypt that night, and I will strike all the firstborn in the land of Egypt, both man and beast, and on all the gods of Egypt I will execute judgment: I am the LORD. The blood shall be a sign for you, on the houses where you are. And when I see the blood, I will pass over you, and no plague will befall you to destroy you, when I strike the land of Egypt."

Exodus 12:12-13 (ESV)

But when Christ appeared as a high priest of the good things that have come, then through the greater and more perfect tent (not made with hands, that is, not of this creation), he entered once for all into the holy places, not by means of the blood of goats and calves but by means of his own blood, thus securing an eternal redemption. For if the sprinkling of defiled persons with the blood of goats and bulls and with the ashes of a heifer sanctifies for the purification of the flesh, how much more will the blood of Christ, who through the eternal Spirit offered himself without blemish to God, purify our conscience from dead works to serve the living God.

Therefore he is the mediator of a new covenant, so that those who are called may receive the promised eternal inheritance, since a death has occurred that redeems them from the transgressions committed under the first covenant.

Hebrews 9:11-15 (ESV)

When Jesus died, it wasn't pretty. A Roman crucifixion would never have been shown on network television. I'm not sure that it would have gotten on the "big screen" with just an "R" rating either. I grew up listening to the gospel accounts being read throughout Holy Week. The writers of the gospels did not have to spell out the ritual to their readers because if you lived in those days under Roman rule, you KNEW and you SAW what a crucifixion was. We have 'cleaned up' our teaching of this account so as not to offend the sensibilities of our students, our congregations.

I wondered if God is offended by us. Is He offended by our lack of interest or caring for what He has done for us? How much do we teach/preach about the sacrifice of Jesus? I confess that this morning was the first time since Good Friday that I meditated on the magnitude of the cost of God's gift. I am humbled.

Paul seems to tell me in Ephesians that I need the power of the Holy Spirit in order to grasp the love that is Jesus, the perfect atonement for my sins. I cannot begin to grasp this love in my own feeble flesh. I need the Holy Spirit to pierce my heart, connect with my spirit, and reveal the truth of God's love. It has SO many facets, like a precious stone that shows me a different color each time I look into it.

The Holy Spirit empowers me, encourages me, to share with others the "free gift" – the horribly beautiful gift – which Jesus holds out to all. I overcome by the Blood of the Lamb, the word of my testimony, and I do not love my life so much as to shrink from death. Hallelujah! To God be the GLORY!

Additional Text: Ephesians 3, Revelation 12

March 31

Jesus said, "There was a rich man who always dressed in the finest clothes and lived in luxury every day. And a very poor man named Lazarus, whose body was covered with sores, was laid at the rich man's gate. He wanted to eat only the small pieces of food that fell from the rich man's table. And the dogs would come and lick his sores. Later, Lazarus died, and the angels carried him to the arms of Abraham. The rich man died, too, and was buried. In the place of the dead, he was in much pain. The rich man saw Abraham far away with Lazarus at his side. He called, 'Father Abraham, have mercy on me! Send Lazarus to dip his finger in water and cool my tongue, because I am suffering in this fire!' But Abraham said, 'Child, remember when you were alive you had the good things in life, but bad things happened to Lazarus. Now he is comforted here, and you are suffering. Besides, there is a big pit between you and us, so no one can cross over to you, and on one can leave there and come here.' The rich man said, 'Father, then please send Lazarus to my father's house. I have five brothers, and Lazarus could warn them so that they will not come to this place of pain.' But Abraham said, 'They have the law of Moses and the writings of the prophets; let them learn from them.' The rich man said, 'No, father Abraham! If someone goes to them from the dead, they would believe and change their hearts and lives.' Abraham said to him, 'If they will not listen to Moses and the prophets, they will not listen to someone who comes back from the dead.' "

Luke 16:19-31 (NCV)

It's been awhile since I read this parable from Jesus. It's been even longer since I heard anyone preach on this text! My focus in the past has been on the blessings Lazarus received for his sufferings and how the rich guy got his 'just desserts'!!! It made me feel better about my 'sufferings'!

Today I'm looking at the rich man's plea to Abraham for his brothers. At the time that Jesus gave the parable, it was the belief of Jews that heaven would be a banquet given by God and Abraham would be the most important guest. Any guest of honor would sit next to Abraham. The rich man, in his present position, sees clearly the true priorities and wants his brothers to get the message that Jehovah God is sovereign and before any idol of wealth or status.

When I think of those that I know who have refused to receive Jesus as Savior and Lord, many times I think like the rich man that if I just get the right messenger to them – they'll turn and accept Jesus. The reality is – it's not the messenger but the message – and the person's willingness to accept the Living Water being offered.

It is often necessary to wander in the desert a long time and become SO parched and desperate that I will give up everything to just not thirst any more. What is that comparison – if the Israelites had not been so stiff-necked the 40-year journey could have been made in 10 days? Something like that! I too could have cut my 40-year journey down to 8-10 years if I had accepted the Holy Spirit's prompting to accept Jesus in faith. The receiving of the salvation message by someone I care about is 70% prayers and 30% example/witness – and <u>ALL</u> in the power of the Holy Spirit.

Additional Text: Isaiah 55

Janet Webb Lister

The oldest of three children with a twin brother and a younger brother, Janet grew up in Florida with gymnastics her focus and a plan to be a coach. Now a wife and mother, she is working in ministry with her husband who is an associate pastor in Ft. Worth, Texas.

..." And behold, I am with you always, to the end of the age."

Matthew 28:20 (ESV)

Trust in the Lord with all your heart,
and do not lean on your own understanding.
In all your ways acknowledge him, and he will make straight your paths.

Proverbs 3:5-6 (ESV)

Despite growing up in a family who attended church every Sunday, my relationship with Christ was "something to do", especially in a crisis or when I needed help in a competition. I attended the Brownsville Revival in Pensacola, Florida when I was 16. That night was when I finally knew Jesus was my Lord and my life and my talent were not my own. I was training for the Junior Olympics and I realized that God had given me that talent and I'd better give it back to Him. I gave God my future, my dreams. For the next five years, I lived off everyone else's relationship with the Lord. I was involved in the day-to-day experiences of that revival and I went to the school of ministry. I was living in a bubble! I wasn't living my life for Jesus with its daily choices of living for Jesus or living for the world. I got married and moved away from Pensacola and my family and the church that had become my spiritual 'home'. My husband and I found it very difficult to find a church that gave us <u>fresh</u> Bread from the Lord and challenged us   I was looking for real fellowship that involves me serving the Lord and also feeds me with accountability, worship, and Bible study. We waited and continued to bring that desire before the Lord for three years. Now we find ourselves blessed to be in a church that has the vision that we were also given, confirming that this is where we are to be.

The 'ordinary' person that has had the greatest influence on my life is our pastor, Rev. Steve Hill. From the first night that I heard him speak at the revival in Pensacola in 1995, he has taken time with me to explain and teach me about the work of the Holy Spirit. He and his wife, Jeri, were there for me as I went through my parents' divorce and my brother's fight with cancer. They have truly taught me what it means to be a servant and to be humble. They are <u>real</u> people with good days and bad days but they have shown me that God is a kind and caring Father who loves me enough to correct and discipline me. I have a moment-to-moment relationship with Jesus that I always wanted. I know the power of the Holy Spirit to walk in faith and live in hope.

April 1

For by grace you have been saved through faith. And this is not your own doing; it is the gift of God, not a result of works, so that no one may boast. For we are his workmanship, created in Christ Jesus for good works, which God prepared beforehand, that we should walk in them. Ephesians 2:8-10 (ESV)

I am given eternal life because of God's undeserved love for me. He loved me first. He saw my sin. He knew that the ONLY WAY that I could be restored and in close relationship with Him was if He gave a perfect sacrifice – His Son.

Indeed, under the law almost everything is purified with blood, and without the shedding of blood there is no forgiveness of sins. Hebrews 9:22 (ESV)

Jesus said to him, "I am the way, and the truth, and the life. No one comes to the Father except through me." John 14:6 (ESV)

It did require a step of faith from me. One step. A step, to believe in someone (Jesus) and something (that He is the Son of God and died for me, a sinner), that I could not reason or fully explain.

And even after that was done, I still cannot balance the scales with my obedience and service to Him. I can't 'get holy enough' to tip the scales even a millimeter. My obedience and service, my wanting to be holy, can only be acceptable to God if I do it out of love. That's it. I do this, Lord, because I love You.

Therefore, we are ambassadors for Christ, God making his appeal through us. We implore you on behalf of Christ, be reconciled to God. For our sake he made him to be sin who knew no sin, so that in him we might becomes the righteousness of God. 2 Corinthians 5:20-21 (ESV)

And so God's love for me makes me SO FULL that I leak! Jesus said that Living Water would flow from me (John 4:13-14) and that I would do even greater things than He did (John 14:12). The 'call' that God has placed on me, and the gifts that He has given to fulfill that call is God's recipe for my success in my life with Him. But it's still all about Jesus. I work to SHOW God, not EARN Him.

Praise the LORD! Praise the LORD! Praise the LORD, O my soul!

I will praise the LORD as long as I live; I will sing praises to my God while I have my being.

Put not your trust in princes, in a son of man, in whom there is no salvation. When his breath departs he returns to the earth; on that very day his plans perish.

Blessed is he whose help is the God of Jacob, whose hope is in the LORD his God, who made heaven and earth, the sea, and all that is in them, who keeps faith forever; who executes justice for the oppressed, who gives food to the hungry.

The LORD sets the prisoners free; the LORD opens the eyes of the blind. The LORD lifts up those who are bowed down; the LORD loves the righteous. The LORD watches over the sojourners; he upholds the widow and the fatherless, but the way of the wicked he brings to ruin.

The LORD will reign forever, your God, O Zion, to all generations. Praise the LORD! Psalm 146 (ESV)

I will bless the LORD at all times; his praise shall continually be in my mouth. My soul makes its boast in the LORD; let the humble hear and be glad. Oh, magnify the LORD with me, and let us exalt his name together!

Psalm 34:1-3 (ESV)

And Mary said, "My soul magnifies the Lord, and my spirit rejoices in God my Savior,..."   *Luke 1:46-47 (ESV)*

To 'magnify' means to *enlarge*. When you're over 40 like me that can be very helpful – even vital – when trying to read something! When something is *magnified*, I can read it, I can understand it.

A focus on God can bring Him into a clearer picture. He becomes larger and everything else becomes less or smaller.

Mary's statement that her *soul* magnified the Lord tells me that the magnification that I seek comes through the Holy Spirit, not MY brain or MY understanding.

[Jesus said,] *"These things I have spoken to you while I am still with you. But the Helper, the Holy Spirit, whom the Father will send in my name, he will teach you all things and bring to your remembrance all that I have said to you."*

John 14:25-26 (ESV)

Jesus knew that we would not remember everything that we would need and so the 'Magnifier', the Holy Spirit, would teach us and remind us of the promises of God. He would remind us of the Truth. He would even help us to separate the truth from the deception that the enemy would try to throw at us.

Do not be unequally yoked with unbelievers. For what partnership has righteousness with lawlessness? Or what fellowship has light with darkness? What accord has Christ with Belial? Or what portion does a believer share with an unbeliever? What agreement has the temple of God with idols? For we are the temple of the living God; as God said, "I will make my dwelling among them and walk among them, and I will be their God, and they shall be my people. Therefore go out from their midst, and be separate from them", says the Lord, "and touch no unclean thing; then I will welcome you, and I will be a father to you, and you shall be sons and daughters to me," says the Lord Almighty.

Since we have these promises, beloved, let us cleanse ourselves from every defilement of body and spirit, bringing holiness to completion in the fear of God.

2 Corinthians 6:14-7:1

Living in holiness, the whole concept of sanctification can be an area of conflict and disagreement among Christians. This is an area where we can certainly use the Holy Spirit's 'magnifying lenses'. By keeping my eyes on Jesus, asking the Holy Spirit to help me 'magnify' Jesus' example to me, I keep the right focus. It's all about the Lord. It's all about HIS magnification – not mine. My sanctification occurs as I see the Lord magnified and submit to cleansing power of the Holy Spirit through Jesus Christ.

Additional Text: Deuteronomy 4, 2 Corinthians 7

But when Christ came as the high priest of the good things we now have, he entered the greater and more perfect tent. It is not made by humans and does not belong to this world. Christ entered the Most Holy Place only once – and for all time. He did not take with him the blood of goats and calves. His sacrifice was his own blood, and by it he set us free from sin forever. The blood of goats and bulls and the ashes of a cow are sprinkled on the people who are unclean, and this makes their bodies clean again. How much more is done by the blood of Christ. He offered himself through the eternal Spirit as a perfect sacrifice to God. his blood will make our consciences pure from useless acts so we may serve the living God.   *Hebrews 9:11-14 (NCV)*

God's word is so powerful, so full of healing, and the ONLY thing that breaks the chains that weigh me down and bind me to the sins in my past. Our Heavenly Father requires that I only ask for His forgiveness. Because of Jesus, because of His perfect sacrifice, I <u>am</u> forgiven.

Jesus not only forgives my sins but it's like they were written on a chalk board and the memory of my sins are <u>erased</u> – never to return. The enemy will continue to attempt to 'resurrect' my sins, my past, by telling me that the sins are still there and that I can NEVER be free from them. WHAT A BOLD-FACED LIE!!! The only thing that can bind me down and hold me back is myself and any lies from the enemy that I choose to believe.

"A thief comes to steal and kill and destroy, but I came to give life – life in all its fullness."   *John 10:10 (NCV)*

The blood of Jesus NEVER loses its power. It saved the apostle, John. It saved me. And if the Lord tarries –it saves my grandchildren. When I take the time to see how far I've come, I MUST sink to my knees and praise God's Holy Name for what He has done for me.

God, be merciful to me because you are loving. Because you are always ready to be merciful, wipe out all my wrongs. Wash away all my guilt and make me clean again.

I know about my wrongs, and I can't forget my sin. You are the only one I have sinned against; I have done what you say is wrong. You are right when you speak and fair when you judge. I was brought into this world in sin. In sin my mother gave birth to me.

You want me to be completely truthful, so teach me wisdom. Take away my sin, and I will be clean. Wash me, and I will be whiter than snow. Make me hear sounds of joy and gladness; let the bones you crushed be happy again. Turn your face from my sins and wipe out all my guilt.

Create in me a pure heart, God, and make my spirit right again. Do not send me away from you or take your Holy Spirit away from me. Give me back the joy of your salvation. Keep me strong by giving me a willing spirit. Then I will teach your ways to those who do wrong, and sinners will turn back to you.

                                        Psalm 51:1-13 (NCV)

Additional Text: John 6, Revelation 22

How is the 'attitude' today? This is one of those subjects that I almost <u>don't</u> want to know what God says! <u>BUT</u> God's truth is always better than the world's deception, isn't it?

...and think the same way that Christ Jesus thought: Christ was truly God. But he did not try to remain equal with God. He gave up everything and became a slave, when he became like one of us. Christ was humble. He obeyed God and even died on a cross. Then God gave Christ the highest place and honored his name above all others. So at the name of Jesus everyone will bow down, those in heaven, on earth, and under the earth. And to the glory of God the Father everyone will openly agree, "Jesus Christ is LORD!" Philippians 2:5-11 (CEV) Dear friends, don't be surprised or shocked that you are going through testing that is like walking through fire. Be glad for the chance to suffer as Christ suffered. It will prepare you for even greater happiness when he makes his glorious return.

Count it a blessing when you suffer for being a Christian. This shows that God's glorious Spirit is with you. But you deserve to suffer if you are a murderer, a thief, a crook, or a busybody. Don't be ashamed to suffer for being a Christian. Praise God that you belong to him. God has already begun judging his own people. And if his judgment begins with us, imagine how terrible it will be for those who refuse to obey his message. The Scriptures say, "If good people barely escape, what will happen to sinners and to others who don't respect God?" If you suffer for obeying God, you must have complete faith in your faithful Creator and keep on doing right. 1 Peter 4:12-19 (CEV)

As a member of the Body of Believers, I do not have much "wiggle room" about my attitude, do I? Paul and Peter share a message from the Lord that we are to set CHRIST as our standard – not our neighbor, friend, boss, or even pastor! Just because I am doing 'better' than they are, doesn't mean that I am in step with Jesus!!! Jesus' standard is HIGH [can we all say "duh"!]! Suffering, humility, obedience, love, and above all else, doing all to the Father's glory — are to be the basic characteristics of my attitude. And it's a DAILY CHOICE, a DAILY RESOLVE on my part to take on Jesus' attitude. Will I fall short? Absolutely! But God's grace and mercy has no end. Like a toddler who is trying to walk, my Heavenly Father will help me up, dust me off, and I will go again — having learned something from Jesus who has gone before me. It's all about spending time with Jesus. You are who you 'hang' with, as the kids say. How much time each day do I hang around Jesus?

"I have used examples to explain to you what I have been talking about. But the time will come when I will speak to you plainly about the Father and will no longer use examples like these. You will ask the Father in my name, and I won't have to ask him for you. God the Father loves you because you love me, and you believe that I have come from him." John 16:25-27 (CEV)

Additional Text: Proverbs 4, Galatians 5

April 5

"For no good tree bears bad fruit, nor again does a bad tree bear good fruit, for each tree is known by its own fruit. For figs are not gathered from thornbushes, nor are grapes picked from a bramble bush. The good person out of the good treasure of his heart produces good, and the evil person out of his evil treasure produces evil, for out of the abundance of the heart his mouth speaks."

Luke 6:43-45 (ESV)

"You have heard that it was said, 'An eye for an eye and a tooth for a tooth.' But I say to you, do not resist the one who is evil. But if anyone slaps you on the right cheek, turn to him the other also. And if anyone would sue you and take your tunic, let him have your cloak as well. And if anyone forces you to go one mile, go with him two miles. Give to the one who begs from you, and do not refuse the one who would borrow from you.

You have heard that it was said, 'You shall love your neighbor and hate your enemy.' But I say to you, love your enemies and pray for those who persecute you, so that you may be sons of your Father who is in heaven. For he makes his sun rise on the evil and on the good, and sends rain on the just and on the unjust. For if you love those who love you, what reward do you have? Do not even the tax collectors do the same? And if you greet only your brothers, what more are you doing than others? Do not even the Gentiles do the same? You therefore must be perfect, as your heavenly Father is perfect."

Matthew 5:38-48 (ESV)

Exodus 21 is a recount of the Lord's instructions to Moses regarding — consequences (*"But if there is serious injury, you are to take life for life, eye for eye, tooth for tooth, hand for hand, foot for foot, burn for burn, wound for wound, bruise for bruise"*). The Lord was instructing His children that there <u>are</u> consequences for their actions but the consequences should be equal to the injury. Historically, someone could be put to death for <u>stealing</u>.

Jesus comes along and tells us He is not going to "abolish" but "fulfill" the Law. He tells us that loving God and loving our neighbors are the "pins" that hold all the other laws in place. He spends a lot of time 'hammering home' His point about our hearts. Out of the goodness, compassion, forgiveness, kindness of our hearts shall there be a flowing out of our mouths. It will spill on to others and change lives. Ah — but revenge, exacting restitution, anger, rage, malice — these too will have an overflow on to others and change lives!

I believe this is another area of trust in God. Do I trust that He sees what someone has done to me? Do I trust that He is keeping a ledger of their wrong doing and that there <u>will</u> be a day of judgment, a day of accounting? Even if I do not see it? Do I want God to measure me and exact His judgment on <u>me</u> with the same single-mindedness and measure that I seek on <u>others</u>? Even when I deserve it? When they deserve it? [shudder] When someone 'commits a crime' against me, do I call a lawyer — or do I call GOD?

"...love your enemies and pray for those who persecute you, so that you may be sons of your Father who is in heaven..."

Additional Text: Matthew 6, Romans 12

April 6

"God loved the people of this world so much that he gave his only Son, so that everyone who has faith in him will have eternal life."　　　John 3:16 (CEV)

God is love and anyone who doesn't love others has never known him. God showed his love for us when he sent his only Son into the world to give us life.
　　　1 John 4:8-9 (CEV)

"Teacher, what is the most important commandment in the Law?"
Jesus answered: "Love the Lord your God with all your heart, soul, and mind. This is the first and most important commandment. The second most important commandment is like this one. And it is, 'Love others as much as you love yourself.' All the Law of Moses and the Books of the Prophets are based on these two commandments."　　　Matthew 22:36-40 (CEV)

A <u>very</u> young, brand new associate pastor at the church I attended preached on these passages. I was struck by the simplicity of this message and yet the 'arrow' of the Lord was sharp and pierced my heart with its truth. I felt the worldly analysis of my professed faith fall away and the exegetical 'hogwash' (pardon me, all you theologians out there!) that even I fall into as I study God's Word in my quiet time be cleansed away with a power sprayer of God's clear truth.

The officials were amazed to see how brave Peter and John were, and they knew that these two apostles were only ordinary men and not well educated. The official were certain that these men had been with Jesus.　　　Acts 4:13 (CEV)

"Unschooled" and "ordinary". As I think about Luke, the author of this book, who certainly <u>was</u> schooled I would guess that his definition of these words would be like a 6th generation Bostonian commenting on a Ph.D. from Alabama! A 'hick' accent and 'different' grammar/slang could flush your Ph.D. down the ol' toilet as far as they are concerned!!! But this passage tells me that it really doesn't matter what the sum total of my education level and my pedigree might be — do people "take note" that I have been and continue to be with Jesus? Do I <u>LIVE</u> the love of God with all my heart, soul, and mind? Do I love others <u>as</u> I love myself? Does everything in my life — including the ministry God has given me to steward hang from these two commandments? Does everything that I teach come back to *"God loved the people of this world so much that he gave his only Son, so that everyone who has faith in him will have eternal life."* If it doesn't, then there is too much of <u>me</u> in it and not enough of Jesus!

Additional Text: 1 Corinthians 2, Galatians 2

April 7

As he was coming close to Jerusalem, on the way the Mount of Olives, the whole crowd of followers began joyfully shouting praise to God for all the miracles they had seen. They said, "God bless the king who comes in the name of the Lord! There is peace in heaven and glory to God!"

Some of the Pharisees in the crowd said to Jesus, "Teacher, tell your followers not to say these things." But Jesus answered, "I tell you, if my followers didn't say these things, then the stones would cry out."

As Jesus came near Jerusalem, he saw the city and cried for it, saying, "I wish you knew today what would bring you peace. But now it is hidden from you. The time is coming when your enemies will build a wall around you and will hold you in on all sides. They will destroy you and all your people, and not one stone will be left on another. All this will happen because you did not recognize the time when God came to save you."   Luke 19:37-44 (NCV)

We call this Palm Sunday. It is the remembrance of Jesus' triumphant entry into Jerusalem before He dies. For those of us who have sat through the 2004 movie, *The Passion of the Christ*, our internal DVD player may spin us through some different pictures than we have seen in the past. I do think that I came away from that movie with a greater sense of how much Jesus truly loves me! As I go through Holy Week, I want to spend extra time in worship. I don't want any 'stones' crying out in worship because I kept silent. I want the worship to come not just out of my mouth but straight from my heart.

It is also a time for me to especially remember those in Jerusalem and across the Middle East who daily live in war conditions that I can only imagine. Jesus wept over the city because they refused to see Him. I hear confirmed reports from China and India and parts of Africa where the Gospel has broken through cultures that have been 'stone cold' in the past. They are FREE in Jesus Christ! Maybe like the Pharisees, there is an 'anger' in the Middle East because the *whole world* is going after Jesus Christ. I pray for a Holy Spirit love and peace that breaks the reactionary rage. I pray for the real war that is going on.

Why are the nations so angry? Why are the people making useless plans? The kings of the earth prepare to fight, and their leaders make plans together against the LORD and his appointed one. They say, "Let's break the chains that hold us back and throw off the ropes that tie us down."

But the one who sits in heaven laughs; the Lord makes fun of them. Then the LORD warns them and frightens them with his anger. He says, "I have appointed my own king to rule in Jerusalem on my holy mountain, Zion."

Now I will tell you what the LORD has declared: He said to me, "You are my son. Today I have become your father. If you ask me, I will give you the nations; all the people on earth will be yours."   Psalm 2:1-8 (NCV)

Additional Text: John 12, Job 42

Give thanks to the LORD and pray to him. Tell the nations what he has done. Sing to him; sing praises to him. Tell about all his miracles. Be glad that you are his; let those who seek the LORD be happy.   *1 Chronicles 16:8-10 (NCV)*

Isn't that a great hymn of praise to God, who is so worthy of praise?! David spoke these words as the Ark of Covenant was brought into Jerusalem. Truly a time of celebration!

But we thank God! He gives us the victory through our Lord Jesus Christ. So my dear brothers and sisters, stand strong. Do not let anything change you. Always give yourselves fully to the work of the Lord, because you know that your work in the Lord is never wasted.   *1 Corinthians 15:57-58 (NCV)*

I am very blessed in my life. I have found our Father God to be faithful. May I briefly testify?

In April 1999, my then 12-year-old son was playing baseball and basketball and had discovered girls weren't as bad as he previously thought. One day, he came to me complaining of a sore throat. I looked. There was…a growth …a tumor. Three weeks later, he was diagnosed with cancer.

Always be joyful. Pray continually, and give thanks whatever happens. That is what God wants for you in Christ Jesus.   *1 Thessalonians 5:16-18 (NCV)*

For the next year, that kind of Scripture was hard for me to read, much less claim and agree. For the next year, my son and I went every week for chemo and every three weeks it would require chemo in the hospital. Four weeks of radiation treatment would cause 2nd degree burns on in the inside of his mouth. No school. No baseball or basketball. No hair. Weight loss. Some visits with friends when he wasn't too sick or too weak or having treatments or transfusions or…whatever. God is faithful and He _is_ worthy of my praise.

Hundreds, no <u>thousands</u> of people prayed. I received emails from all over the world, as one person would tell another. We had compassionate doctors, nurses, technicians, and volunteers, who treated us like we were the only one they would care for that day. We had a family of God that held our arms up (like Aaron and Hur did for Moses) when we were too tired to pray for ourselves. God is faith and He _is_ worthy of my praise.

I know how to live when I am poor, and I know how to live when I have plenty. I have learned the secret of being happy at any time in everything that happens, when I have enough to eat and when I go hungry, when I have more than I need and when I do not have enough. I can do all things through Christ, because he give me strength.   *Philippians 4:12-13 (NCV)*

I will not lie to you and tell you that I live these Scriptures. I continue to press in closer to Jesus to learn from Him and His friends.

My son was healed, miraculously and by God. The enemy, satan, would try to remind us of all that we do not have; of our troubles, all our unanswered questions…especially the 'whys'. But what about all the many, many blessings He gives us? He has given me trust…that step beyond faith…where I believe in Him no matter what I 'see' or what the situation. He gives peace beyond understanding. God is faithful and He <u>is</u> worthy of my praise.

...even as he chose us in him before the foundation of the world, that we should be holy and blameless before him. In love, he predestined us for adoption through Jesus Christ, according to the purpose of his will, to the praise of his glorious grace, with which he has blessed us in the Beloved.
Ephesians 1:4-6 (ESV)

"You did not choose me, but I chose you and appointed you that you should go and bear fruit and that your fruit should abide, so that whatever you ask the Father in my name, he may give it to you. These things I command you, so that you will love one another."
John 15:16-17 (ESV)

God <u>chose</u> me! God chose <u>ME</u>!

I was a good athlete as a child and young adult, not a GREAT one. I was NOT the first picked when choosing up basketball teams, although that was my best sport. (It helped that I was 5'8" and *mean* under the goal!) I was usually about the 3rd or 4th round pick! That's down far enough that I began to sweat or blush just a bit and wonder if I <u>would</u> be chosen before the last round!

Paul, the Scripture scholar, says that I was chosen <u>before</u> the creation of the world, that ALL of us were "predestined" to be saved through Jesus. All I have to do is just say, "Yes!" Jesus says He chose me and told me to go DO something with my freedom – bear 'eternal' fruit. Don't go after the money or fame that won't last but go for something 'eternal', something that will glorify the Father.

God desires that I be holy, that I make good choices that bring 'eternal' fruit into my life.

But the fruit of the Spirit is love, joy, peace, patience, kindness, goodness, faithfulness, gentleness, self-control; against such things there is no law.
Galatians 5:22-23 (ESV)

After assuring me that I am <u>chosen</u> by Him and admonishing me to bear 'eternal' fruit, <u>and</u> promising that the Father will answer my prayers, Jesus wraps it ALL together by telling me again that I am to love EVERYONE!!! There's the 'kicker'. I will be known as HIS disciple when the fruit and power of His name is sealed with that *agape*, unconditional, love for <u>everyone</u>. I am embracing God's desire that I be *HOLY*.

I am <u>chosen</u> because of what God desired and has already done for me. And so...I love Him and love others.

Your steadfast love, O LORD, extends to the heavens, your faithfulness to the clouds. Your righteousness is like the mountains of God; your judgments are like the great deep; man and beast you save, O LORD.

How precious is your steadfast love, O God! The children of mankind take refuge in the shadow of your wings.
Psalm 36:5-7 (ESV)

Additional Text: Psalm 63, Song of Songs 2

I am pleading for your help, O Lord; for I have been honest and have done what is right, and you must listen to my earnest cry! Publicly acquit me, Lord, for you are always fair. You have tested me and seen that I am good. You have come even in the night and found nothing amiss and know that I have told the truth...

Protect me as you would the pupil of your eye; hide me in the shadow of your wings as you hover over me. My enemies encircle me with murder in their eyes.. Lord, arise and stand against them. Push them back! Come and save me from these men of the world whose only concern is earthly gain – these men whom you have filled with your treasures so that their children and grandchildren are rich and prosperous.

But as for me, my contentment is not in wealth but in seeing you and knowing all is well between us. And when I awake in heaven, I will be fully satisfied, for I will see you fact to face.   *Psalm 17:1-3, 8-9, 13-15 (TLB)*

Have you ever wanted vindication? I can raise my hand on that! Whether it's "winning" a discussion with my husband or seeing MY baseball team annihilate a rival, I have desired <u>vindication</u>.

<u>Validation</u> is a close cousin to <u>vindication</u>. Many times they travel together. When I am vindicated, my worth, my integrity, I might even say, my name, is validated.

David, or this psalm writer, humbly cries out to God because He knows THAT is where His vindication will come! Linda Smith, a woman of God who has mentored youth for many years, tells the young people, "What God says about you is the most true thing about you".

Who I am, what I am worth is not defined by my job, my boss, my family, parents, the people I call friends, or even the church that I attend. So anything that they might say against me – what do I care? If God didn't say it – it isn't totally true!

What God says about me – now those are defining words:

For I am God – I only – and there is no other like me who can tell you what is going to happen. All I say will come to pass, for I do whatever I wish. I will call that swift bird of prey from the east – that man Cyrus from far away. And he will come and do my bidding. I have said I would do it and I will.

Isaiah 46:10-11 (TLB)

Dear friends, let us practice loving each other, for love comes from God and those who are loving and kind show that they are getting to know him better. But if a person isn't loving and kind, it shows that he doesn't know God – for God is love.

God showed how much he loved us by sending his only Son into this wicked world to bring to us eternal life through his death. In this act we see what real love is: it is not our love for God, but his love for us when he sent his Son to satisfy God's anger against our sins.   *1 John 4:7-12 (TLB)*

Additional Text: 2 Timothy 2, Isaiah 66

April 11

Therefore remember that at one time you Gentiles in the flesh, called "the uncircumcision" by what is called the circumcision, which is made in the flesh by hands – remember that you were at that times separated from Christ, alienated from commonwealth of Israel and strangers to the covenants of promise, having no hope and without God in the world. But now in Christ Jesus you who were once far off have been brought near by the blood of Christ. For he himself is our peace, who has made us both one and has broken down in his flesh the dividing wall of hostility by abolishing the law of commandments and ordinances, that he might create in himself one new man in place of the two, so making peace, and might reconcile us both to God in one body through the cross, thereby killing the hostility. And he came and preached peace to you who were far off and peace to those who were near. For through him we both have access in one Spirit to the Father. So then you are no longer strangers and aliens, but you are fellow citizens with the saints and members of the household of God, built on the foundation of the apostles and prophets, Christ Jesus himself being the cornerstone, in whom the whole structure, being joined together, grows into a holy temple in the Lord. In him you also are being built together into a dwelling place for God by the Spirit. Ephesians 2:11-22 (ESV)

This is a wonderful passage of God's words that remind me how far I've come since I accepted Jesus as my Savior and chose to walk with Him, serving the Father.

In 1995, I was a successful nurse in a senior management position in a nationally ranked organization. I had been married for 18 years and had 3 great children. And I was empty and lost. There was a hole in my life that you could have driven an entire military division through and I didn't know why.

In July of that year, I followed my two older children to the revival meetings that were being held in Pensacola. I stopped looking in all the wrong places and accepted that I was a sinner in need of a Savior named Jesus. It is impossible for me to describe the healing and filling up of that hole that took place that night. I have never been the same and I am NOT turning back! HALLELUJAH!

Within a year, my earthly father died of cancer and my husband and I divorced. Without the power and strength of the Lord in my life, I would have collapsed because everything that I had leaned on before – was nothing but ashes. Jesus was and is the only one I can count on. He has truly given me 'beauty for ashes' as Isaiah said so many thousands of years ago.

And so having been saved because of God's grace, not because of anything I've done, I answer God's call on my life and share with others about the saving, healing power of Jesus Christ. The healed becomes a healing instrument in the hands of God.

Additional Text: Isaiah 61, Philippians 3

April 12

Robert Murray McCheyne, a Scottish pastor who lived only 30 years in the early 1800's once said: *"I long for love without any coldness, light without dimness, and purity without spot or wrinkle."* Jesus, too, desired this kind of love for us.

This is what I say to all who will listen to me: Love your enemies, and be good to everyone who hates you. Ask God to bless anyone who curses you, and pray for everyone who is cruel to you... Give to everyone who asks and don't ask people to return what they have taken from you. Treat others Just as you want to be treated.

If you love only someone who loves you, will God praise you for that? Even sinners love people who love them. If you are kind only to someone who is kind to you, will God be pleased with you for that? Even sinners love people who love them. If you are kind only to someone who is kind to you, will God be pleased with you for that? Even sinners are kind to people who are kind to them...

But love your enemies and be good to them. Lend without expecting to be paid back. Then you will get a great reward, and you will be the true children of God in heaven. He is good even to people who are unthankful and cruel. Have pity on others, just as your Father has pity on you.

Jesus said: Don't judge others, and God won't judge you. Don't be hard on others, and God won't be hard on you. Forgive others, and God will forgive you. If you give to others, you will be given a full amount in return. It will be packed down, shaken together, and spilling over into your lap the way you treat others is the way you will be treated.   Luke 6:27-28, 30-33, 35-38 (CEV)

WOW! Jesus' standard is high! The reward for obedience was also great!

Be sincere in your love for others. Hate everything that is evil and hold tight to everything that is good. Love each other as brothers and sisters and honor others more than you do yourself. Never give up. Eagerly follow the Holy Spirit and serve the Lord. Let your hope make you glad. Be patient in time of trouble and never stop praying. Take care of God's needy people and welcome strangers into your home.

Ask God to bless everyone who mistreats you. Ask him to bless them and not to curse them. When others are happy, be happy with them, and when they are sad, be sad. Be friendly with everyone. Don't be proud and feel that you are smarter than others. Make friends with ordinary people. Don't mistreat someone who has mistreated you. But try to earn the respect of others, and do your best to live at peace with everyone...Don't let evil defeat you, but defeat evil with good.   Romans 12:9-18, 21 (CEV)

We overcome evil – with love.

Everything will soon come to an end. So be serious and be sensible enough to pray. Most important of all, you must sincerely love each other, because love wipes away many sins.   1 Peter 4:7-8 (CEV)

We are admonished to be wise and clear – but always, ALWAYS cover our words, our actions, and our thoughts with love, mercy, and grace.

Additional Text: 1 John 4, Luke 6

Charles Mackintosh, an Irish preacher in the early 1800's once said, *"The grand business of the servant of Christ is to obey. His object should not be to do a great deal, but simply to do what he is told."* Jesus has shown us by example what it is to be <u>totally</u> obedient to our Heavenly Father.

It was almost time for the Jewish Passover Feast. Jesus knew that it was time for him to leave this world and go back to the Father. He had always loved those who were his own in the world, and he loved them all the way to the end.

Jesus and his followers were at the evening meal. The devil had already persuaded Judas Iscariot, the son of Simon, to turn against Jesus. Jesus knew that the Father had given him power over everything and that he had come from god and was going back to God. So during the meal Jesus stood up and took off his outer clothing. Taking a towel, he wrapped it around his waist. Then he poured water into a bowl and began to wash the followers' feet, drying them with the towel that was wrapped around him.

Jesus came to Simon Peter, who said to him, "Lord, are you going to wash my feet?"

Jesus answered, "You don't understand now what I am doing, but you will understand later."

Peter said, "No, you will never wash my feet."

Jesus answered, "If I don't wash your feet, you are not one of my people."

Simon Peter answered, "Lord, then wash not only my feet, but wash my hands and my head, too!"

Jesus said, "After a person has had a bath, his whole body is clean. He needs only to wash his feet. And you men are clean, but not all of you." Jesus knew who would turn against him, and that is why he said, "Not all of you are clean."

When he had finished washing their feet, he put on his clothes and sat down again. He asked, "Do you understand what I have just done for you? You call me 'Teacher' and 'Lord' and you are right, because that is what I am. If I, your Lord and Teacher, have washed your feet, you also should wash each other's feet. I did this as an example so that you should do as I have done for you. I tell you the truth, a servant is not greater than his master. A messenger is not greater than the one who sent him. If you know these things, you will be happy if you do them." John 13:1-17 (NCV)

Notice that Judas' feet were washed right along with John's feet. They were washed with Peter's, who would <u>deny</u> Jesus three times in just a few short hours.

Jesus is a servant to <u>all</u>. Jesus died for the sins of <u>all</u>. He died for Cain's sins. He died for <u>my</u> sins. He died for my grandsons', Alex and Jaxon, sins and my granddaughter, Anna's sins. Jesus desires that ALL come to the saving knowledge of Him. His love. His compassion. His example is what jumpstarts my obedience. As my love for Him grows – my obedience becomes more and more spontaneous. It becomes my <u>WHOLE</u> life.

Additional Text: Philippians 2, 1 Timothy 2

April 14

It was almost time for the Feast of Unleavened Bread, called the Passover Feast. The leading priests and teachers of the law were trying to find a way to kill Jesus, because they were afraid of the people.

Satan entered Judas Iscariot, one of Jesus' twelve apostles. Judas went to the leading priests and some of the soldiers who guarded the Temple and talked to them about a way to hand Jesus over to them. They were pleased and agreed to give Judas money. He agreed and watched for the best time to hand Jesus over to them when he was away from the crowd.

The Day of Unleavened Bread came when the Passover lambs had to be sacrificed. Jesus said to Peter and John, "Go and prepare the Passover meal for us to eat."...So Peter and John left and fond everything as Jesus had said. And they prepared the Passover meal. Luke 22:1-8, 13 (NCV)

I remember as a child helping my mom prepare the Easter Sunday dinner. Most of the preparation happened on Friday and Saturday because the meal base was ham, potato salad, and deviled eggs. My usual task was to cube all the cooked potatoes. A messy, sticky job!

I suspect there is some preparation needed for a Passover dinner also. If you do not have your own large room then you have to find someone who is willing to 'rent' you one. Peter and John must have been pretty happy to find things already in place for them. Not only a big enough table but enough comfortable couches for everyone to recline. Nice!

Judas had another job. I like Luke's account of this because he puts the primary blame where it belongs – satan! I wonder what was in Judas' mind. What lies were being whispered as a justification for betraying someone who had treated him with kindness and love? When I am tempted and choose to agree – logic doesn't become part of the equation.

The account of Jesus' last supper with His disciples is about their relationship. Jesus knows that time is short and no matter which gospel I read there are important points for me to take into my heart. Matthew and Mark give me a beautiful picture of the breaking of the bread and sharing of the wine as Jesus testifies that He won't personally do this again with us until He returns. He promises He will return in glory. Jesus also reminds me through Peter that I, too, will deny Him but He died for me anyway! Luke reports the question among the disciples as to who is the greatest and He reminds them that He has been their servant. He also tells Peter that there will be a time of sifting but that He has already prayed for him to be strong. What an encouragement that during my times of 'sifting' that Jesus is there praying for me! John tells of the washing of the disciples' feet and then writes four mores chapters worth of encouragement and concludes with Jesus' prayer in chapter 17.

We might think that Holy Thursday or Maundy Thursday is about the Last Supper, Holy Communion. That is the sacrament. A sacrament is "an outward sign of an inward change". Communion is all about the relationship between Jesus and me. It is about OUR communing together. There is so much there for me to receive – if I will just 'recline' with Him and listen.

April 15

I always thank my God as I remember you in my prayers, because I hear about your faith in the Lord Jesus and your love for all the saints. I pray that you may be active in sharing your faith, so that you will have a full understanding of every good thing we have in Christ. Your love has given me great joy and encouragement, because you, brother, have refreshed the hearts of the saints.

Philemon 4-7

As I began praying today, I thought of the people I have met or who have joined this devotion group in the last year. I felt tears burn my eyes at how God continues to reach out to people to <u>come</u> into His Kingdom or continue to enter a deeper knowledge and understanding of Him. He never gives up. God has a heart for His children that have not changed since the day He was willing to allow His only Son to <u>*die*</u> for us.

Two other men, both criminals, were also led out with him to be executed. When they came to the place called the Skull, there they crucified him, along with the criminals—one on his right, the other on his left. Jesus said, "Father, forgive them, for they do not know what they are doing." And they divided up his clothes by casting lots.

The people stood watching, and the rulers even sneered at him. They said, "He saved others; let him save himself if he is the Christ of God, the Chosen One."

The soldiers also came up and mocked him. They offered him wine vinegar and said, "If you are the king of the Jews, save yourself."

There was a written notice above him, which read: THIS IS THE KING OF THE JEWS.

One of the criminals who hung there hurled insults at him: "Aren't you the Christ? Save yourself and us!"

But the other criminal rebuked him. "Don't you fear God," he said, "since you are under the same sentence? We are punished justly, for we are getting what our deeds deserve. But this man has done nothing wrong."

Then he said, "Jesus, remember me when you come into your kingdom.'"

Jesus answered him, "I tell you the truth, today you will be with me in paradise."

It was now about the sixth hour, and darkness came over the whole land until the ninth hour, for the sun stopped shining. And the curtain of the temple was torn in two. Jesus called out with a loud voice," Father, into your hands I commit my spirit." When he had said this, he breathed his last. Luke 23:32-46

Two thieves were given the ultimate invitation as they faced a certain death. One chose eternal life. The other chose to keep his way of doing things that certainly had not worked for him in the past but he was unwilling to take that step of faith that Jesus' way might be better. He refused to give up control and humble himself to receive a gift that he didn't earn or didn't deserve.

Coming to know Jesus as Savior is receiving the truth that it isn't about <u>me</u> but about Jesus. Continuing to know Jesus as Lord and King is receiving the truth that it *continues* to NOT be about me but about God.

Additional Text: Proverbs 9 and 10

[Solomon prays,] *"Everyone sins, so your people will also sin against you. You will become angry with them and hand them over to their enemies. Their enemies will capture them and take them away to their countries far or near. Your people will be sorry for their sins when they are held as prisoners in another country. They will be sorry and pray to you in the land where they are held as prisoners, saying, 'We have sinned. We have done wrong and acted wickedly.' They will truly turn back to you in the land of their enemies. They will pray to you, facing this land you gave their ancestors, this city you have chosen, and the Temple I have built for you. Then hear their prayers from your home in heaven, and do what is right. Forgive your people of all their sins and for turning against you. Make those who have captured them show them mercy. Remember, they are your special people. You brought them out of Egypt, as if you were pulling them out of a blazing furnace.* 1 Kings 8:46-51 (NCV)*

"Sin." Now there is a word that has become politically incorrect! It seems that more and more each day that the 'world' would want to blur the lines between 'right' and 'wrong' and that truly we accept 'The 10 <u>Suggestions</u>' and not burden ourselves with 'Commandments'.

Do I truly understand <u>why</u> I need mercy and grace from God? Do I take the time to stop and look at my filthiness and realize that even though I may be doing "better than ol' Joe over there! After all, I don't have <u>his</u> sin!" JOE isn't my standard, is he?"

[Jesus says,] *"You say, 'I am rich, and I have become wealthy and do not need anything.' But you do not know that you are really miserable, pitiful, poor, blind, and naked."* Revelation 3:17 (NCV)*

You are the only one I have sinned against; I have done what you say is wrong. You are right when you speak and fair when you judge. Psalm 51:4 (NCV)*

I think the hardest words to say, in truth and from the heart, is: "I'm sorry. Forgive me, please?" To say these words, I have to first acknowledge that I <u>have</u> in fact done something wrong. I acknowledge it and acknowledge that I <u>NEED</u> forgiveness. And in my pride, I refuse and so I shove it into my sack of 'stuff' and carry it around with me. After awhile, I am *dragging* it around with me because it has become so heavy! Do I feel the pain in my neck and shoulders? Do I feel the weight in my heart? Do I think that this is 'normal'???

[Jesus said,] *"Accept my teachings and learn from me, because I am gentle and humble in spirit, and you will find rest for your lives. The teaching that I ask you to accept is easy; the load I give you to carry is light."*

Matthew 11:29-30 (NCV)

If this is what Jesus says then any heaviness and weight is <u>not</u> Him and it is time for me to <u>LET IT GO</u>!!! "I'm sorry, Lord. Please forgive me." <u>NOW</u> is the time.

Additional Text: 1 John 1 and 2

April 17

The LORD spoke to Moses, saying, "Speak to Aaron and his sons, saying, Thurs you shall bless the people of Israel: you shall say to them, The LORD bless you and keep you; the LORD make his face to shine upon you and be gracious to you; the LORD lift up his countenance upon you and give you peace."

Numbers 7:22-26 (ESV)

Submit yourselves therefore to God. Resist the devil, and he will flee from you. Draw near to God, and he will draw near to you. Cleanse your hands, you sinners, and purify your hearts, you double-minded. Be wretched and mourn and weep. Let your laughter be turned to mourning and your joy to gloom. Humble yourselves before the Lord, and he will exalt you. James 4:7-10 (ESV)

I know that where God is – there is peace in any storm. Even in the midst of any battle here on earth, if I walk in the footsteps of God, where He has gone before me, there is that 'peace that passes all understanding'. (Philippians 4:7)

Look at the 'blessing' that God Himself gave to Moses to give to Aaron (the priests). Specific words that they were to pray over the people. Words of joy, of hope, of promise, -- of peace. Did God keep those promises of blessings? Yes – <u>when</u> the Israelites were obedient! God's face DID shine on them! He DID give them grace and peace! When they wanted their own way, when they thought they knew better than God how events should progress – then His face was hidden from them and His blessings withheld from them. God tells me that He is <u>infinite</u>; that His ways are not mine. He also tells me His promises are <u>true</u> – 'yes' and 'amen' (2 Corinthians 1).

We have this as a sure and steadfast anchor of the soul, a hope that enters into the inner place behind the curtain, where Jesus has gone as a forerunner on our behalf, having become a high priest forever after the order of Melchizedek.

Hebrews 6:19-20 (ESV)

Let us hold fast the confession of our hope without wavering, for he who promised is faithful. Hebrews 10:23 (ESV)

I don't know who wrote Hebrews. He wrote a lot about hope and faith and promises and testimonies. I'm glad he did! I am glad I have this anchor in God's words.

A friend sent me a bookmark with these words:

We never need to be without hope.
For as we look into the future with the eyes of faith,
We will see that God is already there. -- Roy Lessin

Additional Text: Hebrews 10 and 11

When we were with you, we gave you this rule: "Anyone who refuses to work should not eat."   *2 Thessalonians 3:10 (NCV)*

I didn't know that the sign held by the homeless man I saw yesterday at the highway exit came straight from Scripture. I wonder if he did?

Paul was instructing the ministry workers who seem to be following the Pharisee's example rather than Jesus'. They were idle and expecting others to pay them and feed them because they were – "holy?" – and to do it while they themselves did NOTHING! I seem to remember that Jesus severely rebuked this practice:

"The teachers of the law and the Pharisees have the authority to tell you what the law of Moses says. So you should obey and follow whatever they tell you, but their lives are not good examples for you to follow. They tell you to do things, but they themselves don't do them. They make strict rules and try to force people to obey them, but they are unwilling to help those who struggle under the weight o f their rules."   *Matthew 23:2-4 (NCV)*

When Jesus sent out his disciples, this is what He said:

"There are a great many people to harvest, but there are only a few workers. So pray to God, who owns the harvest, that he will send more workers to help gather his harvest. Go now, but listen! I am sending you out like sheep among wolves. Don't carry a purse, a bag, or sandals, and don't waste time talking with people on the road. Before you go into a house, say, 'Peace be with this house.' If peaceful people live there, your blessing of peace will stay with them, but if not, then your blessing will come back to you. Stay in the peaceful house, eating and drinking what the people there give you. A worker should be given his pay. Don't move from house to house."   *Luke 10:2-7 (NCV)*

When I 'retired' from my 40-hour a week job to go into full time ministry, it was with joy at being released to do the 'call' on my heart. However, I was definitely <u>concerned</u> about the Lord supplying the needs of my family. I certainly never knew that I was going from 40 hours a week to seven days a week; with no two daily schedules the same. And money? Well, I've found peace (most of the time!) in my Lord who DOES supply all my needs. It has been a walk of faith with a whole lotta building going on!!!

As Jesus said, ministers who <u>work</u> for Him deserve their wages. Just as the person who builds my house or stocks the shelves at the local store should not have to beg or apologize for their pay checks that they earned, so a pastor, teacher, evangelist, or anyone else who works to build the kingdom of God should not apologize or beg for the wage that they have earned.

And now, brothers and sisters, we want you to know about the grace God gave the churches in Macedonia. They have been tested by great troubles, and they are very poor. But they gave much because of their great joy. I can tell you that they gave as much as they were able and even more than they could afford. No one told them to do it. But they begged and pleaded with us to let them share in this service for God's people. And they gave in a way we did not expect: They first gave themselves to the Lord and to us. This is what God wants.   *2 Corinthians 8:1-5 (NCV)*

And I will make you to this people a fortified wall of bronze;
they will fight against you, but they shall not prevail over you,
for I am with you to save you and deliver you, declares the LORD.
I will deliver you out of the hand of the wicked, and redeem you from the grasp
of the ruthless"   *Jeremiah 15:20-21 (ESV)*
He [John the Baptist] *said therefore to the crowds that came out to be baptized*
by him, "You brood of vipers! Who warned you to flee from the wrath to come?
Bear fruits in keeping with repentance. And do not begin to say to yourselves,
'We have Abraham as our father.' For I tell you, God is able from these stones
to raise up children for Abraham. Even now the axe is laid to the root of the
trees. Every tree therefore that does not bear good fruit is cut down and thrown
into the fire."   *Luke 3:7-9 (ESV)*

An evangelist I know says there are two kinds of messages: "Twinkie" messages — sweet and full of God's love and mercy and "Brussels sprouts" messages — good for us but not our favorite to taste and hear! This is a Brussels sprout devotion.

Jeremiah cries out to God, whining really, that he has been suffering a long time and where is God in all of this? That's me. Whether I am looking at the global picture and wondering when God is going to put His foot down on those I believe deserve it or whether it is a personal trial and/or torment that I am seeking His relief — I am crying out to God. There is a kingdom principle here that I must look at my end of the bargain. I must repent or if it is a church crying out — members must repent — or a country (like Nineveh did) there must be a cry of repentance from the people.

God says 'if you repent, I will restore you so you can serve Me!' Repent means turn away from. Make a 180-degree turn. Do not just blabber worthless words but be truly repentant and get on track with God's agenda, leaving my personal agenda behind. And then, we will be an example/ambassador for Him. Others may come against us — but God will be with us.

Jesus, very graphically I might add, gives us a stern warning about God's wrath. He tells us that if we have truly repented — we will produce "fruit" from this repentance. The verses in Galatians [19-26] are not an all inclusive list of the evil fruits of the "sinful nature" but when we repent of whatever the Holy Spirit has sent conviction about — we will exhibit: love, joy, peace, patience, kindness, goodness, faithfulness, gentleness, and self-control.

Here is the Brussels sprout part: just because we sit in church every Sunday and serve on committees or sing in the choir — doesn't mean we will escape the wrath of God. Jesus says clearly — if we do not produce good fruit (the ones listed in Galatians and more like mercy and grace), then we will experience the wrath of God. This is not about salvation — believe on the Lord Jesus Christ and you are saved — this is about wrath for the life we chose to live after being saved. [1 Corinthians 3:10-15] Are we living for Jesus or ourselves? Are we serving others for Him or just serving ourselves?

Additional Text: 1 Corinthians 3, Luke 3

"If you remember my laws and commands and obey them, I will give you rains at the right season; the land will produce crops, and the trees of the field will produce their fruit. Your threshing will continue until the grape harvest, and your grape harvest will continue until it is time to plant. Then you will have plenty to eat and live safely in your land. Leviticus 26:3-5 (NCV)*

If you carefully obey the commands I am giving you today and love the LORD your God and serve him with your whole being, then he will send rain on your land at the right time, in the fall and spring, and you will be able to gather your grain, new win, and oil. He will put grass in the fields for your cattle, and you will have plenty to eat. Deuteronomy 11:13-15(NCV)*

There is a time for everything, and everything on earth has its special season.
There is a time to be born and a time to die.
There is a time to plant and time to pull up plants.
There is a time to kill and a time to heal.
There is a time to destroy and a time to build.
There is a time to cry and a time to laugh.
There is a time to be sad and a time to dance.
There is a time to throw away stones and a time to gather them.
There is a time to look for something and a time to stop looking for it.
There is a time to keep things and a time to throw things away.
There is a time to tear apart and a time to sew together.
There is a time to be silent and a time to speak.
There is a time to love and a time to hate.
There is a time for war and a time for peace. Ecclesiastes 3:1-8 (NCV)*

Our Father is the Lord of seasons. This characteristic is one of encouragement and hope for me.

When I am experiencing times of refreshing and the Lord is pouring out His words to me, it is like 'spring' when new plants are just coming forth and each day there is something new! An 'autumn' time is also a time of anticipation as I feel God preparing me to see the harvest of the back-breaking work He and I have been doing during the 'summer' months that are now past. These three 'seasons' are so important to remember and reflect upon as I enter the 'winter' season where my life may appear dormant and at times even desolate. Winter is a time to press in closer to the Lord, finding warmth in His promises and reflect on the testimonies of what He has done in my life and the lives of others, gaining new insight.

God, we thank you; we thank you because you are near. We tell about the miracles you do.

You say, "I set the time for trial, and I will judge fairly. The earth with all its people may shake, but I am the one who holds it steady." Psalm 75:1-3 (NCV)*

Additional Text: Habakkuk 3, Mark 4

April 21

I saw a new heaven and a new earth. The first heaven and the first earth had disappeared, and so had the sea. Then I saw New Jerusalem, that holy city, coming down from god in heaven. It was like a bride dressed in her wedding gown and ready to meet her husband.

I heard a voice shout from the throne: God's home is now with his people. He will live with them, and they will be his own. Yes, God will make his home among his people. He will wipe all tears from their eyes, and there will be no more death, suffering, crying, or pain. These things of the past are gone forever."
Revelation 21:1-4 (CEV)

You were doing so well until someone made you turn from the truth.
Galatians 5:7 (CEV)

Most of us hate commercials. And yet, sometimes I find myself compelled to watch one – almost in fascination at the technical or graphic abilities of the producer <u>or</u> at the absurdity of the message!!! Commercials are very powerful – that's why advertisers are willing to spend so much on a 30 second 'spot'!

There are commercials in my life whether I watch TV or not. A 'spot' spoken by a friend about another can sway me on how I think about another person. Especially if I respect that friend; maybe they are even a Christian! TV, newspapers, books, videos, music, etc. etc. My eyes and ears are rapid pathways into my mind and heart.

I confess to you that I read the Book of Revelation only to remind myself WHO WINS! And how the words apply to me now – I'm not into pre-trib, mid-trib, post-trib, or pan-trib, WHATEVER! I want to be prepared <u>now</u> for whatever is to come!

There are wonderful promises! Powerful, convicting promises! Read <u>all</u> of Revelation 21. It's easy for me to read about 'living water' – what a gift! I do not feel convicted when I read the plan for the 'vile' and 'murderers'. I'm not vile or a murderer! But the 'others' that the Lord mentions – do I feel just as confident? That glass house I'm living in looks a little fragile, doesn't it? Thank You, Lord, that I am covered by Jesus' Blood!

I believe Paul's question in Galatians is the important one. Who or what keeps me from obeying <u>God's</u> truth? Do I spend time in His Word so I <u>KNOW</u> His truth? Frankly, I need to quit blaming the 'commercials' (whether a non-believer acquaintance or my spouse or my pastor, or my best-est friend!) and take ownership of my spiritual life and the responsibility I have to it EVERY day! The best way to get rid of filth on TV is to reach out with that remote and TURN IT OFF!!! I have a remote inside of me, too. "Turn off the trash, Jody, and get in the word. Quit listening to everyone else so much and spend time with Me -- your Father in heaven."

What must I give you, LORD, for being so good to me? I will pour out an offering of wine to you, and I will pray in your name because you have saved me. I will keep my promise to you when your people meet.
Psalm 116:12-14 (CEV)

Additional Text: Revelation 21, Galatians 5

"I can't do it!" "I can't learn…Geometry!" "I can't do this project!" "I can't fit in with his family!"

Remember this saying, "A few seeds make a small harvest, but a lot of seeds make a big harvest." Each of you must make up your own mind about how much to give. But don't feel sorry that you must give and don't feel that you are forced to give. God loves people who love to give. God can bless you with everything you need, and you will always have more than enough to do all kinds of good things for others. 2 Corinthians 9:6-8 (CEV)

Many of us might be familiar with Paul's words to the church at Philippi when he testified that he could *"do everything through him who gives me strength"*. That's true. But in his words to the Church at Corinth, Paul encourages me further when he tells me that if I sow – if I give – I will reap – I will receive. If I ask for help in Geometry – both from the teacher and God, I WILL receive understanding. If I will put time and effort and, yes again, ask for help from God AND maybe someone who wants an opportunity – I can do the project. If I ask the Lord for <u>MORE</u> grace and take the time to find a point of common interest – I can receive my spouse's appreciation and maybe even a smile from an in-law!!! I sow. I reap.

Have you read what Paul said <u>before</u> he announced that he could do everything <u>with</u> God?

But Christ has shown me that what I once thought was valuable is worthless. Nothing is as wonderful as knowing Christ Jesus my Lord. I have given up everything else and count it all garbage. All I want is Christ and to know that I belong to him. I could not make myself acceptable to God by obeying the Law of Moses. God accepted me simply because of my faith in Christ. All I want is to know Christ and the power that raised him to life. I want to suffer and die as he did, so that somehow I also may be raised to life.

I have not yet reached my goal, and I am not perfect. But Christ has taken hold of me. So I keep running and struggling to take hold of the prize. My friends, I don't feel that I have already arrived. But I forgot what is behind, and I struggle for what is ahead. I run toward the goal, so that I can win the prize of being called to heaven. This is the prize that God offers because of what Christ Jesus has done. All of us who are mature should think in this same way. And if any of you think differently, God will make it clear to you. But we must keep going in the direction that we are now headed…

I am not complaining about having too little. I have learned to be satisfied with whatever I have. I know what it is to be poor or to have plenty, and I have lived under all kinds of conditions. I know what it means to be full or to be hungry, to have too much or too little. Christ gives me the strength to face anything.

Philippians 3:7-16, 4:1-13

I sow into my time with God by making it a priority. I reap as I move towards the goal that God has given me, learning and testifying as I go. My spiritual life is a <u>LIVING</u> thing. It is not stagnant or a holding pond. It is a stream of living water with God as its source, pouring into others that they may give God thanks.

I have received many emails and calls from people who are struggling with questions about God and loved ones who are dying. I, too, have experienced some very difficult losses in the last two years and I did not want to hear clichés or be told that I should just "have faith" and "trust God". I KNOW THAT! I guess I wanted to just know that God really saw my grief and felt my bewilderment and confusion.

It is the same with the dead who are raised to life. The body that is "planted" will ruin and decay, but it is raised to a life that cannot be destroyed. When the body is "planted," it is without honor, but it is raised in glory. When the body is "planted" it is weak, but when it is raised, it is powerful. The body that is "planted" is a physical body. When it is raised, it is a spiritual body...

I tell you this, brothers and sisters: Flesh and blood cannot have a part in the kingdom of God. Something that will ruin cannot have a part in something that never ruins. But look! I tell you this secret: We will not all sleep in death, but we will all be changed. It will take only a second – as quickly as an eye blinks – when the last trumpet sounds. The trumpet will sound, and those who have died will be raised to live forever, and we will all be changed. This body that can be destroyed must clothe itself with something that can never be destroyed. And this body that dies will clothe itself with that which can never die. When this happens, this Scripture will be made true: "Death is destroyed forever in victory." "Death, where is your victory? Death, where is your pain?" Death's power to hurt is sin, and the power of sin is the law. But we thank God! He gives us the victory through our Lord Jesus Christ.

1 Corinthians 15:42-44, 50-57 (NCV)

Just as my spirit cannot continue to move closer to God if I choose to live in sin – so my natural body cannot be immortal. I cannot dwell in a spiritual place for eternity while in a natural/mortal body.

OK – so God set up these laws of nature – but even though I accept those laws that doesn't lessen how I loved that person and want them here with me!

God gave me permission to grieve. He validated that it was part of my healing. I was blessed that those that I loved, and now miss so much because they have died, knew Jesus as Savior and Lord. I KNEW by their testimony – both in word and works. What if I'm not sure? If someone I knew and loved died and did NOT know Jesus as Savior – yes that would be the greatest tragedy. But I submit to you both as someone who seeks to know God, know His heart, AND as a nurse who has worked in hospice and critical care units – we do NOT know when a person ceases to receive communication and GOD is certainly not constrained by a coma or disease!!!

Yes, there will come a day when I will put off this perishable shell called my body and I will be given an Imperishable one that will last all eternity! I will be reunited with those who have gone before me.

"...because the Lamb at the center of the throne will be their shepherd. He will lead them to springs of water that give life. And God will wipe away every tear from their eyes."

Revelation 7:17 (NCV)

David Ravenhill, minister and son of the late Leonard Ravenhill, wrote in his book, *The Jesus Letters* that *We, too, err when tolerance takes priority over holiness*.

I'm not sure "tolerance" is the word that I would put in opposition to "holiness" in the Church. I actually think we should be tolerant of others until it causes me to *COMPROMISE* my principles of faith. My principles are the 'bottom lines' that I believe God has placed in my heart. An example would be: I believe that 'sinners' should be in the church I attend. They should be in worship with me. I can hear you laughing! But Jesus said He came for the 'sick' not the well. That means the fornicators and the liars and homosexuals should be in church right next to the rest of us sinners!

However, if I chose to rebelliously continue to sin despite encouragement to do otherwise, then there are consequences for that which could include a loss of a leadership role until I allow the Holy Spirit to get me back on track!

If you tell others that you belong to me, I will tell my Father in heaven that you are my followers. But if you reject me, I will tell my Father in heaven that you don't belong to me.

Don't think I came to bring peace to the earth! I came to bring trouble, not peace. I came to turn sons against their fathers, daughters against their mothers, and daughters-in-law against their mothers-in-law. Your worst enemies will be in your own family.

If you love your father or mother or even your sons and daughters more than me, you are not fit to be my disciples. And unless you are willing to take up your cross and come with me, you are not fit to be my disciples. If you try to save your life, you will lose it. But if you give it up for me, you will surely find it.

Matthew 10:32-39 (CEV)

This may sound harsh but I believe that one of the principles that Jesus taught was straight out of the Bible that HE read and I could start by reading the whole 28th chapter of Deuteronomy where it describes the blessings for obedience and the curses for disobedience. Jesus knew it was going to cause some *tension* in the Body of Believers when we hold each other accountable. Yes, it must be done with the right motivation as Jesus did to encourage and grow disciples into mature belief in God.

Stay away from people who are not followers of the Lord! Can someone who is good get along with someone who is evil? Are light and darkness the same?

2 Corinthians 6:14 (CEV)

In another translation, it says not to be 'yoked' with unbelievers. That is a HARD teaching. After I became a believer in 1995, it was VERY difficult to let go of some close friendships and to also watch some friendships disintegrate because I had changed and my friend had not and did not want to do so.

Because of what Jesus said, many of his disciples turned their backs on him and stopped following him. Jesus then asked his twelve disciples if they were going to leave him. Simon Peter answered, "Lord, there is no one else that we can go to! Your words give eternal life. We have faith in you..." John 6:66-68 (CEV)

Hard choices with consequences.

April 25

And he told them a parable to the effect that they ought always to pray and not lose heart. He said, "In a certain city there was a judge who neither feared God nor respected man. And there was a widow in that city who kept coming to him and saying, 'Give me justice against my adversary.' For a while he refused, but afterward he said to himself, 'Though I neither fear God nor respect man, yet because this widow keeps bothering me, I will give her justice, so that she will not beat me down by her continual coming.' " And the Lord said, "Hear what the unrighteous judge says. And will not God give justice to his elect, who cry to him day and night? Will he delay long over them? I tell you, he will give justice to them speedily. Nevertheless, when the Son of Man comes, will he find faith on earth?"
Luke 18:1-8 (ESV)

My husband, Henry Neufeld, has written a series of articles about *The Hand of God.* You can read the articles in their entirety on his website www.energion.com . Here is an excerpt from the first article:

When people see acts of God and miracles, they say, "God is active. God is showing his power." When there are few such acts, they perceive God as distant or inactive. "Why doesn't God do something?" they ask.

But such acts, in most people's view, need explanations. Why would God intervene in one case and not in another? Shouldn't God always intervene to accomplish the good?

Good questions. Many people, including me, have wondered where was God glorified in the terminal illness or accidental death of a child.

A pastor made an interesting statement one Sunday when he said; "Justice was served by Jesus that day on Calgary". All that was done before that day and all that has happened since or WILL happen – Jesus was justice.

And he judges the world with righteousness; he judges the peoples with uprightness. The LORD is a stronghold for the oppressed, a stronghold in times of trouble. And those who know your name put their trust in you, for you, O LORD, have not forsaken those who seek you.
Psalm 9:8-9 (ESV)

The fear of man lays a snare, but whoever trusts the LORD is safe. Many seek the face of a ruler, but it is from the LORD that a man gets justice.
Proverbs 29:25-26 (ESV)

I believe Jesus gave the parable of the 'persistent widow' because He wanted to tell me where I would find the 'JUSTICE' that I may seek in my life. God is the ONLY ONE qualified to exact justice for and in any situation. And He's already DONE IT! My job is to pray. To persistently *pray* and ask for the Lord's justice in a situation is both a Godly prayer and a prayer that WILL be answered. It's a timing thing…it's a God thing!

After this I heard what seemed to be the loud voice of a great multitude in heaven, crying out, "Hallelujah! Salvation and glory and power belong to our God, for his judgments are true and just;…
Revelation 19:1-2 (ESV)

Additional Text: Psalm 9, John 17

We may make a lot of plans, but the LORD will do what he has decided.
Proverbs 19:21 (CEV)

You mean I don't always get my way! Well, at least I know this was true even BEFORE I was a Christian! The difference is illustrated in the story of Joshua.

One day, Joshua was near Jericho when he saw a man standing some distance in front of him. The man was holding a sword, so Joshua walked up to him and asked, "Are you on our side or on our enemies' side?"

"Neither," he answered. "I am here because I am the commander of the LORD's army."

Joshua fell to his knees and bowed down to the ground. "I am your servant," he said. "Tell me what to do."

"Take off your sandals," the commander answered. "This is a holy place." So Joshua took off his sandals. *Joshua 5:13-15 (CEV)*

Many believe that this was the pre-incarnate Jesus – Jesus BEFORE He came in the flesh to die for my sins. The point of the story is not whether God will bless my plan – it's whether I am on GOD's plan.

I truly dislike backtracking. So it seems like the best path is to ask the Lord FIRST about HIS plan and THEN move on it. "But I always have such GOOD plans!" Sure! Plans that God will have to untangle! "You gave me administrative gifts, Lord!" That's right, Jody, so you can 'administer' MY gifts, in MY timing. "Oh." God's plans are like His promises. I can count on them! They are just and true. They have looked at all the 'angles' and have everyone's best interests. Paul says God works with a Holy Spirit guarantee. That's the kind of warranty I want!

Because I was confident of this, I planned to visit you first so that you might benefit twice. I planned to visit you on my way to Macedonia and to come back to you from Macedonia, and then to have you send me on my way to Judea. When I planned this, did I do it lightly? Or do I make my plans in a worldly manner so that in the same breath I say, "Yes, yes" and "No, no"?

But as surely as God is faithful, our message to you is not "Yes" and "No." For the Son of God, Jesus Christ, who was preached among you by me and Silas and Timothy, was not "Yes" and "No," but in him it has always been "Yes." For no matter how many promises God has made, they are "Yes" in Christ. And so through him the "Amen" is spoken by us to the glory of God. Now it is God who makes both us and you stand firm in Christ. He anointed us, set his seal of ownership on us, and put his Spirit in our hearts as a deposit, guaranteeing what is to come. *2 Corinthians 1:15-22 (NIV)*

"...guaranteeing what is to come". There are a lot of businessmen out there who would like to have that kind of guarantee. Can you imagine what you could do with stock investments if you had GOD'S guarantee of what is to come?

I do have that guarantee. I've read the end of God's book and know what happens to me because I believe that Jesus is my Lord and Savior. No matter what happens between now and then, I have God's promises and guarantees.

Additional Text: Revelation 21 and 22

April 27

I was truly blessed one Sunday to hear two wonderful teachings in two different churches. I would like to share some of what I heard in these two messages today and tomorrow.

I remember your true faith. That faith first lived in your grandmother Lois and in your mother Eunice, and I know you now have that same faith. This is why I remind you to keep using the gift God gave you when I laid my hands on you. Now let it grow, as a small flame grows into a fire. God did not give us a spirit that makes us afraid but a spirit of power and love and self-control.
2 Timothy 1:5-7 (NCV)

I was told that the word "sincere" here means something like 'not hypocritical' faith. What you speak – is what you do – what you see is the real thing! This sincere, un-hypocritical (!) faith was started in Grandma and was taught and passed on to Mom and then to son, Timothy. Pastor Bob called this a good example of the 'three generation principle'. Many times in Scripture we are shown this principle but in a negative way – that with every generation the faith or God's precepts become more 'watered down'. Examples like Abraham, Isaac, and Jacob, who though none were perfect, it seems that each became more weak and less obedient. Or how about David, Solomon, and Rehoboam? They definitely went from weak to worse!

What is the strength level of the faith I am passing on to my children and grandchildren? Is it strong, grounded in the Word of God and my personal, intimate experience of Him? Or is it watered-down faith, guaranteed not to be held to too high a standard that might offend my son/daughter and their friends and their parents? Do I talk the talk and walk the walk? Do I open my cloak and allow my children to see my wounds as Jesus did Thomas? Do I share with them that daily decisions are made with God's help and that He gets all the glory for successes?

When my life is boiled down to its bottom-line common denominator, all that I have to give to my children is my faith. Nothing else is guaranteed! What is my legacy to them?

"Don't store treasures for yourselves here on earth where moths and rust will destroy them and thieves can break in and steal them. But store your treasures in heaven where they cannot be destroyed by moths or rust and where thieves cannot break in and steal them." *Matthew 6:19-20 (NCV)*

Most of us grew up hearing our parents explain that the hard work and commitment they had toward their jobs was to provide us with an inheritance when they died. As a child, I remember that this long-term plan was difficult for me to grasp and I would just like to have Dad home for my concert or play. Now as an adult, I certainly appreciate the concept that my parents were trying to fulfill but I also hear the Lord tell me that I need to 'factor in' what is truly the essential inheritance that is of far greater worth than money or a stock portfolio. I want to pass on an imperishable legacy to my children and grandchildren: the saving grace and mercy of Jesus Christ. I want them to KNOW that Jesus died for them so that they who are perishable will be raised up imperishable for all eternity!

When the sacrifice had been offered, and they had eaten the meal, Hannah got up and went to pray. Eli was sitting in his chair near the door to the place of worship. Hannah was brokenhearted and was crying as she prayed. "LORD All-Powerful, I am your servant, but I am so miserable! Please let me have a son. I will give him to you for as long as he lives, and his hair will never be cut."

Hannah prayed silently to the LORD for a long time. But her lips were moving, and Eli thought she was drunk. "How long are you going to stay drunk?" he asked. "Sober up!"

"Sir, please don't think I'm no good!" Hannah answered. "I'm not drunk, and I haven't been drinking. But I do feel miserable and terribly upset. I've been praying all this time, telling the LORD about my problems." Eli replied, "You may go home now and stop worrying. I'm sure the God of Israel will answer your prayer."   *1 Samuel 1:9-17 (CEV)*

Hannah weeping and wailing for her child, as yet unborn and un-conceived! Hannah does what I have done before – she makes a bargain with God. "If you give me a son, I will give him back to you." AND she continues to pray. To me, it seems she is praying in the Spirit, like Paul said in Romans 8:26. Many times when we see people praying from that deep place in their heart, with words (or with just tears and groans) that the Holy Spirit can discern, we might think them a bit 'off' as Eli thought Hannah was drunk! We might even think that we should stop this! But WAIT! Maybe the wise course of action is to pray <u>for</u> them that God would intervene in HIS way to meet the person's need. That would take the judgmental factor out, wouldn't it? Praise God that Eli does hear the truth of Hannah's words and gives her a pastoral blessing, not a further rebuke!

Hannah takes seriously her promise to God and when God blesses her with a son, she is obedient to bring Samuel to serve in the Lord's temple. My pastor pointed out that Hannah had a strong prayer life. This is a characteristic of a Godly mother. It's not who you are to the world, it's who you are to God. Hannah also spoke intimately to God. She asked from her heart and in her bargain, she gave all she had. Hannah was also learning great patience. She was learning the blessing that comes with waiting on the Lord. She CONTINUED to pray. Waiting on the Lord doesn't mean that I do not continue to pray and talk to God about my need. I learn patience in trials. Patience and persistence in my labor called prayer is a refining fire that brings my prayer weapon from a 'scatter gun' to a 'laser' that pierces the heart of the need. By giving her child to God, Hannah was preparing Samuel for life. She brought him to the House of the Lord and told him that serving God was his primary service or 'call' in life. That didn't make Samuel a preacher. That made him a servant in whatever way God saw fit. I <u>am</u> to teach my children and grandchildren about the Lord, no matter how old <u>they</u> are or <u>I</u> am!!!

Additional Text: Deuteronomy 6, 1 Samuel 2 and 3

April 29

Remember Jesus Christ, risen from the dead, the offspring of David, as preached in my gospel, for which I am suffering, bound with chains as a criminal. But the word of God is not bound! Therefore I endure everything for the sake of the elect that they also may obtain the salvation that is in Christ Jesus with eternal glory. The saying is trustworthy, for: if we have died with him, we will also live with him; if we endure, we will also reign with him; if we deny him, he also will deny us; if we are faithless, he remains faithful – for he cannot deny himself.   *2 Timothy 2:8-13 (ESV)*

My online dictionary (www.m-w.com) defines "freedom" as

- Liberty of the person from slavery, detention, or oppression.
- Exemption from an unpleasant or onerous condition: *freedom from want.*

Do you have freedom, if not, why not?

During the 70's when ERA (Equal Rights Amendment) was being debated with a passion, I found myself asking questions about how the government was going to legislate people's opinions and attitudes. As a nurse, I had been dealing with sexual harassment long before prosecution was ever a threat. It seemed to me that my 'freedom' as a woman was going to have to come from somewhere besides the U.S. legislature. I had no answers. It would be 20 years before I realized the answer.

Since we have such a hope, we are very bold, not like Moses, who would put a veil over his face so that the Israelites might not gaze at the outcome of what was being brought to an end. But their minds were hardened. For to this day, when they read the old covenant, that same veil remains unlifted, because only through Christ is it taken away. Yes, to this day whenever Moses is read a veil lies over their hearts. But when one turns to the Lord, the veil is removed. Now the Lord is the Spirit, and where the Spirit of the Lord is, there is freedom. And we all, with unveiled face, beholding the glory of the Lord, are being transformed into the same image from one degree of glory to another. For this comes from the Lord who is the Spirit.   *2 Corinthians 3:12-18 (ESV)*

From Viet Nam to China to the Bronx, NY to south Los Angeles, people continue to look for freedom. When they look up and look at Jesus, they find it. Jesus is where I found it in 1995. Freedom from 'want'. A 'want' I could not even put a name to – I just had an emptiness that I couldn't fill – but Jesus did. I was set free from a slavery of sins I could not stop in myself alone. The weight of the oppression of my past was about to kill my spirit but Jesus lifted it off of me and filled all the empty places, making me brand new! Fresh and alive with GOD'S Living Water! Once I tasted freedom, I wanted it – 24/7.

Freedom is a journey. It's making choices every day to obey God, not be a slave to the world's opinion. It's allowing God to continue to peel away the past and draw me closer to my future with Him. Jesus said, *"If you hold to my teaching, you are really my disciples. Then you will know the truth, and the truth will set you free."*   *John 8:31-32 (NIV)*

Additional Text: 2 Corinthians 3, John 8

The son said, "Father, I have sinned against God in heaven and against you. I am no longer good enough to be called your son." But his father said to the servants, "Hurry and bring the best clothes and put them on him. Give him a ring for his finger and sandals for his feet. Get the best calf and prepare it, so we can eat and celebrate. This son of mine was dead, but has now come back to life. He was lost and has now been found." And they began to celebrate.

The older son had been out in the field. But when he came near the house, he heard the music and dancing. So he called one of the servants over and asked, "What's going on here?" The servant answered, "Your brother has come home safe and sound, and your father ordered us to kill the best calf." The older brother got so angry that he would not even go into the house.

His father came out and begged him to go in. But he said to his father, "For years I have worked for you like a slave and have always obeyed you. But you have never even given me a little goat,, so that I could give a dinner for my friends. This other son of yours wasted your money on prostitutes. And now that he has come home, you ordered the best calf to be killed for a feast." His father replied, "My son, you are always with me, and everything I have is yours. But we should be glad and celebrate! Your brother was dead, but he is now alive. He was lost and has now been found."   Luke 15:21-32 (CEV)

The story of the prodigal son has been told and preached in many, many, MANY Sunday School classrooms and churches. I haven't heard as much on the "older brother".

The 'Greatest Commandments': "Love the Lord your God with all your heart" and "love your neighbor as yourself" and the 'Great Commission' "Go into all the world and make disciples" may be a good beginning in determining the direction the Church is to go in mission statements and the development of programs. It is clearer for me to apply these to the "prodigals" but do I see the application to the "older son"?

I have met many who have grown up with God in their homes. They begin as small children in Sunday School and continued to have some type of Christian input in their lives through young adulthood, marrying and in turn raising their own children in the Lord. But do we pay attention that if there is LIFE there must be GROWTH? Our Christian LIFE is not a stagnant or plateau situation. Do I as a leader in Christ's Church encourage those who may be "the older son" to grow in their relationship with Jesus – that there is always MORE?!! I believe that this also refreshes their desire to disciple the "prodigals" and lead by example.

I was a "prodigal" that needed unconditional love and acceptance by those who had an ongoing relationship with Jesus and 'knew their way around' the church. I had some wonderful mentors who encouraged me, discipled me. But as the years have passed I find myself now with a better understanding of the "other" son. I want to rejoice – REJOICE – when the prodigals come home to Jesus! It's time for me to disciple and mentor someone, someone that God points out to me. And I want to also REJOICE when a senior saint glows with a new level of intimacy with Jesus! Both are reasons to celebrate!!!

Anne Chancey Dalton

". . . if we hope for what we do not see, we wait for it with perseverance."

Romans 8:25 (NKJV)

Some are called to minister to the masses. But I minister to individuals. I am the mother of two biological children, eight foster children, and about thirty-five other people who have lived with our family. I'm also 'Mom' to some of our church members—a congregation of mixed races where tattooed bikers in black leather sit beside friends in military uniforms.

I grew up in a middle class home in Prattville, Alabama with my twin sister, Nan. Louvenia, our older sister, married and moved away the year we were born. Our parents had a strong faith and attended worship services with us.

My life and Nan's revolved around the church during our teen years. Rev. Charles Britt taught compassion for the less fortunate and instilled in us a desire for social justice. We learned it's not enough to feel sorry for someone—you have to do something about it. The situation or system has to change. We saw our parents show love and compassion to our black neighbors by helping them when they were sick. In return, these neighbors helped our family when we needed it.

I was in college in Montgomery during the Civil Rights Movement, but I didn't join the protests. Perry Dalton and I were dating. We knew we were right for each other, but we had major difficulties solving minor differences. Both of us worked in the Huntingdon College cafeteria and were friends with the black workers. They constantly teased him. They'd say, "You got to treat that girl right!" Years later they still took credit for getting us together.

In 1962, I married Perry, a United Methodist pastor. His foster parents, Dot and Henry Roper took him in at age 17, and eventually their love and care extended to the rest of Perry's family.

We followed the footprints of the Ropers and Rev. Britt. Over the years, we've shared hope and home with a mother and two teenage daughters; youth from juvenile detention facilities; inmates released by the judge; runaways; exchange students, and many others—each with a unique story.

One day Perry called from the church. He'd been counseling a woman and asked if she and her son could come for dinner. I said, "Sure." They stayed six months.

Mark, a homeless alcoholic, lived with us three times. A car hit and killed him in Atlanta. The only address in his pocket was ours, even though we hadn't seen him in over a year.

A church member experienced discrimination on his federal job. He told his superiors, "I've heard 'equal rights' all of my life, but I didn't really know what it meant. Now I've got a white pastor who treats me as an equal—so I know the difference." Changes gradually took place.

Almost all who lived with us were raised in families on welfare. Only a few remain in that vicious cycle.

Cindy and Julie—our daughters by birth—and many of our foster children now open their homes to others when the need arises.

One person after another, year by year—our way of changing the system.

Tell everyone on this earth to shout praises to God!...
Our God, you tested us, Just as silver is tested. You trapped us in a net and gave us heavy burdens. You sent war chariots to crush our skulls. We traveled through fire and through floods, but you brought us to a land of plenty.
I will bring sacrifices into your house, my God, and I will do what I promised when I was in trouble.   *Psalm 66:1, 10-13 (CEV)*

What an awesome song of praise! I wish I had the talent to put it to music.

The psalmist praises God and affirms how mighty and wonderful He is. And then he states that he knows that God tests us and refines us like silver. Refining a metal means to burn out the impurities until you are left with only the pure beautiful silver. If I were a hunk of metal, refining wouldn't hurt so much. God's refining DOES hurt and IS a choice of obedience and submission for me to come out from my sin so I can be more pure than I was before.

On the day the Lord comes, he will be like a furnace that purifies silver or like strong soap in a washbasin. No one will be able to stand up to him. The LORD will purify the descendants of Levi, as though they were gold or silver. Then they will bring the proper offerings to the LORD...   *Malachi 3:2-3 (CEV)*

I am told that a refiner sits and looks at the metal as it is heated. At the moment of cleansing, when all the impurities are gone, the refiner sees his own reflection in the metal. When God refines me to His point of purity, then I will reflect only Him.

This psalm also says that God has allowed burdens to be laid on our backs and men to run over us! It is a true saying that without the 'test'— there is no 'test-i-mony'! Jesus confirms that there will be burdens but He tells me clearly that <u>with</u> Him the yoke is easy and the burden light. (Matthew 11:30) BUT it also testifies that we are brought to a place of abundance. God desires to give us good gifts but like any good parent, He allows us to learn that there are consequences for our choices. He wants it to be blessings but if we choose disobedience the consequence will be discipline.

The last four verses bring assurance that God hears my prayer. As my husband, Henry, says, "God answers our prayer better than we pray them!" And so I praise Him and desire to remain obedient to Him. I lay my petitions and prayers before God and <u>KNOW</u> that God has not rejected my prayer or withheld his love from me!

Shout praises to the LORD! Praise God in his temple. Praise him in heaven, his mighty fortress. Praise our God! His deeds are wonderful, too marvelous to describe.
Praise God with trumpets and all kinds of harps. Praise him with tambourines and dancing, with stringed instruments and woodwinds. Praise God with cymbals, with clashing cymbals.
Let every living creature praise the LORD. Shout praises to the LORD!
           Psalm 150 (CEV)

Additional Text: Psalm 66, 2 Chronicles 20

That very day two of them were going to a village name Emmaus, about seven miles from Jerusalem, and they were talking with each other about all these things that had happened. While they were talking and discussing together, Jesus himself drew near and went with them. But their eyes were kept from recognizing him. And he said to them, "What is this conversation that you are holding with each other as you walk?" And they stood still, looking sad. Then one of them, named Cleopas, answered him. "Are you the only visitor to Jerusalem who does not know the things that have happened there in these days?" And he said to them, "What things?" And they said to him, "Concerning Jesus of Nazareth... And he said to them, "O foolish ones, and slow of heart to believe all that the prophets have spoken! Was it not necessary that the Christ should suffer these things and enter into his glory?" And beginning with Moses and all the Prophets, he interpreted to them in all the Scriptures the things concerning himself.

So they drew near to the village to which they were going. He acted as if he were going farther, but they urged him strongly, saying, "Stay with us, for it is toward evening and the day is now far spent." So he went in to stay with them. When he was at the table with them, he took the bread and blessed and broke it and gave it to them. And their eyes were opened, and they recognized him. And he vanished from their sight. They said to each other, "Did not our hearts burn within us while he talked to us on the road, while he opened to us the Scriptures?" Luke 24:13-19, 28-32 (ESV)

The story of the road to Emmaus opens up a new light in my life. So many times I feel that wave of frustration and despair because some situation in my life was not responding in the way I thought it should! The two disciples are walking along deep in grief and sorrow because Jesus did NOT defeat the Romans and destroy their rule. In fact Jesus is presumed DEAD!

Jesus in turn vents his frustration in v. 25 when He calls them foolish and unbelieving. Jesus is speaking the very words of the Father, fulfilling prophecy after prophecy about Himself and still the 'spiritual blindness' is there! In fact, until the disciples came together and BROKE bread together – they couldn't see Him…I have to believe that unity and reconciliation are key to my spiritual growth.

God <u>desires</u> intimacy with me. How do I build intimacy in my marriage? By spending time together! Intimacy is not just about physical location. That is only the beginning. It is about being *real* with the other person. It is trusting that person to accept me for who I am and loving me anyway. When faced with questions and frustration and despair, I must 'break bread' or 'commune' with Jesus in prayer, reading the Scriptures, singing praise, instead of sitting in my pool of self-pity. In communing with God, I receive the abundant life that He has promised me and all the gifts that go with it.

Additional Text: Psalm 18, Isaiah 40

When they finished eating, Jesus said to Simon Peter, "Simon, son of John do you love me more than these?"
He answered, "Yes, Lord, you know that I love you."
Jesus said, "Feed my lambs."
Again Jesus said, "Simon son of John do you love me?"
He answered, "Yes, Lord, you know that I love you."
Jesus said, "Take care of my sheep."
A third time he said, "Simon son of John do you love me?"
Peter was hurt because Jesus asked him the third time, "Do you love me?"
Peter said, "Lord you know everything; you know that I love you!"
He said to him, "Feed my sheep. I tell you the truth, when you were younger, you tied your own belt and went where you wanted. But when you are old, you will put out your hands and someone else will tie you and take you where you don't want to go." (Jesus said this to show how Peter would die to give glory to God.) Then Jesus said to Peter, "Follow me!"　　John 21:15-19 (NCV)

When I have read this passage before, the point I have looked at is about "Feed my sheep". Feeding the sheep has to do with all of us – not just pastors. Today, however, the Lord really spoke to me about "Do you love me?" Let's look at the three times that Jesus asks the question and put the emphasis in a little different place each time:

1) "Do you truly love me more than these?" Do I? Do I love Jesus? Love Him with His standard – not just more than Susie at work or Billy, my 'Sunday-only' brother? For me, it's do I love Him enough to obey Him in every detail – even when I don't see the point. What if I hear the Lord say, "Jody, I want you to tithe 15% this month." Or "No, don't get the groceries today. Wait."

2) "Do you truly love me?" Do I worship God EVERY DAY? Do I take time – not just a 'drive thru' – but intentional time to thank God specifically for what He's done, doing, and will be doing in my life? Do I hit my knees and WORSHIP Him? Why not? Do I think it's necessary to kneel? I'd like to be able to justify a reason why I cannot kneel but I just can't think of one good reason – so there it is!

3) "Do you love me?" Do I love Jesus more than any other? More than my spouse? More than my children? Many of us read about then President-elect Bush taking 30 minutes to lead a young man to Christ when he could have been doing what the world was calling him to do at the time. If I love Jesus so much, why didn't I tell the lady who cut my hair this morning about Jesus? I felt the Holy Spirit nudge me!

It would seem that Jesus' question "Do you love me?" would be a 'duh' question. But is it really?

Additional Text: 1 John 4, Psalm 103

"I am the vine; you are the branches. Whoever abides in me and I in him, he it is that bears much fruit, for apart from me you can do nothing. If anyone does not abide in me he is thrown away like a branch and withers; and the branches are gathered, thrown into the fire, and burned. If you abide in me, and my words abide in you, ask whatever you wish, and it will be done for you. By this my Father is glorified, that you bear much fruit and so prove to be my disciples."   *John 15:5-8 (ESV)*

Jesus' words do cut like a two-edge sword, don't they? On one side, they cut through the lies of the enemy and bring such hope: If I <u>choose</u>, I am attached to a life-giving vine that will give me ALL that I need to grow and mature. On the other side, (again, it's <u>my</u> choice!) the words bring hard truths and absolute warnings: if I do not attach myself to this vine it is promised that I will be thrown away into the fire and burned.

His words also help to unsnarl some of my 'theological' questions like: "I pray and ask and You don't answer, God, or You didn't answer in the way I thought you would. What's up with that?"

". If you abide in me, and my words abide in you, ask whatever you wish, and it will be done for you."

Most of the time I focus in on the last part: I ask — He gives me! But the first part tells me the <u>truth</u> of the last part: <u>IF</u> I am in Him, implying that I have His mind, His heart, His — everything! — <u>AND</u> His "words" are <u>IN</u> me — I'm learning, I'm growing, I'm seeing with <u>HIS</u> vision, <u>HIS</u> perspective — <u>THEN</u> I'm wishing for the things that are in His agenda and will glorify the Father and will bear much fruit in me and I will be KNOWN as His disciple.

"As the Father has loved me, so have I loved you. Abide in my love. If you keep my commandments, you will abide in my love, just as I have kept my Father's commandments and abide in his love. These things I have spoken to you, that my joy may be in you, and that your joy may be full.

This is my commandment, that you love one another as I have loved you. Greater loves has no one than this that someone lays down his life for his friends. You are my friends if you do what I command you. No longer do I call you servants, for the servant does not know what his master is doing; but I have called you friends, for all that I have heard from my Father I have made known to you. You did not choose me, but I chose you and appointed you that you should go and bear fruit and that your fruit should abide, so that whatever you ask the Father in my name, he may give it to you. These things I command you, so that you will love one another."   *John 15:9-17 (ESV)*

Additional Text: Leviticus 26, Psalm 49

Don't let anyone forget these things. And with God as your witness, you must warn them not to argue about words. These arguments don't help anyone. In fact, they ruin everyone who listens to them. Do your best to win God's approval as a worker who doesn't need to be ashamed and who teaches only the true message.

Keep away from worthless and useless talk. It only leads people farther away from God. That sort of talk is like a sore that won't heal. And Hymenaeus and Philetus have been talking this way by teaching that the dead have already been raised to life. This is far from the truth, and it is destroying the faith of some people.   *2 Timothy 2:14-18 (CEV)*

Everything will soon come to an end. SO be serious and be sensible enough to pray. Most important of all, you must sincerely love each other, because love wipes away many sins. Welcome people into your home and don't grumble about it. Each of you has been blessed with one of God's many wonderful gifts to be used in the service of others. SO use your gift well. If you have the gift of speaking, preach God's message. If you have the gift of helping others, do it with the strength that God supplies. Everything should be done in a way that will bring honor to God because of Jesus Christ, who is glorious and powerful forever. Amen.   *1 Peter 4:7-11 (CEV)*

I am a 'bottom-line' kind of person. The bottom-line in my Christian faith is: there is only one God. Jesus, the Son of God, came to earth and died for my sins. Because of Him, I have eternal life. God's Holy Spirit is the power and communicator in my life. That's it for me.

But Christ has shown me that what I once thought was valuable is worthless. Nothing is as wonderful as knowing Christ Jesus my Lord. I have given up everything else and count it all as garbage. All I want is Christ and to know that I belong to him. I could not make myself acceptable to God by obeying the Law of Moses. God accepted me simply because of my faith in Christ. All I want is to know Christ and the power that raised him to life. I want to suffer and die as he did, so somehow I also may be raised to life...

All of us who are mature should think in this same way. And if any of you think differently, God will make it clear to you.   *Philippians 3:7-11, 15 (CEV)*

I have a difficult time when I hear Christians argue and actually <u>divide</u> over issues such as styles of worship, moving pulpit furniture, and even speaking in tongues or not speaking in tongues. My heart actually aches and more often than not I will weep. Jesus spoke often about love and spoke only in a harsh divisive way with the religious leadership, who showed little love and much manipulation!

Finally, my friends, keep your minds on whatever is true, pure, right, holy, friendly, and proper. Don't ever stop thinking about what is truly worthwhile and worthy of praise.   *Philippians 4:8 (CEV)*

Where are my thoughts and my words and my actions when discussions come up in my home, in committee meetings, or wherever? Are my thoughts on the 'lovely' things of God? Do I ask Him for <u>HIS</u> direction? Do I give up <u>MY</u> agenda and way of thinking?

May 6

You've heard the saying, "You can run but you cannot hide." Growing up and learning that there are consequences for my actions is a difficult lesson, a necessary lesson. It teaches me about sin.

But if you don't do as you have said, then you will have sinned against the Lord, and you may be sure that your sin will catch up with you. Numbers 32:23 (TLB)

If I ride the morning winds to the farthest oceans, even there your hand will guide me, your strength will support me. If I try to hide in the darkness, the night becomes light around me. For even darkness cannot hide from God; to you the night shines as bright as day. Darkness and light are both alike to you.
Psalm 139:9-12 (TLB)

"The sentence is based on this fact: that the Light from heaven came into the world, but they loved the darkness more than the Light, for their deeds were evil. They hated the heavenly Light because they wanted to sin in the darkness. They stayed away from that Light for fear their sins would be exposed and they would be punished. But those doing right come gladly to the Light to let everyone see that they are doing what God wants them to." John 3:19-21 (TLB)

Sin is <u>anything</u> that separates me from God. It is an action. It is words. It is thoughts. Separation from God feels like loneliness, isolation, confusion, and oppression.

There is only ONE remedy for sin. Repentance. Turning 180 degrees away from the sin and walking towards God and His truth and His love. So simple.

So difficult when my pride has produced boulders in the path. The way to blast through the pride boulder is to get naked before God and see myself through His eyes. I see dirt and stains from the sins that I have chosen. I repent. "I am sorry, Father. Please forgive me." I see His love. I am washed clean because of Jesus' perfect sacrifice on the cross. Amazing love. Amazing grace. I am set free in the Light of God's love.

Mark Twain said, "Telling the truth is wonderful because you don't have to remember what you said."

Walking in the Light is walking with God, knowing that everything is done through Him.

Don't ever forget those wonderful days when you first learned about Christ. Remember how you kept right on with the Lord even though it meant terrible suffering. Sometimes you were laughed at and beaten, and sometimes you watched and sympathized with others suffering the same things. You suffered with those thrown into jail, and you were actually joyful when all you owned was taken from you, knowing that better things were awaiting you in heaven, things that would be yours forever.

Do not let this happy trust in the Lord die away, no matter what happens. Remember your reward! You need to keep on patiently doing God's will if you want him to do for you all that he has promised. Hebrews 10:32-36 (TLB)

Additional Text: Numbers 32, Romans 5, 1 John 1

May 7

The time is coming when people won't listen to good teaching, Instead, they will look for teachers who will please them by telling them only what they are itching to hear. They will turn from the truth and eagerly listen to senseless stories.
2 Timothy 4:3-4 (CEV)

They have refused his teaching and have said to his messengers and prophets: Don't tell us what God has shown you and don't preach the truth. Just say what we want to hear, even if it's false. Stop telling us what God has said! We don't want to hear any more about the holy God of Israel.   Isaiah 30:10-11 (CEV)

I think all of us would agree that any given Scripture can be taken out of context and made to mean (or support!) anything that I want. It is significant to me that all the gospel writers tell the story of Jesus' temptation and show us that satan is the master of twisting God's words! So how do I hear the Lord's truth and not be deceived? Henry wrote a paper on this. Here are his seven points:

1) I learn to KNOW God's word. God's word is not limited to the written word. God created through His word and is reflected throughout creation (Psalm 33:6-9, Romans 1:20). Jesus is God's word in the flesh (John 1:1-3, 14). It is God-breathed and is useful (1 Timothy 3:16, 17). God's word is ALIVE and ACTIVE (Hebrews 4:12).

2) I must keep the Word and the Holy Spirit "married" together. The Word of God is not just dry facts. It transforms lives when I allow it into my heart and life through the power of the Holy Spirit. It is not just a matter of reading God's word, but of hearing and obeying.

3) It is NOT just a scholarly study. I must not just study God's Word for facts. I must study in order to know God not just about Him. While reading commentaries or other books can be valuable and even necessary, there is no substitute for studying the Lord for myself (1 Corinthians 2:14-15).

4) I must study ALL God's words, not just a few. Let's face it, some of the Scriptures are just "easy reading"! God loves me. God wants to bless me. Some Scriptures require me to "chew" awhile and pray for the Lord's revelation. Jesus asked the young ruler how he read the Scriptures (Luke 10:26). I put in the time – I receive the reward of God's knowledge.

5) Reading Scripture is NOT just for church events, programs, and Sunday School curricula. *My soul is consumed with longing for your ordinances at all times. Psalm 119:20* It is SO IMPORTANT that as I learn, I pass along to others how to study and receive for themselves – not to be afraid of what they read.

6) I should neither accept EVERY interpretation nor reject every interpretation of God's written or spoken word; this includes prophecy. 1 Thessalonians 5:19-22 tell us to not just arbitrarily reject but put everything to the test, accepting what is good and shove away the evil.

7) I have to ask myself an important question: Am I patient to hear God's word? There are no shortcuts. How important is it to me?

Additional Text: Psalm 119:145-176, 2 Thessalonians 2

Now Jericho was shut up inside and outside because of the people of Israel. None went out, and none came in. And the LORD said to Joshua, "See, I have given Jericho into your hand, with its king and mighty men of valor. You shall march around the city, all the men of war going around the city once. Thus shall you do for six days. Seven priests shall bear seven trumpets of rams' horns before the ark. On the seventh day you shall march around the city seven times, and the priests shall blow the trumpets. And when they make a long blast with the ram's horn, when you hear the sound of the trumpet, then all the people shall shout with a great shout, and the wall of the city will fall down flat, and the people shall go up, everyone straight before him."   *Joshua 6:1-5 (ESV)*

The pastor spoke yesterday about "self-control" as part of his sermon. [Remember I've always said that the Lord 'hammers' ME with the message first and then I JOYFULLY pass it along to you!] Paul was given "self-control" as one of the fruits of the Holy Spirit (Galatians 5:22). These four points gave me clear vision on areas of my life where self-control needs to grow.

1) Timing – Joshua was told and in turn told the people to march around Jericho every day for six days BUT not to speak/shout until the seventh day. How often I want to take the instruction or insight I have received from the Lord and JUMP RIGHT INTO the situation. It's like I turn up the volume of discernment to hear God's answer but there's an internal volume control that automatically kicks in when the word "wait" comes!!! Maybe the knowledge is for me to pray FIRST and God will release "in due season".

2) Talents – Just because I CAN shout – doesn't mean I SHOULD! God knows what he is doing in raising up a BODY of Believers, a well-oiled machine to go out and win the lost for Christ. Do I jump in every time without asking God "Do you want ME?" because He could want to use someone else! Like I told a group the other night, "I don't have control issues – I just want it done RIGHT!" ha! ha!

3) My tongue – uh-oh! It is much easier to hear God say, "Speak!" I actually suspect He says "Hush!" more often. Even when He gives me a word of knowledge or wisdom, sometimes it is for me to pray or study about for "a while" or even forever! What goes IN my spirit only goes OUT when God says so and IF he says so!

4) Treasures – My treasures: that's referring to more than just money. My husband is a 'treasure'. Our children and grandchildren. ALL our 'resources'. They are treasures and they ALL belong to God FIRST!

Self-control is not a 'bad' word and it IS something that I want and can attain – from the Holy Spirit and WITH the Holy Spirit's help!

Additional Text: Joshua 6, Matthew 6

This teaching is true:

If we died with him, we will also live with him. If we accept suffering, we will also rule with him. If we refuse to accept him, he will refuse to accept us. If we are not faithful, he will still be faithful, because he cannot be false to himself. Continue teaching these things, warning people in God's presence not to argue about words. It does not help anyone, and it ruins those who listen. Make every effort to give yourself to God as the kind of person he will accept. Be a worker who is not ashamed and who uses the true teaching in the right way. Stay away from foolish, useless talk, because that will lead people further away from God.

2 Timothy 2:11-16 (NCV)

Jesus told me to *"Go! And make disciples! Baptizing in the name of the Father, Son, and Holy Spirit and teaching them to obey everything that I have commanded you."* (Matthew 28-18-20) He didn't tell me to go and argue over His words, did He?

I believe that by Jesus' words and His example that He wanted me to make my ministry of evangelism – PERSONAL. I believe that while what I teach and share with others must be grounded in Scripture, it is grounded in Scripture because of the time I have spent with Him, listening to Him and learning from Him about what I need to learn first before I can share it with others. The sharing must always have more "I's" and "me's" than "you's"!!! If someone else receives a lesson from God through my sharing – HALLELUJAH! – the Holy Spirit was able to use me! Sometimes what I share may not be specifically for that person but maybe it connected them to something the Lord DID specifically want to them to know so that they in turn can share with others. That is a good thing, too!

God's words are personal to each and every one of us. That is just another facet of His great love for us.

So I bow in prayer before the Father from whom every family in heaven and on earth gets its true name. I ask the Father in his great glory to give you the power to be strong inwardly through his Spirit. I pray that Christ will live in your hearts by faith and that your life will be strong in love and be built on love. And I pray that you and all God's holy people will have the power to understand the greatness of Christ's love – how wide and how long and how high and how deep that love is. Christ's love is greater than anyone can ever know, but I pray that you will be able to know that love. Then you can be filled with the fullness of God.

With God's power working in us, God can do much, much more than anything we can ask or imagine. To him be glory in the church and in Christ Jesus for all time, forever and ever. Amen.

Ephesians 3:14-21 (NCV)

Additional Text: Isaiah 66, John 7

Then Jesus was led up by the Spirit into the wilderness to be tempted by the devil. *Matthew 4:1 (ESV)*

God has anointed and given us so many wonderful pastors and teachers! One Sunday, I went with my sons to *New Dimensions Christian Center* and Pastor Greg Burns was preaching there. His opening question was, "What do you do when you are backed into a corner?" Now I could relate to that! I saw many nods and elbow nudges telling me that there were others who have also felt life's circumstances backing them into a corner. I can even get 'spiritual' in that corner as I lift my eyes to heaven and ask God what He wants me to learn from this situation – so I can MOVE ON! So I can ESCAPE!

Pastor Burn's first point was that I must be willing to be led into the wilderness by the Holy Spirit. God may want to lead me to a place where I have nothing left to distract or to lean on except Him.

[He] who led you through the great and terrifying wilderness, with its fiery serpents and scorpions and thirsty ground where there was no water, who brought you water out of the flinty rock, who fed you in the wilderness with manna that your fathers did not know, that he might humble you and test you, to do you good in the end. Beware lest you say in your heart, 'My power and the might of my hand have gotten me this wealth.' You shall remember the LORD your God, for it is he who gives you power to get wealth that he may confirm his covenant that he swore to your fathers, as it is this day. And if you forget the LORD your God and go after other gods and serve them and worship them, I solemnly warn you today that you shall surely perish, because you would not obey the voice of the LORD your God. *Deuteronomy 8:15-20 (ESV)*

Yes, I know that God led the Israelites in the desert for 40 years to discipline and teach them. Why would I think He wouldn't use the same lesson plan for me? Does He love me less?

Then he led out his people like sheep and guided them in the wilderness like a flock. He led them in safety, so that they were not afraid, but the sea overwhelmed their enemies. *Psalm 78:52-53 (ESV)*

God is a good and gracious father who desires that I 'grow up'. In each stage of my children's development, I have looked upon them with love and, yes, pride. But there is a sense of accomplishment when adult children walk away from you and go out without parental props and are seen by others in the Body as mature, working parts. The time we spent in the desert has produced God's desired fruit!

So then, brothers, we are debtors, not to the flesh, to live according to the flesh. For if you live according to the flesh you will die, but if by the Spirit you put to death the deeds of the body, you will live. For all who are led by the Spirit of God are sons of God. For you did not receive the spirit of slavery to fall back into fear, but you have received the Spirit of adoption as sons, by whom we cry, "Abba, Father. *Romans 8:12-15 (ESV)*

Additional Text: Psalm 78, Romans 8

All my bones shall say, "O LORD, who is like you, delivering the poor from him who is too strong for him, the poor and needy from him who robs him?"
Malicious witnesses rise up; they ask me of things that I do not know. They repay me evil for good; my soul is bereft. But I, when they were sick—I wore sackcloth; I afflicted myself with fasting; I prayed with head bowed on my chest. I went about as though I grieved for my friend or brother; as one who laments his mother, I bowed down in mourning. Psalm 35:10-14 (ESV)

I am continuing today with what Pastor Burns delivered into my heart one Sunday as he preached on the question, "What do you do when you are backed into a corner?"

Point #1 must be willing to be led in the wilderness by the Holy Spirit and stay there until God leads me out.

Point #2 was that I must die to my will. The psalmist brings home this point to my heart in a very specific example to pray, even intercede, for my enemies. Jesus, too, is very clear and plain on this point.

"But I say to you who hear, Love your enemies, do good to those who hate you, bless those who curse you, pray for those who abuse you. To one who strikes you on the cheek, offer the other also, and from one who takes away your cloak do not withhold your tunic either. Give to everyone who begs from you, and from one who takes away your goods do not demand them back. And as you wish that others would do to you, do so to them." Luke 6:27-31 (ESV)

If I am 'backed into a corner' in a situation in my life, looking to Jesus as the answer and example is a good way to cast my eyes, isn't it? However, sometimes His clear answer is not what I really want to hear. I should know that it is going to involve things like "grace" and "mercy", shouldn't I? I should also know that Jesus uses the Father as His standard of action and so what I do in the situation is to complete the circle, reflecting back and glorifying the Father.

So Jesus said to them, "Truly, truly, I say to you, the Son can do nothing of his own accord, but only what he sees the Father doing. For whatever the Father does, that the Son does likewise. For the Father loves the Son and shows him all that he himself is doing." John 5:19-20 (ESV)

Jesus also showed me that He could 'beg' the Father to reconsider His plan. In fact, Jesus could 'beg' three times.

And going a little farther he fell on his face and prayed, saying, "My Father, if it be possible, let this cup pass from me; nevertheless, not as I will, but as you will." Matthew 26:39 (ESV)

Jesus' example is very clear that no matter the difficulty I MUST pray and submit to the will of the Father. Jesus sets the example to walk in faith that 'Abba Father' does see and know the difficulties. He knows what He is asking of me. My response to this 'I'm-backed-into-the-corner-situation' must be "Not my will, Father, but Yours."

Additional Text: Luke 6, John 5

"Always remember what is written in the Book of the Teachings. Study it day and night to be sure to obey everything that is written there. If you do this you will be wise and successful in everything. Remember that I commanded you to be strong and brave. Don't be afraid, because the LORD you God will be with you everywhere you go."   *Joshua 1:8-9 (NCV)*

Pastor Burns #3 point of his sermon Sunday was that "when I am backed into a corner" in a situation in my life – PROCLAIM THE WORD!

Joshua got VERY good advice from the Lord. Duh! When I am in a tough 'season' in my life, my tendency is to pull in and isolate myself from others AND from God. I go out less including accepting excuses NOT to attend Bible study or Wed. night services – even Sunday morning services. Who do I think is whispering in my ear not to go? It sure isn't GOD!

God is telling me to <u>press</u> <u>in</u> closer to Him. He wants to talk to me, encourage me, and hold me in those tough seasons.

They are strong, like a tree planted by a river. The tree produces fruit in season, and its leaves don't die. Everything they do will succeed.
                                                                    Psalms 1:3 (NCV)

From Paul, a servant of God and an apostle of Jesus Christ, I was sent to help the faith of God's chosen people and to help them know the truth that shows people how to serve God. That faith and that knowledge come from the hope for life forever, which God promised to us before time began. And God cannot lie. At the right time God let the world know about that life through preaching. He trusted me with that work, and I preached by the command of God our Savior. To Titus, my true child in the faith we share: Grace and peace from God the Father and Christ Jesus our Savior.   *Titus 1:1-4 (NCV)*

God <u>is</u> all about 'seasons'. He spoke many times through His prophets and Jesus about planting and reaping and the seasons. I believe He wanted me to know that just as He revealed to Joseph, there will be seasons in my life of great prosperity and I should rejoice and bring into my spiritual barn the 'tithes' of faith and trust and hope. I am building an intimate, personal relationship with God. There will be seasons in my life of great spiritual famine, times of testing and trials. I am to go to the storehouse and utilize and 'stand' on that faith and trust and hope that has been built up. The relationship building continues but it has a place to begin in my 'spiritual store house'.

The LORD says, "I will forgive them for leaving me and will love them freely, because I am not angry with them anymore. I will be like the dew to Israel, and they will blossom like a lily. Like the cedar trees in Lebanon, their roots will be firm. They will be like spreading branches, like the beautiful olive trees and the sweet-smelling cedars in Lebanon. The people of Israel will again live under my protection. They will grow like the grain, they will bloom like a vine, and they will be as famous as the wine of Lebanon."   *Hosea 14:4-7 (NCV)*

Additional Text: 2 Corinthians 10, Colossians 4

Jesus told a story to some people who thought they were better than others and who looked down on everyone else:

Two men went into the temple to pray. One was a Pharisee and the other a tax collector. The Pharisee stood over by himself and prayed, "God, I thank you that I am not greedy, dishonest, and unfaithful in marriage like other people. And I am really glad that I am not like that tax collector over there. I go without eating for two days a week, and I give you one tenth of all I earn."

The tax collector stood off at a distance and did not think he was good enough even to look up toward heaven. He was so sorry for what he had done that he pounded his chest and prayed, "God, have pity on me! I am such a sinner."

Then Jesus said, "When the two men went home, it was the tax collector and not the Pharisee who was pleasing to God. If you put yourself above others, you will be put down. But if you humble yourself, you will be honored."

Luke 18:9-14 (CEV)

Behave like obedient children. Don't let your lives be controlled by your desires, as they used to be. Always live as God's holy people should, because God is the one who chose you, and he is holy. That's why the Scriptures say, "I am the holy God, and you must be holy too."   *1 Peter 1:14-16 (CEV)*

God has spoken to my heart many times in the past about holiness. Colossians chapter 3 is a favorite of mine giving very specific instructions about living a holy life. This morning, however, I think God wanted to give me a different perspective on living a holy life. Do I live it as a Pharisee or a tax collector? Just as I was searching and meditating with as much brutal honesty as I could muster, the Lord reminded me of these Scriptures:

God treats everyone alike. He accepts people only because they have faith in Jesus Christ. All of us have sinned and fallen short of God's glory. But God treats us much better than we deserve, and because of Christ Jesus, he freely accepts us and sets us free from our sins.   *Romans 3:22-24 (CEV)*

You were saved by faith in God, who treats us much better than we deserve. This is God's gift to you, and not anything you have done on your own. It isn't something you have earned, so there is nothing you can brag about. God planned for us to do good things and to live as he has always wanted us to live. That's why he sent Christ to make us what we are.   *Ephesians 2:8-10 (CEV)*

So — holiness is the work of the Holy Spirit that begins in my heart and then shows itself outwardly — 'oozing' out — glorifying God, reflecting back to Him. True Godly holiness is characterized through its source, God, motivated by love, and is focused on becoming like Jesus. There is no pride, no wondering what others think, and no vain attempt to earn God's favor. God's standard is the only one that matters and Jesus is the only example that I pattern myself.

As I kneel before my Heavenly Father this morning and allow Him to shine the light on my life, I feel safe in His love. I know that He loves me just where I am but desires more for me. HIS motivation is not condemnation but love and a desire that I succeed in being holy because HE is holy!

Additional Text: Romans 3 and 4

May 14

"I have much more to say to you, but right now it would be more than you could understand. The Spirit shows what is true and will come and guide you into the full truth. The Spirit doesn't speak on his own. He will tell you only what he has heard from me, and he will let you know what is going to happen. The Spirit will bring glory to me by taking my message and telling it to you. Everything that the Father has is mine. That is why I have said that the Spirit takes my message and tells it to you." John 16:12-15 (CEV)

"Watch out for people who will take you to court and have you beaten in their meeting places. Because of me, you will be dragged before rulers and kings to tell them and the Gentiles about your faith. But when someone arrests you, don't worry about what you will say or how you will say it. At that time you will be given the words to say. But you will not really be the one speaking. The Spirit from your Father will tell you what to say." Matthew 10:17-20 (CEV)

I'm a planner. I like to have a plan. It has been a real stretch for me since 1995 to be a part of this "move of the Holy Spirit" because frequently the Holy Spirit does not speak plans in advance! He certainly could! But when working with me, I think the Holy Spirit knows that if He gave me the direction too far in advance (more than 24 hours!) I would attempt to "help" Him and "tweak" His plan in order to make it better!

I also know that the Holy Spirit did not reveal everything in me that needed cleaning and changing at the time that I accepted Jesus as Savior. It certainly would have been more than I could bear. It has been a process. It seems that He keeps me in that balance where I rejoice at what God has DONE and IS DOING in me and in that place like where Paul cries out *"What a wretched man I am! Who will rescue me from this body of death? Thanks be to God--through Jesus Christ our Lord!"* [Romans 7:24-25]

God is so compassionate and loves me so much. He gives me illustrations in His Word that tell me that it is all right to come "hide in the shadow of His wing" or in the "crevice of the rock" or "stand on the Rock". I do not have to 'handle' stuff by myself and, in fact, can even say like Scarlett O'Hara — "I'll think about it tomorrow!" The Holy Spirit will guide me and speak to me and direct me "at the proper time" which means GOD'S TIME. In my flesh that is sometimes very frustrating, but in my moments of intimacy and submission to my Lord, it is comforting and strengthening to know that God does see and does have the larger, more accurate picture that includes His perfect timing.

You cannot fool God, so don't make a fool of yourself! You will harvest what you plant. If you follow your selfish desires, you will harvest destruction, but if you follow the Spirit, you will harvest eternal life. Don't get tired of helping others. You will be rewarded when the time is right, if you don't give up. We should help people whenever we can, especially if they are followers of the Lord. Galatians 6:7-10 (CEV)

Additional Text: John 15 and 16

So Moses stretched out his hand over the sea, and the sea returned to its normal course when the morning appeared. And as the Egyptians fled into it, the LORD threw the Egyptians into the midst of the sea. The waters returned and covered the chariots and the horsemen; of all the host of Pharaoh that had followed them into the sea, not one of them remained. But the people of Israel walked on dry ground through the sea, the waters being a wall to them on their right hand and on their left. Exodus 14:27-29 (ESV)

O God, you are my God; earnestly I seek you; my soul thirsts for you; my flesh faints for you, as in a dry and weary land where there is no water. So I have looked upon you in the sanctuary, beholding your power and glory. Because your steadfast love is better than life, my lips will praise you.

Psalm 63:1-3(ESV)

But Jesus answered them, "You are wrong, because you know neither the Scriptures nor the power of God." Matthew 22:29 (ESV)

"Then will appear in heaven the sign of the Son of Man, and then all the tribes of the earth will mourn, and they will see the Son of Man coming on the clouds of heaven with power and great glory." Matthew 24:30 (ESV)

His divine power has granted to us all things that pertain to life and godliness, through the knowledge of him who called us to his own glory and excellence...

2 Peter 1:3 (ESV)

The Scriptures the Lord took me to this morning seem to require little comment on my part to 'connect the dots' (but <u>of course</u> I will!).

In the story of Egyptians and Israelites, my first reaction was "Well, yeah, Lord — part the sea for me, letting <u>me</u> walk on dry land, and then drown my enemies (every one of them!) behind me — I can see YOUR POWER in that!" Duh! "Hold on, Jody. I've got more to say…"

Psalm 63 has been an experiential song for me. I've been on my face crying before the Lord and then seen and felt His very presence press in on me, bringing calm and peace, and — a holy awe and yes, fear — as He seem to 'show' me that <u>HE</u> is bigger and more powerful than any 'problem' or 'petition' that I have. So, I immediately felt the humbling of His reminder that His 'POWER SHOW' is not just in water and wind and other forms of nature!

And then, just in case I had any arrogance left, I believe God cut me off at the knees with Jesus' reminder to the know-it-all's of His day that they were in error because they did not seek God's Word in truth, nor did they have any kind of intimate relationship with Him so they couldn't possibly know His power either! (gulp!)

Jesus gives me a glimpse in Matthew 24 of what is to come, and it's going to be better than any "Independence Day" space ship blocking out the sun! Praise God I am in the 'elect'!!!

God always leaves me with hope and instructions to draw closer to Him after He has chastised me — and He did that again this morning with 2 Peter. God desires that I be <u>effective</u> and <u>productive</u> in my knowledge of Jesus Christ so I can share with the world — after I have learned it myself!

Psalm 57

Have mercy on me, O God, have mercy on me, for in you my soul takes refuge.
I will take refuge in the shadow of your wings until the disaster has passed.
  [Let's see — 'disasters' in my life…yup, I'm crouching under His wings!]

I cry out to God Most High, to God, who fulfills his purpose for me.
  [Disaster…purpose? Is there a purpose?]

He sends from heaven and saves me, rebuking those who hotly pursue me;
God sends his love and his faithfulness.
  [What a promise and encouragement!]

I am in the midst of lions; I lie among ravenous beasts--
  men whose teeth are spears and arrows, whose tongues are sharp swords.
  [Remember: I am in the world, not of the world.]

Be exalted, O God, above the heavens; let your glory be over all the earth.
  [In everything I do, may You be glorified, Lord.]

They spread a net for my feet -- I was bowed down in distress.
They dug a pit in my path -- but they have fallen into it themselves.
  [Revenge is Mine, says the Lord.]

My heart is steadfast, O God, my heart is steadfast; I will sing and make music.
Awake, my soul! Awake, harp and lyre! I will awaken the dawn.
I will praise you, O Lord, among the nations;
I will sing of you among the peoples.
For great is your love, reaching to the heavens; your faithfulness reaches to the
skies.
Be exalted, O God, above the heavens; let your glory be over all the earth.
  [You are worthy of my praise, Lord!! You are worthy!!!]

Whether David wrote this 'song' or someone else — what a pattern for my prayer and worship life!

In the morning, O LORD, you hear my voice; in the morning I lay my requests
before you and wait in expectation.   *Psalm 5:3*

Morning or evening and in between, I bring my requests before the Lord… and wait in EXPECTATION! Not in despair or doubt, but EXPECTATION! And as I wait, I praise You, Lord, because You are You — and worthy of praise! That is a comforting place to be. God is not only faithful but He is FAITH. And I want to be plugged in to THAT outlet!!!

And the LORD afflicted the child that Uriah's wife bore to David, and he became sick. David therefore sought God on behalf of the child. And David fasted and went in and lay all night on the ground. And the elders of his house stood beside him, to raise him from the ground, but he would not, nor did he eat food with them. On the seventh day the child died. And the servants of David were afraid to tell him that the child was dead, for they said, "Behold, while the child was yet alive, we spoke to him, and he did not listen to us. How then can we say to him the child is dead? He may do himself some harm." But when David saw that his servants were whispering together, David understood that the child was dead. And David said to his servants, "Is the child dead?" They said, "He is dead." Then David arose from the earth and washed and anointed himself and changed his clothes. And he went into the house of the LORD and worshiped. He then went to his own house. And when he asked, they set food before him, and he ate. Then his servants said to him, "What is this thing that you have done? You fasted and wept for the child while he was alive; but when the child died, you arose and ate food." He said, "While the child was still alive, I fasted and wept, for I said, 'Who knows whether the LORD will be gracious to me, that the child may live?' But now he is dead. Why should I fast? Can I bring him back again? I shall go to him, but he will not return to me."

Then David comforted his wife, Bathsheba, and went in to her and lay with her, and she bore a son, and he called his name Solomon. And the LORD loved him...   2 Samuel 12:15-24 (ESV)

Well, Praise the Lord anyway!

I remember a well-meaning friend telling me that when I was going through a difficult time in my life. It did not make me feel holy – it made me feel fleshy! I was like David's servants in the Scripture. I could not imagine praising the Lord or rejoicing at that moment. I was disappointed and depressed because God had not responded the way I thought He should and I couldn't see His glory in my life.

A few years have passed, and there are still tough times in my life but I have found that God has taught me to look beyond the moment and know that He is there the whole time. I receive David's testimony that when times are tough. I am to pray, asking for God's mercy and grace; His undeserved forgiveness and love. Yes, even ask for the way I would like the situation to turn out. Maybe I've even asked the Lord for His will and felt His answer. And then it turned out differently. "Wait! What happened, Lord?" It is so easy at that moment to allow confusion and disbelief to take over. But if I choose to stop and go to my knees again, asking God for His truth and His assurance, peace will come. Maybe even answers. As much as I may want answers, I want peace more. I will have all eternity to receive the answers.

Like David when he received Solomon, the Lord will send more gifts my way. Like Job who after losing everything, received many-fold over what he lost. Did Job forget his children that were killed? I doubt it. But He praised the Lord anyway because He knew the 'eternity' of their life and his.

I have been crucified with Christ. It is no longer I who live, but Christ who lives in me. And the life I now live in the flesh I live by faith in the Son of God, who loved me and gave himself for me. Galatians 2:20 (ESV, emphasis mine)
And he came out and went, as was his custom, to the Mount of Olives, and the disciples followed him. And when he came to the place, he said to them, "Pray that you may not enter into temptation." And he withdrew from them about a stone's throw, and knelt down and prayed, saying, "Father, if you are willing, remove this cup from me. Nevertheless, not my will, but yours be done." And there appeared to him an angel from heaven, strengthening him. And being in an agony he prayed more earnestly; and his sweat became like great drops of blood falling down to the ground. Luke 22:39-44 (ESV, emphasis mine)
Then Jesus said to them, "You will all fall away because of me this night. For it is written, 'I will strike the shepherd, and the sheep of the flock will be scattered.' But after I am raised up, I will go before you to Galilee." Peter answered him, "Though they all fall away because of you, I will never fall away." Jesus said to him, "Truly I tell you, this very night, before the rooster crows, you will deny me three times." Peter said to him, "Even if I must die with you, I will not deny you!" And all the disciples said the same.
Matthew 26:31-35 (ESV)

I was struck that in both of these stories with Jesus that He tries to warn His disciples of temptation and their fleshly ability to "fall". They ignore Him and, in fact, very shortly "fall".

The Gospels tell us on several occasions that Jesus PRAYED. Jesus! God! While on earth, in His earthly body, God yet man, needed to PRAY! Showed us how to pray! Spent time in conversation with God! Speaking AND listening — to God — PRAYER!!! The writers of the gospels thought it important enough — were inspired with conviction — to record Jesus praying. I wonder if there is a connection — increase prayer, decrease "fall" into temptation — duh!!!

The more time I spend in prayer — in conversation with God — the closer we become. In prayer, I come into line with God. I begin to know His ways, His thoughts, and His heart. In prayer, my flesh is crucified. In prayer, my faith increases, my trust in God increases. IN prayer.

Here are some references of prayers:
Genesis 25:21   Isaac prayed for Rebekah
Exodus 9:29   Moses prays to stop one of the plagues
2 Samuel 7:18 David prays
1 Kings 8:22   Solomon prays
Nehemiah 1:8   Nehemiah prays
Job 42:9   Job prays for his friends
Psalms — all of them are prayers — pick some!
Daniel 9:3   Daniel prays
Habakkuk 3:1   Habakkuk prays
John 17   Jesus prays
Acts 1:14 All the disciples and followers met together and prayed
Philippians 1:9   Paul prays

Those people who make idols are nothing themselves, and the idols they treasure are just as worthless. Worshipers of idols are blind, stupid, and foolish. Why make an idol or an image that can't do a thing?

Isaiah 44:9-10 (CEV)

"Don't store up treasures on earth! Moths and rust can destroy them, and thieves can break in and steal them. Instead, store up your treasures in heaven, where moths and rust cannot destroy them, and thieves cannot break in and steal them. Your heart will always be where your treasure is."

Matthew 6:19-21 (CEV)

We are not preaching about ourselves. Our message is that Jesus Christ is Lord. He also sent us to be your servants. The Scriptures say, "God commanded light to shine in the dark." Now God is shining in our hearts to let you know that his glory is seen in Jesus Christ.

We are like clay jars in which this treasure is stored. The real power comes from God and not from us.   *2 Corinthians 4:5-7 (CEV)*

I have been reading a lot about "obedience" and "idolatry" in a book by John Bevere, The Devil's Door. I've always thought idolatry as being gold images like little Buddha dolls. I have never bowed to anything like that! Bevere raises an interesting question to me, however, giving me reason to read and study these Scriptures for myself. When I question God, argue with Him about where He is leading or how He is answering and even decide to 'go my own way' or just sit and pout hoping He will change His mind — am I saying that I know better than Him? Am I implying that in my witness to others? I am 'shaping' my own answer to my petition that I have laid before the Lord instead of being totally open to HIS answer. Bevere encourages me to aspire to be so much like Jesus that I will even do nothing when God is quietly saying, "Wait." It is simple obedience.

"But, Lord, You gave me an intellect and reasoning power, aren't I supposed to use it?"

The LORD said:

Heaven is my throne; the earth is my footstool. What kind of house could you build for me? In what place will I rest? I have made everything; that's how it all came to be. I, the LORD, have spoken.

The people I treasure most are the humble – they depend on me and tremble when I speak.   *Isaiah 66:1-2 (CEV)*

While I use the mind that the Lord has given me and exercise the reasoning that has come from my experience and the tradition of my maturing, in the final analysis do I bow to God's word and His way for me? Do I *tremble* in holy fear and obedience to HIM? Do I lay down ALL idols of myself and give HIM all the glory for my life?

Additional Text: Isaiah 66, 2 Corinthians 4

When I became a Christian, when I made a 180-degree turn and said, "I am living for You, Jesus, and there's no turning back", I wanted to know the truth about God. I wanted to know what HE said, not what a church hierarchy said He said!

All my life I had sat in a church each Sunday and was told what God, through the Bible, said. It was interpreted for me and I swallowed pretty much what I was told. Many of us are lazy enough to be "OK" with being spoon-fed ... UNTIL we reach a crossroad in our life. Maybe it's a big decision, like career or marriage. Maybe it's a tragedy involving someone we love. Maybe it is a decision like, "Should I have sex with this person?" and the answer can have life-changing consequences. In any case, the TRUTH of what someone else has told us comes into question. We have no personal knowledge with which to determine truth or lies – and so we are on shifting sand. Decisions are made. Validation of truth or lies comes after the facts.

I WANT TO KNOW THE TRUTH ABOUT GOD, WHO HE IS AND WHAT HE IS! And that requires WORK on my part. I have to put in the time. I have to put time into studying God's Word, Scripture, for myself. I have to experience God and His presence in my life, for myself. I have to reason with God, holding up what others might say, and see if it lines up with HIS word, HIS truth, and HIS way of doing things.

For thus says the LORD, who created the heavens (he is God!), who formed the earth and made it (he established it; he did not create it empty, he formed it to be inhabited!): "I am the LORD, and there is no other. I did not speak in secret, in a land of darkness; I did not say to the offspring of Jacob, 'Seek me in vain.' I the LORD speak the truth; I declare what is right."   Isaiah 45:18-19 (ESV)

When I spend time with the Lord, study His word, experience His presence, -- well this is what Jesus says:

"...If you abide in my word, you are truly my disciples, and you will know the truth, and the truth will set you free...Truly, truly, I say to you, everyone who commits sin is a slave to sin. The slave does not remain in the house forever; the son remains forever. So if the Son sets you free, you will be free indeed."

John 8:31, 34-35

God has set me free through Jesus Christ. That's a truth I can stand on!

Blessed is he whose help is the God of Jacob, whose hope is the LORD his God, who made heaven and earth, the sea, and all that is in them, who keeps faith forever; who executes justice for the oppressed, who gives food to the hungry.
The LORD sets the prisoners free; the LORD opens the eyes of the blind.
The LORD lifts up those who are bowed down; the LORD loves the righteous.
The LORD watches over the sojourners; he upholds the widow and the fatherless, but the way of the wicked he brings to ruin.
The LORD will reign forever, your God, O Zion, to all generations.
Praise the LORD!   *Psalm 146:5-10 (ESV)*

Additional Text: Romans 6, 2 Corinthians 3

[The context of this story: Esther is the King's wife. Mordecai is her uncle. Both are Jews but no one knows that Esther is. The king has been tricked into a decree by an evil nobleman, Haman that will destroy all the Jews in the kingdom. Mordecai has asked that Esther go to the king and intervene. The law says that going to the king without invitation will end in death. Esther has just reminded her uncle of this…]

Esther's message was given to Mordecai. Then Mordecai sent back word to Esther: "Just because you live in the king's palace, don't think that out of all the Jewish people you alone will escape. If you keep quiet at this time, someone else will help and save the Jewish people, but you and your father's family will all die. And who knows, you may have been chosen queen for just such a time as this." Esther 3:12-14 (NCV)

The apostle Paul says:

I am in prison because I belong to the Lord. God chose you to be his people, so I urge you now to live the life to which God called you. Always be humble, gentle, and patient, accepting each other in love. You are joined together with peace through the Spirit, so make every effort to continue together in this way. There is one body and one Spirit, and God called you to have one hope. There is one Lord, one faith, and one baptism. There is one God and Father of everything. He rules everything and is everywhere and is in everything. Ephesians 4:1-6 (NCV)

And then, Peter teaches us how to build a firm foundation for our calling:

Because you have these blessings, do your best to add these things to your lives: to your faith, add goodness; and to your goodness, add knowledge; and to your knowledge, add self-control; and to your self-control, add patience; and to your patience, add service for God; and to your service for God, add kindness for your brothers and sisters in Christ; and to this kindness, add love. If all these things are in you and are growing, they will help you to be useful and productive in your knowledge of our Lord Jesus Christ. But anyone who does not have these things cannot see clearly. He is blind and has forgotten that he was made clean from his past sins.

My brothers and sisters, try hard to be certain that you really are called and chosen by God. If you do all these things, you will never fall. And you will be given a very great welcome into the eternal kingdom of our Lord and Savior Jesus Christ. 2 Peter 1:5-11 (NCV)

As I was reading these passages I was thinking about 'calls' I have received lately – as in <u>telephone</u> calls! I was remembering how I appreciated 'caller ID' that allows me to pick and choose which calls I accept. There are some 'calls' from God that I wish I did not 'see'. I have a choice to answer or not! In the past, I have been known to *ignore* some 'calls' from God! I am finding it very hard to do that now because I know that even if the 'call' is a tough, serious "outpost" duty – not answering for whatever reason will result in unrest and pain in my soul that I cannot shake until I ask forgiveness. God tells me in 2 Peter to be prepared for my 'call' and remember that there is an <u>eternal</u> reward that goes on forever!

...Respect the LORD your God, and do what he has told you to do. Love him. Serve the LORD your God with your whole being, and obey the LORD's commands and laws that I am giving you today... Deuteronomy 10:12-13 (NCV)

Before I made a decision to let go and turn my life over to God, I allowed it to be SO complicated. It's NOT complicated. It's just not EASY! It is very different than this 'microwave' world I live in. When you eat good ol' white Irish potatoes, do you fix the *instant* kind? Or do you buy the ones in a 5 or 10 lb. sack, take them home and wash them, stand at the sink and peel them, chop them up, stick them in a pot with water and salt, and boil them for about 15 minutes or so, mash them adding milk and butter, then mix them on high with your electric mixer (that you had to take out and dust off!) until they are fluffy with maybe juuuuuust a few little lumps in them so you know they're the 'real McCoy' and then finish them off with just a little pat of butter so it melts and drips down that mountain of potatoes? Makes you want to sneer at the *instant* ones, doesn't it? Making *real* mashed potatoes isn't complicated; it just takes some time and effort! Accepting God for who He is and His Son as Savior and Lord, isn't complicated, it just takes some time and effort!

Moses speaks clearly to us about what the Lord asks of me in this relationship:

- Fear Him. This is a Holy fear, not a 'BOO!' in the dark fear. This isn't about 'when is God going to whack me up side of the head because of what I've done'. This is about grabbing on to the fact that He is Lord, Creator of ALL the universe and HE wants to be in *close* relationship to ME!!!

- Walk in all his ways – be obedient – observe what He tells me to do. Again, not complicated, just takes some time and effort to learn and build a relationship with God that brings forth love that *inspires* me to be obedient. Yes, Holy fear also helps me to be obedient when faced with choices in my life.

- Love him -- It's a relationship thing. It's reading about Him, talking to Him (and being totally honest), and WORSHIPPING Him for who He is. I learn more and more about that as our relationship grows!

- Serve him – In some ways, maybe that is the more difficult. God may ask me to serve in ways that are difficult for me to do. Serving Him requires me to do all the other three things and give God all the credit for it! He may ask me to serve by being quiet and in prayer when I'd rather take ACTION! He may ask me to GO some place that I never considered!

You adulterous people, don't you know that friendship with the world is hatred toward God? Anyone who chooses to be a friend of the world becomes an enemy of God.   *James 4:4*

James calls us 'adulterous people' because we love someone besides the One that we are committed to – married to – are in covenant with – GOD. We find our relationship with the Lord difficult because we are full of PRIDE and IDOLIZE things other than God. And so I am back to simple – a simple choice – to be faithful to God only, to put Him FIRST in my life. To be completely committed to God.

You had my mother give birth to me. You made me trust you while I was just a baby. I have leaned on you since the day I was born; you have been my God since my mother gave me birth. *Psalm 22:9-10 (NCV)*

I have been reading a book, <u>Experiencing the Father's Embrace</u> by Jack Frost. He and his wife minister to pastors and leadership, having a vision that we would all 'see' the total love that our Father has for us. One of the anonymous stories he relates was when a couple came for prayer with two small sons. The woman wept as she confessed that she did not know how to love. She had never experienced the unconditional love of a father and so she had no point of reference to give the same to her children. Her five-year-old son innocently turned to her and told her that <u>he</u> would show her how to love.

I am easily frustrated when I am asked to do something I don't know how to do. I sense this mother was feeling that kind of frustration. Jesus knew I would have days like that and He spoke words just for those times.

At that time the followers came to Jesus and asked, "Who is greatest in the kingdom of heaven?"

Jesus called a little child to him and stood the child before his followers. Then he said, "I tell you the truth, you must change and become like little children. Otherwise, you will never enter the kingdom of heaven. The greatest person in the kingdom of heaven is the one who makes himself humble like this child." *Matthew 18:1-4 (NCV)*

When a child doesn't know something, he/she will tug on your sleeve and ask for help! It is a simple equation to them – "I don't know so I ask someone who does and then I'll know." Period.

When I do not know how to <u>receive</u> the Father's love, I can take my clue from someone who does, a child, and just hold my arms out and take it in. When a child receives a parent's love, there are no barriers or preconceived ideas about how it will be delivered, he/she just knows it's coming and they hold their arms wide open and just receive it!

When I do not know how to <u>give</u> the Father's love, I can take my clue from someone who does, Jesus, who like a child, throws His arms out without any barriers or preconceived ideas about how it will flow out, and He just lets it happen!

Receiving must come before the giving and it is so, SO important that I take the time to allow my Father to pour out His love on me. I need nutrients for my physical body. I need 'Father love' for my spiritual life.

Let's just stop and be quiet and <u>receive</u> our Heavenly Father's love. Shhh.

Additional Text: John 10, Luke 11

2 Samuel Chapter 2 looks at the Lord's response to David's adultery with Bathsheba and the murder of her husband, Uriah. Nathan, the prophet, has gone to David with a story of a rich man who takes the only lamb of a poor man and slaughters it to feed a traveler instead of using one of his many lambs. David has said the rich man should die for what he has done to the poor man.

Then Nathan said to David, "You are the man!...Now there will always be people in your family who will die by a sword, because you did not respect me [the LORD]; you took the wife of Uriah the Hittite for yourself!...
Then David said to Nathan, "I have sinned against the LORD."
2 Samuel 12:7, 10, 13 (NCV)

I was struck by the simplicity of David's answer to Nathan. No excuses. No explanations. Just *"I have sinned against the LORD"*. He didn't blame it on his flesh. He didn't blame satan. *"I have sinned..."*.

Nathan answered, "The LORD has taken away your sin. You will not die. But what you did caused the LORD's enemies to lose all respect for him. For this reason the son who was born to you will die."   *2 Samuel 12:13-14 (NCV)*

When I sin, I say to the world (and to myself!), "I know better than You, God." Contempt is a harsh word but sin comes from rebellion and arrogance before God – and that IS contempt!

Then Nathan went home. And the LORD caused the son of David and Bathsheba,...to be very sick. David prayed to God for the baby. David refused to eat or drink.   *2 Samuel 12:15-16 (NCV)*

David repented for his sin and he asked God for mercy for his son. He KNEW the son's illness was a consequence for his sin. "Why did God allow an innocent child to die?" you might ask. I believe God KNEW that David would be a great servant for Him and leader but David needed to learn discipline and fear of the Lord. This event got his attention and he <u>did</u> learn Godly principles. See what follows after David is told the child is dead:

Then David got up from the floor, washed himself, put lotions on, and changed his clothes. Then he went into the LORD's house to worship..."While the baby was still alive, I refused to eat, and I cried. I thought 'Who knows? Maybe the LORD will feel sorry for me and let the baby live.' But now that the baby is dead,...I can't bring him back to life. Some day I will go to him, but he cannot come back to me."   *2 Samuel 12:20, 22-23 (NCV)*

I don't know that I am in the place that David was. But I want to get there. David saw with 'eternal' eyes. He may have lowered his eyes to the flesh level with Bathsheba but he has learned the lesson and lifted his eyes eternity and grabbed on to the lesson learned. And God sent him a confirmation blessing through Nathan, the prophet, saying their son, conceived in marriage, would be named "Jedidiah" which means, "loved by the Lord".

It was a hard lesson. Being a growing, maturing Christian is not for "weenies"! It's hard. It's eternal. It's AWESOME! It's GOD!!!

Additional Text: 2 Samuel 12, Psalm 42

May 25

O my people, listen to my teaching. Open your ears to what I am saying. For I will show you lessons from our history, stories handed down to us from former generations. I will reveal these truths to you so that you can describe these glorious deeds of Jehovah to your children, and tell them about the mighty miracles he did. Psalm 78:1-4 (TLB)

"I know how many good things you are doing. I have watched your hard work and your patience; I know you don't tolerate sin among your members, and you have carefully examined the claims of those who say they are apostles but aren't. You have found out how they lie. You have patiently suffered for me without quitting.

Yet there is one thing wrong; you don't love me as at first! Think about those times of your first love (how different now!) and turn back to me again and work as you did before; or else I will come and remove your candlestick from its place among the churches." Revelation 2:2-5 (TLB)

"I know you well – you are neither hot nor cold; I wish you were one or the other! But since you are merely lukewarm, I will spit you out of my mouth! You say, 'I am rich, with everything I want; I don't need a thing!' And you don't realize that spiritually you are wretched and miserable and poor and blind and naked...Look! I have been standing at the door and I am constantly knocking. If anyone hears me calling him and opens the door, I will come in and fellowship with him and he with me." Revelation 3:15-17, 20 (TLB)

Memorial Day always strikes at my heart more than Veterans Day. I'm not sure why exactly but maybe it's the giving of all that they had – their very lives that reaches my soul. I've been to Arlington Cemetery. I've wept in front of the Viet Nam War Memorial at the loss of friends and sobbed at the statue of the nurses holding a soldier and looking up for the chopper to come while his blood runs on the ground.

There is much discussion about the memorial that is to be built at "Ground Zero" in New York City. Psychologically I understand the need to do something – a closure for the almost 2,000 who will never be recovered.

These Scriptures seem to give me a more <u>eternal</u> memorial for those who have gone before me, and instruction in the 'memorial' that I leave <u>my</u> children, the next generation:

-- to tell them the deeds of the Lord, what He has done in the past and what He is doing in my life

-- to live out <u>every day</u> in my 'first love' feelings with the Lord. That these feelings never diminish; and that I openly repent when I sin.

-- and most importantly, I think, from my generation (with characteristics of our apathy and ambivalence) to give to the next generation that I <u>AM</u> 'hot' for the Lord, that I not just live a lukewarm, 'yeah, whatever!' life IN the Lord and that I STAND for something so they (my children) won't FALL for just anything!!!

Do I live out a <u>LIVING</u> MEMORIAL to God each day?

Additional Text: Revelation 2 and 3

May 26

Arise, shine, for your light has come, and the glory of the LORD has risen upon you. For behold, darkness shall cover the earth, and thick darkness the people; but the LORD will arise upon you, and his glory will be seen upon you. And nations shall come to your light, and kings to the brightness of your rising.

Isaiah 60:1-3 (ESV)

Is the Light of God in me such that people know it?

The people who walked in darkness have seen a great light; those who dwelt in a land of deep darkness, on them has light shined. *Isaiah 9:2 (ESV)*

In this passage of Isaiah, he is speaking prophetically of the Messiah. If Jesus lives in me, then His Light should be shining out of me like a beacon on a hill drawing all who are in the darkness of the world toward Him. I have been given my 'orders' plain and simple:

"...You shall love the Lord your God with all your heart and with all your soul and with all your mind. This is the great and first commandment. And the second is like it: you shall love your neighbor as yourself. On these two commandments depend all the Law and the Prophets." Matthew 22:37-40 (ESV)

"...All authority in heaven and on earth has been given to me. Go therefore and make disciples of all nations, baptizing them in the name of the Father and of the Son and of the Holy Spirit, teaching them to observe all that I have commanded you. And behold, I am with you always, to the end of the age."

Matthew 28:18-20 (ESV)

These are simple orders. I do not need a college education to grasp them! I am even told that all that I need to fulfill my orders has been given to me – including the constant presence of my Commander-in-Chief! The only obstacle holding me back from fulfilling my orders – is ME! How much longer will I let that excuse hold back the *glory* of God in my life? How much longer will I use excuses that include the responsibilities of my job, the needs of my family, the 'stuff' that I made a commitment to (without asking GOD, by the way!), and the expectations of others on how I should spend my time and talents? Do I think that God is not aware of these things? Do I think that God would have me go do what He is asking of me and let my children starve?!! What message am I sending my children if I am NOT doing the will of God? Now that is worse than starving!

I know, O LORD, that the way of man is not in himself, that it is not in man who walks to direct his steps. Correct me, O LORD, but in justice; not in your anger, lest you bring me to nothing. *Jeremiah 10:23-24 (ESV)*

Additional Text: 1 Corinthians 4, Psalm 14

When Joseph's brothers saw that their father was dead, they said, "It may be that Joseph will hate us and pay us back for all the evil that we did to him." So they sent a message to Joseph, saying, "Your father gave this command before he died, 'Say to Joseph, Please forgive the transgression of your brothers and their sin, because they did evil to you.' And now, please forgive the transgression of the servants of the God of you father." Joseph wept when they spoke to him. His brothers also came and fell down before him and said "Behold, we are your servants." But Joseph said to them, "Do not fear, for am I in the place of God? As for you, you meant evil against me, but God meant it for good, to bring it about that many people should be kept alive, as they are today."...Thus he comforted them and spoke kindly to them.

Genesis 50:15-21 (ESV)

"If your brother sins against you, go and tell him his fault, between you and him alone. If he listens to you, you have gained your brother. But if he does not listen, take one or two others along with you, that every charge may be established by the evidence of two or three witnesses...

Then Peter came up and said to him, "Lord, how often will my brother sin against me, and I forgive him? As many as seven times?" Jesus said to him, "I do not say to you seven times but seventy times seven."

Matthew 18:15-16, 21-22 (ESV)

Do you think Peter was talking about Andrew, his brother? Or maybe another unnamed biological brother? Mark had recorded Jesus' definition of 'brother' in chapter 3 of his gospel: *"Whoever does the will of God, he is my brother and sister and mother." V. 35* So maybe Peter is just talking about general forgiveness and offense and not a specific person or incident.

However when I apply Peter's question and Jesus' words to a specific person and incident in <u>my</u> mind it is much more difficult to say "Yes, Lord" in perfect obedience and the DO IT! It's all about 'rights' and 'fair' in my mind. Ah-Ha! It's about love and forgiveness in GOD'S mind!!!

Joseph's story takes me a step further and asks me to just suppose that what if God had a higher purpose in allowing the circumstance with the person who has 'wronged' me? Could it be even something as basic but SO IMPORTANT to God like love and forgiveness??!!!

And Jesus said, "Father, forgive them, for they know not what they do."

Luke 23:34 (ESV)

Tommy Tenny has said in his book, <u>Secret Source of Power</u>, that the cross should always remind us that forgiveness is not cheap. I might also add – not easy! But look at what forgiveness can do!!!

To whom do I need to GIVE forgiveness today? How much longer will I refuse to freely give?

"...give, and it will be given to you. Good measure, pressed down, shaken together, running over, will be put into your lap. For with the measure you use it will be measured back to you." Luke 6:38 (ESV)

"Heal the sick, raise the dead, cleanse those who have leprosy, drive out demons. Freely you have received, freely give." Matthew 10:8

Behold, how good and pleasant it is when brothers dwell in unity! It is like the precious oil on the head, running down on the beard, on the beard of Aaron, running down on the collar of his robes! It is like the dew of Hermon, which falls on the mountains of Zion! For there the LORD has commanded the blessing, life evermore.   *Psalm 133 (ESV)*

"I do not ask for these only, but also for those who will believe in me through their word, that they may all be one, just as you, Father, are in me, and I in you, that they also may be in us, so that the world may believe that you have sent me. The glory that you have given me I have given to them, that they may be one even as we are one, I in them and you in me, that they may become perfectly one, so that the world may know that you sent me and loved them even as you loved me."   *John 17:20-23 (ESV)*

We who are strong have an obligation to bear with the failings of the weak, and not to please ourselves. Let each of us please his neighbor for his good, to build him up. For Christ did not please himself, but as it is written, "The reproaches of those who reproached you fell on me." For whatever was written in former days was written for our instruction, that through endurance and through the encouragement of the Scriptures we might have hope. May the God of endurance and encouragement grant you to live in such harmony with one another, in accord with Christ Jesus, that together you may with one voice glorify the God and Father of our Lord Jesus Christ. Therefore, welcome one another as Christ has welcomed you, for the glory of God. Romans 15:1-7 (ESV)

Well, gosh, not only does God want me to be in unity with 'my brothers and sisters' but I am to glorify Him by putting up with them [bear with the failings!] AND encouraging them!!! 'Rebuke' or 'discipline' to MY correct way of thinking isn't listed!!! In fact, when I look up those words (rebuke and discipline) in my concordance, the Scriptures eight out of 10 times related those words only to GOD'S authority. When given outside of God, they refer to a rebuke in LOVE (and I hear the loud warning to my intentions in that!), or they refer to the authority of a parent.

Jesus spoke quite clearly and frankly about His expectation that we LOVE and BEAR WITH one another above and beyond what is expected and done by the 'average' person: He said –

"If you love those who love you, what benefit is that to you? For even sinners love those who love them. And if you do good to those who do good to you, what benefit is that to you? For even sinners do the same...But love your enemies, and do good, and lend, expecting nothing in return, and your reward will be great, and you will be sons of the Most High, for he is kind to the ungrateful and the evil. Be merciful, even as your Father is merciful."

                                       Luke 6:32-33, 35-36 (ESV)

And to 'top off' this message to me, God clearly tapped me on the shoulder and pointed His finger in our home to my husband and son. 'Unity' and 'Encouragement' and 'Bearing with' and 'Love' must begin RIGHT HERE!!!! And RIGHT NOW!!!! If I only show Jesus' example to others and leave these two most important ones out -- then that's all it is --- SHOW!!!

The woman said, "Sir, I can see that you are a prophet. My ancestors worshiped on this mountain, but you Jews say Jerusalem is the only place to worship." Jesus said to her: Believe me, the time is coming when you won't worship the Father either on this mountain or in Jerusalem. You Samaritans don't really know the one you worship. But we Jews do know the God we worship, and by using us, God will save the world. But a time is coming, and it is already here! Even now the true worshipers are being led by the Sprit to worship the Father according to the truth. These are the ones the Father is seeking to worship him." John 4:19-23 (CEV)

When my husband, Henry and I began to look for a new church to attend, it was very difficult. I had only attended two churches in my entire 40+ years. I confess that I had a preconceived notion about the church that God would send us to – what it would look like, how the worship would be, who the pastor would be as well as what his (yes, <u>his</u>) giftings would be. Whether or not the Spirit of God was in and flowing through the church would manifest itself by MY standards!

I have heard similar stories from college students, seminary students, and even an adult friend of mine who three years ago felt led to a church (and stayed) but admits that he has been 'bothered' by the fact that there was no cross as a focal point of the sanctuary. Others, including myself, have shared about the need for candles, order of worship, and even the Bible version that is read.

Jesus doesn't mention any of those things in His priorities of what 'true worship' is. He says only that we are to "*worship the Father in spirit and truth*". Now I could rationalize that all those 'things' that I wanted could be manifestations of the Holy Spirit and God's truth. But what I hear in my spirit is – all those 'things' are <u>minors</u> and God is trying to get me to look at <u>major</u> issues. Issue. One '<u>major issue</u>' – "Jody, if I am present for you to worship and you are present worshipping <u>in</u> My Spirit and <u>in</u> My Truth, then the rest are just minor issues."

I think of Hungary (or Eastern Europe in general just a few years ago), China, and other places where Christian worship has been and still is being done in secret and in places that certainly do not LOOK like places of worship. The church that I visited my first Sunday in Hungary looks like an office building. The Communists had allowed the building to be built for a church but they got to plan and determine the architecture inside and out. The enemy used them to make the building as 'un-church-like' as he could get it. Those people didn't care! They were SO HUNGRY (no pun intended!) to worship God that they didn't care what it looked like!!!

...and they were singing the song that his servant Moses and the Lamb had sun. They were singing: "Lord God All-Powerful, you have done great and marvelous things. You are the ruler of all nations, and you do what is right and fair. Lord, who doesn't honor and praise your name? You alone are holy, and all nations will come and worship you, because you have shown that you judge with fairness." Revelation 15:3-4 (CEV)

Then the LORD said to Noah, "Go into the ark, you and all your household, for I have seen that you are righteous before me in this generation...For in seven days I will send rain on the earth forty days and forty nights, and every living thing that I have made I will blot out from the face of the ground." And Noah did all that the LORD commanded him...In the six hundredth year of Noah's life, in the second month, on the seventeenth day of the month, on that day all the fountains of the great deep burst forth, and the windows of the heavens were opened. And rain fell upon the earth forty days and forty nights.

Genesis 7:1,4-5, 11-12 (ESV)

I believe that this really happened. I believe Noah and his wife and sons and daughters-in-law were ridiculed by everyone they knew for building this huge boat. And then the rain came. And came. And came. And the boat began to float. And the cries outside the boat began as people realized that the water was going to continue to rise and the rain was going to continue to fall. Aunts, uncles, cousins, friends – all crying outside the boat "Help!" "Noah!" "Jehovah, help us!" But it was too late.

The apostle, Paul, someone who KNEW the law, also knew we could NOT obtain our eternal salvation by obedience to the law and the works of our own hands.

For by grace you have been saved through faith. And this is not your own doing; it is the gift of God, not a result of works, so that no one may boast. For we are his workmanship, created in Christ Jesus for good works, which God prepared beforehand, that we should walk in them. *Ephesians 2:8-10 (ESV)*

Scripture tells us that *"Noah was a righteous man, blameless among the people of his time, and he walked with God." Genesis 6:9* It doesn't say this inclusively, extending to his wife, sons, and their wives. It seems to imply that they came under Noah's 'umbrella'. If that is so, I wonder what went through their minds as they sat inside this boat hearing the cries of those outside and remembering their own moments of unrighteousness. A reminder to <u>me</u> that *"It is by grace you have been saved."*

I do not know what it is going to be like in the times ahead. There's the rapture where I could be in line at Wal-Mart and then GONE! Will the woman and her 12-year-old son in front of me stay? There's Judgment Day where Jesus calls me as a 'sheep' to come join Him at the wedding feast. Will I notice the 'goats' walking the other way?

Now is the time for me to realize that I have been called to be a part of the 'Heaven Bound Tours'. There may be many who are watching, silently wondering about this huge boat that GOD has built. (HE built it—it's that 'grace thing'!) There may be some who are openly critical and down right UGLY about the invitation! There may be many who are 'clue-less' and seemingly do not care. While God builds the boat, He has sent me to invite others to come. He really doesn't want anyone crying outside after the door is shut. What excuse do I have today for not sharing about this 'grace thing'?

Additional Text: Romans 3, Hebrews 2

How can a young person live a pure life? By obeying your word.
With all my heart I try to obey you. Don't let me break your commands.
I have taken your words to heart so I would not sin against you.
LORD, you should be praised. Teach me your demands.
My lips will tell about all the laws you have spoken.
I enjoy living by your rules as people enjoy great riches.
I think about your orders and study your ways.
I enjoy obeying your demands, and I will not forget your word.
Psalm 119:9-16 (NCV)

One night, I went to Brownsville Assembly of God to attend their weekly service. Rev. Steve Hill was there. One of the Scriptures in his sermon jumped from the page of my Bible and pierced my heart.

If you make a promise to God, don't be slow to keep it. God is not happy with fools, so give God what you promised.   *Ecclesiastes 5:4 (NCV)*

Many times I <u>pray</u> a Scripture. That is a very powerful thing to me – praying God's anointed words. Praying the verses of Psalm 119 *"I will not forget your word"* sounds like a promise or vow to me!

God has given me His own words to advise me and lead me through each day of my life. They are <u>words</u> of Life. They are promises from the Lord Himself. He takes <u>His</u> vows seriously and I can testify that His promises are true. Are my promises to Him taken with the same "covenant mind"?

We set our eyes not on what we see but on what we cannot see. What we see will last only a short time, but what we cannot see will last forever.
2 Corinthians 4:18 (NCV)

We have around us many people whose lives tell us what faith means. SO let us run the race that is before us and never give up. We should remove from our lives anything that would get in the way and sin that so easily holds us back. Let us look only to Jesus, the One who began our faith and who makes it perfect. He suffered death on the cross. But he accepted the shame as if it were nothing because of the joy that God put before him. Now he is sitting at the right side of God's throne. Think about Jesus' example. He held on, while wicked people were doing evil things to him. So do not get tired and stop trying.
Hebrews 12:1-3 (NCV)

"Teacher, which command in the law is the most important?"
Jesus answered, " ' Love the Lord your God with all your heart, all your soul, and all your mind.' This is the first and most important command. And the second command is like the first: 'Love your neighbor as you love yourself.' All the law and the writings of the prophets depend on these two commands."
Matthew 22:36-40 (NCV)

"I will not neglect your word". Jesus said loving the Lord first and foremost with all that I am and loving others as myself is the basis for everything else. How am I doing on 'neglecting' or paying attention to THAT word?

Additional Text: Psalm 90, Matthew 13

Leah Bridges Taylor

Growing up as an Army brat and the youngest of three, Leah accepted Jesus as her Savior in middle school. She was a place kicker on her high school football team and played soccer through college. She became one of the NCAA's Women of the Year. Now a young wife and mother of two, ages 3 and 1 ½, Leah is also a teacher and gifted vocalist.

"I pray that the LORD will bless and protect you, and that he will show you mercy and kindness. May the LORD be good to you and give you peace."

Numbers 6:24-26 (CEV)

The most extra, extra, extraordinary time in my life has been the time I have been pregnant and now a mother of two children. God has allowed me to be a part of that. Linda Smith told me once that 'anyone who wants to enter this life has to enter through the womb of a woman'. It is the gateway of life. I think we have taken that extraordinary experience and we as a nation abort, ignore, or abuse it. I am not 'just' a stay-at-home mom. If my children can know Jesus and affect God's kingdom for Christ, there is nothing more important to me in this world. I pray for my children every night that they would wear those shoes of the gospel of peace and carry the gospel anywhere they go and be forever on their lips. God created me for that. We (women) are not created the same as men. Not greater or less than, we're just created different. And we are able to experience a child move within us. When we 'meet' this child for the first time, we already KNOW this child. It's a miracle.

I don't want to be one of those overbearing, over protective mothers but I also know that there is just a window here when they are so young and they need us. That is the most important thing that I can be doing is give myself to them. I have plenty of time to do a job later on. As long as we are able and my husband agrees that I can stay at home, I am going to do that. That is what personally works for us. My husband is a minor league baseball player and we have to move around a lot. I am always there when the children go to sleep and wake up in the morning, whether we are in a hotel on the road or in an apartment in Virginia or Oklahoma. I am able to be there and be the home base. God has taught me that the state or condition of my house is not as important as the condition of my heart. My heart creates the feeling of a haven for people to come here and be welcome.

We need to allow ourselves as a 'new' mom to receive a lot of grace because our quiet time does not exist for a while! There will be 'seasons' when our schedule is interrupted because of the demands put on our time. It works for me to get up in the morning and walk before anyone is awake and then come home and be in the Word. And, yes, there was also a time that I was so exhausted with the second pregnancy that I couldn't get up that early. My time with the Lord is not to be legalistic but a relationship and God knows my heart and that I desire to spend time with Him.

Let them give thanks to the LORD for his love and for the miracle he does for people. Let them offer sacrifices to him. With joy they should tell what he has done.

Others went out to sea in ships and did business on the great oceans. They saw what the LORD could do, the miracles he did in the deep oceans. He spoke, and a storm came up, which blew up high waves...In their misery they cried out to the LORD, and he saved them from their troubles. He stilled the storm and calmed the waves. They were happy that it was quiet, and God guided them to the port they wanted. Let them give thanks to the LORD for his love and for the miracles he does for people. Let them praise his greatness in the meeting of the people; let them praise him in the meeting of the older leaders.

Psalm 107:21-25, 28-32 (NCV)

One day Jesus and his followers got into a boat, and he said to them, "Let's go across the lake." And so they started across. While they were sailing, Jesus fell asleep. A very strong wind blew up on the lake, causing the boat to fill with water, and they were in danger. The followers went to Jesus and woke him, saying, "Master! Master! We will drown!" Jesus got up and gave a command to the wind and the waves. They stopped, and it became calm. Jesus said to his followers, "Where is your faith?" The followers were afraid and amazed and said to each other, "Who is this that commands even the wind and the water, and they obey him?"

Luke 8:22-25 (NCV)

Both of these Scriptures tell us clearly that God commands the storms, even creates them. It is hard for me sometimes to accept that God not only knows about the storms in my life – He has the power to create <u>and</u> the ability to calm them and chooses not to do so!

I believe I was created by God to worship Him and have intimate fellowship with Him. That was His original plan with Adam and Eve and that is His plan with me. That's the "Big Picture" as near as I can wrap my little finite mind around it. God may use 'storms' in my life (and those that I love) to cause me (and them!) to cry out to Him – to come closer to Him, leaving behind the things that are separating us; knowing that only <u>HE</u> can calm the storm and make all things new.

And so I wait and trust in the One who can calm my storms. Meanwhile, I pray –

I ask only one thing from the LORD. This is what I want:

Let me live in the LORD's house all my life. Let me see the LORD's beauty and look with my own eyes at his Temple. During danger he will keep me safe in his shelter. He will hide me in his Holy Tent, or he will keep me safe on a high mountain.

Psalm 27:4-5 (NCV)

When I <u>choose</u> to 'dwell' so close to God that I am actually in His house, the storms may rage outside but I am safe with Him, standing firm on the Rock, Jesus Christ.

Additional Text: 2 Corinthians 12, Hebrews 13

Praise be to the God and Father of our Lord Jesus Christ, the Father of compassion and the God of all comfort, who comforts us in all our troubles, so that we can comfort those in any trouble with the comfort we ourselves have received from God. For just as the sufferings of Christ flow over into our lives, so also through Christ our comfort overflows. If we are distressed, it is for your comfort and salvation; if we are comforted, it is for your comfort, which produces in you patient endurance of the same sufferings we suffer. And our hope for you is firm, because we know that just as you share in our sufferings, so also you share in our comfort.   *2 Corinthians 1:3-8*

I know I have read this passage many times but today I just received how many solid truths and points I can meditate and stand on:

- God is the Father of compassion and all comfort. It is not in our human nature to be compassionate or comforting – it all comes from His Holy Spirit.

- the comfort that I receive from Him has a two-fold purpose: to comfort me and to be passed on to others who need comfort.

- the sufferings I am going through – Jesus has already passed that way. Yes, every one that I can list, He has gone through something similar. So, I can stand on the promise that the comfort will come, too.

- sometimes it's hard to step back and see the bigger picture that my distresses CAN benefit others. CAN be a testimony and encourage THEIR faith in the Lord. I can honestly say that sometimes I didn't even CARE if it would benefit others – I didn't want to go through it and I didn't want to see the 'redeeming value' of it!!! That's when my 'pity party' would reach its peak!!! I'm going to meditate on this part for a while. I have a feeling that there may be a connection to Paul's other truth about being "content in all circumstances" [Phil. 4:11] ouch!

- Sharing our hardships with one another is IMPORTANT! A burden shared is less of a burden! And as Paul testified, it recognizes that when we are weak, God is strong. I will also meditate on how often I rely on myself instead of God. I know that God is not saying that I should lie around like a slug and wait for Him to do EVERYTHING but I suspect that I am not where I am suppose to be on reliance on Him vs. me! Note: Paul states clearly that they were in such despair as they thought they would die. God will allow us to reach the 'end of our rope' so that He gets all the glory/credit for pulling us up!

- Because of these hardships, hope is firmly planted through the testimony of the experience.

- Paul recognizes the part that the Prayer Partners played. When going through the hardship, the power of prayer from the Body of Christ is extraordinary! It is knowing that there IS an Aaron and Hur on either side of me, holding up my arms when I grow weary! [Exodus 17:10-13]

- And the testimony continues as more people catch on to the power of God! We KNOW that He will not leave us nor forsake us!!! We KNOW it!!!

- Never forget to give thanks IN ALL THINGS! From hardship to resolution, give thanks! (1 Thessalonians 5:16-17)

One day late in June, when I was thirty years old, the heavens were suddenly opened to me and I saw visions from God.   Ezekiel 1:1 (TLB)

I've stood beside some rivers and looked up at the sky, admiring the beautiful clouds and bright blue sky. Can you imagine what it would be like to see the clouds part and "TA-DA!!!"? Like Ezekiel, I would spend time later trying to describe what I had seen – GOD! I encourage you to look at the next 24 verses in the first chapter of Ezekiel and how this prophet, as the apostle John did later in Revelation, <u>TRIED</u> to describe something that defied human words and dimensions.

For high in the sky above them was what looked like a throne made of beautiful blue sapphire stones, and upon it sat someone who appeared to be a Man.

From his waist up, he seemed to be all glowing bronze, dazzling like fire; and from his waist down he seemed to be entirely flame, and there was a glowing halo like a rainbow all around him. That was the way the glory of the Lord appeared to me. And when I saw it, I fell face downward on the ground, and heard the voice of someone speaking to me: Ezekiel 1:26-28 (TLB)

Yes, I think I might fall face down, too. And this was just the <u>glory</u> of the Lord!! Ezekiel doesn't say this was the Lord Himself that made him fall to the ground!!!

"Son of dust," he said, "I am sending you to the nation of Israel, to a nation rebelling against me. They and their fathers have kept on sinning against me until this very hour. For they are hardhearted, stiff-necked people. But I am sending you to give them my messages – the messages of the Lord God. And whether they listen or not (for remember, they are rebels), they will at least know they have had a prophet among them. Son of dust, don't be afraid of them; don't be frightened even though their threats are sharp and barbed and sting like scorpions. Don't be dismayed by their dark scowls. For remember, they are rebels! You must give them my messages whether they listen or not (but they won't, for they are utter rebels). Listen, son of dust, to what I say to you. Don't you be a rebel, too! Open your mouth and eat what I give you."

                                                    Ezekiel 2:3-8 (TLB)

Can you hear the Lord saying –

"Do not be afraid"

"You <u>must</u> speak my words to them"

"It doesn't matter whether they listen or not"

"<u>You</u>! YOU, Jody, be obedient to the words I tell you. Whether any one else is obedient – <u>you</u> be obedient!"

This really does strike an arrow to my heart about these devotions. They are for <u>ME</u>! Sharing them with others is the <u>second</u> order God gives me and will mean <u>nothing</u> in my spiritual life if I do not obey the first!

Additional Text: Ezekiel 36 and 37

June 4

When a person's steps follow the LORD, God is pleased with his ways. If he stumbles, he will not fall, because the LORD holds his hand. I was young, and now I am old, but I have never seen good people left helpless or their children begging for food.   *Psalm 37:23-25 (NCV)*

My child, hold on to wisdom and good sense. Don't let them out of your sight. They will give you life and beauty like a necklace around your neck. Then you will go your way in safety, and you will not get hurt. When you lie down, you won't be afraid; when you lie down, you will sleep in peace. You won't be afraid of sudden trouble; you won't fear the ruin that comes to the wicked, because the LORD will keep you safe. He will keep you from being trapped.
Proverbs 3:21-26 (NCV)

Taking a step in faith. Seems simple. Basic.

Faith means being sure of the things we hope for and knowing that something is real even if we do not see it.   *Hebrews 11:1 (NCV)*

Taking a step of faith means that I am stepping out into a place (a decision) that I am only <u>hoping</u> for and I CERTAIN-LY do <u>not</u> see!

The psalmist says, however, that though I might stumble – I won't fall. In his many years of experience, he testifies that he has <u>NEVER</u> seen those who seek the Lord and are obedient, forsaken by God and He has always met their needs. ALWAYS! With that, I am admonished to ask the Lord for 'sound judgment' and 'discernment'. They are tools given by God as I listen to Him and take my 'steps of faith'.

I love that verse *"You won't be afraid of sudden trouble"*. It does not give me an ironclad promise that there will not be 'sudden trouble'. It says I shouldn't <u>fear</u> it! God is there before me. I am not alone. <u>HE</u> will guide me through and give me HIS strength and wisdom. WOW! God is SO GOOD!!! SO FAITHFUL!!!

King Ahab told Jezebel everything Elijah had done and how Elijah had killed all the prophets with a sword. So Jezebel sent a messenger to Elijah, saying, "May the god punish me terribly if by this time tomorrow I don't kill you just as you killed those prophets."

When Elijah heard this, he was afraid and ran for his life, taking his servant with him. When they came to Beersheba in Judah, Elijah left his servant there. Then Elijah walked for a whole day into the desert. He sat down under a bush and asked to die. "I have had enough, LORD," he prayed..."LORD God All-Powerful, I have always served you as well as I could. But the people of Israel have broken their agreement with you, destroyed your altars, and killed your prophets with swords. I am the only prophet left, and now they are trying to kill me, too."

The LORD said to Elijah, "Go, stand in front of me on the mountain, and I will pass by you."   *1 Kings 19:1-4, 10-11*

No matter the circumstances of my life, the Lord is there.

Additional Text: 1 Kings 19, John 10

The things that happened to those people are examples. They were written down to teach us, because we live in a time when all these things of the past have reached their goal. If you think you are strong, you should be careful not to fall. The only temptation that has come to you is that which everyone has. But you can trust God, who will not permit you to be tempted more than you can stand. But when you are tempted, he will also give you a way to escape so that you will be able to stand it...

"We are allowed to do all things," but all things are not good for us to do. "We are allowed to do all things," but not all things help others grow stronger. Do not look out only for yourselves. Look out for the good of others also.

1 Corinthians 10:11-13, 23-24 (NCV)

Are there things in my life that are "permissible" but not beneficial or constructive to my life? I could qualify that and say my 'spiritual' life but my spiritual life IS my life. Maybe it makes me feel better to try to separate my 'spiritual' life from the rest of my life but there really isn't any separation possible. If I want God to be in my life (guide, director, protector) then do I separate my life into rooms and invite Him into some but then turn and say, "Hey, Lord, uh...I gotta go do something in here so why don't You just hang out over there?!"

So as I look at the TOTAL rooms in my life are there 'hairballs' under the bed and 'cobwebs' in the upper corners that while not causing an overt health problem, they are not inviting the Lord into a clean house. AND when I invite others in (to hang around me) whether they are believers or not, they notice the 'dirt' and wonder just what kind of spiritual housekeeper I am!

I don't want my life to be just a place for 'SHOW'. I want my life to be a place that the Lord desires to use it as His dwelling. God is holy. There is no compromise. He comes closer to me as I leave behind the 'sin that so easily entangles' (Hebrews 12:1) and move closer to His holiness. God does not force His glory or His presence on me. He allows me to refuse His invitation. He desires that I choose Him and choose to be holy. He gives me the Holy Sprit that is the 'voice' inside of me reminding me of the Father's words and wisdom. I have all I need to build a temple where God lives. It is a 'glass' temple that allows God to shine forth so that all others see, all that they remember, is Him.

So prepare your minds for service and have self-control. All your hope should be for the gift of grace that will be yours when Jesus Christ is shown to you. Now that you are obedient children of God do not live as you did in the past. You did not understand, so you did the evil things you wanted. But be holy in all you do, just as God the One who called you, is holy. It is written in the Scriptures: "You must be holy, because I am holy." 1 Peter 1:13-16 (NCV)

Additional Text: Hebrews 12, Revelation 22

June 6

The high and lofty one who inhabits eternity, the Holy One, says this: I live in that high and holy place where those with contrite, humble spirits dwell; and I refresh the humble and give new courage to those with repentant hearts. For I will not fight against you forever, nor always show my wrath; if I did, all mankind would perish – the very souls that I have made. I was angry and smote these greedy men. But they went right on sinning, doing everything their evil hearts desired. I have seen what they do, but I will heal them anyway! I will lead them and comfort them, helping them to mourn and to confess their sins. Peace, peace to them, both near and far, for I will heal them all.

Isaiah 57:15-19 (TLB)

Isaiah had a tough job. Most prophets do! Isaiah would bring a word of stern, I mean stern (!), rebuke to Israel but then when the people would respond with repentance and contrite hearts, God would give a word of restoration and encouragement. I receive that, too!

In this passage, God says that He lives in the 'heavenlies' but also with those who are humble (Micah 6:8). He promises He will not stay angry with me for He knows my weakness, my human frailties. He even explains what make Him angry with me, especially my rebellion and 'willful ways'. And then, the <u>best</u> part, He states His promises to <u>heal</u> me, <u>guide</u> me, and <u>comfort</u> me. God knows what I need to be restored. He knows what I need to know His peace. He knows what will produce PRAISE for <u>HIM</u> in me! He KNOWS!

O loving and kind God, have mercy. Have pity upon me and take away the awful stain of my transgressions. Oh, wash me, cleanse me from this guilt. Let me be pure again. For I admit my shameful deed – it haunts me day and night. It is against you and you alone I sinned, and did this terrible thing. You saw it all, and your sentence against me is just. But I was born a sinner, yes, from the moment my mother conceived me. You deserve honesty from the heart; yes, utter sincerity and truthfulness. Oh, give me this wisdom.

Sprinkle me with the cleansing blood and I shall be clean again. Wash me and I shall be whiter than snow. And after you have punished me, give me back my joy again. Don't keep looking at my sins – erase them from your sight. Create in me a new, clean heart, O God, filled with clean thoughts and right desires. Don't toss me aside, banished forever from your presence. Don't take your Holy Sprit from me. Restore to me again the joy of your salvation and make me willing to obey you. Then I will teach your ways to other sinners, and they – guilty like me – will repent and return to you. Don't sentence me to death. O my God, you alone can rescue me. Then I will sing of your forgiveness, for my lips will be unsealed – oh, how I will praise you.

You don't want penance; if you did, how gladly I would do it you aren't interested in offerings burned before you on the altar. It is a broken spirit you want – remorse and penitence. A broken and contrite heart, O God, you will not ignore.

Psalm 51:1-17 (TLB)

Additional Text: Micah 6, Psalm 69

Much has certainly been written about the 'prayer of Jabez':

Jabez called upon the God of Israel, saying, "Oh that you would bless me and enlarge my border, and that your hand might be with me, and that you would keep me from harm so that it might not bring me pain!" And God granted what he asked.   *1 Chronicles 4:10 (ESV)*

I have taken some time to read the follow-up book to the Prayer of Jabez, by Bruce Wilkinson, which is called Secrets of the Vine, which looks at John 15. Bear with me as I share the Scripture the Lord took me to this morning. [God, or Yahweh, is speaking.]

"Enlarge the place of your tent, and let the curtains of your habitations be stretched out; do not hold back; lengthen your cords and strengthen your stakes. For you will spread abroad to the right and to the left, and your offspring will possess the nations and will people the desolate cities. Fear not, for you will not be ashamed; be not confounded, for you will not be disgraced; for you will forget the shame of your youth, and the reproach of your widowhood you will remember no more. For your Maker is your husband, the LORD of hosts is his name; the Holy One of Israel is your Redeemer, the God of the whole earth he is called.   *Isaiah 54:2-5 (ESV)*

The prayer that Jabez made is important, or significant, to me for two reasons. First, in the midst of pages (in my NIV) of genealogies there is a prayer – AND it says that, "*God granted what he asked*". That does seem to 'highlight' the thought conveyed.

Second, I have spoke to many people that are praying that prayer and commented that they didn't pray consistently for themselves before they had read Mr. Wilkinson's book. While I do not see any one prayer as a 'good luck' talisman, praying is good! And God will handle the rest!

In taking me to Isaiah 54, I felt the Lord speaking to me in a very similar context as the 1 Chronicles 4 passage. ANY Scripture can be spoken by me as a prayer to the Lord. I felt His delight that I would use HIS words to pray to Him. He just wants me to pray – to have a conversation with Him, right?

If I think of prayer as just that, a conversation with God, I can begin with 10 minutes. Rarely do I sit down with any new friend and have a two-hour non-stop conversation. My relationship builds as I make the commitment to talk to God every day and I see the fruit that comes from that time like answered prayer and the courage, peace, and wisdom for each day. God is faithful and ready to talk. The question is: am I? What is my excuse today for missing time with God?

Additional Text: Deuteronomy 30, Proverbs 12

But you, man of God, flee from all this, and pursue righteousness, godliness, faith, love, endurance and gentleness. Fight the good fight of the faith. Take hold of the eternal life to which you were called when you made your good confession in the presence of many witnesses. In the sight of God, who gives life to everything, and of Christ Jesus, who while testifying before Pontius Pilate made the good confession, I charge you to keep this command without spot or blame until the appearing of our Lord Jesus Christ, which God will bring about in his own time--God, the blessed and only Ruler, the King of kings and Lord of lords, who alone is immortal and who lives in unapproachable light, whom no one has seen or can see. To him be honor and might forever. Amen.

1 Timothy 6:11-16

Jesus <u>did</u> testify before Pilate [John 18:28-19:16]. He testified to the <u>truth</u> knowing that the consequence was death. I, too, am to testify to the truth of Jesus and what He has done in my life and the consequence is the death of self. If I testify and yet live my life the way <u>I</u> want then my testimony has no power and is nothing but "show". When I die to my own plan and control, then my testimony takes on power from the Holy Spirit and will pierce hearts with the love and changing power of God.

"I tell you the truth, whoever hears my word and believes him who sent me has eternal life and will not be condemned; he has crossed over from death to life. I tell you the truth, a time is coming and has now come when the dead will hear the voice of the Son of God and those who hear will live... Do not be amazed at this, for a time is coming when all who are in their graves will hear his voice and come out--those who have done good will rise to live, and those who have done evil will rise to be condemned. By myself I can do nothing; I judge only as I hear, and my judgment is just, for I seek not to please myself but him who sent me. If I testify about myself, my testimony is not valid. There is another who testifies in my favor, and I know that his testimony about me is valid... I do not accept praise from men, but I know you. I know that you do not have the love of God in your hearts. I have come in my Father's name, and you do not accept me; but if someone else comes in his own name, you will accept him. How can you believe if you accept praise from one another, yet make no effort to obtain the praise that comes from the only God? But do not think I will accuse you before the Father. Your accuser is Moses, on whom your hopes are set. If you believed Moses, you would believe me, for he wrote about me. But since you do not believe what he wrote, how are you going to believe what I say?"

John 5:24-25, 28-32, 41-47

Many times in my testimony I feel I have to <u>convince</u> someone that what I say is true. Jesus tells me in this passage that I need only accept the praise of the Father not the praise of men. I testify with the power and guidance of His Holy Spirit and let Him do the rest. Jesus gives me the example that Moses testified about Him and the leaders and scholars of His time did not believe MOSES so He is not surprised that they didn't believe "the carpenter's son". It's all about having an open heart and listening ears wrapped in an obedient spirit that will speak or 'hush' by the power of God's Holy Spirit.

I will extol you, my God and King, and bless your name forever and ever. Every day I will bless you and praise your name forever and ever. Great is the LORD, and greatly to be praised, and his greatness is unsearchable.
One generation shall commend your works to another, and shall declare your mighty acts. On the glorious splendor of your majesty, and on your wondrous works, I will meditate.   *Psalm 145:1-5 (ESV)*

Jesus said to them, "Truly, I say to you, in the new world, when the Son of Man will sit on his glorious throne, you who have followed me will also sit on twelve thrones, judging the twelve tribes of Israel. And everyone who has left houses or brothers or sisters or father or mother or children or lands, for my name's sake, will receive a hundredfold and will inherit eternal life. But many who are first will be last, and the last first."   *Matthew 10:28-30 (ESV)*

Glorious. When I think of the word "glorious", earthly things just do not come up to that indescribable word. Brides and babies are beautiful and wondrous in their glow and perfection — but "glorious"? No, that word doesn't come to me.

I think "glorious", "reverence", and "adoration" are exclusively God-words to me. I can't imagine an earthly person or object to connect with those words.

Brothers, join in imitating me, and keep your eyes on those who walk according to the example you have in us. For many, of whom I have often told you and now tell you even with tears, walk as enemies of the cross of Christ. Their end is destruction, their god is their belly, and they glory in their shame, with minds set on earthly things. But our citizenship is in heaven, and from it we await a Savior, the Lord Jesus Christ, who will transform our lowly body to be like his glorious body, by the power that enable shim even to subject all things to himself.   *Philippians 3:17-21 (ESV)*

Now that really is hard for me to wrap my mind around — I am going to be "GLORIOUS"! It's all about Jesus and what <u>HE</u> did and <u>HE</u> is doing in me, and for me. His righteousness. His blood, covering my "<u>un</u>-glorious-ness"!!! I will be a reflection of Jesus. Laying my "glorious-ness" from Him down at the Father's feet in adoration and reverence. WOW!

After this I looked; and behold, a door standing open in heaven! And the first voice, which I had heard speaking to me like a trumpet, said, "Come up here, and I will show you what must take place after this." At once I was in the Spirit, and behold, a throne stood in heaven, with one seated on the throne...Around the throne were twenty-four thrones, and seated on the thrones were twenty-four elders, clothed in white garments, with golden crowns on their heads...

And whenever the living creatures give glory and honor and thanks to him who is seated on the throne, who lives forever and ever, the twenty-four elders fall down before him who is seated on the throne and worship him who lives forever and ever. They cast their crowns before the throne, saying, "Worthy are you, our Lord and God, to receive glory and honor and power, for created all things, and by your will they existed and were created."   *Revelation 4:1-2, 4, 9-11 (ESV)*

Additional Text: Revelation 5, Psalm 111

"And it shall come to pass afterward, that I will pour out my Spirit on all flesh; your sons and your daughters shall prophesy, your old men shall dream dreams, and your young men shall see visions. Even on the male and female servants in those days I will pour out my Spirit."   *Joel 2:28-29 (ESV)*

"Prophesy" to "*speak for*". I am told the original word had nothing to do with predictions. I am not surprised, however, that we humans desire to <u>know</u> what's coming in the future and so we expect to hear — pardon my <u>un</u>godly metaphor — a "900 psychic" word from God!

I think as I look at the passages talking about prophecy that God maybe wanted us to see this gift from Him in a different light.

Love never ends. As for prophecies, they will pass away; as for tongues, they will cease; as for knowledge, it will pass away. For we know in part and we prophesy in part, but when the perfect comes, the partial will pass away...So now faith, hope, and love abide, these three; but the greatest of these is love. Pursue love, and earnestly desire the spiritual gifts, especially that you may prophesy. For one who speaks in a tongue speaks not to men but to God; for no one understands him, but he utters mysteries in the Spirit. ON the other hand, the one who prophesies speaks to people for their <u>upbuilding</u> and <u>encouragement</u> and <u>consolation</u>. The one who speaks in a tongue builds up himself, but the one who prophesies <u>builds up the church</u>. Now I want you all to speak in tongues, but even more to prophesy. The one who prophesies is greater than the one who speaks in tongues, unless someone interprets, so that the church may be built up.   *1 Corinthians 13: 8-10, 13-14:5 (ESV)*

[Jesus said,] *"Not everyone who says to me, 'Lord, Lord,' will enter the kingdom of heaven, but the one who does the will of my Father who is in heaven. On that day many will say to me, 'Lord, Lord, did we not prophesy in your name, and cast out demons in your name, and do many mighty works in your name?' And then will I declare to them, 'I never knew you; depart from me, you workers of lawlessness.'"*   *Matthew 7:21-23 (ESV)*

And he [Jesus] said to him, "You shall love the Lord your God with all your heart and with all your soul and with all your mind. This is the great and first commandment. And a second is like it: You shall love your neighbor as yourself. On these two commandments depend all the Law and the Prophets."

Matthew 22:37-40 (ESV)

Wow — Jesus even said not only the Law, but the <u>Prophets</u> are pinned on these two commandments. Every word spoken for Him must be able to trace its origin or its root from these two commandments. Any 'word' from God whether it be an encouragement or rebuke MUST come from the root of these two commandments.

I think I will look at "Prophecy" in a different light — uh, Light.

Additional Text: Romans 12, Jeremiah 1

I am the LORD. There is no other God; I am the only God. I will make you strong, even though you don't know me, so that everyone will know there is no other God. From the east to the west they will know I alone am the LORD. I made the light and the darkness. I bring peace, and I cause troubles. I, the LORD, do all these things.   *Isaiah 45:5-7 (NCV)*

God pointed this passage out to me recently. I don't remember ever reading it before although I'm sure I have. It 'popped' for me for this day.

It tells me that God is sovereign. There is no one else. There is no 'minor god' like we speak about 'minor prophets'. There is only one God, creator of all.

God acknowledges my weaknesses. He says here as He has told me in other passages that He gives <u>first</u> – not in response to something I've done. Here it is 'strength' that He gives to me even though I haven't acknowledged Him! <u>HE</u> gives first. He gives to me so that I may receive His strength and then have an opportunity to acknowledge <u>where</u> my strength comes from. Others will hear my testimony and look to Him for <u>their</u> strength and know the source. Paul said it well in his letter to the Philippians:

Because I am in prison, most of the believers have become more bold in Christ and are not afraid to speak the word of God.   *Philippians 1:14 (NCV)*

And then God says in Isaiah that He creates 'light' and 'prosperity', which I joyfully receive! BUT – God says that He also creates 'darkness' and 'disaster'. That is a little unsettling. Initially I think I would rather know that <u>satan</u> created the evil. But then I remember that <u>GOD</u> is sovereign. There is no other God but Him! God is the only One who can create and so He is the One who can <u>stop</u> or <u>destroy</u> or <u>overcome</u> the evil. He has the ultimate power, the final answer. If there is to be evil in this world, I want <u>GOD</u> to be ultimately in charge of it or have control of it – not satan!   This is a troubling passage to think of God connected to evil but I believe that we as Christians should not just ignore such a passage or throw it out or dismiss it as something that was only for Isaiah's time. God is sovereign and there is no other!

[Jesus said,]*"The Father himself loves you. He loves you because you loved me and believed that I came from God. I came from the Father into the world. Now I am leaving the world and going back to the Father...*
I told you these things so that you can have peace in me. In this world you will have trouble, but be brave! I have defeated the world."

                              John 16: 27-28, 33 (NCV)

Yes, there is evil in this world. There is disease and suffering and disasters that occur. But I <u>do</u> take heart; I do have <u>hope</u> because <u>GOD</u> <u>IS</u> <u>IN</u> <u>CONTROL</u>! I trust <u>HIM</u>!

Additional Text: Job 1 and 2

How much do I need to do whatever God has called me to do? How much education do I need? How much time do I need? How much money do I need? Let's see what Gideon and Naaman needed.

Early in the morning Gideon and all his men set up their camp at the spring of Harold. The Midianites were camped north of them in the valley at the bottom of the hill called Moreh. Then the LORD said to Gideon, "You have too many men to defeat the Midianites. I don't want the Israelites to brag that they saved themselves. So now, announce to the people, 'Anyone who is afraid may leave Mount Gilead and go back home.'" So twenty-two thousand men returned home, but ten thousand remained. Then the LORD said to Gideon, "There are still too many men. Take the men down to the water, and I will test them for you there..."

Then the LORD said to Gideon, "Using the three hundred men who lapped the water, I will save you and hand Midian over to you. Let all the others go home..." That night the LORD said to Gideon, "Get up. Go down and attack the camp of the Midianites, because I will give them to you."

Judges 7:1-4, 7, 9 (NCV)

And He did. God did – not Gideon's army. Gideon's army was successful because they were obedient to God. Let's look at Naaman.

Naaman was commander of the army of the king of Aram. He was honored by his master, and he had much respect because the LORD used him to give victory to Aram. He was a mighty and brave man, but he had a skin disease... [leprosy]
So Naaman went with his horses and chariots to Elisha's [the prophet] *house and stood outside the door. Elisha sent Naaman a messenger who said, "Go and wash in the Jordan River seven times. Then your skin will be healed, and you will be clean."*
Naaman became angry and left. He said, "I thought Elisha would surely come out and stand before me and call on the name of the LORD his God. I thought he would wave his hand over the place and heal the disease..."

2 Kings 5:1, 9-11 (NCV)

Sometimes what God is calling me to do is just too simple for me! Maybe there's a big storm brewing in my church and I want God to change my pastor's mind or give me a great 'word' to give the church council or deacon board! Maybe God says, "Jody, I want you to pray every day for wisdom for my people. And I want you to do something you've never done before – I want you to fast on Wed. before the meeting on Wed. night. That's it. That's what I want you to do." But – now why would I think I need to improve on God's plan?

God just wants me to be obedient. He has done so much for me! I KNOW He sees the situation and knows the needs. Why do I think He needs help with the solution? Do I think He's not doing enough like in Gideon and Naaman's stories? Well, like in Gideon and Naaman's stories, He did <u>EXACTLY</u> what needed to be done! (Naaman was healed, by the way!)

So how much do I need to do when God has called me to do something? Exactly as much as He says. He asks me only for a willing and obedient heart. Hallelujah!

June 13

Jesus and his followers went to Capernaum. When they went into a house there, he asked them, "What were you arguing about on the road?" But the followers did not answer, because their argument on the road was about which one of them was the greatest. Jesus sat down and called the twelve apostles to him. He said, "Whoever wants to be the most important must be last of all and servant of all."

Then Jesus took a small child and had him stand among them. Taking the child in his arms, he said,"Whoever accepts a child like this in my name accepts me. And whoever accepts me accepts the One who sent me."   Mark 9:33-37 (NCV)

Jesus makes it very clear that children are important. In these verses from Mark's gospel, He holds the child in His strong, protective arms as He looks all the adults in the eye and tells them that if they're going to be one of His followers, then pay attention to the needs of this child. And in fact, these children are not only important to Him – but to His Father.

So – where do children rank in our church budget? When we plan special events in our church, how many are geared with special consideration for our children? Does the event give them an opportunity to praise God in their way with their music or must they be quiet and sit through an hour of more of music and text that is relevant to ME?!!

Jesus said to his followers, "Things that cause people to sin will happen, but how terrible for the person who causes them to happen! It would be better for you to be thrown into the sea with a large stone around your neck than to cause one of these little ones to sin. So be careful!

If another follower sins, warn him, and if he is sorry and stops sinning, forgive him. If he sins against you seven times in one day and says he is sorry each time, forgive him."   Luke 17:1-4 (NCV)

I hear Jesus remind me that His children are young – in age but also in their relationship to Him. They are looking to ME to be HIS example. I am warned to be careful about the example, about the message I send to these children. Jesus doesn't qualify these children and my responsibility to them only as it applies to my biological children and grandchildren. I am to look with Jesus' eyes to ALL His babies in the faith whether they are 6 or 60!!!

Jesus takes it further, making it clear that while His children NEED discipline, learning obedience and submission to the Father, they also NEED to know the Father's unconditional love and forgiveness. When this younger brother or sister in the Lord SINS and then asks forgiveness, I am to be there with open arms and speak those words of forgiveness, even if that is seven times in one day!

...but Jesus said, "Let the little children come to me. Don't stop them, because the kingdom of heaven belongs to people who are like these children."

Matthew 19:14 (NCV)

Additional Text: Isaiah 11, Matthew 7

June 14

George Mueller, a man of great faith who worked with orphans during the 1800's said,

"The most important part of my prayers are the fifteen minutes after I say 'Amen' ".

But even so, the quiet words of a wise man are better than the shout of a king of fools.   *Ecclesiastes 9:17 (TLB)*

Being quiet before the Lord. Getting on my knees, whether figuratively or in reality, and just waiting – minutes or hours – just waiting. Just being.

Have you even set a timer for five minutes and just sat quietly in a chair without a book or music – just quiet. It seems like FOREVER, doesn't it? I think that's why I have such a struggle to wait and just listen. Like Elijah...

"Go out and stand before me on the mountain," the Lord told him. And as Elijah stood there the Lord passed by, and a mighty windstorm hit the mountain; it was such a terrible blast that the rocks were torn loose, but the Lord was not in the earthquake. And after the earthquake, there was a fire, but the Lord was not in the fire. And after the fire, there was the sound of a gentle whisper. When Elijah heard it, he wrapped his face in his scarf and went out and stood at the entrance of the cave. And a voice said, "Why are you here, Elijah?" He replied again, "I have been working very hard for the Lord God of the armies of heaven, but the people have broken their covenant and have torn down your altars; they have killed everyone of your prophets except me; and now they are trying to kill me, too."   *1 Kings 19:11-14 (TLB)*

Time passes much more quickly when I am in a high-charged worship service with God pouring out His Holy Spirit with lots of JOY and SHOUTS of praise! An hour can slip by like a few minutes!

What about those quiet times when there is just me and the Lord with few words needed if I am really listening?

God came to Elijah in a gentle whisper to hear all about Elijah's troubles. He heard every word that Elijah said and then God spoke and took care of Jezebel and Ahab! AND gave him Elisha, an attendant and a 'brother' he could count on. It is in those quiet times that my relationship with God finds the strong bonds that bind us together, giving me the spiritual strength that I need to run the really long race, the marathon that I've been given.

In your day of trouble, may the Lord be with you! May the God of Jacob keep you from all harm. May he send you aid from his sanctuary in Zion. May he remember with pleasure the gifts you have given him, your sacrifices and burnt offerings. May he grant you your heart's desire and fulfill your plans. May there be shouts of joy when we hear the news of your victory, flags flying with praise to God for all that he has done for you. May he answer all your prayers! "God save the king" – I know he does! He hears me from highest heaven and sends great victories. Some nations boast of armies and weaponry, but our boast is in the Lord our God.   *Psalm 20:1-7 (TLB)*

Additional Text: Habakkuk 2 and 3

"Be strong and brave. Don't be afraid or worried because of the king of Assyria or his large army. There is a greater power with us than with him. He only has men, but we have the LORD our God to help us and to fight our battles." The people were encouraged by the words of Hezekiah king of Judah.

2 Chronicles 32:7-8 (NCV)

The king of Assyria had a reputation. He would lay siege to a city and slaughter all the inhabitants and take whatever he wanted. So far nothing was stopping him. We could compare him to General Sherman and his march to the sea during the Civil War. The people of Judah were understandably afraid. But King Hezekiah had a 'secret weapon' and he KNEW the power of his weapon. He must have spoke with such confidence that the people gained confidence FROM him. Now that's a testimony!

Jesus gave a testimony many times about the power of God. After the Last Supper, when His time with His disciples was running out, He prayed for them and in that prayer He asked the Father to protect them. He asked the One who could do it. He asked the One who had the power over the evil that would come against them. Jesus said,

"All I have is yours, and all you have is mine. And my glory is shown through them. I am coming to you; I will not stay in the world any longer. But they are still in the world. Holy Father, keep them safe by the power of your name, the name you gave me, so that they will be one, just as you and I are one."

John 17:10-11 (NCV)

Robert Leighton, a 17th century Scottish preacher said, "Adversity is the diamond dust Heaven polishes its jewels with." Because it is so hard, in order to polish a diamond, you have to use diamond dust. I admit that God DOES have to use diamond dust to polish me! Adversity or troubles, difficult troubles, may TRY to overwhelm me – but I have the same 'secret weapon' that King Hezekiah had; that Jesus had. There is NOTHING more powerful than my Heavenly Father. He gave me my earthly life and my eternal life. And so much more. When I feel alone and isolated – well, that's a bold-faced lie! I combat that feeling by turning to my Father's Words, to a song of worship, and to many memories of what He has done in my life and those I love.

Our Lord is great and very powerful. There is no limit to what he knows.

Psalm 147:5 (NCV)

When I want to throw my own pity party and say, "No one understands me!" God does. He knows me inside and out. He will even meet with me and sit down and listen to my woes and hold my hand and sort out the emotions from the truth. He will direct my path. He is FOR me so who can be against me? – and WIN?!!!

This God is our God forever and ever. He will guide us from now on.

Psalm 48:14 (NCV)

Additional Text: Psalm 48 and 145

And Elijah came near to all the people and said, "How long will you go limping between two different opinions? If the LORD is God, follow him; but if Baal, then follow him." And the people did not answer him a word.

1 Kings 18:21 (ESV)

Oooo. That last phrase is a cut to the heart, isn't it? *"And the people did not answer..."*! Elijah, like Joshua before him, told his people flat out to CHOOSE whom they would serve. Choice A: God, Jehovah, the great I AM or Choice B: Baal, made by man out of stone, silent, able to be manipulated by anyone with a few gold coins. Seems like a no-brainer question, doesn't it?

Many believe, as I once did, that making NO choice is an option. It's not. By making no choice, I've made a choice NOT to serve God. Much as I wanted to "waver and waffle", sitting on the fence, by choosing NOT to jump God's way – I jumped the enemy's way. Jesus said:

"No one can serve two masters, for either he will hate the one and love the other, or he will be devoted to the one and despise the other. You cannot serve God and money."

Matthew 6:24 (ESV)

and

The plans of the heart belong to man, but the answer of the tongue is from the LORD. All the ways of a man are pure in his own eyes, but the LORD weighs the spirit...

The heart of man plans his way, but the LORD establishes his steps.

Proverbs 16:1-2, 9 (ESV)

There's the point. If I choose God, then I am <u>giving up</u> myself, my plans, and my secret inner control of my life. Jesus told the rich young ruler when he asked what he had to do to get eternal life to "give up" his riches, his idol, himself and then follow Jesus. There's the question: Am I ready to give up WHATEVER God asks so I will be 'light' and able to follow Jesus. God knows my heart. He knows my secret sin. He loves me any way and wants me to be with him, 24 – 7. SWEET! Now is the time. No more excuses. No more hiding behind church leadership or my spouse or my parents. Let Jesus shine the light on me and examine me. May Jesus prune me or discipline me as He sees fit.

"I am the true vine, and my Father is the vinedresser. Every branch of mine that does not bear fruit he takes away, and every branch that does bear fruit he prunes, that it may bear more fruit."

John 15:1-2 (ESV)

Now's the time to let the Lord determine my steps! No more living on another's relationship with the Lord!

"...Whoever abides in me and I in him, he it is that bears much fruit, for apart from me you can do nothing."

John 15:5 (ESV)

Additional Text: Colossians 1, 2 Thessalonians 1

Then Nebuchadnezzar, in a terrible rage, ordered Shadrach, Meshach, and Abednego to be brought in before him. "Is it true, O Shadrach, Meshach, and Abednego," he asked, "that you are refusing to serve my gods or to worship the golden statue I set up? I'll give you one more chance. When the music plays, if you fall down and worship the statue, all will be well. But if you refuse, you will be thrown into a flaming furnace within the hour. And what god can deliver you out of my hands then?"

Shadrach, Meshach, and Abednego replied, "O Nebruchadnezzar, we are not worried about what will happen to us. If we are thrown into the flaming furnace, our God is able to deliver us; and he will deliver us out of your hand, Your Majesty. But if he doesn't, please understand, sir, that even then we will never under any circumstance serve your gods or worship the golden statue you have erected."   *Daniel 3:13-18 (TLB)*

This is one of those days when I wondered about God!!! I mean, more than usual!!!

This Scripture from Daniel is one of my favorites that I need to read more often. Here were three men who are seemingly without power in their lives, at the mercy of a foreign king. They were ordered to do something that they KNOW they are not going to do. There is no 'wiggle room' here! Refusing to worship the king's god means they were going to die! These three men came back to the king with three short points: 1) They were not worried about defending themselves – they were not pleading for mercy. 2) They said, "Our God Jehovah is able to save us and He WILL do it. And 3) IF it is our God Jehovah's will not to do so, -- we will not serve your god any way"!!!

The story continues with the king REALLY getting angry and heating the furnace so hot that it kills his guards. The three men walk among the flames with a 'mysterious' 4th man and come out of the furnace without even the smell of smoke on their clothes. The king receives an AWESOME testimony and is changed as well as the three men receiving leadership positions in the country.

But all these things that I once thought very worthwhile – now I've thrown them all away so that I can put my trust and hope in Christ alone. Yes, everything else is worthless when compared with the priceless gain of knowing Christ Jesus my Lord.   *Philippians 3:7-8 (TLB)*

Paul shares his heart. He TOTALLY opens up and reveals that all that he was and is – counts for NOTHING – ZERO – in the presence of his relationship to Christ. Paul knows that his faith in Christ, the salvation that came from that and everything else is from God and THAT is all that matters in his life. He confesses that he has not truly grabbed on to all that the gift of salvation means – but he wants to grab on to it – he wants the prize! That spoke to me today that NOTHING – NOTHING – NOTHING – in my life could compare to the Good News. Zip. Nuttin', honey! As I sit here today and look around at my home, family pictures, the peace of living in the USA, having an income that provides…I consider it a 'throwaway' compared to *knowing* that Jesus is MY Lord and Savior.

What is it that I must let go of – so I can grab on to Jesus FIRST?

June 18

God is fair and righteous. This word He gave to Ezekiel in Chapter 7 for Israel also applies to me:

Again the LORD spoke his word to me, saying: "Human, the Lord GOD says this to the land of Israel: An end! The end has come on the four corners of the land. Now the end has come for you, and I will send my anger against you. I will judge you for the way you have lived, and I will make you pay for all your actions that I hate. I will have no pity on you; I will not hold back punishment from you. Instead, I will make you pay for the way you have lived and for your actions that I hate. Then you will know that I am the LORD."

Ezekiel 7:1-4 (NCV)

Jesus warns us about running after wealth and spending our time 'worrying' about worldly things over our spiritual 'status'.

"And why do you worry about clothes? Look at how the lilies in the field grow. They don't work or make clothes for themselves. But I tell you that even Solomon with his riches was not dressed as beautifully as one of these flowers. God clothes the grass in the field, which is alive today but tomorrow is thrown into the fire. So you can be even more sure that God will clothe you. Don't have so little faith!...
Don't judge other people, or you will be judged. You will be judged in the same way that you judge others, and the amount you give to others will be given to you. Why do you notice the little piece of dust in your friend's eye, but you don't notice the big piece of wood in your own eye? How can you say to your friend, 'Let me take that little piece of dust out of your eye'? Look at yourself! You still have that big piece of wood in your own eye. You hypocrite! First, take the wood out of your own eye. Then you will see clearly to take the dust out of your friend's eye." *Matthew 6:28-30, 7:1-5 (NCV)*

It is so much easier for me to judge where I believe others are in their walk with Jesus. God will judge me with the same measuring stick and will 'repay me for my conduct'.

Isn't there a common thread here? My loving and wonderful Redeemer will be my Judge. He will open the Book and look at my life and fairly judge my practices and conduct. Jesus will look at my life and shine a light on what I chose as priorities. He will hold up the measure that I judged others, the love that I extended to them and use the same measure for me.

If we say we have no sin, we are fooling ourselves, and the truth is not in us. But if we confess our sins, he will forgive our sins, because we can trust God to do what is right. He will cleanse us from all the wrongs we have done. If we say we have not sinned we make God a liar, and we do not accept God's teaching.
My dear children, I write this letter to you so you will not sin. But if anyone does sin, we have a helper in the presence of the Father – Jesus Christ, the One who does what is right. He is the way our sins are taken away, and not only our sins but the sins of all people. *1 John 1:8-2:2 (NCV)*

Additional Text: Luke 12, Romans 2

Love the LORD your God and always obey his orders, rules, laws, and commands. Remember today it was not your children who saw and felt the correction of the LORD your God. They did not see his majesty, his power, his strength, or his signs and the things he did in Egypt to the king and his whole country. They did not see what he did to the Egyptian army, its horses and chariots, when he drowned them in the Red Sea as they were chasing you. The LORD ruined them forever. They did not see what he did for you in the desert until you arrived here. They did not see what he did to Dathan and Abiram, the sons of Eliab the Reubenite, when the ground opened up and swallowed them, their families, their tents, and everyone who stood with them in Israel. It was you who saw all these great things the LORD has done. So obey all the commands I am giving you today so that you will be strong and can go in and take the land you are going to take as your own. Deuteronomy 11:1-8 (NCV)

I have seen. Yes, I have seen God's miracles. Not just in 'stories' in the Bible or in the visual screen of my mind but in the actual, reality of my life. I have witnessed physical healings that cannot be explained away with modern medical knowledge. I have seen angry, bitter people become peaceful, loving individuals not because of years of counseling but because of supernatural healing that went on inside their hearts. I've seen the wonder come into someone's eyes when a changed heart suddenly occurs and they are incredulous with what has happened! I have seen drug addicts and alcoholics and addicted smokers take that faith step toward God and never turn back to their chain of addiction again. Years later, they are still walking in freedom! Yes, miracles from God are still happening!

Brothers and sisters, think about the things that are good and worthy of praise. Think about the things that are true and honorable and right and pure and beautiful and respected. Do what you learned and received from me, what I told you, and what you saw me do. And the God who gives peace will be with you.
Philippians 4:8-9 (NCV)

I have choices throughout each day. I can be a witness for God – or not! There is no in-between! I can be a conduit of the Light which is in me because of Jesus or I can hide that Light, thinking I am keeping it all for myself. Have you even put a candle inside a closed jar? It goes out when it uses up the oxygen inside the jar. Jesus' Light will go out inside me if I do not allow the 'oxygen' (the Holy Spirit) to flow through me. If I do not daily take in the Breath of God and allow it to flow out of me, the Light becomes dimmer each day. I'm a conduit of God, not a closed vault!

First I want to say that I thank my God through Jesus Christ for all of you, because people everywhere in the world are talking about your faith.
Romans 1:8 (NCV)

I tell my children about You, Lord. I tell my parents, my brother and sisters. It seems like so little and yet how did those 12 men in Jerusalem get the news to this continent? One person at a time! Throw a pebble in a pond and watch the ripple spread throughout the whole body of water! I can be a witness today for God – or not. Which will it be?

June 20

I want them to be strengthened and joined together with love so that they may be rich in their understanding. This leads to their knowing fully God's secret, that is, Christ himself. In him all the treasures of wisdom and knowledge are safely kept. I say this so that no one can fool you by arguments that seem good, but are false. Though I am absent from you in my body, my heart is with you, and I am happy to see your good lives and your strong faith in Christ. As you received Christ Jesus the Lord, so continue to live in him. Keep your roots deep in him and have your lives built on him. Be strong in the faith, just as you were taught, and always be thankful. Be sure that no one leads you away with false and empty teaching that is only human, which comes from the ruling spirits of this world, and not from Christ. All of God lives in Christ fully (even when Christ was on earth), and you have a full and true life in Christ, who is ruler over all rulers and powers. Colossians 2:2-10 (NCV)

I am blessed that the 'New Age Movement' never tempted me. When I was in college I remember a girl in my dorm that was really absorbed by 'TM', transcendental meditation. I was young and didn't see the 'harm' in it so I went with two other girls one day to her room and tried it! After she explained what she thought was the purpose and benefits of the upcoming session, we proceeded to sit on the floor in the required 'lotus' position and watched while she lit the incense. I closed my eyes and the 'hum' or 'chant' began. At first I had a hard time keeping a 'spiritual' attitude and external face because, frankly, I thought the chant was silly! Then the incense started to get to me. (I was a smoker at the time, too, but always in a well-ventilated place!) When my legs began to cramp, I released my screaming muscles as quietly as possible and left the room. No one ever asked me about the session. Maybe they all left!

I don't feel particularly proud that I did get involved in that type of spirituality because I also didn't go to <u>any</u> church! I was disillusioned about God and anything related so I avoided and denied all need or existence of that part of my life as best as I could! That was pretty easy since I do not remember <u>anyone</u> speaking to me about my faith or lack thereof the entire four years I was absent. I was actually absent <u>more</u> than those four years as I spent my preteen and teen years sitting in church with my parents in body but the mind and spirit never went there!

When I receive an email from someone asking for help, asking for prayer, my response is to ask God how I can help and then when I respond, I always include a point encouraging the person to be in church and seeking an accountability partner. More often than not, the person has been where I was and is backing away from their life in a local church body and may not have even shared their need with the pastor or any leadership person.

Jesus showed us by His example that it is absolutely <u>VITAL</u> to be part of a church body! Being a part of a church that keeps Jesus as the Head and focuses on being a servant like Jesus keeps <u>me</u> from being distracted by deceptive doctrine and teaching that I may accept because it happens to be what I want to hear!!! I want to <u>always</u> be pointed in the path that is going in right relationship with God. I want to be <u>plugged in</u> to God's conduit!

Philemon, each time I mention you in my prayers, I thank God. I hear about your faith in our Lord Jesus and about your love for all of God's people. As you share your faith with others, I pray that they may come to know all the blessings Christ has given us. My friend, your love has made me happy and has greatly encouraged me. It has also cheered the hearts of God's people.

Philemon 4-7 (CEV)

As I began praying today, I thought of the people I have met or who have joined this devotion group in the last year. I felt tears burn my eyes at how God continues to reach out to people to <u>come</u> into His Kingdom or continue to enter a deeper knowledge and understanding of Him. He never gives up. God has a heart for His children that have not changed since the day He was willing to allow His only Son to <u>die</u> for us.

Two criminals were led out to be put to death with Jesus. When the soldiers came to the place called "The Skull", they nailed Jesus to a cross. They also nailed the two criminals to crosses, one on each side of Jesus.

Jesus said, "Father, forgive these people! They don't know what they're doing."...Above him was a sign that said, "This is the King of the Jews."

One of the criminals hanging there also insulted Jesus by saying, "Aren't you the Messiah? Save yourself and save us!" But the other criminal told the first one off, "Don't you fear God? Aren't you getting the same punishment as this man? We got what was coming to us, but he didn't do anything wrong." Then he said to Jesus, "Remember me when you come into power!" Jesus replied, "I promise that today you will be with me in paradise."

Around noon the sky turned dark and stayed that way until the middle of the afternoon. The sun stopped shining, and the curtain in the temple split down the middle. Jesus shouted, "Father, I put myself in your hands!" Then he died.

Luke 23:32-35, 38-46 (CEV)

Two thieves were given the ultimate invitation as they faced a certain death. One chose eternal life. The other chose to keep his way of doing things that certainly had not worked for him in the past but he was unwilling to take that step of faith that Jesus' way might be better. He refused to give up control and humble himself to receive a gift that he didn't earn or didn't deserve.

Coming to know Jesus as Savior is receiving the truth that it isn't about <u>me</u> but about Jesus. Continuing to know Jesus as Lord and King is receiving the truth that it *continues* to NOT be about me but about God.

Think how much the Father loves us. He loves us so much that he lets us be called his children, as we truly are. But since the people of this world did not know who Christ is, they don't know who we are. My dear friends, we are already God's children, though what we will be hasn't yet been seen. But we do know that when Christ returns, we will be like him, because we will see him as he truly is. This hope makes us keep ourselves holy, just as Christ is holy.

1 John 3:1-3 (CEV)

Additional Text: Romans 2 and 3

June 22

'Religion' -- Belief in and reverence for a supernatural power or powers regarded as creator and governor of the universe. A personal or institutionalized system grounded in such belief and worship.

Webster's Revised Unabridged, 1998

The Christian who is pure and without fault, from God the Father's point of view, is the one who takes care of orphans and widows, and who remains true to the Lord – not soiled and dirtied by his contacts with the world.

James 1:27 (TLB)

Religion that pleases God the Father must be pure and spotless. You must help needy orphans and widows and not let this world make you evil.

James 1:27 (ESV)

Well there it is, from Miriam-Webster's newest edition to the apostle James, I have some ways of looking at religion. When I stand behind the dictionary's definition and look, I am more than a little uncomfortable with the word 'religion'. How can the system of belief and worship be both personal <u>and</u> an institution and yet hold the integrity of the Founder?

James gives me a more narrow look in that he says that he is defining the word from Father God's point of view. It is all about agape love and holiness. This definition is easier to apply to me personally but much more difficult to bring to an institution that defines its beliefs by committee and is influenced by the current 'wind' blowing in from the world. The words 'politically correct' come to mind.

'Faith' adds another viewpoint.

Confident belief in the truth, value, or trustworthiness of a person, idea, or thing. The theological virtue defined as secure belief in God and a trusting acceptance of God's will. A set of principles or beliefs.

Webster's Revised Unabridged, 1998

Faith makes us sure of what we hope for and gives us proof of what we cannot see. It was their faith that made our ancestors pleasing to God.

Hebrews 11:1-2 (ESV)

By faith we have been made acceptable to God. And now, because of our Lord Jesus Christ, we live at peace with God.   *Romans 5:1 (ESV)*

But we live by faith, not by what we see.   *2 Corinthians 5:7 (ESV)*

Webster's says that faith is something that I have confidence in and that it is secure and is based on principles. The writers of the Bible do not put such 'concrete' words to it. They do not use words that seem to grow the word from <u>within</u> ME. Faith is given from God that I cannot see, about God that I cannot see, and continues because of God that I cannot see. How weird is that! And yet when times are unbelievably difficult and the world tells me I have no options and all is lost – faith tells me that there is something MORE – and faith is proven correct.

Additional Text: 2 Chronicles 20, Mark 11

Jesus and his disciples sailed across Lake Galilee and came to shore near the town of Gerasa. As Jesus was getting out of the boat, he was met by a man from that town. The man had demons in him. He had gone naked for a long time and no longer lived in a house, but in the graveyard...

Then the demons left the man and went into the pigs. The whole herd rushed down the steep bank into the lake and drowned. When the men taking care of the pigs saw this, they ran to spread the news in the town and on the farms. The people went out to see what had happened, and when they came to Jesus, they also found the man. The demons had gone out of him, and he was sitting at the feet of Jesus. He had clothes on and was in his right mind. But the people were terrified. Then all who had seen the man healed told about it. Everyone from around Gerasa begged Jesus to leave, because they were so frightened. When Jesus got into the boat to start back, the man who had been healed begged to go with him. But Jesus sent him off and said, "Go back home and tell everyone how much God has done for you." The man then went all over town, telling everything that Jesus had done for him. Luke 8:26-27, 33-39 (CEV)

I cannot imagine what it must have been like for the demon-possessed man. I do remember a woman that I met when I was in nursing school and taking my practicum in psychiatry at the large institute that was there. This woman had been treated for depression most of her life. In fact, as I remember it, she had lived in an institute off and on since she was a teenager and she was now in her 60's. There was a meeting that I attended to determine whether she was to be remanded permanently to the state institution. As I read this story, how awesome it would have been if she had met <u>Jesus</u> at the meeting and 'pigs' would have been sent to the institution, not her! There certainly would have been some doctors and nurses and technicians <u>frightened</u> by a scene where a 'man' stood up and commanded whatever had been tormenting her all those years to "Go!". Seeing the woman stand up and clearly begin speaking would have scared a bunch of us out of our wits!

It was important that the <u>former</u> demon-possessed man stay and walk out his life in front of his family and peers. <u>He</u> would be the one that others would see Jesus in. Jesus would become healer and friend as the man became part of the community again. I think it would have been *easier* for him to have gone with Jesus. Staying behind and working day-to-day to bring in the 'harvest' of that town for God was a difficult plot of ground to dig in! Many times, my close family and friends don't want to hear about my life in Jesus. However, <u>living</u> my life in Jesus is a testimony that is quiet yet powerful! Allowing my loved ones to see struggles and who I lean on gives them hope and a direction to look for their strength. I may never know they are watching. That's good because then God gets <u>all</u> the credit! It is also true, unfortunately, that people who knew me 'BJ' (before Jesus) do not always allow me to move forward, forgetting the past, which <u>Jesus</u> has forgiven. It is with the power of the Holy Spirit, providing sufficient grace (unconditional love), and Jesus showing me the way, that I <u>live</u> my new life in Christ.

Wait for the LORD and keep his way. He will exalt you to inherit the land;
when the wicked are cut off, you will see it.
I have seen a wicked and ruthless man flourishing like a green tree
in its native soil, but he soon passed away and was no more;
though I looked for him, he could not be found.
Consider the blameless, observe the upright;
there is a future for the man of peace.
But all sinners will be destroyed; the future of the wicked will be cut off.
The salvation of the righteous comes from the LORD;
he is their stronghold in time of trouble.
The LORD helps them and delivers them; he delivers them from the wicked
and saves them, because they take refuge in him.   *Psalm 37:34-40*

God never ceases to amaze me! I thought that I was just 'cruising' the psalms today, just soaking up the joy and words of praise. I was thinking about how I should be praising God out of just an overflowing of love and devotion for all that He has done and not out of a duty or obligation. And then He brought me to these verses.

I felt God tell me again to 'be content where you are now and wait to see what I am going to do'!!! I even felt a shrug coming on …when I went on to read about those who are 'wicked' and seem to be getting so much! Now, 'wicked' for me is more than just a sinner. I'm a sinner! 'Wicked' to me is a sinner who knows he/she is doing wrong and is enjoying it! There is no repentance or receiving of conviction! I started to rejoice (yes, I admit rejoicing!) when I saw that the 'wicked' would be no more! And then I felt the conviction of the Holy Spirit and tears came to my eyes for the obliteration of those who do not turn from wickedness!

"…*there is a future for the man of peace.*" Another translation uses 'prosperity' in place of 'peace'. Am I a woman of peace? Do I trust God that He knows my present state and has plans for my future? Isn't that where my strength lies?

This is what the LORD says:

"Let not the wise man boast of his wisdom or the strong man boast of his strength or the rich man boast of his riches, but let him who boasts boast about this: that he understands and knows me, that I am the LORD, who exercises kindness, justice and righteousness on earth, for in these I delight," declares the LORD.   *Jeremiah 9:23-24*

No matter what I perceive to be the success of others or whether I think that is fair or right, God tells me that REAL SUCCESS and REAL BLESSINGS are in my understanding and knowing HIM! God is the kind and 'RIGHT' judge.

That is a good place that I 'cruised' in today!

Additional Text: Mark 4, Psalm 119: 97-120

After these things God tested Abraham's faith. God said to him, "Abraham!" And he answered, "Here I am." Then God said, "Take your only son, Isaac, the son you love, and go to the land of Moriah. Kill him there and offer him as a whole burnt offering on one of the mountains I will tell you about." Abraham got up early in the morning and saddled his donkey. He took Isaac and two servants with him. After he cut the wood for the sacrifice, they went to the place God had told them to go. On the third day Abraham looked up and saw the place in the distance. He said to his servants, "Stay here with the donkey. My son and I will go over there and worship, and then we will come back to you."

Genesis 22:1-5 (NCV)

Abraham said that he and Isaac were going to *WORSHIP!!* Some might say that Abraham told the servants that to deceive them so they wouldn't know what he was really planning to do. I think they might have caught on anyway when Abraham came back and Isaac didn't! I believe Abraham just spoke the truth. He was going to worship God because he was worshipping by obedience. He was in absolute agreement with God, committed to Him. There was no music, no singing, no preaching, no weekly bulletin, just radical, nothing-held-back obedience!

Then I looked, and I heard the voices of many angels around the throne, and the four living creatures, and the elders. There were thousands and thousands of angels, saying in a loud voice: "The Lamb who was killed is worthy to receive power, wealth, wisdom, and strength, honor, glory, and praise!" Then I heard all creatures in heaven and on earth and under the earth and in the sea saying: "To the One who sits on the throne and to the Lamb be praise and honor and glory and power forever and ever." The four living creatures said, "Amen," and the elders bowed down and worshiped. *Revelation 5:11-14 (NCV)*

The word 'amen' is directly tied to worship as it means that there is complete agreement with the words spoken. "So be it!" Some of us have been known to speak out an 'Amen' when our pastor or another gives forth a truth straight from God. By speaking 'Amen', I am not only agreeing with the words given but I am also speaking a receiving and acceptance of the word and agreeing to be obedient to that word.

David, like Abraham, was given a difficult 'word' from the Lord that his child from his adulterous affair would die. David repented and begged God to change His mind as he fasted and prayed. When the child died, David got up and *worshipped* God; affirming with an 'amen' heart that God's will was right and just. No wonder David is described as a man after God's own heart (Acts 13:22). He worshipped God perfectly with total abandonment of himself.

God is looking for worshippers who will be radical and totally abandon 'self' for Him. True worship is when I say 'yes' to God's will no matter how difficult the request. There is no objection, no resistance in my spirit, just an 'amen' of total agreement.

Additional Text: John 4, Romans 11

Then Jesus' mother and brothers arrived. Standing outside, they sent someone in to tell him to come out. Many people were sitting around Jesus, and they said to him, "Your mother and brothers are waiting for you outside." Jesus asked, "Who are my mother and my brothers?" Then he looked at those sitting around him and said, "Here are my mother and my brothers! My true brother and sister and mother are those who do what God wants."   Mark 3:31-35 (NCV)

Most of us with long-distance family are really happy when we are able to be together, especially for holidays as it brings back memories of other family feasts! With our parents both in heaven, my brother and I have become very aware of the importance of <u>making time</u> to be together with each other, our children and in-laws.

Standing near his cross were Jesus' mother, his mother's sister, Mary the wife of Clopas, and Mary Magdalene. When Jesus saw his mother and the follower he loved standing nearby, he said to his mother, "Dear woman, here is your son." Then he said to the follower, "Here is your mother." From that time on, the follower took her to live in his home.   John 19:25-27 (NCV)

Our heavenly Father desires to give me 'good gifts'. He brings people into my life whom He chooses that I will build a relationship. They become brothers and sisters that love me unconditionally and encourage me and hold me accountable to God's standard, not their own. Sounds almost too good to be true, doesn't it? If I seek this gift from God and am willing to be open to whomever He sends, I will be blessed! This is important to God. It is no coincidence that one of the last acts that Jesus did was establishing such a relationship with His mother and John. It wasn't just for them and their circumstances. It was for me and <u>my</u> circumstances. Jesus spent most of His ministry teaching me about <u>relationships</u>. My relationship to Him, my relationship to my parents, my relationship within the Body of Christ <u>and</u> with unbelievers! Jesus is all about relationships!

Dear friends, we should love each other, because love comes from God. Everyone who loves has become God's child and knows God. Whoever does not love does not know God, because God is love. This is how God showed his love to us: He sent his one and only Son into the world so that we could have life through him. This is what real love is: It is not our love for God; it is God's love for us in sending his Son to be the way to take away our sins.

Dear friends, if God loved us that much we also should love each other. No one has ever seen God, but if we love each other, God lives in us, and his love is made perfect in us...And so we know the love that God has for us, and we trust that love. God is love. Those who live in love live in God, and God lives in them. This is how love is made perfect in us: that we can be without fear on the day God judges us, because in this world we are like him. Where God's love is, there is no fear, because God's perfect love drives out fear. It is punishment that makes a person fear, so love is not made perfect in the person who fears.

We love because God first loved us...And God gave us this command: Those who love God must also love their brothers and sisters.

1 John 4:7-12, 16-19, 21 (NCV)

Let brotherly love continue. Do not neglect to show hospitality to strangers, for thereby some have entertained angels unawares. Remember those who are in prison, as though in prison with them, and those who are mistreated, since you also are in the body. Hebrews 13:1-3 (ESV)

Almost every day I receive a letter or bulletin in the mail describing a financial need somewhere in the Body of Christ. Somewhere a ministry is seeking those who do not know Jesus as Lord and Savior and serving them, leading them into the Kingdom of God. Most of them I recognize and know they are legitimate, God-glorifying ministries. What can I do for them? What does <u>God</u> want me to do?

This passage tells me to love them and remember them. That doesn't always involve money. I can take a few minutes of my time and lift them in prayer. I can leave that letter or pamphlet on my desk that day and just offer prayers throughout the day. I could pin that picture up on my bulletin board for the week. I could write their name in my prayer journal. I could pass their need along to someone who has been given the gift of giving. <u>I</u> could send them an offering. I know that I can't out-give God!

There are many ways that God can use me to lift up members of the Body. "I can't do anything!" is a lie from hell that brings discouragement and frustration. Neither of those is from God, are they?

Pray for us, for we are sure that we have a clear conscience, desiring to act honorably in all things. I urge you the more earnestly to this in order that I may be restored to you the sooner. Now may the God of peace who brought again from the dead our Lord Jesus, the great shepherd of the sheep, by the blood of the eternal covenant, equip you with everything good that you may do his will, working in us that which is pleasing in his sight, through Jesus Christ, to whom be glory forever and ever. Amen. Hebrews 13:18-21 (ESV)

Prayer has power. How do I know that a car that I see on a dealer's lot has power? I start it and take it out for a test drive. I need to take my prayers out for more test drives! I want to see how God works when I speak to Him and lay my requests before Him, expecting to see His power! (Psalm 5)

Rejoice always, pray without ceasing, give thanks in all circumstances; for this is the will of God in Christ Jesus for you. 1 Thessalonians 5:16-18 (ESV)

Is anyone among you suffering? Let him pray. Is anyone cheerful? Let him sing praise. Is anyone among you sick? Let him call for the elders of the church, and let them pray over him, anointing him with oil in the name of the Lord. And the prayer of faith will save the one who is sick, and the Lord will raise him up. And if he has committed sins, he will be forgiven. Therefore, confess your sins to one another and pray for one another, that you may be healed. The prayer of a righteous person has great power as it is working. James 5:13-16 (ESV)

Has someone been on your mind lately? Wondering how they are doing? Lift them in prayer now! 'The prayer of someone in right relationship with God is powerful and effective.' AND prayer *brings* me into an intimate right relationship with God!

June 28

"You priests should be eager to spread knowledge, and everyone should come to you for instruction, because you speak for me, the LORD All-Powerful. But you have turned your backs on me. Your teachings have led others to do sinful things, and you have broken the agreement I made with your ancestor Levi. So I caused everyone to hate and despise you, because you disobeyed me and failed to treat all people alike."   *Malachi 2:7-9 (CEV)*

Well. Those words should strike Holy Fear in all of us who preach, teach a Sunday School class, a Bible study, or even teach on a radio program! Seriously, those of us that teach, preach, share, WHATEVER – have a HOLY responsibility to our 'students'. Preparing or delivering the information should be done ONLY with prayerful preparation and Holy Fear.

My friends, we should not all try to become teachers. In fact, teachers will be judged more strictly than others...

My dear friends, with our tongues we speak both praises and curses. We praise our Lord and Father, and we curse people who were created to be like God, and this isn't right. Can clean water and dirty water both flow from the same spring? Can a fig tree produce olives or a grapevine produce figs? Does fresh water come from a well full of salt water?

Are any of you wise or sensible? Then show it by living right and by being humble and wise in everything you do. But if your heart is full of bitter jealousy and selfishness, don't brag or lie to cover up the truth. That kind of wisdom doesn't come from above. It is earthly and selfish and comes from the devil himself. Whenever people are jealous or selfish, they cause trouble and do all sorts of cruel things. But the wisdom that comes from above leads us to be pure, friendly, gentle, sensible, kind, helpful, genuine, and sincere. When peacemakers plant seeds of peace, they will harvest justice.

James 3:1, 9-18 (CEV)

For me, James gives 'flesh' to the words recorded in Malachi. First James warns me that I will be judged closely. Further in the chapter, he discusses the power that my tongue has and when this is applied to me as a teacher, I am convicted not only by the words I speak but also by my actions AND my heart! CHECK MY EGO AT THE DOOR!!! Pride that gives impetus to ambition is not of God. Envy for someone else or what they teach or the 'success' of their ministry is also not of God. Remember that the writer of Proverbs tells me that Fear of the Lord is the beginning of wisdom. James says that wisdom from the Lord is <u>pure</u> and peace-loving (that means NOT divisive!) and has good fruit. I was struck by the word "submissive". Submissive to what GOD wants me to teach and how He wants me to teach it. That combines with mercy and sincerity in producing that 'good fruit'. Check the fruit – is the harvest good.

One of the wisest teachers I have ever met, Dr. Alden Thompson, said, "The test of my ministry is not <u>what</u> I teach you. It's whether I leave you loving God and each other more." I think he's taken these Scriptures into his heart, don't you?

Additional Text: James 4, 3 John

June 29

Immediately Jesus made the disciples get into the boat and go on ahead of him to the other side, while he dismissed the crowd. After he had dismissed them, he went up on a mountainside by himself to pray. Matthew 14:22-23

Priorities. Jesus was a busy man. He had twelve guys to train in the ministry, literally thousands of people who were hungry and hurting (legitimate needs!) who were clamoring for Him to help them, and during this particular week, his cousin, John, had just been murdered by the local spineless leader for no other reason than he was telling the truth.

Jesus deals with the immediate priorities in an interesting way. He sends the twelve ministers-in-training out into a boat by themselves instead of doing what they wanted Him to do which was listen to more stories about how they made the demons flee and rallied the local villages to 'our cause'. The twelve probably thought it was time to talk battle strategies against the guy who had just murdered John. "Come on, Jesus, we're ready to strike back!" Jesus also dismisses the crowd. Five thousand people had come from their villages to hear Him speak and receive His healing touch without thought or even a plan to eat. They just wanted to be with Him. They wanted to hear His words of life. "Minister to us, Jesus!" Most ministers would be excited to have 5,000 people come to a revival service! Jesus sends them away while He does – what? Make a note of it… *he went up on a mountainside by himself TO PRAY.*

Wait for the LORD; be strong and take heart and wait for the LORD.

Psalm 27:14

When will I learn from Elijah that God is in the whisper? When will I learn from David that God is there even when His hand is heavy on me and I cry rivers of tears on my bed at night? When will I learn from Isaiah that God desires mercy from me and not the sacrifice of thousands of bulls (or thousands of service hours)? There are no shortcuts to relationships. I cannot spend one hour a week with my husband, Henry, and expect that he will understand my needs and support me. I cannot expect to know God if I hear one twenty minute sermon a week and thank him for His blessings at every meal. Unanswered questions and insight into how God works are priorities in my life because I am at the point in my life where I can identify with the sick woman and Jarius (Luke 8) and the father and son (Luke 9) and Paul (2 Corinthians 12) and his thorn. I have no other options and I will not GO BACK to the way things were in my life. So I must press on and climb up the mountain (meaning I will have to put forth some effort and some sweat!) and spend time alone with the Father and talk. Priority #1 in my life.

But whatever was to my profit I now consider loss for the sake of Christ. What is more, I consider everything a loss compared to the surpassing greatness of knowing Christ Jesus my Lord, for whose sake I have lost all things. I consider them rubbish, that I may gain Christ and be found in him, not having a righteousness of my own that comes from the law, but that which is through faith in Christ—the righteousness [a right relationship] *that comes from God and is by faith.* Philippians 3:7-9

I now place you in God's care. Remember the message about his great kindness! This message can help you and give you what belongs to you as God's people. I have never wanted anyone's money or clothes. You know how I have worked with my own hands to make a living for myself and my friends. By everything I did, I showed how you should work to help everyone who is weak. Remember that our Lord Jesus said, "More blessings come from giving than from receiving."   *Acts 20:32-35 (CEV)*

God's grace is undeserved love. It is sufficient for any circumstance and His love is an extravagant inheritance for me.

Paul says that he was not only minister by telling the Good News of Jesus Christ and Him crucified as the perfect atonement but he was to work – as in physical labor – to supply his needs and the needs of his associates. He was also to work to help those in need. Paul reminds us that Jesus promised blessings to those who GIVE.

Jesus was sitting in the temple near the offering box and watching people put in their gifts. He noticed that many rich people were giving a lot of money. Finally, a poor widow came up and put in two coins that worth only a few pennies. Jesus told his disciples to gather around him. Then he said: I tell you that this poor widow has put in more than all the others. Everyone else gave what they didn't need. But she is very poor and gave everything she had. Now she doesn't have a cent to live on."   *Mark 12:41-44 (CEV)*

Isn't it interesting that Jesus – BOLDLY I would say – sat down and watched the offerings come in to the temple treasury? I wonder, as people were tossing in their offerings if anyone noticed or was intimidated by His examination. Do I feel Jesus' eyes on me when I give? After all, His opinion is the only one that matters, right? Hmmm.

Jesus is quite clear on who gave an amount that received His blessing. While many gave from their excess, it was the widow, giving a fraction of a penny, who received the Lord's approval. She gave out of FAITH. She gave in spite of her needs. She gave from her heart.

What is at the root of my giving to the lord, whether that is money, time, or talent? Do I give only out of obligation? Sort of covering my bases? Do I give so that the family in the pew behind me or anyone else will see me and think how 'holy' I am, or be jealous? Do I give with joy and the peace that I know the will of God or do I give grudgingly and with worry about tomorrow?

Think how much the Father loves us. He loves us so much that he lets us be called his children, as we truly are. But since the people of the world did not know who Christ is, they don't know who we are.   *1 John 3:1 (CEV)*

How extravagant is God's love!

Additional Text: Exodus 32, Ephesians 2

Linda Bullard
1949 - 2002

*We know that in everything God works for the good of those who love him…
In all these things we have full victory through God who showed his love for us.
Yes, I am sure that neither death, nor life, nor angels, nor ruling spirits, nothing
now, nothing in the future, no powers, nothing above us, nothing below us, nor
anything else in the whole world will ever be able to separate us from the love of
God that is in Christ Jesus our Lord.* Romans 8:28, 37-39 (NCV)

Linda was one of those people who came into my life for too short a time but
left 'footprints' that impacted my life and the ministry of encouragement and
healing that I was given.

She was born in North Carolina and had a strong faith foundation in her
parents. Linda met her husband, Ron, through friends in school and
interestingly they have the exact same birthday. They raised two children and
have five grandchildren. After some years in Denver, they came to Pensacola
when Linda had an opportunity to transfer after her TDY (that's temporary duty
for all of us non-military people!) had brought her to that base. She told her
husband that "they treat me like family" which is very unusual in a civil service
job. The move also brought them closer to family in North Carolina, which
would be important in the coming years.

Linda and Ron had returned to their faith roots as they raised their own
children. Linda was active in drama and outreach in various churches they
attended across denominational lines. They sought a church with "the presence
of God". Linda's friend and boss invited them to her church, Pine Forest United
Methodist Church in Pensacola, FL. They came back and stayed when the
'Pensacola Outpouring' revival of 1995 made such a tangible change in the
power of God's word and joy of worship in that church.

In 1999, Linda was diagnosed with lymphoma. This began a "journey" through
various facilities for treatments, numerous tests, and even a bone marrow
transplant. The conviction and depth of Linda's faith and the changes in her
heart and life came before the illness. God was NOT taken by surprise but in
fact, prepared her for the journey that was to come. He brought her to a place of
connection with many people of prayer and support. He brought her as a
witness to doctors and patients, friends and acquaintances. Many described
Linda as having a "charisma" and ability to find ways to bring people to a place
where they are comfortable, allowing them to talk. It was a diverse group of
older women, young men, teens…all meeting with this woman with gentle eyes
and a ready smile.

From her journal: *Life can be tough for all those around a cancer patient day
to day. Whether it's the reality of what can take place or the trying to be
positive all the time, it has to get you down from time-to-time. That's when you
cry out to God the most; it's also when He is there the most…when we are upset
we can't hear from God. We have to be able to hang on to our trust in God.
Then we can shake off the problem and go on. You know you can change by
speaking and believing God's word…He who began a good work in me will be
faithful to complete it! He never lets us down.*

"But now I must obey the Holy Spirit and go to Jerusalem. I don't know what will happen to me there. I know only that in every city the Holy Spirit tells me that troubles and even jail wait for me. I don't care about my own life. The most important thing is that I complete my mission, the work that the Lord Jesus gave me – to tell people the Good News about God's grace."

Acts 20:22-24 (NCV)

Paul was resolved and armed with the Spirit of God. He was not in denial and he was not a masochist. He knew, because the Holy Spirit told him, what was in his future. That helped Paul seek the Lord for the strength needed; the Godly assurance that brings divine peace.

You are God's children whom he loves, so try to be like him. Live a life of love just as Christ loved us and gave himself for us as a sweet smelling offering and sacrifice to God. *Ephesians 5:1-2 (NCV)*

Scripture tells us in 1 Peter 4 that Jesus lives for the will of God because He suffered. As an imitator of Jesus, I will experience suffering – knowing this, I set my face toward the New Jerusalem; the HOPE I have in Jesus. No matter what comes through my life, I have hope and promises in Jesus Christ.

Father, in the name and authority of Jesus, I pray on the armor of God. The Helmet of Salvation *that I know with certainty that I am bought with a price and the child of a King.* The Breastplate of Righteousness *not anything I can earn. It is a free gift. It is Jesus' righteousness, given to me. I can enter the Holy of Holies and be with You, Father.* The Belt of Truth *seal it on me with the Blood of Jesus. I want to hear and know only Your voice. All others are deceivers.* The Shoes of Peace *ready to take the Gospel into all the world. I speak peace into all my storms, all winds and waves – peace.* The Shield of Faith *Father, increase my faith. Increase the shield above my head, below my feet, and around my body. Holy Spirit, be my rear guard.* The Sword of the Spirit, the Word of God *Lord, increase my hunger for your Word. May it be nourishment to my spirit. Lord, wrap me in the cloak of humility. ALL glory, honor, and praise belong to You. I am only an ordinary instrument in the hands of an extra-ordinary God. Seal me in the Blood of Jesus. I charge warrior angels around me. I consecrate all that I steward to You, Lord. Use me this day as You will.* *Ephesians 6:10-18 (personal translation)*

Ephesians chapter 6 is a Scripture that I believe we should pray every day. Have you ever prayed a Scripture? Praying the very words of God-inspired truth is POWERFUL. Praying on the Armor of God EVERY DAY is powerful. It is truth. It is God.

We have a bookmark produced at *Pacestters Bible School* that has the Ephesians 6 text as I pray it in my time with my Father. I would like to share that with you. I have found it to be a good 'mark' in my Bible for each day. If you would like one of these bookmarks sent to you FREE – just email me: bible@biblepacesetter.org.

Additional Text: 2 Samuel 22, Isaiah 26

July 2

And now, brothers and sisters, we want you to know about the grace God gave the churches in Macedonia. They have been tested by great troubles, and they are very poor. But they gave much because of their great joy. I can tell you that they gave as much as they were able and even more than they could afford. No one told them to do it. But they begged and pleaded with us to let them share in this service for God's people. And they gave in a way we did not expect: They first gave themselves to the Lord and to us. This is what God wants.

2 Corinthians 8:1-5 (NCV)

Have you ever been on vacation and visited a church only to find out that the pastor is preaching on tithing? Paul gave a testimony to Corinth on the giving of the Macedonian churches. Giving is a message I need to meditate on more often. Paul acknowledges the trials that come our way making the giving of our time or money difficult. But he is applauding the Macedonians giving despite the difficulties and says they gave "*beyond their ability*". They gave in **faith**. *And they did not do as we expected, but they gave themselves first to the Lord and then to us in keeping with God's will.* Paul may have expected the Macedonians to give – but he is obviously overwhelmed that they gave to God all their concerns about their own needs, their fears maybe of famine, or loss of their jobs because they were Christians. They gave themselves to God and THEN gave to Paul's ministry knowing the assurance of their Lord that He would take care of them. That seems like a good precept when I am asked to give to a mission or when I get read to write my tithe check to my home church. I have heard many testimonies from friends and fellow members of my church of how God has provided when they step out in faith and give as God is directing. "I felt God telling me to give the $50 I was going to use for groceries next week to the youth mission trip. I did and the next week I received a $100 check in the mail from a rebate I sent in three months ago and forgot about." or "I kept tithing even when my rent increased and my salary didn't! And I have always had groceries and even money for extras that I didn't have before."

Remember this: The person who plants a little will have a small harvest, but the person who plants a lot will have a big harvest. Each one should give as you have decided in your heart to give. You should not be sad when you give, and you should not give because you feel forced to give. God loves a person who gives happily. And God can give you more blessings than you need. Then you will always have plenty of everything – enough to give to every good work.

2 Corinthians 9:6-8 (NCV)

And so after talking it over with the Lord whether it is my time I am asked to donate to a mission trip or money for tithes or a special offering to another ministry – I am to give cheerfully – with **JOY** – because God gave me the means and He put the 'call' in my heart to give and it's all about Him, any way. That alone is a reason to give *cheerfully*.

Additional Text: Psalm 126, Galatians 6

And the disciples were filled with joy and with the Holy Spirit. Acts 13:52 (ESV)

Jesus' disciples did not just have some joy. They were <u>filled</u> with joy <u>AND</u> the Holy Spirit! I am a disciple of Jesus, too. Does this describe my life? Now before I deceive myself in thinking that my life has more difficulties, let me read this text in context.

The next Sabbath almost the whole city gathered to hear the word of the Lord. But when the Jews saw the crowds, they were filled with jealousy and began to contradict what was spoken by Paul, reviling him. And Paul and Barnabas spoke out boldly, saying, "It was necessary that the word of God be spoken first to you. Since you thrust it aside and judge yourselves unworthy of eternal life, behold, we are turning to the Gentiles. For so the Lord has commanded us, saying, " ' I have made you a light for the Gentiles, that you may bring salvation to the ends of the earth.' "

And when the Gentiles heard this, they began rejoicing and glorifying the word of the Lord, and as many as were appointed to eternal life believed. And the word of the Lord was spreading throughout the whole region. But the Jews incited the devout women of high standing and the leading men of the city, stirred up persecution against Paul and Barnabas, and drove them out of their district. But they shook off the dust from their feet against them and went to Iconium. <u>And the disciples were filled with joy and with the Holy Spirit.</u>

Acts 13:44-52 (ESV)

Paul and Barnabas were not given a 'sweet' message to deliver. From my perspective it was GREAT! -- salvation for the Gentiles! That's me! But to be a Jew and have to deliver that message to the Jews was a TOTALLY 'broccoli' message – not very palatable! The description that the leading people of the city "stirred up persecution" and "drove them out of their district was more than just a committee showing up and politely asking them to leave! And yet, they "were filled with joy and with the Holy Spirit". David Ravenhill says, "A joy-filled Church is a powerful witness to a joy-starved world." God's joy in me is a testimony to His power to raise me above the 'happenings' of this world that define 'happiness' and give me eyes to 'see' my momentary troubles (even though they may last years!) are fleeting when I understand the concept of eternity. Conflicts with others and that need to be seen as 'right' shrink to their <u>true</u> size when I understand the standard of <u>God's judgment</u> and His clear sight in all situations.

Beloved, I pray that all may go well with you and that you may be in good health, as it goes well with your soul. For I rejoiced greatly when the brothers came and testified to your truth, as indeed you are walking in the truth. I have no greater joy than to hear that my children are walking in the truth.

Beloved, do not imitate evil but imitate good. Whoever does good is from God; whoever does evil has not seen God.   *3 John 2-4, 11 (ESV)*

I want to 'see' God today and be filled with His joy.

Additional Text: Acts 13, Colossians 4

July 4

The Lord is the Spirit, and where the Spirit of the Lord is, there is freedom. Our faces, then, are not covered. We all show the Lord's glory, and we are being changed to be like him. This change in us brings ever greater glory, which comes from the Lord, who is the Spirit. God, with his mercy, gave us this word to do, so we don't give up.   *2 Corinthians 3:17-4:1 (NCV)*

That evening, Jesus said to his followers, "Let's go across the lake." Leaving the crowd behind, they took him in the boat just as he was. There were also other boats with them. A very strong wind came up on the lake. The waves came over the sides and into the boat so that it was already full of water. Jesus was at the back of the boat, sleeping with his head on a cushion. His followers woke him and said, "Teacher, don't you care that we are drowning!"

Jesus stood up and commanded the wind and said to the waves, "Quiet! Be still!" Then the wind stopped, and it became completely calm. Jesus said to his followers, "Why are you afraid? Do you still have no faith?"

The followers were very afraid and asked each other, "Who is this? Even the wind and the waves obey him!"   *Mark 4:35-41 (NCV)*

4th of July! A day to celebrate the birth of America – freedom – and for those of us who *are* Christians, -- freedom to worship our Lord in whatever way the Holy Spirit leads us.

Oswald Chambers strikes me with the truth when he says that worry comes from wanting my own way instead of following Jesus' example. Jesus was never bothered by worry because He was not trying to accomplish His own goals but instead He was here to fulfill the Father's goals.

It would be easy for me today to look back on what God <u>did</u> through our forefathers and rejoice at the wars He has already brought us through.

Recently, my cousin gave me a book of family history. A genealogy "thing". I was excited to read of the faith of my – let's see – my great, great, great-grandmother and father's faith as they came from Prussia in 1847. I found out that daily morning devotions were a part of their lives. We celebrate and others, even on an international level, see the freedom of our Christian faith that is the foundation of our national freedom. Mark's gospel tells me that there were 'other boats' who also must have heard Jesus' commands and were witnesses to His power in the one true God.

And so I rejoice today and pray for this nation. I receive Paul's message that <u>God</u> has given me this work to do and I will not worry or tire but live victoriously in Him. Let's stop right now and lift our country's leadership to the Lord and pray for God's divine guidance in all things. Father,…

Additional Text: Romans 13, 1 Timothy 2

Now there was a day when the sons of God came to present themselves before the LORD, and satan also came among them. The LORD said to satan, "From where have you come?" Satan answered the LORD and said, "From going to and fro on the earth, and from walking up and down on it." And the LORD said to satan, "Have you considered my servant Job, that there is none like him on the earth, a blameless and upright man, who fears God and turns away from evil?" Job 1:6-8 (ESV)

And satan then complains to God that He has set Job apart and protected him. He speculates that if God allowed Job to be 'struck' that Job would curse God.

And the LORD said to satan, "Behold, all that he has is in your hand. Only against him do not stretch out your hand." So satan went out from the presence of the LORD. Job 1:12 (ESV)

Clearly, the Lord is giving satan <u>permission</u> to do what he wants with anything that Job stewards, including his family. In Job chapter 2, God gives satan permission to do what he wants with Job himself – he just can't kill him!

That can be a tough concept – satan can only do to me what God allows. When I think of some of the events in my life, I must reconcile myself that God allowed them to happen. He didn't create the cancer in my son, James, but He allowed it to happen. God didn't choose divorce for me but He allowed it to happen. Let's look at Job's reaction after all his children are dead and all his livestock and possessions are destroyed:

Then Job arose and tore his robe and shaved his head and fell on the ground and worshiped. And he said, "Naked I came from my mother's womb, and naked shall I return. The LORD gave, and the LORD has taken away; blessed be the name of the LORD." In all this Job did not sin or charge God with wrong. Job 1:20-22 (ESV)

I noticed that it did not say that Job had a great revelation on <u>WHY</u> all this had happened to him. It just says that Job acknowledged that everything had come from God in the first place and was His to do with as He pleased. Job may not have understood but he trusted God. He continued to TRUST God and gave Him praise.

Now the account of Job continues with less than helpful counsel from his wife and his three friends. In fact, around chapter 38, God gets tired of 'chatter' of Job and his three friends and says:

"Who is this that darkens counsel by words without knowledge? Dress for action like a man; I will question you, and you make it known to me. Where were you when I laid the foundation of the earth? Tell me, if you have understanding." Job 38:2-4 (ESV)

God clarifies to Job that He is in control of the universe and knows all things. Job may not understand why all this is happening to him but God does. (Chapters 38-42).

The account of Job ends with the Lord prospering Job again with TWICE what he had before. Does that mean that Job forgot about the children who died? I don't think so. Job received the blessings of the Lord and let the questions rest in the Lord's hands.

Yesterday, we looked at the story of Job and how God allowed satan to strike at Job by killing all his children and destroying all that he stewarded. Let's look at how God uses satan.

First, God uses satan to refine us, the believers. I have been infected with the devil's disease: PRIDE and even in my most meek moments, I still tend to think of myself too highly. Apparently, Paul had the same problem as he shared in 2 Corinthians 12:

So that I would not become too proud of the wonderful things that were shown to me, a painful physical problem was given to me. This problem was a messenger from satan, sent to beat me and keep me from being too proud. I begged the Lord three times to take this problem away from me. But he said to me, "My grace is enough for you. When you are weak, my power is made perfect in you." So I am very happy to brag about my weaknesses. Then Christ's power can live in me.   *2 Corinthians 12:7-10 (NCV)*

While I don't know the nature of the problem, I am told plainly that it was to keep Paul humble! I am also told quite clearly that it was "*a messenger of satan*" that was to torment him <u>AND</u> that the messenger was under God's control. Satan was used to strengthen God's servant.

In his book, <u>America Looks Up</u>, Max Lucado says that satan loses even when he seems to win. As satan wields his sword and tries to give me a fatal blow, the One who is <u>really</u> in control causes satan's sword to in fact cut away the weeds and 'refine' those of us who faithfully believe in the Lord.

The prophet Malachi tells us that we will be refined:

No one can live through that time; no one can survive when he comes. He will be like a purifying fire and like laundry soap. Like someone who heats and purifies silver, he will purify the Levites and make them pure like gold and silver. Then they will bring offerings to the LORD in the right way. And the LORD will accept the offerings from Judah and Jerusalem, as it was in the past.   *Malachi 3:2-4 (NCV)*

John sees in the vision given to him that we, as the Bride of Christ, will be spotless.

Then I heard what sounded like a great many people, like the noise of flooding water, and like the noise of loud thunder. The people were saying:

"Hallelujah! Our Lord God, the Almighty, rules. Let us rejoice and be happy and give God glory, because the wedding of the Lamb has come, and the Lamb's bride has made herself ready. Fine linen, bright and clean, was given to her to wear." (The fine linen means the good things done by God's holy people.)   *Revelation 19:6-8 (NCV)*

The torment and trials that satan and his world lays on me can be used to refine me as I trust the Lord more and myself and my ways less.

Additional Text: Isaiah 48, Daniel 12

How does God use even satan? Yesterday we read that God uses satan to refine the believers. God also uses satan to WAKE UP the sleeping!

When you meet together in the name of our Lord Jesus, and I meet with you in spirit with the power of our Lord Jesus, then hand this man over to satan. So his sinful self will be destroyed, and his spirit will be saved on the day of the Lord.
1 Corinthians 5:4-5 (NCV)

They knew God, but they did not give glory to God or thank him. Their thinking became useless. Their foolish minds were filled with darkness. They said they were wise, but they became fools. They traded the glory of God who lives forever for the worship of idols made to look like earthly people, birds, animals, and snakes. Because they did these things, God left them and let them go their sinful way, wanting only to do evil. As a result, they became full of sexual sin, using their bodies wrongly with each other. They traded the truth of God for a lie. They worshiped and served what had been created instead of the God who created those things, who should be praise forever. Amen.
Romans 1:21-25 (NCV)

Timothy, my child, I am giving you a command that agrees with the prophecies that were given about you in the past. I tell you this so you can follow them and fight the good fight. Continue to have faith and do what you know is right. Some people have rejected this, and their faith has been shipwrecked. Hymenaeus and Alexander have done that, and I have given them to satan so they will learn not to speak against God.
1 Timothy 1:18-20 (NCV)

These are tough words. Frankly, these are some of those Scriptures I would rather not read. *"It's not the Scriptures I don't know that bother me. It's the ones I do know!"* said Mark Twain. So now I know these Scriptures. What do I do with them? I wake up! – and ask the Holy Spirit to discuss it with me.

From Job to Paul I am told that God controls satan's actions. He 'allows' him to have input in my life. I see it as "the world" and evil. It may begin as temptation. It may be just a downright attack!

Jesus encouraged His disciples in Gethsemane to *"pray so that you will not fall into temptation" (Matthew 26:41).* He knew that satan was 'prowling' that night.

If you think you are strong, you should be careful not to fall. The only temptation that has come to you is that which everyone has. But you can trust God, who will not permit you to be tempted more than you can stand. But when you are tempted, he will also give you a way to escape so that you will be able to stand it.
1 Corinthians 10:12-13 (NCV)

Satan may tempt me but my Father has already marked out an escape path!

"So no weapon that is used against you will defeat you. You will show that those who speak against you are wrong. These are the good things my servants receive. Their victory comes from me", says the LORD.   Isaiah 54:17 (NCV)

I may receive an attack from satan's little minions but they can NOT stand against me AND my Lord! I am awake and ready for battle!

Additional Text: Psalm 108, 2 Corinthians 10

How does God use satan? First, God uses satan to refine the believers. He also uses satan to wake up the sleeping. Finally, God uses satan to teach the Church.

[Jesus said,] *"Simon, Simon, satan has asked to test all of you as a farmer sifts his wheat. I have prayed that you will not lose your faith! Help your brothers be stronger when you come back to me."*   *Luke 22:31-32 (NCV)*

[Jesus is praying to His Father.] *I am praying for them. I am not praying for people in the world but for those you gave me, because they are yours. All I have is yours, and all you have is mine. And my glory is shone through them. I am coming to you; I will not stay in the world any longer. But they are still in the world. Holy Father, keep them safe by the power of your name, the name you gave me, so they may be one, just as you and I are one."*

John 17:9-11 (NCV)

Isn't it awesome that Jesus <u>knew</u> us even 2000 years ago and spoke to the Father about us. He prayed and interceded for us then and He continues to do so now. We have God's strength to get through the 'sifting'. I told a group at a conference that Jesus is coming back for His BRIDE – not a girlfriend! We as a Church must see ourselves as THE BRIDE – and as a bride, desire to be SO BEAUTIFUL before our Groom. A bride does not come to her wedding without combing her hair or taking a shower! The dress that a bride wears isn't dirty with mud from a recent run through a field. It won't have old stains from 'unimportant' past games. A bride is as beautiful as she can be and will do whatever it takes to be a 'vision' of loveliness. That means – acknowledging our sin, repenting, accepting God's freely given mercy, and turning towards holiness, which is where HIS strength comes in.

[Joseph said to his brothers,] *"You meant to hurt me, but God turned your evil into good to save the lives of many people, which is being done."*

Genesis 50:20 (NCV)

God is SO GLORIFIED and satan is SO FRUSTRATED through these times!

I remember when my oldest son was around 18 mos. old and I was baking 'something' in the oven. He kept 'toddling' over and wanting to touch the oven door. I told him "NO!" and slapped his little hand with a "NO!" but he stood there, waiting for a chance to touch it any way. I knew it wouldn't <u>burn</u> him but I also knew it would hurt. I finally turned my back – and there he went. "Waaaa!!!" He had finally gotten what he wanted and it HURT! He looked up at me with those big blue eyes full of tears like "Mama, how could you let that happen?!" He never touched a hot stove again. God 'allows' me to learn because He loves me SO much.

The Father has loved us so much that we are called children of God. And we really are his children. The reason the people in the world do not know us is that they have not known him.   *1 John 3:1 (NCV)*

Additional Text: Matthew 16, Romans 15

"Why do you keep on saying that I am your Lord, when you refuse to do what I say?" Luke 6:46 (CEV)

Ouch. When the Lord took me to this Scripture, I confess that the first half of the verse was very familiar but the context last half was conveniently un-familiar. Jesus' question is obviously right on target. If I call him "Lord", then obedience should follow, right? A little man named Zachaeus met Jesus one day and showed me what blessings will come with obedience.

Jesus was going through Jericho, where a man named Zacchaeus lived. He was in charge of collecting taxes and was very rich. Jesus was heading his way, and Zacchaeus wanted to see what he was like. But Zacchaeus was a short man and could not see over the crowd. So he ran ahead and climbed up into a sycamore tree. When Jesus got there, he looked up and said, "Zacchaeus, hurry down! I want to stay with you today." Zacchaeus hurried down and gladly welcomed Jesus.

Everyone who saw this started grumbling, "This man Zacchaeus is a sinner! And Jesus is going home to eat with him."

Later that day Zacchaeus stood up and said to the Lord, "I will give half of my property to the poor. And I will now pay back four times as much to everyone I have ever cheated."

Jesus said to Zacchaeus "Today you and your family have been saved, because you are a true son of Abraham. The Son of Man came to look for and to save people who are lost." Luke 19:1-10 (CEV)

Zacchaeus – chief IRS man. He wouldn't be loved any more in our time than he was in 31 A.D.! Zacchaeus was curious. Zacchaeus got more than he bargained for. He got a personal visit with the One he was seeking. Zacchaeus got convicted about his cheating ways. And then comes the important part. He called Jesus 'Lord' but he was also OBEDIENT!

Jesus came to seek and save the lost and Zacchaeus received eternal salvation and blessings because of his obedience.

"I am the LORD All-Powerful, and I challenge you to put me to the test. Bring the entire ten percent into the storehouse, so there will be food in my house. Then I will open the windows of heaven and flood you with blessing after blessing. Malachi 3:10 (CEV)

Obedience brings blessings. It's a God promise! God's words to the prophet Malachi are most often heard when our pastors or elders teach about stewardship. The words encourage us to tithe ten percent of our income to the work of the Lord. Some of us have struggle with obedience to tithing when it seems we have more days than money at the end of each month. Some of us struggle with giving our time or talents to a local mission or even committing to a Sunday School class. "I'm not sure that is what the Lord really wants me to do." That excuse is usually just that – an excuse. God's word and Jesus' example and the Holy Spirit are not shy about confirming the direction they want me to move. Obedience is a sweet gift to the Lord that brings back a flood of blessings from the Lord.

God, I look to you for help. I trust in you, LORD. Don't let me die. Protect me from the traps they set for me and from the net that evil people have spread. Let the wicked fall into their own nets, but let me pass by safely.

Psalm 141:8-10 (NCV)

James B. Crooks said, "A man who wants to lead the orchestra must turn his back on the crowd." Wise words. I believe this is the pit that most of us in Church leadership fall and then wonder how we got there. It is a pit that is full of those who are anxious to criticize EVERYTHING and yet do little or NOTHING themselves when the 'call' comes to work outside the USUAL.

Jesus worked outside – the usual. Jesus healed on the Sabbath (even in the Temple) and THAT was a DIFFERENT Sabbath service. Jesus allowed His disciples to glean grain from a field on the Sabbath and THAT was considered UNNECESSARY work. Jesus told the Church to pay the taxes to Caesar (even if they were unfair) and THAT was when the leadership WANTED Him to be RADICAL and He was not!

Don't depend on your own wisdom. Respect the LORD and refuse to do wrong. Then your body will be healthy, and your bones will be strong.

Proverbs 3:7-8 (NCV)

I am very familiar with verse 6 of this Proverb that tells me to trust in God and not in my own understanding and yet I miss the second part of the admonition and continue to try to 'reason out' my walk with God instead of letting go of my own wisdom and accepting that God is God and walk on His path, away from evil and confusion, letting God direct the path with HIS ALL-KNOWING eyes.

Paul and those with him went through the areas of Phrygia and Galatia since the Holy Spirit did not let them preach the Good News in the country of Asia. When they came near the country of Mysia, they tried to go into Bithynia, but the Spirit of Jesus did not let them. So they passed by Mysia and went to Troas. That night Paul saw in a vision a man from Macedonia. The stood and begged, "Come over to Macedonia and help us." After Paul had seen the vision, we immediately prepared to leave for Macedonia, understanding that God had called us to tell the Good News to those people. Acts 16:6-10 (NCV)

I've never heard a sermon on this passage. I wonder why. Paul, a smart man, schooled in the languages and spiritual wisdom of his time, changes his evangelism plan because "*the Spirit of Jesus would not allow them*" to enter a region. They went to a different city. And then, 24 hours later, Paul has a vision and goes to yet another place. His ministry is directed and redirected by the Spirit of God. Now, I bet the Holy Spirit also gave Paul some long-range visions also. But the point would be that Paul went with whatever was on GOD'S plan for today or next year, not what statistics dictated. Did Paul have people who were what I would call 'accountability brothers'? I don't know. It doesn't say that specifically but there were some notes in Acts and in his letters where Paul speaks of the concept of accountability and if Paul was teaching that I make the assumption that he also lived it. As I should live what I teach!

Hand to the plow. Eyes on Jesus. Moving ahead. Let the dogs bark – but the train moves on. THAT is God's way.

Let's see what God says about anger:

A gentle answer will calm a person's anger, but an unkind answer will cause more anger.   *Proverbs 15:1 (NCV)*

Foolish people lose their tempers, but wise people control theirs.
                                                Proverbs 29:11 (NCV)

Love is not rude, is not selfish, and does not get upset with others. Love does not count up wrongs that have been done.   *1 Corinthians 13:5 (NCV)*

You were taught to leave your old self – to stop living the evil way you lived before. That old self becomes worse, because people are fooled by the evil things they want to do. But you were taught to be made new in your hearts, to become a new person. That new person is made to be like God – made to be truly good and holy. So you must stop telling lies. Tell each other the truth, because we all belong to each other in the same body. When you are angry, do not sin, and be sure to stop being angry before the end of the day.
                                                Ephesians 4:22-26 (NCV)

Anger, unfortunately, has always been a part of my life. One of my earliest memories on the farm was a day when we were bailing hay. A steel pin holding a wagon to the tractor broke and my grandfather took the pieces and threw them (narrowly missing two heads!) and cursed a 'blue cloud' over everyone in a five-mile radius! My father had a very volatile temper that erupted much greater than the circumstance warranted, including during times of discipline. I, too, have battled with anger, and lost too often until I received the 'cure' in Jesus Christ. Jesus is God's perfect example of unconditional love. Love 'cures' anger.

It would be easy for me to put forth a 'generational curse' argument on why I can erupt in anger. Including the point that <u>sometimes</u> anger is justified! BUT – with Jesus and His Holy Spirit in my life, I have the <u>power</u> to CHOOSE how I will respond to a given situation. It is not an uncontrollable – I have a choice – response. I can walk FREE in God's VICTORY!

I can do all things through Christ, because he gives me strength.
                                                Philippians 4:13 (NCV)

This is also an area where an "accountability" partner, a brother or sister in the Lord, can pray with me and ask me: "How did it go this week?" He or she may be able to help identify a "trigger" in my flesh that the enemy knows how to set off. With prayer and further leaning on the Lord, I can walk the path to freedom and in turn, show others what God can do.

Be humble under God's powerful hand so he will lift you up when the right time comes. Give all your worries to him, because he cares about you.
                                                1 Peter 5:6-7 (NCV)

What is <u>your</u> burden or cross that is weighing you down today? Is it anger or rage? Jealousy? Paranoia? Depression? Fear? Our Heavenly Father wants to set you FREE! Ask and you SHALL receive!

Additional Text: Exodus 4, James 4

"Command the people of Israel to bring you pure olive oil, made from pressed olives, to keep the lamps on the lampstand burning. Aaron and his sons must keep the lamps burning before the LORD from evening till morning. This will be the Meeting Tent, outside the curtain which is in front of the Ark. The Israelites and their descendants must obey this rule from now on."

Exodus 27:20-21 (NCV)

It was one of the <u>important</u> jobs of the Levites, the priests, to keep the lamps burning in the tabernacle. That required some diligence to keep the oil level up and the wicks trimmed.

In the New Testament, we have Jesus, the Great High Priest, showing us how to make <u>our</u> tabernacles worthy for God to dwell inside.

Later, Jesus talked to the people again, saying, "I am the light of the world. The person who follows me will never live in darkness but will have the light that gives life."

John 8:12 (NCV)

[Jesus said,] *"You are the light that gives light to the world. A city that is built on a hill cannot be hidden. And people don't' hide a light under a bowl. They put it on a lampstand so the light shines for all the people in the house. In the same way, you should be a light for other people. Live so that they will see the good things you do and will praise your Father in heaven."*

Matthew 5:14-16 (NCV)

Jesus shows me how to keep myself filled with the oil of the Holy Spirit that will allow His light to shine <u>through</u> me. I must press in to an intimate relationship, allowing the Holy Spirit to filter me like the Levites filtered the olive oil until it was clearer and burned brightly in the lamp. There are times when He will 'trim' me like a wick is trimmed so the light is bright and piercing. Remember how Jesus was seen by John walking among the lampstands (the churches) in Revelation? He pointed out the areas that needed trimming in each church. And at the end of each note for a church, Jesus said, *"He who has an ear, let him hear what the Spirit says to the churches."* Will I hear what Jesus has to say to the lampstand named 'Jody'? How bright does His light burn in me?

Now may God himself, the God of peace, make you pure, belonging only to him. May your whole self – spirit, soul, and body – be kept safe without fault when our Lord Jesus Christ comes. You can trust the One who calls you to do that for you.

1 Thessalonians 5:20-21 (NCV)

'Sanctify' is just one of those 'church' words that means that God wants me to be 'in shape' to burn brightly for Him like a lamp on a stand, giving HIS light to the WHOLE world! Am I willing to submit to my Great High Priest, Jesus, and be trimmed and pressed so that the lampstand that is me burns brightly in the Holy of Holies that I take every where I go?

Additional Text: Nehemiah 8 and 9, Colossians 3

July 13

Gather all the people: the men, women, children, and foreigners living in your towns so that they can listen and learn to respect the LORD your God and carefully obey everything in this law.   *Deuteronomy 31:12 (NCV)*

Wisdom begins with respect for the LORD; those who obey his orders have good understanding. He should be praised forever.   *Psalm 111:10 (NCV)*

George Whitefield, that great 18th century evangelist said, "It is good to be humbled. I am never better than when I am brought to lie at the foot of the cross. It is a certain sign God intends that soul a greater crown." Humility comes with the fear of God. The older I am and the longer that I am a Christian the more I learn that I am NOTHING and know NOTHING in comparison to my Lord. I am becoming more and more "a sponge for Jesus" as my friend, Linda Smith says. I soak up His love and grace and mercy and He squeezes me out on others. The Christian life is truly ALL ABOUT Him and not about me!

[Jesus said,] *"I will show you the one to fear. Fear the one who has the power to kill you and also to throw you into hell. Yes, this is the one you should fear."*
Luke 12:5 (NCV)

These words from Jesus have taken on a deeper, richer, truer meaning to me since Sept. 11, 2001. In the days following the bombings, the conversations of most of us held tones of fear and uncertainty. Our nation is now faced with the possibility of war. I remember war. I remember my friends being drafted. I remember refusing college financial help from the military because I knew there was the distinct possibility that I could end up in Southeast Asia when I got out. My male friends went to Viet Nam. Some did not return but are now names on a wall of granite. War has no winners, just those who lose more.

It is not a time for fear. It is a time for TRUTH. It is a time to 'fish or cut bait' – meaning who do I stand for? Will I stand for the one who attempts to frighten me with the death of my physical body or will stand for the One who holds my ETERNAL life in His hands? Those who went to work as usual on September 11th 2001, testify to me that I can no longer straddle the fence and worry about it tomorrow!

We are workers together with God, so we beg you: Do not let the grace that you received from God be for nothing. God says, "At the right time I heard your prayers. On the day of salvation I helped you." (Isaiah 49:8) I tell you that the "right time" is now, and the "day of salvation "is now.
2 Corinthians 6:1-2 (NCV)

Accepting Jesus as my Lord and Savior means I walk in confidence knowing what is in store for me ETERNALLY! I walk in VICTORY!

Additional Text: Psalm 111, Luke 12

All Israel was listed in the genealogies recorded in the book of the kings of Israel. The people of Judah were taken captive to Babylon because of their unfaithfulness.   *1 Chronicles 9:1*

God allowed an entire nation to be taken into captivity because they were unfaithful to <u>Him</u>. His chosen people were held captive by heathens – tortured and killed by them – because of their <u>unfaithfulness</u>. God takes idolatry very seriously.

The first commandment as stated in Exodus chapter 20 is:

And God spoke all these words:

"I am the LORD your God, who brought you out of Egypt, out of the land of slavery. You shall have no other gods before me."   *Exodus 20:1-3*

That's idolatry. Idolatry is anything or anyone that I put in front of God or His plans and will in my life. When I must make a decision about a job promotion – do I ask my best friend or God? Do I base the decision on His ways or my ambition? When deciding whom I am going to marry or even who are my friends, do I ask God or base it only on what I <u>see</u> or what <u>I</u> want?

God says: *For I know the plans I have for you," declares the LORD, "plans to prosper you and not to harm you, plans to give you hope and a future. Then you will call upon me and come and pray to me, and I will listen to you. You will seek me and find me when you seek me with all your heart. I will be found by you," declares the LORD, "and will bring you back from captivity. I will gather you from all the nations and places where I have banished you," declares the LORD, "and will bring you back to the place from which I carried you into exile."*   *Jeremiah 29:11-14*

Jesus says: *"No one can serve two masters. Either he will hate the one and love the other, or he will be devoted to the one and despise the other. You cannot serve both God and Money."*   *Matthew 6:24*

Look at John's recording of his encounter with the Living God:

I turned around to see the voice that was speaking to me. And when I turned I saw seven golden lampstands, and among the lampstands was someone "like a son of man," dressed in a robe reaching down to his feet and with a golden sash around his chest. His head and hair were white like wool, as white as snow, and his eyes were like blazing fire. His feet were like bronze glowing in a furnace, and his voice was like the sound of rushing waters. In his right hand he held seven stars, and out of his mouth came a sharp double-edged sword. His face was like the sun shining in all its brilliance. When I saw him, I fell at his feet as though dead. Then he placed his right hand on me and said: "Do not be afraid. I am the First and the Last. I am the Living One; I was dead, and behold I am alive for ever and ever! And I hold the keys of death and Hades."

Revelation 1:12-18

Additional Text: Joshua 24, Isaiah 29

My mother was born in 1919. In her lifetime, she saw many changes in her home. Electricity was probably the biggest as well as too many appliances to count including the microwave. Transportation went from a horse/mule to cars to planes to landing on the moon.

My mother was also Catholic. She saw many changes in her denomination including a service that went from Latin to English and in the last few years, Bible study and healing services. Yes, she lived through many changes.

I, too, have seen many changes in my life – most are subtle and, yes, I would say insidious. There has always been electricity and telephones – it has just moved into fiber optics. There have always been movies – they're just more violent and pornographic.

Changes – some big – some – not so big.

What can I count on? Who can I trust to always be there?

LORD, your word is everlasting; it continues forever in heaven. Your loyalty will go on and on; you made the earth, and it still stands. All things continue to this day because of your laws, because all things serve you. I had not loved your teachings, I would have died from my sufferings. I will never forget your orders, because you have given me life by them. I am yours. Save me. I want to obey your orders. Wicked people are waiting to destroy me, but I will think about your rules. Everything I see has its limits, but your commands have none.

Psalm 119:89-96 (NCV)

Yes! I can count on God. He is First and Last. He is eternal. He has always been and HE will always be. Period. (Revelation 1 and 22)

Looking for happiness? My Heavenly Father desires to give me good gifts. (Luke 11) He gave His only Son so I would have eternal life! (John 3)

Looking for a spouse that I KNOW is the right one? God knows the hidden secrets of a person's heart. He knows which one will match mine. (Psalm 19 and 139)

How do I raise my kids? God knows the importance of honoring my father and mother AND that parents should not frustrate their children. (Ephesians 6)

Each day is different. Each day has changes. Jesus is the anchor that I can count on to hold me steady in any storm. (Hebrews 6)

You, LORD, give true peace to those who depend on you, because they trust you
So, trust the LORD always, because he is our Rock forever.

Isaiah 26:3-4 (NCV)

Additional Text: (See the above references!)

The earth belongs to the LORD, and everything in it – the world and all its people. He built it on the waters and set it on the rivers.   Psalm 24:1-2 (NCV)
But I do not need bulls from your stalls or goats from your pens, because every animal of the forest is already mine. The cattle on a thousand hills are mine.
Psalm 50:9-10 (NCV)

It's always good to know who owns the house I am in or the car I drive or the store where I shop. I can usually know some things about the quality of the product or the integrity and reputation of the company if I know its origins.

God owns it all. There is not a drop of water, leaf on a tree, or puppy born today that doesn't belong to God. He made it all. It's His. I also belong to Him. Unlike the other things mentioned, I have a choice on whether I will belong to God. After I make that choice, the assurance comes.

Then Joshua said to the people, "Now respect the LORD and serve him fully and sincerely. Throw away the gods that your ancestors worshiped on the other side of the Euphrates River and in Egypt. Serve the LORD. But if you don't want to serve the LORD, you must choose for yourselves today whom you will serve...As for me and my family, we will serve the LORD."
Joshua 24:14-15 (NCV)

When our dog, Barnabas, came to us, he was only 6 weeks old. He is now 5 years old. There is no doubt, no question in his little mind who his 'daddy' is – it is not my husband or me – it is our son, James. When James comes home from school, Barnabas jumps up and greets him at the door. He KNOWS who provides him with food and a warm, dry place to live, and treats and toys. It's a good life and it's provided by his 'daddy'!!!

God provides for all of MY needs. There is nothing that God cannot do for me. Every day I have an opportunity to "consider what great things He has done" for me. Just waking up in the morning able to breathe fresh air and worship Him in freedom is pretty great!!!

Let's take time today and count some blessings.

Several times you sent me things I needed when I was in Thessalonica. Really, it is not that I want to receive gifts from you, but I want you to have the good that comes from giving. And now I have everything, and more. I have all I need, because Epaphroditus brought your gift to me. It is like a sweet-smelling sacrifice offered to God, who accepts that sacrifice and is pleased with it. My God will use his wonderful riches in Christ Jesus to give you everything you need. Glory to our God and Father forever and ever! Amen.
Philippians 4:16-20 (NCV)

Additional Text: Genesis 12, Mark 11

The soldiers brought the apostles to the meeting and made them stand before the Jewish leaders. The high priest questioned them, saying, "We gave you strict orders not to continue teaching in that name. But look, you have filled Jerusalem with your teaching and are trying to make us responsible for this man's death." Peter and the other apostles answered, "We must obey God, not human authority!" Acts 5:27-29 (NCV)

Obedience to the Lord has MANY pluses, doesn't it? When I obey the Lord, He GIVES me His Spirit that speaks to me, empower me, and guides me in FURTHER obedience to my Heavenly Father. Those are blessings.

Disobedience to God has consequences also. It brings sorrow, illness, confusion, and alone-ness. Some would call those consequences "curses".

Deuteronomy 28 is a 68-verse chapter of the Bible that deals with blessings and curses. Moses came down from the mountain, after a lengthy conversation with God and delivered this message to the Israelites and ME. Can you just imagine hearing this from the Lord and knowing it's the truth. It brings a diverse mixture of joy and holy fear.

You must completely obey the LORD your God, and you must carefully follow all his commands I am giving you today. Then the LORD your God will make you greater than any other nation on earth. Obey the LORD your God so that all these blessings will come and stay with you: You will be blessed in the city and blessed in the country. Your children will be blessed, as well as your crops; your herds will be blessed with calves and your flocks with lambs. Your basket and your kitchen will be blessed. You will be blessed when you come in and when you go out. Deuteronomy 28:1-6 (NCV)

That's the joy part. It goes on for 14 verses. Here's just a part of the other 54 verses:

But if you do not obey the LORD your God and carefully follow all his commands and laws I am giving you today, all these curses will come upon you and stay: You will be cursed in the city and cursed in the country. Your basket and your kitchen will be cursed. Your children will be cursed, as well as your crops; the calves of your herds and the lambs of your flocks will be cursed. The LORD will send you curses, confusion, and punishment in everything you do. You will be destroyed and suddenly ruined because you did wrong when you left him... You will have to feel around in the daylight like a blind person. You will fail in everything you do. People will hurt you and steal from you everyday, and no one will save you. Deuteronomy 28:15-20, 29 (NCV)

Whew! Tough words! Tough love! God doesn't sit up on His golden throne, waiting for me to mess up so He can slap the back of my head with a curse! In fact, many "lesser things" prick my conscience trying to get me to turn away from temptation and sin. God sends people into my life to speak His truth and love. I always have the choice to listen or ignore the warning.

Today I ask heaven and earth to be witnesses. I am offering you life or death, blessings or curses. Now, choose life! Then you and your children may live. Deuteronomy 30:19-20 (NCV)

Life – The Lord is my life! The best choice!

July 18

Since therefore Christ suffered in the flesh, arm yourselves with the same way of thinking, for whoever has suffered in the flesh has ceased from sin, so as to live for the rest of the time in the flesh no longer for human passions but for the will of God.　　　　　　　　　　　　　　　　　　　　　　　*1 Peter 4:1-2 (ESV)*

What a phrase "*...has ceased from sin, so as to live for the rest of the time in the flesh no longer for human passions but for the will of God.*". I need to 'write that on my forehead' (Jeremiah 31:33). But wait, it says that Jesus lives this way because of the His <u>suffering</u>.

From that time Jesus began to show his disciples that he must go to Jerusalem and suffer many things from the elders and chief priests and scribes, and be killed, and on the third day be raised. And Peter took him aside and began to rebuke him, saying, "Far be it from you, Lord!" This shall never happen to you." But he turned and said to Peter, "Get behind me, Satan! You are a hindrance to me. For you are not setting your mind on the things of God, but on the things of man." Then Jesus told his disciples, "If anyone would come after me, let him deny himself and take up his cross and follow me. For whoever would save his life will lose it, but whoever loses his life for my sake will find it. For what will it profit a man if he gains the whole world and forfeits his life? Or what shall a man give in return for his life? For the Son of Man is going to come with his angels in the glory of his Father, and then he will repay each person according to what he has done. Truly, I say to you, there are some standing here who will not taste death until they see the Son of Man coming in his kingdom."　　　　　　　　　　　　　　　　　*Matthew 16:21-28 (ESV)*

Notice that Jesus did not rebuke <u>Peter</u>. He identified the one whispering in Peter's ear that was getting him off track and trying to influence God's plan. Deny <u>myself</u>. Get my mind in tune with an <u>eternal</u> God-plan and not short-term plan or instant gratification that is all this world has to offer.

Is not this what we said to you in Egypt, 'Leave us alone that we may serve the Egyptians'? For it would have been better for us to serve the Egyptians than to die in the wilderness."　　　　　　　　　　　　　　　　　　　*Exodus 14:12 (ESV)*

The Israelites said, "*It would have been better for us...*" There's that self-centered pride thing again! So many times in looking at situations in my life I only look with narrow vision at how it affects m<u>e</u>. Help me, Lord! I want to look with God's eyes that see a bigger picture: how can <u>GOD</u> be glorified? How can others be helped and brought closer to God, healed, comforted, etc?

And then there is the point that "going back to Egypt" is NOT the best thing! Isn't it strange how sometimes I want to go back to the slavery of my past instead of moving forward? The past can be comfortable. It has some known factors where the future has many more "unknowns". I must remember that God goes before me and I follow HIS lead!

Teach me to do your will, for you are my God!
Let your good Spirit lead me on level ground!　　　　　　　　　　*Psalm 143:10 (ESV)*

Additional Text: Psalm 143, Deuteronomy 5

"When our minds are filled with God, suffering will become full of sweetness, of unction, and of quiet joy."   Brother Lawrence (1611-1691)

Brother Lawrence speaks rightly about suffering. The only glory in it comes with a focus on God. Now that's a choice and often it is a difficult choice. It is making a choice in my spirit over my flesh. Let's see what Paul said to the Romans about spirit and flesh:

For those who live according to the flesh set their minds on the things of the flesh, but those who live according to the Spirit set their minds on the things of the Spirit... You, however, are not in the flesh but in the Spirit, if in fact the Spirit of God dwells in you. Anyone who does not have the Spirit of Christ does not belong to him... For all who are led by the Spirit of God are sons of God. For you did not receive the spirit of slavery to fall back into fear, but you have received the Spirit of adoption as sons, by whom we cry, "Abba, Father!" The Spirit himself bears witness with our spirit that we are children of God, and if children, then heirs – heirs of God and fellow heirs with Christ, provided we suffer with him in order that we may also be glorified with him.

Romans 8:5, 9, 14-17 (ESV)

Paul tells me, bottom line, I have a choice. I can live in the "me" life and do what I want to do, when I want to do it, and how I want to do it – or I can choose God's way. Now choosing God's way means that I won't always understand what He's doing and why He's doing it. That is not a reflection on my lack of intelligence or understanding. It just means that my understanding of God is the same as my 4-year-old grandson's understanding of me. He doesn't know all the facts that I do. I don't know all the facts that God does. Sometimes the 4-year-old must trust and obey without understanding. In fact he may NEVER understand why I did something the way I did. I have to apply that same principle to my relationship to God. That's difficult. I don't like to think of myself as some snotty-nosed kid who needs a "parent". But I do because I don't know everything! I need guidance. I need unconditional love. I need Someone who knows more than I do and has my best interests in mind even when I can't see that. It's a trust 'thing'. It's a heart 'thing'.

Paul's words end with the promise that as I share in Jesus' sufferings, I share in His glory also. Just as my children have had to share in the tough times that we have been through, they are also now sharing in the 'good' times, the times of plenty. That's a promise I can hang on to when we go through future difficulties. It encourages me to choose God's way again, even when I cannot see the 'why'. It is a simple – but difficult – choice.

"And if it is evil in your eyes to serve the LORD, choose this day whom you will serve, whether the gods your fathers served in the region beyond the River, or the gods of the Amorites in whose land you dwell. But as for me and my house, we will serve the LORD."   Joshua 24:15 (ESV)

Additional Text: John 7, Romans 8

But do not overlook this one fact, beloved, that with the Lord one day is as a thousand years, and a thousand years as one day. The Lord is not slow to fulfill his promise as some count slowness, but is patient with you, not wishing that any should perish, but that all should reach repentance. But the day of the Lord will come like a thief, and then the heavens will pass away with a roar, and the heavenly bodies will be burned up and dissolved, and the earth and the works that are done on it will be exposed.

Since all thing are thus to be dissolved, what sort of people ought you to be in lives of holiness and godliness, waiting for and hastening the coming of the day of God, because of which the heavens will be set on fire and dissolved, and the heavenly bodies will melt as they burn! But according to his promise we are waiting for new heavens and a new earth in which righteousness dwells.

2 Peter 3:8-13 (ESV)

God doesn't tell time like I learned in kindergarten! I've always been a time conscious person. After becoming a nurse, I found myself graduate to being <u>obsessive</u> about time. It is totally 'un-cool' for a nurse to give a patient medication more than 15 minutes before or after the time it was ordered to be given!!! Even if I had 20 patients who were to receive medication at 9 a.m. – get it to them ALL between 8:45 and 9:15 a.m.! There are no good excuses for not accomplishing my task!

Talk about trying to teach an old dog new tricks ... God desires that I move on HIS schedule – not mine. Let's look at that definition of a 'God day' that Peter spoke of: *...with the Lord one day is as at thousand years, and a thousand years as one day.*

When I am on God's timing my 'full' day can become an opportunity to watch God take this frantic day and slow it down to what He wants. All of a sudden, I have time to pray with people, write a note of encouragement, or just 'be'. OR God can shift me into high gear as He goes before me and brings up the rear and I accomplish certainly more than I asked or imagined!!! For me, it is much more difficult to hear and obey God when He tells me to be quiet before Him. I am much more comfortable serving in a more <u>active</u> capacity!

God's timing is perfect. Today I choose to obey and trust <u>Him</u> for the schedule!

Additional Text: Psalm 119

July 21

So that I would not become too proud of the wonderful things that were shown to me, a painful physical problem was given to me. This problem was a messenger from Satan, sent to beat me and keep me from being too proud. I begged the Lord three times to take this problem away from me. But he said to me, "My grace is enough for you. When you are weak, my power is made perfect in you." So I am happy to brag about my weaknesses. Then Christ's power can live in me. For this reason I am happy when I have weaknesses, insults, hard times, sufferings, and all kinds of trouble for Christ. Because when I am weak, then I am truly strong.   *2 Corinthians 12:7-10 (NCV)*

I grew up in the Midwest and learned about tornadoes. Now I've lived in Florida for over 20 years. I've learned a lot about hurricanes. A wind blowing at over 120 mph can drive a pinecone through my windshield or a pine needle into the trunk of a tree like it was an arrow! It's all about force.

'Grace' is about power but it's not about force. I don't think I can receive God's grace unless I want it. Grace is unconditional love. There is much speculation about this 'thorn' that Paul speaks about. It could be a physical condition or it could be a person or situation. Paul says he pleaded with God to remove the torment. He didn't ask – he PLEADED! God responded that HIS unconditional love was enough. ENOUGH – SUFFICIENT!!! ALL that Paul needed! If grace was what Paul needed, maybe the 'thorn' was a person or a situation involving a person or group of people. God says His 'unconditional love' was enough but would Paul be weak enough – OPEN ENOUGH – to let God's unconditional love fill him up so that he could receive the POWER of Christ's unconditional love, His 'grace'.

But God's mercy is great, and he loved us very much. Though we were spiritually dead because of the things we did against God, he gave us new life with Christ. You have been saved by God's grace.   *Ephesians 2:4-5 (NCV)*

I was 'saved' because I was weak and so lost, having no where else to go and opened myself to receive only what God could give me – LIFE – ETERNAL LIFE! God could not force that unconditional love on me. I had to open the door and say, "YES! I want it!" So easy – yet, so hard, because it has nothing – NOTHING – to do with any worthiness or strength within me – it's about being too weak to do anything else!

Since we have a great high priest, Jesus the Son of God, who has gone into heaven, let us hold on to the faith we have. For our high priest is able to understand our weaknesses. When he lived on earth, he was tempted in every way that we are, but he did not sin. Let us, then, feel very sure that we can come before God's throne where there is grace. There we can receive mercy and grace to help us when we need it.   *Hebrews 4:14-16 (NCV)*

The *power* of grace comes straight from the throne room of God. It is not a *little* gift or a *cheap* gift. I believe it is a gift of POWER that works MIRACULOUSLY every time! I open my arms WIDE because I need a lot of 'grace' today!

Additional Text: Acts 6, Ephesians 2

July 22

Dwight L. Moody, an evangelist of the 19th century said, *"If we teach our children as we ought to do, instead of Sunday being the dreariest, dullest, tiresomest day of the week to them, it will be the brightest, happiest day of the whole seven."*

Train children how to live right, and when they are old, they will not change.

Proverbs 22:6 (NCV)

Moses admonished the Israelites and now me also with these words:

Look, I have taught you the laws and rules the LORD my God commanded me. Now you can obey the laws in the land you are entering, in the land you will take. Obey these laws carefully, in order to show the other nations that you have wisdom and understanding. When they hear about these laws, they will say, "This great nation of Israel is wise and understanding." No other nation is as great as we are. Their gods do not come near them, but the LORD our God comes near when we pray to him. And no other nation has such good teachings and commands as those I am giving to you today. But be careful! Watch out and don't forget them as long as you live, but teach them to your children and grandchildren. *Deuteronomy 4:5-9 (NCV)*

Paul warned us in Ephesians chapter 6 not to "exasperate" our children but instead to "train" them:

Fathers, do not make your children angry, but raise them with the training and teaching of the Lord. *Ephesians 6:4 (NCV)*

There's that word again – like from Proverbs – train. I <u>train</u> someone when I lead by example. I'm not commanding – I'm not <u>just</u> instructing. I'm "training". When I am truthful and open and clear – by example. This God-system perpetuates itself. I train someone – they train someone else.

I believe that also means that I should be transparent before my children – that my life with it's trials and tests be an example of having an "INTIMATE" walk with the Lord. Not perfect – in fact, what an awesome lesson to my children when they see Mom struggle – even repent – and then walk forward in victory! Always in victory because I know whose I am! Who I belong to!

Jesus said to let the children come to Him – May I not be a stumbling block to the children with <u>my</u> rules and regulations that say before they can come to Jesus – they have to wear their hair a certain way or only listen to a certain kind of music. May my example show them that I <u>CHOOSE</u> to live the way GOD directs <u>ME</u> BECAUSE – I love Him! I choose to please <u>JESUS</u> (not man) because I LOVE Him because <u>HE</u> loved ME <u>FIRST</u>!!!

Additional Text: Titus 2, Hebrews 5

July 23

God may kill me, but still I will trust him and offer my defense.

Job 13:15 (CEV)

Job's words are very familiar to us. Job's children are dead and he has lost all of his worldly possessions. The only thing he has left is his life and his hope in God. And one more thing. Job says that he will defend himself to God. I only feel the need to defend myself to those I care about, those whose opinion I value. Job loves God. AND he knows God loves him. Still.

Your worshipers will see me, and they will be glad that I trust your word.

Psalm 119:74 (CEV)

When cancer came to my son, James, I was often asked "How do you do it?" meaning – go on with life, function, laugh, I guess basically do anything except weep and ask "why". "God" is the only answer. Sometimes I would share specifically about the ways God was working in our lives but it still came back to – God. There is no other way to survive that kind of battle with joy and life instead of despair and loss.

And this hope is what saves us. But if we already have what we hope for, there is no need to keep on hoping.

Romans 8:24 (CEV)

Hope. Faith. Love. Given by God in sufficient quantities for the task in front of me. All I have to do is ask for it. Sometimes I ask not so much in words but in my spirit where I know that I can not go through what is in front of me without help from the Lord. I must keep the goal in front of me – eternal life through Jesus Christ.

This hope is like a firm and steady anchor for our souls. In fact, hope reaches behind the curtain and into the most holy place.

Hebrews 6:19 (CEV)

Time with the Lord, every day, is vital to me. Prayer, reading His words, worshiping Him in song or just quiet before Him. It is the living water and fresh bread that keeps me well and strong. That keeps 'hope' a strong and sure anchor.

[Jesus said,] *"Heal the sick, raise the dead, cleanse those who have leprosy, drive out demons. Freely you have received, freely give."*

Matthew 10:8

Freely I share with you today that Jesus is the answer no matter what the pain or loss. He who is God and has <u>everything</u> came to earth with <u>nothing</u> and gave <u>me</u> ALL He had so that I, too, might have <u>everything</u> that is eternal. Hope, an anchor that will bring me through every storm.

There is a wonderful song, *The Anchor Holds*, by Ray Boltz and Lawrence Chewning. You can go to www.rayboltz.com and listen to the song that is on his *The Concert of a Lifetime* CD. It is a song that will be a classic in my library along with *It is Well With My Soul*.

Additional Text: Psalm 42, Romans 4

The kind of sorrow God wants makes people change their hearts and lives. This leads to salvation, and you cannot be sorry for that. But the kind of sorrow the world has brings death. *2 Corinthians 7:10 (NCV)*

John Welch, a 16th century Scottish clergyman, was devoted to prayer and ministry. He often woke during the night and wailed in prayer about the condition of his flock. He said about Godly sorrow, *"There is Godly sorrow which leads a man to life, and this sorrow is wrought in a man by the Spirit of God, and in the heart of the godly, that he mourns for sin because it has displeased God, who is so dear and so sweet a Father to him."*

As I continue to walk with the Lord and grow in the knowledge and experience of Him, I am 'cut to the heart' about two things: 1) God's faithfulness and loving mercy and 2) my sin and unworthiness. When God's 'godliness' meets with my 'humanness' – each becomes very apparent!!! It brings repentance to my heart. It brings me to my knees, with tears, asking my Father to forgive. He does. Every time.

I believe these are the moments when I hear His voice inviting me 'to be holy because I am holy'. If I want to draw closer to God, it will happen when I repent – or turn away – from sin – and take deliberate steps to God, to holiness. It will involve sorrow, Godly sorrow, for the condition that I had chosen to live in. Like the prodigal son who lived among the pigs, he had to go to his father and repent in order to find himself in a better condition. His father received his repentance, forgave him, and then showed him how to celebrate and LIVE in the victory of that forgiveness. The son did not have to live as a slave the rest of his life. He was restored to the full life as the son of the Father.

Brothers and sisters, we want you to know about those Christians who have died so you will not be sad, as other who have no hope. We believe that Jesus died and that he rose again. So, because of him, God will raise with Jesus those who have died... And we will be with the Lord forever. So encourage each other with these words. *1 Thessalonians 4:13-14, 17-18 (NCV)*

Godly sorrow comes for my sins but also for other events in my life that bring grief. I experience 'losses' when people that I love move geographically far away as well as when they die. Separations through divorce and custody disputes bring sorrow that tears at my heart. Paul acknowledges the very real sorrow that comes but he reminds me that because of Jesus I have something that others do not have if they do not have Jesus – I have HOPE.

Sorrow will certainly be a part of the 'human condition' of this life. As I grieve the losses that come my way, may I remember that the same grace and mercy that allows me to accept God's forgiveness when I have grieved HIM with my sin and moves me on to a new time of life with Him will also lift me from the grief of losses and move me on to a new time of life with Him. It is Godly sorrow. It ends in victory every time!

Then your light will shine like the dawn, and your wounds will quickly heal. Your God will walk before you, and the glory of the LORD will protect you from behind. *Isaiah 58:8 (NCV)*

Additional Text: 1 Thessalonians 4 and 5

July 25

Surely you know. Surely you have heard. The LORD is the God who lives forever, who created all the world. He does not become tired or need to rest. No one can understand how great his wisdom is. He gives strength to those who are tired and more power to those who are weak. Even children become tired and need to rest, and young people trip and fall. But the people who trust the LORD will become strong again. They will rise up as an eagle in the sky; they will run and not need rest; they will walk and not become tired.

Isaiah 40:28-31 (NCV)

How are your Mondays? Do you rest and relax over the weekend and truly enjoy a Sabbath or are the days just another two workdays?

My husband and I went on a vacation one week. It was our first in three years. I knew I was tired but I didn't realize how exhausted until I slept 10 hours the first night.

God doesn't grow tired or exhausted. He goes non-stop, 24 – 7. He is watching over me 24 – 7. God also GIVES strength. Remember, Paul testified that in MY weakness, God is strong! (2 Corinthians 12)

"There is nothing more deceitful than your estimate of your own strength." said Robert McCheyne, a 19th century Scottish pastor. And George Swinnock, a 17th century English clergyman said, *"Satan watcheth for those vessels that sail without a convoy."*

I never knew how important being 'plugged in' to an alive church body was until I was away from it for almost six months. Do you belong to a local church? I mean really belong. I am so blessed by my home church. I know my pastor and he preaches 'fresh bread' from his own time with the Lord and holds me accountable. I am involved in the prayer ministry of the church. And I tithe give offerings as God directs. I share what God is doing in my life and learn more about Him from the others in this 'Body' of Christ.

Our growing Christian life is fed by God's Holy Spirit. He POURS OUT His life and nourishment individually, yes, but He saturates me as I come together with others in the Body of Christ and worship and serve Him. It's a multiplication thing! If you are NOT involved in a local church, get rid of the analysis and excuses that you've used and get 'plugged in' **NOW**!

As iron sharpens iron, so people can improve each other.

Proverbs 27:17 (NCV)

Happy are those who listen to me, watching at my door every day, waiting at my open doorway. Those who find me find life, and the LORD will be pleased with them. Those who do not find me hurt themselves. Those who hate me love death.

Proverbs 8:34-36 (NCV)

Additional Text: Proverbs 25 and Hebrews 10

July 26

When you have all you want to eat, then praise the LORD your God for giving you a good land. Be careful not to forget the LORD your God so that you fail to obey his commands, laws, and rules that I am giving you today. When you eat all you want and build nice houses and live in them, when your herds and flocks grow large and your silver and gold increase, when you have more of everything, then your heart will become proud. You will forget the LORD your God, who brought you out of the land of Egypt, where you were slaves...

If you forget the LORD your God and follow other gods and worship them and bow down to them, I warn you today that you will be destroyed. Just as the LORD destroyed the other nations for you, you can be destroyed if you do not obey the LORD your God.   *Deuteronomy 8:10-14, 19-20 (NCV)*

Everything that I have – God gave me. Why do I have a problem accepting that without a "Yes, but..."? Well, for one thing – PRIDE! Yup, I think to myself: "I went to school and I studied and I am here now to reap what I deserve. I earned it!!!" BUT if I continue to trace the things that I have accomplished I will find God standing there through every test, every bit of tuition I paid or scholarship that I won! "But, but...," I say. Now here's is what is at the core of the problem...below what personal pride is covering up...an inability to accept the Father's <u>unconditional</u> love. Yes, it's true...I <u>don't</u> deserve it! That is absolutely correct! He gives it anyway. And it's bigger than any 'love experience' I have ever had or will have!

I ask the Father in his great glory to give you the power to be strong inwardly through his Spirit. I pray that Christ will live in your hearts by faith and that your life will be strong in love and be built on love. And I pray that you and all God's holy people will have the power to understand the greatness of Christ's love – how wide and how long and how high and how deep that love is. Christ's love is greater than anyone can ever know, but I pray that you will be able to know that love. Then you can be filled with the fullness of God.

Ephesians 3:16-19 (NCV)

It will take Holy Spirit power for me to grasp the dimensions of God's love. It surpasses all knowledge, all points of reference. The text from Deuteronomy is very <u>STRONG</u> on how important it is for me to give God all the credit for all that I am and all that I have. God desires so much for me to accept His love and feel that joy (only that is really not a strong enough word!) when I accept His love and become filled with Him!

I am going to just stop for a few minutes and consider some of the MANY things God has given me just in the past few days or weeks or months. I'm going to just put a few notes down so I can come back at the end of the year and see how much more there is: _____

_____

_____

Additional Text: Psalm 112, Acts 20

Faith means being sure of the things we hope for and knowing that something is real even if we do not see it. Hebrews 11:1 (NCV)

Then Paul stood before the meeting of the Areopagus and said, "People of Athens, I can see you are very religious in all things. As I was going through your city, I saw the objects you worship. I found an altar that had these words written on it: TO A GOD WHO IS NOT KNOWN. You worship a god that you don't know, and this is the God I am telling you about! The God who made the whole world and everything in it is the Lord of the land and the sky. He does not live in temples built by human hands. This God is the One who gives life, breath, and everything else to people. He does not need any help from them; he has everything he needs. God began by making one person, and from him came all the different people who live everywhere in the world. God decided exactly when and where they must live. God wanted them to look for him and perhaps search all around for him and find him, though he is not far from any of us: 'We live in him. We walk in him. We are in him.' Some of your own poets have said: 'For we are his children.' Acts 17:22-28 (NCV)

I am originally from Missouri. Some would say that my personality is typical of the state motto, "Show Me"! I like things that I can quantify. I like my desk organized and carry a calendar with me at all times. I think God likes to mess with me on this!

At that time Jesus said, "I praise you, Father, Lord of heaven and earth, because you have hidden these things from the people who are wise and smart. But you have shown them to those who are like little children. Yes, Father, this is what you really wanted." Matthew 11:25-26 (NCV)

God wants me to walk in <u>faith</u>. He tells me His <u>grace</u> is sufficient. His <u>love</u> is everlasting. I should be joyful in <u>hope</u>. How do I quantify those things?

And we speak about these things, not with words taught us by human wisdom but with words taught us by the Spirit. And so we explain spiritual truths to spiritual people. A person who does not have the Spirit does not accept the truths that come from the Spirit of God. That person thinks they are foolish and cannot understand them, because they can only be judged to be true by the Spirit. 1 Corinthians 2:13-14 (NCV)

Oh. Guess it doesn't matter where I've come from – only where I am going with God. Today is a brand new day on the journey. What will I choose to do with my Lord today?

Additional Text: Matthew 17, Romans 14

I am happy in my sufferings for you. There are things that Christ must still suffer through his body, the church. I am accepting, in my body, my part of these things that must be suffered. I became a servant of the church because God gave me a special work to do that helps you, and that work is to tell fully the message of God. This message is the secret that was hidden from everyone since the beginning of time, but now it is made known to God's holy people. God decided to let his people know this rich and glorious secret which he has for all people. This secret is Christ himself, who is in you. He is our only hope for glory.
Colossians 1:24-27 (NCV)

A mystery. I love reading or watching a good mystery. It is unfortunate that too many of Today's writers think they have to add gallons of gore and sex in order to make the story interesting. Maybe if they just picked an interesting subject and true hero that would hold the reader's attention – even after 2000 years!

God's plan of salvation, now THERE'S a mystery. MAN turns his back on God. Man has everything – and turns 180 degrees and chooses to disobey. Man is lost. What sacrifice can make up or atone for such sin?

God has a plan. Nothing takes God by surprise. Only the Son of Man – God Incarnate – God in the flesh – Emmanuel – can atone for my sin. And there is the mystery.

WHY would Jesus die for me? Because of what I can say to Him? I don't think so. Here is what God said to Job:

"Who is this that makes my purpose unclear by saying things that are not true?"
Job 38:2 (NCV)

Or maybe it's because of what I can do for Him? Look at what God said to Isaiah: *The LORD says, "Shout out loud. Don't hold back. Shout out loud like a trumpet. Tell my people what they have done against their God; tell the family of Jacob about their sins. They still come every day looking for me and want to learn my ways. They act just like a nation that does what is right, that obeys the commands of its God. They ask me to judge them fairly. They want God to be near them. They say, 'To honor you we had special days when we gave up eating, but you didn't see. We humbled ourselves to honor you, but you didn't notice.' "*
Isaiah 58:1-3 (NCV)

Can I stand before you and the Lord today and tell you that everything I have said or done today was to first and foremost glorify God? I wish I could.

So why? Explain the mystery of salvation to me, Lord.

It is so simple. Look. Listen. Here it is:

"I love you people with a love that will last forever. That is why I have continued showing you kindness."
Jeremiah 31:3 (NCV)

The Spirit and the bride say, "Come!" Let the one who hears this say, "Come!" Let whoever is thirsty come; whoever wishes may have the water of life as a free gift.
Revelation 22:17 (NCV)

God loves me. God loves you. Let us open our hearts and receive His love. Tear down the walls, Lord. Let us receive your love – receive it in truth today – because of the sacrifice of Jesus. Thank You, Lord.

Here are two gospel stories about healing and faith:

Later Jesus went to Jerusalem for a special Jewish feast. In Jerusalem there is a pool with five covered porches, which is called Bethzatha in the Jewish language. This pool is near the Sheep Gate. Many sick people were lying on the porches beside the pool. Some were blind, some were crippled, and some were paralyzed. A man was lying there who had been sick for thirty-eight years.

John 5:1-5 (NCV)

When Jesus was leaving there, two blind men followed him. They cried out, "Have mercy on us, Son of David!" After Jesus went inside, the blind men went with him. He asked the men, "Do you believe that I can make you see again?" They answered, "Yes, Lord." Then Jesus touched their eyes and said, "Because you believe I can make you see again, it will happen." Then the men were able to see. But Jesus warned them strongly, saying, "Don't tell anyone about this."

Matthew 9:27-30 (NCV)

Faith. Does God answer prayer according to <u>our faith</u>? Is the <u>will</u> of the Almighty contingent upon what I believe and how much I believe about Him?

Faith means being sure of the things we hope for and knowing that something is real even if we do not see it. Faith is the reason we remember great people who lived in the past. *Hebrews 11:1 (NCV)*

One of the most well-known verses in the Bible about faith. The next 36 verses tell us about these wonderful 'great people' and their faith, implying that they were extra-ordinary, void of doubt. Hmmmm.

Abel – well, he ends up murdered.

Abraham – let's see: he lied to a king about his wife, he doubted God and manipulated His promise, causing a whole mess of problems with the begetting of Ishmael <u>and</u> Isaac, <u>and</u> he dodged the bullet in sacrificing Isaac.

Jacob – manipulated his brother, his father and lived most of his adult years in exile

Joseph – sold as a slave, is wrongfully accused of adultery, and ends up in prison and then becomes #2 man in Egypt – then manipulates <u>his</u> brothers out of revenge

Moses – whined his way through his 'call' from God until God's anger 'burned' against him

Israelites – whined and complained for 40 years on a trip that should have been done in a couple of weeks

The walls of Jericho – fell down because of <u>Joshua's</u> obedience to God and the people's love and obedience to <u>Joshua</u> it seems to me, not God.

We have around us many people whose lives tell us what faith means. SO let us run the race that is before us and never give up...Let us look only to Jesus, the One who began our faith and who makes it perfect. *Hebrews 12:1-2 (NCV)*

And, for me, here is the answer to my original question. It is not <u>my</u> faith that is counted when I petition God. It is my complete weakness in Jesus. I come to God asking for healing and mercy and help, stinky in my sins, and Jesus steps in front of me so that all the Father sees is a beautiful daughter with a request. Ahhh – here comes my faith!

Is God welcome in <u>every</u> room of my life, every 'part' of my life? Or do I compartmentalize my life into 'mine' and 'His'?

Then the Pharisees went and plotted how to entangle him in his talk. And they sent their disciples to him, along with the Herodians, saying, "Teacher, we know that you are true and teach the way of God truthfully, and you do not care about anyone's opinion, for you are not swayed by appearances. Tell us, then, what you think. Is it lawful to pay taxes to Caesar, or not?" But Jesus, aware of their malice, said, "Why put me to the test, you hypocrites? Show me the coin for the tax." And they brought him a denarius. And Jesus said to them, "Whose likeness and inscription is this?" They said, "Caesar's." Then he said to them, "Therefore render to Caesar the things that are Caesar's, and to God the things that are God's." Matthew 22:15-21 (ESV)

So what part of my life is 'God's'? ALL OF IT!!! Good answer! "That's hard. He may decide to do something with my life that isn't on my agenda!" I say. Let's look at the alternative. This story was sent in an email to me. I apologize to the earthly author and appreciate his/her illustration.

"Once there was a very wealthy young man. He lived in an elaborate house with dozens of beautiful rooms. One day he decided to invite the Lord to come home and stay with him. When the Lord arrived, this young man offered him the very best room in the house. It was upstairs and at the end of the hall. 'This room is yours, Jesus! Stay as long as you like and you can do whatever you want, Jesus. It's yours!'

That evening the young man retired for the night when a loud knocking came at the front door. He pulled on his robe and went to open the door. There stood three of satans' demons ready to spring in and attack. He quickly tried to shut the door but one of the demons kept sticking his foot inside the frame. Sometime later, after a great struggle, he was able to shut and lock the door. He returned to his room, totally exhausted. 'Can you believe that?' he thought. 'Jesus is just down the hall and while I was battling demons, He slept. Oh, well. Maybe He didn't hear.'

The next day things went along normally in his life and the young man retired early, very tired. About midnight, a ruckus could be heard outside the man's front door that he KNEW would tear the door down! He stumbled down and opened the door to find DOZENS of demons trying to get into his home. For nearly three hours, the man fought and struggled against the demons and finally was able to slam the door shut on them.

He really didn't understand this at all! 'Why won't the Lord come to my rescue? Why does He allow me to fight all by myself? I feel so alone.' Troubled, he found his way to the sofa and fell asleep. In the morning, he quietly went to the bedroom door where he had left Jesus and knocked. 'Jesus. Lord, I don't understand. For the last two nights I have been battling demons away from my door while You laid here sleeping. Don't You care? I gave you the best room! I really thought that once I invited you to live with me that you would take care of me. What more can I do?' With tears in His eyes, Jesus quietly said, 'My precious child, I am Lord of this room but I am not Master of this house. I can only protect what you release into my care.' 'Lord, please forgive me! Take my <u>entire</u> house – it is yours. I am so sorry that I never offered you <u>all</u>.' With this, the young man flung open the bedroom door and knelt at Jesus' feet. All was given <u>and</u> forgiven in that moment.

That night the young man went to bed wondering if the demons would return. 'But Jesus said He would take care of all that I have given Him.' About midnight, the banging on the front door began. The young man slipped out of his room in time to see Jesus going down the stairs. 'No need to be afraid,' He said. He watched in awe as Jesus swung open the door. Satan stood at the door with his demons surrounding him. 'What do you want, satan?' the Lord asked. The devil bowed low in the presence of God. 'So, sorry, I seem to have gotten the wrong address.' And with that, he and his minions ran away."

Jesus wants all of me not just a part. He will take all that I give Him, but nothing more. How much of my heart have I given to the Lord? Am I keeping a portion of it away from Him? Why not let the Lord fight the battles for me? He is <u>always</u> victorious!

~

I have not reached my goal, and I am not perfect. But Christ has taken hold of me. So I keep on running and struggling to take hold of me. So I keep on running and struggling to take hold of the prize. My friends, I don't feel that I have already arrived. But I forget what is behind, and I struggle for what is ahead. I run toward the goal, so that I can win the prize of being called to heaven. This is the prize that God offers because of what Christ Jesus has done.

Philippians 3:12-14 (CEV)

I am a very goal-oriented person. I find comfort when I get up in the morning and I know just what tasks I need to tackle in order to accomplish my goals of the day. Yes, I am more than a bit of a control freak!

God is goal-oriented, too. It is truly a wondrous thing when He and I have the same goal!!! Unfortunately, I cannot say that is always true. In fact, I suspect God alternates between rolling His eyes and laughing and shaking His head and pounding His fist down on the golden arm of His throne as He watches me 'struggling' and 'running' toward my goals. What is God's goal for me?

2 Corinthians 5:9 says, *So we make it our goal to please him.* O-KAY. How do I do that?

The LORD God has told us what is right and what he demands: "See that justice is done, let mercy be your first concern, and humbly obey your God."

Micah 6:8 (CEV)

When asked what is the greatest commandment, Jesus answered a Pharisee, an expert in law, *"Love the Lord your God with all your heart, soul, and mind. This is the first and most important commandment. The second most important commandment is like this one. And it is, "Love others as much as you love yourself." All the Law of Moses and the Books of the prophets are based on these two commandments."* *(Matthew 22:37-40 CEV)*

Love the Lord with all that I am. Everything! Hold nothing back! Everything I do – Everything I say – EVERYTHING is to reflect back on God and how much I love Him!

Love others like I do myself. That means I love myself without conditions. Love myself whether I get that promotion or not. Love who I am – even if no one else seems to – because – God does! And then – love others the same way – no conditions – just love.

Remember, we are told to 'forget the past' – all the junk – all the reasons – all the excuses – FORGET IT! It is my choice and once I make the choice to let the baggage go – God will be there to LIFT me UP! Sending me to press on and strain toward HIS goal for my day, for my life, for eternity – pleasing Him.

Additional Text: 2 Corinthians 5, 1 Timothy 1

Linda B. Smith

The oldest of seven children, Linda accepted Jesus as her Savior when she was five-years-old at a tent meeting that she attended with her grandmother, Nana Webb. In those early years, Linda, along with her sisters, was raised in the Catholic Church while her brothers went to the Methodist Church with their father. Their home was blended together with God always in the center.

Nana Webb continued to be an important influence in Linda's spiritual life as she listened to Nana's stories of tent revivals and healing services that had been a part of her life. Nana had a vision that Linda would attend Asbury Theological Seminary, which she shared with Linda after she had made the decision to attend the Kentucky school, majoring in journalism. While there, Linda learned about the 1949 Asbury Revival. It was during this time that she became interested in revival history. Leonard Ravenhill's book, *Why Revival Tarries*, was an encouragement to continue 'watching for God'.

"I kept my ear to the ground, reading all the revival history I could find. I watched and read about Dr. Billy Graham, Benny Hinn, and Kathyrn Kuhlman. I still strain to see the horizon to catch a glimpse of what God is going to do next. 'God-watchers' are usually unknown, like undercover operatives. We have a voracious appetite for God."

After college, Linda toured with Campus Crusade for Christ under Bill Bright. Utilizing the music style of the day, teams of Christian youth toured both the United States and Europe singing Christian songs and giving testimonies with their invitation to choose Jesus as Savior and Lord.

Linda has been a high school English teacher and a co-owner of a Bible bookstore. She is the mother of three daughters and two sons. Her husband is a local church pastor. Through it all, she has continued to teach and mentor children and youth, encouraging them to seek a mature and intimate relationship with Jesus. During her time as a youth pastor at Pine Forest United Methodist Church in Pensacola, FL, the wonderful and rocky days of the Pensacola Outpouring occurred. Many of the youth were radically changed by this revival. The pastor and Linda had the daunting task to attempt to answer questions from both the youth and their parents about the changes. Today the majority of those youth are still growing and serving the Lord as pastors, teachers, worship leaders, and leaders of uncommon lives in a common workplace.

"It is not so much what you do in your life but who and what you are to God that is important."   *-- Linda Smith*

After the Israelites heard the report from the twelve men who had explored Canaan, the people cried all night and complained to Moses and Aaron, "We wish we had died in Egypt or somewhere out here in the desert! Is the LORD leading us into Canaan, just to have us killed and our women and children captured? We'd be better off in Egypt." Then they said to one another, "Let's choose our own leader and go back." Numbers 14:1-4 (CEV, emphasis mine)

Among some church goers, the concept of 'going back to Egypt' is a popular one. The idea simply stated is: "Let's go back to our <u>known</u> captivity. Let's go back to the way things <u>were</u>." Most people who know me, if pressured, would put me into the more charismatic, progressive pile of Christians. However, the 'back to Egypt virus' can infect me, too.

It <u>is</u> a matter of trust. Do I trust God to lead me forward, free from the captivity that keeps me from following Him without question, into the Promise Land to live with Him forever? Do I trust that GOD knows where He is going? Do I trust Him to prepare a place for me that is SO MUCH BETTER than anything I can imagine?

My granddaughter, Anna, and grandson, Jaxon, were recently visiting. Like most children they <u>LOVE</u> to ride in the car. I have a minivan that affords them large side windows where they can see where we are going and all the people and dogs who happen by on the way! Anna is from Ft. Worth. Jaxon is from Phoenix. Do they know where they are going when we all get in the car in Pensacola? Nope. They do not know where they are going. They do not recognize any streets or houses or stores we pass by...except maybe Wal-mart or Target! Are they concerned that they are riding in unknown territory? Nope. Why is that? Why is there no anxiety? Because they <u>trust</u> Mom and Dad; maybe even Nanna and Poppa to know the way home.

Abraham had faith and obeyed God. He was told to go to the land that God had said would be his, and he left for a country he had never seen. Because Abraham had faith, he lived as a stranger in the promised land. He lived there in a tent, and so did Isaac and Jacob, who were later given the same promise. Abraham did this, because he was waiting for the eternal city that God had planned and built. Hebrews 11:8-10 (CEV)

[Jesus said,] *"There are many rooms in my Father's house. I wouldn't tell you this, unless it was true. I am going there to prepare a place for each of you. After I have done this, I will come back and take you with me. Then we will be together. You know the way to where I am going...I am the way, the truth, and the life!...Without me, no one can go to the Father."* John 14:2-4, 6 (CEV)

Jesus also said in verse one to trust the Father and trust Him also. Good advice as I travel this road towards the Promise Land. I don't have a map. I've never been there before but the Father has. I trust God to show me the road home.

Additional Text: Hebrews 11, John 14

August 2

For you did not receive the spirit of slavery to fall back into fear, but you have received the Sprit of adoption as sons, by whom we cry, "Abba! Father!" The Spirit himself bears witness with our spirit that we are children of God, and if children, then heirs – heirs of God and fellow heirs with Christ, provided we suffer with him in order that we may also be glorified with him.

Romans 8:15-16 (ESV)

It is truly hard for me to think that God sees me <u>as His child</u>. I KNOW all the feelings I have inside for <u>my</u> children. There is not a question that I would do <u>anything</u> to take away any pain from one of them. I rejoice at their accomplishments and yet my love for them was birthed when all they could do was just lay there on the bed randomly moving their arms and legs and seemingly unable to focus on <u>anything</u> much less <u>my</u> face. My prayers for them come from <u>deep</u> within my spirit. I 'see' them as individuals with unique and wonderful gifts and yet we are a family 'unit' that is incomplete when <u>one</u> is absent from the group. Why would <u>GOD</u> feel this way about <u>me</u>?

Blessed be the God and Father of our Lord Jesus Christ, who has blessed us in Christ with every spiritual blessing in the heavenly places, even as he chose us in him before the foundation of the world, that we should be holy and blameless before him. In love he predestined us for adoption through Jesus Christ, according to the purpose of his will, to the praise of his glorious grace, with which he has blessed us in the Beloved.   *Ephesians 1:3-6 (ESV)*

God didn't adopt or choose me because I was good-looking or rich or terribly wise. The first time I saw my children I <u>KNEW</u> they were beautiful and wonderful and perfect! No one could have told me different! I also knew that they would be a lot of work, cost more money than I could imagine, and break my heart. I loved them …no, I LOVE THEM more now than I did that morning when I first saw them. I didn't think that could be possible.

God <u>adopted</u> me. He <u>chose</u> me. He saw all the trouble and cost I would be and yet signed His name over mine and took me to His heart and said, "Hey, Jody. You can call me 'Abba'. Daddy." God didn't need <u>me</u> to complete <u>Him</u> and yet He gave me life any way and loves me any way. God's commitment to me is greater than my commitment to Him. I understand that. All of my children at some point during their growing up years got disgusted with my rules, stomped their feet, and said, "I hate you!" They rejected me as their parent. I've done the same to God. My rejection of Him did not sever His love for me any more than my child's rejection and anger toward me severed my love for him/her.

For I am sure that neither death nor life, nor angels nor rulers, nor things present nor things to come, nor powers, nor height nor depth, nor anything else in all creation, will be able to separate us from the love of God in Christ Jesus our Lord.   *Romans 8:38-39 (ESV)*

My Abba Father will <u>never</u> turn away from me. The doors to the home He has for me will never be closed to me. When other people fail me or hurt me or I fail myself, Father is always waiting to hold me, love me, and remind me that <u>His</u> love never fails. He is Father.

Two blind men were sitting beside the road and when they heard that Jesus was coming that way, they began shouting, "Sir, King David's Son, have mercy on us!" The crowd told them to be quiet, but they only yelled the louder.
When Jesus came to the place where they were he stopped in the road and called, "What do you want me to do for you?"
"Sir, they said, "we want to see!"
Jesus was moved with pity for them and touched their eyes. And instantly they could see, and followed him. Matthew 20:30-34 (TLB)

What were the followers thinking??!! Two people obviously in need of a Savior and the crowd tells them to "SHUT UP!" How could any follower of Jesus keep someone from getting close to Jesus? Unfortunately, we do it a lot.

Have you ever heard someone say, "Well, I don't go to church because this church believes 'this' and another one believes 'that'. So how do I know who's right?" Or someone tells you, "Yes, I used to go to that church but when I raised some questions about why we do such-and-such…well, I got the cold shoulder after that." We spend our time scrutinizing how someone approaches Christ, making sure they 'do it right' and miss the point that Jesus just desires that they come…any way they can!

Jesus was on His way to Jerusalem. Matthew tells this story of the two blind men. Mark relates the story of the blind man, Bartimaeus. Luke remembers Jesus' parable of the ten minas and the investment that Jesus as made in us so that we may produce more 'servant fruit' to glorify the Father. John tells of another who had been in need of a Savior and wanted to express her gratitude to Jesus and so she anointed Jesus' feet and wiped them with her hair, another example of a 'ritual' that didn't meet the followers' standards but met Jesus instead!

So don't criticize each other any more. Try instead to live in such a way that you will never make your brother stumble by letting him see you doing something he thinks is wrong…In this way aim for harmony in the church and try to build each other up. Romans 14:13, 19 (TLB)

Whether it is a 'brother' Christian or a 'brother' still looking for a Savior, Jesus reminds me that He was always open to those with a seeking heart. It was only the 'closed', self-centered Pharisees of the Church that He showed NO patience. How can I clear a path to Jesus for someone today?

Additional Text: Daniel 12, Matthew 15

August 4

I saw in the night visions, and behold, with the clouds of heaven there came one like a son of man, and he came to the Ancient of Days and was presented before him. And to him was given dominion and glory and a kingdom, that all peoples, nations, and languages should serve him; his dominion is an everlasting dominion, which shall not pass away, and his kingdom one that shall not be destroyed. Daniel 7:13-14 (ESV)

The Son of Man in power and in glory is the image that 'rallies' me; pumps me up! The picture of the Messiah in VICTORY is what I want to see and what the Jews of Jesus' day searched with eager anticipation. The 'good guys' win – the 'bad guys' get their 'just rewards'! For Jesus' day it was Rome falling; for me it is satan's eternal defeat!

And as Jesus was going up to Jerusalem, he took the twelve disciples aside, and on the way he said to them, "See, we are going up to Jerusalem. And the Son of Man will be delivered over to the chief priests and scribes, and they will condemn him over to the Gentiles to be mocked and flogged and crucified, and he will be raised on the third day."...
But Jesus called them to him and said, "You know that the rulers of the Gentiles lord it over them, and their great ones exercise authority over them. It shall not be so among you. But whoever would be great among you must be your servant, and whoever would be first among you must be your slave, even as the Son of Man came not to be served but to serve, and to give his life as a ransom for many." Matthew 20:17-19, 25-28 (ESV)

Jesus is <u>trying</u> to get His disciples and me to *understand* that God's plan for glory and VICTORY is different than what I (and the disciples) think it will be. VICTORY will come through serving. Warfare will be fierce <u>on my knees</u>. I will be the STRONGEST soldier when I am weakest and fall to my knees. When I reach out and extend Jesus' unconditional love – my enemy is defeated! God's Kingdom will be extended and grow when I serve and love.

I, Paul myself entreat you, by the meekness and gentleness of Christ – I who am humble when face to face with you, but bold toward you when I am away! – I beg of you that when I am present I may not have to show boldness with such confidence as I count on showing against some who suspect us of walking according to the flesh. For though we walk in the flesh, we are not waging war according to the flesh. For the weapons of our warfare are not of the flesh but have divine power to destroy strongholds. We destroy arguments and every lofty opinion raised against the knowledge of God, and make every thought captive to obey Christ,... 2 Corinthians 10:1-5 (ESV)

That last phrase there "*...and make every thought captive to obey Christ,..*" tells me where I start in my days as Christ's soldier. Even my thoughts are put <u>under</u> obedience to Jesus so that when He, my Commander-in-Chief, gives an order – it doesn't occur to me to question or analyze. I just 'do it'! I <u>know</u> my Commander. I have a day-to-day relationship with Him. I trust Him. I obey Him. The VICTORY is assured. I <u>LOVE</u> being on the WINNING TEAM!

Additional Text: 2 Corinthians 10, Revelation 18

Blessed is the one whose transgression is forgiven, whose sin is covered. Blessed is the man against whom the LORD counts no iniquity, and in whose spirit there is no deceit.   *Psalm 32:1-2 (ESV)*

David tells us — he confessed — and God forgave him. A done deal. But let's look at another story in 1 Samuel 15:

* King Saul is told by the prophet Samuel that the LORD wants him to go WIPE OUT the Amalekites for what they had done to Israel. v.3 *"Now go, attack the Amalekites and totally destroy everything that belongs to them. Do not spare them; put to death men and women, children and infants, cattle and sheep, camels and donkeys.' "*

* So Saul takes 210,000 men and attacks. BUT —v. 8 *"Saul and the army spared Agag (the king) and the best of the sheep and cattle, the fat calves and lambs--everything that was good. These they were unwilling to destroy completely, but everything that was despised and weak they totally destroyed."*

* And what was God's response to that? v. 11-12 *"I am grieved that I have made Saul king, because he has turned away from me and has not carried out my instructions." Samuel was troubled, and he cried out to the LORD all that night. Samuel interceded for his disobedient king. The next morning, he got up and went to look for him.*

* v.13 *When Samuel reached him, Saul said, "The LORD bless you! I have carried out the LORD's instructions."* LIAR!

* Saul goes on to add lie after lie on top of his disobedience! EXCUSES, EXCUSES, EXCUSES!!!

* Finally Samuel says, "STOP!" He tells Saul what the Lord told him during the night — the <u>truth</u> of what Saul had done.

* Saul <u>again</u> makes excuses and tries to weasel around make it sound like he <u>had</u> obeyed the Lord — technically — like he <u>knew</u> the Lord would not want him to kill the 'good stuff'!!!

* Samuel cuts to the bottom line and says, *"Has the LORD as great delight in burnt offerings and sacrifices, as in obeying the voice of the LORD? Behold, to obey is better than sacrifice, and to listen than the fat of rams. For rebellion is as the sin of divination, and presumption is as iniquity and idolatry. Because you have rejected the word of the LORD, he has also rejected you from being the king."*   *vv.22-23*

And that was it for Saul. I don't believe that God was harsh because Saul was disobedient — it was because Saul refused to repent — turn away and admit he had disobeyed.

Mercy by definition is undeserved forgiveness. Every sin I commit requires God's forgiveness. Any attempt to defend myself is worthless and is a mockery to God. When I first feel the conviction, may I fall on my face at the feet of our Savior, confess my sin and plead His great mercy --- and <u>receive it</u>! He does not hold it back when I humble myself and ask!

Additional Text: 1 Samuel 15, Psalm 32

When Jesus, Peter, James, and John came back to the other followers, they saw a great crowd around them and the teachers of the law arguing with them. But as soon as the crowd saw Jesus, the people were surprised and ran to welcome him. Jesus asked, "What are you arguing about?"
A man answered, "Teacher, I brought my son to you. He has an evil spirit in him that stops him from talking. When the spirit attacks him, it throws him on the ground. Then my son foams at the mouth, grinds his teeth, and becomes very stiff. I asked your followers to force the evil spirit out, but they couldn't."
Jesus answered, "You people have no faith. How long must I stay with you? How long must I put up with you? Bring the boy to me."
So the followers brought him to Jesus. As soon as the evil spirit saw Jesus, it made the boy lose control of himself, and he fell down and rolled on the ground, foaming at the mouth. Jesus asked the boy's father, "How long has this been happening?" The father answered, "Since he was very young...If you can do anything for him, please have pity on us and help us." Jesus said to the father, "...All things are possible for the one who believes." Immediately the father cried out, "I do believe! Help me to believe more!"...When Jesus went into the house, his followers began asking him private, "Why couldn't we force that evil spirit out?" Jesus answered, "That kind of spirit can only be forced out by prayer."   *Mark 9: 14-24, 28-29 (NCV)*

Let's look at this scripture and see what the Lord will show us:

— It's important to note that this miracle is recorded just after the Transfiguration. Jesus, James, Peter, and John have just come down the mountain to find — what? The other disciples in an argument! [Have you ever noticed how many arguments in your family take place as you are getting ready to go to a worship service, or Bible study or you come home from a wonderful retreat weekend, walk in the door to your house and BLAM! A "police action" is going on in your kitchen and someone forgot to warn you!]

— I like the way the father cuts to the chase and tells Jesus just how bad his son's condition has become — it was an emergency to him.

— Do you hear the frustration — the edge in Jesus' voice? When are the disciples — when are <u>we</u> going to catch on?!?!?

— Jesus asks the father how long the son had been like this. I think Jesus probably already knew the answer — He just wanted the disciples to know!

— Over and over in Jesus' teaching, He tells us that if we would just <u>BELIEVE</u> —ANYTHING — is possible!

— The boy's father speaks words that we must take in today and imprint upon our hearts — *"help my unbelief"* — give me MORE faith, MORE trust in You, Lord.

— And at the end, Jesus tells us the most powerful part of the whole event — *"this kind can come out only by prayer"* some translations say "prayer and fasting". To do God's work, I must look to <u>His</u> power. I <u>know</u> His power when I spend time <u>listening</u> and <u>learning</u>, growing in Jesus.

August 7

Do you ever feel like you get NO RESPECT from the people closest to you? Parents, children, siblings, 'best friends'? Well, neither did Jesus!

Jesus left and returned to his hometown with his disciples. The next Sabbath he taught in the Jewish meeting place. Many of the people who heard him were amazed and asked, "How can he do all this? Where did he get such wisdom and the power to work these miracles? Isn't he the carpenter, the son of Mary? Aren't James, Joseph, Judas, and Simon his brothers? Don't his sisters still live here in our town?" The people were very unhappy because of what he was doing. But Jesus said, "Prophets are honored by everyone, except the people in their own family." Jesus could not work any miracles there, except to a few sick people by placing his hands on them. He was surprised that the people did not have any faith.   *Mark 6:1-6 (CEV)*

A phenomenon that many of us have experienced as parents is [and if we are truthful, we experienced the <u>other</u> side of it as teenagers ourselves] the "Mom dumb — Mom Genius" phenomenon. [Dads, just plug your name in here, OK?] The phenomenon goes something like this:

"When I was 15, Mom was sooooo dumb!" How dumb was she? And the tale-teller will impart a couple of incidents that usually involve sneaking out of the house or when 'Mom' showed how she was soooo CLUELESS about fashion or music or whatever.

Now, fast forward to about age 19, — or at whatever age the previously mention child has spent at least a year away from home, in college or the service. "Mom, how did you <u>do</u> all of this? You are one in a million, Mom!"

As usual we do not know the wisdom available to us through our parents, our teachers, our pastors, our friends, and yes, our children, until they have moved on. "Oh, but if <u>Jesus</u> was here among us, I wouldn't MISS HIM!!!"

But He <u>IS</u> here among us in the people just listed, maybe even trying with loud shouts to get our attention!!! I wonder if Jesus isn't "amazed at {our} lack of faith"!!!!

My child, listen carefully to everything I say. Don't forget a single word, but think about it all. Knowing these teachings will mean true life and good health for you. Carefully guard your thoughts because they are the source of true life. Never tell lies or be deceitful in what you say. Keep looking straight ahead, without turning aside. Know where you are headed, and you will stay on solid ground. Don't make a mistake by turning to the right or the left.

Proverbs 4:20-27 (CEV)

I know several people who read a chapter in Proverbs every day. If it is August 7[th,] then they read Proverbs 7. Since there are 31 chapters in Proverbs that works out pretty well! No matter what or how the Lord leads me to study in His word each day, my goal is to pull in every crumb of wisdom that He wants to give me. Some days those words are difficult. God is faithful and will 'simmer' them inside of me to bring His truth clearly to me if I will only be open to His teaching. Some days the words are like a healing ointment to my bruised spirit, renewing and restoring me! My strength comes from my Heavenly Father, the only opinion that counts!

Do you look for peace in your life? Do the words: "calm", "tranquility", "harmony", and "serenity" seem foreign in your world? They are in my world, too. Maybe it's because like — love — we're looking for it in all the wrong places. Here is what the Lord said to Isaiah, the prophet:

"The mountains may disappear, and the hills may come to an end, but my love will never disappear; my promise of peace will not come to an end," says the LORD who shows mercy to you.   *Isaiah 54:10 (NCV)*

This speaks to my soul my inmost place, telling me that even when a 'HURRICANE' is blowing through my life, maybe even backs up, in case it missed something! — God's love is still there. He promises me peace — inner peace — no matter what. It's my choice. When I'm running late for an appointment, there's no gas in the car, and I have no cash in my purse, and the cell phone rings with the person I am to meet wondering where I am — I can choose to turn 'left' and TOTALLY lose it — maybe throw something — at the very least experience chest pain or the burn of an ulcer — OR — I can turn 'right' and say, "Help me, Lord! <u>What</u> do I do now? Truly, only You have the answer to that! I will trust in You, Lord!"

Let's see what <u>Jesus</u> says about peace:

"I have told you all these things while I am with you. But the Helper will teach you everything and will cause you to remember all that I told you. This Helper is the Holy Spirit whom the Father will send in my name. I leave you peace; my peace I give you. I do not give it to you as the world does. So don't let your hearts be troubled or afraid."   *John 14:25-27 (NCV)*

This is good. In fact, Jesus goes on to say in chapter 15 of John's gospel that He is the vine and if we stayed plugged into Him, we will bear "much fruit". That sounds REALLY good!!!

Let's also look at what ELSE Jesus says about 'peace':

"Don't think that I came to bring peace to the earth. I did not come to bring peace, but a sword. I have come so that 'a son will be against his father, a daughter will be against her mother, a daughter-in-law will be against her mother-in-law. A person's enemies will be members of his own family.' Those who love their father or mother more than they love me are not worthy to be my followers. Those who love their own son or daughter more than they love me are not worthy to be my followers. Whoever is not willing to carry the cross and follow me is not worthy of me. Those who try to hold on to their lives will give up true life. Those who give up their lives for me will hold on to true life."

         Matthew 10:34-39 (NCV)

I guess we would have to say that Jesus came with a sword, didn't He? He certainly divided the church of His day — the Pharisees and Sadducees and Rome against this new idea that was later called "Christian". But remember, Jesus said that He gives us 'peace' — but not like we know it in the world. We will not find peace in making the 'perfect family' or the most 'successful career'. Jesus says I must lay down my life — I must lose my life — lose my way of doing things — and follow <u>HIS</u> way. When I make Him #1, then the peace will be <u>RIGHT</u> <u>THERE</u>! No line — No waiting!

"Evil" is defined by Webster as "Morally bad or wrong; wicked; depraved, causing pain or trouble: harmful, injurious; offensive or disgusting". Since September 2001, we have heard a lot about 'good' and 'evil'. We have drawn pictures in our own minds about what is 'good' and what is 'evil'. I feel pretty good about myself and shift my eyes to "OTHERS" who are certainly evil — not like me!! "Am I glad I am not like 'THEM'!"

'Sin' according to Webster is an "offense against God". uh – oh.

"Either make the tree good and its fruit good, or make the tree bad and its fruit bad, for the tree is known by its fruit. You brood of vipers! How can you speak good, when you are evil? For out of the abundance of the heart the mouth speaks. The good person out of his good treasure brings forth good, and the evil person out of his evil treasure brings forth evil. I tell you, on the day of judgment people will give account for every careless word they speak, for by your words you will be justified, and by your words you will be condemned."

Matthew 12:33-37 (ESV)

Fruit — words, careless words. Of course, I could emphasize that Jesus was speaking about the Pharisees at the time. But can I really argue it through that those words are NOT for me?!? Jesus speaks about "good" being stored up in a person. That implies that I have been taking in 'good' stuff — not trash. So I look inward and check: Have I been taking in 'good' in what I read, what I listen to, what I watch on TV, the conversation of the crowd I hang around, — how is my internal warehouse? Am I storing up 'good' so that 'good' will overflow?

Paul speaks right out in Romans chapter 2, verse 5: *But because of your hard and impenitent heart you are storing up wrath for yourself on the day of wrath when God's righteous judgment will be revealed. He will render to each one according to his works: to those who by patience in well-doing seek for glory and honor and immorality, he will give eternal life; but for those who are self-seeking and do not obey the truth, but obey unrighteousness, there will be wrath and fury. There will be tribulation and distress for every human being who does evil, the Jew first and also the Greek, but glory and honor and peace for everyone who does good, the Jew first and also the Greek. For God shows no partiality.*   *Romans 2:5-11 (ESV)*

My loving Savior will be a righteous and true Judge one day and I WILL be called to account for careless words and un-loving acts. Today is the day for me to repent of the 'sin' in my life and begin again — walking in New LIFE because of God's grace.

Heavenly Father, I ask for your forgiveness today in Jesus' name. I want to begin again, always keeping You #1 in my life. I also ask forgiveness for careless words and thoughtless acts that have hurt others. Forgive me for my lack of love, even for those who seem unlovable. After all, You loved me when I was unlovable! It is because of Jesus that I can ask this — AMEN.

Additional Text: Matthew 12, Romans 3

August 10

Then Jesus took the children in his arms and blessed them by placing his hands on them.

As Jesus was walking down a road, a man ran up to him. He knelt down, and asked, "Good teacher, what can I do to have eternal life?" Jesus replied, "Why do you call me good? Only God is good. You know the commandments. 'Do not murder. Be faithful in marriage. Do not steal. Do not tell lies about others. Do not cheat. Respect your father and mother.'" The man answered, "Teacher, I have obeyed all these commandments since I was a young man." Jesus looked closely at the man and loved him. Mark 10:16-21 (CEV)

Have you ever experienced Jesus' look of love? It's a moment when I have felt — wrapped — in Him. There is no condemnation for the past and — there is hope and peace — about the future — but all I want to do is stay right there, in the present, in His arms. "He loves me!" And then — in a blinding second — I know the truth about what stands between me and Jesus. A sin. Something that has been more important than Jesus in my life. Little or big. Sin has no size. It's there.

I am the LORD your God, and you must dedicate yourselves to me and be holy, just as I am holy. Don't become disgusting by eating any of these unclean creatures. I brought you out of Egypt so that I could be your God. Now you must become holy, because I am holy! Leviticus 11:44-45 (CEV)

This is a passage that speaks a detail about Levitical law. The larger picture or point is: Be holy — because the LORD is holy. I draw close to God and can be intimate with Him ONLY as I move toward more holiness and away from sin.

You have been raised to life with Christ. Now set your heart on what is in heaven, where Christ rules at God's right side. Think about what is up there, not about what is here on earth. You died, which means that your life is hidden with Christ, who sits beside God. Christ gives meaning to your life, and when he appears, you will also appear with him in glory. Colossians 3:1-4 (CEV)

Colossians 3 continues on to encourage me to 'kill' the temptations that are a part of my life, a part of the world that I live. How do I avoid those temptations that lead to sin? I focus my eyes, my thoughts in another direction. That means making conscious, deliberate choices on who I keep close company with and what I 'consume' in the books I read, the programs I watch, and the music, even the advice, I may listen to. God wants to spend time with me so I must make a choice in my priorities.

Let the message about Christ completely fill your lives, while you use all your wisdom to teach and instruct each other. With thankful hearts, sing psalms, hymns, and spiritual songs to God. Whatever you say or do should be done in the name of the Lord Jesus, as you give thanks to God the Father because of him. Colossians 3:16-17 (CEV, emphasis mine)

Additional Text: Colossians 2 and 3

Jesus knew on the evening of Passover Day that it would be his last night on earth before returning to his Father. During supper the devil had already suggested to Judas Iscariot, Simon's son, that this was the night to carry out his plan to betray Jesus. Jesus knew that the Father had given him everything and that he had come from God and would return to God. And how he loved his disciples! So he got up from the supper table, took off his robe, wrapped a towel around his loins, poured water into a basin, and began to wash the disciples' feet and to wipe them with the towel he had around him. When he came to Simon Peter, Peter said to him, "Master, you shouldn't be washing our feet like this!" Jesus replied, "You don't understand now why I am doing it; some day you will." "No!" Peter protested, "you shall never wash my feet!" "But if I don't you can't be my partner," Jesus replied. Simon Peter exclaimed, "Then wash my hands and head as well – not just my feet!"...

"You call me 'Master' and 'Lord,' and you do well to say it, for it is true. And since I, the Lord and Teacher, have washed your feet, you ought to wash each other's feet. I have given you an example to follow: do as I have done to you. How true it is that a servant is not greater than his master. Nor is the messenger more important than the one who sends him. You know these things – now do them! That is the path of blessing."   John 13:1-9, 13-17 (TLB)

This is John's account of the passion of Jesus Christ. The apostle, John, was the only one who wrote about Jesus washing his disciples feet. John seems to really want us to grab hold of the immense scope of Jesus' love.

In looking at several versions of this scripture passage, I did not find any clear statement that Judas left the room prior to the foot washing or the breaking of the bread for communion. It is difficult for me to accept that Jesus got down on His hands and knees and washed the feet of the man He KNEW was going to betray Him. And yet, that is why Jesus came. To love the unlovable. To be a servant to those who hated Him, even betrayed Him.

"And so I am giving a new commandment to you now – love each other just as much as I love you. Your strong love for each other will prove to the world that you are my disciples."   John 13:34-35 (TLB)

Who is the Judas in my life? I suspect we all have at <u>least</u> one. It may be an ex-spouse. It may be a child who has stolen from us, betrayed us. It may be a parent who has abused us. It may be a co-worker who 'set us up', made us look bad, took credit for our idea. It may even be a member of our church who has betrayed us, treated us worse than a non-believer! Jesus is asking <u>ME</u> to wash Judas' feet. Wash them tenderly, thoroughly, and anoint them with God's oil of love.

Father, I need Your grace here. I receive Your 'call' to this service. I ask, Father, that You show me Jesus washing <u>MY</u> feet. My dirty, unworthy feet. Father, You know me. You know, that like Peter, I need my head and hands washed, too! Wash me clean, Father, of my pride and self-righteousness, that I may truly be Your servant, glorify <u>YOU</u> in everything that I do. I ask this in Jesus' name. AMEN.

August 12

You see my shame and disgrace. You know all my enemies and what they have said. Insults have broken my heart and left me weak. I looked for sympathy, but there was none; I found no one to comfort me. They put poison in my food and gave me vinegar to drink. Psalm 69:19-21 (NCV)

These words are prophetic words about the events in Jesus' death. Let's go to Luke's gospel:

As they led Jesus away, Simon, a man from Cyrene, was coming in from the fields. They forced him to carry Jesus' cross and to walk behind him. A large crowd was following Jesus, including some women who were sad and crying for him. But Jesus turned and said to them, "Women of Jerusalem, don't cry for me. Cry for yourselves and for your children."...

When they came to a place called the Skull, the soldiers crucified Jesus and the criminals – one on his right and the other on his left. Jesus said, "Father, forgive them, because they don't know what they are doing."...

The soldiers also made fun of him, coming to Jesus and offering him some vinegar. They said, "If you are the king of the Jews, save yourself!"...

[One of the criminals said,] "Jesus, remember me when you come into your kingdom." Jesus said to him, "I tell you the truth, today you will be with me in paradise."

It was about noon, and the whole land became dark until three o'clock in the afternoon because the sun did not shine. The curtain in the Temple was torn in two. Jesus cried out in a loud voice, "Father, I give you my life." After Jesus said this, he died. Luke 23:26-28, 33-34, 36-37, 42-46 (NCV)

John records Jesus' last words as *"It is finished."* As with two people and any one incident or accident in our present world, witnesses remember what impresses or strikes them personally. Luke saw Jesus releasing His spirit to the Father. John heard the completion of the mission. Both knew the sacrifice was complete. It was perfect.

Christ did not go into the Most Holy Place made by humans, which is only a copy of the real one. He went into heaven itself and is there now before God to help us. The high priest enters the Most Holy Place once every year with blood that is not his own. But Christ did not offer himself many times. Then he would have had to suffer many times since the world was made. But Christ came only once and for all time at just the right time to take away all sin by sacrificing himself. Just as everyone must die once and be judged, so Christ was offered as a sacrifice one time to take away the sins of many people. And he will come a second time, not to offer himself for sin, but to bring salvation to those who are waiting for him. Hebrews 9:24-28 (NCV)

Let us bow today and see the scope of Jesus' sacrifice for our sins. He did it all for me. He did it all for you. PRAISE THE LORD FOR HIS INDESCRIBABLE LOVE!

Christ's love is greater than anyone can ever know, but I pray that you will be able to know that love. Then you can be filled with the fullness of God. Ephesians 3:19 (NCV)

Aliens. It brings to my mind weird, sometimes monstrous looking creatures that salivate a lot and breathe REALLY heavy! OK, maybe I've watched too much TV and movies in my life!

God clearly says from Old Testament to New Testament that, as His children, we are ALIENS of this world; that HEAVEN is our home.

But you are God's chosen and special people. You are a group of royal priests and a holy nation. God has brought you out of darkness into his marvelous light. Now you must tell all the wonderful things that he has done. The Scriptures say, "Once you were nobody. Now you are God's people. At one time no one had pity on you. Now God has treated you with kindness." Dear Friends, you are foreigners [aliens] **and strangers on this earth.** *So I beg you not to surrender to those desires that fight against you. Always let others see you behaving properly, even though they may still accuse you of doing wrong. Then on the day of judgment, they will honor God by telling the good things they saw you do.* 1 Peter 2:9-12 (CEV)

My friends, I want you to follow my example and learn from others who closely follow the example we set for you. I often warned you that many people are living as enemies of the cross of Christ. And now with tears in my eyes, I warn you again that they are headed for hell! They worship their stomachs and brag about the disgusting things they do. All they can think about are the things of this world. But we are citizens of heaven and are eagerly waiting for our Savior to come from there. Our Lord Jesus Christ has power over everything, and he will make these poor bodies of ours like his own glorious body. Dear friends, I love you and long to see you. Please keep on being faithful to the Lord. You are my pride and joy. Philippians 3:17 – 4:1(CEV)

That sounds really good to me! But --- do I live in this world like an alien or do I try to 'fit in'? Jesus tells us clearly —

"If the people of this world hate you, just remember that they hated me first. If you belonged to the world, its people would love you. But you don't belong to the world. I have chosen you to leave the world behind, and that is why its people hate you." John 15:18-19 (CEV)

So --- just how 'comfortable' do I feel in this world? The Lord tells me that if I am hated (for my beliefs, my lifestyle) --- I'm on the right track!!! Sometimes that 'hate' comes as criticism — even from family and friends. Remember that Jesus' brothers did not initially believe in Him.

The 'hate' also comes when I take a stand for the Lord. By not participating in gossip and destructive talk and behavior, I may be considered 'strange' or 'stupid' or 'naïve'. O-KAY — so be it! If I am an ALIEN, people should wonder from what planet I just dropped in! Maybe I should see it as an opportunity to share about my homeland!!!

The price of being an 'alien' to this world is seeing all the temporary success and glory that this world may offer and saying "No – that is not my focus. That is not my priority." I must be about my Heavenly Father's business. Even in my day-to-day life, my 'job' — I am about my Heavenly Father's business. I am about kingdom building and glorifying the Lord FIRST!

August 14

Never stop praying, especially for others. Always pray by the power of the Spirit. Stay alert and keep praying for God's people.   *Ephesians 6:18 (CEV)*

There have been difficult times in my life. Looking back, I can see the 'season' of difficulty had a beginning and end and between there were wonderful messengers of God who encouraged me to keep going – I <u>could</u> make it to the end of the current race! Right now, this season is the <u>most</u> difficult that I could ever had imagined. The life-threatening illness of my son is a journey we have been on for several years now but our current 'season' appears to be the most difficult as I watch my child walk through a journey I never thought <u>I</u> would see and that he wouldn't take for another 60 years.

Many people want to <u>do</u> something. I have heard more about various health-promoting diets and various vitamin and minerals supplements than I knew existed or learned about in nursing school.

It is those people who send me a note or touch my hand or arm and say, "I pray for your son every day" that brings encouragement and keeps my eyes on the Hope that we have in Jesus. As one that has been in the medical profession 'way too many years, I <u>know</u> just how little that it is about pills and procedures and how much it is about prayer and God!

"Never stop praying". *"Always pray by the power of the Spirit"*. It seems that <u>every</u> prayer would be under Holy Spirit guidance. I had a friend come to me just the other day and say, "I was praying for you and 'felt led' to pray, not for you at that time but for your doctor. I don't know who he is but I prayed for 15 minutes just about him." She didn't know that we had a meeting with him that day and it was wonderful the way he spoke to my son and encouraged him. Praying with the Holy Spirit means prayers may take a path that wasn't in <u>my</u> plan but was known by God to be accurate and perfect!

So the sisters sent word to Jesus, "Lord, the one you love is sick."   *John 11:3*

This comes from the story of Lazarus. We aren't told who the messenger is but he must have been someone that the sisters <u>really</u> trusted to get the message through and convey it with the right tone of urgency and importance. A petition, a prayer is sent to Jesus about a need. The prayer reminds Jesus that it is <u>not</u> about "…the one who loves <u>You</u>, Lord" but rather it is about *"the one <u>you</u> love is sick"*. God hears and answers prayers out of <u>HIS</u> great love, not mine. God <u>hears</u> and <u>answers</u> prayers out of <u>HIS</u> <u>great</u> <u>love</u>.

And so today, I am encouraged and comforted to know that many people <u>are</u> helping today – they are praying. And I am encouraged and comforted to know that <u>GOD</u> hears and answers my prayers and their prayers because of <u>HIS</u> love. I have ALL I need.

Additional Text: Luke 11, Ephesians 3

August 15

...whatever you do, do all to the glory of God.　　*1 Corinthians 10:31 (ESV)*

Whatever? Whatever.

[Jesus said,] *"In the same way, let your light shine before others, so that they may see your good works and give glory to your Father who is in heaven."*

Matthew 5:16 (ESV)

My light? My message to others that comes through my life, my words, ...what and who I am.

In him also, when you heard the word of truth, the gospel of your salvation, and believed in him, were sealed with the promised Holy Spirit, who is the guarantee of our inheritance until we acquire possession of it, to the praise of his glory.

Ephesians 1:13-14 (ESV)

My salvation, that <u>free</u> gift, that came because <u>God</u> 'wooed' me and never gave up on me, is an opportunity to glorify Him.

Or do you not know that your body is a temple of the Holy Spirit within you, whom you have from God? You are not your own, for you were bought with a price. So glorify God in your body.　　*1 Corinthians 6:19-20 (ESV)*

I was cruising along here pretty good until this one! Those of you who personally know me know that I am overweight. This is an area that I need to allow the Holy Spirit to strengthen me and guide me in <u>His</u> way so that God may be glorified! Praise God that He has not given up on me yet!

For it is all for your sake, so that grace extends to more and more people it may increase thanksgiving, to the glory of God so we do not lose heart. Though our outer nature is wasting away, our inner nature is being renewed day by day.

2 Corinthians 4:15-16 (ESV)

And so my struggles also glorify God because the <u>victory</u> is all about Him. And when 'success' comes in my natural life, God gets all the glory there, too.

Honor the LORD with your wealth and with the firstfruits of all your produce; then y our barns will be filled with plenty, and your vats will be bursting with wine.　　*Proverbs 3:9-10 (ESV)*

Therefore David blessed the LORD in the presence of all the assembly.　And David said: "Blessed are you, O LORD, the God of Israel our father, forever and ever. Yours, O LORD, is the greatness and the power and the glory and the victory and the majesty, for all that is in the heavens and in the earth is yours. Yours is the kingdom, O LORD, and you are exalted as head above all. Both riches and honor come from you, and you rule over all. In your hand are power and might, and in your hand it is to make great and to give strength to all. And now we thank you, our God, and praise your glorious name."

1 Chronicles 29:10-13 (ESV)

Beware lest you say in your heart, 'My power and the might of my hand have gotten me this wealth.' You shall remember the LORD your God, for it is he who gives you power to get wealth that he may confirm his covenant that he swore to your fathers, as it is this day.　　*Deuteronomy 8:17-18 (ESV)*

God is the source. I am just a reflection of Him and what He can do.

Additional Text: Colossians 3 and 4

August 16

Epaphras, who is one of you and a servant of Christ Jesus, sends greetings. He is always wrestling in prayer for you, that you may stand firm in all the will of God, mature and fully assured.   *Colossians 4:12*

Have you ever 'wrestled' in prayer with God? Have you ever come to Him with prayer and asked and asked and asked and asked? "Why don't You answer, Lord?" "Do You hear me?"

Prayer, earnest, persistent prayer comes upon us in different ways. It isn't about how long or loud we become but it is an intense cry of our heart aimed at the heart of God. It is not about emotion but about motion TOWARD God that will not be stopped until we hear directly from the Lord.

Someone recently sent me this story: A voyaging ship was wrecked during a storm at sea and only two of the men on it were able to swim to a small, desert like island. The two survivors, not knowing what else to do, agreed they had no other recourse but to pray to God. However, to find out whose prayer was more powerful, they agreed to divide the territory between them and stay on opposite sides of the island. The first thing they prayed for was food. The next morning, the first man saw a fruit-bearing tree on his side of the land, and he was able to eat its fruit. The other man's parcel of land remained barren.

After a week, the first man was lonely and he decided to pray for a wife. The next day, another ship was wrecked, and the only survivor was a woman who swam to his side of the land. On the other side of the island, there was nothing.

Soon the first man prayed for a house, clothes, and more food. The next day, like magic, all of these were given to him. However, the second man still had nothing

Finally, the first man prayed for a ship, so that he and his wife would leave the island. In the morning, he found a ship docked at his side of the island.

The first man boarded the ship with his wife and decided to leave the second man on the island. He considered the other man unworthy to receive God's blessings, since none of his prayers had been answered.

As the ship was about to leave, the first man heard a voice from heaven booming, "Why are you leaving your companion on the island?"

"My blessings are mine alone, since I was the one who prayed for them," the first man answered. "His prayers were all unanswered and so he does not deserve anything."

"You are mistaken!" the voice rebuked him. "He had only one prayer, which I answered. If not for that, you would not have received any of my blessings."

"Tell me," the first man asked the voice, "What did he pray for that I should owe him anything?"

"He prayed that all your prayers be answered."

For all we know, our blessings are not the fruits of our prayers alone, but those of another praying for us. It is not the length of my prayer or the volume. All of that is for my benefit. God answers in His perfect timing and with His perfect answer. I need to wait not just on any answer but on God's best answer.

Additional Text: Psalm 39, Luke 6

Peter said, "Remember, we have left everything to be your followers! What will we get?"   *Matthew 19:27 (CEV)*

When you were growing up and teams were chosen for spelling or sports or school projects, were you on the front half that was chosen or the back half that was chosen? There was a moment in the choosing when everyone just <u>knew</u> that the people <u>now</u> left standing were the ones that wouldn't be chosen at all if that were an option. You could feel the blush come to your face, couldn't you? I imagine most of us have been in the last group for some category of 'picking'. Very few people are popular, smart, AND athletic! In some category that life throws out…we all find ourselves on the 'lesser' side at some time or another.

In a culture that certainly had its share of classes and prejudices, Jesus' words were RADICAL!!! Jesus had already 'rocked' His listeners in Matthew 19:23. Jesus told the 'rich young man/ruler' that there was nothing he could <u>do</u> to have eternal life but instead he would have to <u>give up</u> his wealth. Jesus said it was <u>hard</u> to be wealthy and have eternal life. He mentions camels and needles. The disciples couldn't believe it! The rich Pharisees had been telling them for centuries that the more 'perfectly expensive' offerings would gain God's attention and for a price they would pray their 'holier' prayers for them! If the wealthy couldn't be guaranteed a place in heaven, then who could? Now Jesus says the 'first will be last and the last first'. What kind of cock-eyed religion is that? A loving one.

In the next chapter of Matthew, Jesus goes on to give them the parable of the vineyard workers. He applies His 'last shall be first' statement in vivid color to something everyone of that day and this could understand. Most of us know that if we are hired for an 8-hour day at $10/hour, we have to be there for eight hours to get $80. If some guy came to my workplace for only one hour and got paid the same as me, I wouldn't be happy. Jesus says it's different in His world. In this case, since I am one of the 'late-comers'…I am A-OK with the equal pay policy!

In Jesus' world, if you are a '<u>first</u>-chooser' and you chose to follow Jesus since…well, you can't remember a time when you didn't! Jesus has <u>always</u> been Savior and Lord to you. Your parents told you about Him while you were in the crib. You grew up knowing that you were less than perfect, a sinner, and that God LOVED YOU <u>SO MUCH</u> that He gave His Son, Jesus as a perfect sacrifice <u>for YOU</u>. You've been a worker in the vineyard…all your life. Maybe you had times that you 'took vacation' or slacked a bit in your work but you have <u>always</u> known that you were His child. Some of us…weren't in that same place. We kept leaving the 'choosing line' and running off to play our own game and gave Jesus' game little or NO attention! We waited to mid- or late afternoon or evening …maybe even late NIGHT to decide to accept Jesus' invitation to be on His team! How patient He is to wait for us to turn our eyes to Him and say, "OK, I'll let you be the captain and owner of the team!" We are the 'last' half but receive the same reward. God's 'equal opportunity' GIFT – eternal life.

Additional Text: Matthew 19, Ephesians 2

August 18

So if there is any encouragement in Christ, any comfort from love, any participation in the Spirit, any affection and sympathy, complete my joy by being of the same mind, having the same love, being in full accord and of one mind. Do nothing from rivalry or conceit, but in humility count others more significant than yourselves. Let each of you look not only to his own interests, but also to the interests of others. Have this mind among yourselves, which is yours in Christ Jesus, ...   Philippians 2:1-5 (ESV)

This would have to be listed as one of my favorite passages in the Bible. Paul speaks plainly to me to be '*like-minded*' with Christ. It gives me a standard of humility and love that I saw Jesus walk out in His life. It is a standard that I see in so many men and women of faith both in the Bible and in every day life. It speaks of my '*attitude*,' which usually needs a daily adjustment! You know that piece of equipment that a house framer uses? A level? It has that bubble in it and you move the ends up or down until the bubble settles just in the middle of the cylinder and then you know that you are 'level'. Jesus is my bubble. He is the point of reference that keeps me level.

BUT there is more to this passage than I receive at first glance. If I go to the verses just before it in chapter 1, I will see that there is a reason that Paul mentions the 'comfort' of Christ. Because if I am to enjoy being '*like-minded*' with Christ, there is another piece of that fellowship.

For it has been granted to you that for the sake of Christ you should not only believe in him but also suffer for his sake, engaged in the same conflict that you saw I had and now hear that I still have.   Philippians 1:29-30 (ESV)

The suffering and pain and problems that come into my life each and every day have a purpose. It is not to glorify ME! It is not to show others what I can do! The struggles have only one purpose...to glorify GOD. Remember what Jesus said when His disciples asked why a man was born blind? They wanted to know who had sinned and 'caused' the problem.

Jesus answered, "It was not that this man sinned, or his parents, but that the works of God might be displayed in him."   John 9:3 (ESV)

I bet Paul had heard this story or had seen others like it and spoke the words to the Philippian church to help them (and me!) to hang in there during the struggles of life.

"For it has been granted to you that for the sake of Christ you should not only believe in him but also suffer for his sake..." It's been '*granted*' to me. That sounds like a gift, doesn't it? And that's where my eyes must come up and OFF of me and look *eternally* into what is REALLY important...glorifying God with my walk of faith that comes out of my weakness and gives Him ALL the credit for getting through the struggle.

You have kept count of my tossings; put my tears in your bottle. Are they not in your book? Then my enemies will turn back in the day when I call. This I know, that God is for me. In God, whose word I praise, in the LORD, whose word I praise, in God I trust; I shall not be afraid. What can man do to me?   Psalm 56:8-11 (ESV)

Additional Text: Psalm 56, John 16

August 19

Jesus left the city and went to the Mount of Olives, as he often did, and his followers went with him. When he reached the place, he said to them, "Pray for strength against temptation." Then Jesus went about a stone's throw away from them. He kneeled down and prayed, "Father, if you are willing, take away this cup of suffering. But do what you want, not what I want." Then an angel from heaven appeared to him to strengthen him. Being full of pain, Jesus prayed even harder. His sweat was like drops of blood falling to the ground. When he finished praying, he went to his followers and found them asleep because of their sadness. Jesus said to them, "Why are you sleeping? Get up and pray for strength against temptation."   *Luke 22:39-46 (NCV)*

I was given a little 'gift book' last Christmas and I've just now picked it up to read...after Henry had read it. Many might say that those books tend to be 'soft' or 'fluff' but God bless those who are able to say what God wants them to say in less than 350 pages! The book is *Wrestling With God by Greg Laurie*. In it the author says that only what is outside God's will is outside the power of prayer. He reminds me that prayer is getting me to move toward God not the other way around! I learn when I pray.

Jesus asked God for another way for Him to fulfill His mission. He asked that God would allow Him to step away from the plan that was being carried out. BUT He also told the Father that He wanted to be in His will. God heard that prayer and answered with an angel. God did not change the plan. God did not lower the bar for what had to be done as atonement for our sins but He heard the cry of His Son and sent Him the <u>best</u> answer. God <u>always</u> answers my prayers with the <u>best</u> answer.

How do I pray 'in the will' of God? By spending time in His presence. A lot. More than once a day for 10 minutes. By making my life a 'conversation with God'. Sounds a little over the top, doesn't it? Maybe I am just speaking for myself but I need to be talking to God every day, all day. With these conversations my will bends to <u>His will</u>. My attitude becomes <u>His attitude</u>. I begin to see circumstances with <u>His eyes</u>. That is my goal.

[Jesus said,] *"If you remain in me and follow my teachings, you can ask anything you want and it will be given to you. You should produce much fruit and show that you are my followers, which brings glory to my Father. I loved you as the Father loved me. Now remain in my love. I have obeyed my Father's commands, and I remain in his love. In the same way, if you obey my commands, you will remain in my love. I have told you these things so that you can have the same joy I have and so that your joy will be the fullest possible joy."*

John 15:7-11 (NCV)

Additional Text: Deuteronomy 10, Psalm 40

August 20

This is what the LORD says: I will answer your prayers because I have set a time when I will help by coming to save you. I have chosen you to take my promise of hope to other nations. You will rebuild the country from its ruins, then people will come and settle there. You will set prisoners free from dark dungeons to see the light of day. Isaiah 40:8-9 (CEV)

God 'saves' me. The word 'save', when used in the same breath as 'God', has three descriptions.

"Christ Jesus came into the world to save sinners." This saying is true, and it can be trusted. I was the worst sinner of all! 1 Timothy 1:15 (CEV)

Jesus came as the <u>perfect</u> sacrifice to cover my sins. It took the Son of God to spill <u>His</u> blood so that my sins could disappear when I accept that I am a sinner and ask God to 'save' me. Jesus saved me.

The Spirit of the LORD God has taken control of me! The LORD has chosen and sent me to tell the oppressed the good news, to heal the brokenhearted, and to announce freedom for prisoners and captives. This is the year when the LORD God will show kindness to us and punish our enemies. The LORD has sent me to comfort those who mourn, especially in Jerusalem. He sent me to give them flowers in place of their sorrow, olive oil in place of tears, and joyous praise in place of broken hearts. They will be called "Trees of Justice," planted by the LORD to honor his name. Then they will rebuild cities that have been in ruins for many generations. Isaiah 61:1-4 (CEV)

God is full of grace and pours that grace and mercy on me through His Holy Spirit. When I am in need, He comforts me and heals my heart. He raises my eyes when I despair in this world and shows me the 'eternal' picture, giving me a hope and a future. God saves me.

I saw a new heaven and a new earth. The first heaven and the first earth had disappeared, and so had the sea. Then I saw New Jerusalem, that holy city, coming down from God in heaven. It was like a bride dressed in her wedding gown and ready to meet her husband. I heard a loud voice shout from the throne: God's home is now with his people. He will live with them, and they will be his own. Yes, God will make his home among his people. He will wipe all tears from their eyes, and there will be no more death, suffering, crying, or pain. These things of the past are gone forever. Revelation 21:1-4 (CEV)

God saves me ultimately for an eternal life with Him in paradise. I weep when I think of eternity with Him!

God's Spirit makes us sure that we are his children. His Spirit lets us know that together with Christ we will be given what God has promised. We will also share in the glory of Christ, because we have suffered with him. I am sure that what we are suffering now cannot compare with the glory that will be shown to us...And this hope is what saves us. But if we already have what we hope for, there is no need to keep on hoping. However, we hope for something we have not yet seen, and we patiently wait for it. Romans 8:16-18, 24-25 (CEV)

God saved me. God continues to save me. God will save me from eternal death and bring me to live with Him FOREVER! GOD IS GOOD AND MIGHTY TO SAVE!

August 21

"His master replied, 'Well done, good and faithful servant! You have been faithful with a few things; I will put you in charge of many things. Come and share your master's happiness!'"   Matthew 25:23

This is the most common answer people give when asked what they would like to hear God say to them when they reach heaven. I want to know that God is pleased with me.

This statement was given by Jesus in a parable that He gave while answering the disciples questions about Jesus' return, the signs that will come just prior to that. I've heard many people give their thoughts, ideas, and interpretations of Matthew 24, Mark 13, Luke 12 and 17, Daniel, Ezekiel, and Revelation. It seems to be in our human nature to want to know some kind of 'time line' for the 'end times'. I wonder if it is because we want to be the first to say, "Look, here is the Christ!" or "There He is!" or if we just can't stand being out of the 'loop'? Since every time I have heard or read these passages discussed I've been told something different…I have to conclude that no one really knows!

[Jesus said,] *"No one knows when that day or time will be, not the angels in heaven, not even the Son. Only the Father knows…So always be ready, because you don't know the day your Lord will come."*   Matthew 24:36, 42 (NCV)

Jesus tells me that it is NOT for me to know the 'when' but that I am to be ready. I am to be a 'witness' that NOW is the time to turn to the truth that is in Jesus.

There is a website, www.classmates.com where you can list your name for your high school. You can also pay a fee and then you can exchange information and contact others who have paid the fee who were in your high school class. I ran through the list of classmates and there was about 50% of the class listed. It was interesting that as I read the list the names, faces, and images of events would pop into my head as I recalled that person. I do not have any particular desire to travel back in time or in miles to attend a high school reunion. I am not a 'looking back' kind of person but I did wonder how many of these childhood friends I would see in heaven. We never talked about God in high school that I remember. I think we were too convinced that we were invincible and would never die. Until one Friday night in my junior year four young men went to a concert and only one of them survived a head-on collision on their way home. We cried and mourned their death but then went on with our lives.

"Be dressed, ready for service, and have your lamps shining. Be like servants who are waiting for their master to come home from a wedding party. When he comes and knocks, the servants immediately open the door for him. They will be blessed when their master comes home, because he sees that they were watching for him. I tell you the truth, the master will dress himself to serve and tell the servants to sit at the table, and he will serve them. Those servants will be happy when he comes in and finds them still waiting, even if it is midnight and or later."   Luke 12:35-38 (NCV)

It is not for me to know the day or hour that the Lord will call me home or will return. I am just to live my life here in readiness.

August 22

Do you not know that in a race all the runners compete, but only one receives the prize? So run that you may obtain it.   *1 Corinthians 9:24 (ESV)*

"I'm running. Running. I'm running from room to room. There is a terrible thunderstorm and the rain is coming in the roof. The ceiling is falling in. Water is everywhere. Carpet is sopping wet. In some places the water is ankle deep. Where is my cell phone? If I just find the phone I can call and get someone out to fix the problem. Kids! They are friends of my son and they need to leave. Go on! Go home! Got to find the phone. Running. Running from room to room. Just find the phone and call someone to come fix the roof. Running. Running. Where is the phone?"

That is the dream I had. I laid down for a one-hour nap. I rarely dream or remember a dream. I awoke from this 'nap' – EXHAUSTED! I was more tired and disoriented <u>after</u> the nap. "Help me, Lord! Clear my mind!" I felt that I was told to go get my Bible and look up this verse about running.

Notice how Paul says that all the runners run, <u>but</u>…it isn't about running for the sake of running. It is about running to win. It is about running for a prize. It is about running <u>smart</u>!

Brothers, I do not consider that I have made it my own. But one thing I do: forgetting what lies behind and straining forward to what lies ahead, I press on toward the goal for the prize of the upward call of God in Christ Jesus.
                                        Philippians 3:13-14 (ESV)

Sometimes I lose sight of the goal. What is my focus? Glorifying God.

Sometimes I lose sight of the path of the race. How do I get to my goal?

Follow Jesus' example. Follow the path of the saints who have gone before me. It may not always be an easy path. It may have struggles and obstacles that God may show me a way around <u>but</u> He also may be leading me THROUGH them. I need to be talking and listening to Him more to hear the guidance and instruction to make it THROUGH.

You have faith in God, whose power will protect you until the last day. Then he will save you, just as he has always planned to do. On that day you will be glad, even if you have to go through many hard trials for a while. Your faith will be like gold that has been tested in a fire. And these trials will prove that your faith is worth much more than gold that can be destroyed. They will show that you will be given praise and honor and glory when Jesus Christ returns. You have never seen Jesus, and you don't see him now. But still you love him and have faith in him, and no words can tell how glad and happy you are to be saved. That's why you have faith.   *1 Peter 1: 5-9 (CEV)*

I <u>am</u> running a race but I want to run a <u>smart</u> race, turning to Jesus first and following in HIS footsteps.

Additional Text: Matthew 13, Luke 9

And Mary said, "My soul magnifies the Lord, and my spirit rejoices in God my Savior, for he has looked on the humble estate of his servant. For behold, from now on all generations will call me blessed; for he who is mighty has done great things for me, and holy is his name." Luke 1:46-49 (ESV)

What a beautiful prayer! If you haven't read it recently, take time today to do that. It struck me this morning that Mary was a young probably minimally educated girl and yet this prayer is...poetry. And it is poetry because it came straight from her heart! She was...inspired! Her heart is full because God – GOD! – knows her and has blessed HER!

Blessed is the one whose transgression is forgiven, whose sin is covered. Blessed is the name against whom the LORD counts no iniquity, and in whose spirit there is no deceit. For when I kept silent, my bones wasted away through my groaning all day long. For day and night your hand was heavy upon me; my strength was dried up as by the heat of summer. I acknowledged my sin to you, and I did not cover my iniquity; I said, "I will confess my transgressions to the LORD," and you forgave the iniquity of my sin. Psalm 32:1-5 (ESV)

What a beautiful prayer! An intimate prayer! Maybe this is the prayer that David said when he committed his multiple sins of lust, adultery, and murder. I don't know. I hear the same anguish that I feel when I have sinned and I am reluctant to admit it and ask God for forgiveness. I feel 'low' and blanketed by terrible pain. The release of that pain when the forgiveness comes is like being in a vise that is suddenly released and I am FREE!

Prayer isn't beautiful because of the words that are said. It is beautiful because of the unfiltered truth that is expressed. It is the <u>intimacy</u> of coming face-to-face with my Father and knowing that He is looking at me not with condemnation but with love and joy that I have come to Him.

[Jesus said,] *"What man of you, having a hundred sheep, if he has lost one of them, does not leave the ninety-nine in the open country, and go after the one that is lost, until he finds it? And when he has found it, he lays it on his shoulders, rejoicing,. And when he comes home, he calls together his friends and his neighbors, saying to them, 'Rejoice with me, for I have found my sheep that was lost.' Just so, I tell you, there will be more joy in heaven over one sinner who repents than over ninety-nine righteous persons who need no repentance."* Luke 15:4-7 (ESV)

Maybe today is one of those days when you don't know what is out of 'sync but you feel a little 'blue', a bit down. Go get with the Lord. He's waiting for you.

Maybe it is a day to rejoice because you have a new grandchild or you've just found out you are pregnant! Maybe God has blessed you with some needed wisdom or maybe He just feels *so close* to you, so tangible! Take some time right now and pour out your heart to Him. If you are at work, close your office door for a few minutes or take a bathroom break! Don't miss an opportunity to tell God what is truly on your heart! It <u>is</u> a beautiful thing!

Additional Text: Mark 3, John 7

A friend of mine died <u>totally</u> unexpectedly one weekend. We had known each other for about 15 years. Judi was my age. It's hard to believe that she went to sleep on Friday night and woke up in heaven. Her blatant love for the Lord, her willingness to serve Him in whatever way He asked, and her steadfast prayer life will be missed. There is a hole where she stood in my life.

This is my second letter to you, dear brothers, and in both of them I have tried to remind you – if you will let me – about facts you already know: facts you learned from holy prophets and from us apostles who brought you the words of our Lord and Savior...

But don't forget this, dear friends, that a day or a thousand years from now is like tomorrow to the Lord. He isn't really being slow about his promised return, even though it sometimes seems that way. But he is waiting, for the good reason that he is not willing that any should perish, and he is giving more time for sinners to repent...

Dear friends, while you are waiting for these things to happen and for him to come, try hard to live without sinning; and be at peace with everyone so that he will be pleased with you when he returns. And remember why he is waiting. He is giving us time to get his message of salvation out to others. Our wise and beloved brother Paul has talked about these same things in many of his letters. Some of his comments are not easy to understand, and there are people who are deliberately stupid, and always demand some unusual interpretation – they have twisted his letter to mean something quite different from what he meant, just as they do the other parts of the Scripture – and the result is disaster for them

I am warning you ahead of time, dear brothers, so that you can watch out and not be carried away by the mistakes of these wicked men, lest you yourselves becomes mixed up, too. But grow in spiritual strength and become better acquainted with our Lord and Savior Jesus Christ. To him be all glory and splendid honor, both now and forevermore. Good-bye.   Peter

2 Peter 3:1-2, 8-9, 14-18 (TLB)

God meant for us to have friends. He sends people into my life that teach me and love me. They are wonderful 'gifts' from God. These friends are to be cherished and appreciated like the precious jewels they are. I remember the words to a song that I sang as a child: "Make new friends, but keep the old. One is silver. The other is gold." I have a friend, Jean that I have known since first grade. She <u>is</u> gold. I have another friend, Laney, who has become gold to me, as we have walked through these last 10 years together. God continues to refine me and refine them. He continues to pour out His good gifts.

Dear friend, don't let this bad example influence you. Follow only what is good. Remember that those who do what is right prove that they are God's children; and those who continue in evil prove that they are far from God...I have much to say but I don't want to write it, for I hope to see you soon and then we will have much to talk about together.   *3 John 11, 13-14 (TLB)*

The time apart from my friend is minuscule compared to the eternity that we will spend together. And so today, I praise God for my friend, Judi.

Before those people lived in darkness, but now they have seen a great light. They lived in a dark land, but a light has shined on them...

A child has been born to us; God has given a son to us. He will be responsible for leading the people. His name will be Wonderful Counselor, Powerful God, Father Who Lives Forever, Prince of Peace. Power and peace will be in his kingdom and will continue to grow forever. He will rule as king on David's throne and over David's kingdom. He will make it strong by ruling with justice and goodness from now on and forever. The LORD All-Powerful will do this because of his strong love for his people.   *Isaiah 9:2, 6-7 (NCV)*

God came to earth, loving us so much that He would leave <u>His</u> throne and <u>His</u> kingdom to dwell among us. Jesus, God-in-the-flesh, Immanuel, living here on earth with all of its pain and suffering so that when that same pain and suffering comes to us…we can walk in the same steps that He did.

He [Herod] sent soldiers to the prison to cut off John's head. And they brought it on a platter and gave it to the girl, and she took it to her mother. John's followers came and got his body and buried it. Then they went and told Jesus. When Jesus heard what had happened to John, he left in a boat and went to a lonely place by himself.   *Matthew 14:10-13 (NCV)*

When Jesus saw Mary crying and the Jews who came with her also crying, he was upset and was deeply troubled. He asked, "Where did you bury him?"

"Come and see, Lord," they said. Jesus cried.

So the Jews said, "See how much he loved him." But some of them said, "If Jesus opened the eyes of the blind man, why couldn't he keep Lazarus from dying?"   *John 11:33-37 (NCV)*

There's no great hidden theological point to these two passages. Jesus was moved to grief for the death of His cousin and friend and needed time away with Father. Jesus was moved to compassionate tears for those grieving even when He <u>knew</u> what was to happen next…Lazarus being restored to life.

Jesus said, "Don't let your hearts be troubled. Trust in God, and trust in me. There are many rooms in my Father's house; I would not tell you this if it were not true. I am going there to prepare a place for you. After I go and prepare a place for you, I will come back and take you to be with me so that you may be where I am...

If you love me you will obey my commands. I will ask the Father, and he will give you another Helper to be with you forever – the Spirit of truth...   *John 14:1-3, 15-17 (NCV)*

"I told you these things so that you can have peace in me. In this world you will have trouble, but be brave! I have defeated the world."   *John 16:33 (NCV)*

No matter what path I am currently walking, Jesus has been there before. No matter what pain I feel in my heart, the Holy Spirit is there to hold me and heal me. No matter what it is that has brought tears to my eyes, my Father is there to wipe them away and hold me because I am His Child.

Additional Text: Revelation 21 and 22

Then he returned from the region of Tyre and went through Sidon to the Sea of Galilee, in the region of the Decapolis. And they brought to him a man who was deaf and had a speech impediment, and they begged him to lay his hand on him. And taking him aside from the crowd privately, he put his fingers into his ears, and after spitting touched his tongue. And looking up to haven, he <u>sighed</u> and said to him, "Ephphatha," that is, "Be opened." And his ears were opened, his tongue was released, and he spoke plainly. Mark 7:31-35 (ESV, emphasis mine) The Pharisees came and began to argue with him, seeking from him a sign from heaven to test him. And he <u>sighed</u> deeply in his spirit and said, "Why does this generation seek a sign? Truly, I say to you, no sign will be given to this generation." And he left them, got into the boat again, and went to the other side.   Mark 8:11-13 (ESV, emphasis mine)

It's interesting to me that Mark uses the word 'sigh' in recalling these two stories. It makes me wonder why here. Maybe it was because <u>5,000</u> people had just witnessed an extraordinary miracle (are there "ordinary" ones?) <u>and</u> had their bellies filled in the process. It would seem that with 5,000 witnesses it would be hard to keep Jesus a secret any longer even given the lack of high-tech communication in this time!

Maybe Jesus was displaying a very human characteristic of frustration...that's when <u>I</u> sigh! Certainly in the second story that seems true. No 'sign' was given to the close-hearted Pharisees and Jesus turns on His heel and gets back in the boat.

Frustration can be a good thing. Yes, a <u>good</u> thing when it spurs me on to put forth more effort and not just sit back on my heels waiting for something to be handed to me.

For I consider that the sufferings of this present time are not worth comparing with the glory that is to be revealed to us. For the creation waits with eager longing for the revealing of the sons of God. For the creation was subjected to futility, not willingly, but because of him who subjected it, in hope that the creation itself will be set free from its bondage to decay and obtain the freedom of the glory of the children of God. For we know that the whole creation has been groaning together in the pains of childbirth until now. And not only the creation, but we ourselves, who have the firstfruits of the Spirit, groan inwardly as we wait eagerly for adoption as sons, the redemption of our bodies. For in this hope we were saved. Now hope that is seen is not hope. For who hopes for what he sees?   Romans 8:18-24 (ESV)

When I become stagnant by the complacency of where I am in Jesus and decide that I 'have arrived', my spiritual life begins to decay. God desires that I continue to move forward <u>toward</u> Him and so He does allow obstacles or difficult paths that will frustrate me into moving forward, reaching out for Him.

I see Jesus' sighs as a human manifestation of His heart's desire that I continue to move forward in Him. I will learn more about His mind and His heart and His power. I will become more like Him, a disciple of Jesus.

Additional Text: 2 Timothy 2, Hebrews 6

Don't use bad language. Say only what is good and helpful to those you are talking to, and what will give them a blessing. Don't cause the Holy Spirit sorrow by the way you live. Remember, he is the one who marks you to be present on that day when salvation from sin will be complete. Stop being mean, bad-tempered and angry. Quarreling, harsh words, and dislike of others should have no place in your lives. Instead, be kind to each other, tenderhearted, forgiving one another, just as God has forgiven you because you belong to Christ. Follow God's example in everything you do just as a much loved child imitates his father. Be full of love for others, following the example of Christ who loved you and gave himself to God as a sacrifice to take away your sins. And God was pleased, for Christ's love for you was like sweet perfume to him.

Ephesians 4:29-5:2 (TLB)

My world would certainly be a different kind of place if I did what was in the above God-breathed words. I would like to walk in my life speaking words that would only build up others. There would be correction but the tone of the words would be full of God's love. The Holy Spirit will rejoice as I continue to move with Him, listening to Him with an open, obedient heart. My life would be so full of the fruit of God (Galatians 5:22) that there would be no room for the fruit of my flesh like getting even with anyone or anything that I had determined was unfair! FORGIVENESS! God's forgiveness, which has NO conditions would flow from me because I would be full of His sufficient grace!

Living a life of love that is defined and given by God is not an impossible task. God is always willing to supply all that I need of His love, grace, and mercy. He will not "stuff it in me". He will give and give as long as I hold the door open to my heart and get rid of anything that is taking up space that is not from Him!

Blessings on all who reverence and trust the Lord – on all who obey him! Their reward shall be prosperity and happiness. Psalm 128:1-2 (TLB)

For me, it is not only spending time in His presence through prayer and worship but it is also taking time when I am in a given situation to pause and let God be God in that moment. Allow God to take the lead instead of my tongue and my thoughts.

O LORD, hear me praying; listen to my plea, O God my King, for I will never pray to anyone but you. Each morning I will look to you in heaven and lay my requests before you, praying earnestly. I know you get no pleasure from wickedness and cannot tolerate the slightest sin. Therefore proud sinners will not survive your searching gaze, for how you hate their evil deeds. You will destroy them for their lies; how you abhor all murder and deception...

But make everyone rejoice who puts his trust in you. Keep them shouting for joy because you are defending them. Fill all who love you with your happiness. For you bless the godly man, O Lord; you protect him with your shield of love.

Psalm 5:1-6, 11-12

And so, today, I pick up my cross and walk forward again, knowing that being an imitator of Jesus means the 'yoke' (connection to Him) is easy and the 'burden' (choosing to be like Him) is light. Being 'righteous' is choosing a relationship with God. With His continued help, I can do that!

Give ear to my words, O LORD, consider my groaning. Give attention to the sound of my cry, my King and my God, for to you do I pray. O LORD, in the morning you hear my voice; in the morning I prepare a sacrifice for you and watch.

For you are not a God who delights in wickedness; evil may not dwell with you. The boastful shall not stand before your eyes; you hate all evildoers. You destroy those who speak lies; the LORD abhors the bloodthirsty and deceitful man.

But I, through the abundance of your steadfast love, will enter your house. I will bow down toward your holy temple in the fear of you. Lead me, O LORD, in your righteousness because of my enemies; make your way straight before me.

For there is no truth in their mouth; their inmost self is destruction; their throat is an open grave; they flatter with their tongue. Make them bear their guilt, O God; let them fall by their own counsels; because of the abundance of their transgressions cast them out, for they have rebelled against you.

But let all who take refuge in you rejoice; let them ever sing for joy, and spread your protection over them, that those who love your name may exult in you. For you bless the righteous, O LORD; you cover him with favor as with a shield.

Psalm 5 (ESV)

The verses I typed in **bold** are about those who are wicked and arrogant, liars and deceivers. Sometimes I want to just leave those words out of my reading. "That's not <u>me</u>!" (arrogance?) But it is good to read <u>all</u> the words, the warnings, and allow the Holy Spirit to examine my heart. Examine the place that I may successfully hide from all others except Him.

...and at the end of your life you groan, when your flesh and body are consumed, and you say, "How I hated discipline, and my heart despised reproof! I did not listen to the voice of my teacher, or incline my ear to my instructors. I am at the brink of utter ruin in the assembled congregation."...

For a man's ways are before the eyes of the LORD, and he ponders all his paths. The iniquities of the wicked ensnare him, and he is held fast in the cords of his sin. He dies for lack of discipline, and because of his great folly he is led astray.
Proverbs 5:11-14, 21-23 (ESV)

I was recently on a long flight from Amsterdam to Memphis, TN. I went to these two chapters in Psalms and Proverbs because...it was July 5th! And here I found these words about discipline and correction! The writer of Proverbs is RIGHT! I <u>don't</u> like discipline and I'd rather <u>NOT</u> be corrected! But I hate mistakes and missteps that lead to sin more. Feeling God's displeasure and that sense of distance because I have chosen MY way and refused His...is NOT a good place to be!

And all these blessings shall come upon you and overtake you, if you obey the voice of the LORD your God.
Deuteronomy 28:2 (ESV)

Blessings for obedience!

Additional Text: Leviticus 26, Deuteronomy 28

Then the Spirit of the LORD entered Jahaziel. (Jahaziel was Zechariah's son. Zechariah was Benaiah's son. Benaiah was Jeiel's son, and Jeiel was Mattaniah's son.) Jahaziel, a Levite and a descendant of Asaph, stood up in the meeting. He said, "Listen to me, King Jehoshaphat and all you people living in Judah and Jerusalem. The LORD says this to you: 'Don't be afraid or discouraged because of this large army. The battle is not your battle, it is God's.'   *2 Chronicles 20:14-15 (NCV)*

Battles are part of my everyday life in this world. Some battles are easily identified. They are familiar and frequent battles that come from my flesh like control and pride. Some battles are more camouflaged like trust and hope that hide under discouragement and lies. In each case, my Commander-in-chief, Jehovah the Lord, is aware of it <u>ALL</u>. He did not fall asleep while the enemy made a 'sneak attack' against me. He sees it all and has the battle strategy all laid out if I am willing to come to Him and await His orders.

Gates, open all the way. Open wide, aged doors so the glorious King will come in. Who is this glorious King? The LORD, strong and mighty. The LORD, the powerful warrior. Gates, open all the way. Open wide, aged doors so the glorious King will come in. Who is this glorious King? The LORD All-Powerful – he is the glorious King.   *Psalm 24:7-10 (NCV)*

"*the LORD, the powerful warrior*". Yes, that is my God. There is none other like Him. When the enemy rises up with fangs and claws and large amounts of drool – God is already standing there! I am NOT alone!

Elisha's servant got up early, and when he went out, he saw an army with horses and chariots, all around the city. The servant said to Elisha, "Oh, my master, what can we do?"

Elisha said, "Don't be afraid. The army that fights for us is larger than the one against us." The Elisha prayed, "LORD, open my servant's eyes, and let him see." The LORD opened the eyes of the young man, and he saw that the mountain was full of horses and chariots of fire all around Elisha.
       2 Kings 6:15-17 (NCV)

I do not 'fight' with guns and knives and 'smart bombs' but with prayer and praise of my God Almighty. I do not 'fight' with persuasive words or debate but with prayers of blessings and the same grace and mercy that God has extended to me. The 'secret weapon' of God's unconditional love and my faith, which may be only the size of a seed will destroy my enemy and glorify my Commander-in-Chief!

Mighty God! HALLELUJAH!

Additional Text: Psalm 24 and 150

I pray that the Lord, who gives peace, will always bless you with peace. May the Lord be with all of you.   *2 Thessalonians 3:16 (CEV)*

That is a good prayer to speak over anyone, isn't it? God's peace is not a blessing of 'Utopia' or Shangri-La, however.

"I came to set fire to the earth, and I wish it were already on fire! I am going to be put to a hard test. And I will have to suffer a lot of pain until it is over. Do you think that I came to bring peace to earth? No indeed! I came to make people choose sides."   *Luke 12:49-51 (CEV)*

The disciples were afraid of the Jewish leaders, and on the evening of that same Sunday they locked themselves in a room. Suddenly, Jesus appeared in the middle of the group. He greeted them and showed them his hands and his side. When the disciples saw the Lord, they became very happy. After Jesus had greeted them again, he said, "I am sending you, just as the Father has sent me." Then he breathed on them and said, "Receive the Holy Spirit. If you forgive anyone's sins, they will be forgiven. But if you don't forgive their sins, they will not be forgiven."   *John 20:19-23 (CEV)*

Jesus seems very clear to me that He was not promising me an easy life if I believed in Him. He, in fact, tells me that there will be 'division' and that life in this world will bring 'trouble' (John 16:33). No matter how hard I search and try to stretch Scripture, I do not find God promising me a life here without hardship, disease, or troubles. But what about all the times when Jesus says, "Peace be with you!"?

Jesus' peace goes past the 'feel good' of my present world. He wants me to have a peace that <u>does</u> go past my understanding in any situation (Philippians 4:7). In the midst of the most terrible circumstances when NOTHING makes sense – there is God's peace…His Holy Spirit peace. That 'peace' doesn't come easily. As I read again the gospel accounts of Jesus' death, I see the temple curtain torn in two and the barrier between God and me destroyed. It is into that Holy Place that Jesus provides that I find His perfect peace. It came with the highest price ever paid. And it was for <u>me</u>.

Jesus said to his disciples, "Don't be worried! Have faith in God and have faith in me. There are many rooms in my Father's house. I wouldn't tell you this, unless it was true. I am going there to prepare a place for each for you. After I have done this, I will come back and take you with me. Then we will be together. You know the way to where I am going."   *John 14: 1-3 (CEV)*

The place of God's perfect peace is where I want to <u>live</u>. I reject the chaos and despair of this world and I <u>choose</u> to step toward Jesus where there is peace that only <u>HE</u> can provide. I thank my Lord that He knew all that my life would be and saw the need for His peace 'way before I did.

You are my God and protector. Please answer my prayer. I was in terrible distress, but you set me free. Now have pity and listen as I pray…

There are some who ask, "Who will be good to us?" Let your kindness, LORD, shine brightly on us. You brought me more happiness than a rich harvest of grain and grapes. I can lie down and sleep soundly because you, LORD, will keep me safe.   *Psalm 4:1, 6-8 (CEV)*

About this time, Hezekiah got sick and was almost dead. Isaiah the prophet went in and told him, "The LORD says you won't ever get well. You are going to die, so you had better start doing what needs to be done..."
Isaiah replied, "The LORD will prove to you that he will keep his promise. [Hezekiah would be healed] Will the shadow made by the setting sun on the stairway go forward ten steps or back ten steps?"
"It's normal for the sun to go forward," Hezekiah answered. "But how can it go back?" Isaiah prayed, and the LORD made the shadow go back ten steps on the stairway built for King Ahaz.   *2 Kings 20:1, 9-11 (CEV)*

There are many accounts in the Bible telling me the ways that God sent signs to His children to <u>prove</u> that He would do what He said or that the voice or order that the person heard was *really* God speaking to them. He used burning bushes, thunder and lightening, wet and dry fleece, whales, and vivid visions just to name a few.

Some people, even within God's Church, would say that He doesn't do those things anymore. I wonder if it isn't more likely that we have fooled ourselves into believing that. Have we taken our great scientific knowledge and applied it to an infinite God deceiving ourselves into thinking that there is <u>always</u> an explanation for events, even voices that we hear? Have we lost the wonderment that we had as a child when we saw our first firefly or our first shooting star? Must everything in my life have form and reason applied to it? Am I afraid that God <u>does</u> speak to me, and so that means He is closer and more aware of me and all that I do than I would like? I want God to be close in the difficult times to protect and comfort me but I'd rather He keep His distance so I do not feel His conviction when I want things to be <u>MY</u> way. When I think that my life is <u>totally</u> out of my control and I can't see the 'reason' for events and circumstances, what then? Am I willing to admit that my life was NEVER in my control? Am I willing then to *SEE* God?

The LORD said, "Ezekiel, son of man, I want you to stand up and listen." After he said this, his Spirit took control of me and lifted me to my feet. Then the LORD said: Ezekiel, I am sending you to the people of Israel. They are just like their ancestors who rebelled against me and refused to stop. They are stubborn and hardheaded. But I, the LORD God, have chosen you to tell them what I say. Those rebels may not even listen, but at least they will know that a prophet has come to them. Don't be afraid of them or of anything they say. You may think you're in the middle of a thorn patch or a bunch of scorpions. But be brave and preach my message to them, whether they choose to listen or not. Ezekiel, don't rebel against me, as they have done. Instead, listen to everything I tell you."
Ezekiel 2:1-8 (CEV)

"Do not be rebellious but receive what I have for you." God has many signs and wonders for me...today...and every day. Do I have eyes to see them?

Additional Text: John 4, 1 Corinthians 2

Susan Lewis

Born in Selma, Alabama, Susan was an Air Force 'brat' with two sisters and a brother. She is a registered nurse in the labor and delivery where she is finding many opportunities to serve her Lord.

You have turned for me my mourning into dancing; you have loosed my sackcloth and clothed me with gladness, that my glory may sing your praise and not be silent, O LORD my God, I will give thanks to you forever!

Psalm 30:11-12

I've been an atheist. I've been married. I've been divorced. Around the time of my divorce, my mother also died of cancer. At one time I was 'in a relationship' with a drug addict that of course had nowhere to go but down! I was self-sufficient and yet so lost and broken. My sister, Cheryl, invited me to her church. She said there was a group of young people there, *Broken Vessels* that sang and led the congregation in worship. It was wonderful! My experience with church before had been stiff and boring. I began to go every week and then 2-3 times a week. There were people there who prayed with me. The cold, hard wall around my heart broke and I received the love of God and believed that Jesus died for ME! I wept and wept with the tenderness of God's love!

Dancing began for me at age 27 when I was looking for an exercise class. I progressed into ballet productions and modern dance. After accepting Jesus as my Savior, I felt God asking me, "Make a choice: dance for them (and the applause) or dance for Me". I chose to make a change and dance for God. He opened many doors! He did not mean for the talent He gave me to be wasted when He knew where to use it in His kingdom. I've taught dance in many churches, especially how to incorporate it as part of worship in a way that is joyful and pleasing in God's eyes.

I have also picked up the flute again after laying it down in high school in order to be the drum major! He has allowed me to play at a level that I never had! Who ever knew that I would be playing and dancing like Miriam?!

My life has been like a rough ocean where God takes me 10 feet under to the quiet, the peace. I look up and see the waves still rolling but I'm in God's shelter and there is peace. I'm still weeping with the joy of God's love!

September 1

About the middle of the feast Jesus went up into the temple and began teaching. The Jews therefore marveled, saying, "How is it that this man has learning, when he has never studied?" So Jesus answered them, "My teaching is not mine, but his who sent me. If anyone's will is to do God's will, he will know whether the teaching is from God or whether I am speaking on my own authority. The one who speaks on his own authority seeks his own glory, but the one who seeks the glory of him who sent him is true, and in him there is no falsehood."   *John 7:14-18 (ESV)*

Teach me your way, O LORD, that I may walk in your truth; unite my heart to fear your name. I give thanks to you, O Lord my God, with my whole heart, and I will glorify your name forever. For great is your steadfast love toward me; you have delivered my soul from the depths of Sheol.   *Psalm 86:11-13 (ESV)*

When our children would have their first tests of a new school year, they would say that those were the 'good' kind because they were essentially reviewing information from last year. No new concepts.

Even though at my "extreme age" I haven't taken a test since Flo Nightingale and I were in school together (!), but I remember the feelings like it was yesterday. Some tests were 'good' in that I went in feeling confident and prepared for the test and expected to do well. Most were tests that I studied and went in 'wired' but feeling prepared. A few (fortunately only a few) were tests that caused sweaty palms and an increased heart rate because I did not study and I was not prepared! And then one stands out in a class by itself (NURSING BOARDS!!!) — I had studied all through college and 'crammed' for the first time in my life — and still I was sweaty and nervous.

Life has its tests. I don't think I am exaggerating by saying — DAILY tests. Have I studied? Am I prepared? Studying requires: 1) the right resources/teachers — The Bible (the standard for all others) and the One who inspired it, other authors, church leadership and brothers and sisters in the Lord 2) the right environment to study — worship, my private devotion time, study groups and 3) my attitude and desire to grow and learn.

Being prepared begins with knowing that there will be tests. I don't know if I had my first test in first grade or if it was second grade. I just remember being so taken by surprise and — PANICKED! — and — so out of control! Now I know that all that analysis comes from an adult looking back on a childhood memory — but I can certainly see parallel truths in my adult life.

Yes, life has its tests and I need to be prepared DAILY for these tests. I need to do my part in daily study and then plant my feet FIRMLY on the other part — that GOD is there and has in fact already gone before me! Big or small — I will never take another test alone. Some may be 'pop' tests — some may be 'end of the semester' EXAMS — but I am not alone.

What is the 'test' today? OK, God, let's go do it! Lord, I want to glorify You!

Additional Text: 2 Samuel 14-15, John 14

September 2

We are blessed in this country that we are allowed to seek employment and earn a wage, providing for our families. Most of us grow up believing that if we just work hard enough and achieve educational or technical certifications that we will be "successful", making lots of money and rising in status and making us feel good.

"Remember that the Sabbath Day belongs to me. You have six days when you can do your work, but the seventh day of each week belongs to me, your God. No one is to work on that day – not you, your children, your slaves, your animals, or the foreigners who live in your towns. In six days I made the sky, the earth, the oceans, and everything in them, but on the seventh day I rested. That's why I made the Sabbath a special day that belongs to me."

Exodus 20:8-11 (CEV)

"Do your work in six days and rest on the seventh day, even during the seasons for plowing and harvesting." *Exodus 34:21 (CEV)*

God does encourage us to 'labor', not expecting a 'free ride'. (2 Thessalonians 3:10) God does, however, teach us a balance as He makes it clear that we do not achieve in and of ourselves. Our 'success' is ABSOLUTELY dependent upon our relationship to Him. Worldly success has no eternal impact.

And so we celebrate LABOR DAY today. What is my Sabbath celebration? Do I celebrate what the Lord is doing for my ETERNAL SUCCESS? Do I honor God with my Sabbath rest? Do I give Him more than just an hour or two? Is it a day just for Him?

Don't have anything to do with worthless, senseless stories. Work hard to be truly religious. As the saying goes, 'Exercise is good for your body, but religion helps you in every way. It promises life now and forever.' These words are worthwhile and should not be forgotten. We have put our hope in the living God, who is the Savior of everyone, but especially of those who have faith. That's why we work and struggle so hard. *1 Timothy 4:7-10 (CEV)*

A young man gave me a plaque he made and it said: "Working for the Lord doesn't pay much but the retirement is out of this world". It is a struggle between God's words that tell me to give Him the Sabbath, not working and focusing on Him and the world's view that I should make the most of every opportunity no matter when it comes. For me it comes down to trust. Do I trust God that He knows what is asked of me and the tasks that need to be done? Will I give Him what He asks because I KNOW that He will take care of the rest? That should be an easy question to answer.

Additional Text: 1 Kings 3, Matthew 16

September 3

What can we say about all this? If God is on our side, can anyone be against us?   *Romans 8:31 (CEV)*

What <u>can</u> we say? Let's look at the <u>statement</u> of the question: GOD IS FOR US!

I read some interesting thoughts about this statement in a book by Max Lucado called *America Looks Up*. Pastor Lucado reminds me that <u>God</u> is for me. My parents may be gone or want to forget me. Teachers may not even remember that I was in their class, and so-called friends may think I'm strange but GOD is still on my side.

And then, God <u>is</u> for me. That's a powerful statement. No "if's" or "but's". God IS! He doesn't claim me just when I win an award or make A's. And He doesn't ignore me when I make a mistake – which I do!

Then there is the thought that God is <u>for</u> me. God is the one cheering me on. He's not waiting to criticize me. He's actually willing to carry me when the race becomes long and hard.

And finally, God is for <u>me</u>. As Max said, "Had he (God) had a calendar, your birthday would be circled. If he drove a car, your name would be on His bumper. We know he has a tattoo, and we know what it says; *"I have written your name on my hand."*   *Isaiah 49:16*

God is with me so who CAN be against me?

God did not keep back his own Son, but he gave him for us. If God did this, won't he freely give us everything else? If God says his chosen ones are acceptable to him, can anyone bring charges against them? Or can anyone condemn them? No, indeed! Christ died and was raised to life, and now he is at God's right side, speaking to him for us. Can anything separate us from the love of Christ? Can trouble, suffering, and hard times, or hunger and nakedness, or danger and death?   *Romans 8:32-35 (CEV)*

All those things are tough. No doubt about it. They CAN NOT separate me from God, however. Only I have that power. Me? Yup, me. Father God wants me to be joined with Him, in connection with Him. It's my choice today.

You were the weakest of all nations, but the LORD chose you because he loves you and because he had made a promise to your ancestors. Then with his mighty arm, he rescued you from the king of Egypt, who had made you his slaves. You know that the LORD your God is the only true God. So love him and obey his commands, and he will faithfully keep his agreement with you and your descendants for a thousand generations.   *Deuteronomy 7:7-9 (CEV)*

God is faithful to His promises and He has promised that I am His and He promised this to 1, 000 generations! We have a ways to go before that runs out on the Lord's covenant promise!

I speak to you as my friends, and I have told you everything that my Father has told me. You did not choose me. I chose you and sent you out to produce fruit, the kind of fruit that will last. Then my Father will give you whatever you ask for in my name. So I command you to love each other.   *John 15:15-17 (CEV)*

Jesus reaffirms that I am chosen. He reaffirms that He is for me. God is for me.

September 4

"Come now, let us reason together," says the LORD: "though your sins are like scarlet, they shall be white as snow; though they are red like crimson, they shall become like wool."   *Isaiah 1:18 (ESV)*
"Come, everyone who thirsts, come to the waters; and he who has no money, come, buy and eat! Come, buy wine and milk without money and without price."   *Isaiah 55:1 (ESV)*
"Come to me, all who labor and are heavy laden, and I will give you rest."
                    Matthew 11:28 (ESV)
"Again he sent other servants, saying, 'Tell those who are invited, See, I have prepared my dinner, my oxen and my fat calves have been slaughtered, and everything is ready. Come to the wedding feast.' But they paid no attention, and went off, one to his farm, another to his business..."   *Matthew 22:4-5 (ESV)*

God has sent out many invitations to me. He has sent these invitations throughout my life. They did not just begin when I became a believer in Him. The invitations came so I <u>would</u> come to believe in Him. God has desired that I <u>come</u> to Him and <u>become</u> more intimate and close to Him every day. It is not a one-time invitation; it continues until I see His hand extended as He brings me into the final wedding banquet that Jesus spoke in Matthew 22.

I like to have choices. I like the feeling of control that comes when I have a <u>choice</u>. There are not many choices in this world. I did not have a choice about my nose and finances limit my changing it! Until I decided to use Clairol, I had no say in my hair! Some people change jobs; some change spouses in order to feel some resemblance of control in a life that seems out of control!

God gives me the ULTIMATE choice of <u>where</u> I will spend eternity. God allows me to decide not where I am going to spend a measly 75 years but where I am going to spend ETERNITY!!! FOREVER!!! The choice is mine. The choice is freely given.

And Jesus said to them, "Follow me, and I will make you become fishers of men."   *Mark 1:17 (ESV)*

God also gives me the opportunity to be used to extend His invitation to others. God gave His all – I have a choice to give ALL of me to serve Him. In serving Him, I extend the invitation to others, some I know, and some I do not but the circle continues to grow, as we become *'fishers of men'*.

There is an invitation that has arrived in my 'Inbox' today. God has extended His invitation to 'Come' and spend time with Him today. Will I accept or not? The choice is mine.

Additional Text: Hosea 11, Joel 2

September 5

Then the king will say to those on his left, "Get away from me! You are under God's curse. Go into the everlasting fire prepared for the devil and his angels!"

Matthew 25:41 (CEV)

In the middle of Jesus' description of Judgment Day where He describes the separation of the 'sheep' and 'goats', He tells us clearly that hell, or the 'eternal fire', was created not for us but for satan and his followers. I find that comforting and a confirmation of what Paul said to Timothy:

This kind of prayer is good, and it pleases God our Savior. God wants <u>everyone</u> to be saved and to know the whole truth... 1 Timothy 2:3-4 (CEV, my emphasis)

God is a good parent. He desires that His children come to Him out of love and the joy of being with Him but He is also willing to apply some 'negative' discipline, teaching me that there <u>are</u> consequences for making poor choices. 'Hell' is the consequence for NOT <u>choosing</u> God as the Lord of my life. Hell was not made for people. For a person to go to hell that person must <u>choose</u> to go against God's destiny.

God doesn't intend to punish us, but to have our Lord Jesus Christ save us.

1 Thessalonians 5:9 (CEV)

God's plan and desire has <u>always</u> been for me to live with Him for all eternity. Hell is <u>my</u> choice, not God's. To choose hell means that I love myself more than God. I love sin more than the Savior who died for me. And I love <u>this</u> world more than the eternal world that God created <u>for</u> me. Judgment is that moment in time when God will look at me and say, "Your choice is now honored." Will heaven be <u>my</u> choice or will hell be <u>my</u> choice?

The first recorded sermon or teaching that Jesus gave was on a mountainside. He spoke of those who are 'blessed' (the Beatitudes) and ended with a clear warning about the judgment. He describes it in Matthew 7 as a 'wide and narrow gate'. His last sermon or teaching in Matthew 25 also speaks of judgment in the description of the 'sheep and the goats'. Jesus did not want me to be wondering about Judgment. Jesus wanted me to understand my two choices. He wanted me to be informed. He wanted me to choose wisely. Jesus wanted me to choose...Him.

We die only once, and then we are judged. So Christ died only once to take away the sins of many people. But when he comes again, it will not be to take away sin. He will come to save everyone who is waiting for him.

Hebrews 9:27-28 (CEV)

My friends, the blood of Jesus gives us courage to enter the most holy place by a new way that leads to life! And this way takes us through the curtain that is Christ himself...We should keep on encouraging each other to be thoughtful and to do helpful things. Some people have gotten out of the habit of meeting for worship, but we must not do that. We should keep on encouraging each other, especially since you know that the day of the Lord's coming is getting closer.

Hebrews 10:19-20, 24-25 (CEV)

Let us truly continue to meet together and encourage each other to make <u>good</u> choices, GOD choices. I want to live <u>eternally</u> with God AND with <u>you</u>!

September 6

Heavens and earth, be happy. Mountains, shout with joy, because the LORD comforts his people and will have pity on those who suffer. Isaiah 49:13 (NCV)
The LORD says, "I am the one who comforts you. So why should you be afraid of people who die? Why should you fear people who die like grass? Have you forgotten the LORD who made you, who stretched out the skies and made the earth? Why are you always afraid of those angry people who trouble you and who want to destroy? But where are those angry people now? People in prison will soon be set free; they will not die in prison, and they will have enough food. I am the LORD your God, who stirs the sea and make the waves roar. My name is the LORD All-Powerful. Isaiah 51:12-15 (NCV)

I live along the Gulf Coast and hurricanes are a part of our world. In the Midwest, it is tornadoes. In California, it is earthquakes. In the extreme north, there are snowstorms and avalanches. When what we call 'natural disasters' occur, it is interesting, and yes puzzling, to see one home or family completely destroyed and the next home not be touched. The 'why' of it cannot be explained here on earth. Death and destruction may seem random and horrific, without sense or reason.

On the other side of this coin is the outpouring of kindness and assistance that comes when disaster hits. I have watched neighbors who had never spoke a dozen words to each other share water, food supplies, tools, and manpower; helping each other and forging lasting relationships that may never have occurred without this common point of need and help. Bible study groups that took the 'book learning' and put it into action by just showing up at a home to clear the yard and cover the roof on a house, bringing food and candles.

Praise be to the God and Father of our Lord Jesus Christ. God is the Father who is full of mercy and all comfort. He comforts us every time we have trouble, so when others have trouble, we can comfort them with the same comfort God gives us. We share in the many sufferings of Christ. In the same way, much comfort comes to us through Christ. If we have troubles, it is for your comfort and salvation, and if we have comfort, you also have comfort. This helps you to accept patient the same sufferings we have. 2 Corinthians 1:3-6 (NCV)

To accept that suffering comes to me so that I <u>may</u> turn to the Lord and receive His comfort and <u>then</u> pass that same comfort along to others in need is a hard lesson to accept. I must suffer – in order to learn. And yet, that certainly worked on a much smaller scale in school, didn't it? Would I have studied and learned my multiplication tables if tests were not given, even tests of standing before the class and reciting a table? Would I have learned how to balance a chemical equation if I had not been tested? NO!!! I admit this with some measure of shame! Would I have learned that <u>GOD</u> is the *only one* with the true comfort and some portion of answers I can understand to the questions that seem to have no answers if I had not experienced the suffering and pain of death and disasters? NO!!! I would have avoided those situations and the people involved with them.

"Blessed are those who mourn, for they will be comforted." Matthew 5:4
I know God's promises are true … because I have experienced them.

That day a man named Simeon, a Jerusalem resident, was in the Temple. He was a good man, very devout, filled with the Holy Spirit and constantly expecting the Messiah to come soon... "Lord," he said, "Now I can die content! For I have seen him as you promised me I would. I have seen the Savior you have given to the world. He is the Light that will shine upon the nations, and he will be the glory of your people in Israel!"...

Simeon blessed them but then said to Mary, "A sword shall pierce your soul, for this child shall be rejected by many in Israel, and this to their undoing. But he will be the greatest joy of many others. And the deepest thoughts of many hearts shall be revealed."   *Luke 2:25, 29-31, 34-35 (TLB)*

Mary had been told many hard things in her life...by reputable sources! God sends an angel to tell her she is going to have a baby <u>before</u> she has been with her husband! I'm sure there were some busybodies even in those days that could count and spread the rumor that it wasn't Joseph's child! THEN a 'righteous and devout' man of God tells Mary that her newborn son will cause great upheaval in Israel. He didn't say her son would be a hero or a great leader. God's message through Simeon was not easy! The <u>truth</u> of a man's heart would be revealed for what it truly was. That doesn't sound like a message of peace, does it? And, then, just in case Mary was holding on to some kind of hope that this message from God about her son was going to have a silver lining...Simeon tells Mary that the *pain* of what was going to happen to her son was going to be like a sword piercing her heart.

God's messages are true. God's messages are wise. God's messages will always keep the BIG PICTURE as the standard. The BIG PICTURE is His sacrifice of atonement through Jesus and that ALL would come to a saving relationship with Him because of God's willingness to give … His Son. If you think that message isn't difficult, see the 2004 movie, *The Passion of the Christ*.

...and he [Jesus] said, "I have looked forward to this hour with deep longing, anxious to eat this Passover meal with you before my suffering begins. For I tell you now that I won't eat it again until what it represents has occurred in the Kingdom of God." Then he took a glass of wine, and when he had given thanks for it, he said, "Take this and share it among yourselves. For I will not drink wine again until the Kingdom of God has come."   *Luke 22:15-18 (TLB)*

Jesus knew what must be done. It was a hard message to receive. It was a difficult order to obey.

"Father, if you are willing, please take away this cup of horror from me. But I want your will, not mine."   *Luke 22:42 (TLB)*

Jesus came to live in this world just as you and I did. He kept in mind that this was not the place where He would receive His reward. This world would be difficult. Obedience to God was the only path Jesus would walk. He didn't do it in even HIS own strength.

Then an angel from heaven appeared and strengthened him... Luke 22:43 (TLB)

Our Father is faithful and He <u>will</u> give us whatever it is that we need for each day ...when we receive His message with an open and obedient heart.

A friend of mine died this week. I know he is with Jesus. I miss him. I ache for his family. Sorrow. Grief.

LORD, have mercy, because I am in misery. My eyes are weak from so much crying, and my whole being is tired from grief. My life is ending in sadness, and my years are spent in crying. My troubles are using up my strength, and my bones are getting weaker.   Psalm 31:9-10 (NCV)

The psalmists wrote of grief and sorrow about as many times as they wrote of joy and the goodness of the Lord. In fact, even when writing about sorrow they always come back to their belief that God hears them and WILL answer:

But I trust in you, O LORD; I say, "You are my God."   Psalm 31:14

Solomon in Ecclesiastes expresses what he has learned as truth. Solomon asked the Lord for wisdom. He is the human example for wisdom. He tells us in the first chapter that wisdom and knowledge came with a high cost.

Then Jesus went with his followers to a place called Gethsemane. He said to them, "Sit here while I go over there and pray." He took Peter and the two sons of Zebedee with him, and he began to be very sad and troubled. He said to them, "My heart is full of sorrow, to the point of death. Stay here and watch with me." After walking a little farther away from them, Jesus fell to the ground and prayed, "My Father, if it is possible, do not give me this cup of suffering. But do what you want, not what I want."   Matthew 26:36-39 (NCV)

And finally Matthew records in his gospel Jesus' own point of *overwhelming* grief. Jesus reaches out and asks – expects – His friends, His disciples, to stay close to Him and comfort Him, pray with Him. He finds out that when it comes down to it – it is just He and God, the only One that He can truly count on. God does not 'let the cup pass' but He walks the Via dolorosa [the painful road] with Him.

God walks painful roads with me. I may want to avoid them and take the Easy Highway but as Solomon learned, they do bring wisdom and knowledge. When I consider the price too high, I also consider the alternative and KNOW that price is too high.

And so I stand on the testimony of others before me and claim the promises that God is there every step of the way and I keep walking, one step at a time.

But I will sing about your strength. In the morning I will sing about your love. You are my defender, my place of safety in times of trouble. God, my strength, I will sing praises to you. God, my defender, you are the God who loves me.

Psalm 59:16-17 (NCV)

Additional Text: Psalm 31, Luke 22

September 9

At that time King Herod caused terrible suffering for some members of the church. He ordered soldiers to cut off the head of James, the brother of John. When Herod saw that this pleased the Jewish people, he had Peter arrested during the Festival of Thin Bread. He put Peter in jail and ordered four squads of soldiers to guard him. Herod planned to put him on trial in public after the festival. While Peter was being kept in jail, the church never stopped praying to God for him.   *Acts 12:1-5 (CEV)*

"The road to heaven is soaked with the tears and blood of the saints", so said William Plumer, 19th century American minister. Even today, there are Christian believers who are persecuted and put to death. Some estimate the number of martyrs to be in the thousands each year.

I've often wondered as I read this passage in Acts about how it was noted that James was killed and Peter was imprisoned. Peter was later supernaturally released. Peter was put to death several years later. What was God's thinking in His plan and timing? I don't know. What is God's thinking and timing when anyone dies be it a 13-year-old child, a 35-year-old father, or a 95-year-old widow? I don't know.

Each of us has opportunities to serve God. God "*wants all men to be saved and to come to a knowledge of the truth*" (1 Timothy 2:4). I know that everything He does is about saving souls and growing up more believers and worshiping Him. Sometimes how He does that is difficult and seems more than I can bear.

God's Spirit doesn't make cowards out of us. The Spirit gives us power, love, and self-control.

Don't be ashamed to speak for our Lord. And don't be ashamed of me, just because I am in jail for serving him. Use the power that comes from God and join with me in suffering for telling the good news. God saved us and chose us to be his holy people. We did nothing to deserve this, but God planned it because he is so kind. Even before time began God planned for Christ Jesus to show kindness to us. Now Christ Jesus has come to show us the kindness of God. Christ our Savior defeated death and brought us the good news. It shines like a light and offers life that never ends. My work is to be a preacher, an apostle, and a teacher. That's why I am suffering now. But I am not ashamed! I know the one I have faith in, and I am sure that he can guard until the last day what he has trusted me with.   *2 Timothy 1:7-12 (CEV)*

Paul tells Timothy, his young student and believer, that he IS suffering. He doesn't gloss it over. Paul says he is NOT ashamed and he KNOWS whom he believes in AND – here's the biggie – Paul says he TRUSTS God. Despite all the above, Paul continues to take a step of faith – it's not a one time 'step' – and put his trust in the Lord. THAT is a testimony!

Additional Text: Isaiah 53, Mark 8

September 10

"Comfort! Comfort my People!" God says. Speak to Jerusalem's heart, and cry out to her that her warfare is completed, that her iniquity is paid for ... For she has received from the hand of the LORD, double for all her sins. Do you not know? Have you not heard? The LORD, the eternal God, Creator of the world from end to end, does not grow weary or get tired, there's no searching out his wisdom. He gives strength to the weary, to the one without power he multiples strength. Even young men become tired and grow weary, and youths will surely stumble. But those who put their hope in the LORD renew their strength, they will climb with wings like eagles. They will run and not get weary. They will walk, and not be exhausted. Isaiah 40:1-2, 28-31 (HNT)

I went to a friend's funeral today and this was one of the Scriptures that I was asked to read. Isn't that an awesome statement there in those beginning verses – my *"warfare is completed,"* and my *"iniquity is paid for"* and finally, *"from the hand of the LORD"* I will receive *"double"* for ALL my sins! WOW! What a promise! As the Bride of Christ, this is the promise! In the context of my friend's death, after battling cancer for many years, he ran the race, he kept the faith, and next is the prize for which he ran. AWESOME!

Verses 28-31 give me hope and encouragement for the race that I still have to run. God's promise is true that He does not tire in the race. He is with me every step of the way and I can rely on Him to hold me up. In fact, not just hold me up but allow me to SOAR!!! So why don't I feel like I'm soaring? Uh, maybe it's 'cause I have so many un-Godly burdens piled on my back? Why do I carry all these burdens? "If I don't – who will?" [all together now --] GOD!!! Provided they are burdens that ARE to be carried by someone! Ooops!

Another point that was made in this AWESOME worship service today is that THE most common Scripture quoted by pastors, teachers, and other Church leadership when asked a question that they do not know the answer to [like why me? Or why suffering?] is --- (drum roll, please!)

"For my thoughts are not your thoughts, and your ways are not my ways," *declares the LORD.* Isaiah 55:8 (HNT)

Yes, I use it frequently, too!!!

Maybe, just maybe, the burdens that I carry are NOT meant to be carried. Maybe God is dealing with that person – or ME! – and a 'test' is being given and a GREAT testimony is going to come from it – IF I will get out of the way and let God do what God NEEDS to do!!! His 'way' has a much bigger perspective!!!

I want to soar. I want to be an eagle, not a ground hog!

Additional Text: 1 Kings 18, Hebrews 9

September 11

For the same God who said, "Let light shine out of darkness!" has made light shine in our hearts. That light is the knowledge of the glory of God in the face of Jesus Christ. We have this treasure in clay jars, so that this is from God, and not from us.   *2 Corinthians 4:6-7 (HNT)*

Christianity for me is belief in God and following Christ's example or imitating Jesus in that belief that brings eternal life. I was looking at the words 'light' and 'darkness' in the Bible and in every passage I read 'light' is associated with knowledge of God and His truth whereas 'darkness' is where God is not and denotes a lack of the knowledge of God. This makes sense in the practical application in my life. When I am on <u>God's</u> path, no matter what the circumstances, there is 'right-ness' and peace. The picture of the moment is clear even though I may not be able to see past the moment. When I am 'off' God's path, my world seems gray and lacks light to provide a clear image. I confess that when I am in that gray place that I stumble around and feel a 'panic' rise up in me and yet I hesitate to walk toward the 'light' that is <u>always</u> there because that means I will have to walk away from <u>my</u> way or what <u>I</u> want. I even have wonderful brothers and sisters who reflect God's light to me, consciously or unconsciously leading me towards His light and still I hesitate to leave <u>my</u> darkness. Funny, huh? No, not really.

Open to me, gates of righteousness, I will enter them and I will praise the LORD. This is the gate for the LORD, those who are righteous will enter it. I will praise you because you have answered me, and you will be a savior for me. The stone that the builders rejected has become the key cornerstone. This is something that comes from the LORD, it is marvelous in our eyes. This is the day that the LORD has made, let's rejoice and be glad in it. We ask you, LORD, save us! We ask you, LORD, prosper us! Blessed is the one who comes in the name of the LORD. We bless you from the house of the LORD. The LORD is God and he will shine for us. Join together in a feast with tree branches to the horns of the altar. You are my God and I will praise you My God, I will exalt you. Ascribe praise to the LORD for he is good. For his graciousness is eternal.
Psalm 118:19-29 (HNT)

Notice it says here that God "<u>made</u> his light shine upon us". It is no coincidence. God <u>wants</u> me to walk in His light. He <u>wants</u> me to know the Truth. It is not a game to Him. My life in Him is something He <u>wants</u> me to be successful in doing! He puts His way, His truth, His life out there with bright lights and big signs that say, "This way! Over here!" When I am on a trip down an unknown highway, I will not miss the exit <u>when I am LOOKING for it</u>! It's when I am talking and paying little attention or paying attention is secondary to what <u>I</u> am doing – that is when I miss the exit and end up lost and back-tracking!

" I am the LORD who called you in righteousness, I have also taken you by your hand. I gave you a covenant of people, to be a light to the nation, to open the eyes of the blind, to bring forth the captives from the dungeon, from prison those who live in darkness."   *Isaiah 42:6-7 (HNT)*

How great is the love that the Father has for us, His children!

At this time the whole world spoke one language, and everyone used the same words. As people moved from the east, they found a plain in the land of Babylonia and settled there.
They said to each other, "Let's make bricks and bake them to make them hard."
So they used bricks instead of stones, and tar instead of mortar. Then they said to each other, "Let's build a city and a tower for ourselves, whose top will reach high into the sky. We will become famous. Then we will not be scattered over all the earth."
The LORD came down to see the city and the tower that the people had built. The LORD said, "Now, these people are united, all speaking the same language. This is only the beginning of what they will do. They will be able to do anything they want. Come, let us go down and confuse their language so they will not be able to understand each other."
So the LORD scattered them from there over all the earth, and they stopped building the city. The place is called Babel since that is where the LORD confused the language of the whole world. So the LORD caused them to spread out from there over the whole world.   Genesis 11:1-9 (NCV, emphasis mine)

So much for man's ingenuity and plan! Look at how we meet together and talk and discuss the options and possibilities and do it all with the goal of what <u>we</u> will achieve!

Our pastor told us Sunday of a church where the members would bring the Christ Candle into whatever meeting was convening. The Christ Candle is a large candle representing the presence of Christ in the sanctuary. This church brought this candle into every meeting, Administrative Board, Trustees, etc., to remind every member Who is present and Who is truly in charge. Good idea!

The stench of PRIDE and SELF-SERVICE was so *DISGUSTING* to God that He didn't care if they were building a tower or a monument <u>to</u> Him – their hearts were SO FAR away from Him that He knew this was just the beginning of their evil!

Pride will ALWAYS bring disunity and destroy my relationship with God. Yes, <u>destroy</u>.

The LORD hates those who are proud. They will surely be punished...
Good people stay away from evil. By watching what they do, they protect their lives. Pride will destroy a person; a proud attitude leads to ruin.
*   Proverbs 16:5, 17-18 (NCV)*

Humility before God means that I KNOW who is in charge of my life and who gets all the glory for whatever I accomplish.

[Jesus said,] "Whoever is your servant is the greatest among you. Whoever makes himself great will be made humble. Whoever makes himself humble will be made great."   Matthew 23:11-12 (NCV)
Are there those among you who are truly wise and understanding? Then they should show it by living right and doing good things with a gentleness that comes from wisdom.   James 3:13 (NCV)

Additional Text: 1 Peter 5, 2 John

My enemies will turn away when I cry out, I know this, because God is for me.
In God (I praise his word); In the LORD (I praise his word)
In God I trust, I will not fear what mortal man may do to me.
I acknowledge my vows to you, God. I will offer thank offerings to you.
For you saved my soul from death, did you not save my feet from stumbling?
So I could walk before God in the light of life.   *Psalm 56:9-13 (HNT)*

   The NIV Exhaustive Concordance has about four pages of references for the words 'know', 'knew', 'knows', 'knowledge', etc.   The majority of the references deal directly with what <u>God</u> knows and what I <u>will know</u> or <u>do know</u> because of God.

   I am not surprised about the references to what <u>GOD</u> knows. He knows a lot! Like…EVERYTHING! But the way I sometimes live my life you'd think that I have doubts about what God knows!   I cry and weep before Him over circumstances like I think He fell asleep and got surprised or turned His head and didn't care! Hogwash! He knows the circumstances before they happen and I believe He puts His arm around me a little tighter, helping me to brace for the blow before I even know it is coming! He strengthens my shield of faith and tightens the straps on my helmet of salvation and belt of truth and sharpens my sword with new insight into His words, His very mind.

   And that brings me into what I <u>will know</u> or <u>do know</u> because of God. He has guided my steps and brought me into His library of knowledge whenever I ask and take the time to learn. It is my choice. Those of you who are teachers of elementary and secondary students KNOW that you can NOT *CRAM* the knowledge into a child's head who doesn't want to learn or take the time to listen! Boy, does that speak to <u>ME</u> as a child of God???!!! Am I willing to spend the time in God's classroom? Am I willing to embrace <u>HIS</u> concepts or am I convinced that I already know everything? Ouch!

And Moses said to the LORD, "Look, you keep saying to me, 'Lead this people up to the land,' but you have not let me know who you will send with me. Yet you say, 'I know you by name, and you have also found favor in my eyes.' So now, if I have really found favor in your eyes, let me know your ways, so that I will know you. In that way I will find favor in your eyes. And note this: This nation is your people!'" And God said, "My presence (literally face) will go along with you, and I will give you rest."   *Exodus 33:12-14 (HNT)*

   Moses asks for God to teach him. LOOK at what God answers! He doesn't just say, "Sure, Moses! Sit down and listen to me." God says MORE than that! God says He will be right THERE with Moses <u>AND</u> that Moses will receive <u>rest</u> with the knowledge that He receives. WOW! God will tell him <u>exactly</u> what he needs to hear and know and it will be such <u>perfect</u> knowledge that he will relax, secure in the knowledge and presence of his Lord. No wonder the psalmist mentions 'thank offerings' and 'praise offerings' so much. God is WORTHY to receive them!

Additional Text: Nehemiah 12, Philippians 4

...So Joseph followed them to Dothan and found them [his brothers] *there. But when they saw him coming, recognizing him in the distance, they decided to kill him! "Here comes that master-dreamer," they exclaimed. "Come on, let's kill him and toss him into a well and tell father that a wild animal has eaten him. Then we'll see what will become of all his dreams!"* Genesis 37:17-20 (TLB)

Then Judas Iscariot, one of the twelve apostles, went to the chief priests, and asked, "How much will you pay me to get Jesus into your hands?" And they gave him thirty silver coins. From that time, on, Judas watched for an opportunity to betray Jesus to them...

At that very moment while he was still speaking, Judas, one of the Twelve, arrived with a great crowd armed with swords and clubs, sent by the Jewish leaders. Judas had told them to arrest the man he greeted, for that would be the one they were after. So now Judas came straight to Jesus and said, "Hello, Master!" and embraced him in friendly fashion.

Jesus said, "My friend, go ahead and do what you have come for." Then the others grabbed him. Matthew 26:14-16, 47-50 (TLB)

I was wrestling this morning with the knowledge that I am going to have to go to someone who has been untrustworthy and deceitful to me and ask them for their help. After flipping the situation around in my mind a bit and trying to think of a way to achieve the goal without involving the person, I know that I will have to go to the person. I also know that there is an opportunity here for God to be glorified. But that will involve repentance on my part for my hard heart.

Jesus knew that Judas was the one to betray Him. Did He know from the moment He met him? Jesus was God. Besides Judas was a thief. I imagine Jesus was aware that Judas was stealing from their 'ministry fund'. Certainly all the gospels tell us that Jesus knew at the last supper that Judas would betray Him and yet He washed Judas' feet along with the others. Jesus sets agape love, unconditional love, as His example to me. That doesn't make me stupid or unwise, just compassionate.

Are we insane? If so, it is to bring glory to God. And if we are in our right minds, it is for your benefit. Whatever we do, it is certainly not for our own profit, but because Christ's love controls us now. Since we believe that Christ died for all of us, we should also believe that we have died to the old life we used to live...So stop evaluating Christians by what the world thinks about them or by what they seem to be like on the outside. Once I mistakenly thought of Christ that way, merely as a human being like myself. How differently I feel now! When someone becomes a Christian he becomes a brand new person inside. He is not the same any more. A new life has begun!

2 Corinthians 5:13-14, 16-17 (TLB)

And so in the days ahead, I will be asking God for His grace and mercy. I will be asking Him to remind me of how much HE has forgiven me. I stand on His promise that His grace is sufficient and that when the time arrives for me to go to this person for the help, it will be Jesus that she sees and hears...not me.

September 15

So early in the morning the chief priests and elders of the people entered into consultation against Jesus so as to kill him. So they bound him and handed him over to Pilate the governor. Then Judas, who had betrayed him, saw that Jesus had been condemned. He was deeply regretful and returned the thirty silver coins to the high priests and the elders. He said, "I have sinned by betraying an innocent person." But they said, "How does that concern us? You deal with it!" And he threw the silver coins into the temple, went away and then hanged himself. But the high priests took the silver coins and said, "It's not legal to throw these into the offering box, since it was paid for blood. So they consulted together and bought the Potter's field with it, to be used as a burial ground for foreigners. That is why that field is called "Blood Field" to this day. Then the word that was spoken through Jeremiah the prophet was fulfilled, "I took thirty silver coins, the value set by the children of Israel, and I gave it for the potter's field, as the Lord commanded me." Jesus stood before the governor, who asked him, "Are you the king of the Jews?" But Jesus said, "You said it!"

Matthew 27:1-11 (HNT)

Judas' suicide has always been a Scripture of interest to me even in my elementary, parochial years. It was a part of the passion of Christ that was hurriedly read over. I think my teachers hoped that we wouldn't notice it. It is a part of the passion that is troublesome to most of us as Judas is shown to be a man who had no choice in what he did. He was 'doomed to destruction' is the way Jesus Himself describes him (John 17:12). I am uncomfortable with a rigid pre-destination theology so Judas' lack of choice is troublesome to me.

Mary took a Roman pound (about 12 ounces) of strong perfume, oil of nard, pure and very valuable, and she anointed Jesus' feet and wiped them with her hair. The whole house was filled with the smell of the perfume. Now Judas Isacriot, who was about to betray him, said, "Why wasn't this perfume sold for three hundred denarii and the money given to the poor?" He said this not because he was concerned about the poor, but because he was a thief and he carried the common purse, and helped himself to what was put in it.

John 12:3-6 (HNT)

Though I do not find any information in the Scripture about Judas' life before his designation as a disciple, Judas does seem to come into the picture as a man who has made choices in his life prior to his meeting with Jesus that have set the 'tone' of his life. He is self-centered and shows a moral code that puts him in the center with whatever <u>he</u> wants. He is a liar and a thief with a thin veneer of self-righteousness.

Judas clearly shows remorse for what he has done and cries out his repentance for having "*betrayed innocent blood*". Was he forgiven and will walk the streets of heaven with Peter and John once again?

Jesus is our judge (John 5:19-23) and He is just and true in His judgment. I believe that I have many opportunities in my life to choose a road that honors God and humbles me. I believe that God desires that I be saved and come to a knowledge of the truth about Him (1 Timothy 2:4).

September 16

Blessed is the man who walks not in the counsel of the wicked, nor stands in the way of sinners, nor sits in the seat of scoffers; but his delight is in the law of the LORD, and on his law he meditates day and night. Psalm 1:1-2 (ESV)

Blessed is the one who considers the poor! In the day of trouble the LORD delivers him; the LORD protects him and keeps him alive; he is called blessed in the land; you do not give him up to the will of his enemies. The LORD sustains him on his sickbed; in his illness you restore him to full health.
Psalm 41:1-3 (ESV)

Blessed are those who dwell in your house, ever singing your praise! Blessed are those whose strength is in you, in whose heart are the highways to Zion.
Psalm 84:4-5 (ESV)

Blessed is the man who fears the LORD, who greatly delights in his commandments! Psalm 112:1 (ESV)

Blessings are on the head of the righteous, but the mouth of the wicked conceals violence. The memory of the righteous is a blessing, but the name of the wicked will rot. The wise of heart will receive commandments, but a babbling fool will come to ruin. Whoever walks in integrity walks securely, but he who makes his ways crooked will be found out. Proverbs 10:6-9 (ESV)

'Blessings' or 'to be blessed'. What does it mean? Scripture uses it a lot and I sure throw it around a lot. But what does it mean? I went to Webster's and when I read "to invoke divine care" – that shot into my heart. Instead of the word 'blessed' in the previous Scripture, what if I put those words in?

Divine care comes to the man who does not walk in the counsel of the wicked
Divine care comes to he who has regard for the weak
Divine care comes to those who dwell in your house, Lord
Divine care comes to those whose strength is in you, Lord
Divine care comes to the man who fears the LORD
Divine care crowns the head of the righteous (those in right relationship with You)

When I am obedient to God, a 'covering' of 'divine care' comes over me. It is another 'shield' in my armor that God has given me. It is God's hand on me. His seal is on my thoughts and actions.

Look at the Beatitudes in Matthew 5. God's divine care is on those who are 'poor in spirit', those who 'mourn', etc. Read it! I can feel God's hand on that passage. It is a hand of comfort but also a hand of power and of strength!

It is not unusual for me to hug someone and say, "Blessings!" without even thinking. I will not be doing that again. When I say "Blessings!" or "Be blessed!" it will be with the knowledge that I have asked God to put His hand on this person. It is the best gift I can give anyone.

Additional Text: Leviticus 26, Ephesians 4

Don't be deceived, my beloved brothers and sisters. Every good and complete gift comes down from above, from the Father of lights, with whom there is no variation or even a shadow of turning. James 1:16-17 (HNT)

I've been thinking about blessings lately. Counting my blessings is taking time to have an intimate, personal 'testimony' time with my Lord. I need to do it every day. But do I miss recognizing some of the blessings? My 'world' of sight and sound is a deluge of what advertisers and others think I should have and so my mind easily makes a LONG list of what I don't have. BUT – I AM rich!

God raised us up and made us sit in heavenly places with Christ Jesus, so that he might show in the ages to come the superabundant riches of his grace in kindness to us through Christ Jesus. Ephesians 2:6-7 (HNT)

Yes, I have LIFE in Jesus. That in itself would be enough but there is more. And this is where the victory comes for me. In my day-to-day, moment-to-moment life, I confess that I need to 'see' a tangible blessing that has a 'now' pay off. I know that is shallow of me and shows that my eyes are not always looking with eternal rewards but ... there it is! I am blessed:

- ✓ with friends. These friends call me or email me at just the right moment. They pray for me and usually don't tell me.
- ✓ with family. I have a true-blue husband who is not only there in the good days and the victory days but all the days in between. I have children that continue to surprise me with the depth of their lives. I have a brother who even after 50 years still loves his little sister.
- ✓ with a home. I have a car. I am able to go to the grocery store this week.
- ✓ that this morning I didn't spill the sugar. I don't mean a teaspoon. It was almost 2 lbs.!

Blessings come in many sizes and with immediate and long-term consequences. Blessings are gifts from God. They are the manifestation of His grace and mercy. They are gifts just for me. Gifts are nothing when they are left in the bag or kept wrapped up in pretty paper and a bow. Gifts are true gifts when they are opened and appreciated and thanksgiving is given. AND when the gift is seen or used each day. A good reason to think about my blessings every day, isn't it? I bet my conscious list of what I should have or don't have will get smaller and smaller!

So since we have been made right by faith, we have peace with God through our Lord Jesus Christ, through whom we also have received access by faith into this grace by which we stand and boast in the hope of the glory of God. And not in this alone, but we also boast in our tribulations, since we know that tribulation brings out patience, and patience creates character and character produces hope. But hope is not ashamed, because the love of God has been poured out in our hearts through the Holy Spirit which was given to us. Romans 5:1-5 (HNT)

Additional Text: Genesis 12, John 20

September 18

Jesus said, "Don't let your hearts be troubled. Trust in God, and trust in me."
John 14:1 (NCV)

"Don't let this throw you. You trust God, don't you? Trust me."
John 14:1 (The Message, Peterson, Eugene. NavPress. 1993)

"Trust me" Period. Jesus had just washed the disciples' feet and had released Judas to leave and do what he was going to do. The revelation that there was a betrayer among them must have been a jaw-dropper and a heart-sinker. And then He says more:

When Judas was gone, Jesus said, "Now the Son of Man receives his glory, and God receives glory through him. If God receives glory through him, then God will give glory to the Son through himself. And God will give him glory quickly. My children, I will be with you only a little longer. You will look for me, and what I told the Jews, I tell you now: Where I am going you cannot come. I give you a new command: Love each other. You must love each other as I have loved you. All people will know that you are my followers if you love each other...
Peter asked, "Lord, why can't I follow you now? I am ready to die for you!"
Jesus answered, "Are you ready to die for me? I tell you the truth, before the rooster crows, you will say three times that you don't know me."
John 13:31-35, 37-38 (NCV)

Notice that there is no comment about the 'new command'. The disciples are immediately filled with grief and worry. The 'big guy', Peter, the one who is looked on as a leader, is told that HE will deny Jesus. I can only imagine how the disciples were reeling! I bet they were hoping that Jesus would JUST SHUT UP because they couldn't take any more! But He does tell them more. He tells them not to worry but trust Him.

I have a 'worry' today. I admit that there is scarcely a day goes by that I don't have something come across my mind that I would define as a 'worry'. Jesus is very specific here about my 'worry'. Trust Him. That's it. No prayer strategy. No discussion. Don't worry – trust Jesus.

"If you love me, you will obey my commands. I will ask the Father, and he will give you another Helper to be with you forever – the Spirit of truth. The world cannot accept him, because it does not see him or know him. But you know him, because he lives with you and he will be in you. I will not leave you alone like orphans; I will come back to you. In a little while the world will not see me anymore, but you will see me. Because I live, you will live, too. On that day you will know that I am in my Father, and that you are in me and I am in you. Those who know my commands and obey them are the ones who love me, and my Father will love those who love me. I will love them and will show myself to them."
John 14:15-21 (NCV)

And so Jesus tells me that He knows that trust will be a difficult thing for me but He desires so much that I be obedient to His commands that He sends me a helper who will speak to me, speak the <u>truth</u> to me. Right now is the time for me to listen to Him.

Additional Text: Acts 1, Ephesians 1

He is the LORD our God, his judgments are in the whole world. Remember his covenant forever, the word he commanded for a thousand generations. Which he made with Abraham, and was also his oath to Isaac. He established it to Jacob as a statute, to Israel as an eternal covenant. Saying, "To you I will give the land of Canaan, the full measure of your inheritance."

1 Chronicles 16:14-18 (HNT)

The LORD turns the counsel of the nations around, he thwarts the peoples' plans. The LORD's counsel stands forever, the plans he makes are for generations. *Psalm 33:10-11 (HNT)*

What does 'forever' mean? Webster's says, "for a limitless time" and "at all times: continually". Even those definitions have little meaning to me. I grew up in a country that celebrates that it has been in existence for 228 years and considers that a long time! My world celebrates youth, not the wisdom of age. Warranties are given for three years. A million-dollar home expects to be paid off in 30 years. No, I really don't think I have any point of reference to understand 'forever' and yet that is the timeframe for the Lord I believe in and I serve. He actually takes it even a step further into 'eternal' because not only does He have no end – He has always been so He also has no beginning. Now there is a philosophical circle to contemplate!

I am the living bread that came down from heaven. If anyone eats some of this bread, he will live forever, and the bread that I will give him is my flesh, which I offered so that the world may live. *John 6:51 (HNT)*

God really plays with our heads, doesn't He? The very brain and intelligence that He gave us…is too limited by its very input mechanisms of senses and concepts of reason to explain His words. I don't consider myself a genius (by IQ definition) but I am also not a stupid person. No matter how much I may read and reason somewhere along the way I must take a step *out into the abyss* that has nothing connecting it! All I have is *FAITH* that this Jesus is who He says He is and that the 'forever' He promises is true.

I did that in 1995. I remember my heart pounding and my breathing was rapid. I was scared! What if I was wrong? It would definitely be the biggest letdown of my life! There is a scene in the third Indiana Jones' movies, *Indiana Jones and the Last Crusade*, where Indy's father lay dying and Indy is going forward to find the Holy Grail, Jesus' cup from the Last Supper. Indy must cross this HUGE abyss – just sheer rock wall on each side – and he must believe that there is a path there only because the 'legend' papers say so. His love for his father, the possibility that water poured from the Holy Grail might save him, is bigger than his fear and so he steps out…and finds his foot planted on ROCK! A step of faith saves his father. A step of faith saves my soul…'forever'. Go figure! You won't be able to figure it. I personally know men and women smarter than me who have tried and they all tell me that it ultimately came down to a step of faith. Most took it because they felt they had no other choice. The hole in their life or the emptiness was a 'sickness' that was killing them. They wanted to live and so they took the step of faith and found …LIFE.

Now when Jesus heard this, he withdrew from there in a boat to a desolate place by himself. But when the crowds heard it, they followed him on foot from the towns. When he went ashore he saw a great crowd, and he had compassion on them and healed their sick. Matthew 14:13-14 (ESV)

Since then we have a great high priest who has passed through the heavens, Jesus, the Son of God, let us hold fast our confession. For we do not have a high priest who is unable to sympathize with our weaknesses, but one who in every respect has been tempted as we are, yet without sin.

Hebrews 4:14-15 (ESV)

Jesus was God. Jesus was human. He had every weakness that I have and yet did not sin. The words from the Book of Hebrews are a passage of hope and give me the standard, Jesus.

The story from Matthew, however, makes me pause and realize that if I had been on that shore, I would not have reacted the same as Jesus. Why is that? There must be something important for me to learn from this passage because except for the crucifixion, it is the only story that is recounted in all <u>four</u> gospels (Mark 6:30, Luke 9:10, John 6:5). It is an introduction to the feeding of the five thousand.

Matthew, Mark, and Luke tell me that Jesus had learned that Herod the tetrarch had beheaded his cousin and forerunner, John the Baptist. Now Herod was concerned with Jesus' popularity and wanted to meet with Him. I doubt that it was a 'social summons'. The disciples had also been sent out and were returning excited by all that God had done through them: healings, demons cast out, and preaching the Good News. Jesus wanted some quiet time. I imagine He had the idea for a quiet meal, listening to His disciples and then some alone time with the Father and to bed. Instead He got a huge crowd that was not slowed by a three-mile hike around the lake. They wanted something from Him and they were determined to get it!

I have days like that. It seems everyone wants something from me. Everyone expects something from me. No one is offering to <u>do</u> something for me. It's like running into a school of piranhas! How does Jesus react with *compassion*? It would be easy for me to 'cop out' and say, "Well, He's God!" The writer of Hebrews is almost redundant in trying to tell me that Jesus isn't *almost* like me but <u>is</u> like me in EVERY weakness and in EVERY temptation and yet does not sin. In some ways, being God would make it even tougher. Jesus had compassion and healed the sick that came. Not just those *worthy* to be healed or who <u>thanked</u> Him or who 'asked' (or prayed!) correctly or enough – He just healed them. Jesus knew their hearts and their pasts and yet saw them with compassion. They were valuable in His sight. THAT is the important point in this passage for me. People are <u>valued</u> by God, individually AND as a whole. We each have worth. He made me. He made you. God does not make junk! He did not make one person more or less valuable than another any more than I love one of my children more than the others.

Additional Text: Isaiah 43, 1 Peter 2

September 21

So be very careful how you live. Do not live like those who are not wise, but live wisely. Use every chance you have for doing good, because these are evil times. So do not be foolish but learn what the Lord wants you to do. Do not be drunk with wine, which will ruin you, but be filled with the Spirit.

Ephesians 5:15-18 (NCV)

Wise living comes from more than the education I have accumulated and how I have applied that education. Wisdom is also the ability to discern qualities and information that may not be quantitative by mere physical or intellectual means. Wisdom is being thirsty for knowledge while at the same time knowing that knowledge will not always give me the answers I need. Paul says I will avoid being foolish if I learn what the Lord wants me to do. I would say it is then doing what the Lord wants me to do. That brings me to the sticky point of giving up what I may want and choosing God's way instead. And there is a point of wisdom: God knows more than me so His way is the better way.

Where is the wise person? Where is the educated person? Where is the skilled talker of this world? God has made the wisdom of the world foolish. In the wisdom of God the world did not know God through its own wisdom. So God chose to use the message that sounds foolish to save those who believe. The Jews ask for miracles, and the Greeks want wisdom. But we preach a crucified Christ. This is a big problem to the Jews, and it is foolishness to those who are not Jews. But Christ is the power of God and the wisdom of God to those people God has called – Jews and Greeks. Even the foolishness of God is wiser than human wisdom, and the weakness of God is stronger than human strength.

Brothers and sisters, look at what you were when God called you. Not many of you were wise in the way the world judges wisdom. Not many of you had great influence. Not many of you came from important families. But God chose the foolish things of the world to shame the wise, and he chose the weak things of the world to shame the strong. He chose what the world thinks is unimportant and what the world looks down on and thinks is nothing in order to destroy what the world thinks is important. God did this so that no one can brag in his presence. Because of God you are in Christ Jesus, who has become for us wisdom from God. In Christ we are put right with God, and have been made holy, and have been set free from sin. So, as the Scripture says, "If someone wants to brag, he should brag only about the Lord."

1 Corinthians 1:20-31 (NCV)

Living wisely is an attainable goal when my eyes are on Jesus. My standard, my example, in all things, is right here in plain sight. There is no situation that does not have a 'Jesus answer' to follow. It may not be the answer I want to hear or see but it is there. It may not be an easy answer but even in that God provides His Spirit to strengthen me and give me courage and peace to follow His path. It would be wise of me to keep the 'fuel' I need to be prepared for the arrival of Jesus, my Bridegroom. Jesus says I am to be a 'light' in the world. I continue to receive from His Spirit the fuel that comes from obedience and worship of Him. THAT is living wisely!

September 22

And their hearing was immediately opened up, and the bonds of their tongues were broken, and they spoke clearly. And Jesus commanded them not to tell anyone, but the more he commanded the more they proclaimed. And the crowd was amazed beyond all measure and said, "He has done everything well, and he makes the deaf hear and the dumb speak."   *Mark 7:35-37 (HNT)*

Do you find something every day that you would term 'amazing'? It occurred to me this morning that I may have become a little jaded in my 21st century thinking. My mind quickly flips through my folders of knowledge and attempts to explain most of the things that come to my eyes' attention. There are not many occasions that I am stopped with a stunning blow of 'amazement'. That is unfortunate because there are still many amazing things in my life.

I took a trip this past week in my van to visit my son and his family. It was amazing that I drove about 150 miles on a highway with thousands of other vehicles and reached my destination safely in about two hours. When my parents were the age of my children, the same trip would have been done in a vehicle that would have taken six hours. Amazing.

I go into my living room and turn on a screen that gives me pictures of events and people around the world. I receive information from my television minutes after it happens. I can send a message through my computer to someone thousands of miles around the world from me and they will receive it in minutes. I can listen to my son play a baseball game through my computer. Amazing.

I look at my children and see myself or their father and yet they are individuals with physical and emotional characteristics all their own. I can look at my grandchildren and see my parents and yet they, too, are unique. Amazing.

Then I go lay down in my bed and reach out to hold the hand of a man who is very wise and yet loves me and is committed to me out of all the women in the world. I am blessed that I get to be with him for a lifetime. Amazing.

In the morning, I will begin another day and see more amazing things. I am learning not to take them for granted. God brings 'amazing' things in my life many of which won't be here again tomorrow so I must savor them today.

And suddenly there was a sound from heaven like a strong wind blowing, and it filled the whole house where they were staying and something like flames of fire appeared, divided and settled on each one of them, and they were all filled with the Holy Spirit and began to speak in different kinds of languages just as the Spirit caused them to speak. And there were Jewish men of good reputation staying in Jerusalem. They were from every nation under heaven. And when this noise came about, the crowd came together and were confused, because each one was hearing them speaking in their own language.   *Acts 2:2-6 (HNT)*

Though many witnessed this event that day and many heard Peter's words of repentance that came after this event, Scripture does not tell us that <u>all</u> acknowledged Jesus as Savior and not <u>all</u> gave God the credit for the amazing happenings of the day. Things haven't changed much in 2,000 years. I want to be open to 'see' the amazing events that come from God and acknowledge Him as the author and creator of amazing things…every day. What would go on my 'amazing list' today?

September 23

The disciples were afraid of the Jewish leaders, and on the evening of that same Sunday they locked themselves in a room. Suddenly, Jesus appeared in the middle of the group. He greeted them...A week later the disciples were together again, This time, Thomas was with them. Jesus came in while the doors were still locked and stood in the middle of the group. He greeted his disciples...

John 20:19, 26 (CEV)

Theophilus, I first wrote to you about all that Jesus did and taught from the very first until he was taken up to heaven. But before he was taken up, he gave orders to the apostles he had chosen with the help of the Holy Spirit. For forty days after Jesus had suffered and died, he proved in many ways that he had been raised from death. He appeared to his apostles and spoke to them about God's kingdom.

Acts 1:1-3 (CEV)

On the day of Pentecost all the Lord's followers were together in one place. Suddenly there was a noise from heaven like the sound of a mighty wind! It filled the house where they were meeting. Then they saw what looked like fiery tongues moving in all directions, and a tongue came and settled on each person there. The Holy Spirit took control of everyone, and they began speaking whatever languages the Spirit let them speak.

Acts 2:1-4 (CEV)

As I read these words this morning, I am reminded that these 11-12 men, some of whom defined themselves by their brawn and some by their intellect and even others by their heritage, huddled behind locked doors like children scared of the 'boogie man'. They were God's plan to spread the Good News into <u>all</u> <u>the</u> <u>world</u>. Was God surprised by their fear? No, Jesus told them during those intense hours before He died (John 14-16) that He would send them the Holy Spirit that would counsel them, comfort them, and remind them of all that He had said and done. Jesus knew that they would allow the enemy to whittle away at their faith. He knew that their flesh was weak and that they would rely too much on what they could <u>see</u> and what the 'nay-sayers' would chip away from their experience with HIM. Jesus sent <u>HIS SPIRIT</u> to inspire, restore, and rebuild.

It was already late in the afternoon, and they arrested Peter and John and put them in jail for the night. But a lot of people who had heard the message believed it. So by now there were about five thousand followers of the Lord...The officials were amazed to see how brave Peter and John were, and they knew that these two apostles were only ordinary men and not well educated. The officials were certain that these men had been with Jesus.

Acts 4:3-5, 13 (CEV)

Our Father has a plan. He sent His Son, Jesus, as the PERFECT atonement sacrifice for the sins of His children so that we <u>could</u> live in a right relationship with Him. God wanted <u>all</u> His children that <u>HE</u> created to have this opportunity. And so He takes 'ordinary' people and sends them out to tell others the Good News. BUT He also gives us His Spirit to continually 'infuse' us with whatever we need to be obedient to His direction and guidance. And so the story continues...

Jesus left that place and traveled to the region of Tyre and Sidon, where a Canaanite woman from the area met them and cried out, saying, "Sir! Son of David! Have mercy on me! My daughter is badly tormented by a demon. But he didn't give her even a single word in response. His disciples approached him and said, "Send her away, because she is following us and crying out." But Jesus answered, "I was sent only to the lost sheep of the house of Israel." But she continued to follow along, bow down before him and say, "Sir! Show me mercy!"   Matthew 15:21-25 (HNT)

Believe it or not I think this is a scenario that anyone who is a parent can relate. I have three biological children and four more that have come to be very important in my life and the lives of our family. In each one, there have been times when I watched them struggle and make decisions. I admit that many times I wanted to jump into the middle of their struggle and shake them, scream and wave my hands, but heard clearly from the Lord, "No!" There is no <u>action</u> for me … but pray. That is not the last resort but the first. Like the woman of Phoenicia, I fall to my knees to the One who can and <u>will</u> DO something. Jesus said to me, "…*Do not let your hearts be <u>troubled</u> and do not be afraid.*" (John 14:27, emphasis mine). Worry and panic is not living where God is. That unbelievable peace comes when I kneel before the Lord of Lords and cast my burden at His feet, knowing He answers.

Then he answered, "It's not good to give the children's bread to the dogs." But she said, "Yes sir! Even the dogs eat of the crumbs which fall from their master's table." Then Jesus answered her, "Oh woman! Your faith is great! Let what you wish happen for you!" Her daughter was healed from that hour.

Matthew 15:26-28 (HNT)

Was Jesus being a cruel smart aleck with his remark about dogs? No. Jesus is always looking for opportunities in my life to build my faith and allow me to proclaim what I know to be true about Him. I can trust Jesus.

Concerning which we have much to say that is difficult to understand, since your hearing has become lazy. For you ought to be teachers by now, yet you again need someone to teach you the elements of the foundation of God's message. But you now need milk and not solid food. For everyone who needs milk is untested in the message of righteousness, since he is still an infant. Solid food is for the mature, for those who through practice have exercised their understanding to distinguish good and evil.   Hebrews 5:11-14 (HNT)

Training is never easy. Not only is it physically or spiritually difficult and exhausting, many times it feels mundane and repetitive. Whether I am practicing scales and chord progressions on a musical instrument or attempting to improve my proficiency and understanding of a computer program or training day after day for the Olympics or to become a professional athlete, the path to excel is long and often requires solitude. Growing in God requires the same commitment. Time on my knees is time to worship <u>through</u> the seemingly overwhelming odds to get close to Jesus and say, "Help me, Lord!" And then listen for His answer, "You have great faith, Woman!"

September 25

But the Pharisees went out and conspired against him, how to destroy him. Jesus, aware of this, withdrew from there. And many followed him, and he healed them all and ordered them not to make him known. This was to fulfill what was spoken by the prophet Isaiah [42]: "Behold, my servant whom I have chosen, my beloved with whom my soul is pleased. I will put my Spirit upon him, and he will proclaim justice to the Gentiles. He will not quarrel or cry aloud, nor will anyone hear his voice in the streets; a bruised reed he will not break, and a smoldering wick he will not quench, and he brings justice to victory; and in his name the Gentiles will hope." Matthew 12:14-21 (ESV)

What got the Pharisees 'hot' enough to want to kill Jesus? He rebuked them because they were more interested in keeping the letter of the Law than the Spirit. They thought it was more important that you not 'work' (i.e., heal someone!) on the Sabbath than show love/compassion. Matthew, being a tax collector, knew a lot about lack of love/compassion from both sides of the equation. He was certainly scorned and ridiculed for his job. He also knew how to take the 'letter of the Law' and work it to his advantage to get the maximum tax from someone. I can see how this incident made an impression on him and made it into the Good News. Matthew was educated enough or inspired to remember the passage from Isaiah that spoke of the Messiah and His perfect, tender love.

Have you had times of feeling 'bruised'? Are there times when the 'fire' inside seems to just a 'smoldering wick' where once there had been a bonfire blazing for the Lord? Sin and the battles in this world can do that to me.

God knows the true inside picture of my life and He is the One who can restore! He is the One who restores me and then teaches me how to lead others to that place of restoration.

And you were dead in the trespasses and sins in which you once walked, following the course of this world, following the power of the air, the spirit that is now at work in the sons of disobedience – among whom we all once lived in the passions of our flesh, carrying out the desires of the body and the mind, and were by nature children of wrath, like the rest of mankind. But God, being rich in mercy, because of the great love with which he loved us, even when we were dead in our trespasses, make us alive together with Christ – by grace you have been saved – and raised us up with him and seated us with him in the heavenly places in Christ Jesus, so that in the coming ages he might show the immeasurable riches of his grace in kindness toward us in Christ Jesus. For by grace you have been saved through faith. And this is not your own doing; it is the gift of God, not a result of works, so that no one may boast. For we are his workmanship, created in Christ Jesus for good works, which God prepared beforehand, that we should walk in them. Ephesians 2:1-10 (ESV)

Additional Text: Luke 6, Ephesians 2

September 26

In the crowd was a woman who had been bleeding for twelve years. She had gone to many doctors, and they had not done anything except cause her a lot of pain. She had paid them all the money she had. But instead of getting better, she only got worse. The woman had heard about Jesus, so she came up behind him in the crowd and barely touched his clothes. She had said to herself, "If I can just touch his clothes, I will get well." As soon as she touched them, her bleeding stopped, and she knew she was well. Mark 5:25-29 (CEV)

Jesus was on His way to the home of a synagogue ruler. He has requested that Jesus heal his daughter. Matthew 9 and Luke 8 also record the same two events together.

As a nurse and woman, I am able to fill in a few blanks in my own mind about this woman. She has not only had to live with being ostracized by her community because her illness made her 'unclean' but she also lived with the moment-to-moment reality that she is unclean. The bleeding never stops. She must change 'bandages' several times a day and she can smell the discharge. If she had a husband or children, they have long ago been 'released' from caring for her. It had become a chronic illness and not many people are going to stay with no end in sight! She has run out of money for cures, probably even for food and shelter. It wouldn't surprise me to be told that suicide seems like the only alternative. She wouldn't be welcome even in the leper colonies!

And then…she hears about a holy man named Jesus. How did she hear about Him? In those days, there wasn't glass over the windows of the houses. Maybe she heard people talking as they passed her home. Maybe she heard it from someone she had known who was ALSO sick and 'unclean' like her. She was desperate. She heard this Jesus didn't even charge anything! That was in her price range!

The woman was taking a BIG CHANCE by going out and coming near a crowd. Chances were good that she would touch someone. Chances were good that someone would recognize her. Can't you just hear the squeal? "Ah!!! The UNCLEAN WOMAN touched me!!!"

She thought she would be 'stealth'. She thought she would only just *touch* Jesus' hem. Just a glance-touch! Did she change her mind and walk up to Jesus with her request? Was it the beauty of her prayer that healed her? NO! She was HEALED BEFORE Jesus knew ANYTHING about her! God reached down and even bypassed the humanity of Jesus and just … healed … her!

After her healing, as Jesus inquired about who had been 'hit by the Power' – Jesus says something to her that is not said to ANYONE ELSE in the Gospels. He calls her, "*Daughter*". He addresses her in the familiar way, signifying her importance to the Father.

There are legends that say that this woman, like the 12 apostles before her, left everything and followed Jesus, serving Him and His children the rest of her life. There is even speculation that she is Veronica who was reported to have wiped the face of Jesus as He walked to Calvary. I don't know but I do know that ever since Jesus touched *me* and healed *me*, I have followed Him and will continue to do so the rest of my life.

And they brought the boy to him....Jesus asked his father, "How long has this been happening to him?" And he said, "From childhood... But if you can do anything, have compassion on us and help us." And Jesus said to him, "IF you can! All things are possible for one who believes." Immediately the father of the child cried out and said, "I believe; help my unbelief!" And when Jesus saw that a crowd came running together, he rebuked the unclean spirit, saying to it, "You mute and deaf spirit, I command you, come out of him and never enter him again." And after crying out and convulsing him terribly, it came out, and the boy was like a corpse, so that most of them said, "He is dead." But Jesus took him by the hand and lifted him up, and he arose. And when he had entered the house, his disciples asked him privately, "Why could we not cast it out?" And he said to them, "This kind cannot be driven out by anything but prayer."

Mark 9:20-29 (ESV)

I am often asked to pray with and for people. And, yes, I have looked into eyes that reflected a 'being' that was not of God. I believe in God. I believe in satan. I believe in God's army and I believe in satan's army that live in a spiritual realm. So I've often wondered about Jesus' statement that "*This kind can come out only by prayer.*" Whose prayer?

Jesus had just come down off the mountain from the transfiguration. He had spent time with Elijah and Moses in the heavenly realm. He came down off the mountain and immediately was greeted with 'a problem'. Something that apparently the rest of the apostles couldn't handle. Maybe at that moment, JESUS uttered a prayer! It sounds like His patience was wearing thin! But the gospel doesn't tell us that. Jesus' words sound like orders given succinctly to an underling – which is certainly what the demon was!

Maybe the Pharisees that were standing around went to the temple to pray and intercede for the boy? And miss an opportunity to see/hear Jesus 'blaspheme' again as they determined in <u>their</u> mind? Not likely!

The only one uttering a prayer was…the boy's father. From his heart, from years of dealing with the illness or demon, the father speaks his heart's desire: "*But if you can do anything, take pity on us and help us.*" The prayer isn't pretty. The prayer does not RING with faith! "*…if you can…*" the father says. And then when Jesus gives him the reassurance that with God all things are possible, the father responds with another prayer, "*I do believe; help me overcome my unbelief*". He asks for help even in his doubt and unbelief.

God gives us 'nuggets' of pure…gold, for lack of a better word, throughout our lives. A prayer warrior named Terrie spoke God's words to me when she counseled me that in some cases God tells us that His way is "maximum prayer – minimum contact". In other words, pray for someone more than I try to convince them with <u>my</u> words! A wise woman named Linda taught my children (and through them – me!) that "the truest thing about you is what <u>God</u> says about you". My husband, Henry, has given a 'nugget' applicable to this story of Jesus: "God answers our prayers better than we pray them!". My prayers are the utterances of my heart to my Father who keeps His ears tuned to hear my cries. He knows how best to answer and <u>that</u> IS the answer.

September 28

Later Jesus went to Jerusalem for a special Jewish feast. In Jerusalem there is a pool with five covered porches, which is called Bethzatha in the Jewish language. This pool is near the Sheep Gate. Many sick people were lying on the porches beside the pool. Some were blind, some were crippled, and some were paralyzed. A man was lying there who had been sick for thirty-eight years. When Jesus saw the man and knew that he had been sick for such a long time, Jesus asked him, "Do you want to be well?"   John 5:1-6 (NCV)

It's interesting to think about the 'feasts' or 'celebrations' I observe as a Christian. Easter, Christmas, Pentecost are all days that I usually celebrate inside a church building. Jesus did not always seclude Himself <u>inside</u> a building. He was OUT spending time with the sinners and the 'unclean' that would not have felt comfortable and maybe not even felt *welcome* inside the church. Jesus is outside the temple walking carefully among the sick. He hears the moans of pain. He doesn't isolate Himself from the sinners and the sick that He came to heal.

I will tell about the LORD's kindness and praise him for everything he has done. I will praise the LORD for the many good things he has given us and for his goodness to the people of Israel. He has shown great mercy to us and has been very kind to us. He said, "These are my people; my children will not lie to me." So he saved them. When they suffered, he suffered also. He sent his own angel to save them. Because of his love and kindness, he saved them. Since long ago he has picked them up and carried them.   Isaiah 63:7-9 (NCV)

My Savior, the example of my life, did not just <u>pray</u> for the sick. He ministered to them. He served them. Pain and suffering and disease were not just a theory or a point of discussion. People had names and faces that were forever in His heart. I believe that is one of the images that went before Him as He walked towards Calvary and the Cross.

Family of Jacob, listen to me! All you people from Israel who are still alive, listen! I have carried you since you were born; I have taken care of you from your birth. Even when you are old, I will be the same. Even when your hair has turned gray, I will take care of you. I made you and will take care of you. I will carry you and save you.   Isaiah 46:3-4 (NCV)

Additional Text: Isaiah 46, Luke 23

Three days later there was a wedding in Cana, Galilee, and Jesus' mother was there. Jesus and his disciples were also invited to the wedding. And they ran out of wine, and Jesus' mother told him that they didn't have any more wine. Jesus said to her, "What does that have to do with us, woman? My time hasn't come yet!" His mother told the servers, "Whatever he says, do it!" Now there were six stone water jars there, used for the Jewish ceremonial washing, each one of which could hold 20 gallons or so. Jesus said to them, "Fill the jars with water." So they filled them up to the brim. And he said to them, "Now draw some out and carry it to the master of the feast." So they took some to him. Now when the master of the feast tasted the water which had become wine, he didn't know where it came from (though the servants who had drawn the water did) he called the bridegroom, and said to him, "Everybody serves the good wine first, and when people are drunk, the poorer wine, but you have kept the good wine till now." Jesus did this first sign in Cana of Galilee and revealed his glory, and his disciples put their faith in him. John 2:1-11 (HNT)*

"*My time hasn't come yet!*" What did Jesus mean by that? It makes me think that there was a heavenly plan and timetable for Jesus' first miracle and a wedding of an unknown couple in Cana wasn't it!

Matthew records healings as the first miracles in his gospel (Matthew 4:23). Mark tells me that while Jesus was teaching in a synagogue in Capernaum He tossed out an evil spirit that had possessed a man (Mark 1:21). Luke also tells that story (Luke 4:31) just after he repeats the rejection of Jesus because of His teaching.

John's story of the wedding at Cana seems to reflect a time before Jesus became known outside His 'home' or local area. When I look at the four gospels it makes sense to me that Jesus would spend some initial time with just that inner circle of disciples, the twelve. He would want to establish a relationship with them so that they would know Him more intimately.

A wedding feast in this culture was a several-day affair. Food and wine were to be provided to the guests for that whole time. It was not a "Let's get drunk and weird!" kind of party. That would be considered TOTALLY inappropriate! A wedding was a great celebration, however, and the family would have been FOREVER embarrassed if the wine ran out before the party was to be over.

To consider that there was a 'sovereign timetable' that Jesus changed to provide a miracle for no other reason than…kindness…is an amazing concept. Before throwing the idea out as being impossible theologically, look at what God says about His love for His children:

And if we're children, we are also heirs--God's heirs, and also Christ's co-heirs. If indeed we share in his suffering so we also may share in his glory.
Romans 8:17 (HNT)*

Now Yahweh has declared today that you are his treasured people just as he has told you, and he told you to keep his commandments as well. (19) He also promised to make you higher than all the nations which he made, praiseworthy, famous and honorable, and so you would be a holy people for Yahweh your God just as he promised. Deuteronomy 26:18-19 (HNT)*

September 30

When Joseph awoke, he did as the angel commanded, and brought Mary home to be his wife...   *Matthew 1:24 (TLB)*

One of my favorite writers, Max Lucado, talks a lot about the unanswered questions and information that we do not have that appears in the white spaces between the words. He's right. There <u>are</u> many unanswered questions especially about the <u>people</u> and their life and their relationship with God. We see them in print like looking through a knothole in a fence...just a part, not the whole picture.

Joseph has always been of great interest to me. I always felt a connection since my name is – a nickname – of his name. There is little written about him except for this first chapter and then again for 2-3 verses in Jesus' trip to the temple at age 12. He is never mentioned again and so we conclude that he died before Jesus was 30 and began His ministry. Joseph would not have been an old man when he died, even by the day's standard.

I would think that Joseph would have many questions for God regarding the circumstances surrounding the birth of the Messiah and especially the setting for His entrance into the world.

"Where are the midwives and temple priests and even our family?"

"Why didn't Mary go into labor before we left home where at least she would have a bed and clean linens?"

"Who is going to celebrate with us?"

I, too, have many questions about the circumstances that God leads me through. "Why this way? Why not another way?" "Are You SURE You know what You are doing?"

When Abraham was ninety-nine years old, God appeared to him and told him, "I am the Almighty; obey me and live as you should."   *Genesis 17:1 (TLB)*

"Stand Silent! Know that I am God! I will be honored by every nation in the world!"   *Psalm 46:10 (TLB)*

"For I am the Lord your God, your Savior, the Holy One of Israel. I gave Egypt and Ethiopia and Seba [to Cyrus] in exchange for your freedom, as your ransom. Others died that you might live; I traded their lives for yours because you are precious to me and honored, and I love you."   *Isaiah 43:3-4 (TLB)*

"I am the A and the Z, the Beginning and the Ending of all things," says God, who is the Lord, the All Powerful One who is, and was, and is coming again!   *Revelation1:8 (TLB)*

When I saw him, I fell at his feet as dead; but he laid his right hand on me and said, "Don't be afraid! Though I am the First and Last, the Living One who died, who is now alive forevermore, who has the keys of hell and death – don't be afraid!   *Revelation 1:17-18 (TLB)*

Yes, I have many questions but the perspective changes when I remember that He is <u>GOD</u>. He is <u>SOVEREIGN</u>! He is <u>ETERNAL</u>! He is <u>ALIVE</u>! And He loves <u>ME</u>!

Additional Text: Genesis 18 and 19

Myrtle Blabey Neufeld

This is my mother-in-law. I was blessed with the 'bonus' of a wonderful friend and 'mother'' when I married my Henry later in life.

I will instruct thee and teach thee in the way which thou shalt go: I will guide thee with mine eye.   *Psalm 32:8 (KJV)*

Born in Manitoba, Canada in 1918, Myrtle Blabey Neufeld was the eighth of eleven children. As she shares with a ready smile and steady gaze the many stories from her life, I understood why her children describe her as a woman who 'always puts a constructive spin on things'. Two of her older siblings died at age 2 and 6 weeks from a whooping cough epidemic. In the years of post-war depression, all the children were expected to work for the daily necessities of their life, which included Myrtle hiring on as a housekeeper in nearby homes.

She left home and family traveling to Kentucky to attend nursing school. The schools of nursing at that time used students as 'free' labor to staff and care for patients while gaining valuable training. Her older sister also graduated from the same school and was, for a time, her supervisor.

She married Ray Neufeld in 1946 while he was still in medical school. This covenant marriage marked the beginning of a partnership that would send them across the United States to Cheopas, Mexico and on to Georgetown, Guyana as they taught and ministered to whoever was in need. Children came and became a part of the team despite their young age. Arriving in Mexico, their four children were 14, 12, 10, and 5.

Myrtle's faith was a constant throughout her life. Every need was brought before the Lord, whether financial and provisional needs for a growing family, ongoing health needs as her husband battled chronic illness, or just a need for peace as family members moved to far points of the globe and communication was scarce.

" When times were difficult, I would go outside and look up at the stars and ask, 'Are You there?' and then I would know that He created the stars, the heavens, the flowers, and me. I would lay out the problems before God ...and let it rest there." *Directed Paths* by Myrtle Neufeld, a story of faith, is available from Energion Publications.

Six days later Jesus took Peter, James, and his brother John to the top of a high and lonely hill, and as they watched, his appearance changed so that his face shone like the sun and his clothing became dazzling white. Suddenly Moses and Elijah appeared and were talking with him...a bright cloud came over them, and a voice from the cloud said, "This is my beloved Son, and I am wonderfully pleased with him. Obey him." At this the disciples fell face downward to the ground, terribly frightened. Jesus came over and touched them. "Get up," he said, "don't be afraid."   Matthew 17: 1-3, 5-7 (TLB)

Recently, a pastor friend of mine did a "Moment with the Children" during a service in which he showed them his cell phone. In answer to his questions, the children said that a cell phone was a way you could talk to people anywhere, any time. About that time, his cell phone rang and noting the caller ID, the pastor told the children it was God. He attempted to encourage at least one of them to take the phone and say, "Hello" but not one of the six children would do so. Of course, it would be reasonable to assume that they were a bit embarrassed or constrained to do so in front of many people but I thought to myself, "That will preach!" My friend did a good job of continuing with the teaching by talking to "God" himself and passing along His message that He loves them and is <u>always</u> ready to talk – that's called 'prayer'.

How often is God ready and more than willing to talk to me and I refuse? When the world presses in with its trials and confusion, God is <u>right there</u> – ready to listen, <u>really</u> listen – and even more wonderful – He has the wisdom and the knowledge to untangle and straighten the path before me, bringing His peace and comfort into my spirit.

The crux of the matter is that I have to choose to make the call – choose to accept <u>His</u> call. Many times I am in such a SPIN that I do not even realize that HE is calling me – trying to reach out and touch ME when I don't pick up the phone and call Him. I want to ALWAYS call Him first. He is and wants to be my first call for help!

"Don't be afraid, Jody. Call me. I am always here. We can talk this through. I will NEVER leave you nor forsake you."

One day he gave this illustration to a large crowd that was gathering to hear him..."A farmer went out to his field to sow grain. As he scattered the seed on the ground, some of it fell on a footpath and was trampled on; and the birds came and ate it as it lay exposed. Other seed fell on shallow soil with rock beneath. This seed began to grow, but soon withered and died for lack of moisture. Other seed landed in thistle patches, and the young grain stalks were soon choked out. Still other fell on fertile soil, this seed grew and produced a crop one hundred times as large as he had planted." As he was giving this illustration he said, "If anyone has listening ears, use them now!" His apostles asked him what the story meant.   Luke 8:4-8 (TLB)

Take time now to go to Luke 8 and read Jesus' explanation. God wants to talk to me and to you – today.

Additional Text: Luke 8, Matthew 17

October 2

Now that same day two of them were going to a village called Emmaus, about seven miles from Jerusalem. They were talking with each other about everything that had happened. As they talked and discussed these things with each other, Jesus himself came up and walked along with them; but they were kept from recognizing him.

He asked them, "What are you discussing together as you walk along?" They stood still, their faces downcast. One of them, named Cleopas, asked him, "Are you only a visitor to Jerusalem and do not know the things that have happened there in these days?"

"What things?" he asked.

"About Jesus of Nazareth," they replied. "He was a prophet, powerful in word and deed before God and all the people. The chief priests and our rulers handed him over to be sentenced to death, and they crucified him; but we had hoped that he was the one who was going to redeem Israel. And what is more, it is the third day since all this took place. In addition, some of our women amazed us. They went to the tomb early this morning but didn't find his body. They came and told us that they had seen a vision of angels, who said he was alive. Then some of our companions went to the tomb and found it just as the women had said, but him they did not see."

He said to them, "How foolish you are, and how slow of heart to believe all that the prophets have spoken! Did not the Christ have to suffer these things and then enter his glory?" And beginning with Moses and all the Prophets, he explained to them what was said in all the Scriptures concerning himself.

Luke 24:13-27

There are many Scriptures, like this one, that are just FULL of good stuff! A pastor or teacher could make a good long 'series' out of it!

Today, God pointed out this question to me: *Did not the Christ have to suffer these things and <u>then</u> enter his glory?"* (emphasis mine). The disciples are grieving, depressed, and not understanding what has happened to their leader, teacher, a prophet, a righteous man. "Why did this happen?" and "How <u>could</u> it happen?" Certainly questions I have asked about situations of suffering in my life!

And Jesus' answer? He reminds them that NOTHING has happened by mistake or caught <u>GOD</u> unawares! EVERYTHING – EVERYTHING – even the <u>suffering</u> and <u>death</u> of the Messiah was foretold. The disciples just didn't want to remember that part. They had <u>selective</u> memory about what was God's plan for the atonement of His children. The disciples forgot that it was going to take a *<u>blood sacrifice</u>* for a perfect atonement. Did they think there was going to be 'blood' WITHOUT there being blood? They just didn't reason it out because that would have led them to some hard places <u>before</u> they would get to the V-I-C-T-O-R-Y!

Jesus said these things and <u>more</u> (emphasis mine):

"Do not let your hearts be troubled. <u>Trust in God</u>; <u>trust also in me</u>." John 14:1

"I am the way and the truth and the life. <u>No one</u> comes to the Father except through me." John 14:6

When Jesus noticed that some of the guests were choosing the best places to sit, he told this story: "When someone invites you to a wedding feast, don't take the most important seat, because someone more important than you may have been invited. The host, who invited both of you, will come to you and say, 'Give this person your seat.' Then you will be embarrassed and will have to move to the last place. So when you are invited, go sit in a seat that is not important. When the host comes to you, he may say, 'Friend, move up here to a more important place.' Then all the other guests will respect you. All who make themselves great will be made humble, but those who make themselves humble will be made great."

Luke 14:7-11 (NCV)

I have often read this Scripture and I have heard wonderful preaching on the 'rightness' of being humble and having the characteristic of humility. It wasn't until I was meditating today on another Scripture that I felt the 'click' of understanding occur.

Anyone who speaks should speak words from God. Anyone who serves should serve with the strength God gives so that in everything God will be praised through Jesus Christ. Power and glory belong to him forever and ever. Amen.

1 Peter 4:11 (NCV)

"For thine is the kingdom and the power and the glory forever and ever Amen." As Christians, this has become part of what we call The Lord's Prayer. It reminds me that above all else, God is sovereign and He receives <u>all</u> the praise because only <u>He</u> has all the power. This connects me to humility. I understand that it is not a false humility that rises with an "Aw, Gee Shucks! But I really <u>do</u> want you to notice and applaud how humble I am about how GREAT I am!" Being humble isn't about me. It is keeping my eyes and my heart focused on how GREAT is my Lord! That's it. No comparing me to Him because there IS no comparison of me to Him!!! If my focus is on God and my desire is to point everyone around me to God, then neither my eyes nor theirs will be on me. Humility and being humble comes as a natural result, not a manufactured result.

Then Jesus said to the man who had invited him, "When you give a lunch or dinner, don't invite only your friends, your family, your other relatives, and your rich neighbors. At another time they will invite you to eat with them, and you will be repaid. Instead, when you give a feast, invite the poor, the crippled, the lame, and the blind. Then you will be blessed, because they have nothing and cannot pay you back. But you will be repaid when the good people rise from the dead."

Luke 14:12-14 (NCV)

Jesus completes the circle of His teaching by reminding me of His example of love. He came to heal those who were sick. He came to love those who seemed unlovable. He loved me <u>before</u> I loved Him. He receives <u>my</u> love when I become a conduit for <u>His</u> love.

This is how God showed his love to us: He sent his one and only Son into the world so that we could have life through him. This is what real love is: It is not our love for God; it is God's love for us in sending his Son to be the way to take away our sins. Dear friends, if God loved us that much we also should love each other.

1 John 4:9-11 (NCV)

Hear me, O LORD, and listen to the voice of my adversaries. Should good be repaid with evil? Yet they have dug a pit for my life. Remember how I stood before you to speak good for them, to turn away your wrath from them. Therefore deliver up their children to famine; give them over to the power of the sword; let their wives become childless and widowed. May their men meet death by pestilence, their youths be struck down by the sword in battle. May a cry be heard from their houses, when you bring the plunderer suddenly upon them! For they have dug a pit to take me and laid snares for my feet. Yet you, O LORD, know all their plotting to kill me. Forgive not their iniquity, nor blot out their sin from your sight. Let them be overthrown before you; deal with them in the time of your anger. Jeremiah 18:19-23 (ESV)

Well. That pretty well covers it, doesn't it? That is an example of an ANGRY prayer! Jeremiah has been beaten up and ridiculed and he is NOT taking it any more. He wants God to exact some revenge! NOW!

Now the word of the LORD came to me saying, "Before I formed you in the womb I knew you, and before you were born I consecrated you; I appointed you a prophet to the nations." Jeremiah 1:4-5 (ESV)

God didn't make a mistake when He chose Jeremiah. He knew what He was doing. Jeremiah is tired. He has 'reasons' for his anger.

"But I say to you that everyone who is angry with his brother will be liable to judgment; whoever insults his brother will be liable to the council; and whoever says, 'You fool!' will be liable to the hell of fire." Matthew 5:22 (ESV)

"But I say to you who hear, Love your enemies, do good to those who hate you, bless those who curse you, pray for those who abuse you." Luke 6:27-28 (ESV)

I need help walking this road with God. I need the Holy Spirit to give me those extra measures of love, peace, patience, kindness, goodness, gentleness, and self-control that allows me to treat those as Jesus would. In my flesh I might be able to avoid murder but anger can be a daily battle.

A fool gives full vent to his spirit, but a wise man quietly holds it back.

Proverbs 29:11 (ESV)

Know this, my beloved brothers: let every person be quick to hear, slow to speak, slow to anger; for the anger of man does not produce the righteousness that God requires. Therefore put away all filthiness and rampant wickedness and receive with meekness the implanted word, which is able to save your souls. But be doers of the word, and not hearers only, deceiving yourselves. For if anyone is a hearer of the word and not a doer, he is like a man who looks intently at his natural face in a mirror. For he looks at himself and goes away and at once forgets what he was like. But the one who looks into the perfect law, the law of liberty, and perseveres, being no hearer who forgets but a doer who acts, he will be blessed in his doing. James 1:19-25 (ESV)

Let us turn to God and allow the Holy Spirit to strengthen us in our weakness. He is the One that Jesus promised.

Additional Text: Jeremiah 1, James 1

Simon Peter, Thomas, Nathanael, the sons of Zebedee, and two others of his disciples were together. Simon Peter said to them, "I am going fishing." They said to him, "We will go with you." They went out and got into the boat, but that night they caught nothing.

Just as day was breaking, Jesus stood on the shore; yet the disciples did not know that it was Jesus. Jesus said to them, "Children, do you have any fish?" They answered him, "No." He said to them, "Cast the net on the right side of the boat, and you will find some." So they cast it, and now they were not able to haul it in, because of the quantity of fish. The disciple whom Jesus loved therefore said to Peter, "It is the Lord!" When Simon Peter heard that it was the Lord, he put on his outer garment, for he was stripped for work, and threw himself into the sea. The other disciples came in the boat, dragging the net full of fish, for they were not far from the land...   *John 21:2-8 (ESV)*

Peter was grieving. He was grieving, not only for the death of his teacher and friend, but for the dream that JESUS was the Messiah. And so he did what I have done when I grieve…tasks that are familiar and comforting. Fishing had been his way of making a living all of his life. It was also where he first met Jesus. (Matthew 4:18) There was comfort in visiting that place again.

Casting the net, pulling it in, casting it again. There was a rhythm and a good sweat that comes with the work. And just like that time some three years ago, Peter was having no luck fishing. I can see him shaking his head and the sheen of tears that comes to his eyes. "What else? I can't even catch fish!" Peter had just been through the worse days and nights of his life beginning with Jesus' arrest and going straight to the pits when he denied that he knew Jesus not just once but THREE TIMES! I bet he could still see the look that he exchanged with Jesus across Pilate's courtyard. (Luke 22:61) His salty tears mix with the salt spray of the sea.

Once again, Jesus inquires about Peter's luck fishing. Once again, Jesus asks Peter to throw his unsuccessful net back into the sea. "Try it again – this time with me!" is His unstated command. And once again, Peter and his fishing buddies come up with a catch that is SO HUGE it almost sinks the boat!

John's cry, "It is the Lord!" sends Peter over the side of the boat because he cannot wait another minute to get near his Savior, the Savior that once again has saved him and is now going to serve him. Again.

The story doesn't end here. John goes on to tell us that Jesus receives Peter back and the slate is wiped clean. All denials are forgotten. Simon is once again Peter, the rock.

This is the disciple who is bearing witness about these things, and who has written these things, and we know that his testimony is true. Now there are also many other things that Jesus did. Were every one of them to be written, I suppose that the world itself could not contain the books that would be written.   *John 21:24-25 (ESV)*

The world is not big enough to tell the many stories of how Jesus heals and restores. These devotions are not big enough to tell the many times that Jesus has healed <u>me</u> and restored <u>me</u>. JESUS CHRIST BE PRAISED!

"I want to be like Jesus!" Reality: Have three years of intense ministry including rejection by the church leadership and then get crucified.

"I want to be like Mary!" Reality: Get a 'call from God' that your family and friends would never believe, give birth to your firstborn in a stable, have your heart ripped out as you watch your son fulfill his destiny, and then watch him die on a cross.

"I want to be Jesus' disciple!" Well, let's see: one committed suicide, 11 were martyred, one lived to old age but isolated on an island. It wasn't just the 'state' that hated them...the church leadership thought they were heretics!

When Jesus noticed how large the crowd was growing, he instructed his disciples to get ready to cross to the other side of the lake. Just then one of the Jewish religious teachers said to him, "Teacher, I will follow you no matter where you go!" But Jesus said, "Foxes have dens and birds have nests, but I, the Messiah, have no home of my own – no place to lay my head." Another of his disciples said, "Sir, when my father is dead, then I will follow you." But Jesus told him, "Follow me now! Let those who are spiritually dead care for their own dead." Matthew 8:18-22 (TLB)

"...don't be afraid of those who threaten you. For the time is coming when the truth will be revealed: their secret plots will become public information. What I tell you now in the gloom, shout abroad when daybreak comes. What I whisper in your ears, proclaim from the housetops! Don't be afraid of those who can kill only your bodies – but can't touch your souls! Fear only God who can destroy both soul and body in hell...If anyone publicly acknowledges me as his friend, I will openly acknowledge him as my friend before my father in heaven. But if anyone publicly denies me, I will openly deny him before my Father in heaven. Don't imagine that I came to bring peace to the earth! No, rather, a sword...If you refuse to take up your cross and follow me, you are not worthy of being mine. If you cling to your life, you will lose it; but if you give it up for me, you will save it." Matthew 10:26-28, 32-34, 38-39 (TLB)

Being a disciple of Jesus can truly ONLY be done by the power of the Holy Spirit. My feeble mind, spirit, and body can withstand neither the demands nor the assault that comes. You may think I am being overly dramatic but our history tells us differently, doesn't it? The cost of being a disciple is high.

Dear friends, don't be bewildered or surprised when you go through the fiery trials ahead, for this is no strange, unusual thing that is going to happen to you. Instead, be really glad – because these trials will make you partners with Christ in his suffering, and afterwards you will have the wonderful joy of sharing his glory in that coming day when it will be displayed. 1 Peter 4:12-13 (TLB)

Peter brings it all into focus for me. It isn't about me. It isn't about what I might 'suffer'. It's about the lost. It is about all those who don't know Jesus and His sustaining power and unchanging, eternal love. Whatever the cost for me, Jesus already paid it. So -- "GO!"

Additional Text: Matthew 10, 1 Peter 4

October 7

God said, *"Now we will make humans, and they will be like us. We will let them rule the fish, the birds, and all other living creatures." So God created humans to be like himself; he made men and women.* **Genesis 1:26-27 (CEV)**

I have been blessed to be able to travel some and see the Rocky Mountains, the Gulf of Mexico, the Atlantic Ocean, and a Missouri field filled with ripe wheat and corn. I've lived in a home that seemed to be strategically placed in the path of the cardinals' migration and watched then fly across my lawn like small streaking red flags. I have stood on the shore and watch dolphins jump and flip on waves that sparkled like diamonds in the sun. I've seen a waterfall inside a cave that comes from an undiscovered river and flows on to an undiscovered place. And yet none of these 'wonders' is made in God's image. It is only in us that He put something of Himself. He gave us choice.

The LORD God put the man in the Garden of Eden to take care of it and to look after it. But the LORD told him, "You may eat fruit from any tree in the garden, except the one that has the power to let you know the difference between right and wrong. If you eat any fruit from that tree, you will die before the day is over!" **Genesis 2:15-17 (CEV)**

From the very beginning, God gave us a choice to obey...or not to obey. He gave us a choice to love...or not to love. Being God He knew all that would be. And He had a plan. From the beginning, He loved us with a perfect Father's love, willing even to <u>die</u> for us. Because death is what it would take to make the perfect atonement for our sin of <u>dis</u>obedience. Nothing less would be enough.

In the beginning was the one who is called the Word. The Word was <u>with</u> God and <u>was</u> truly <u>God</u>. And with this Word, God created <u>all</u> things. <u>Nothing</u> was made without the Word. <u>Everything</u> that was created received its <u>life</u> FROM him, and his life gave light to everyone. The light keeps shining in the dark, and darkness has never put it out...The Word was in the world, but no one knew him, though God had made the world with his Word. He came into his own world, but his own nation did not welcome him. Yet some people accepted him and put their faith in him. So he gave them the <u>right</u> to be the children of God. They were not God's children by nature or because of any human desires. God himself was the one who made them his children. **John 1:1-5, 10-13 (CEV)**

Jesus was God in the flesh. Jesus was in the Garden when I became the image of God. He was there when that ...something called 'choice' was placed inside of me. Jesus was there when I made the choice to <u>reject</u> Him. He was there when I made the choice to <u>accept</u> Him and for the time between. His Spirit has been working inside of me that time to continue to make choices of obedience and slap me on the back of the head when I turn towards <u>dis</u>obedience.

Jesus said to his disciples, "Don't be worried! Have faith in God and have faith in me. There are many rooms in my Father's house. I wouldn't tell you this, unless it was true. I am going there to prepare a place for each of you." **John 14:1-3 (CEV)**

From beginning to end God has been there and continues to be there <u>just</u> for me. That is a true story of eternity.

And he [Jesus] said to all, "If anyone would come after me, let him deny himself and take up his cross daily and follow me. For whoever would save his life will lose it, but whoever loses his life for my sake will save it. For what does it profit a man if he gains the whole world and loses or forfeits himself? For whoever is ashamed of me and of my words, of him will the Son of Man be ashamed when he comes in his glory and the glory of the Father and of the holy angels...Now about eight days after these sayings he took with him Peter and John and James and went up on the mountain to pray and as he was praying, the appearance of his face was altered, and his clothing became dazzling white. And behold, two men were talking with him, Moses and Elijah,... Luke 9:23-26, 28-30 (ESV)*

Jesus was teaching 'brussel sprouts' here, a tough message. These words followed by the transfiguration are recorded in Matthew 17 and Mark 9 also. Time was growing short and the cross was coming closer. Jesus had been teaching about love and forgiveness but now it was time to begin to separate those who were just 'sunny day friends' and those who would be there through storms and yet continue to spread the Good News. Jesus reminds me that it is about Him and not about me. It seems that there is such <u>urgency</u> in His words. He seems to be directing my eyes toward the bigger picture – eternal life through Him. When choices become difficult, there is really no choice. There is only Him. Jesus knows the Truth. Sometimes standing with the Truth means standing in a lonely place.

Eight days and eight nights later, Jesus goes up on a mountain to pray. Up on a mountain, sitting on a beach in the early morning or late evening, even sitting on my back porch can be a place to meet with the Father and receive His strength and peace for the journey ahead. And whom does the Father send to speak to Jesus and encourage Him? It struck me this morning that we do not know where Moses is buried. (Deuteronomy 34:5-6) Elijah was taken by whirlwind to heaven, not buried. (2 Kings 2:11-12) It seems right that these two came to Jesus to speak to Him. Jesus is the conqueror of death!

"Fear not, I am the first and the last, and the living one. I died, and behold I am alive forevermore, and I have the keys of Death and Hades. Write therefore the things that you have seen, those that are and those that are to take place after this." Revelation 1:18-19 (ESV)*

And I heard a loud voice from the throne saying, "Behold, the dwelling place of God is with man. He will dwell with them, and they will be his people, and God himself will be with them as their God. He will wipe away every tear from their eyes, and death shall be no more, neither shall there be mourning nor crying nor pain anymore, for the former things have passed away."

And he who was seated on the throne said, "Behold, I am making all things new." Also he said, "Write this down, for these words are trustworthy and true." And he said to me, "It is done! I am the Alpha and the Omega, the beginning and the end. To the thirsty I will give from the spring of the water of life without payment. The one who conquers will have this heritage, and I will be his God and he will be my son." Revelation 21:1-7 (ESV)*

October 9

Naaman, commander of the army of the king of Syria, was a great man with his master and in high favor, because by him the LORD had given victory to Syria. He was a mighty man of valor, but he was a leper. Now the Syrians on one of their raids had carried off a little girl from the land of Israel, and she worked in the service of Naaman's wife. She said to her mistress, "Would that my lord were with the prophet who is in Samaria! He would cure him of his leprosy."... So Naaman came with his horses and chariots and stood at the door of Elisha's house. And Elisha sent a messenger to him, saying, "Go and wash in the Jordan seven times, and your flesh shall be restored, and you shall be clean." But Naaman was angry and went away, saying, "Behold, I thought that he would surely come out to me and stand and call upon the name of the LORD his God, and wave his hand over the place and cure the leper."

2 Kings 5:1-3, 9-11 (ESV)

Physical healing and how God works and does not work is a subject that has had Bible scholars studying and arguing for decades. Since I have not studied that many years and do not have any 'bragging credentials', I am not going to get in to any arguments! Like Naaman, I do get frustrated when God does not choose to SHOW OFF with a spectacular WOW miracle! I want to see the miraculous acts that were told in the Bible and foretold in the Bible. I want to see them in my own life!

As he passed by, he saw a man blind from birth. And his disciples asked him, "Rabbi, who sinned, this man or his parents, that he was born blind?" Jesus answered, "It was not that this man sinned, or his parents, but that the works of God might be displayed in him. We must work the works of him who sent me while it is day, night is coming, when no one can work. As long as I am in the world, I am the light of the world." *John 9:1-5 (ESV)*

"that the works of God might be displayed in him.." Now there is a definitive answer to the question: Why did this happen? Jesus tells me several times that all His work is to glorify <u>the Father</u>. He arrived 'late' to heal Lazarus and instead brought him out of the grave so that the Father would get the praise for it. (John 11) Jesus said in His prayer that His death was for God's glory (John 17). It is not just in the easily understood and received healings that God is glorified.

These all died in faith, not having received the things promised, but having seen them and greeted them from afar, and having acknowledged that they were strangers and exiles on the earth. *Hebrews 11:13 (ESV)*

I continue to struggle to realize that as a child of God – I am not 'at home' here. My home is with my Father in heaven. The psalmist speaks of 70 or 80 years as our life span in Psalm 90 but begins the psalm by telling the Lord that <u>HE</u> has been our dwelling place for generations. My home, my goal is with the Lord, coming to Him on His timetable. His time for me may be very different than what I have planned or what the world says is 'normal'.

"...God so loved the world, that he gave his only Son,..." *John 3:16 (ESV)*

That is what I am promised. No conditions. No clauses. A promise. An <u>ETERNAL</u> promise.

"Pray along these lines: 'Our Father in heaven, we honor your holy name. We ask that your kingdom will come now. May your will be done here on earth, just as it is in heaven. Give us our food again today, as usual ... "

Matthew 6:9-11 (TLB)

It is interesting, and yes, a bit troubling, that Jesus instructs me to pray – for bread enough for…today. Only. In this prayer, my past is only brought up to forgive my sins. My future is only about the temptations that may come my way and the assurance that God is not surprised by that either. My present, my today – God will provide enough 'bread', of everything that I need…for today.

And don't make me either rich or poor; just give me enough food for each day.

Proverbs 30:8 (NCV)

Jesus said the same thing that the 'Wisdom' of Proverbs said, *'enough food for each day'*! It is a trust issue. Trust God that He knows what I need for today and knows even what tomorrow will bring and has that in His hand also.

When things are going well, the 'bread' that God provides are like 'Twinkies' or 'Oreos' on my plate! The time is sweet. I want to just spend a lot of time with the Lord and enjoy the meal He has prepared for me. This is God's kitchen not His restaurant where I receive my 'daily bread'. It's not a restaurant because I don't come in expecting a menu that I order what I want but it is God's kitchen where He plans what He knows what I need. Some days have more vegetables where I receive lessons and some days have meat that I have to 'chew' and 'chew' and swallow in small bites so I don't choke! God's lessons of His love and mercy to me are sweet. His lessons of unconditional love and mercy that I extend to others in the same way that I want to receive it…are sometimes as palatable as cauliflower! The larger lessons of how He works and His way of wisdom require some 'chewing' on my part and take a little longer to 'digest'. And then there are those cups of suffering and pain that are sometimes so vile and difficult to look at. Jesus was given a cup like that. What did He do?

Jesus who knew the Father and trusted Him completely, looked at what the Father was giving Him that day for His 'bread' and said, "Oh, no! PLEASE give me something else! … But, I'll drink it ... with your help." (Matthew 26:39)

Yes, sometimes what is on my plate for this day is difficult to consume. The 'cup' may contain suffering and hardship that seems impossible to drink: the loss of a job, wrongful accusations of co-workers or even family and friends, the loss of someone you love and it hurts so much you may think you will never 'eat' again. Jesus has been there and He even asked the Father to take the cup from Him. Look at the Father's response:

An angel from heaven appeared to him and strengthened him.   *Luke 22:43*

Whatever the Father serves me this day, I must take that step of trust in faith and know from my past experiences with Him that He will send me the strength I need…for today. I may never be exonerated in this world. I may never have all the answers to my questions in this world. But I will always have Jesus before me and His Holy Spirit surrounding me and my 'Abba Father' who loves me. I have what I need…for today.

As a baseball fan, Spring Training is an especially wonderful time of year for me. I love to hear the *crack* of the bat (yes, a wooden one!) and that *thunk* that a baseball makes as it hits the glove – a *STRIKE*! These are wonderful details that bring a smile to my face and joy in my heart! God has been teaching me lately, through His Spirit, to be aware of Him in details.

In the beginning God created...   Genesis 1:1

Would you stop right there and turn to Genesis 1? Read the first ... 25 verses. If you can, go outside and sit on the steps or in a chair on the porch and read those verses. I hope it's a pretty day and you hear birds chirp and dogs bark. Listen and look for God's details in everything that is around you.

I look up at birds that I see and wonder what my world would be like if God had decided that birds wouldn't have any 'vocal cords' and so there would be no chirping or singing. There wouldn't be different 'songs' and sounds, would there? I look at the clouds, the leaves, even snowflakes. All are different with shades and colors and shapes. Why would God do that? He could have just as easily made everything different shades of black and white! But God didn't. He made waterfalls (even as big as Niagara!) and even orange trees that have fragrant flowers and delicious fruit!

Then God said, "Let us make man in our image, in our likeness, and let them rule over the fish of the sea and the birds of the air, over the livestock, over all the earth, and over all the creatures that move along the ground." So God created man in his own image, in the image of God he created him; male and female he created them.   Genesis 1:26-27

How wonderful are all of these details that God gave to me! He gave me 'rule' status over them. That gives me something to think about when I consider good stewardship and how I use resources. And He made me – in HIS image; to be His reflection to others.

Let's take time this week and appreciate the details that God has given. Get up early, take a lunch break outside, or watch the sunset and thank our Father for His many, MANY blessings. He is a God of details and does NOT make mistakes!

October 12

Then Jesus went about a stone's throw away from them [his disciples]. *He kneeled down and prayed, "Father, if you are willing, take away this cup of suffering. But do what you want, not what I want."* Luke 22:41-42 (NCV)

I was praying recently with some college students and each of them expressed their need to 'know God's will' in different areas of their lives. Early in our maturing relationship with Jesus we learn about Jesus' desire and joy in 'doing the Father's will'. Jesus tells us that He came to glorify the Father and that He could do nothing apart from the Father. It didn't take me long to figure out that if I too did God's will, followed His plan, that I would be in a much better place. How do I know God's will?

Speaking the truth in love, we will grow up in every way into Christ, who is the head...Each part does its own work to make the whole body grow and be strong with love. Ephesians 4:15-16 (NCV)

I learn God's will through the words of other Christians. I see the 'fruit' in their lives, peace in adversity, joy in worship and worship in daily life and so I listen to them and hear what God has done or said in their life. God has given each member of the Body an assignment and He reveals His will through His Body. It could happen in a Bible study or small group or choir practice or over dessert. For as many members of the Body, God will use that many methods of revelation. And THAT is why ol' satan would like to keep me out of the church when I am in a spiritual slump. When things are tough in my life, I can 'hear' many 'reasons' why I can't make it to church or why I have to leave the service early and avoid any conversation. Since God reveals Himself through His children, the enemy will pull out all the stops to keep me away from the Body!

God also reveals His will through His Word. If I am seeking to know God's will in my life, I can rest assured that the answer will be in line with His God-breathed Word.

It is God's will that His children be saved. If I want to know which profession to choose, the question I can use is which one will allow me to have a greater impact for His kingdom? Who should I marry? Does this person in my life help me bring glory to God? If God has the Big Picture, He also has the details.

God shows me His will as we build our relationship. When my husband and I first started dating, I knew by the end of our first conversation that he was a vegetarian. (I wondered if this was God's will right then as I love meat!) After a year of courtship and five years of marriage, I know that even though Henry is a vegetarian, that doesn't mean he eats all vegetables. The same is true with my time with God. As I spend more time with Him, I begin to know His heart. He is a gentleman and He will not force His way into my life. God spends time with me in conversation when I invite Him. He will come any time!

What is God's will in my life? What ignites a passion in my heart? (Jeremiah 20) Is it singing? Orphans? The inner city or the forgotten country? LISTEN to that FIRE! God will open the door. Jesus was not only a wildfire, torching heart after heart after heart, but He was also a warm, welcoming candle. His fire cleansed the destructive infection in my soul and gave me a light to illuminate my steps so I could follow His will.

"Our Father in heaven, hallowed be your name."   *Matthew 6:9 (ESV)*

Jesus gave me an eyewitness picture of who my Father is. My Father <u>lives</u> in heaven and His name, His identity, is <u>holy</u>; it is to be revered. From Moses to Job to John, those who have had a personal encounter with the Father have come away changed, altered.

When the LORD saw that he turned aside to see, God called to him out of the bush, "Moses, Moses!" And he said, "Here I am." Then God said, "Do not come near; take your sandals off your feet, for the place on which you are standing is holy ground." And he said, "I am the God of your father, the God of Abraham, the God of Isaac, and the God of Jacob." And Moses hid his face, for he was afraid to look at God.   *Exodus 3:4-6 (ESV)*

Then Job answered the LORD and said: "I know that you can do all things, and that no purpose of yours can be thwarted. 'Who is this that hides counsel without knowledge?' Therefore I have uttered what I did not understand, things too wonderful for me, which I did not know. 'Hear, and I will speak; I will question you, and you make it known to me.' I had heard of you by the hearing of the ear, but now my eye sees you; there I despise myself, and repent in dust and ashes."   *Job 42:1-6 (ESV)*

I, John, your brother and partner in the tribulation and the kingdom and the patient endurance that are in Jesus, was on the island called Patmos on account of the word of God and the testimony of Jesus. I was in the Spirit on the Lord's day, and I heard behind me a loud voice like a trumpet...Then I turned to see the voice that was speaking to me,...When I saw him, I fell at his feet as though dead. But he laid his right hand on me, saying, "Fear not. I am the first and the last, and the living one..."   *Revelation 1:9-10, 12, 17-18 (ESV)*

It is interesting to me that John had spent three years with Jesus and never ended up on his face! Now he has an encounter with a risen dwelling-in-heaven Jesus and he knows 'holy'. He, too, knows that 'hallowed' be His Name.

I believe that it is so <u>important</u> that I take time to center or focus on the holiness of my <u>Father</u> in heaven. When the storms of life rage, when the 'insanity' of this world is blasted across the news media and splashed in bright, blazing colors on screens and printed media – my <u>Father</u> is still 'in heaven' and His name is still 'hallowed'. The only – ONLY – question is: Where will I turn my eyes and thoughts?

"Be still, and know that I am God."   *Psalm 46:10 (ESV)*

"Fear not, for I am with you; be not dismayed, for I am your God; I will strengthen you, I will help you, I will uphold you with my righteous right hand."   *Isaiah 41:10 (ESV)*

Additional Text: John 1, Revelation 1

In you, O LORD, do I take refuge; let me never be put to shame! In your righteousness deliver me and rescue me; incline your ear to me, and save me! Be to me a rock of refuge, to which I may continually come; you have given the command to save me, for you are my rock and my fortress. Rescue me, O my God, from the hand of the wicked, from the grasp of the unjust and cruel man.

Psalm 71:1-4 (ESV)

This psalm is a <u>wonderful</u> prayer! He starts out as I usually do, telling God that I KNOW He is God and so I also KNOW that since He <u>is</u> God – He can do the 'miracle stuff' and pull me out of whatever fire pit I've has gotten into and show His 'God-power' by kicking my enemies to the curb!

Do not cast me off in the time of old age; forsake me not when my strength is spent. For my enemies speak concerning me; those who watch for my life consult together and say, "God has forsaken her; pursue and seize her, for there is none to deliver her." O God, be not far from me; O my God, make haste to help me! May my accusers be put to shame and consumed; with scorn and disgrace may they be covered who seek my harm. *vv. 9-13 (ESV)*

Sometimes I think I've been at this 'ministry-business' a long time and I feel tired and run down. I'd like to blame that feeling on everyone else but the truth is…I am shouldering burdens that aren't mine to carry! I may or may not be spending the time I need with the Lord but I surely am <u>not</u> leaving the burdens <u>with Him</u> when I leave His presence!

But I will hope continually and will praise you yet more and more. My mouth will tell of your righteous acts, of your deeds of salvation all the day, for their number is past my knowledge. With the mighty deeds of the Lord GOD I will come; I will remind them of your righteousness, yours alone. O God, from my youth you have taught me, and I still proclaim your wondrous deeds. So even to old age and gray hairs, O God, do not forsake me, until I proclaim your might to another generation, your power to all those to come. *vv. 14-18 (ESV)*

Passing my faith, my experiences with God, along to my children and all 'children' of God is being obedient to Jesus' command to "Go! and make disciples…". These 'disciples' are not <u>my</u> disciples but His. If those that I share my faith with, mentor, move on and become 'busy' with the Lord's work and never visit me or give me a thought again – then I've done what I was called to do. God is still going to be there with me and will <u>never</u> 'forsake me'. God has called me to hand out <u>His</u> water of life to the marathon runners that pass my way. With <u>His</u> power, they will continue on, never remembering the one who handed them the water…just remembering the water itself!

You who have made me see many troubles and calamities will revive me again; from the depths of the earth you will bring me up again. *v. 20*

There it is again. God doesn't promise me a 'perfect' life here on earth without trouble or suffering. He just promises that He is faithful and will always be there with me <u>every</u> step of the way. What He does in my life is 'right' and good. Even those who do not believe in Him, see the 'fruit' in my life and feel the power of His touch even if they deny it! God is God. And yet, He loves me and is intimate and personal with me. WOW.

October 15

I thank God as I always mention you in my prayers, day and night. I serve him, doing what I know is right as my ancestors did. Remembering that you cried for me, I want very much to see you so I can be filled with joy. I remember your true faith. That faith first lived in your grandmother Lois and in your mother Eunice, and I know you now have that same faith. This is why I remind you to keep using the gift God gave you when I laid my hands on you. Now let it grow, as a small flame grows into a fire. God did not give us a spirit that makes us afraid but a spirit of power and love and self-control.

So do not be ashamed to tell people about our Lord Jesus, and do not be ashamed of me, in prison for the Lord. But suffer with me for the Good News. God, who gives us the strength to do that, saved us and made us his holy people. That was not because of anything we did ourselves but because of God's purpose and grace. That grace was given to us through Christ Jesus before time began, but it is now shown to us by the coming of our Savior Christ Jesus. He destroyed death, and through the Good News he showed us the way to have life that cannot be destroyed. I was chosen to tell that Good News and to be an apostle and a teacher. I am suffering now because I tell the Good News, but I am not ashamed, because I know Jesus, the One in whom I have believed. And I am sure he is able to protect what he has trusted me with until that day.

2 Timothy 1:3-12 (NCV)

Today is my mother's birthday. She was very active all of her life until about four years before she died and it was necessary that she have constant care. She wanted to "go to heaven and see Jesus and Bob (my dad)". I am so blessed to know that she and Dad did KNOW Jesus as Lord and Savior.

My mother's testimony of her faith was not a verbal one. (I'm sure my parents were both very puzzled by their daughter's zealous faith!) My mother taught my brother and me to pray, before meals, before bedtime. I remember one morning I ran to my mother as she was preparing breakfast upset because I had fallen asleep before finishing my prayers. I remember my mother saying, "Don't worry, Jo, your Guardian Angel finished for you." I don't know if that statement is 'theologically' correct but I do believe it is a good and true answer for a young child. It made me believe that God's interest in me was close and loving and protective. It is a belief that I have returned to and found to be true even now.

My mother's faith was lived out in her prayer life. I remember seeing her pray early in the morning and before she went to bed at night. I have a French provincial chair of hers in my home. It certainly does NOT fit my style but it's "Mom's Prayer Chair". I know that during my high school and college years when I walked to the edge of many decision 'cliffs' and peered over – my mother was at home praying for me. I suspect that same Holy Spirit-sent Guardian Angel was straining with all her might to pull me back from the cliff!!!

My mother and I did not have a "Leave it to Beaver" relationship but I am grateful to God for His sufficient grace that reminds me of my own imperfections as a mother and allows me to extend His mercy to Mom and others as He has extended His mercy to me. God is SO good!

Some interesting points have come to my attention in the gospel account of Jesus' crucifixion:

About noon the sky turned dark and stayed that way until around three o'clock. Then about that time Jesus shouted, "Eloi, Eloi, lema sabachthani?" which means, "My God, my God, why have you deserted me? Some of the people standing there heard Jesus and said, "He is calling for Elijah." One of them ran and grabbed a sponge. After he had soaked it in wine, he put it on a stick and held it up to Jesus. He said, "Let's wait and see if Elijah will come and take him down!" Jesus shouted and then died. At once the curtain in the temple tore in two from top to bottom. A Roman army officer was standing in front of Jesus. When the officer saw how Jesus died, he said, "This man really was the Son of God!"   *Mark 15:33-39 (CEV)*

...the other criminal told the first one off. "Don't you fear God? Aren't you getting the same punishment as this man? We got what was coming to us, but he didn't do anything wrong." Then he said to Jesus, "Remember me when you come into power!" Jesus replied, "I promise that today you will be with me in paradise."   *Luke 23:40-43 (CEV)*

"God-in-a-box". I've heard that expression a lot to describe someone who limits God; particularly in the way He may manifest Himself in a situation (answer a prayer, 'respond' to our worship).

When I am pondering a 'snarl-ly' question about God, I have felt drawn to the gospels, searching for Jesus' words or actions. In this instance, I see God, through Jesus, acting in a way not expected by those watching. He is submissive to the Father's plan. He died in a humiliating, cruel way. But...

Forgiveness is spoken once again, at this painful, awful time. Once more, a soul is given rest and promised eternal life. That's why Jesus came. That's why He died. I wonder if those standing at a distance saw Jesus talking to the thief or was it 'shown' to them by the Holy Spirit later?

The centurion who was standing closer had witnessed the quiet submission during the crucifixion and 'cat call' while Jesus hung on the cross. Now he sees the earth and sky's reaction to His death. Mark records the centurion's description as "*Son of God*". Luke says "*righteous man*". Either way, the unbeliever proclaims his belief! Jesus may not have acted as I (a church-going believer) expected but I cannot explain away the fruit that I see.

First of all, I ask you to pray for underline{everyone}. Ask God to help and bless them all, and tell God how thankful you are for each of them. Pray for kings and others in power, so that we may live quiet and peaceful lives as we worship and honor God. This kind of prayer is good, underline{and} it pleases God our Savior. God want underline{everyone} to be saved and to know the whole truth...

1 Timothy 2:1-4 (CEV, emphasis mine)

I want my heart to be like Jesus' heart and burn for souls, willing to submit any of my preconceived notions and personal doctrines to Him. I want to keep my eyes on Jesus. Only Jesus. "Watch me work!" He says. "Do what I do!" "Give ME all the praise!" Right on!

Comfort me with your love, as you promised me, your servant.

Psalm 119:76 (NCV)

Heaven and earth, be happy. Mountains, shout with joy, because the LORD comfort his people and will have pity on those who suffer.   Isaiah 43:19 (NCV)

Today is going to be a very difficult day for a friend of mine. There are circumstances in the lives of those I love that leaves me ... speechless. There is really <u>nothing</u> I can say that can 'fix it' or 'make it better'. Some might say that claiming that the 'answer' is JESUS – is a cliché. Maybe clichés come about from truths!

Today won't be the end of her pain as she walks on learning to <u>live</u> with her loss. The loss of someone we love, the loss of the stability or familiarity of our lives because of divorce or job change we did not expect even the loss of our health is a painful, seemingly long journeys. I've been through those journeys and I <u>desperately</u> wanted someone to say SOMETHING that would make everything 'right'. When someone would try, it usually came in the form of "I know how you feel and I ..." No, actually the person did NOT know how <u>I</u> felt! Or I would hear familiar Scriptures. Now that <u>can</u> be helpful but more often than not God's words came on <u>His</u> timing when the words came quietly into my spirit and <u>not</u> when someone said them because that's all they could think of to say.

Instead of saying a bunch of words to my friend today, I think I am going to take the Holy Spirit's GOOD ADVICE and just keep praying that Jesus ... our Savior, our Friend, our Redeemer, and the One who <u>truly</u> knows her heart ... will just be closer to her today. Maybe instead of saying <u>my</u> words to her, Jesus' words and <u>His</u> Holy Spirit will do all the comforting. And I'll just quietly pray and be there close by as she needs me.

Does your life in Christ give you strength? Does his love comfort you? Do we share together in the spirit? DO you have mercy and kindness? If so, make me very happy by having the same thoughts, sharing the same love, and having one mind and purpose. When you do things, do not let selfishness or pride be your guide. Instead, be humble and give more honor to others than to yourselves. Do not be interested only in your own life, but be interested in the lives of others

Philippians 2:1-4 (NCV)

Take some time today and do the <u>BEST</u> for someone you love ... including taking time to <u>pray</u> for them. Each day is an opportunity to lay my cares and concerns for those I love before the Lord. I <u>KNOW</u> that He will hear and with wise and loving hands He will separate the wheat from the chaff and answer the prayer so much better than I could ever pray it!

Additional Text: Psalm 61 and 62

[Jesus said,] *"God loved the world so much that he gave his one and only Son so that whoever believes in him may not be lost, but have eternal life. God did not send his Son into the world to judge the world guilty, but to save the world through him...They are judged by this fact: The Light has come into the world, but they did not want light. They wanted darkness, because they were doing evil things. All who do evil hate the light and will not come to the light, because it will show all the evil things they do. But those who follow the true way come to the light, and it shows that the things they do were done through God."*

John 3:16-21 (NCV)

Do you remember the day (or night) that you said, "Yes, Jesus, I need You as Savior and Lord"? Take some time today and think about it. Maybe you have been blessed to grow up always knowing about Jesus and His love and it seems He has always been there for you. But I bet there was a moment, a time, when the *enormity* of what He did for you struck a chord inside you that changed your walk with Him forever.

I don't remember a time when I didn't know the name Jesus and that He was born in a manger in Bethlehem and died on a cross on Calvary. But it took over 40 years until I admitted, accepted, the fact that Jesus did it … for me. My personal pride and at the same time my feelings of no self-worth had me rejecting the idea that Jesus did it all for me. No way! I could not accept that GOD loved me so much that He sent His Son to die for me. That I needed His Son to die for me.

My walk to freedom happened on a July night in 1995 when a preacher said, *"What good is it for a man to gain the whole world, and yet lose or forfeit his very self? If anyone is ashamed of me and my words, the Son of Man will be ashamed of him when he comes in his glory and in the glory of the Father and of the holy angels." (Luke 9:25-26 NIV, emphasis mine).* The truth ran through me like Drain-o through a clogged pipe. I was ashamed of God. I was ashamed that I needed Him and so had rejected Him ALL MY LIFE. Well…He was going to reject ME if I didn't turn around, lay that pride of mine down, and walk toward Him. It was no coincidence that I was in a room with about 2000 people. The 'ashamed factor' was going to be dealt with right then! All of this went through my mind in the three seconds after the preacher read that Scripture. I got to my feet and stepped out into the aisle and I've never looked back. My life since than has been more like the 'via dolorosa' than the 'mount of transfiguration'! It has taken me awhile to understand that walking with Christ means walking with Christ. His life here was not easy or beautiful. It was with eyes on eternity that Jesus walked this earth in peace and joy. I'm learning.

I look at my walk to Jesus and my heart is FULL and overflowing with love and gratitude for the One, the only One, who loves me, loves me without conditions and desires that I grow closer and closer to Him. My walk to freedom on that July night continues each day: "Free at last! Free at last! Thank God Almighty! I am free at last!"

Additional Text: 2 Corinthians 3, Ephesians 3

October 19

Tear open the skies and come down to earth so that the mountains will tremble before you. Like a fire that burns twigs, like a fire that makes water boil, let your enemies know who you are. Then all nations will shake with fear when they see you. You have done amazing things we did not expect. You came down, and the mountains trembled before you. From long ago no one has ever heard of a God like you. No one has ever seen a God besides you, who helps the people who trust you. You help those who enjoy doing good, who remember how you want them to live. But you were angry because we sinned,. For a long time we disobeyed, so how can we be saved? All of us are dirty with sin. All the right things we have done are like filthy pieces of cloth. No one worships you or even asks you to help us. That is because you have turned away from us and have let our sins destroy us. But LORD, you are our father. We are like clay, and you are the potter; your hands made us all. LORD, don't continue to be angry with us; don't remember our sins forever. Please, look at us, because we are your people.   *Isaiah 64:1-9 (NCV)*

There is a lot to consider in this passage. Isaiah, the prophet had been sent by God to Judah. Because of the rottenness of this society, Isaiah foresaw its collapse. But he also knew and offered an alternative to tragedy: his people's survival depended on their acceptance <u>again</u> of the Lord's precepts and laws. By returning to God's ways, they might be saved. Because Isaiah spoke for God and of God, his goal was to redirect his people into the ways acceptable to the God whom by their conduct they had alienated, and so to save them from catastrophe. Isaiah's words spoken in the 700 B.C. era also come clearly to us in the 21st century.

Terrible tragedies come to us both personally and as a people. We as <u>God's</u> people are not exempt. It is foolish to think that just because I believe and serve God that no tragedy or tragic events will ever enter my life. No one in Biblical history was exempt from pain or suffering. As I read from Abraham to Zephaniah, from Jesus to Paul and John, there is an unfolding of events and the struggle to connect our God with His unfailing love to the suffering that occurs. In this chapter Isaiah reminds me of the miraculous power of God that is manifested in the AWESOME things He has done! He calls on God to manifest His power that we as a people would <u>TURN</u> from our sin in holy fear and be reconciled once again to our Father. Once again, we would submit to the Father and become the true work of His hands, His people.

Each day, I must begin with looking to my Father. As I walk through the day, He is there to direct my steps and give me <u>His</u> light to follow the path that is found with a 'right relationship' to Him. And at the end of each day, whatever has come my way, I have the opportunity to accept and <u>know</u> that God is <u>STILL</u> God and walk that much closer in fellowship with my Lord.

God is strong and can help you not to fall. He can bring you before his glory without any wrong in you and can give you great joy. He is the only God, the One who saves us. To him be glory, greatness, power, and authority through Jesus Christ our Lord for all time past, now, and forever. Amen.

Jude 24-25 (NCV)

October 20

When the day of Pentecost arrived, they were all together in one place. And suddenly there came from heaven a sound like a mighty rushing wind, and it filled the entire house where they were sitting. And divided tongues as of fire appeared to them and rested on each one of them. And they were all filled with the Holy Spirit and began to speak in other tongues as the Spirit gave them utterance...But Peter, standing with the eleven, lifted up his voice and addressed them, "Men of Judea and all who dwell in Jerusalem, let this be known to you, and give ear to my words." Acts 2:1-4, 14 (ESV)

I've often thought about this scene. What would I have done if I had been there? To be with a group of fellow believers, in prayer and experience God's presence in such an intimate tangible way is a GLORIOUS experience. How could I not go out and tell everyone? But do I?

Every Tuesday night, a group has been meeting at a local church. We came together because we were all looking for more time for prayer ministry and musical worship in our individual churches. We 'checked' ourselves and yes, we were faithful to our personal time with the Lord but with more discussion it was clear that what we felt we were missing was the corporate time that allows God to bring together the Body with its different gifts to worship Him and be used by Him to minister to each other. Was there any reason why we couldn't meet? This did not mean we weren't committed to our home churches and loved that fellowship. We could do both! And so we have. And God is there. Each time is different. God directs the time. There is such <u>PEACE</u> in the chapel. One night, a friend of mine came who leads praise and worship all over the country and she didn't know it but playing piano wasn't the only reason she was to be there. God began healing her that night from years of heartache and loss. Her ministry of worship is moving forward and growing! Another night, I received such sweet, encouraging prayer that I felt like a well that was just bubbling over and I have slept *so well* ever since!!!

If any of you live in the Pensacola, Florida area and want to know more or get directions, email me at jody@biblepacesetter.org and join us as we meet with God! If you live away and are looking for such a time, ask God to show you a group of believers and the meeting that He has on His calendar! I <u>know</u> there is one near you!

"You shall keep my Sabbaths and reverence my sanctuary; I am the LORD. If you walk in my statutes and observe my commandments and do them, then I will give you your rains in their season, and the land shall yield its increase, and the trees of the field shall yield their fruit. Your threshing shall last to the time of the grape harvest, and the grape harvest shall last to the time for sowing. And you shall eat your bread to the full and dwell in your land securely. I will give peace in the land, and you shall lie down, and none shall make you afraid...I will make my dwelling among you, and my soul shall not abhor you. And I will walk among you and will be your God, and you shall be my people.
Leviticus 26:2-6, 11-12 (ESV)

Additional Text: Psalm 95, Ephesians 5

In the morning, as he was returning to the city, he became hungry. And seeing a fig tree by the wayside, he went to it and found nothing on it but only leaves. And he said to it, "May no fruit ever come from you again."

Matthew 21:18-19 (ESV)

And when those who were around him saw what would follow, they said, "Lord shall we strike with the sword?" And one of them struck the servant of the high priest and cut off his right ear. But Jesus said, "No more of that!" And he touched his ear and healed him.

Luke 22:49-51 (ESV)

When times in my life become <u>very</u> difficult, I find myself coming back to the Scriptures that cover Jesus' last week on this earth. I look at what I think of <u>His</u> toughest week and ask, "What can I learn from Him?" There's a lot there. What isn't there are the spectacular miracles that I had read in the previous twenty chapters. From the time that Jesus came into Jerusalem on a donkey until He died, only these two 'miracles' are recorded. Even His resurrection from the dead isn't noted by shepherds on a hillside hearing angels singing in a chorus. Maybe there is something to learn from that. When events in my life bring the hardest questions and the heaviest loads, it is then that instead of looking for the spectacular I need to look for the promises. I must 'plug in' to the points of faith that I <u>KNOW</u> are true and that have proven to me over and over. When my world here tilts, I hang on to the anchors of faith that hold my <u>spiritual</u> world in balance.

"When the Son of Man comes in his glory, and all the angels with him, then he will sit on his glorious throne. Before him will be gathered all the nations, and he will separate people one from another as a shepherd separates the sheep from the goats. And he will place the sheep on his right, but the goats on the left. Then the King will say to those on his right, 'Come, you who are blessed by my Father, inherit the kingdom prepared for you from the foundation of the world."

Matthew 25:31-34 (ESV)

"Do not let your hearts be troubled. Trust in God; trust also in me." John 14:1

"Now is your time of grief, but I will see you again and you will rejoice, and no one will take away your joy...I have told you these things, so that in me you may have peace. In this world you will have trouble. But take heart! I have overcome the world."

John 16:22, 33

Many homes have 'Irish blessings' in frames on their walls. Bedrooms and studies have university banners and bobble-head dolls that proclaim loyalty and allegiance to a team. I'm a baseball fan myself so I am not going to throw away my pictures of my favorite player BUT maybe framing a few Scripture 'anchors' and spending more time in committing THOSE words to my heart and memory will achieve the more permanent goals that I am <u>really</u> seeking.

So we do not lose heart. Though our outer nature is wasting away; our inner nature is being renewed day by day. For this slight momentary affliction is preparing for us an eternal weight of glory beyond all comparison, as we look not to the things that are seen but to the things that are unseen. For the things that are seen are transient, but the things that are unseen are eternal.

2 Corinthians 4:16-18 (ESV)

[Daniel prays,] *"Please show mercy to your chosen city, not because we deserve it, but because of your great kindness. Forgive us! Hurry and do something, not only for your city and your chosen people, but to bring honor to yourself."*
[Daniel writing about his vision:] *I was still confessing my sins and those of all Israel to the LORD my God, and I was praying for the good of his holy mountain, when Gabriel suddenly came flying in at the time of the evening sacrifice. This was the same Gabriel I had seen in my vision, and he explained: "Daniel, I am here to help you understand the vision…"* Daniel 9:18-22 (CEV)

What a wonderful passage of hope and encouragement! I <u>love</u> reading Daniel, not so much for its metaphorical perspective because I don't begin to understand all the possible prophetic nuances of Daniel's visions but just taking the words at face value, Daniel encourages me with his 'conversations' with God. Here is Daniel, in exile, isolated from all the 'stuff' and corporate rituals that makes his faith firm and comfortable, and he is faced with difficult choices and difficult visions and messages that are to be delivered to his people and to the kings who hold them captive. Prophets were <u>never</u> given 'easy' messages! Daniel also never sees himself as better than the rest of Israel. He numbers himself among the transgressors, just like Jesus did.

Daniel gives me the message of hope as he says to God that the requests are made to the Lord Jehovah not because <u>I</u> am righteous but because <u>GOD</u> is merciful. No request is too small or insignificant to bring before the Lord. Jesus says the same thing.

Suddenly a Canaanite woman from there came out shouting, "Lord and Son of David, have pity on me! My daughter is full of demons." Jesus did not say a word. But the woman kept following along and shouting, so his disciples came up and asked him to send her away. Jesus said, "I was sent only to the people of Israel! They are like a flock of lost sheep." The woman came closer. Then she knelt down and begged, "Please help me, Lord!" Jesus replied, "It isn't right to take food away from children and feed it to dogs."
"Lord, that's true," the woman said, "but even dogs get the crumbs that fall from their owner's table." Jesus answered, "Dear woman, you really do have a lot of faith, and you will be given what you want." At that moment her daughter was healed. Matthew 15:21-29 (CEV)

This Canaanite woman was not 'right' with God. She was not a Jew. She had no 'righteous' prayer. She was only a desperate mother whose child was suffering. So she asked for help from God. I bet her concept of God was different than those surrounding Jesus that day. She didn't care what they thought of her. She had a desperate need. God saw her heart. God saw the <u>real</u> place that her faith came. It was not in the ritual or the words of how she asked. It was from her heart. God responded with mercy.

I offer you my heart, LORD God, and I trust you…Show me your paths and teach me to follow; guide me by your truth, and instruct me. You keep me safe, and I always trust you. Psalm 25:1, 4-5 (CEV)

Additional Text: Psalm 25, Daniel 9

October 23

William Law, a 17th century English clergyman, said, *"For there is nothing that makes us love a man so much as praying for him; and when you can once do this sincerely for any man, you have fitted your soul for the performance of everything that is kind and civil towards him."*

It's hard to be angry with someone if I am praying for them! The apostle Paul shared in the opening remarks in many of his letters about how he was praying for that particular church.

My friends, I want you to know what a hard time we had in Asia. Our sufferings were so horrible and so unbearable that death seemed certain. In fact, we felt sure that we were going to die. But this made us stop trusting in ourselves and start trusting God, who raises the dead to life. God saved us from the threat of death, and we are sure that he will do it again and again. Please help us by praying for us. Then many people will give thanks for the blessings we receive in answer to all these prayers. 2 Corinthians 1:8-11 (CEV)

I have heard about your faith in the Lord Jesus and your love for all of God's people. So I never stop being grateful for you, as I mention you in my prayers. I ask the glorious Father and God of our Lord Jesus Christ to give you his Spirit. The Spirit will make you wise and let you understand what it means to know God. My prayer is that light will flood your hearts and that you will understand the hope that was given to you when God chose you. Then you will discover the glorious blessings that will be yours together with all of God's people. I want you to know about the great and mighty power that God has for us followers. Ephesians 1:15-19 (CEV)

I noticed that in both of these prayers Paul does not ask the Lord to make them do something. He doesn't pray a manipulative prayer. For the Corinthian church it is a prayer for thanksgiving and praise. He asks the Lord to give the Ephesian church a blessing of wisdom and revelation – GOD'S wisdom and revelation! Not his! If there is correction needed, Paul prays that God will do that.

When I come to a place where I am at odds with someone, I pray more freely when my prayer is a prayer of blessing to that person. I think prayer may need to begin and end with ME. Sounds selfish, doesn't it? But if I begin a prayer with MY praise and thanksgiving to God and asking Him to create in ME a pure heart FIRST – my spirit is ready to pray for the other person or a church or ministry with an open heart, full of the fruit of God. When I end the prayer with thanksgiving and praise that God has allowed me to lift this person and receive the blessing of watching the Lord work in this person's life or a ministry – it keeps the focus on God, giving Him all the glory for the answered prayer. As my husband says, **"God answers our prayer better than we pray it!"**

Additional Text: Psalm 66, 2 Corinthians 1

October 24

It has been wonderful to 'hear' from so many people that while most of us have more questions than answers in regards to God and healing – we are also walking in faith <u>and</u> in the hope and joy of tomorrow. We <u>know</u> God's promises are true! Thank you for all who have responded so far.

I had an opportunity to talk to someone about their observations after spending some time in studying about Paul. Paul spoke a lot about healing.

...even though I have received wonderful revelations from God. But to keep me from getting puffed up, I was given a thorn in my flesh, a messenger from Satan to torment me and keep me from getting proud. Three different times I begged the Lord to take it away. Each time he said, "My gracious favor is all you need. My power works best in your weakness." So now I am glad to boast about my weaknesses, so that the power of Christ may work through me. Since I know it is all for Christ's good, I am quite content with my weaknesses and with insults, hardships, persecutions, and calamities. For when I am weak, then I am strong.
2 Corinthians 12:7-10 (NLT)

Many believe that the 'thorn' was a sore or chronic, severe pain. Others believe the 'thorn' was metaphorical and not an actual physical problem. Whatever it was, Paul says he *"begged the Lord"* three times to heal him of this problem. God didn't. God's answer was that <u>He</u> would provide the grace sufficient to hold Paul up as he endured this pain.

Not that I was ever in need, for I have learned how to get along happily whether I have much or little. I know how to live on almost nothing or with everything. I have learned the secret of living in every situation, whether it is with a full stomach or empty, with plenty or little. *Philippians 4:11-12 (NLT)*

Sounds like Paul <u>did</u> find that God's grace was sufficient to produce contentment *"in every situation"*. I want that. I want God's peace and contentment in whatever situation I am in. I believe that is being so far <u>into</u> God that there is nothing between us!

Since God did not spare even his own Son but gave him up for us all, won't God, who gave us Christ, also give us everything else?...

And I am convinced that nothing can ever separate us from his love. Death can't and life can't. The angels can't and the demons can't. Our fears for today, our worries about tomorrow, and even the powers of hell can't keep God's love away. Whether we are high above the sky or in the deepest ocean, nothing in all creation will ever be able to separate us from the love of God that is revealed in Christ Jesus our Lord. *Romans 8:32, 38-39 (NLT)*

Additional Text: Romans 8, Philippians 4

When someone becomes a Christian he becomes a brand new person inside. He is not the same any more. A new life has begun! All these new things are from God who brought us back to himself through what Christ Jesus did. And God has given us the privilege of urging everyone to come into his favor and be reconciled to him. For God was in Christ, restoring the world to himself, no longer counting men's sins against them but blotting them out. This is the wonderful message he has given us to tell others. We are Christ's ambassadors. God is using us to speak to you: we beg you, as though Christ himself were here pleading with you, receive the love he offers you – be reconciled to God...

For God says, "Your cry came to me at a favorable time, when the doors of welcome were wide open. I helped you on a day when salvation was being offered." Right now God is ready to welcome you. Today he is ready to save you.   *2 Corinthians 5:17-20, 6:2 (TLB, emphasis mine)*

"*Christ's ambassadors*". Has a ring of importance to it, doesn't it? It is important as 'ambassadors/disciples' is God's Plan A for spreading the Good News and winning souls…and there is no Plan B!

God made us in His image to be the perfect people to share all that He had created. Sin separates us from that eternal life. We who have been reconciled through Jesus have been 'called' to the ministry of reconciliation. It is the important ring in my life. This is the reason I ask God for more of His love, compassion, and mercy for His children. I do not have to know someone personally to pray for them and be an example, an 'ambassador', for Jesus.

Sometimes I think God has put us apostles at the very end of the line, like prisoners soon to be killed, put on display at the end of a victor's parade, to be stared at by men and angels alike. Religion has made us foolish, you say, but of course you are all such wise and sensible Christians! We are weak, but not you! You are well thought of, while we are laughed at…We have replied quietly when evil things have been said about us. Yet right up to the present moment we are like dirt under foot, like garbage.   *1 Corinthians 4:9-10, 13 (TLB)*

In this Scripture, Paul speaks of 'apostles' specifically. Not all of us are called to be apostles or operate in the office of apostle. But when we walk in the footsteps of Christ, we become a '*spectacle*' in the eyes of the universe. We no longer are 'normal'. "*We are fools for Christ*" turning away from relying on the wisdom and strength and honor of the world! God reminds us that we are aliens in this world and do not act like those who belong to this world but we belong to Him.

When we are cursed, we bless; when we are persecuted, we endure it; when we are slandered, we answer kindly.   *1 Corinthians 4:12*

Yes, this is the life of an ambassador for Christ. Sounds like an important job, doesn't it?

Additional Text: Ezekiel 1, Colossians 3

October 26

"Blessed are the poor in spirit, for theirs is the kingdom of heaven. Blessed are those who mourn, for they will be comforted. Blessed are the meek, for they will inherit the earth. Blessed are those who hunger and thirst for righteousness, for they will be filled. Blessed are the merciful, for they will be shown mercy. Blessed are the pure in heart, for they will see God. Blessed are the peacemakers, for they will be called sons of God. Blessed are those who are persecuted because of righteousness, for theirs is the kingdom of heaven. Blessed are you when people insult you, persecute you and falsely say all kinds of evil against you because of me. Rejoice and be glad, because great is your reward in heaven, for in the same way they persecuted the prophets who were before you."   *Matthew 5:3-12*

E. Stanley Jones, a 19th-century missionary in America, Japan, Europe and India, called this passage the Christian's "working philosophy of life". Jesus' words were not just a hopeless ideal or something just to <u>be</u> in His eternal kingdom. His words are for then <u>and</u> NOW! Jesus was giving us a <u>new</u> ethic to live by.

"the poor in spirit" Those who realize their spiritual need for a Savior. The kingdom of heaven is now mine because I know that I am a sinner and Jesus has saved me.

"those who mourn" Isaiah said that I would be comforted by the Messiah (Isaiah 61). Jesus came to comfort (save) suffering humanity.

"the meek" Not the greedy but the humble and trusting will inherit the earth. Accepting God's will and His plan instead of doing it <u>my way</u>.

"those who hunger and thirst for righteousness" 'Righteousness' means lining up with <u>God's will</u> in ALL aspects of my life. In desiring a <u>right relationship</u> with Him, it becomes a 'hunger and thirst' that can only be quenched when I give up my own 'food' and take what is only good for me.

"the merciful" This was a real eye-opener because the Jews believed that those who suffered were being rightly punished for some sin. Like me, they had skipped over some of God's words *"For I desire mercy, not sacrifice"* (Hosea 6:6) when it did not fit their daily way of life.

"the pure in heart" Sin is like dust that clouds the vision and causes me to see only in part. Only with true worship, a true desire to be one with God, will I <u>see</u> Him.

"the peacemakers" A 'son' has the nature of the Father, desiring peace and reconciliation with His children and between His children. The Father desires that we display His divine nature of love.

"the persecuted" Ridicule and social pressure are sure to come when I move in 'right relationship' with God. I must look with 'eternal eyes' and keep in step with Jesus.

"great is your reward in heaven" Sounds great, doesn't it? Someone once said, "pie in the sky when you die!" Well, hoping for a reward in the future <u>is</u> a good incentive for the work I do now. But my future reward is also something that I possess here and now as I <u>live</u> with Christ each day. Powerful words from my powerful Savior!

Then the LORD appeared to Solomon at night and said to him, "I have heard your prayer and have chosen this place for myself to be a Temple for sacrifice. I may stop the sky from sending rain. I may command the locusts to destroy the land. I may send sickness to my people. Then if my people, who are called by my name, are sorry for what they have done, if they pray and obey me and stop their evil ways, I will hear them from heaven. I will forgive their sin, and I will heal their land. Now I will see them, and I will listen to the prayers prayed in this place. I have chosen this Temple and made it holy. So I will be worshiped there forever. Yes, I will always watch over it and love it.

2 Chronicles 7:12-16 (NCV)

I have heard many people ridicule those who spend time each day in prayer. "Why bother? God already knows what you need!" True. But prayer is not for God's benefit but for mine!

When I pray, I have an opportunity to lay out all my thoughts before God. All my emotions and feelings that may twist and turn the truth in my life are laid out before God and He who is truth sifts them and brings them back to me in clarity. Keeping all of that deep inside of me only causes an 'infection' that sickens my soul and spirit, causing me to see things with limited or no true vision. I need God's healing power in all parts of my life.

[Jesus said,] *"When you pray, don't be like the hypocrites. They love to stand in the synagogues and on the street corners and pray so people will see them. I tell you the truth, they already have their full reward. When you pray, you should go into your room and close the door and pray to your Father who cannot be seen. Your Father can see what is done in secret, and he will reward you. And when you pray, don't be like those people who don't know God. They continue saying things that mean nothing, thinking that God will hear them because of their many words. Don't be like them, because you Father knows the things you need before you ask him."*   *Matthew 6: 5-8 (NCV)*

Jesus gives us 'guidelines' for prayer. In John 17, He even gives us a personal example by allowing us to listen as He makes His final prayer to His Father before He is separated from Him for the first time in all eternity. Here in Matthew, Jesus tells me to praise the Father for just who He is.

"Our Father in heaven, may your name always be kept holy. May your kingdom come and what you want be done here on earth as it is in heaven."

vv.9-10 (NCV)

Then Jesus says to ask for what I need for this day:

"Give us the food we need for each day. Forgive us for our sins, just as we have forgiven those who sinned against us. And do not cause us to be tempted, but save us from the Evil One."   *vv. 11-13 (NCV)*

I believe that when I speak out what I think I need, I find out what I really do need. One of the things that I need every day is to forgive others. This is definitely one of the ways that the evil one does tempt me.

Prayer. The power in my life that is there for me 24/7. It has everything that I need!

"There but for the grace of God, go I." I have thought and said that so often. Did you ever wonder about the origin of that saying? George Whitefield, an 18th-century evangelist, was heard to say this as he watched a man walking to the gallows. Forgiving a sinner is remembering that I, too, am a sinner.

The law of the LORD is perfect, reviving the soul.
The decrees of the LORD are trustworthy, making wise the simple.
The commandments of the LORD are right, bringing joy to the heart.
The commands of the LORD are clear, giving insight to life.
The reverence for the LORD is pure, lasting forever.
The laws of the LORD are true; each one is fair.
They are more desirable than gold, even the finest gold.
They are sweeter than honey, even honey dripping from the comb.
They are a warning to those who hear them;
There is great reward for those who obey them.
How can I know all the sins lurking in my heart?
Cleanse me from these hidden faults.
Keep me from deliberate sins! Don't let them control me.
Then I will be free of guilt and innocent of great sin.
May the words of my mouth and the thoughts of my heart be pleasing to you, O LORD, my rock and my redeemer.   *Psalm 19:7-14 (NLT)*

God is gracious and good to me. He sets His commandments before me and teaches me His way. He desires that I obey out of love for Him. He has forgiven me of SO MUCH.

It is His Holy Spirit that softens my heart and causes me to bow my head in adoration. It is His Holy Spirit that touches my spirit, making mercy and grace real to me. Then I know, just a little, about God's great love and forgiveness. As that mercy and grace flows in me, there is an opportunity for it to just continue to flow OUT of me and bathe others with its life-giving power. Forgiveness, the chain-breaking freedom of forgiveness, is revealed.

[Jesus said,] *"If you forgive those who sin against you, your heavenly Father will forgive you. But if you refuse to forgive others, your Father will not forgive your sins.*   *Matthew 6:14-15 (NLT)*

Mercy is forgiveness without criticism or contempt. It is when I begin to understand the truth that except for the grace of GOD there I would be.

Additional Text: Psalm 30, Luke 10

October 29

I am writing these things to you now, even though I hope to be with you soon, so that if I can't come for a while, you will know how people must conduct themselves in the household of God. This is the church of the living God, which is the pillar and support of the truth.   *1 Timothy 3:14-15 (NLT)*

"household of God". Other translations call it "God's family". "Family". Does the word bring pictures to your mind of the *Waltons*? *Leave it to Beaver*? I would guess that most of us <u>wish</u> that were our family experience! Even with God as the 'head of the household', I'm afraid that as a member of His family I would have to describe us as more like the *Family Feud* than *Father Knows Best*!

'Family' is one of those tricky concepts that are wonderful and perfect on paper but sticky and <u>imperfect</u> in practical application. God has given us precepts that show us how we *"ought to conduct themselves in God's household"* but too often my eyes are looking directly at MYSELF and MY requirements for daily life and so my place in the family becomes a territorial battle!

Is there any encouragement from belonging to Christ? Any comfort from his love? Any fellowship together in the Spirit? Are your hearts tender and sympathetic? Then make me truly happy by agreeing wholeheartedly with each other, loving one another, and working together with one heart and purpose.   *Philippians 2:1-2 (NLT)*

Take time today and read Philippians 2:1-16. It's worth reading a second or third time. As head of our household, God gave us His First Born as an example of humility and right focus within the family. He is not asking anything of me that Jesus did not walk through, even family relationships. Jesus' natural brothers and sisters were no more or less than mine. His 'brothers' and 'sisters' in the *Family of God* didn't wear shiny halos all day and pluck harps on clouds. They were real people with 'fleshy' desires and sharp tongues!

Then the mother of James and John, the sons of Zebedee, came to Jesus with her sons. She knelt respectfully to ask a favor. "What is your request?" he asked.

She replied, "In your Kingdom, will you let my two sons sit in places of honor next to you, one at your right and the other at your left?"...

But Jesus called them together and said, "You know that in this world kings are tyrants, and officials lord it over the people beneath them. But among you it should be quite different. Whoever wants to be a leader among you must be your servant, and whoever wants to be first must become your slave. For even I, the Son of Man, came here not to be served but to serve others, and to give my life as a ransom for many."   *Matthew 20:20-21, 25-28 (NLT)*

Yes, families are tricky things. I am grateful that my husband has placed God as head of our household. When I have concerns or I'm unhappy, I know Who to take my complaints to! When things are going well, I know Who to thank!

Even in families there can be a struggle to be the one served instead of desiring to serve. A servant heart is a place where Jesus can live and grow in every family.

Additional Text: Philippians 2, 1 Corinthians 13

Then Jacob made a vow, saying, "If God will be with me and will keep me in this way that I go, and will give me bread to eat and clothing to wear, so that I come again to my father's house in peace, then the LORD shall be my God, and this stone, which I have set up for a pillar, shall be God's house. And of all that you give me I will give a full tenth to you." Genesis 28:20-22 (ESV)

"*a tenth*". There's that 'tithe' thing! Tithing, to me, is where the 'rubber meets the road' in my walk of faith. Faith in God is no longer just a theory that, of course, I agree with…in theory. Committing 10% of everything that God gives to me, just as Jacob said, sounds like an easy thing until the everyday realities of a 7% cost of living increase and a 3% raise in salary. Since I've been in ministry and without an every two-week check that I can literally count, tithing has reached a new level of faith!

Now concerning the collection for the saints: as I directed the churches of Galatia, so you also are to do. On the first day of every week, each of you is to put something aside and store it up, as he may prosper, so that there will be no collecting when I come. 1 Corinthians 16:1-2 (ESV)

Paul implies here that the tithe comes before the expenses of the week are paid. That I am relying on God for the whole…not just the 10%. A step of faith. My choice.

The point is this: whoever sows sparingly will also reap sparingly, and whoever sows bountifully will also reap bountifully. Each one must give as he has made up his mind, not reluctantly or under compulsion, for God loves a cheerful giver. And God is able to make all grace abound to you, so that having all sufficiency in all things at all times, you may abound in every good work.

2 Corinthians 9:6-8 (ESV)

It's not a 'Pharisee' thing, this tithing. Tithing does <u>not</u> impact my salvation. That is <u>sealed</u> when I accepted Jesus as Savior and Lord. But when I walk with Jesus, I am given assurance and faith and strength for the day. Giving back to God is giving what He is going to keep giving and giving and giving to me. I <u>cannot</u> out-give God!

And God is able to make all grace abound to you, so that having all sufficiency in all things at all times, you may abound in every good work.

'*abound*' …to be fully supplied, says *Webster's*. I <u>do</u> have all that I need. All that I <u>want</u>? Well, God and I will continue to work on that list each day, won't we? ☺

Additional Text: Genesis 29, Isaiah 60

I would like to spend a moment, just one-to-one with each of you. And before you ask, "How can you think that you are talking just to me, Jody? You don't even know me!" No, I don't but God does. And that is really the point of His Words, isn't it? God speaks to each one of us...everyday. The devotions that we share together...it is God's words for me that day. They were not words spoken to me for Jane Smith. They were for me. When I dismiss God's words as only given for someone else, that is the very time that He will bring them back around to me again and again because I missed the point, didn't I? Here is an example: God spoke to Jonah about 3000 years ago. He brought it around to me again last night.

Now the word of the LORD came to Jonah the son of Amittai, saying, "Arise, go to Nineveh, that great city, and call out against it, for their evil has come up before me." Jonah 1:1-2 (ESV)

The Assyrians were a nasty group of folks. They were pagans. They liked to do human sacrifices, including children. They were disgusting! And God sent one of His prophets to call them to repentance. He sent Jonah.

We may know the Sunday School story of how Jonah was not in agreement with God's plan and had a 'change of heart' in the belly of a whale. I did not know the history behind it and so did not really appreciate the why of Jonah's refusal to go to Nineveh. Some would say that was irrelevant and that Jonah was just disobedient, end of story. That's true but it speaks to me when I feel I have 'reasons' for arguing with God about what He is saying to me. Jonah and his people had been treated badly...more than badly...by the Assyrians. The fact that they would 'rot in hell' one day was maybe a comforting thought while Jonah and his people were being persecuted by them! Call these blood-suckers to repentance??!! Pshaw!

Jonah was finally obedient because God was rather insistent! And what do you know? The king of Assyria and all the people heard the voice of God...and repented. But Jonah got angry that the people of Nineveh did not get punished!

GET OVER IT, JODY, (I mean) JONAH! The story of Jonah isn't just about a whale and how God used it to change a prophet's mind to be obedient! The lesson doesn't stop when the whale burps him out on the shore! Jonah still didn't get it!

When God tells me to go, that's the first step. I am to be obedient to that. When God tells me that I've done what I was supposed to do, places His hand on me in blessing, I am to rejoice! I do not 'tweak' the situation a bit more or tell God how to improve or finish the project! I am part of God's Body through Jesus Christ. I am part. Like Jonah, I may find that difficult because the people He calls me to minister may not show me what I want to see happen. I may not think they repent enough! I may think they got 'off' too lightly! GET OVER IT, JODY! YOU'RE NOT THE JUDGE! YOU'RE NOT ME (GOD)!!!!

God has the situation under control. He gives me a job for a season. I am obedient to that. I move on and rejoice over what has been whether I saw the outcome I expected or not. I don't want to get stuck looking back but instead to look forward to what God will do next!

Janet Wilkie, LCSW

Born in Center Point, Alabama, Janet's parents were divorced when she was two. Her mother was "a praying mom" who gave her a foundation that brought Janet back to her spiritual roots when she became very ill with stress and stomach problems just a few years ago. She attended a Joyce Meyers crusade and stood when prayer was offered for healing. "I felt a warmth flow through me from my throat to my stomach. I have not needed <u>any</u> prescription medication since. God truly healed me!" Janet has been used by God to touch many others with His power to heal and comfort through her work with hospice patients and bereaved families... God has given Janet <u>large</u> amounts of compassion and wisdom that have certainly helped me through some difficult times. I asked her to share with you also.

God blesses those who grieve. They will find comfort!   Matthew 5:4 (CEV)

There are many 'loss scenarios'. A 'loss' is defined by <u>my</u> perception. It could be a death or divorce but it could also be a loss of a job, financial security, my home, a friend or relationship, my health, even a child moving away to college or getting married. That type of 'loss' while expected <u>can</u> cause feelings of grief.

Mourning begins with the anticipation that a loss <u>might</u> occur. The word 'cancer' may immediately bring on feelings of grief. Anticipatory grief does not <u>lessen</u> the intensity of the grief at the time of the event but the healing after the loss may have a shorter 'acute' stage. An example that I see often in hospice work is the spouse who begins to mourn the loss of their loved one several months or weeks <u>before</u> the death. They see that person grow weaker and they begin to mourn the losses that may be occurring daily... When the loved one actually dies, the mourner doesn't feel less grief at the time but the acute pain they feel may not last as long as someone who's loved one died suddenly.

Grief is prolonged when it is avoided. It is important to share our grief and walk through it with others. Unresolved grief <u>will</u> manifest itself in broken relationships, irritability, frustration, lack of concentration, confusion, and physical symptoms including nausea, headaches, insomnia, loss of appetite, prolonged depression, high blood pressure and heart palpitations.

How can I as a Christian help? Be a good listener. Quoting Scripture for comfort and sharing how God helped <u>you</u> comes only <u>after</u> the listening. Every person grieves differently. Even the strongest Christian may have questions and issues with God, including ANGER! That does <u>not</u> equal a lack of faith on their part. It means there is a new aspect in their relationship with God and they will need to work through it. Don't tell them how to feel or what they should or should not be doing. Being present and listening is so much more helpful. Include the bereaved in activities but respect their wishes for time alone also. Do not judge the person. The book of Job is a good example of what <u>not</u> to do! Job's friends spent too much time giving advice and too little time just listening! (See 'References' for recommended books.)

November 1

Yet among the mature we do impart wisdom, although it is not a wisdom of this age or of the rulers of this age, who are doomed to pass away. But we impart a secret and hidden wisdom of God, which God decreed before the ages for our glory. None of the rulers of this age understood this, for if they had, they would not have crucified the Lord of glory. But, it is written, "What no eye has seen nor ear heard, nor heart of man imagined, what God has prepared for those who love him"—these things God has revealed to us through the Spirit. For the Spirit searches everything, even the depths of God.   *1 Corinthians 2:6-10 (ESV)*

I have recently been reading about some of the early "warriors" of the Church: Joan of Arc, a French peasant girl, who around 1429 obeyed the Holy Spirit's call to lead her country's army against the English. She had no military training, military leadership by a female was unheard of, and yet, the army <u>did</u> rally around her and defeated the enemy, allowing Charles the VII to be crowned king. Her "voices" later became her downfall as she was accused of heresy when she testified before a Church tribunal that "I answer nothing from my own head, what I answer is by command of my voices. They do not order me to disobey the Church, but God must be served first." She was burned at the stake in 1431.

Vibia Perpetua, a young noblewoman of northern Africa in the 2nd century, had visions that she recorded and shared with others while in prison as a Christian. Apparently, Perpetua was a widow and mother of a nursing child. Her father came to the prison, asking her to renounce her faith for the sake of her child. Pointing to a water vessel, Perpetua asked her father, "Can that vessel, which you see, change its name?" When he shook his head negatively, Perpetua is reported to have said, "Nor can I call myself any other than I am, that is to say, a Christian." She was to be 'exposed to wild beasts' at the emperor's 'games'. She was attacked but not killed there but later was executed by gladiators.

I do not feel God is calling me to lead the US Army in the War on Terrorism nor do I believe that I will be in an arena to be mauled by wild animals. HOWEVER, while walking in obedience to God's Holy Spirit I do find myself walking against the flow of this world and the 'norms' that many people ascribe. God has given me instructions that take me to places that are definitely <u>OUT</u> of my comfort zone, after all, I <u>am</u> an 'alien' to this world! God also takes me to places of peace and rest for my soul in the midst of this world. He meets me on the battlefield and shows me the tent He has set up and invites me in for rest and a 'conference' with His Holy Spirit. There I seek to see more of the "height, depth, and width of God's love" for me and all of His children. I seek His Holy Spirit counsel for <u>each step</u> I take.

I ask the Lord for courage today.

Be watchful, stand firm in the faith, act like men, be strong. Let all that you do be done in love.   *1 Corinthians 16:13-14 (ESV)*

Additional Text: Proverbs 15, 1 Corinthians 2

November 2

Hallelujah! Thank you, Lord! How good you are! Your love for me continues on forever. Who can ever list the glorious miracles of God? Who can ever praise him half enough? Happiness comes to those who are fair to others and are always just and good.   Psalm 106:1-3 (TLB)

Don't let evil get the upper hand but conquer evil by doing good.

Obey the government, for God is the one who has put it there. There is no government anywhere that God has not placed in power. So those who refuse to obey the laws of the land are refusing to obey God, and punishment will follow.
                                                   Romans 12:21-13:2 (TLB)

Remind your people to obey the government and its officers, and always to be obedient and ready for any honest work. They must not speak evil of anyone, nor quarrel, but be gentle and truly courteous to all.   Titus 3:1-2 (TLB)

We are truly blessed to have an opportunity to exercise our right AND responsibility to vote. When I first began to vote my decisions on which candidate or on the resolutions were based on whatever my friends said or what my parents said (sometimes I would vote opposite of my parents, after all what did they know?!) or who was cute or charismatic. Good reasoning, huh?!

Now almost 30 years later, I would have to testify that PRAYER is the ONLY way to know God's will and His knowledge of the true hearts of those who are running or the truth of the resolutions. It is unfortunate that mentioning religious beliefs has become a plus in getting votes whether it is the truth or not. It is also true that a candidate may have some views that are different than mine but his/her heart is truly seeking God's will and maybe we both have something to learn from that!

I will pray each time that I go to the voting booth for God's wisdom. I ask that He confirm to me His will regardless of the candidate's party affiliation. I ask that I read clearly the resolutions and issues that are before me, seeing with God's eyes and heart.

Let us also remember to pray each day for our President and leadership, not that they do MY will but that they do GOD'S will and be obedient and answerable to the Lord. May they be blessed with God's wisdom, strength, and understanding that is far greater than man's. May the leaders of our country and city look for Godly solutions. Praying blessings on our government leaders and officials is certainly something they will be grateful to receive!

Jesus told us to 'give to the government what is the government's and to God the things that are God's'. Good advice.

Additional Text: Luke 12, Ephesians 6

Blessed is the one who does not walk in the counsel of the wicked, nor takes his stand in the same place as sinners, nor sits down in the seat of the scornful. But his pleasure is found in the LORD's instruction, and he meditates in it day and night. He will be like a tree planted by springs of water that gives his fruit in season. His leaves do not wither, and whatsoever he does prospers.

Psalm 1:1-3 (HNT)

With the tongue we praise the Lord and Father and with it we curse people who are made in God's likeness. Out of one mouth come blessing and cursing. It's not right, brothers and sisters, for things to be this way! It's not possible for a fountain to pour forth from the same opening both sweet and bitter, is it? It's not possible, my brothers and sisters, for a fig tree to produce olives or a grapevine to produce figs, is it? Neither can a salt spring produce sweet water.

James 3:9-12 (HNT)

This morning I was sitting and looking out on the trees in my backyard. I noticed that some saplings were straight and seemed to be stretching toward the sun. Some older trees appeared strong with many branches reaching out in all directions. Some trees were bent and almost convoluted in the ways their branches were spread. Some had many roots, easily detected as they popped up above the earth and then went down again. Others had no trace of roots on the surface but by the circumference of the tree, I could tell it was an old tree and its roots must be deep and strong.

Jesus knew that His disciples (and future disciples) would understand the truths that He expressed in the metaphor of "Vine and Branches". As I look at the trees in my yard, I can sketch a picture in my mind of the tree that I want to be called "Jody". I want my tree to never lose the characteristic of the sapling, stretching up towards the Son, always wanting more nourishment and light in my life. I want my roots to be deep, a strong anchor in any storm. I want my branches to be long, reaching in all directions and yet balanced with the height and depth of the tree. I want the leaves and fruit to be rich in color and more fruit to be on the tree each season.

Trees must be tended and provided with the nutrients and light that they need in order for all these things to happen. It's a daily task. My parents had a beautiful yard and gardens and people would stop and ask them for their 'secret' and Dad obliged them some of his ideas about mulch and fertilizer but looking back on it – I know what the 'secret' was. He WORKED every day – sometimes an hour – sometimes several hours – EVERY DAY!!!

What is MY commitment to tending and working so that the tree that I am may glorify its Maker?

I myself am the vine, you are the branches. The one who remains in me and I in him, this one bears much fruit, because without me you can do nothing... In this is the father glorified, so that you might bear much fruit and you might be my disciples. Just as the father loved me, so also I love you. Remain in my love. If you keep my commands, you will remain in my love just as I have kept my father's commands and I remain in his love."

John 15:5, 8-10 (HNT)

Just as our bodies have many parts and each part has a special function, so it is with Christ's body. We are all parts of his one body, and each of us has a different work to do. And since we are all one body in Christ, we belong to each other, and each of us needs all the others. Romans 12:4-5 (NLT)

I don't know if I ever paid attention to that last phrase, "*and each of us needs all the others*". From the beginning, it was God's plan and Jesus' example that we be in fellowship. That's a 'church-y' kind of word but in this case, I think, accurate.

Luke recounts in *Acts* that the replacement of Judas was not done by a quorum of the Believers that felt like showing up that night and had nothing better to do. They heard God say, "This is important! Be there!" and they were. When Pentecost occurred, *Acts 2* says, *When the day of Pentecost came, they were all together in one place.* 'All together'. They were in fellowship. Not just in a physical place but they desired to be TOGETHER with the LORD!

The eye can never say to the hand, "I don't need you." The head can't say to the feet, "I don't need you." In fact, some of the parts that seem weakest and least important are really the most necessary...So God has put the body together in such a way that extra honor and care are given to those parts that have less dignity. This makes for harmony among the members, so that all the members care for each other equally. If one part suffers, all the parts suffer with it, and if one part is honored, all the parts are glad. Now all of you together are Christ's body, and each one of you is a separate and necessary part of it.
1 Corinthians 12:21-22, 24-27 (NLT)

We, Jesus' disciples, the Saints of God, (whatever!) NEED each other. We need each other as Aaron and Hur to hold each other up. We need each other as the friends of the lame man to carry each other before the Lord. We need each other as David and Miriam to dance with praise and rejoice before the Lord. We need each other as we listen to the 'Ezra's' share the Word of God with us as a Body.

We are the Body and are challenged when we reject parts that are different from us. We COULD be a 'well oiled' Body if we came together in the unity of the Holy Spirit and committed to continue to BUILD the Body as God planned.

But you, Timothy, belong to God; so run from all these evil things, and follow what is right and good. Pursue a godly life, along with faith, love, perseverance, and gentleness. Fight the good fight for what we believe. Hold tightly to the eternal life that God has given you, which you have confessed so well before many witnesses. 1 Timothy 6:11-12 (NLT)

Additional Text: 1 Corinthians 12, 1 Timothy 6

November 5

Then Moses led the people of Israel away from the Red Sea, and they moved out into the Shur Desert. They traveled in this desert for three days without water. When they came to Marah, they finally found water. But the people couldn't drink it because it was bitter. Then the people turned against Moses. "What are we going to drink?" they demanded. So Moses cried out to the LORD for help, and the LORD showed him a branch. Moses took the branch and threw it into the water. This made the water good to drink. Exodus 15:22-25 (NLT)

God's chosen people, His children, have been given sweet water to drink where there had been bitter water. A miracle. God provided what His children needed. And not <u>one</u> "Thank you" was given. Before I start throwing stones let me exam my own glass house!

Each and every day, God gives me everything that I need. "BUT" the inner voice says, "I <u>WORKED</u> and made money and bought the food in my frig and pay the utilities so I have electricity and don't have garbage. I <u>worked</u> for MY food!"

It is easy to begin to justify the 'good things' that have come into my life. I see them as the result of my hard work and perseverance. The question then comes regarding the source of the opportunities that were given and the focus that was needed. Just how 'wonderful' do I think I am? Not as wonderful and loving and giving as my God!

In all things and in all ways, the source of the gifts given to me is a Heavenly Father that I have only begun to know. I give of my time and talents to His plan for His kingdom and He gives back to me many times over! He allows me to see 'fruit' in my labors and even receive thanks from His children. It all belongs to <u>Him</u>!

It took the Israelites 40 years and Moses many trips up mountains before they learned God's ways for them, including thanksgiving in <u>all</u> things. And in looking at Bible history, Christian history, as a whole, I find it VERY comforting that God has been so gracious to accept repentance for our pride when it was truly all about what HE has done! I think it was George Patton that said if we don't learn from history we are going to <u>repeat</u> history. I want to LEARN from Job and the rest and not go <u>through</u> what they went through!

Therefore, since we are surrounded by such a huge crowd of witnesses to the life of faith, let us strip off every weight that slows us down, especially the sin that so easily hinders our progress. And let us run with endurance the race that God has set before us. We do this by keeping our eyes on Jesus, on whom our faith depends from start to finish. He was willing to die a shameful death on the cross because of the joy he knew would be his afterward...Think about all he endured when sinful people did such terrible things to him, so that you don't become weary and give up. Hebrews 12:1-3 (NLT)

One of the problems the Israelites had was that they only encouraged each other to rebel and whine! One of the <u>best</u> ways that I can please God and serve Him is to <u>encourage</u> His children to <u>do good</u>. If I will allow God to use me to be His voice and hands to LIFT His children up to do even MORE GOOD than they thought they could...God smiles on that work!

Judas had given them a prearranged signal: "You will know which one to arrest when I go over and give him the kiss of greeting. Then you can take him away under guard." As soon as they arrived, Judas walked up to Jesus. "Teacher!" He exclaimed, and gave him the kiss. Then the others grabbed Jesus and arrested him. But someone pulled out a sword and slashed off an ear of the high priest's servant. Jesus asked them, "Am I some dangerous criminal, that you come armed with swords and clubs to arrest me? Why didn't you arrest me in the Temple? I was there teaching every day. But these things are happening to fulfill what the Scriptures say about me."

Meanwhile, all his disciples deserted him and ran away. There was a young man following along behind, clothes only in a linen nightshirt. When the mob tried to grab him, they tore off his clothes, but he escaped and ran away naked.

Mark 14:44-52 (NLT)

The disciples, the eleven who had been with Jesus, in His presence, for three years, day and night, ran like scared rabbits. The disciples, who had seen five loaves and three fish feed FIVE THOUSAND, ran. The disciples, who had seen Lazarus come out of a tomb after three days without smell or decay, ran off in the bushes and didn't even care if they had their clothes!

The next day the council of all the rulers and elders and teachers of religious law met in Jerusalem... They brought in the two disciples and demanded, "By what power, or in whose name, have you done this?" Then Peter, filled with the Holy Spirit, said to them..., "Let me clearly state to you and to all the people of Israel that he was healed in the name and power of Jesus Christ from Nazareth, the man you crucified, but whom God raised from the dead...."The members of the council were amazed when they saw the boldness of Peter and John, for they could see that they were ordinary men... *Acts 4: 5, 7-8, 10,13 (NLT)*

Here are the disciples again in front of the same high priest and rulers that seized Jesus that night in Gethsemane. What made them run that night when Jesus was standing right there with them and now, Jesus is gone, and yet they stand in front of the Sanhedrin alone and loudly proclaim the very words that make the rulers *furious*?!! What happened to change fear to fear-less-ness?

In one of these meetings as he [Jesus] was eating a meal with them, he told them, "Do not leave Jerusalem until the Father sends you what he promised. Remember, I have told you about this before. John baptized with water, but in just a few days you will be baptized with the Holy Spirit...But when the Holy Spirit has come upon you, you will receive power and will tell people about me everywhere..." *Acts 1:4-5, 8 (NLT)*

Yes, Pentecost. But how does that extraordinary day come and apply into my everyday life? Jesus' words are eternal. When events and people in my life try to knock me down and throw 'fear' over me like a cloak, the Holy Spirit is already there. Putting that 'cloak' on every morning (i.e., the armor of God, Ephesians 6:10-18) is good preparation, like keeping an umbrella in my car. Fear is a sneaky, insidious enemy that trips me up or grabs me around the throat sometimes when I least expect, just like it did Peter and the other ten. Jesus knows that and gives me the power of the Most High God.

November 7

LORD, my God, I prayed to you, and you healed me. You lifted me out of the grave; you spared me from going down to the place of the dead...
You changed my sorrow into dancing. You took away my clothes of sadness, and clothed me in happiness. I will sing to you and not be silent. LORD, my God, I will praise you forever.   *Psalm 30:2-3, 11-12 (NCV)*

"Mourning" *an outward sign of grief for a person's death; a period of time during which signs of grief are shown*   *-- Miriam-Webster Dictionary*

Contrary to company policies that allow three days 'bereavement leave' or supervisors who may allow their employees some 'slack' for four to six weeks with the death of a spouse, child, or parent, 'mourning' is not a period of time that we leave behind because we made a decision to do so.

When my 17-year-old son died, the outward signs of grief were seen by many at first, some later, and GOD continues to know the pain in my heart. It is GOD who is able to touch that pain with His Spirit and <u>know</u> the exact 'ointment' I need at that particular moment. It is GOD who is able to hear the words that sometimes aren't even <u>words</u> but groanings in my spirit for the loss of the son that I love. It is GOD who knows that I <u>know</u> where James is and that we will be together for *eternity* but the pain of this time of separation is sharp and penetrating. It is GOD that also knows how I wonder about HIS plan and James' role in it. GOD is the <u>only</u> One who has any valid answers to any 'why' questions.

Blessed are those who mourn, for they <u>will be</u> comforted.   *Matthew 5:4*

God doesn't leave me when times are tough. I may move away because I am hurt that <u>HE</u> allowed the circumstances. I may move away because my focus becomes <u>me</u> and <u>my</u> pain instead of continuing to look to God for His guidance, His plan, His healing. God's words about grief and mourning are difficult when I am in that place of mourning because they ask me to LOOK UP and get focused again on God's <u>eternal</u> vision and that is a perspective that is moving forward, not stalling. I've listed some of the passages and it would be well for us to look at these now so that we bring those words, God's words, into our hearts and spirits NOW. When our time of mourning comes, we will have these words within us to draw from and allow them to <u>carry</u> us THROUGH that 'period of time'.

Additional Text: Ecclesiastes 3, Isaiah 61, Romans 12:9-21
1 Corinthians 7:29-31, James 4 and 5, Revelation 21

November 8

Every king in all the earth shall give you thanks, O Lord, for all of them shall hear your voice. Yes, they shall sing about Jehovah's glorious ways, for his glory is very great. Yet though he is so great, he respects the humble, but proud men must keep their distance. Though I am surrounded by troubles, you will bring me safely through them. You will clench your fist against my angry enemies! Your power will save me. The Lord will work out his plans for my life – for your loving kindness, Lord, continues forever. Don't abandon me – for you made me.   *Psalm 138:4-8 (TLB)*

I share with you the day-to-day struggles and victories that God brings me through. I share not for sympathy. I share for two reasons: 1) Even though some may consider me a leader and a 'mature' Christian, I struggle. I desire to come closer to God every day. As I get closer to His holiness, there is another layer of my un-holiness to shed! Sometimes I gladly throw off the 'chains that bind'. Sometimes I am reluctant to give up what is familiar and comfortably uncomfortable! And 2) I need prayer from the Body of Believers. I need uplifting in prayer and there are no 'God reasons' for me not to ask! There is a Proverbs statement (27:17) about 'iron striking iron' and how we help each other with our discussions (not arguments!). We have an opportunity to build each other's faith.

...the disciples were together again, and this time Thomas was with them. The doors were locked; but suddenly, as before, Jesus was standing among them and greeting them. Then he said to Thomas, "Put your finger into my hands. Put your hand into my side. Don't be faithless any longer. Believe!"

"My Lord and my God!" Thomas said. Then Jesus told him, "You believe because you have seen me. But blessed are those who haven't seen me and believe anyway."   *John 20:26-29 (TLB)*

Jesus opens His cloak and shows me His wounds so that I may believe. I believe and follow Him because I KNOW that He has suffered and yet is faithful and obedient to God. The Son shows me the truth of the Father. I want to do the same. I want to open my cloak and let the world see my wounds AND see that it is JESUS that brings me through!

The LORD will work out his plans for my life. God is faithful and His promises are true. What a wonderful statement and promise to know that God already has a plan for my life and that if I keep an open heart and mind, God will show me the best plan for my life. I DO have a solid ROCK to stand on no matter what the storm! Struggles and victories are part of my life but traveling through is going to be better when I allow Jesus to be not just a 'part' but the leader and guide of my life.

Additional Text: Proverbs 27, Acts 2

[Jesus said,] *"And why worry about a speck in your friend's eye when you have a log in your own? How can you think of saying, 'Friend, let me help you get rid of that speck in your eye,' when you can't see past the log in your own eye? Hypocrite! First get rid of the log from your own eye; then perhaps you will see well enough to deal with the speck in your friend's eye!"* Luke 6:41-42 (NLT) *Don't worry about the wicked. Don't envy those who do wrong. For like grass, they soon fade away. Like springtime flowers, they soon wither. Trust in the LORD and do good. Then you will live safely in the land and prosper. Take delight in the LORD, and he will give you your heart's desires...Be still in the presence of the LORD, and wait patiently for him to act. Psalm 37:1-4, 7 (NLT)*

It is interesting to me when the Lord leads me to two passages of Scripture that seem to me to be unrelated – at first. Then as I wait and read them both again and even a third or forth time, I hear His voice begin to speak to me specifically about some 'thing' in my life that I am currently 'fretting' about. ☺

When it seems 'all hell is breaking loose' in my life, it is easy to look around and see the 'peace' in others lives. If it is finances that are vexing me, I see others buying new cars or a house or having a big birthday bash for their child and...it makes me 'fret'! I can pull out my trusty finger and point out the weaknesses in their lives and wonder why I – I who am walking with my Lord – why I do not have the same 'luck'! (I am laughing and shaking my head as I write this!)

This is where God connected the Psalm to Jesus' parable of the speck of sawdust and the board. I am looking at the 'speck' in someone else's life. I am looking at their 'speck' of peace or good fortune OR their 'speck' of weakness. I am ignoring my own 'BOARD' of jealousy or envy. I am ignoring my own 'BOARD' of *BLESSINGS*!!! Yes, *BLESSINGS*!!! No matter WHAT is going on in my life, I can make a HUGE list of blessings EVERY DAY that God is giving me.

I can now hear God say to me, "Jody, Jody, Jody. I love you with an everlasting love. I want so many things for you. Look at the many blessings and gifts I have given to you and Henry and your children and grandchildren. Look at what I've done for you." And I look...and my eyes fill with tears of thanksgiving. Washing the plank out of my eye.

Every year, I watch the movie, *White Christmas*, at least six times during the holiday season. There's a song in there that Bing Crosby and Rosemary Clooney sing about counting blessings when I am worried. Bing tells Rosemary that if she will count her blessings, she'll fall asleep.

Maybe that movie is a bit 'cheesy' for some but I think one of the reasons I watch it is for that song. Counting my blessings brings Holy Spirit peace to me every day.

Additional Text: Psalm 37, Proverbs 15

Don't worry about anything; instead, pray about everything. Tell God what you need, and thank him for all he has done. If you do this, you will experience God's peace, which is far more wonderful than the human mind can understand. His peace will guard your hearts and minds as you live in Christ Jesus.

Philippians 4:6-7 (NLT)

When I am out teaching about prayer and intimacy with God whether in the U.S. or Europe, I think the most frequently asked questions are, "How do I know it is God talking to me?" and "How do I know that I am following the will of God?" Good questions. I don't think the answers are difficult but their application is contrary to my nature!

God is truthful. His words today do not negate His words of 2000 years ago. So when I believe I hear His voice, what He is saying to me will line up with what He said to Paul two centuries ago. God will not tell me that it is OK for me to worry about my children. He will not tell me that what I am dealing with now is more difficult than anything Paul had to do so my worry is justified. No, God is able to take care of my concerns just like He did Paul's.

I believe that I <u>know</u> I am in the will of God because that place has a very *distinctive* characteristic: peace. The will of God may be a place that is outside my 'nature' or my 'flesh' but my spirit recognizes it and it is a place of peace for my spirit. Recently, my family and I went through a very difficult 'season' when my youngest son had a recurrent cancer. Through every step as we decided about doctors, place of treatment, path of treatment, and timing, God directed each step. The difficult task was to 'wait' on Him. We might have a question at 8 a.m. on Tuesday morning and the clear answer did not show itself until Thursday at noon. When it came, it was clear and it came with such peace! Waiting was difficult! I wanted the answer on Tuesday at 8:05 a.m.!!! But waiting brought the *perfect* answer and the *perfect peace*!!!

Those who love your law have great peace and do not stumble.

Psalm 119:165 (NLT)

May the Lord of peace himself always give you his peace no matter what happens. The Lord be with you all.   *2 Thessalonians 3:16 (NLT)*

*[Jesus said,] "...and he will give you all you need from day to day if you live for him and make the Kingdom of God your **primary** concern.*

Matthew 6:33 (NLT, emphasis mine)

Jesus' words during the Sermon on the Mount are often quoted in discussions about God's will and obedience until the words seem almost cliché. They are NOT cliché. They are succinct and true!

Additional Text: Psalm 119: 89-112, Galatians 5

November 11

Then I turned to the Lord God and prayed and asked him for help. I did not eat any food. To show my sadness, I put on rough cloth and sat in ashes. I prayed to the LORD my God and told him about all of our sins.   *Daniel 9:3-4 (NCV)*

A few years ago, when it seemed <u>everyone</u> was talking about the one verse prayer that a man named Jabez said in 1 Chronicles 4, I decided to do a study on prayers in the Bible. It was a LONG study because there is a fair amount of prayer going on! It was very encouraging to me, however, because it really brought to my heart that these were ordinary people like me just talking to God. They were sharing their feelings and everyday concerns with the One True God, Jehovah, who they <u>knew</u> would hear. Their prayers displayed anguish, despair, anger, joy in victory, and even their desire that God bring down some wrath and destroy their enemies!

Some of the prayers were beautifully reassuring:

[Jesus said,] *"I am coming to you [Father] now. But I pray these things while I am still in the world so that these followers can have all of my joy in them. I have given them your teaching. And the world has hated them, because they don't belong to the world, just as I don't belong to the world. I am not asking you to take them <u>out</u> of the world but to <u>keep them safe from the Evil One</u>. They don't <u>belong</u> to the world, just as I don't belong to the world. Make them ready for your service through your truth: your teaching is truth. I have sent them into the world, just as you sent me into the world. For their sake, I am making myself ready to serve so that they can be ready for their service of the truth.*
John 17:13-19 (NCV)

Some were sad, full of pain: *By the rivers in Babylon we sat and cried when we remembered Jerusalem. On the poplar trees nearby we hung our harps.*
Psalm 137:1-2 (NCV)

And some were FULL of joy, rejoicing at what God had done: *"The LORD lives! May my Rock be praised! Praise God, the Rock, who saves me! God gives me victory over my enemies and brings people under my rule. He frees me from my enemies. You set me over those who hate me. You saved me from cruel men. SO I will praise you, LORD, among the nations. I will sing praises to your name. The LORD gives great victories to his king. He is loyal to his appointed king, to David and his descendants forever."*   *2 Samuel 22:47-51 (NCV)*

God is SO willing to meet with me and hear ALL that is in me. He takes all my feelings and sifts them for me so that I will know what is true and what is just…stuff! God listens to me and then gently turns me toward His right path when I am open to His will and wisdom. There is always time in my Father's day to meet with me. I choose to make the time to be quiet and listen to <u>Him</u>!

Additional Text: 2 Samuel 22, Psalm 54

November 12

Thank the LORD for all the glorious things he does; proclaim them to the nations. Sing his praises and tell everyone about his miracles. Glory in the Lord; O Worshipers of God, rejoice. Search for him and for his strength, and keep on searching! Think of the mighty deeds he did for us, his chosen ones – descendants of God's servant Abraham, and of Jacob. Remember how he destroyed our enemies. He is the Lord our God. His goodness is seen everywhere throughout the land.   *Psalm 105:1-7 (TLB)*

The words of this 'song' do not qualify <u>when</u> I am to give thanks, sing, praise, and tell. It says to just DO IT! It's easy to dance around and tell all the wonderful things that God has done in my life when things are going well. Words just flow and it all seems to just 'bubble out'! My testimony is good to give but those who hear it may think, "I wish my life was just full of blessings like her life is." The testimony is good but...

When life is tough and all is not Paradise, praise and thanksgiving becomes a choice. It is then that I go to my quiet place and seek God's face, looking for the truth in His eyes. It is a time to look to God and accept His strength. I choose to recall the 'wonders' and miracles He has done in my life and those I love. I remember times when I did not understand what God was doing and followed the situation through until I could see that God's judgment was right and true. I remember. And I lift my head in the tough times and I cling to the hope that is fueled by faith and the testimonies. God gives me strength for today.

He will keep in perfect peace all those who trust in him, whose thoughts turn often to the Lord! Trust in the Lord God always, for in the Lord Jehovah is your everlasting strength.   *Isaiah 26:3-4 (TLB)*

For you must worship no other gods, but only Jehovah, for he is a God who claims absolute loyalty and exclusive devotion.   *Exodus 34:14 (TLB)*

My pastor exhorted me with this Scripture from Exodus, saying that God was <u>passionate</u> about His relationship to me. Am I passionate about my relationship to Him? If I hold my emotions back from God, that may be something to explore. God is the best place to put my emotions because He will sift through them and return to me the 'true emotions', void of flesh, pure and worthy of trust.

I want to be <u>passionate</u> about God. If that makes me different or weird, well, God's opinion is the only one that matters. I praise Him today...because He is worthy!

Additional Text: Psalm 9, Zechariah 8

November 13

Mourn, you priests who serve at the altar of my God. Spend your days and nights wearing sackcloth. Offerings of grain and wine are no longer brought to the LORD's temple. Tell the leaders and people to come together at the temple. Order them to go without eating and to pray sincerely. Joel 1:13-14 (CEV)

I learned about fasting at a young age. To me it meant fish sticks and macaroni and cheese on Fridays...EVERY Friday. EEIISH! (That means 'yuk' in Midwest kid language!) I did not really know why we had to 'not eat meat' except that it had something to do with church and Jesus dying on a Friday. When I became independent and out on my own I seem to take perverse pleasure out of eating steak or a hamburger on Fridays. (Yes, rebellion is a word that comes to mind!) Over the years I have known many people who said they were fasting in addition to praying for a particular request. My impression was that this somehow added power to a prayer. I was embarrassed that I never fasted because I could not connect the dots between my childhood experiences of fasting and how that could in any way add power to a prayer!

Shout the message! Don't hold back. Say to my people Israel: You've sinned! You've turned against the LORD. Day after day, you worship him and seem eager to learn his teachings. You act like a nation that wants to do right by obeying his laws. You ask him about justice, and say you enjoy worshiping the LORD. You wonder why the LORD pays no attention when you go without eating and act humble. But on those same days that you give up eating, you think only of yourselves and abuse your workers. Isaiah 58:1-3 (CEV)

And then I read Isaiah 58. God's words to Isaiah and His people about their ritual of fasting spoke to me and the mist of the past and the fog of my present understanding disappeared! 'Fasting' was a sacrament! Just like baptism and communion! Now, before I am hung for heresy...a sacrament is an outward sign of an inward change...God <u>does</u> 'call' me to fast. He calls me to <u>turn</u> my heart more to Him, to draw closer to Him. That is going to happen in 'prayer' or in conversation with Him, right? I 'fast' as an outward sign that my heart is turned completely to God and desire nothing more than to be in <u>His</u> presence and 'converse' about what <u>HE</u> wants. Recently, this 'call' to fast came, as my son was to have surgery. Because I 'fasted' does that mean that my prayer was more powerful? I believe that the 'fast' turned my heart more toward God as I 'gave up' my choice to eat that day and I also found I could 'give up' my worry and fear and KNOW that God was in control with all the true answers.

In the story of Jonah, the people of Nineveh were warned by Jonah that God was going to destroy the city. The people believed the message and began a fast for repentance. Did God spare Nineveh because they fasted or because they <u>changed</u> from their wickedness? The fast was the outward sign of their changed hearts. They stopped their narcissistic, me-centered lives and turned their hearts and lives to God and His ways. Am I willing to 'give up' so God 'can do' in my life?

Additional Text: Isaiah 58, Jonah (it's a small book!)

November 14

That evening a rich man named Joseph, a follower of Jesus from the town of Arimathea, came to Jerusalem. Joseph went to Pilate and asked to have Jesus' body. So Pilate gave orders for the soldiers to give it to Joseph. Then Joseph took the body and wrapped it in a clean linen cloth. He put Jesus' body in a new tomb that he had cut out of a wall of rock, and he rolled a very large stone to block the entrance of the tomb...

The next day, the day after Preparation Day, the leading priests and the Pharisees went to Pilate. They said, "Sir, we remember that while that liar was still alive he said, 'After three days I will rise from the dead.'...

Pilate said, "Take some soldiers and go guard the tomb the best way you know." So they all went to the tomb and made it safe from thieves by sealing the stone in the entrance and putting soldiers there to guard it.

Matthew 27: 57-60, 62-63, 65-66 (NCV)

"...*guard the tomb the best way you know*". And we, as humans, have been trying to do that for over 2000 years. I try closing Jesus and all that He is inside a tomb so that He won't cause any more trouble in my life. Take Him out on Easter with a shiny white robe or on Christmas with His cute, baby cheeks all wrapped up in a blanket but don't let His words of loving discipline or His bloody beaten body mess up my tidy world. How can I talk like this as a believing Christian? Because I look in the mirror and see the truth that Jesus KNOWS me and KNOWS my heart and loves me anyway! But He wants MORE for me! He wants me to be closer to Him and closer to the Father so Jesus doesn't let me get away with my bad attitude and my shallow life.

[Jesus said,] *"A thief comes to steal and kill and destroy, but I came to give life – life in all its fullness. I am the good shepherd. The good shepherd gives his life for the sheep."* John 10:10-11 (NCV)

Jesus came so that MY life may be full and complete. That happens when I accept ALL of Jesus' way and let go of MY way.

Jesus answered, "I tell you the truth, you aren't looking for me because you saw me do miracles. You are looking for me because you ate the bread and were satisfied. Don't work for the food that spoils. Work for the food that stays good always and gives eternal life. The Son of Man will give you this food, because on him God the Father has put his power."

The people asked Jesus, "What are the things God wants us to do?" Jesus answered, "The work God wants you to do is this: Believe the One he sent."..

Then Jesus said, "I am the bread that gives life. Whoever comes to me will never be hungry, and whoever believes in me will never be thirsty...Those who see the Son and believe in him have eternal life, and I will raise them on the last day. This is what my Father wants." John 6:26-29, 35, 40 (NCV)

I've heard that Mark Twain said, "It's not the Scripture I don't know that bothers me. It's the Scripture I do know." I guess I could shut Jesus and what I don't know about Him up and just coast along for the next 40 years. I'd be 'saved' and go to heaven...but I wouldn't be living that 'full life' He promised, would I? That's what I want. Nothing less than Jesus' definition of a 'full life'!

November 15

Now the sons of Eli were evil men who didn't love the Lord...So the sin of these young men was very great in the eyes of the Lord; for they treated the people's offerings to the Lord with contempt.   *1 Samuel 2:12, 17 (TLB)*

    Eli's sons were <u>priests</u> in the House of the Lord. Eli had taught his sons the rituals from an early age. Eli's sons knew 'about' God but they did not KNOW HIM. Hophni and Phinehas embraced the deception that since they had the High Priest for a father and were priests themselves, they had all they needed. They knew the rituals. They knew how to 'work the system'. They did NOT know God. They did NOT know <u>His</u> character.

I am the Lord! That is my name, and I will not give my glory to anyone else; I will not share my praise with carved idols.   *Isaiah 42:3 (TLB)*

You shall be holy to me, for I the Lord am holy, and I have set you apart form all other people, to be mine.   *Leviticus 20:26 (TLB)*

But be holy now in everything you do, just as the Lord is holy, who invited you to be his child. He himself has said, "You must be holy, for I am holy."   *1 Peter 1: 15-16 (TLB)*

    The gifts of the Spirit, the anointing of God, and even pastoral (evangelistic, prophetic, etc.) authority can be given by the laying on of hands. BUT nowhere in the Old Testament or the New Testament does it say that God's character can be 'imparted' by the laying on of hands. There is NO SHORT CUT! David Ravenhill said, *"It is the anvil of experience and the hammer of obedience to God and His Word."*

    Eli's sons wanted short cuts. They wanted to have all the blessings and 'perks' of being a priest in the House of God without knowing who they served and representing Him in Spirit and Truth. Their sin *"was very great in the eyes of the Lord"*.

But you are not like that, for you have been chosen by God himself – you are priests of the King, you are holy and pure, you are God's very own – all this so that you may show to others how God called you out of the darkness into his wonderful light. Once you were less than nothing; now you are God's own. Once you knew very little of God's kindness; now your very lives have been changed by it.   *1 Peter 2:9-10 (TLB)*

    The Question of the Day: Am I willing to receive God's gift of self-control and put it to use in prioritizing my life to spend time with Him so that I KNOW Him?

Additional Text: 1 Samuel 2, 1 Peter 2

My friends, be glad, even if you have a lot of trouble. You know that you learn to endure by having your faith tested.   *James 1:2-3 (CEV)*

I haven't reached the spiritual level where *"be glad"* comes to mind when I am going through troubles. I do realize that I have more perseverance inside me than I did 10 years ago so I know that some good DID occur!

God will bless you, if you don't give up when your faith is being tested. He will reward you with a glorious life, just as he rewards everyone who loves him.   *James 1:12 (CEV)*

Here is where I need to grow more and develop my 'eternal eyesight' and 'eternal heart'. When trials come into my day, I want to be able to 'see' the marathon race that I am currently in and look up and 'see' the finish line, however far off it may be. I want to keep God's goal for me in mind every moment of the day so that I do not <u>focus</u> on the hurdle but instead focus on the point beyond each hurdle and I believe that will keep my steps within Jesus' steps and allow me to make it over the hurdle and keep running toward the <u>goal</u>. The hurdles are not the goal. They are part of the trials and part of the run. I may be moving through each day, not knowing God's specific ultimate goal for me or maybe not <u>accepting</u> His goal, but if my heart is desiring to <u>be</u> in God's will and direction, then I can put one step in front of another and stay in the race and on track.

We know that God is always at work for the good of everyone who loves him. They are the ones God has chosen for his purpose, and he has always known who his chosen ones would be. He had decided to let them become like his own Son, so that his Son would be the first of many children.   *Romans 8:28-29 (CEV)*

"We know…" there is a key phrase. To have the assurance that I KNOW God's true nature and character places a seed of trust and faith and hope that is the beginning and end of any and all other questions I may have. The "know" part comes with daily conversations with God, building each day in our relationship.

The "good" that God works to place in me does NOT guarantee me a stress-free, no-problem life. God brought good out of David's adultery and murder. He brought good out of Joseph's confinement in Egypt. God brought the <u>perfect</u> good out of Jesus' suffering and physical death on the cross. God's purpose in my life is greater than my problems, pain, and even my sin.

God's purpose in my life is that I become like Jesus, the first fruit. Everything that God allows points toward this purpose. Am I willing to run the race? Am I willing to take the next step? When my lungs ache and my feet are raw and swollen, will I choose to trust Him and stay on course?

His Spirit lets us know that together with Christ we will be given what God has promised. We will also share in the glory of Christ, because we have suffered with him. I am sure that what we are suffering now cannot compare with the glory that will be shown to us.   *Romans 8:17-18 (CEV)*

And so I keep running…today.

November 17

And now they came to an olive grove called the Garden of Gethsemane, and he instructed his disciples, "Sit here, while I go and pray." He took Peter, James, and John with him and began to be filled with horror and deepest distress. And he said to them, "My soul is crushed by sorrow to the point of death; stay here and watch with me."   *Mark 14:32-34 (TLB)*

Three verses that say so much to me when *"My soul is crushed..."*. Jesus, the Son of God, felt crushed by sorrow! I usually think of Jesus being 'crushed' by the horrific journey He was facing. I wonder if He was seeing the HUGE cloud of sins about to descend upon Him and knew it would separate Him from the Father.

Jesus asked His three most trusted and closest disciples (friends, brothers: Mark 3:34) to *"...watch"*. He <u>needed</u> them with Him as He prayed. He wasn't asking them to join Him in chains when He was arrested. He was asking them to just be with Him as He PRAYED! And what happened?

He went a little further and fell to the ground and prayed that if it were possible the awful hour awaiting him might never come. "Father, Father," he said, "everything is possible for you. Take away this cup from me. Yet I want your will, not mine." Then he returned to the three disciples and found them asleep.
                                                                 Mark 14:35-37 (TLB)

Jesus turned to the three men He knew the best and asked them to 'watch' with Him. Jesus sets an example for <u>me</u> that tell me to 'call' those He has given <u>me</u> to 'watch' with me when I am *"overwhelmed"*. "Do not be stubborn or let your pride get in the way, Jody. Call your sisters to pray!"

But what about the 'failure' of the disciples to stay awake? Why should I call anyone when they might forget to pray even if I ask them? I don't think that's my part of the obedience equation. I'm just to ask. When I am on the <u>other side</u> of the scenario and someone has called <u>me</u> to pray or 'watch' with them, then that is my part of the obedience equation to <u>remember</u> and be strong to 'watch' and pray. I would imagine that there were many things about this night that replayed over and over in the disciples' minds for the rest of their lives.

About that time King Herod moved against some of the believers, and killed the apostle James (John's brother). When Herod saw how much this pleased the Jewish leaders, he arrested Peter during the Passover celebration...
                                                                 Acts 12:1-3 (TLB)

James died. Peter would be released from prison by a MIRACLE. Was the Church praying for Peter more often or more accurately? Later, Peter would die much like his Savior, by crucifixion. I am 'called' to pray not because I have the power to evoke the ultimate outcome of the scenario (that's God's sovereign job!) but because I do <u>affect</u> the journey of me and my sister or brother. Jesus teaches me to 'watch and pray'.

Additional Text: Acts 7, James 5

The story of Gideon is one that speaks to me. An 'ordinary' kind of guy who gets a 'call' from God!

Then once again the Israelites started disobeying the LORD, so he let the nation of Midian control Israel for seven years...The Midianites took almost everything that belonged to the Israelites, and the Israelites begged the LORD for help.

Judges 6: 1, 6 (CEV)

The key word here, I think is "*again*". In reading the Old Testament, it is easy for me to begin to roll my eyes and mutter, "Here we go again!" The Israelites played out that two-verse scenario over and over and over and...over. But so do I! "Evil?" you say? Sin is evil. When I make the choice to succumb to the temptation, I have chosen evil. I get myself in a fix and feel that distance from God and cry out for help. Here we go again!

The angel appeared and spoke to Gideon, "The LORD is helping you, and you are a strong warrior!" Gideon answered, "Please don't take this wrong but if the LORD is helping us, then why have all of these awful things happened?"...

Then the LORD himself said, "Gideon, you will be strong, because I am giving you the power to rescue Israel from the Midianites."

"Gideon," the LORD answered, "you can rescue Israel because I am going to help you! Defeating the Midianites will be as easy as beating up one man."

Gideon said, "It's hard to believe that I'm actually talking to the LORD. Please do something so I'll know that you really are the LORD."

Judges 6:12-13, 16-17 (CEV)

Yes, sir, been there and done that! Especially if I 'hear' God asking me to do something that is unexpected or something I really do not want to do! "Is that really You, Lord?!!" God then proceeds to prove that He is the I AM by performing the 'tests' that Gideon asks of Him: turning a fleece from dry to wet one night and wet to dry the next, with the ground around it producing the opposite! If this were 'reality TV' there would be a disclaimer not to try this at home!

The LORD said, "Gideon, your army is too big. I can't let you win with this many soldiers. The Israelites would think that they had won the battle all by themselves and that I didn't have anything to do with it.   *Judges 7:2 (CEV)*

And so God takes His handpicked commander from leading 32,000 men to 10,000 to 300. And God's reasoning on this is very clear that no one else is going to get the credit for what happens except HIM! I have often wondered why things happen in my life that is SO overwhelming! My son doesn't just get cancer. It is a cancer that has a 25% success rate the first time it occurs and decreases by 50% each time after that! GOD is the only One to get the credit for the success of the chemo or the surgery! Science says even with that the statistics are less than 'poor'! GOD gets all the glory!

The Midianites had been defeated so badly that they were no longer strong enough to attack Israel. And so Israel was at peace for the remaining forty years of Gideon's life...Soon after Gideon's death, the Israelites turned their backs on God again. They set up idols of Baal and worshiped...   *Judges 8:28, 33 (CEV)*

"Here we go again!"

November 19

I pray to you, LORD! Please listen. Don't hide from me in my time of trouble.
Pay attention to my prayer and quickly give an answer.   Psalm 102:1-2 (CEV)

I wonder what the cries of all His children sound like to God? From my fleshly perspective, it seems like it would be like being inside the largest nursery I could imagine with infants and toddlers and teenagers all yelling at the same time! But even at that, you can ask any parent if it is not true that they can distinguish and KNOW their child's cry over all the rest! God has shown that He is able to see the 'big picture' of His people AND see the need of the one also.

I am blessed to have 'sisters' in my life who allow me to share my joys and my needs with them. I am also blessed that others feel they can call me during their difficult times. I wish sometimes I could call them all together from different parts of the country and sit them down together and say, "You are NOT alone. You ARE loved by God because He has given you people to stand with you and the inner strength to move on. Take it, grab on to Him, and we'll all make the first step together as a family of believers!"

Our LORD, you are King forever and will always be famous…
Our LORD, the nations will honor you, and all kings on earth will praise your
glory. You will rebuild the city of Zion. Your glory will be seen, and the prayers
of the homeless will be answered.   Psalm 102: 12, 15-17 (CEV)

The proclamation of these verses have Israel's name on it but it could easily have yours or mine! God is sovereign and His reputation and history of compassion and favor is known! I received a family history book, compiled by a cousin, about four years ago and it was awesome to read that my GREAT-grandmother who came from Prussia in the 1830's was known to always have a time with God every morning before the rest of her day began. Four generations have passed and God is still hearing and answering.

Let us grab on today that GOD DOES HEAR ME! He is faithful! If we are 'lame' or 'paralyzed' by something in our lives…Jesus tells us to pick up our mat and WALK! It is a step of faith! Did the man in Luke 5 keep looking back with *longing* to where he had laid for years? Let us move forward today and not delay any longer.

[Jesus said,] *Can worry make you live longer?…*
But more than anything else, put God's work first and do what he wants. Then
the other things will be yours as well. Don't worry about tomorrow. It will take
care of itself. You have enough to worry about today.
*   Matthew 6:27, 33-34 (CEV)*

God is smarter than I am, right? Maybe NOW is the time for me to take His advice??!!!

Additional Text: 1 Kings 22, Luke 19

The soldiers nailed Jesus to a cross and gambled to see who would get his clothes. Then they sat down to guard him. Above his head they put a sign that told why he was nailed there. It read, "This is Jesus, the King of the Jews." The soldiers also nailed two criminals on crosses, one to the right of Jesus and the other to his left. People who passed by said terrible things about Jesus. They shook their heads and shouted, "So you're the one who claimed you could tear down the temple and build it again in three days! If you are God's Son, save yourself and come down from the cross!" The chief priests, the leaders, and the teachers of the Law of Moses also made fun of Jesus. They said, "He saved others, but he can't save himself. If he is the king of Israel, he should come down from the cross! Then we will believe him. He trusted God, so let God save him, if he wants to. He even said he was God's Son."

Matthew 27:35-44 (CEV)

Robbers and criminals insulting me are tolerable and easily ignored but church leadership…is painful and not so easy to forgive. My pastor recently pointed out this Scripture to me as he drove home his point about forgiveness. I admit that it leapt off the page at me with an arrow zinging straight to my heart. I'm sure I must be one of the few people in the world of Christianity that has been truly hurt by church leadership (there is a <u>ton</u> of sarcasm in those words!) but I receive this Word about forgiveness for me today. When I read the gospels and see something as specific as this happening to Jesus and 'see' the same scenario in my own life…I know that God inspired the writer to put it down just for me!

[Jesus said,] *"You did not choose me. I chose you and sent you out to produce fruit, the kind of fruit that will last…If the people of this world hate you, just remember that they hated me first. If you belonged to the world, its people would love you. But you don't belong to the world. I have chosen you to leave the world behind, and that is why its people hate you."*

John 15:16, 18-19 (CEV)

Yes, God desires that I bear good fruit that will last…like 'forgiveness' and 'grace' and 'mercy'…all of which He gives me in abundant measure. To be obedient to God, I have no choice but to accept His grace and mercy for all MY sins and then let it flow out of me to those who hurt and hurl insults my way, no matter who they are. If I am 'crucified with Christ', then I am up there on that cross getting the insults on the Fridays of my life long before the glory of Sunday comes!

"The time will come and is already here when all of you will be scattered. Each of you will go back home and leave me by myself. But the Father will be with me, and I won't be alone. While you are in the world, you will have to suffer. But cheer up! I have defeated the world."   *John 16:32-33 (CEV)*

I am <u>not</u> alone. *"…my Father will be with me."* Yes, He is! And Jesus HAS (already done!) defeated this world of trouble. There is peace when I press in close to Him. Jesus covers me when we are on that Cross. I am with Him and He is with me. Those are words that I say when I take Communion. It is my time of affirming that <u>we</u> are one and it <u>is</u> well with my soul. HALLELUJAH!

Oh, Timothy, you are God's man. Run from all these evil things and work instead at what is right and good, learning to trust him and love others, and to be patient and gentle. Fight on for God. Hold tightly to the eternal life which God has given you, and which you have confessed with such a ringing confession before many witnesses.   *1 Timothy 6:11-12 (TLB)*

Discipline and self-control are two words that have never been comfortable to me. I can hear some say, "Well, they're not supposed to be, Jody!" Actually they are if I want to win the prize!

Paul uses the metaphor of an athlete and a race to give me an accurate picture of my spiritual life. The first truth to know about this race is that it is a marathon, not a sprint! If I prepare and think that I need to study God's word, pray, and submit to God's will and guidance for 'just a short time', I will become discouraged and ill-equipped to run what is in reality a long and difficult race. I must bring into my life more nourishment that only can be found in His presence and more disciplined 'exercise' in God's word <u>every day</u> so that I can have endurance not just for the moment but to finish the race and gain the prize.

I must also realize that an athlete <u>disciplines</u> his/her life and uses <u>self-control</u> to make CHOICES that benefit their training. An athlete does not make these choices thinking that losing is even a possibility! Why go through the pain of pulled muscles and sweat and workouts if you thought you would lose? The really wonderful thing about the race that I am in...I KNOW I WIN!!!

I have fought long and hard for my Lord, and through it all I have kept true to him. And now the time has come for me to stop fighting and rest. In heaven a crown is waiting for me, which the Lord, the righteous Judge, will give me on that great day of his return. And not just to me, but to all those whose lives show that they are eagerly looking forward to his coming back again.
     1 Timothy 4:7-8 (TLB)

Jesus, Paul, Mary, Deborah, and all the others are 'athletes' that set the example of what worked and what didn't. I do not have to rewrite the 'play book'. I do not have to run around trying every fad diet and workout plan. I do not have to wonder if what Jesus said or Paul said would work.

For the free gift of eternal salvation is now being offered to everyone; and along with this gift comes the realization that God wants us to turn from godless living and sinful pleasures and to live good, God-fearing lives day after day, looking forward to that wonderful time we've been expecting, when his glory shall be seen – the glory of our great God and Savior Jesus Christ. He died under God's judgment against our sins, so that he could rescue us from constant falling into sin and make us his very own people, with cleansed hearts and real enthusiasm for doing kind things for others.   *Titus 2:11-14 (TLB)*

I want to wear Jesus' jersey. When I wear Jesus' team jersey, I walk out on the field of life *confident* that I have used the practice time wisely and I know Jesus' plays that <u>work</u> against whatever the opposing team may throw at me! I see the 'payoff' for the discipline and self-control...a winning season!

Then Jesus led them out along the road to Bethany, and lifting his hands to heaven, he blessed them, and then began rising into the sky, and went on to heaven. And they worshiped him, and returned to Jerusalem filled with mighty joy, and were continually in the Temple, praising God.   *Luke 24:50-53 (TLB)*

These verses were shared with me during a meeting and it just suddenly jumped out at me that those who witnessed Jesus' ascension into heaven worshipped Him <u>after</u> He left their sight! This really made me think about the times I don't feel that 'praise' just BUBBLE OUT because everything around me is difficult or sad or empty.

These men and women had <u>Jesus</u> right there with them for three years and now He was gone! He was tangible…and then He wasn't. The feeling of loss and loneliness <u>could</u> have been justifiably great but instead…there was praise!

Then the eleven disciples left for Galilee, going to the mountain where Jesus had said they would find him. There they met him and worshiped him – but some of them weren't sure it really was Jesus! He told his disciples, "I have been given all authority in heaven and earth. Therefore go and make disciples in all nations, baptizing them into the name of the Father and of the Son and of the Holy Spirit, and then teach these new disciples to obey all the commands I have given you; and be sure of this – that I am with you always, even to the end of the world."   *Matthew 28:16-20 (TLB)*

Matthew wanted me to know that the original 11 disciples were there at the ascension. He, too, says they worshiped but he admits there were some doubters. "How can 'this' continue without Jesus?" "Can <u>I</u> keep going?" So Matthew records that Jesus reiterates exactly what He wants them to 'go on' doing and that <u>He</u> <u>WILL</u> <u>be</u> <u>with</u> <u>them</u>!!!

And I suppose that if all the other events in Jesus' life were written, the whole world could hardly contain the books!   *John 21:25 (TLB)*

Most scholars believe Mark's gospel was written last and he gives me the perspective that the disciples <u>did</u> continue the work.

John reminds me that not everything was committed to ink and papyrus! The rest is given to me now through the Holy Spirit. And <u>that</u> is a point for praise and worship! Jesus continues to be tangibly ALIVE to me now, in this century, by the power of the Holy Spirit. Every day, there is reason for me to praise because God is in and around me whether I am on top of a mountain full of joy or climbing out of a pit of difficulties. God is <u>there</u> and worthy of my praise!

Additional Text: Acts 1, Revelation 22

He suffered and endured great pain for us, but we thought his suffering was punishment from God. He was wounded and crushed because of our sins; by taking our punishment, he made us completely well. Isaiah 53:4-5 (CEV)

The usual interpretation of these verses has been quoted to me many times with regards to sickness and disease. I agree that my Lord is the Great Physician but the illness of my physical body is not what put Jesus through the last 12 hours of His earthly life. *The Passion of the Christ* by Mel Gibson is a movie I will probably never view again but I will also never read these verses in Isaiah with a lukewarm feeling in my heart either.

[Jesus said,] *"The Father loves me, because I give up my life, so that I may receive it back again. No one takes my life from me. I give it up willingly! I have the power to give it up and the power to receive it back again, just as my Father commanded me to do."* John 10:17-18 (CEV)

Throughout the movie the phrase, "See how much I love you, Jody" kept running through my mind. I heard it watching Jesus pray in the garden with sweat pouring off Him and remembered the times I wept and prayed in the middle of the night. I heard it as He stumbled through the streets of Jerusalem dazed with pain. I heard it as Jesus crushed the snake under the heel of His sandal. "I love you, Jody." Jesus, the Son of God, came to earth to die for me. If there had been no one else, Jesus still would have had to go to the cross for ME. If there had been no one else, Jesus still would have done it…for me. "See how much I love you, Jody."

Christ died for us at a time when we were helpless and sinful. No one is really willing to die for an honest person, though someone might be willing to die for a truly good person. But God showed how much he loved us by having Christ die for us, even though we were sinful. Romans 5:6-8 (CEV)

While I was still a sinner, Jesus died for me. And He did it not because of any accusations by the Jews of His day or because of the power of the Roman Empire. Jesus died because I was a sinner and only He could be a sacrifice big enough and perfect enough for my sins.

We are careful not to judge people by what they seem to be, though we once judge Christ in that way. Anyone who belongs to Christ is a new person. The past is forgotten, and everything is new. God has done it all! He sent Christ to make peace between himself and us, and he has given us the work of making peace between himself and others…We were sent to speak for Christ, and God is begging you to listen to our message. We speak for Christ and sincerely ask you to make peace with God. 2 Corinthians 5: 16-18, 20 (CEV)

Additional Text: Isaiah 53, Romans 5

Jesus told him, "I am the way, the truth, and the life. No one can come to the Father except through me. If you had known who I am, then you would have known who my Father is. From now on you know him and have seen him!"
Phillip said, "Lord, show us the Father and we will be satisfied."
Jesus replied, "Philip, don't you even yet know who I am, even after all the time I have been with you? Anyone who has seen me has seen the Father! SO why are you asking to see him? Don't you believe that I am in the Father and the Father is in me? The words I say are not my own, but my Father who lives in me does his work through me. Just believe that I am in the Father and the Father is in me. Or at least believe because of what you have seen me do."

John 14:6-11 (NLT)

When I think of the Father, what image comes to my mind? Is God the Father the angry Disciplinarian and Jesus the good Intercessor who throws Himself between me and the Father when I sin?

When I sin, am I afraid to come to the Father confessing and seeking forgiveness? Do I try to 'hide' by returning to an addiction or throw myself into a religious frenzy to 'make up' for my sin? Am I showing that I have accepted a 'religion' of fear and intimidation? Religion and the religious have often misrepresented my Father and made Him into something He is not.

Jesus said that HE came to show me the Father. If I want to know the Father's <u>true</u> feelings when I sin, I need to look to Jesus. The Father, Son, and Holy Spirit <u>are</u> One! Phillip asks the question that I ask, "Who is the Father? Show Him to me!" And Jesus does.

Christ is the visible image of the invisible God. He existed before God made anything at all and is supreme over all creation.　　　*Colossians 1:15 (NLT)*
Such love has no fear because perfect love expels all fear. If we are afraid, it is for fear of judgment, and this shows that his love has not been perfected in us. We love each other as a result of his loving us first.　　　*1 John 4:18-19 (NLT)*

When I take those steps toward the Father, spend time with Him in Word and prayer, I begin to <u>really</u> know Him and know His heart for me. I get rid of that unhealthy fear and stop jumping through hoops to please Him. When I sin, I can turn to Him because I <u>know</u> that I will see NOTHING BUT LOVE in His eyes. I crawl up into my Father's lap and find His love and forgiveness.

"Let's spend time together today, Dad?!"
"OK. Let's."

Additional Text: Colossians 1, 1 John 3

November 25

[Jesus said,] *"I have told you this, so that you might have peace in your hearts because of me. While you are in the world, you will have to suffer. But cheer up! I have defeated the world."* John 16:33 (CEV)

Some things do not turn out like I planned. Some things are really hard for me to understand and fathom. Maybe someday, we can all get together and have a round table theological discussion about all of this. I don't have any theology to share today. All I have is what I know to be true:

God is real.

God cares.

God love me and you and all those that we love.

I know this is all true not just because of an ancient translated manuscript but so many of you have told me over and over that I have been "so strong" and that "James has such courage". The reality is that neither James nor I have these traits because we have good genes or strong mental health. We have it because we needed it and asked God for it and God gave it to us each and every day.

I'd like to be able to assure you that cancer won't ever happen to you or someone you love. I'd like to tell you that this wouldn't happen if you eat the right things or exercise enough or pray enough or even avoid getting too fanatical about God! If you do the 'right' things, nothing 'bad' will every happen to you! The truth is... seemingly unfair things happen to good, even innocent people.

When Herod found out that the wise men from the east had tricked him, he was very angry. He gave orders for his men to kill all the boys who lived in or near Bethlehem and were two years old and younger. This was based on what he had learned from the wise men.

So the Lord's promise came true, just as the prophet Jeremiah had said, "In Ramah a voice was heard crying and weeping loudly. Rachel was mourning for her children, and she refused to be comforted, because they were dead."
Matthew 2:16-18 (CEV)

I have a choice: go through the time with God or without Him.

[Jesus said,]*"I am the vine, and you are the branches. If you stay joined to me, and I stay joined to you, then you will produce lots of fruit. But you cannot do anything without me. If you don't stay joined to me, you will be thrown away. You will be like dry branches that are gathered up and burned in a fire. Stay joined to me and let my teachings become part of you. Then you can pray for whatever you want, and your prayer will be answered. When you become fruitful disciples of mine, my Father will be honored."* John 15:5-8 (CEV)

With God is the better choice. Notice the order of Jesus' words: He says that we are to be connected to Him and that whatever I ask will be given. Then Jesus says that I will have 'trouble' in this world but to be encouraged that this world is not where the victory is! I must see this world and its 'trouble' with *eternal* eyes. As I am walking through both good times and difficult times, I must keep the bigger picture before me!

Additional Text: Ruth 4, 1 John 4

November 26

LORD, have you completely rejected Judah? Do you really hate Jerusalem? Why have you wounded us past all hope of healing? We hoped for peace, but no peace came. We hoped for a time of healing but found only terror. LORD, we confess our wickedness and that of our ancestors, too. We all have sinned against you. For the sake of your own name, LORD, do not abandon us. Do not disgrace yourself and the throne of your glory. Do not break your covenant with us. Please don't forget us! Can any of the foreign gods send us rain? Does it fall from the sky by itself? No, it comes from you, the LORD our God! Only you can do such things. SO we will wait for you to help us. Jeremiah 14:19-22(NLT)

I do not read our local newspaper or watch televised news except when someone else has control of the remote. The inaccuracies of which I have personal knowledge have made me a cynic toward the press. However, I am also not an ostrich so I am aware that we are engaged in wars both here and abroad that are like nitroglycerin riding in a 1950 Chevy without shocks just waiting to escalate and explode!

I am alternately amused and frustrated at the numbers that are quoted by pollsters who claim to have their 'finger on the pulse of the people'. They have <u>never</u> called my house! Nor do I know anyone who has ever received a call from Gallup! It feeds the voice inside my head that tells me that I have NO CONTROL over my world and NO ONE CARES what I think!

I am half right. I DO NOT have control over my world. I have choices. I choose how I will act or react to situations. It is a LIE that no one cares, however.

God <u>is</u> sovereign. He <u>is</u> the One with control. He <u>is</u> the One who cares…about ME. Whether I live in the United States or am flying across the world in response to military orders or I live in a small village in the Ukraine, God knows me and those I love and He cares. Because He sees us ALL, His response to <u>my</u> situation may be quite different than what I anticipate and request in my prayers. He sees how an answer to my prayer affects the soldier in Iraq and the child in the Ukraine. He sees how to bring it together for the good of those who love Him and what will glorify Him as Lord and Savior.

In times of trouble, may the LORD respond to your cry. May the God of Israel keep you safe from all harm. May he send you help from his sanctuary and strengthen you from Jerusalem. May he remember all your gifts and look favorably on your burnt offerings. May he grant your heart's desire and fulfill all your plans. May we shout for joy when we hear of your victory, flying banners to honor our God. May the LORD answer all your prayers. Now I know that the LORD saves his anointed king. He will answer him from his holy heaven and rescue him by his great power. Some nations boast of their armies and weapons, but we boast in the LORD our God. Those nations will fall down and collapse, but we will rise up and stand firm. Give victory to our king, O LORD! Respond to our cry for help.   *Psalm 20 (NLT)*

Additional Text: Isaiah 50, Acts 4

Then he [Jesus] called together his twelve apostles and sent them out two by two with power over evil spirits...The apostles left and started telling everyone to turn to God. They forced out many demons and healed a lot of sick people by putting olive oil on them...

After the apostles returned to Jesus, they told him everything they had done and taught. But so many people were coming and going that Jesus and the apostles did not even have a chance to eat. Then Jesus said, "Let's go to a place where we can be alone and get some rest." They left in a boat for a place where they could be alone. But many people saw them leave and figured out where they were going. So people from every town ran on ahead and got there first. When Jesus got out of the boat, he saw the large crowd that was like sheep without a shepherd. He felt sorry for the people and started teaching them many things.

Mark 6:7, 12-13, 30-34 (CEV)

Sending *"them out two by two"*. It's a great concept and one that we in the Church should be doing. I wonder why it is that we want to keep talent/gifted people in the church instead of encouraging them to minister outside the church. Why are we proud if one answers the 'call' to pastor in five years? Seems like in a church of 500+ we would have at least one a year!! Are we equipping people to 'find' and 'hear' their call from God?   It begs the question: Do we really WANT a New Testament church?

Can't you just 'see' the apostles coming up the road, dusty and tired, and then seeing Jesus sitting over under a tree, their steps quicken and they drop down in front of Him, all talking at once about what they had done and said? I can see Jesus' eyes; proud of what the 'children' had done, passing around the skin of water. And then he looks up and sees that a crowd is beginning to gather and so He suggests that they take this somewhere private and quiet so that they can 'debrief' and physically refresh themselves...maybe even take a bath!

I have always felt the 'wisdom' of rest ... even for those in ministry! Jesus, however, did NOT rest but began to teach and Mark connects this teaching with the feeding of the 5000. Since I haven't reached Jesus' level of supernatural strength, I am going to believe that He DOES give me time off for rest. It is right that I say 'no' to requests, even ministry requests, when what God is telling me to do is rest! It's a listening and obedience 'thing'! ☺

[Jesus said,] *"If you are tired from carrying heavy burdens, come to me and I will give you rest."*   *Matthew 11:28 (CEV)*

Rest in the Lord in ALL things and you WILL have a good night's sleep!

Additional Text: Psalm 62, Hebrews 4

Just as each of us has one body with many members, and these members do not all have the same function, so in Christ we who are many form one body, and each member belongs to all the others.   Romans 12:4-5

I can't let God's message go that we <u>need</u> each other. There are too many of us that take our church fellowship for granted and figure that missing one or two or three or four weeks away from our church family won't matter. It becomes easier and easier to be away, actually. And if I know that for myself…do I give it a priority to encourage, pray, and do whatever I am asked to do to bring others into 'the Family'? Ah…there may be a sticking point. I <u>know</u> it's important to me but maybe I am reluctant to stick my nose into another's 'business'.

Jesus brought together 12 disciples and they were identified <u>with</u> Him. He said in John 13:35 that they would be known as His disciples by their love. This is the primary purpose for a church body (showing the love of Christ in the world) and I am identified with that as a member.

Peter and Paul were a wonderful early Church example of how to get along for the good of the Body (2 Peter 3:15) while having our differences (Galatians 2:11).

I can grow and mature in my Christian walk as I <u>discuss</u> my beliefs and allow others to 'test' those beliefs while I listen and discuss their beliefs. Maturity comes in relationships, not in isolation.

I am given gifts to use <u>in the Body</u> and it begins locally before it begins globally. Just like a child learns to talk and interact at home first and then increases his/her scope, so I must begin in my home church, saving myself from sticking my foot in my mouth in front of those less forgiving!

Anyone who has ever been on a mission trip, whether to a local inner city or across the world will tell you that taking the mission with familiar companions, a Paul and Silas and Barnabas, is the best way to go.

When God puts someone on my heart that is struggling and absent from the Body, I do have a responsibility to answer that 'call' to <u>go</u> and encourage them back into the fellowship that loves them. (James 5:19)

I believe that every one of us knows at least one person or family that is away from a supportive 'family' or local church. Am I praying for them faithfully? Am I doing whatever God has told me to do? Or am I hearing a deceitful voice that says it is not my business?

Consequently, you are no longer foreigners and aliens, but fellow citizens with God's people and members of God's household, built on the foundation of the apostles and prophets, with Christ Jesus himself as the chief cornerstone. In him the whole building is joined together and rises to become a holy temple in the Lord. And in him you too are being built together to become a dwelling in which God lives by his Spirit.   Ephesians 2:19-22

Additional Text: Matthew 18, 2 Timothy 3

[Jesus said,]*"Again you have heard it was said to those of old, 'You shall not swear falsely, but shall perform to the Lord what you have sworn.' But I say to you, do not take an oath at all, either by heaven, for it is the throne of God, or by the earth, for it is his footstool, or by Jerusalem, for it is the city of the great King. And do not take an oath by your head, for you cannot make one hair white or black. Let what you say be simply 'Yes' or 'No'; anything more than this comes from evil."*   *Matthew 5:33-37 (ESV)*

As I was reading this, at first I heard what I always hear about this passage, "Jody, don't swear/curse." I could swear like a sailor when I was in college. (Pardon me, all you navy folks!) My vocabulary was limited and colorful. Why I thought that was 'cool' or something that was in any way admirable is a mystery to me now!

I look at this Scripture now and it speaks to me on a different level. "Jody, you don't have to 'swear' that what you say is true. Just speak the truth and I (God) will stand witness to it by my Spirit. If someone believes you or not, I will know the truth and that is all that matters." WOW! I don't have to convince someone that I am right and they are wrong! ☺ My true word is enough for God and everyone else can believe or not – it does not change my true status!

This next Scripture is a little long but worth reading as I meet opportunities to share my faith with others and feel the temptation to 'convince' them: *"Therefore, O King Agrippa, I was not disobedient to the heavenly vision, but declared first to those in Damascus, then in Jerusalem and throughout all the region of Judea, and also to the Gentiles, that they should repent and turn to God, performing deeds in keeping with their repentance. For this reason the Jews seized me in the temple and tried to kill me. To this day I have had the help that comes from God, and so I stand here testifying both to small and great, saying nothing but what the prophets and Moses said would come to pass: that the Christ must suffer and that, by being the first to rise from the dead, he would proclaim light both to our people and to the Gentiles."...*
And Agrippa said to Paul, "In a short time would you persuade me to be a Christian?" And Paul said, "Whether short or long, I would to God that not only you but also all who hear me this day might become such as I am – except for these chains."   *Acts 26:19-23, 28-29 (ESV)*

I am not aware of any historical evidence that tells me that King Agrippa became a believer after Paul's testimony. I'll put him on my list of folks I am going to look for when I get to heaven! Nevertheless, Paul was obedient to speak the Good News and did so with the power of the Holy Spirit, not his human power or oaths.

Conduct yourselves wisely toward outsiders, making the best use of the time. Let your speech always be gracious, seasoned with salt, so that you may know how you ought to answer each person.   *Colossians 4:5-6 (ESV)*

God's 'salt' in my words means full of <u>His</u> flavor that enhances a picture of Him to others. It is truth and it is agape love.

Additional Text: Acts 26, Colossians 4

November 30

I cry out to God; I call to God, and he will hear me. I look for theLlord on the day of trouble. All night long I reach out my hands, but I cannot be comforted. When I remember God, I become upset; when I think, I become afraid. You keep my eyes from closing. I am too upset to say anything. I keep thinking about the old days, the years of long ago. At night I remember my songs. I think and I ask myself: "Will the Lord reject us forever? Will he never be kind to us again?"

Psalm 77:1-7 (NCV)

When I am in a tough place in my life asking questions that seem to have no answers or unsettling answers, I find myself looking at God in the same way as David. "Are You NEVER going to bless me with peace and joy again?" "Where is all the 'stuff' You promised?" "Where is Your mercy and compassion?" As long as I am turning to God and asking questions, I am actually in the right place. I am turning to the ONLY One who has answers. God doesn't mind the questions. In fact, I believe He welcomes them. It's when I turn away and look only within myself or to some self-help guy that I step away from God. I am choosing something or someone else (including myself) to guide and direct me.

I remember what the LORD did; I remember the miracles you did long ago. I think about all the things you did and consider your deeds. God, your ways are holy. No god is as great as our God. You are the God who does miracles; you have shown people your power. By your power you have saved your people, the descendants of Jacob and Joseph.

Psalm 77:11-15 (NCV)

Testimony. Remembering the deeds of the LORD. Remembering when He came and spoke to me or guided me in right paths. Yes, many of those times were in the middle of the night. Many of those times seem to be 'at the last minute'! David is saying to me, "Wait! Look at what God has <u>done</u> in your life. He's still there and He <u>does</u> hear and <u>is</u> going to answer. Wait. He's done it for generations and generations. He isn't going to stop now. Wait."

There are three answers: yes, no, and wait. Am I willing to accept any of the three that God gives? God builds patience in me whether I ask for it or not! God's 'wait' is a measure of time using His <u>eternal</u> timeline not my idea of hours, days, weeks, months, or years. Yes, the wait could *possibly* be YEARS. So that leaves the question: Am I willing?

Today, I am pressing in closer. I am staying before the Lord and persistently seeking <u>His</u> answers and <u>His</u> ways.

HEAR ME, LORD, AND ANSWER ME! TO YOU I CRY OUT! I TRUST YOU, ONLY YOU!

Additional Text: Psalm 78, Acts 20

More Ordinary People

As iron sharpens iron, so people can improve each other.

Proverbs 27:17 (NCV)

Henry Neufeld – born in British Columbia, Canada, to missionary parents with a brother and two sisters, Henry spent his early years learning about servant hood and 'being content in all things.' His thirst for knowledge had him continuing his graduate studies in Biblical Languages and coming out of that <u>not</u> believing in God. He took a ten-year tour through the military doing Special Operations and earning the nickname of 'Little Hitler' for his ability to do personnel reviews and cut people down to size! To meet this gentle man now is to come into contact with the power of God to <u>totally</u> change people and make 'head knowledge' <u>about</u> Him become 'heart knowledge' <u>of</u> Him. Henry loves me even in the un-lovable times. He supports me and God's 'call' on <u>my</u> life. He is truly my covenant marriage partner with the Lord.

Rev. Perry Dalton – from a broken home, God brought this man out of the ashes and called him to be a pastor and an apostle to many of His children. It's not easy to be my pastor as Perry was for over ten years! God used him to harness my aggressive personality into a path of learning to trust and submit to my heavenly Father. (Notice I said, 'learning'. God is not done with me yet!) Pastoring a church that is hit with the power of God's revival is a slippery slope that is not for the faint of heart. I praise God that Perry was willing to say, "Yes" when that day came in July 1995. Because he was obedient, my children and I and literally countless others were touched by God and will never be the same again.

Laney Beard – born in rural Florida in a strong family of faith, Laney grew up in the middle of a sister and three brothers. She has had many different and powerful experiences within the Body of Christ that have given her unique knowledge of how churches fulfill their 'call' with Christ's Church. When I began to pray for an 'accountability sister', I pictured us sitting at a table with a tea pot between us and our Bibles open. I knew that our time together would be uplifting and joyous! God sent me a 'sister' that would hold my feet to the fire because <u>He</u> desired that I <u>grow up</u> and leave behind my selfish desires and ambitions. He sent Laney to me who looks at me with love and compassion and tells me the truth, straight from the Father's heart. I praise God for all the tears and laughter that we have shared and look forward to what God is going to do next in our lives.

Janet Butler – a wife and mother of two beautiful grown daughters, Janet is *passionate* about her relationship with Jesus. We met while attending the same church and watched our children change from rebellious to reverent when God touched their lives during the 1995 'Pensacola Outpouring'. Those of us who know her know that Janet is wonderfully gifted by God in the area of prayer. She has been given a tender, compassionate heart especially toward the children of God who are hurt and/or lost. Janet would tell you that she certainly is just an "ordinary" woman used by her "extraordinary" God.

December 1

Dear friend who loves God: Several biographies of Christ have already been written using as their source material the reports circulating among us from the early disciples and other eyewitnesses. However, it occurred to me that it would be well to recheck all these accounts from first to last and after thorough investigation to pass this summary on to you, to reassure you of the truth of all you were taught. My story beings with a Jewish priest, Zechariah...Zechariah and Elizabeth were godly folk, careful to obey all of God's laws in spirit as well as in letter. But they had no children, for Elizabeth was barren; and now they were both very old.   *Luke 1:1-7 (TLB)*

I'm trying to decide if I feel encouraged by these opening words from Luke or not. Being a physician, a scientist, I'm sure Luke DID investigate the events he recorded. So Zechariah and Elizabeth were upright and blameless in God's sight and yet they had not received what I am sure was their heart's desire – a child.

Many times in my own life, I have asked from the Lord and hear NOTHING in response. "Lord, are You listening?" With time, He answers. Some questions I am still waiting for His answer but I have heard and I do testify with the psalmist that –

This poor man called, and the LORD heard him; he saved him out of all his troubles. Taste and see that the LORD is good; blessed is the man who takes refuge in him.   *Psalm 34:6, 8 (TLB)*

Let's continue on with what Luke says about Zechariah and Elizabeth:

Zechariah was in the sanctuary when suddenly an angel appears, standing to the right of the altar of incense! Zechariah was startled and terrified. But the angel said, "Don't be afraid, Zechariah! For I have come to tell you that God has heard your prayer, and your wife Elizabeth will bear you a son! And you are to name him John... He will be a man of rugged spirit and power like Elijah, the prophet of old; and he will precede the coming of the Messiah, preparing the people for his arrival He will soften adult hearts to become like little children's, and will change disobedient minds to the wisdom of faith."

Luke 1:11-13, 17 (TLB)

And so their prayer WAS answered – more than they could have asked or imagined. THEIR son was to be the Elijah that would come before the Messiah – preparing the way. WOW!

The Lord DOES answer. He does HONOR His upright and blameless servants. It takes faith and trust. And faith and trust grows in me as I read and absorbed the story of Elizabeth and Zechariah as well as stories of people I know today who have asked and waited with faith and trust in the Lord – and He answers – more than they could ask or imagine. I wait in faith and trust and God answers – more than I could ask or imagine. Praise the Lord!

Additional Text: 2 Kings 4, Daniel 9

December 2

I can do all things through him who strengthens me.   Philippians 3:14 (ESV)

I've always thought that the gospel writer and physician, Luke, sat down with Mary and 'interviewed' her about the events of the birth of Jesus. His gospel is such a true and beautiful picture of this time.

This 15-year-old girl, named Mary, was a girl who had an obedient and humble heart – just what God was looking for in the mother of His Son. She was also a practical girl as she asks the angel how she is going to have a baby since she was a virgin.

And the angel answered her, "The Holy Spirit will come upon you, and the power of the Most High will overshadow you; therefore the child to be born will be called holy – the Son of God.   Luke 1:35 (ESV)

When God calls me to do a task for Him, do I put Him off because I don't see how it can be done? Why do I think God will have a problem supplying the money for a mission trip or tuition for school? Would the One who made the heavens and earth and everything between be stumped in finding a way for me to attend a Bible study EVERY Monday night? Or maybe God could locate Moses to lead His people to the Promised Land but surely He can't find a life mate for me without my going 'hunting' on my own!

So when they had come together, they asked him, "Lord, will you at this time restore the kingdom to Israel?" He said to them, "It is not for you to know times or seasons that the Father has fixed by his own authority. But you will receive power when the Holy Spirit has come upon you, and you will be my witnesses in Jerusalem and in all Judea and Samaria, and to the end of the earth." And when he had said these things, as they were looking on, he was lifted up, and a cloud took him out of their sight.   Acts 1:6-9 (ESV)

Jesus promised me the Holy Spirit and the power that would come with Him. The Holy Spirit reveals to me the very thoughts of God

But, as it is written, "What no eye has seen, nor ear heard, nor the heart of man imagined, what God has prepared for those who love him" – these things God has revealed to us through the Spirit. For the Spirit searches everything, even the depths of God. For who knows a person's thoughts except the spirit of that person, which is in him? So also no one comprehends the thoughts of God except the Spirit of God. Now we have received not the spirit of the world, but the Spirit who is from God, that we might understand the things freely given us by God. And we impart this in words not taught by human wisdom but taught by the Spirit, interpreting spiritual truths to those who are spiritual. The natural person does not accept the things of the Spirit of God, for they are folly to him, and he is not able to understand them because they are spiritually discerned.
1 Corinthians 2:9-14 (ESV)

God gave me Scripture. He gave me a mind to reason things out. He has given me history to teach me how things went with those before me. But He didn't stop there. He desired that He and I have a <u>personal</u> experience together. That HIS Holy Spirit touches my spirit and the experience would be eternal.

Additional Text: 1 Thessalonians 1, Hebrews 2

December 3

Mary responded, "Oh, how I praise the Lord. How I rejoice in God my Savior! For he took notice of his lowly servant girl, and now generation after generation forever shall call me blest of God. For he, the mighty Hoy One, has done great things to me. his mercy goes on from generation to generation, to all who reverence him. How powerful is his mighty arm! How he scatters the proud and haughty ones! He has torn princes from their thrones and exalted the lowly. He has satisfied the hungry hearts and sent the rich away with empty hands. And how he has helped his servant Israel! He has not forgotten his promise to be merciful. For he promised our fathers – Abraham and his children – to be merciful to them forever." Luke 1:46-55 (TLB)

What an example of humility and obedience! For those of us who stand with Joyce Meyers and Liz Curtis Higgs and say "Well, this isn't me on a good day!" – we can still take home some of Mary's heartfelt words as our own.

Mary says that she can only glorify God in her spirit – He is too marvelous for mere words. He knows she is unworthy and yet takes her to use her to answer the cry of generations for a Messiah. BUT she knows it is ALL <u>GOD</u> and that personal pride has no place here and in fact is to be severely punished. God will raise the humble and give His nourishment to those who are hungry for it. She ends with an affirmation that God has honored His generational covenants. She grabs on, I think, to this testimony of faith that will hold her up in the days ahead.

Mary knew how she would be harassed and shamed because she was a woman who was pregnant before she was married -- IF Joseph didn't desert her! There would always be whispers about the timing of Jesus' birth.

Later, there were whispers about her fanatic son, Jesus, AND his fanatic cousin, John. They did things that could get them all thrown out of the synagogue, which was the social "kiss of death" and would affect their entire lives.

Yes, Mary was the perfect example of humility and obedience but she was also a <u>real</u> woman with questions and needs that she laid before the Lord and received His blessings in return.

About a month ago, I began to lay everything down before the Lord each night. As I lay down in my bed and with the light turned off, I mentally review the day. Each event, each conversation, each emotion – I lay it down and ask God to forgive me, bless someone I bumped in to, or sift through the feelings that a particular event brings and put the light of HIS truth on it. I am sleeping better! In the morning, I wake up and say, "OK, Lord, what do you want me to do today?" Yes, I have appointments and responsibilities – but God knows better than I do what is important and should receive priority. Beginning the day with prayer and submission to God's schedule is a lesson from Mary's life that even I can do!

Additional Text: 1 Kings 3, Titus 3

December 4

In the beginning was the Word, and the Word was with God, and the Word was God. He was with God in the beginning. Through him all things were made; without him nothing was made that has been made. John 1:1-3

How good and pleasant it is when brothers live together in unity! Psalm 133:1

When God speaks about unity, He knows what He is talking about! He has been 'One' since ... FOREVER! Over and over in Scripture, God tells me that I must always move towards unity within the Body of Believers. The whole denomination or non-denomination 'thing' is not HIS 'thing'!!!

I saw a sign outside a local Unitarian Universalist church prior to Easter that said, "Resurrection for all!" Now I do not personally believe that the Bible, God's Word, supports the idea that everyone will die and live in heaven with Jesus. So, no, I do not believe in a 'resurrection for all'. But my disagreement is not with the person who has embraced this belief. The 'battle' is with the enemy who has deceived the person into a fear that they cannot be 'good enough' or 'better than' someone else and so there is a decision to believe everyone will be saved from hell by a benevolent God who will not judge ANYONE! By keeping the focus on the true enemy, I can work with and communicate with any number of people and yet still not compromise the truth that God has spoken to me. I don't have to force a giving in or compromise; I can let the Holy Spirit do His job WITHOUT interfering!

"A new command I give you: Love one another. As I have loved you, so you must love one another. By this all men will know that you are my disciples, if you love one another." John 13:34-35

Doesn't get much clearer than this! Unbelievers will know me as a disciple of Jesus if I love others as He did. It will not be great worship or great miracles that will bring people into the Kingdom; it will be my love for others.

"He who hates me hates my Father as well. If I had not done among them what no one else did, they would not be guilty of sin. But now they have seen these miracles, and yet they have hated both me and my Father." John 15:23-24

Unity also comes with the cloak of humility wrapped around it. God resists those who are proud but pours out His grace on the humble (James 4:6).

Be completely humble and gentle; be patient, bearing with one another in love. Make every effort to keep the unity of the Spirit through the bond of peace. Ephesians 4:2-3

Paul tells me to "Make every effort to keep the unity of the Spirit". I always told my children that they should not EVER start a fight, but if they could finish it. They should always look for alternatives and really seek God's command about whether this was a 'fight' for them. If God was telling them to take a stand, they should be obedient and take the stand to finish the battle.

God's Words, including Jesus' example, and the Holy Spirit guide me in all things, on all days.

However, as it is written: "No eye has seen, no ear has heard, no mind has conceived what God has prepared for those who love him" ... 1 Corinthians 2:9

Let us focus on how we can come together to build the Kingdom God!

December 5

When God began creating the heavens and the earth, the earth was at first a shapeless, chaotic mass, with the Spirit of God brooding over the dark vapors. Then God said, "Let there be light." And light appeared. And God was pleased with it, and divided the light from the darkness. So he let it shine for a while, and then there was darkness again. He called the light "daytime," and the darkness "nighttime." Together they formed the first day. Genesis 1:1-5 (TLB)

I was one of those little kids who asked a lot of questions. I remember waking up one night frightened from a dream when I was in pre-school. I was crying and Mom was holding me. I was sobbing, "Why did God make it dark?"

As I've gotten older, I have sometimes still wondered about that question. God made darkness before Adam and Eve fell into sin so I know it wasn't about that. It's easy for me to think that darkness is 'bad' because I have been a nurse and a mother and I know how sickness seems to get worse in the middle of the night and 'help' seems much farther away! When I have gone through difficulties in my life, I feel more alone when I am awake at 3 a.m. than at 3 p.m.

[David said,] *"O Lord, you are my light! You make my darkness bright. By your power I can crush an army; by your strength I leap over a wall."*
2 Samuel 22:29-30 (TLB)

Maybe that is one of the reasons for the night. When situations seem desperate, God is the One who can and will rescue me. It is God that I can turn to like a child who calls for their mother in the darkness of night.

For though once your heart was full of darkness, now it is full of light from the Lord, and your behavior should show it! Because of this light within you, you should do only what is good and right and true. Ephesians 5:8-9 (TLB)

Another reason for darkness is that when I get off track in my walk with the Lord it does feel like that I am stumbling around in a dark unfamiliar room, banging my shins and anticipating that something REALLY BAD is going to jump out and grab me! I want to move towards the light that is coming through the crack in the door. I want to move back towards what I know is Truth. I want to move towards the Light of Christ.

So be careful how you act, these are difficult days. Don't be fools; be wise: make the most of every opportunity you have for doing good. Don't act thoughtlessly, but try to find out and do whatever the Lord wants you to. Don't drink too much wine, for many evils lie along that path; be filled instead with the Holy Spirit, and controlled by him. Ephesians 5:15-18 (TLB)

Live as a child of the Light of God where darkness has no power or appeal. Because of God's great mercy, I AM a child of His Light!

Additional Text: Proverbs 28, Ephesians 6

December 6

This Scripture is part of Jesus' conversation with the Jews who had believed in Him. Jesus is telling them that if they believe and act on His teaching that the truth of the teaching will set them free. They are insulted that Jesus is declaring that they are sinners in need of saving. They felt that because they were descendants of Abraham they did not need Jesus to make them 'right with God'. They did not want to <u>hear</u> the Truth.

Jesus answered: If God were your Father, you would love me, because I came from God and only from him. He sent me. I did not come on my own. Why can't you understand what I am talking about? Can't you <u>stand to hear</u> what I am saying? Your father is the devil, and you do exactly what he wants. He has always been a murderer and a liar. There is nothing truthful about him. He speaks on his own, and everything he says is a lie. Not only is he a liar himself, but he is also the father of all lies. Everything I have told you is true, and you still refuse to have faith in me. Can any of you accuse me of sin? If you cannot, why won't you have faith in me? After all, I am telling you the truth. Anyone who belongs to God will listen to his message. But you refuse to listen, because you don't belong to God."   *John 8:42-47 (CEV, emphasis mine)*

I believe that Jesus is my Lord and Savior. He died for my sins, past and present. I am a Child of God. But sometimes I don't want to hear what God has to say. I admit that sometimes it has even been a conscious choice. He was telling me, disciplining me, and like a stereotypical teenager, I slammed the door on my mind and refused to listen! I can now recall vividly the consequences of that choice. It isn't pretty! I felt so ALONE and ISOLATED. The comfort and peace of God's presence was GONE! I had stepped away from Him! AAAGH!

I believe that as we continue to move toward the 'End Times' that the *hearing* of God's voice both audibly and through His Word will become more and more apparent. We will find ourselves 'aglow' with the revelation of God speaking to us, individually and corporately. We will stand in silence in our worship without being conscious of the passage of time just so we can *hear*! We will find ourselves so *HUNGRY* and we don't want to miss the fresh bread that God will give us!

Yet not everyone has believed the message. For example, the prophet Isaiah asked, "Lord, has anyone believed what we said?"

No one can have faith without hearing the message about Christ.
                                                        Romans 10:16-17 (CEV)

Lord, give me ears to hear and a heart to receive You.

Additional Text: Isaiah 53, Romans 11

December 7

As the deer pants for flowing streams, so pants my soul for you, O God. My soul thirsts for God, for the living God. When shall I come and appear before God? My tears have been my food day and night, while they say to me continually, "Where is your God?" These things I remember, as I pour out my soul: how I would go with the throng and lead them in procession to the house of God with glad shouts and songs of praise, a multitude keeping festival. Why are you cast down, O my soul, and why are you in turmoil within me? Hope in God for I shall again praise him, my salvation and my God.   *Psalm 42:1-5 (ESV)*

The 'why' of things comes up fairly often in this world. Why am I sick? Why has my job been 'cut'? Why didn't I get the promotion? Why do my husband and I seem to have this discussion/fight over and over? Why do these 'bad things' happen to me or those I love?

The psalmist starts out proclaiming how much he loves God. He has an intimate relationship with Him. He's a 'Believer' in a LIVING, personal God.

Then he tells me that he is going through some 'bad thing' that has reduced him to many tears and has his 'buddies' asking, "Where is your God that you've been telling us about?"

He remembers the worship that he has experienced with the Church, the Body. He remembers how awesome and extra-ordinary it was. Which brings him to the question of why he is feeling 'down' when maybe he thought that the awesome worship and intimate relationship would keep all the 'bad things' away! He asks the 'why' questions -- and then succinctly answers: Put your hope in God and praise Him anyway! He states that God is SAVIOR and GOD! The only answer to the 'why' is continuing to place my trust in God and hope. Experience and history of my relationship tells me God will come through. Scripture, like this psalm, confirms that, too. There are many of us that can testify that our faith and hope in God came with many 'discussions' with God, even a 'wrestling match' or two like Jacob had. When days or nights or weeks are difficult, there is nothing else for me to do – except push in closer to God until the answer, the peace comes.

Hope in the LORD in the 'bad things' and praise Him for what He is going to do!

Those who sow in tears shall reap with shouts of joy! He who goes out weeping, bearing the seed for sowing, shall come home with shouts of joy, bringing his sheaves with him.   *Psalm 126:5-6 (ESV)*

Additional Text: Esther 4, Isaiah 40

December 8

"Therefore, say to the Israelites: 'I am the LORD, and I will bring you out from under the yoke of the Egyptians. I will free you from being slaves to them, and I will redeem you with an outstretched arm and with mighty acts of judgment. I will take you as my own people, and I will be your God. Then you will know that I am the LORD your God, who brought you out from under the yoke of the Egyptians. And I will bring you to the land I swore with uplifted hand to give to Abraham, to Isaac and to Jacob. I will give it to you as a possession. I am the LORD.' "

Moses reported this to the Israelites, but they did not listen to him because of their discouragement and cruel bondage. Exodus 6:6-9

God speaks to the Israelites through Moses but they don't listen. God tells the people that He will set them free from the tyranny of the Egyptians, the #1 thing they probably want in their lives, and they don't listen. God says that He is taking them as <u>HIS</u> people and will bring them into the beautiful land that He promised to their leaders for generations and they don't listen. THAT preaches to me 3,300 years later!

God comes to me <u>every day</u> and tells me He loves me. If there is a 'worry' in my life, He wants to handle it for me. And I don't listen. If there is a sickness in my life, He wants to make it better. And I don't listen. Even when I DID NOT KNOW HIM, He wanted to know <u>ME</u>. And I didn't listen for over 40 years. Hey, the Israelites don't have anything on me!

But do not forget this one thing, dear friends: With the Lord a day is like a thousand years, and a thousand years are like a day. The Lord is not slow in keeping his promise, as some understand slowness. <u>He is patient with you</u>, not wanting anyone to perish but everyone to come to repentance. 2 Peter 3:8-9

God is <u>patient</u> with me. Ya' think?!! But there is also a 'time' coming that will not be held back for my stubbornness. Now is the time for me to <u>let go</u> of MY way and <u>LISTEN</u> to God. Hear His voice. Follow and ACCEPT His love.

But the day of the Lord will come like a thief. The heavens will disappear with a roar; the elements will be destroyed by fire, and the earth and everything in it will be laid bare.

Since everything will be destroyed in this way, what kind of people ought you to be? You ought to live holy and godly lives as you look forward to the day of God and speed its coming. That day will bring about the destruction of the heavens by fire, and the elements will melt in the heat. But in keeping with his promise we are looking forward to a new heaven and a new earth, the home of righteousness.

So then, dear friends, since you are looking forward to this, make every effort to be found spotless, blameless and at peace with him. Bear in mind that our Lord's patience means salvation, just as our dear brother Paul also wrote you with the wisdom that God gave him. 2 Peter 3:10-15

The time is now. No more excuses for keeping the un-Godly ways in my life. "Speak, Lord, your servant is listening."

Additional Text: Isaiah 46, Romans 2

December 9

Early the next morning Joshua and all the Israelites left Acacia. They traveled to the Jordan River and camped there before crossing it. After three days the officers went through the camp and gave orders to the people: "When you see the priest and Levites carrying the Ark of the Agreement with the LORD your God, leave where you are and follow it. That way you will know which way to go since you have never been here before. Joshua 3:1-4 (NCV)

Here are thousands of people who have been traveling 40 years and they come to the river that is the doorway to where they want to be. The doorway to the PROMISE that God has given them. The end of a long journey is there. They can see it. And they camp THREE MORE DAYS. Why? What did they DO for three days? Were they waiting on some 'natural' phenomena like the high river to recede? Were they praying and readying themselves spiritually? I don't know but they didn't move until the ARK -- or God -- went before them and said, "COME! NOW!"

Some of us may be more likely to 'tarry' and even wait too long. Some, like me, may jump ahead and strain at the 'bit' in my mouth. Either is out of step with God. God has brought me through some discipline that has now placed my heart where He wants it -- DESIRING to be in step with Him more than myself! Now I must continue to grow in His ways so that my eyes and ears are ready to receive His timing and move accordingly. God is gracious to continue to teach me.

The LORD said, "How terrible it will be for these stubborn children. They make plans, but they don't ask me to help them. They make agreements with other nations, without asking my Spirit. They are adding more and more sins to themselves." ...

The LORD wants to show his mercy to you. He wants to rise and comfort you. The LORD is a fair God, and everyone who waits for his help will be happy. Isaiah 30:1, 18 (NCV)

When I move in HIS time, there are promises He gives. I can count on that I will be WITH HIM all the way, no matter that the way may have its difficulties. Going in God's timing does NOT promise me smooth sailing.

When you pass through the waters, I will be with you. When you cross rivers, you will not drown. When you walk through fire, you will not be burned, nor will the flames hurt you. This is because I, the LORD, am your God, the Holy One of Israel, your Savior..." Isaiah 43:2-3 (NCV)

It is a 'safe sanctuary' that God creates around me that assures me that He is still on the throne and NOTHING takes Him by surprise. He is with me every step of the way. He even sent Jesus, God in the flesh, to walk the same roads with the same temptations to show me the 'how' of my walk through this life. Each day is an opportunity for me to spend time with God and prepare for the journey, the plan He has for me. How much time do I give each day for the most important research I will ever do?

Additional Text: Isaiah 30, Mark 8

December 10

Jesus also spoke of friends. He gave us the command for unconditional love.

"Now I tell you to love each other, as I have loved you. The greatest way to show love for friends is to die for them. And you are my friends, if you obey me." *John 15:12-14 (CEV)*

This passage could be used to describe the Body of Christ, the Church, but it certainly shows us true friendship. There is a trust that must be there with a friend that assures me that I do not have to 'watch my own back' because my friend is already there! She is sensitive to my interests and more often than not, has already prayed for me before I even request it! The Holy Spirit KNEW who to wake up and say, "PRAY FOR JODY!"

Paul said, *Christ encourages you, and his love comforts you. God's Spirit unites you, and you are concerned for others. Now make me completely happy! Live in harmony by showing love for each other. Be united in what you think, as if you were only one person. Don't be jealous or proud, but be humble and consider others more important than yourselves. Care about them as much as you care about yourselves.* *Philippians 2:1-4 (CEV)*

This passage could be used to describe the Body of Christ, the Church, but it certainly shows us true friendship. There is a trust that must be there with a friend that assures me that I do not have to 'watch my own back' because my friend is already there! She is sensitive to my interests and more often than not, has already prayed for me before I even request it! The Holy Spirit KNEW who to wake up and say, "PRAY FOR JODY!"

You people aren't faithful to God! Don't you know that if you love the world, you are God's enemies? And if you decide to be a friend of the world, you make yourself an enemy of God. *James 4:4 (CEV)*

Here again is that hard 'Word' that my friends <u>must</u> be God-chosen. Even as I write this …I remember friends that continue to be of the world and reject God. Tears come to my eyes as I pray for them, asking God to continue to extend to them the mercy that He has shown me. I want eternity for these friends and family that are lost now. I want Jesus for them! God is gracious and good. He desires … even more than I do … that ALL come to the saving knowledge of Him (1 Timothy 2). It is because of this truth that I can allow God to choose my friends and be obedient to His choices. His way is perfect and He has proven that to me over and over. It is a Rock I stand on.

Do I have friends who do not know or do not accept Jesus as Savior and Lord? Sure. But they aren't my close friends. They aren't the ones that I turn to first. That was a difficult lesson for me to wrestle. Jesus had twelve disciples. Did He take all of them everywhere? No. Only Peter, James, and John were present when He raised the little girl from the dead. They were the only ones to actually <u>see</u> their transfigured Lord. And they were the ones next to Him in the Garden.

Who are the God-chosen friends in my life? They are certainly a 'pearl of great price' and I stop now to lift them in prayer.

Additional Text: Exodus 24, Nehemiah 1

December 11

For while we were still weak, at the right time Christ died for the ungodly. For one will scarcely die for a righteous person – though perhaps for a good person one would dare even to die – but God shows his love for us in that while we were still sinners, Christ died for us. Romans 5:6-8 (ESV)

In this the love of God was made manifest among us, that God sent his only Son into the world, so that we might live through him. In this is love, not that we have loved God but that he loved us and sent his Son to be the propitiation for our sins. Beloved, if God so loved us, we also ought to love one another. No one has ever seen God; if we love one another, God abides in us and his love is perfected in us. 1 John 4:9-12 (ESV)

God loves me. Most days I can't even begin to understand what that means. On the days that I do think about how Jesus died for me and how He walks with me, I can't help but tear up and weep at the all-consuming love that I feel.

"Amazing love, how can it be? That Thou, my God, would die for me!"

God's love ... that thing called 'grace' or unconditional love ... is so indescribable and yet once I felt it, I knew what it was! The Bible provides me with a wonderful source to 'study' what God's love is truly all about.

A few years ago, Max Lucado wrote a book that to me is SO RIGHT ON target about God's love. The book is called *In the Grip of Grace.* Max points out that God came to earth and walked roads and ate food and became sweaty under the Middle East sun so that He could show me that He understands and He cares. On the cross, with blood and unspeakable pain, Jesus showed me that His love for me would last for eternity. He was the ONLY ONE who could be the sacrifice that would allow me to have an eternal life with God Himself.

I'm all for reading thought provoking, challenging study guides that encourage me to mature in my walk with God. I also need words of encouragement and that 'rain of blessings' that refresh me and also produce growth in my intimacy with my Heavenly Father who loves me with an everlasting love. This book does that well.

Beloved, I pray that all may go well with you and that you may be in good health, as it goes well with your soul. 3 John 2 (ESV)

Additional Text: 1 John 4, 3 John 2

December 12

"I will ask the Father and he will give you another Comforter, and he will never leave you. He is the Holy Spirit, the Spirit who leads into all truth. The world at large cannot receive him, for it isn't looking for him and doesn't recognize him, But you do, for he lives with you now and some day shall be in you.
John 14:16-17 (TLB)

Have you ever watched the evening news or walked down the hall of a hospital after your son's surgery and asked the question, "Where is God in all of this?" I have. As much as I may be looking for a different kind of answer, here is Jesus' answer to my question in John 14. I have often thought that John 14-17 were VERY IMPORTANT chapters (maybe even deserving heavier emphasis than that!) because these are the words recorded just prior to His death. These are the subjects, the 'points', the lessons that Jesus was delivering, in some cases reviewing, with the twelve men that had the responsibility to continuing Jesus' ministry. There was no Plan B and I believe that Jesus understood how vital it was that He conveys the essential lessons. Here is an essential lesson: God dwells in me. When I look around for God in fear or panic – I need to look no further than inside myself.

"Can a mother forget her little child and not have love for her own son? Yet even if that should be, I will not forget you. See, I have tattooed your name upon my palm and ever before me is a picture of Jerusalem's walls in ruins.
Isaiah 49:15-16 (TLB)

From Old Testament to New, God assures me that He is right HERE. He doesn't forget me or 'miss' my birthday or even a day that might be special only to me, like when I see the azaleas bloom for the first time each year! He is aware when someone disappointments me. He sees the hurt. He sees the nonchalant shrug. He's ready to heal when I ask.

I love the Lord because he hears my prayers and answers them. Because he bends down and listens, I will pray as long as I breathe!...

His loved ones are very precious to him and he does not lightly let them die. O Lord, you have freed me from my bonds and I will serve you forever. I will worship you and offer you a sacrifice of thanksgiving. Here in the courts of the Temple in Jerusalem, before all the people, I will pay everything I vowed to the Lord. Praise the Lord.
Psalm 116:1-2, 15-19 (TLB)

Through my life, including my death, God is there. It's a promise and it's a fact that has already been proven through the lives of those who have gone before me. God is real. God is here.

Additional Text: 1 Chronicles 16, Psalm 116

Now the Philistines attacked Israel, forcing the Israelites to flee. Many were slaughtered on the slopes of Mount Gilboa. The Philistines closed in on Saul and his sons, and they killed three of his sons – Jonathan, Abinadab, and Malkishua.   *1 Samuel 31:1-2 (NLT)*

Then David composed a funeral song for Saul and Jonathan. Later he commanded that it be taught to all the people of Judah. It is known as the Song of the Bow, and it is recorded in The Book of Jashar. "Your pride and joy, O Israel, lies dead on the hills! How the mighty heroes have fallen!... How the mighty heroes have fallen in battle! Jonathan lies dead upon the hills. How I weep for you, my brother Jonathan! Oh, how much I loved you!

2 Samuel 1:17-19, 25-26 (NLT)

I was brought to these passages this morning and recalled how many difficulties that David had in his life. His was not an easy life. I read about David in Hebrews 11 as one of the 'ancients' who was 'commended' for his faith and it's easy for me to think that he had some 'special relationship' with God or was given special insight that allowed him to rise above the difficulties. That is the weakness I have because I have studied the Old Testament with much <u>less</u> time and fervor than the New Testament. David's story begins in 1 Samuel 16 and goes through 1 Kings 2. During this time David endures many personal hardships and losses, builds a kingdom larger than anything up to that time which required many bloody battles, and had sons and wives that plotted and schemed to seize as much power as they could. David made decisions that were <u>not</u> obedient to God's plan. And David did some things that showed he <u>was</u> the man after God's heart.

The men and women of faith that we have been given in the Bible are not <u>perfect</u> saints, just forgiven ones. It is their humility and willingness to seek the Lord's heart and desire in <u>all</u> things in their lives. It is in seeking forgiveness in their disobedience that makes them SAINTS.

Jesus, the Son of God, is shown to me in His humanity with tears (John 11:35) and grief (Matthew 23:37, 26:38) and yes, anger (John 2:13). My human emotions and frailty <u>are</u> part of who God made me to be! It is in these weaknesses that God said He would be STRONG for me. In times of deep emotional wounds when I feel I have been brought to my knees that God is able to put HIS arms out and I can lean on Him and let HIM do ALL the work! It is in those times that I learn the most from God because I have nothing to say! I spend more time LISTENING!

As you endure this divine discipline, remember that God is treating you as his own children. Whoever heard of a child who was never disciplined?... No discipline is enjoyable while it is happening – it is painful! But afterward there will be a <u>quiet harvest</u> of <u>right living</u> for those who are trained in this way.

Hebrews 12:7, 11 (NLT, emphasis mine)

Hardships will bring a HARVEST (a plenty) of peace and a more intimate, 'right living' with my Lord and Savior. That is a hope and a place of encouragement for me.

December 14

Discouragement is one of the key tools of the enemy to get me to give up! Peter knew about being discouraged, until a carpenter came along and talked him into trying ... one more time.

Stepping into one of the boats, Jesus asked Simon, its owner, to push it out into the water...When he had finished speaking, he said to Simon, "Now go out where it is deeper and let down your nets, and you will catch many fish."

"Master," Simon replied, "we worked hard all last night and didn't catch a thing. But if you say so, we'll try again." And this time their nets were so full they began to tear! Luke 5: 3-6 (NLT)

Peter must have been bone-tired that morning. They had been out since dusk trying to make a living and provide for their families. I imagine SOMEONE was catching fish that night, but it wasn't them! Discouragement. Jesus came along and taught Peter about starting over. Giving it a try...one more time. Peter <u>forgot</u> the lesson, too.

About an hour later someone else insisted, "This must be one of Jesus' disciples because he is a Galilean, too." But Peter said, "Man, I don't know what you are talking about." And as soon as he said these words, the rooster crowed. At that moment the Lord turned and looked at Peter. Then Peter remembered that the Lord had said,"Before the rooster crows tomorrow morning, you will deny me three times." And Peter left the courtyard, crying bitterly. Luke 22: 59-62

As he was weeping, maybe <u>then</u> Peter remembered that morning on the shore in Galilee when Jesus taught him about overcoming discouragement. But...what he had done this time, well, that was just too big to overcome! Right?

Simon Peter said, "I'm going fishing."

"We'll come, too," they all said. So they went out in the boat, but they caught nothing all night. At dawn the disciples saw Jesus standing on the beach, but they couldn't see who he was...Then he said, "Throw out your net on the right-hand side of the boat, and you'll get plenty of fish!" So they did, and they couldn't draw in the net because there were so many fish in it.

John 21:3-4, 6 (NLT)

Do you think Peter had a moment of déjà vu? I think that when he felt the pull of all those fish on the net Peter had a flash of knowledge that God had just RE-created a miracle. He had done it – AGAIN! This time the lesson stuck with Peter and he went out and shared that knowledge again, and again, and AGAIN!!!

Be strong and courageous! Do not be afraid of them! The LORD your God will go ahead of you. He will neither fail you nor forsake you."

Deuteronomy 31:6 (NLT)

Additional Text: Deuteronomy 31, John 21

First, I tell you to pray for all people, asking God for what they need and being thankful to him. Pray for rulers and for all who have authority so that we can have quiet and peaceful lives full of worship and respect for God. This is good, and it pleases God our Savior, who wants all people to be saved and to know the truth. 1 Timothy 2:1-4 (NCV)

April 15<u>th</u> is probably the day when more complaining and whining occurs than any other day in the United States. Some may have their day earlier in the year if they file their taxes sooner. Others may experience this phenomenon more often if they file taxes quarterly and/or read their accountant's report. Most of us in America enjoy our freedom and prosperity but we hate paying the price! We are quick to find fault with 'the system' or 'the President' or 'Congress'.

Paul and Timothy lived in a time where whining and complaining against the government could get you imprisoned, even killed. It is unfortunate that there are still places where that is true today. Paul suggests prayers of thanksgiving and petitions for change be given to <u>God</u> who is able to bring about the changes that produce that righteousness (right relationship) which in turns brings holiness and godliness to the land.

I don't know the spiritual state of my local or national figures. I cannot make that determination even by what they claim. No matter who they are or what they claim, God says I should pray for them. I should pray for them whether I like their policies or not. I should ask God to bless them with His presence and wisdom and mercy whether I like them or not!

[The Pharisees said,] *"So tell us what you think. Is it right to pay taxes to Caesar or not?" But knowing that these leaders were trying to trick him, Jesus said, "You hypocrites! Why are you trying to trap me? Show me a coin used for paying the tax." So the men showed him a coin. Then Jesus asked, "Whose image and name are on the coin?" The men answered, "Caesars." Then Jesus said to them, "Give to Caesar the things that are Caesar's, and give to God the things that are God's." When they heard what Jesus said, they were amazed and left him and went away.* Matthew 22:17-22 (NCV)

When God blessed me with provision to care for my family, did I think He didn't realize that there was an 'income tax' involved? Is God's hand so short that He is not going to provide for me in <u>every</u> way?

In another passage in Matthew 17, Peter comes to Jesus when the collectors come to him to get the Temple Tax. Peter, I suspect, is hoping that Jesus will give them a good Scripture that will say that because they are doing 'ministry for the Lord' they are not subject to pay. Let's be clear here. The passage is talking about the tax that was required by the <u>temple</u> for its upkeep. That being said, Jesus infers that He doesn't approve of the way the tax is levied but He also does <u>not</u> sanction disobedience. God provides the way to pay it.

I want to pray for the leadership in my city, my county, my state, and my country each day that God will guide and direct them in <u>His</u> ways. Most of all that we continue to have FREEDOM of faith so that <u>all</u> will have the opportunity to know Him and come to the knowledge of His truth.

December 16

Now Daniel so distinguished himself among the administrators and the satraps by his exceptional qualities that the king planned to set him over the whole kingdom. At this, the administrators and the satraps tried to find grounds for charges against Daniel in his conduct of government affairs, but they were unable to do so. They could find no corruption in him, because he was trustworthy and neither corrupt nor negligent. Finally these men said, "We will never find any basis for charges against this man Daniel unless it has something to do with the law of his God."   *Daniel 6:3-5*

This is the 'set-up' scene for the well-known story of Daniel in the lion's den. Although King Darius soon realized that he was being manipulated and did NOT want Daniel killed, he followed the law but as Daniel was thrown to the lions King Darius said, *"May your God, whom you serve continually, rescue you!" (6:16)*

Live such good lives among the pagans that, though they accuse you of doing wrong, they may see your good deeds and glorify God on the day he visits us.
                                                                1 Peter 2:12

These two verses of Scripture written hundreds of years apart are so powerful to me! I am exhorted to <u>just</u> LIVE my life without fanfare or fire and brimstone arguments to defend my God. So that people, who do not even <u>believe</u>, will glorify God who <u>I believe</u>!!! Too often I feel I must rush to defend God when in fact, God does not need <u>my</u> defense arguments. God gave my life to me and when I choose Him, declare that it is <u>He</u> that I love and will obey and accept as Savior and Lord, then living my life by <u>His</u> principles is all that I have to do. Easy? Not hardly but it is simple.

So ever since we first heard about you we have kept on praying and asking God to help you understand what he wants you to do; asking him to make you wise about spiritual things; and asking that the way you live will always please the Lord and honor him, so that you will always be doing good, kind things for others, while all the time you are learning to know God better and better.

We are praying, too, that you will be filled with his mighty, glorious strength so that you can keep going no matter what happens – always full of the joy of the Lord, and always thankful to the Father who has made us fit to share all the wonderful things that belong to those who live in the kingdom of light. For he has rescued us out of the darkness and gloom of Satan's kingdom and brought us into the kingdom of his dear Son, who bought our freedom with his blood and forgave us all our sins.   *Colossians 1:9-14 (TLB)*

God gave me so much and all He asks is that I live my life to please Him and serve Him. Others may seem to attack me but they're not really, they're attacking my <u>leader</u> and HE can handle it! He will also 'handle it' much better than I can strategize! I need to just keep walking forward serving and loving His children.

Set your minds on things above, not on earthly things. For you died, and your life is now hidden with Christ in God.   *Colossians 3:2-3*

Additional Text: Daniel 5 and 6

Beside the rivers of Babylon, we sat and wept as we thought of Jerusalem. We put away our lyres, hanging them on the branches of the willow trees. For there our captors demanded a song of us. Our tormentors requested a joyful hymn: "Sing us one of those songs of Jerusalem!" But how can we sing the songs of the LORD while in a foreign land?

If I forget you, O Jerusalem, let my right hand forget its skill upon the harp. May my tongue stick to the roof of my mouth if I fail to remember you, if I don't make Jerusalem my highest joy.   *Psalm 137: 1-6 (NLT)*

The words of this song bring sadness to my heart. I cannot imagine what it must be like to live all my life with, not just fear, but the knowledge that my town, the marketplace, my home, my children's school could be bombed at any moment. Death and destruction are a part of life. The people of Israel have lived with war since the time of Abraham, Isaac, and Ishmael.

For hundreds of years the descendants of Abraham, Isaac, and Jacob have prayed and fought for a 'Jerusalem' that would be 'home' or the Promised Land. The descendants of Abraham and Ishmael have been just as determined that much of that same land would be their home. Much blood has been shed with both sides secure in the knowledge that GOD is on their side.

I do not have the gift of discernment or prophetic knowledge in this area that reveals the Scripture to me regarding God's plan for His Jewish children. I just know that He wants all of His children with Him and that He loves all of them. I pray for all who reject Jesus as Savior and Lord with the assurance that my desire is minuscule compared to God's love for them!

A few minutes later some Pharisees said to him, "Get out of here if you want to live, because Herod Antipas wants to kill you!" ...

[Jesus said,] "O Jerusalem, Jerusalem, the city that kills the prophets and stones God's messengers! How often I have wanted to gather your children together as a hen protects her chicks beneath her wings, but you wouldn't let me. And now look; your house is left to you empty. And you will never see me again until you say, 'Bless the one who comes in the name of the Lord!"

Luke 13:31, 34-35 (NLT)

Jesus would not be intimidated by church leadership OR the threatening overlord of the area. He wanted His chosen people to turn to Him but Jesus also did not lower the standard – acknowledge Him as the Son of God.

I pray for the descendants of Isaac, the Jewish people, and I pray for the descendants of Ishmael, the Muslims, AND I pray for my people, the Gentiles. ALL are children of God and have an open invitation from The Shepherd. (John 10:1-18)

Additional Text: John 10, 1 Timothy 2

December 18

Someone came to Jesus with this question: "Teacher, what good things must I do to have eternal life?"

"Why ask me about what is good?" Jesus replied. "Only God is good. But to answer your question, you can receive eternal life if you keep the commandments."

"Which ones?" the man asked. And Jesus replied, "'Do not murder. Do not commit adultery. Do not steal. Do not testify falsely. Honor your father and mother. Love you neighbor as yourself.'"

"I've obeyed all these commandments," the young man replied. "What else must I do?"

Jesus told him, "IF you want to be perfect, go and sell all you have and give the money to the poor, and you will have treasure in heaven. Then come, follow me." But when the young man heard this, he went sadly away because he had many possessions.

Matthew 19:16-22 (NLT) also in Mark 10:17-22, Luke 18:18-23

All three of these gospels carry the same story, almost verbatim. There must be something <u>really</u> important for me to learn! Actually I think there are MANY things for me to learn here.

By looking at all three accounts, I see that this was a young RICH man who is also referred to as a 'ruler'. He had accomplished A LOT in his young life. By that days' standard and even by ours, he was SUCCESSFUL. He was what most of us want to be. But he felt that he LACKED something. He recognized that it was ETERNAL LIFE! He was aware that despite ALL that he had accumulated...it was fleeting. It was not going to be there forever.

In Mark's account it says that Jesus 'looked at him and LOVED him'. I believe that when the man turned and walked away 'sad' that no one was more sad than Jesus. I believe His heart broke that the young man refused His gift of eternal life and chose things...instead. Just like I must choose to LET GO of 'things' in my life that leave no room for Jesus. That could be something relatively recognizable like my job or some hobby that has begun to *consume* my 'free' time so that I am out of balance with not only God but also possibly my family. I must LET GO so that Jesus can come in and set my priorities, giving me balance.

Do you have loved ones that so much want 'ETERNAL LIFE' however they define it? Maybe they see it as Jesus and want so much to believe! Maybe they only know that there is an emptiness somewhere inside of them that they cannot seem to fill with 'stuff' that they are able to BRING HOME. There is a sadness and a lack, isn't there?

Sometimes I just weep and weep over those I love who don't know the assurance of Jesus' love. Sometimes I just want to body slam them to the floor and 'stuff it in'! That won't work! Prayer is the best answer I know. I just keep at it like the persistent widow (look that parable up!) and keep lifting those people before the Lord. I KNOW that God wants them even more than I do!

Additional Text: Luke 18, 2 Peter 1

December 19

One month later God sent the angel Gabriel to the town of Nazareth in Galilee with a message for a virgin named Mary. She was engaged to Joseph from the family of King David. The angel greeted Mary and said, "You are truly blessed! The Lord is with you."

Mary was confused by the angel's words and wondered what they meant. Then the angel told Mary, "Don't be afraid! God is pleased with you, and you will have a son. His name will be Jesus. He will be great and will be called the Son of God Most High. The Lord God will make him king, as his ancestor David was. He will rule the people of Israel forever, and his kingdom will never end."

Luke 1:26-33 (CEV)

So Joseph had to leave Nazareth in Galilee and go to Bethlehem in Judea. Long ago Bethlehem had been King David's hometown, and Joseph went there because he was from David's family. Mary was engaged to Joseph and traveled with him to Bethlehem. She was soon going to have a baby, and while they were there, she gave birth to her first-born son. She dressed him in baby clothes and laid him on a bed of hay, because there was no room for them in the inn.

Luke 2:4-7 (CEV)

Many who go to malls are professional shoppers. I have a few of those in my family. My husband is grateful that I am not one of them! I am a people watcher. I am the one you want to take with you if you are a shopper. I will walk around with you for about an hour and then I'll take your packages, find a bench, and be very happy to just watch people or read a book for however long you want to stay.

In watching people, I have seen a lot of pain. I have seen a lot of 'alone-ness' and sadness. So many hurting people who seem to be *desperately* hunting for something to anesthetize the pain or cure what they see as the 'inevitability' of their lives.

We, as Christians, try so hard to attract them into the warmth that we have found in Jesus. We know the pain, many times from first-hand experience, but since we have found the warmth we are reluctant to expose ourselves to the cold again. I mean that we post our service schedules and put our ads in newspapers and phonebooks and then expect someone who is injured and bleeding to find their own way into the place that will heal them! Is that what Jesus did? No!

God did not continue to sit on His soft throne, smiling benevolently and wave His hand like that would attract my attention. He CAME to me and breathed the same air and felt the same pain and experienced sorrow just like me. Then, He died for MY SINS so that I would know the way to the warmth of eternal life.

What excuse do I continue to use to justify my avoiding God's commands to *GO*??!!

Additional Text: Isaiah 7, Mark 1

December 20

I know that you sincerely trust the Lord, for you have the faith of your mother, Eunice, and your grandmother, Lois.   *2 Timothy 1:5 (NLT)*

I think the hardest job in the world is being a 'mom'. I know that my view might be prejudiced since I have that job. Please notice that I said 'mom', not 'mother'. To be a 'mother' or 'father' is a biological term. If you have been given the right set of cells you can accomplish procreation. A 'mom' to me is someone who takes responsibility to teach, nurture, care, and covers it all with that indefinable wrapping called 'love'. The 'love' may be difficult to define but ask any child if they are loved by their mom and they can say "yes" or "no" rather quickly.

Being a 'mom' also covers such things like discipline and boundaries. It may mean making hard choices that forever impact your child and his/her life but the decisions are made with the conviction to do anything else in the situation will mean worse pain and destruction. It's easy to play 'Monday morning quarterback' 10-20 years later but I am convinced that any decision made with love <u>for</u> the <u>child</u> is not a WRONG decision. Hindsight brings wisdom and maybe *better* decisions in the future.

Not very long after I began my job as 'mom' in which I had had NO formal training or practice, I, like many in a new job, began to look for a manual. The shelves in any given bookstore or library is filled with people who believe they have the *FORMULA* to raise a healthy, well-adjusted child. If that were true, these writers would have received the Nobel Peace Prize by now! But there <u>is</u> a book that CAN BE of vital importance. Yes, the Bible.

It has become clear to me, however, that the <u>book</u> is not enough. What brings a child up to love God, obey God, and follow Jesus in everything that he/she does must include – EXAMPLE. It is not enough for me to TEACH my children <u>about</u> God. I must <u>walk</u> <u>out</u> MY life <u>every</u> <u>day</u> in front of my children. If I tell my child one thing and do another then all I have taught them is the definition of a hypocrite. Following Jesus' example both <u>in</u> my house and with everyone I meet: boss, co-workers, relatives, spouse, is how I pass along MY FAITH to my child and KNOW that seeds have been planted.

But when the Holy Spirit controls our lives, he will produce this kind of fruit in us: love, joy, peace, patience, kindness, goodness, faithfulness, gentleness, and self-control. Here there is no conflict with the law.   *Galatians 5:22-23 (NLT)*
Fix your thoughts on what is true and honorable and right. Think about things that are pure and lovely and admirable, excellent and worthy of praise. Keep putting into practice all you learned from me and heard from me and saw me doing, and the God of peace will be with you.   *Philippians 4:8-9 (NLT)*

"Whatever you have learned, received, heard, or seen in me – put into practice. If you do that, God's peace will be with you." Scary stuff! If my children, (remember, biology may have no part in those I know as 'my children') will put into practice what they have learned from me then God's peace will be a part of them. My children must learn not only about my 'victories' but also they must see my 'struggles' when God's peace is really there and making a difference. By God's grace, I <u>am</u> a 'mom'.

December 21

John begins his gospel with these words: *In the beginning was the Word, and the Word was with God, and the Word was God. He was in the beginning with God. All things were made through him, and without him was not any thing made that was made. In him was life, and the life was the light of men. The light shines in the darkness, and the darkness has not overcome it...*

The true light, which enlightens everyone, was coming into the world. He was in the world, and the world was made through him, yet the world did not know him. He came to his own, and his own people did not receive him. But to all who did receive him, who believed in his name, he gave the right to become children of God, who were born, not of blood nor of the will of the flesh, nor of the will of man, but of God. And the Word became flesh and dwelt among us, and we have seen his glory, glory as of the only Son from the Father, full of grace and truth.

John 1:1-5, 9-14 (ESV)

God has always been three in one – the Trinity – Father, Son, and Holy Spirit. Genesis 1:26 says:

Then God said, "Let us make man in our image, after our likeness..."

Genesis 1:26 (ESV)

God, all-powerful, all-knowing, creator of all that is and will be came to earth as God IN THE FLESH! It brings me back to the question: <u>WHY</u> did God make me?

Did He need the company? I mean, was He bored? Am I just an experimentation in molecules? Did He wonder what would happen if He put a soul into this creation and make it above the other animals? Did He make me so that there would be someone to worship Him?

I do not believe that any of these questions, or the hundreds of others that may come to mind, hold up against what we know about God. All of these questions give God human traits that would imply frailty or lack on His part. GOD doesn't lack anything! GOD isn't fragile!

The answer to the question: Why did God make me is simple and yet deflating: HE LOVES ME!

From OT to NT, prophets and apostles testify that God loves me with a love that defies words and description. I am told over and over that God cares for me. He protects me. He loves me. Jesus Himself gave me the most often quoted Scripture, telling me why God would make me – and make me with the intention that we would be together FOREVER!

[Jesus said,] *"For God so loved the world, that he gave his only Son, that whoever believes in him should not perish but have eternal life. For God did not send his Son into the world to condemn the world, but in order that the world might be saved through him."* *John 3:16-17 (ESV)*

When I look into the manger and see the infant Messiah – God loves ME! GOD LOVES <u>ME</u>!!!!

Additional Text: John 1 and 3

December 22

Love, to me, is the most misunderstood word and concept in the world. I really had no clue as to how to start to understand what 'Love' is until I began to read and see how GOD shows His love. It gave me the TRUE standard to hold my ideas about love and to judge another's love for me.

Because of Jesus and His perfect sacrifice and relationship with the Father, I kneel now before the Father who is the head of the Family of Believers. We are all identified by His family name. Our Father owns all the cows on the hills (Psalm 50) and has all the gifts we really need in our lives. I pray that He will strengthen that place deep inside of you with these gifts by the power of His Holy Spirit, so that Jesus may live inside you not because you earned Him but because you took a single step of faith. You took that step of faith when you accepted and received His unconditional love. I pray that you may have power to just be able to understand and appreciate HOW BIG -- HOW HUGE -- is the love of Jesus for you and all His saints.

This love is beyond our human ability to define or know it but I pray that you will be surrounded by the very Presence of God so much in your life until He is all you have inside of you.

Now God is truly able to do so much more inside of me than I can ever imagine He could or I could even ask Him to do. I give all the glory to Him as the Church follows Jesus' example and teaching and more and more people come to Him and follow Him forever and ever. Amen.

Ephesians 3:14-21 (my translation)

Love is made up of patience, kindness, humility, and a lack of anger, envy, or pride. Love certainly does not keep a ledger of 'rights' and 'wrongs' and doesn't manipulate people for its own agenda or take satisfaction when terrible things happen to others. The truth of God is a reason to rejoice. Love protects, trusts, and provides hope to the one it is given and it <u>always</u> perseveres.

Love doesn't fail no matter what the circumstances and will live on beyond all of our important words or thoughts. 1 Corinthians 13:4-8 (my translation)

Love. So beautiful and so exquisite when copied from Jesus.

"A new command I give you: Love one another. As I have loved you, so you must love one another. By this all men will know that you are my disciples, if you love one another." John 13:34-35

Additional Text: Song of Solomon 4, Luke 7

"Be still, and know that I am God;
I will be exalted among the nations, I will be exalted in the earth."

Psalm 46:10

It's that simple. I have spent my life in various ways asking these and other questions:

Who is 'God'?
What does He want?
What is my purpose in being born?
Why am I here?
What does all 'this' mean?
What will happen tomorrow?
Why is this happening?
Where will I go next?

The answer to these and all other questions is:

"Be still, and know that I am God..."

Making it more complicated or more deeply philosophical or more pragmatic produces mental exercises but no true substance.

"Be still, and know that I am God..."

The real question after that is...do I have the 'guts' to step closer, taking the phrase at face value and give it a test. Just be still and know God. Shh! Be quiet! God can explain Himself if I am willing to hush long enough to hear and listen! Whether I am a proclaimed atheist, a new Christian that has hit my first 'doubt', or a long-time, 'mature' Christian who is experiencing a 'crisis of faith', God IS the only one who can explain Himself!

The king was distressed, but because of his oaths and his dinner guests, he ordered that her request be granted and had John beheaded in the prison. His head was brought in on a platter and given to the girl, who carried it to her mother. John's disciples came and took his body and buried it. Then they went and told Jesus.

When Jesus heard what had happened, he withdrew by boat privately to a solitary place.   *Matthew 14:9-13*

John the Baptist, cousin, probably childhood friend, and fellow minister was killed. He was killed because of the manipulation and whim of a spoiled girl and a spineless king.

"Be still, and know that I am God..."
Simple truth.

Additional Text: Zephaniah 3, 1 Thessalonians 4

December 24

[Jesus said,] *"So if you are about to place your gift on the altar and remember that someone is angry with you, leave your gift there in front of the altar. Make peace with that person, then come back and offer your gift to God.*

Matthew 5:23-24 (CEV)

Jesus, the Son of God, tells me clearly that offerings, service, communion, is not acceptable to the Father without love and unity. *But even if we don't feel at ease, God is greater than our feelings, and he knows everything.*

1 John 4:20 (CEV)

Brothers. Cain and Abel. Did you ever wonder why God didn't like Cain's offering? Did He just like meat over grain? Let's look at that Scripture passage: *Adam and Eve had a son. Then Eve said,"I'll name him Cain because I got him with the help of the LORD." Later she had another son and named him Abel. Abel became a sheep farmer, but Cain farmed the land. One day, Cain gave part of his harvest to the LORD, and Abel also gave an offering to the LORD. He killed the first-born lamb from one of his sheep and gave the LORD the best parts of it. The LORD was pleased with Abel and his offering, but not with Cain and his offering. This made Cain so angry that he could not hide his feelings.*
The LORD said to Cain: What's wrong with you? Why do you have such an angry look on your face? If you had done the right thing, you would be smiling. But you did the wrong thing, and now sin is waiting to attack you like a lion. Sin wants to destroy you, but don't let it! Cain said to his brother Abel, "Let's go for a walk." And when they were out in a field, Cain killed him.

Genesis 4:1-8 (CEV)

It seems like it was Abel's heart that found favor with God. He gave the best of what was his. Cain just gave 'part'.

I think God looks at my heart the same way. How do I really feel about my "brother" or "sister"? [Note: Remember whom Jesus said was my "neighbor" and "brother/sister"! Luke 8:19-21 and 10:26-37] I have a picture of standing in front of Jesus on Judgment Day and on a video screen behind Him scenes are playing of every thought and action I have had with those whom the Lord put in my path and how compassionately and lovingly I responded. It's not a pretty picture!

Many of us are going to go to Communion services or Candlelight services tonight and then we will go eat dinner with our family. Is there something I need to see or call my "brother" about BEFORE I go to Communion? Maybe this will be a good prelude to any New Year's resolutions?

It is truly wonderful when relatives live together in peace. *Psalm 133:1 (CEV)*

Additional Text: Psalm 50, Romans 15

December 25

For the wages of sin is death, but the gift of God is eternal life in Christ Jesus our Lord.
Romans 6:23

Today is Christmas Day. My heart is full for what God has done for me. Just a few short years ago Christmas was all about presents. Every year, I felt such a let down after all the gifts were opened. I would think to myself, "Is that all?" I had spent hundreds of dollars – and I still wondered – is that all? How many times have I watched children tear into gifts and then cry when there was no more to open!

Over the last few years, money has been pretty scarce in our family. The question is no longer how much did we spend but is there ANY money to spend for gifts or a special dinner?

God is good. He wants me to understand what Christmas really is. To accept something new into my heart, I have to be willing to let go or flush out the old. So today, I speak to you as someone who has a full heart because I now grasp that GOD has given and continues to give me all that I need – salvation – eternal life – a new life through Jesus – who came as a baby – grew into a man – showing me how to live an abundant life – and then giving ALL that He had – to be the perfect blood sacrifice for MY sins – and then showed me His power and victory over sin and death as He rose from the dead three days later.

I look around our house today and see a home where Mom and Dad KNOW Jesus as their Savior and we work in His vineyard. I see two grown children who know Jesus as their Savior and desire to raise THEIR children to know Him. I see a teenager who also knows Jesus and has been miraculously healed of cancer not once but TWICE and we believe that the Lord has even more miracles in mind for his life!

Yes, my heart is full today. This full heart is not a gift to stay wrapped up. I am to share that good news of an abundant life through Jesus. The next few days will be opportunities to share with family members who may not know Jesus or know the victorious life that He desires for us. I believe that sharing with family is the most difficult evangelism of all IF I try to do it all myself. If I let the Holy Spirit fill me first with grace and mercy and patience and joy and His peace – well, my family, who think they know me so well are surely going to wonder what happened to me!!! I must remember to allow God to flow through me – overflow from me – giving God all the glory for what will happen. *This service that you perform is not only supplying the needs of God's people but is also overflowing in many expressions of thanks to God.*
2 Corinthians 9:12

As we celebrate Jesus' birth, let us keep our eyes focused on our Savior who came in the power of the Holy Spirit and became our perfect example.

God bless each one of you with the gifts of God that will last eternally and fill every empty space, every wound in your life.

Joy to the world! The Lord has come! Let earth receive her King!
Let every heart prepare Him room. And heaven and nature sing!
And heaven and nature sing! And heaven and heaven and nature sing!

December 26

I wish that everyone were like me, but each person has his own gift from God. One has one gift, another has another gift.   *1 Corinthians 7:7 (NCV)*

The day after Christmas! When I was a child, this was the time to REALLY have fun! Christmas Day is when you had to wear good clothes and sit around at Grandma's and not get dirty and listen to the adults talk about the "old days" – which included telling embarrassing stories about your children! The day after Christmas meant I could go find all my friends and compare 'loot'. Yes, it was a time of trying not to admit that Debbie got something more 'groovy' than me – but I also remember being grateful that I didn't get those 'dorky shoes' that she got!!!

Paul in speaking to the Corinthian church is addressing the bottom line problem that the members were not affirming and encouraging each other in their different gifts. They were jostling for the 'greater seat' – seeking to be 'king of the hill'. Paul even admits that it would be easier for him if everyone was like him – in this case, single instead of married – but he acknowledges that all gifts from God are worthy and needed in the church.

This is why I remind you to keep using the gift God gave you when I laid my hands on you. Now let it grow, as a small flame grows into a fire. God did not give us a spirit that makes us afraid but a spirit of power and love and self-control.   *2 Timothy 1:6-7 (NCV)*

Here Paul tells me not to take my God-given gift and stick it in the back of my closet. God doesn't give us some disgusting 'fruitcake-like' gift. Jesus told us that the Father only gives good gifts to His children. I should use my God-given gifts to build God's kingdom in whatever way His Holy Spirit leads me.

Like the Magi who visited Jesus with their gifts, I am to lay the gifts He has given me down at His feet and say, "Speak, Lord, your servant is listening!"

Jesus was born in the town of Bethlehem in Judea during the time when Herod was king. When Jesus was born, some wise men from the east came to Jerusalem. They asked, "Where is the baby who was born to be the king of the Jews? We saw his star in the east and have come to worship him."

When King Herod heard this, he was troubled, as well as all the people in Jerusalem. Herod called a meeting of all the leading priests and teachers of the law and asked them where the Christ would be born. They answered, "In a town of Bethlehem in Judea. The prophet wrote about this in the Scriptures: 'But you, Bethlehem, in the land of Judah, are important among the tribes of Judah. A ruler will come from you who will be like a shepherd for my people Israel.'"...

After the wise men heard the king, they left. The star they had seen in the east went before them until it stopped above the place where the child was. When the wise men saw the star, they were filled with joy. They came to the house where the child was and saw him with his mother, Mary, and they bowed down and worshiped him. They opened their gifts and gave him treasures of gold, frankincense, and myrrh.   *Matthew 2:1-6, 9-11 (NCV)*

Additional Text: Isaiah 9, 1 Samuel 3

December 27

Happy is the man who doesn't give in and do wrong when he is tempted, for afterwards he will get as his reward the crown of life that God has promised those who love him. And remember, when someone wants to do wrong it is never God who is tempting him, for God never wants to do wrong and never tempts anyone else to do it. Temptation is the pull of man's own evil thoughts and wishes. These evil thoughts lead to evil actions and afterwards to the death penalty from God. So don't be misled, dear brothers.   James 1:12-16 (TLB)

Wouldn't it be great if we could reach a level of 'holiness' where we would never be tempted again??!! I think John Wesley actually thought that level of 'Christian Perfection' existed. I personally do not agree. I do not find any reference in the Bible to ANYONE including Jesus who did not have to battle temptations. While Enoch and David were commended as pleasing God and Abraham was righteous, none of them were without their temptations and even often failed the test!

All these things happened to them [who have gone before us] *as examples – as object lessons to us – to warn us against doing the same things; they were written down so that we could read about them and learn from them in these last days as the world nears its end.*
So be careful. If you are thinking, "Oh I would never behave like that" – let this be a warning to you. For you too may fall into sin.
1 Corinthians 10:11-12 (TLB)

Temptation is the lure to sin, not the sin itself. I ALWAYS have a choice. I was recently faced with the option to have a beer with my dinner. Now, I do not find anywhere in the Bible that it tells me NOT to drink alcohol. Jesus even turned water into wine so that there could be wonderful, tasty wine at the wedding He attended in Cana. HOWEVER, drunkenness and the over-indulgence of alcohol or even the gluttony of food IS sin. So even though God has not forbidden me to have that beer He has put a warning in my heart that I tend to be easily 'tempted' to overindulge – so since I have a choice – I don't drink even one beer because it would not be just one beer for me – it would be six or eight. It would happen not once in a while but every week and then more often. God has given me a way of escape from this sin of drunkenness and gluttony – listen to His voice saying "No" to the one beer and turn away from the path that you know will end where you do NOT want to be! Give God credit for knowing best!

"Keep alert and pray. Otherwise temptation will overpower you. For the spirit indeed is willing, but how weak the body is!"   Matthew 26:41 (TLB)

Jesus said this to His disciples as they were in the Garden of Gethsemane. He knew their weakness because He Himself was experiencing it right at that moment! Prayer and time with God each and every day is the only way that temptations begin to appear with 'red flags' and 'bells and whistles' attached! God's voice becomes stronger and clearer in my life. For every minute I spend with Him, His voice speaks to me with the power of His Spirit and Truth. Temptation becomes clear in the Light of HIS Presence in my life. HALLELUJAH!

The LORD is my shepherd, I shall not be in want.
He makes me lie down in green pastures, he leads me beside quiet waters,
he restores my soul.
He guides me in paths of righteousness for his name's sake.
Even though I walk through the valley of the shadow of death,
I will fear no evil, for you are with me; your rod and your staff, they comfort me.
You prepare a table before me in the presence of my enemies.
You anoint my head with oil; my cup overflows.
Surely goodness and love will follow me all the days of my life,
and I will dwell in the house of the LORD forever.   *Psalm 23*

Most people in the Judeo-Christian world are familiar with this Scripture. The words flow like a well-loved poem.

However, since I am not a shepherd and know little about sheep the words miss a little for me. I grew up in the 60's with its anger, rebellion, and many questions. But I also grew up in the mid-west and spent a lot of time on my grandparents' farm with milk cows, Angus cattle, chickens, a pond, and a creek. There were woods where my dad taught me to hunt. Psalm 23 sounds like THIS to me:

"Lord, You are the landowner of all there is. Since I am Your child, I will never be in need. Because the land is Yours and You watch over me, I feel safe to just lie in the beautiful grass under a shade tree. The creek runs nearby, like the Living Water that flows through me, constantly refreshing me, from the River of Life that is You.

I can count on You because You ARE integrity and lead me on the right paths through life. Some of those paths ARE going to be tough as things happen in this world that bring terrible grief, pain, and even despair. I won't be afraid of this dark time because You are with me, ready and able to guide me THROUGH!

You lay out a table, a feast, for me every day. Those who are jealous and mean to me watch as I am filled by Your love and grace and mercy until it overflows -- even on them.

All that You are will be with me each and every day of my life and I will live forever with You, Lord."   *Psalm 23 (my paraphrase)*

God is my Shepherd. It pleases Him when I grow and mature under His care, learning His wisdom, receiving all that He provides. What a gift I have been given!

Additional Text: Isaiah 17, Matthew 13

'Studying' the Bible or Scriptures isn't always an exciting prospect in and of itself, especially to those of us who studied only enough in school settings to get through and reach our goals. We were not the kids that exhibited a thirst for knowledge through the written word. One of the ways that I knew my life had changed when I accepted Jesus as Savior and Lord was that I truly LIKED to read the Bible. My reading up until 4-5 years ago was significantly heavier in the New Testament than the Old. I thought it was more relevant to my modern day-to-day life! As God continues to be patient with me and pour out His understanding of His Word to me, I find myself...hungry for my time with Him through the Scriptures. He has also taught me some of His 'tricks' to making it more interesting and challenging.

I was reading my NIV one day and I 'felt/heard' God in my spirit say, "What do those words mean to you?" I mentally shrugged. I wasn't sure. Then He said, "Put that passage in your own words. Think about what you would hear if we were sitting across the table and I said this to you. What would it sound like? What words would you hear?" And so that started with me taking a passage, usually the really familiar ones, and 'translating' it into conversation language that is revealing. Here is one that recently came to me:

Blessed are the humble for God's Kingdom is THEIR kingdom as a child of the King. Blessed are those who experience grief and loss of loved ones, jobs, their health, or in many other ways in this world. The Holy Spirit will comfort them TOTALLY in ways they cannot imagine. Blessed are the meek for they will INHERIT the earth, not having to fight and scrape for it. Blessed are those who are SO HUNGRY and THIRSTY for a right relationship with God above ALL else -- they will receive it! Blessed are those who, without conditions, are loving and forgiving and merciful to others for they will receive back the same. Blessed are those who have pure intentions in their hearts without manipulation or greed for their own way -- they will be looking with God's eyes. Blessed are those who see reconciliation with God for EVERYONE! They are ministering just like Jesus. Blessed are those who are persecuted in all the ways Jesus was because they also have a right relationship with the Father -- they have the eternal kingdom with God. Blessed are you when you are insulted and persecuted in many ways -- including with lies and gossip and innuendos-- because of the life you walk in Jesus every day. Get excited! Your riches and glory will be the same as Jesus Christ! Matthew 5:1-12 (my paraphrase)

I've been to wonderful Holy Spirit revival services and weeklong conferences where it seems like I have spent time trying to 'drink from a fire hose'! Taking notes, even just short bullet-like jottings, is a good way to bring back to my quiet time, things that I would like to ponder with the Lord. It's like bringing home homework. There is another one of those words that do not bring to mind wonderful memories but MAYBE it is time to replace those memories with something new and FRESH! It is time for me to GET EXCITED about my NEW CREATION life in Jesus Christ! It is time for me see what a wonderful opportunity I have to spend time with the best Teacher who knows many, many ways to explain the same concept to me!

December 30

God planned for us to do good things and to live as he has always wanted us to live. That's why he sent Christ to make us what we are.   Ephesians 2:10 (CEV)

My pastor said this week that I was "made to make a <u>contribution</u>, not just to consume!" It was a wonder that I could walk to my car when the worship was complete an hour later! My toes hurt SO BAD from him stepping on them!

To live and become like Jesus is about love and being a servant. It's not about how many Scriptures I have memorized unless they are in my heart and manifest themselves through a filter of love and compassion as they did in Jesus. It's not about how many times I go to church in a week or how many committees I am a member or what 'offices' I hold unless I am obedient to how <u>God</u> wants me to serve, and serve with humility. Is God pleased with how I represent <u>Him</u>?

...and think the same way that Christ Jesus thought: Christ was truly God. But he did not try to remain equal with God. He gave up everything and became a slave, when he became like one of us. Christ was humble. He obeyed God and even died on a cross.   Philippians 2:5-8 (CEV)

In the mid-90's, there was a bracelet phenomena that I was a part – WWJD. I wore a black cloth bracelet with the letters "WWJD" stamped into it for over a year. "<u>W</u>hat <u>W</u>ould <u>J</u>esus <u>D</u>o"? WWJD. As 'cheesy' as many thought the idea was, it <u>did</u> make an impact on my lifestyle. It was difficult to make a nasty, snide remark and shake my finger at someone with the bracelet sliding down my arm! I had a hard time slamming the phone down with that hand, too!

Now I need a pair of sunglasses, maybe, with the letters "WAJA" glazed on them so that I would have to look <u>through</u> it: <u>W</u>hat <u>A</u>bout <u>J</u>esus' <u>A</u>ttitude? If the bracelet helped my actions, maybe the glasses would help my attitude!

I was <u>created</u> to worship and serve God. But if I serve only out of duty and with my eyes on the <u>world's</u> response, then I am not following Jesus but, in fact, serving <u>myself</u>. An interesting way to read through the gospels is to look at each scene and 'see' it as answering the question: What was Jesus' attitude in this situation?

Two blind men were sitting beside the road. And when they heard that Jesus was coming their way, they shouted, "Lord and Son of David, have pity on us!" The crowd told them to be quiet, but they shouted even louder, "Lord and Son of David, have pity on us!"

When Jesus heard them, he stopped and asked, "What do you want me to do for you?"   Matthew 20:30-32 (CEV)

Jesus stopped. I guess He didn't mind being interrupted when He was busy! (Ouch!)

And when the chief priests and leaders brought their charges against him, he [Jesus] did not say a thing.   Matthew 27:12 (CEV)

Jesus also didn't feel like He had to justify Himself to everyone who accused Him falsely. I guess He also didn't feel He had to show them that He was <u>right</u> and they were <u>wrong</u>. (Double ouch!!)

WAJA. Will I choose to make Jesus' attitude <u>my</u> attitude today? It's a choice.

Additional Text: Matthew 20, Ephesians 2

Therefore, if anyone is in Christ, he is a new creation; the old has gone, the new has come! All this is from God, who reconciled us to himself through Christ and gave us the ministry of reconciliation: that God was reconciling the world to himself in Christ, not counting men's sins against them. And he has committed to us the message of reconciliation. We are therefore Christ's ambassadors, as though God were making his appeal through us. We implore you on Christ's behalf: Be reconciled to God. God made him who had no sin to be sin for us, so that in him we might become the righteousness of God. As God's fellow workers we urge you not to receive God's grace in vain. For he says,
"In the time of my favor I heard you, and in the day of salvation I helped you."
I tell you, now is the time of God's favor, now is the day of salvation.
2 Corinthians 5:17-6:2

As I come to the end of another year, I cannot help but review the events in my life. I have found that it's important to ask the Lord to shed His light of truth on this reflection but I think it's a good thing – a time of praise for all that the Lord has done. It is an opportunity to walk away from another layer of the 'old woman' in me and press on to the new creation that God is doing inside of me. God does a reconciliation inside of me, using the experiences in my past to refine the new woman that is in my future. Only God can do that so perfectly!

God's grace is always sufficient, sufficient for every experience – every circumstance. What is grace? It is that undeserved love that Jesus showed when He submitted to the Father's plan and walked that *Via Delarosa* – way of pain – to Calvary. Not only walked the way but also did it without anger or complaint. That same grace is right here for me. All day. Every day. Is my boss being unfair? Is my spouse being unreasonable? God's grace is sufficient. Did my church family forget to visit me when I had surgery? Was my name omitted from the list of choir members in the cantata? God's grace is sufficient. It's not a candy coating – it's a heart changing, real deal, eternal fix. It's God's grace.

Jesus told us that we are to love each other. And not just love those we like – but love our enemies, too!!! I need God's grace to do that! I surely cannot do it in my own strength!

Dear friends, let us love one another, for love comes from God. Everyone who loves has been born of God and knows God. Whoever does not love does not know God, because God is love. This is how God showed his love among us: He sent his one and only Son into the world that we might live through him. This is love: not that we loved God, but that he loved us and sent his Son as an atoning sacrifice for our sins. Dear friends, since God so loved us, we also ought to love one another. No one has ever seen God; but if we love one another, God lives in us and his love is made complete in us.
1 John 4:7-12

It's a complete circle. God loves me. He pours that love into me and it flows out of me onto and into others. They, in turn, see God's love in me and in turn love Him for what He has done. God's grace is sufficient for me AND everyone else I allow it to run through! GIVE GOD THE GLORY!!!

Additional Text: Matthew 5, Romans 5

References

God continues to inspire His children to write and share His wisdom and knowledge with each other. These are some of the authors who are mentioned within the texts of the devotions. I pray that with your own Bible in hand, that you will utilize the wonderful resources that we have been given!

Bevere, John. The Devil's Door. Creation House. ISBN# 0884194426. 1997.

Chambers, Oswald. My Utmost for His Highest. Discovery House Publishers. Updated edition. ISBN# 0929239571. July 1992.

Dobson, James. The New Dare to Discipline. Tyndale House Publishers. ISBN# 0842305068. 1996.

Hill, Rev. Stephen. Daily Awakenings. Regal Books. ISBN# 0830725121. 2000.

Joyner, Rick. Final Quest. Whitaker House. ISBN# 0883684780. 1997.

Lucado, Max. America Looks Up. W Publishing Group. ISBN# 0849917476. 2001.

Lucado, Max. In the Grip of Grace. W Publishing Group. ISBN# 0849911435. 1996.

Manning, Doug. Don't Take My Grief Away. Harper San Francisco. ISBN# 0060654171. 1984.

Omartian, Stormie. Praying Through Life's Problems. Integrity Publishers. ISBN# 1591450578. 2003.

Omartian, Stormie. The Power of the Praying Wife.
Harvest House Publishers, Inc. ISBN # 1565075722. 1997.

Omartian, Stormie. The Power of the Praying Husband.
Harvest House Publishers, Inc. ISBN # 0736905324. 2001.

Omartian, Stormie. The Power of the Praying Parent.
Harvest House Publishers, Inc. ISBN# 1565073541. 1995.

Ravenhill, David. The Jesus Letters. Destiny Image.
ISBN# 076842173X. 2002.

Tatelbaum, Judy. The Courage to Grieve. Perennial.
ISBN# 0060911859. 1984.

Tenny, T.F. and Tenny, Tommy. Secret Sources of Power.
Destiny Image Publishers. ISBN# 0768450004. 2000.

Warnke, Mike. Friendly Fire: A Recovery Guide for Believers
Battered by Religion. Destiny Image. ISBN# 0768421241.
2002.

Westberg, Granger. Good Grief. Fortress Press.
ISBN# 0800611144. 1979.

Wilkinson, Bruce. Prayer of Jabez. Multnomah Publishers Inc.
ISBN# 1576737330. 2000.

Wilkinson, Bruce. Secrets of the Vine.
Multnomah Publishers Inc. ISBN# 1576739759. 2001.

Coming in Spring 2007 from Jody Neufeld:

Grief: Finding a Candle of Light

As a nurse and a mother, I found that the hours between 1 and 6 a.m. can be very dark and frightening. Just before light breaks through the clouds is when a child's fever or the amount of my tears and fears become the greatest. And a 'day' or 'night' may not always be measured in a twelve hour period. During a life-threatening illness or any other life-changing situation, joy may seem very fleeting while sadness or grief may take months or years to journey through.

I met Janet Wilkie, LCSW, (and co-author) while working as a nurse for a hospice. At first I thought it was just her 'sweet Southern ways' that encouraged people to open up and let go of their burdens. As she became my friend and walked with me through my son's illness and death, I found out that her 'ways' also included a deep caring and an ability to give me practical options for coping and moving forward in my journey of grief.

I asked Janet to join me in developing a *simple* book that could be helpful in those first days and months following a loss when the pain is so sharp and fresh that all you want to do is go to bed and pull the covers over your head. And yet, you want **desperately** for the ability to move forward even just a step, in the hope that the pain might be relieved even a little bit. The vision that God gave me for this book is that those who are experiencing grief from whatever source **and** those who want to help those who are grieving might find some words of wisdom and practical application within the pages.

-- *Jody Neufeld*

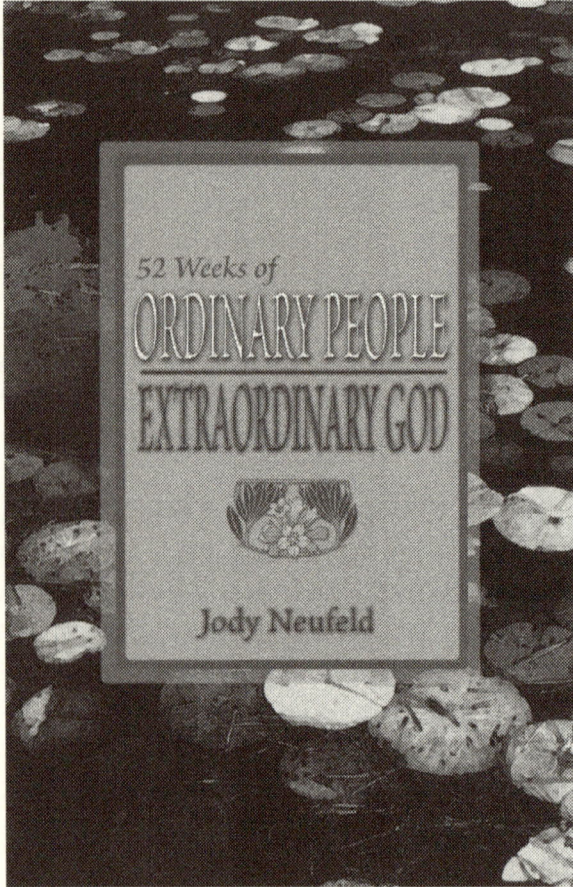

52 Weeks of

ORDINARY PEOPLE

EXTRAORDINARY GOD

Jody Neufeld

Ideal for prayer and study groups!

Jody Neufeld's daily devotional book, Daily Devotions of
Ordinary People – Extraordinary God has become a favorite of
many for individual devotional reading. This small, weekly book
has 52 devotions along with study and discussion questions for
small groups that meet weekly. Call us at (805) 968-1001 or see
our web site (http://www.energionpubs.com) for quantity
discounts. Suggested Retail: $7.99.